Consumer Reports®

BUYING GUIDE 2003

THE EDITORS OF
CONSUMER REPORTS MAGAZINE

Consumers Union • Yonkers, New York

TABLE OF CONTENTS

Dryers
page 66

Autos
page 142

Camcorders
page 20

SHOP SMART

How-tos, tips, and shortcuts that can help you find what you want—fast and at a good price

HOME ENTERTAINMENT

KITCHEN & LAUNDRY

Home theater
in a box
page 38

Barbecue grills
page 94

CONSUMER REPORTS BUYING GUIDE 2003

CONSUMER REPORTS (ISSN 0010-7174) is published 13 times a year by Consumers Union of U.S., Inc., 101 Truman Avenue, Yonkers, N.Y. 10703-1057. Second-class postage paid at Yonkers, N.Y., and at additional mailing offices. Canadian postage paid at Mississauga, Ontario, Canada. Canadian publications registration no. 2665247-98. Title CONSUMER REPORTS registered in U.S. Patent Office. Contents of this issue copyright © 2002 by Consumers Union of U.S., Inc. All rights reserved under International and Pan-American copyright conventions. Reproduction in whole or in part is forbidden without prior written permission (and is never permitted for commercial purposes). CU is a member of the Consumers International. Mailing lists: CU rents or exchanges its customer postal lists so it can be provided to other publications, companies, and nonprofit organizations. If you wish your name deleted from such exchanges, send your address label with a request for deletion to CONSUMER REPORTS, P.O. Box 2127, Harlan, IA 51593-0316. Postmaster: Send address changes to O. Box 2109, Harlan, IA 51593-0298. Back issues: Single copies of 12 preceding issues, $7.95 each; Buying ide, $10 each. Write Back Issues, CONSUMER REPORTS, Customer Relations, 101 Truman Avenue, Yonkers, 10703 Consumer Reports Buying Guide 2003 (ISBN 0-89043-970-2)

Buying Guidance at Your Fingertips

The Consumer Reports Buying Guide helps you find value and quality in today's marketplace. Start with "Shop Smart" on page 7 to find general tips and strategies for shopping in stores, through catalogs, and online. Later in the book, you'll find "Shop Smart" tips at the head of each product Ratings chart with specific guidance for buying particular products.

Products for your home

➤ **Home entertainment**
➤ **Kitchen & laundry**
➤ **Home & yard**
➤ **Home office**

In these sections, you'll find key trends and what's new, followed by concise, informative articles that cover major purchases all around the house. **When you go into the store, you'll know what to ask and what to look for.**

Autos

Look here for tips on getting the best value in a new or used car. Read what's new about the 2003 models, along with Ratings and reviews of more than 200 cars, minivans, pickups, and SUVs. You'll also find Reliability forecasts available only from CONSUMER REPORTS. Also check out the best and worst used cars based on which have been the most (or least) reliable. Plus: reliability histories for 216 models.

Brand-name Ratings & reference

In the Reference Section you'll find Ratings of 897 models in 33 product categories, from barbecue grills and camcorders to vacuum cleaners and washing machines. Also in this section, you'll find:

➤ Consumer Reports' unique brand repair histories for TV sets, computers, refrigerators, lawn mowers, and other big-ticket household products.

➤ Brand Locator, a list of manufacturers' telephone numbers and web addresses.

➤ An index of the last test report as published in issues of CONSUMER REPORTS magazine.

➤ A list of cars and other products recalled during the past year, plus information on how to find out more about product recalls.

About the Consumer Reports family of products

Founded as a magazine in 1936, CONSUMER REPORTS now brings you its unbiased, trusted information in many formats. Its products and publications include CONSUMER REPORTS magazine; buying guides and magazines from Consumer Reports Special Publications; two newsletters, Consumer Reports On Health and Consumer Reports Travel Letter; and Consumer Reports TV, a nationally syndicated consumer news service.

ConsumerReports.org offers site subscribers a searchable version of our test findings and advice, now with wireless PDA accessibility. Auto prices and custom reports are available through the Consumer Reports New Car Price Service and Consumer Reports Used Car Price Service. You can find prices, subscription rates, and more information on these products and services at our www.ConsumerReports.org. Go to "Our Publications" on the home page, then click onto "More Products."

CONSUMER REPORTS specializes in head-to-head, brand-name comparisons of cars and household products. It also provides informed, impartial advice on a broad range of topics from health and nutrition to personal finance and travel.

CONSUMER REPORTS buys all the products it tests and accepts no free samples. We accept no advertising from outside entities nor do we let any company use our information or Ratings for commercial purposes.

CONSUMER REPORTS is published by Consumers Union, an independent, nonprofit testing and information organization—the largest such organization anywhere in the world.

Since 1936, Consumers Union's mission has been to test products, inform the public, and protect consumers. Our income is derived solely from the sale of our publications and services, and from nonrestrictive, noncommercial contributions, grants, and fees.

Shop Smart

How-to's, tips, and shortcuts that can help you find what you want fast and at a good price.

Whatever your shopping style—diligent researcher, casual browser, or determined time-saver—the current shopping scene holds new and expanding options. You can surf web sites, leaf through catalogs, and visit every variety of store, from specialized boutiques to giant warehouse clubs. As the web increasingly influences retailing, chances are you'll use a combination of shopping strategies. Even if you want the immediacy of buying in a store, you may want to check models, prices, and availability online.

Retailers themselves are using more than one venue. Catalog companies, traditional retailers, and brand-name manufacturers have established Internet incarnations. And Internet companies are now publishing catalogs as selling tools.

While shopping alternatives have grown, the basic rules for smart shopping remain the same: Do your homework and determine the best value for your needs. The Consumer Reports Buying Guide, with more than 800 product Ratings plus brand repair histories for many product categories, is a good place to start a search. Here are other shopping tips.

Each month, CONSUMER REPORTS magazine can help with new product reviews and comparisons, test results, and Ratings. Our web site, *ConsumerReports.org*, gives site subscribers access to the latest Ratings and archives of CONSUMER REPORTS, plus online-only content such as e-Ratings of shopping web sites.

Store strategies

Traditional retailers are still the principal shopping choice of consumers. Bricks-and-mortar stores allow what online or catalog shopping can't—an in-person judgment of

overall appearance and important sensory qualities. Researching your purchase before you set off for the store can pay off in valuable product knowledge, time saved, and—maybe—a lower price.

Specialty stores, special service. Need help selecting a product in a category you're not familiar with? Just want a real person to help you? Smaller stores, such as audio boutiques and Main Street shops, can provide a knowledgeable staff and personal service, including special-ordering. These perks may be offset by higher prices. Determine a fair price before you go, using the web or a larger retailer's catalog. Then decide how much the extra service is worth to you. When customization is important, as with computers, online can be the way to go. A recent CONSUMER REPORTS survey found that people purchasing computers over the Internet or through a catalog were generally more satisfied than people who bought them at a bricks-and-mortar retailer.

> ■ **E-RATINGS**
> See Consumer Reports.Org (www.Consumer Reports.org) for exclusive e-Ratings of shopping web sites based on their usability, content, and policies.

Bottom-line basics. Is finding the type of product you want at a good price more important than the latest technology and a large selection? Mass merchandisers such as Wal-Mart, Kmart, and Target cover many categories, with a selection of moderately priced brands from well-known manufacturers, along with their own store-brands. (Wal-Mart and Kmart together account for a huge share of total sales in many categories of appliances and electronic items.) In a recent CONSUMER REPORTS survey, Sears, Target, and Wal-Mart all got high scores for product selection. Some chains, such as JCPenney, have an auction site, where shoppers can bid on merchandise the company wants to move.

Though return policies at most mass merchandisers are usually liberal, returns may entail time and hassle.

Big stores, big selection. Specialty chains such as Circuit City and Best Buy account for three-quarters of home-electronics sales. Home Depot and Lowe's control one-fourth of the home-improvement product market. CompUSAs inhabit strip malls across the country. Sears has a network of stores and a web site with lots of product choices for major appliances and other home products.

These chains may also feature special services, such as viewing/listening rooms for home-theater demonstrations. And although sales-staff expertise may vary, you can generally get questions answered.

Join the club. If you're willing to be flexible on brand and model, check a warehouse club: Costco, BJ's Wholesale Club, or Sam's Club (Wal-Mart's warehouse sibling). Since these stores emphasize value, not service or selection, expect long lines and little sales help. Prices are consistently low, though not necessarily the lowest. Costco was ranked among the highest in a CONSUMER REPORTS survey for quality in several categories of merchandise: electronics; books, music, and videos; hardware and tools; and small appliances.

Clubs charge an annual membership fee (generally $35 to $45). If you don't shop there frequently, that fee can undo much of your savings. Most will issue a limited-time shopping pass, allowing you to browse without joining.

Catalog strategies

Catalogs offer selection and convenience, often from established companies with proven track records and top-notch customer service, plus 24/7 access. Many catalog merchants are also online.

The catalog-web connection can give you the best of both venues. You can browse the catalog (leafing through pages can be quicker than waiting for screens to redraw) and then order online using a catalog's "quick search" feature.

Online catalogs typically feature more merchandise than expensive-to-mail paper catalogs. You'll often find merchandise from an entire year's worth of catalogs online. Web sites frequently feature lines not available in the paper catalog, online-only sales and bargains, even product-selection tips. Habitues of online catalog venues can snap up specials and closeouts before items go out of stock.

Ordering from a catalog over the phone or the web is usually quick, but popular items can still be on back-order, even if they seemed to be in stock when you placed the order. If you don't receive your purchase within the promised time, check back. And before you order, check shipping fees: They can vary widely and add significantly to the cost of the order. See "Secure ordering," on page 10, for precautions that apply to both catalog and web buying.

Web strategies

You can hunt down just about anything on the web, from potato chips to vacation homes, but you'll find that some items are more e-commerce-compatible than others. Books, music, videos, DVDs, and software are big online successes because they're standardized products and no bricks-and-mortar store can stock every title. Branded electronics items also lend themselves to online shopping because it's handy to select them by manufacturer and specific features. Shipping is another factor: Small, lightweight purchases—books as opposed to, say, refrigerators—are top online sellers.

Perhaps even more than for buying, the web is immensely useful for researching a purchase. Information that would previously have taken many hours and many phone calls (if it could be found at all) is now available via a mouse click. Thus armed, you can make better decisions about where to buy, what to buy, and what to pay.

> ▓ OFF THE LIST
> To remove your name from most mailing, telemarketing, and e-mail lists, go to the web site of the Direct Marketing Association at *www.dmaconsumer.org* and then click on "Consumer Assistance."

➤ BUYING THROUGH AUCTIONS

Internet auction sites deal in anything people want to sell. Though sellers provide descriptions (and, often, digital images), details may be fuzzy. Except for sites operated by retailers or businesses, most auction sites do not verify item condition—or whether it really exists. Thus the largest Internet auction site, eBay, suggests you get a written statement from the seller detailing condition and value, return policy, warranty information, promised delivery date, and an address and telephone number.

If you buy something at an auction site, use a credit card (not a debit card) or work out terms with an online escrow service, such as Escrow.com, which processes transactions. (Fees are based on the amount of the transaction, method of payment, and, sometimes, shipping costs.)

At pick-your-own-price sites, you name a price for, say, airline tickets, hotels, or a mortgage, and merchants come to you. Priceline originated this type of "reverse auction." The catch: You must provide a credit-card number up front. If Priceline finds the item at your price, your credit card is charged immediately, usually with no cancellation option. Nor can you request a specific brand.

Secure ordering

Catalogers or e-tailers, retailers should provide complete information about their business and policies. Here's what to look for:

Complete contact information, including a real-world location. Look for a toll-free number, e-mail and postal addresses, and 24-hour customer service. (See Brand Locator for web addresses and phone numbers of major brands.)

Clear shipping, handling, and return policies. Review options and prices before you place an order. Shipping is extra with most catalog orders; some e-tailers offer free shipping when your total reaches a specified amount. When catalog ordering, remember sales tax, charged if the catalog company operates a store in your state.

A 100 percent satisfaction guarantee. Look for a merchant that allows returns for any reason, with no restocking fee. (Custom items and special orders may be excluded.) A good merchant will tell you as you order when items will arrive—or if they'll be delayed.

Security and privacy. At a web site, look for the Trust-e symbol or a Better Business Bureau Online seal, both indicating that the merchant's business practices have passed an audit. As soon as you start the buying process, the site should show a symbol like a key or a lock, or a web address with an "s" (for secure) after the "http." The best sites also cover the $50 maximum that credit-card companies charge if a card is used without authorization.

When catalog ordering, look for a clearly stated list-sharing policy, with an easy way to opt out. If there is no statement, ask for details—or assume that the company rents its customer lists to other merchants.

After the purchase

After you've opened up the box, take a moment to look through the owner's manual. Some products come with a short, handy reference guide. CONSUMER REPORTS Ratings sometimes point out exceptionally clear—

REGULATIONS

Consumer protection online and off

Whenever you shop at home—online, on the phone, or by mail—you have the same safety net against theft of your credit-card number as when you shop in person. If you report misuse right away, you're liable for only $50, even on international transactions. Some web merchants will even reimburse that $50. (Check individual site policies.)

If a product is misrepresented, web shoppers and catalog patrons have the same protection and recourse. Unfortunately, if the merchant—web or otherwise—is not in your state or within 100 miles of your home, some federal protections won't apply. For example, you may not be able to withhold credit-card payment if you have a dispute over product quality. However, many credit-card issuers try to mediate, or will at least credit your account until the dispute is settled. Barring that, you'll have to file a complaint with your state attorney general's office or local consumer-protection bureau.

Note that these protections don't apply to purchases made with a debit card.

Online shopping tools

➤ SEARCH ENGINES, PORTALS, AND DIRECTORIES

These are the places where you can start your online shopping trips.

AltaVista *(www.altavista.com)* has more than 350 million web pages indexed.

AOL Search *(www.search.aol.com)*, available to non-AOL members too, provides returns from several other search engines and services. AOL is also a portal, which is a multifaceted site that combines search capabilities with other services such as shopping, weather, news, chat rooms, and much more.

AskJeeves *(www.askjeeves.com)* is a human-powered search service that returns answers (from a database of 7 million answers) to questions asked in plain English. Also offers access to other search engines.

Excite *(www.excite.com)* has more than 250 million web pages indexed. Also a portal.

Go *(www.go.com)*, affiliated with Disney, uses the Infoseek search service.

Google *(www.google.com)* has 560 million indexed pages and ranks pages according to the number of links that point to each page's site.

HotBot *(www.hotbot.com)* offers "power-searching" features.

Inktomi *(www.inktomi.com)* searches results from more than 2 billion documents.

Open Directory *(www.dmoz.org)* uses a volunteer army of 28,000 "editors" to compile more than 300,000 categories and 2 million links.

Yahoo! *(www.yahoo.com)*, with links to between 1.5 and 1.8 million sites, is the leading referral web site—18 percent of all traffic to e-commerce sites originates there. Also a portal.

➤ METASEARCH SITES

These query other search engines:

Dogpile *(www.dogpile.com)*

Ixquick *(www.ixquick.com)*

Mamma *(www.mamma.com)*

MetaCrawler *(www.metacrawler.com)*

The BigHub *(www.thebighub.com)*

➤ SHOP BOTS

These compare prices, but beware of possible commercial ties to recommended merchants.

www.amazon.com offers price comparisons within the "all products" category of its search box. Goods sold directly by Amazon are listed before those sold by others.

www.consumerworld.org has its own price-comparison search as well as links to other shop bots.

www.dealtime.com searches for the best price in 17 categories, and provides helpful shopping guides. You can also elect to shop local stores, or receive an e-mail notification when a particular item's price drops.

www.mysimon.com lists 17 product categories, allows sorting by price.

www.shopper.com is part of CNET, a web site focusing on computers, consumer electronics, and software. You can rank results by price, and also find shipping charges, availability, and merchant phone numbers.

www.shopping.com, part of the AltaVista search engine, will compare prices and features in 18 categories.

www.streetprices.com is particularly good for consumer electronics and computers.

www.webmarket.com, the shopping channel of www.go2net.com, lets you search for products in 21 categories, including seasonal merchandise and items offered by discounters, outlets, and liquidators.

or unclear—instructions.

Warranty cards. If you fill out the warranty card, the manufacturer can notify you in case of a product recall—especially important for safety-related items such as tires and child car seats. You can omit answering all the market-research questions.

Extended warranties. Retailers may urge you to buy an extended warranty, or "protection plan." The pitch may be powerful, since retailers often make more money on these warranties than they do on the items covered.

But an extended warranty, whether offered online, in a store, or through a catalog, usually amounts to expensive and unnecessary insurance. You're betting the product will break while the extended warranty is in place and that the warranty will cost less than the repair. That's pretty unlikely. A CONSUMER REPORTS survey of owners' experiences showed that few of the products broke during the warranty period and, typically, repairs cost about the same as the warranty.

If you buy with a credit card, you may automatically double the factory warranty anyway; check with the card's issuer for details or limitations. Some manufacturers also offer a warranty extension.

Some expensive and troublesome products might make an extended warranty worthwhile. Computers break a lot (almost 1 in 10 in the survey had a problem just in the first month) and are expensive to have fixed ($200, typically, in the survey).

If you do buy a warranty, read the fine print. All warranties carry a clause excluding repairs due to "abuse" or "misuse." Since cases are reviewed individually, you may or may not be covered.

Some protection plans allow the company to cancel the contract and refund its price instead of covering an expensive repair, which defeats the purpose of a contract. Other plans are automatically renewed unless you decline. Determine if you can leave the item at any of the store's branches, or must send it to a service center. Since the cost of an extended warranty varies widely and high profit margins allow some wiggle room, you may be able to bargain down the price. For more on repairing products, see "Buy Reliable, Fix Smart."

HOME ENTERTAINMENT

What's New in Home Entertainment

A look inside a consumer-electronics store reveals a transformation that can be described in one word: digital. In recent years, digital entertainment products such as DVD players, digital video recorders (DVRs), and satellite-TV receivers have made their mark on the marketplace. Other products, such as camcorders, cameras, receivers, and some TV sets, have moved from analog to digital and in the process have made leaps in what they promise and often can deliver.

CONSUMER REPORTS tests of this new equipment show that digital capability often results in giant leaps in performance. Audio CD players consistently reproduce sound better than turntables did. The typical digital camcorder provides much clearer video than the best of their older, analog cousins. Receivers supporting digital audio can provide more realism when you're watching movies at home than those with earlier, analog-audio standards. High-definition TV shows not just the football game but the sweat glistening on the arms of the players.

But despite digital's superiority over the analog ways of cassette tape, videotape, and traditional NTSC-standard TV, analog products will still be sold for some time to come. If industry infighting and consumer reluctance are any indication, it may be a long time to come. Here's what you can see in today's home-entertainment products:

Movies go digital, but not the set. DVDs, with their capacity for extra features and director commentary tracks, are well on the way to replacing videotapes as the home movie choice. Meanwhile, DVD players have quickly become almost a commodity, with excellent performance the norm and prices dipping below $100.

Despite the record pace of DVD adoption, analog TVs and VCRs are still by far the most-sold home entertainment products, and the best of them are fine performers despite their "nondigitized" nature. VCRs still are a mainstay, though digital recorders, sold under the TiVo, Replay, and other names, can do that with greater speed and commercial-erasing finesse.

Recordable DVD is growing more slowly than predicted because of high cost, technical difficulties, and wrangles over copy-protection concerns. TiVo, Replay, and others still require you to transfer material to videotape for permanent storage.

The digital revolution in audio keeps rolling. It turns out that the introduction of CD players in 1982 was just part one of the digital revolution in consumer audio —the playback part. Part two: the current boom in digital recording options. Audio CD player/recorders, which allow you to create your own CDs for a dollar or two each, have been dropping in price; you can now buy one for a few hundred dollars. New MP3 players offer huge capacity —5 to 20 gigabytes—in very small packages. Digital-music options make music "liquid"—you can pour out what you want to hear, in the order you want, in the format you choose, at home, in the car, or while jetting to Bermuda.

Improvements in digital audio technology, such as DVD-Audio and Super Audio CD (SACD), take full advantage of the surround-sound speaker systems developed for movies. Such capability has worked its way into some high-end DVD players.

Surround sound marches on. To get the most out of a DVD, you need surround sound. Dolby Digital is the surround sound most common on DVD movies. To take full advantage of it, you need a home-theater speaker system and a Dolby Digital receiver to manage them, in addition to your TV and DVD player.

You can buy those components separately or you can buy a system, speakers only or a "home theater in a box," which often includes a receiver sometimes with a built-in DVD player as well. See "Setting Up a Home Theater" on the following page for more information.

Products grow smaller ... yet again. Manufacturers continue to shrink hard drives, batteries, and other parts of audio and video components. The MP3 player can be as small as an ink pen. Portable CD and DVD players can be as thin as 1 inch. "Executive sound systems" have shrunk minisystems into microsystems that fit readily on a desk or into flat systems that hang on a wall.

More options but fewer providers. Even as consumers' ability to control how they see and hear content continues to expand, corporate mergers are further shrinking the number of companies that control the flow of content. Content providers now own media organizations and vice versa, with Internet service in the mix as well. General Electric owns NBC; Viacom owns CBS, MTV, VH1, and Blockbuster; Walt Disney owns ABC; Sony owns Columbia and Tristar; AOLTime Warner includes Warner Brothers and Turner/TNT. BMG owns Napster, and Vivendi Universal Net owns MP3.com and rollingstone.com, among others. These deals mean that, more than ever, forces other than viewer preference can affect what's available.

Copyrights and wrongs. At the same time, copyright issues are limiting control of content—and possibly increasing prices. The creators and publishers of content such as movies and music have legitimate claims to legal protection of what belongs to them. But copyright concerns have led to hardware that blocks you from copying a DVD title you've purchased onto a VHS tape for your personal use. (Expect similar roadblocks when DVD recorders go mainstream.) Blank CDs for recording music include a surcharge to cover royalties the music industry believes would otherwise be denied to musicians.

Less privacy. Every company with which you contract for your home entertainment seems to have gone full-throttle into data mining. Rent a videotape or DVD from Blockbuster or order pay-per-view on cable, and the transaction is recorded in some way. Ditto when you buy a CD off the web, choose a channel on your cable or satellite setup, or fill out a warranty card. You'd expect the original company to use that information to offer related products and services to you. But it's another thing to be bombarded with phone calls, letters, e-mail, and other offers from companies you've never heard of, simply because they have purchased data on you.

More complex choices all around. One more effect of the so-called digital revolution is that it's even harder to be an informed consumer. Products are more complicated, requiring you to study to make a smart choice.

More products involve a service provider—not just computers and cell phones but now some video equipment. Not only do you have to choose between competing services, but once you've chosen and bought the hardware, you're committed to that provider—switching can involve paying hundreds of dollars more to buy new, provider-specific gear, as with satellite-TV equipment or DVRs.

More and more electronics components need to connect with one another, requiring compatible video and audio connections for best results. And competing formats mean that early adopters are betting that the format they choose will be the one that prevails, as manufacturers invent new media formats, music-encoding schemes, and connection specifications.

All this, of course, means a greater challenge for consumers shopping for home-entertainment products. That's where CONSUMER REPORTS can help.

SETTING UP A HOME THEATER

Adding surround sound to a TV can transform the viewing and listening experience even more than buying a bigger set.

Most TV sound can be improved by adding external speakers—a pair of self-powered speakers is a simple, easy way to do that. But for a real home-theater experience, you need a big TV, a video source (hi-fi stereo VCR or DVD player), a surround-decoding receiver/amplifier, and five speakers plus a subwoofer. For details on the components that make up a home-theater system, including home theater in a box and minisystems, see the articles later in this chapter. Here's an overview of the whole system:

➤ SURROUND SOUND EXPLAINED

Surround sound adds additional channels to familiar two-channel sterophonic sound for stronger movie-theater realism, allowing additional speakers to carry the multi-channel sound found on movies.

What you'll hear depends on three things: the format used for the source (a TV show or DVD, for instance), the software decoder (on the receiver or DVD player) used to decipher the format, and the number of speakers you have. If your gear lacks the latest, most sophisticated decoder, it can still handle the TV broadcast or DVD, but it will do so with fewer audio channels and less dramatic effect. Conversely, state-of-the-art hardware can only play older material because new decoders are generally backward-compatible with early formats. Again, you'll hear fewer channels.

Here's a rundown on the major formats:

Dolby Surround, an early version of surround sound, is an analog encoding scheme used mostly for VHS movies and TV shows. It combines four channels into stereo soundtracks. With no decoder—say, on a TV—you'll hear stereo.

With a **Dolby Pro Logic** decoder, you'll hear four channels: left, right, center, and one limited-range surround channel. A newer version, **Pro Logic II,** has the same left, right, and center channels, but also has two discrete, full-range surround channels for a total of five channels. Most new receivers have Pro Logic II ; older models may have only Pro Logic. You'll need four or five speakers for optimal sound.

The next step up is **Dolby Digital**, a digital encoding scheme that's also called Dolby Digital 5.1. Like Pro Logic II, it has full-range left and right channels in front and rear plus a center channel; it adds a subwoofer channel for deep bass (called ".1" because it's limited to low-frequency effects). Dolby Digital is used on digital media such as DVDs, digital cable, digital broadcast TV, and satellite transmissions. It can also decode material that uses Dolby Surround. Virtually all new receivers and some DVD players have Dolby Digital decoders. You'll need five full-range speakers and a subwoofer for optimal sound.

DTS (Digital Theater Systems) is a rival to Dolby Digital, also with six channels. It's offered on most new receivers and on some DVD players. It calls for the same speaker setup as Dolby Digital.

Dolby Digital EX and **DTS-ES** are "extended surround" formats that add either a center-rear surround channel or an extra pair of rear-surround speakers that go behind the listener. With Dolby Digital EX, the two flavors are referred to, respectively, as Dolby Digital 6.1 (with three surround speakers) and 7.1 (with four surround speakers). Both formats are still relatively new and not widely used on either equipment or programming. At this stage, they are mostly for video enthusiasts. You'll need seven or eight speakers for the full effect.

THX is a certification by Lucasfilm (owner of the standard). It indicates that a multichannel audio product has passed certain performance and ergonomic tests and can process sound to stimulate movie-theater acoustics.

➤ **CONNECTING THE COMPONENTS**
Video connections. The way you connect your audio and video equipment can affect the quality of the sound and images you receive. Here's a primer on the various kinds of connections you'll find on your equipment and what you can expect from each:

Even the best TV set won't live up to its potential without a high-quality video source and a high-quality connection. TV sets can have four different types of inputs, each of which accepts a specific kind of signal. Most TVs 25 inches and larger have an antenna/cable, composite-video, and S-video input; a component-video input is found mostly on higher-end models.

The **antenna/cable input,** sometimes called a UHF input, is the most common connection. It's the easiest to use because it's the only one that carries both sound and picture on one cable—in this case, the familiar coaxial cable. (The other video inputs carry only the picture, requiring the use of a separate pair of audio inputs to carry the sound.) The antenna/cable input is used with video sources such as antennas, cable boxes, and VCRs.

The **composite-video input** offers a small step up in quality. It uses a single standard RCA-style jack, a round jack (frequently yellow) with a single pin, to pass video signals. Two separate RCA jacks are used to pass the stereo audio signals. Most video sources have a composite video connection, including cable boxes and VCRs, as well as DVD players.

The **S-video input,** a round jack with four pins, accepts even better-quality signals. This input separates the signal into two signals—color and luminance (black and white)—which improves the image quality. This can be used to connect your TV to DVD players, satellite receivers, and digital-cable boxes, along with digital, S-VHS, or Hi-8 camcorders.

The **component-video input,** a three-cable connection found on some higher-end TVs, carries potentially the best-quality signals. It separates the video signal into three signals, two color and one luminance (black and white). This input is used primarily with DVD players. On HD-ready sets, this input is specially designed to handle signals from HDTV tuners and progressive-scan DVD players.

Some TVs have more than one S-video, composite-video, or component-video input so that you can connect several devices. On many sets, a composite-video or S-video input is on the front of the set for easy access.

Audio connections. The picture is only half the story. You also need to hook up your sound equipment. To obtain the audio from devices such as a VCR, DVD player, cable or satellite receiver, or camcorder, you generally connect one or a pair of **audio inputs** to your receiver, which routes sound to the speakers. Stereo analog audio inputs are labeled L and R for left and right. Newer multichannel receivers will also have **coaxial** or **optical digital-audio inputs** for providing surround sound; some have both. These are used for connecting a DVD player and some digital-cable and satellite receivers. Make sure the receiver's input matches the output of any device you want to connect—in other words, to use an optical output on the DVD player, you need to have an optical input on the receiver.

To output the sound, every multichannel receiver will have at least six speaker terminals so it can accommodate a surround-sound system with six speakers. You don't have to use all six terminals; you can use only two of these for a stereo setup, for instance. Some receivers also have a **subwoofer pre-amp out,** an output that carries unamplified low-frequency

signals to an active (powered) subwoofer.

Some receivers have **5.1 inputs,** six connectors that accept multichannel analog audio signals that another device, such as a DVD player that has a built-in Dolby Digital or DTS decoder or that plays DVD-Audio or SACD discs æhas already decoded through a process that splits a signal into six or more audio channels. The inputs are typically marked Front L and R, Rear (or Surround) L and R, Center, and Subwoofer (which also may be labeled LFE, for low-frequency effects).

User manuals should take you through much of the setup process. Hang on to them. Give yourself easy access to the back of the receiver and other components. You'll need good lighting to read the labeling on the back panels, so have a flashlight ready. Connect audio devices first, using the cables that came with each component.

To connect speakers, you typically strip off enough insulation from the ends of the wires to connect them without shorting to adjacent wires. Observe proper polarity; like a battery, a speaker has "+" and "–" terminals. (The insulation of one wire in each pair should have a distinguishing feature, such as color or striping.) Reversing polarity will cause a loss of bass.

You can plug almost all of your components into a two-prong AC power strip —preferably a unit with surge suppression. The exceptions are the three high-powered devices—the TV, receiver, and powered subwoofer. Plug those into the wall or into a three-prong AC power strip. Or you can plug all of your components into a power control center, which controls the entire system and can include surge suppression.

ARRANGING THE EQUIPMENT

Make sure your room has enough distance between you and the TV for comfortable viewing. The ideal for viewing a conventional, 30- to 40-inch set: 8 to 12 feet. That gives your eyes enough distance to visually knit the scan lines into a unified picture. A high-definition TV screen has no scan lines, so you can sit closer. For sets larger than 40 inches—flat panel or projection sets—figure on sitting more than 10 feet away. Another way of looking at it: The bigger the room, the bigger the TV can be.

Receivers generate more heat than other audio and video components, so they need to go on the top of the stack or on their own shelf, with at least a couple of inches of head space and a path for the heat to escape. If a receiver's surface becomes hot to the touch, try one of the following: turn down the volume; provide more cooling, perhaps with a small fan; use speakers with a higher impedance; or play only one set of speakers at a time.

➤ MATCHING SPEAKERS & RECEIVER

Speakers and the receiver must match in two ways: power and impedance.

Power. Generally, the more power (measured in watts) a receiver delivers, the louder you can play music with less distortion. Each doubling of loudness uses about 10 times as much power. Most models these days provide plenty of power, at least 60 watts per channel.

Here's a quick guide to power requirements for various room sizes: 80 to 100 watts per channel for a large living room (15x25 feet or more with an 8-foot ceiling); 40 to 80 for an average living room (12x20 feet); 20 to 40 for a bedroom (12x14 feet). A "live" (echoey) room will need less power than a "dead" (muffled-sounding) room.

Impedance. Materials that conduct electrical current also resist the current's travel to varying degrees. This resistance, or impedance, is measured in ohms. Standard speaker impedance is 8 ohms, which all receivers can handle. Many speakers have an impedance as low as 4 ohms, according to CONSUMER REPORTS tests. All else being equal, 4-ohm speakers demand more current than 8-ohm speakers. The use of the former generally doesn't pose a problem at normal listening levels but may eventually cause a receiver to overheat or trip its internal overload switch when music is played very loud. Before buying 4-ohm speakers to regularly play loud music, check the manual or back panel of your receiver to confirm that the unit is compatible.

Some speakers overemphasize various frequencies when placed against the wall or tucked in a bookshelf. Manufacturers' recommendations can help you decide on optimal placement.

The best position for the main front speakers is an equilateral triangle whose points are the left speaker, the right speaker, and you, the listener. Try to place them at about the same height as your ears. The center speaker should be atop or below the TV and aligned with, or only slightly behind, the main speakers. The left and right surround speakers can be placed alongside the seating, facing each other or the back wall. The subwoofer can go anywhere convenient—under a table, behind the sofa. Watch out for corners, though. They accentuate the bass, often making it unacceptably boomy.

➤ THE FINE-TUNING

You can optimize the system by properly setting audio levels and taking advantage of some of your components' features.

DVD audio settings. A DVD player can output each disc's audio signal in a number of ways. The raw "bitstream" signal is undecoded; use this setting if your receiver decodes Dolby Digital and DTS audio. If you have only a digital-ready (or DVD-ready) receiver and your DVD player has a built-in Dolby Digital or DTS decoder, use the "analog 6-channel output" setting, which outputs decoded audio to the receiver. And if you have only a stereo receiver or TV (or just stereo speakers), set the DVD player for "analog 2-channel"; this downmixes the multiple channels into two.

Subwoofer adjustments. Most powered subwoofers have two controls: cut-off frequency and volume level. The former is the frequency above which the subwoofer won't reproduce sound. If your main speakers are regular, full-range types (not satellites), set the subwoofer to the lowest setting, typically 80 hertz. If they're satellites with no woofers, see the manual regarding how to set up the satellite and subwoofer combination. Adjust the subwoofer's volume so its contribution is noticeable but subtle.

Receiver settings. Using your receiver's user manual as a guide, adjust the receiver, speaker by speaker, according to each speaker's size, distance from the listener, and sound level relative to the other speakers. With most audio systems, you should be able to sit where you will be listening and make the proper adjustments by using the receiver's remote control.

CAMCORDERS

Fine picture quality and easy editing have improved the functionality of these movie makers. That's especially true of digital models, which are replacing analog.

Home movies—those grainy, jumpy productions of yesteryear—have been replaced by home movies shot on digital or analog camcorders that you can edit and embellish with music using your PC and play back

on your VCR, or even turn into video shorts to e-mail.

Digital camcorders generally offer very good to excellent picture quality, along with very good sound capability, compactness, and ease of handling. Making copies of a digital recording won't result in a loss of picture or sound quality.

Analog camcorders generally have good picture and sound quality and are less expensive. Some analog units are about as compact and easy to handle as digital models, while others are a bit bigger and bulkier.

➤ WHAT'S AVAILABLE

Sony dominates the camcorder market, with multiple models in a number of formats. Other top brands include Canon, JVC, Panasonic, and Sharp.

Most digital models come in one of two formats: MiniDV or Digital 8. New formats such as the disc-based DVD-RAM and DVD-R and tape-based MicroMV have also appeared. Some digital models weigh as little as one pound.

MiniDV. Don't let the size deceive you. Although some models can be slipped into a large pocket, MiniDV camcorders can record very high-quality images. They use a unique tape cassette, and the typical recording time is 60 minutes at SP (standard play) speed. Expect to pay $7 for a 60-minute tape. You'll need to use the camcorder for playback—it converts its recording to an analog signal, so it can be played directly into a TV or VCR. If the TV or VCR has an S-video input jack, you can use it to get the best possible picture. Price range: $475 to more than $2,000.

Digital 8. Also known as D8, this format gives you digital quality on Hi8 or 8mm cassettes, which cost $6.50 or $3.50 respectively, less than MiniDV cassettes. The Digital 8 format records with a faster tape speed, so a "120-minute" cassette lasts only

60 minutes at SP. Most models can also play your old analog Hi8 or 8mm tapes. Price range: $500 to $900.

Disc-based. Capitalizing on the explosive growth and capabilities of DVD movie discs, these formats offer benefits tape can't offer: long-term durability, a compact medium, and random access to scenes as with a DVD. The 3¼-inch discs record standard MPEG-2 video, the same format used in commercial DVD videos. The amount of recording time varies according to the quality level you select: from 20 minutes per side at the highest-quality setting for DVD-RAM, up to about 60 minutes per side at the lowest setting. DVD-RAM discs are not compatible with many DVD players, but the discs can be reused. DVD-R is compatible with most DVD players and computer DVD drives, but the discs are write-once. Expect to pay $25 for a blank disc.

Most analog camcorders come in one of three formats: VHS-C, Super VHS-C, and Hi8. They usually weigh around 2 pounds. Picture quality is generally good, though a notch below that of digital.

VHS-C. This format uses an adapter to play in any VHS VCR. Cassettes most commonly hold 30 minutes on SP and cost $3.50. Price range: $280 to $500.

Super VHS-C. S-VHS-C is the high-band variation of VHS-C and uses special S-VHS-C tapes. (A slightly different format, S-VHS/ET-C, can use standard VHS-C tapes.) The typical S-VHS-C tape yields 30 minutes at SP and costs $6.50. JVC is the only brand that offers models in this format. Price range: $300 to $500.

Hi8. This is the "high-band" variant of 8mm (an analog format that is virtually extinct). For full benefits, you need to use Hi8 tape and watch on a TV set that has an S-video input. A 120-minute cassette tape costs about $6.50. Price range: $200 to $400.

➤ KEY FEATURES

A flip-out **LCD viewer** is becoming commonplace on all but the lowest-priced camcorders. You'll find it useful for reviewing footage you've shot and easier to use than the eyepiece viewfinder for certain shooting poses. Some LCD viewers are hard to use in sunlight, a drawback on models that have only a viewer and no eyepiece.

Screens vary from 2½ to 4 inches measured diagonally, with a larger screen offered as a step-up feature on higher-priced models. Because an LCD viewer drains the battery pack faster than an eyepiece viewer does, you don't have as much recording time when using an LCD viewer.

> ▦ **TECH TIP**
> If your camcorder has an S-video jack, treat the connection with care. The jacks of two models in past tests made only intermittent contact with the plugs, crippling connections.

An **image stabilizer** automatically reduces most of the shakes from a scene you're capturing. Most stabilizers are electronic; a few are optical. Either type can be effective, though mounting the camcorder on a tripod is the surest way to get steady images. Designing a camcorder means trying to strike the proper balance between picture quality, low-light performance, and image stabilization; we've seldom seen a camcorder that excels in all three areas. If you need a camcorder with very good low-light capability, check the specs.

Full auto switch essentially lets you point and shoot. The camcorder automatically adjusts the color balance, shutter speed, focus, and aperture (also called the "iris" or f-stop with camcorders).

Autofocus adjusts for maximum sharpness; manual focus override may be needed for problem situations, such as low light. (With some camcorders, you may have to tap buttons repeatedly to get the focus just right.) With many camcorders, you can also control exposure, shutter speed, and white balance.

The **zoom** is typically a finger control—press one way to zoom in, the other way to widen the view. (The rate at which the zoom changes will depend on how hard you press the switch.) Typical optical zoom ratios range from 10:1 to 26:1. The zoom relies on optical lenses, just like a film camera (hence the term "optical zoom"). Many camcorders offer a digital zoom to extend the range to 400:1 or more, but at a lower picture quality.

Regardless of format, analog or digital, every camcorder displays **tape speeds** the same way as a VCR. Every model includes an SP (standard play) speed. MiniDV and Digital 8 types have a slower, LP (long play) speed, which adds 50 percent to the recording time. A few 8mm and Hi8 models have an LP speed that doubles the recording time. All VHS-C and S-VHS-C camcorders have an even slower, EP (extended play) speed that triples the recording time. With analog camcorders, slower speeds can worsen picture quality. Slow-speed picture quality doesn't suffer on digital camcorders. Using slow speed, however, means sacrificing some seldom-used editing options and may restrict playback on other camcorders. Disc-based formats offer different "quality" levels, such as Fine and Standard, to provide a choice of recording times.

Quick review lets you view the last few seconds of a scene without having to press a lot of buttons. For special lighting situations, preset **auto-exposure settings** can be helpful. A "snow & sand" setting, for example, adjusts shutter speed or aperture to accommodate the high reflectivity of snow and sand.

A **light** provides some illumination for close-ups when the image would otherwise be too dark. **Backlight** compensation increases the exposure slightly when your subject is lit from behind and silhouetted. **An infrared-sensitive recording mode** (also known as "night vision," "zero lux," or "MagicVu") allows shooting in very dim or dark situations, using infrared emitters. You may use it for nighttime shots, although colors won't register at all in this mode.

Some camcorders can double as a **digital still** camera. Digital cameras, however, are far better for still photos.

Audio/video inputs let you record material from another camcorder or from a VCR, useful for copying part of another video onto your own. (A digital camcorder must have such an input jack if you want to record analog material digitally.) Unlike a built-in microphone, an external microphone that is plugged into a **microphone jack** won't pick up noises from the camcorder itself, and it typically improves audio performance.

Features that may aid editing include a **built-in title generator,** a **time and date stamp,** and a **time code,** which is a frame reference of exactly where you are on a tape—the hour, second, and frame. A **remote control** helps when you're using the camcorder as a playback device or when using a tripod. **Programmed recording** ("self-timer") starts the camcorder recording at a preset time.

➤ HOW TO CHOOSE

Performance differences. Digital camcorders get high marks in CONSUMER REPORTS picture-quality tests. The top-performing models yield pictures that are sharp and free of streaks and other visual "noise" and have accurate color. Audio quality is not quite as impressive, at least using the built-in microphone. Still, digitals record pleasing sound that's devoid of audio flutter (a wavering in pitch that can make sounds seem thin and watery), if not exactly CD-like, as some models claim.

Typically, the best analog models we've tested are good—on a par with the lowest-scoring digitals. The lowest-scoring analog models delivered soft images that contained noticeable video noise and jitter, and they reproduced colors less accurately than any digital model. And while sound for 8mm and Hi8 analog camcorders is practically free of audio flutter, all the VHS-C analog camcorders suffered from some degree of that audio-signal problem.

Recommendations. If you don't want to spend a lot, an analog camcorder is a good value—many are now priced at about $300. Analog models may also appeal to you if you have little interest in video editing. If you want to upgrade, however, consider a digital model. Prices are as low as $500 and are continuing to fall.

Try before you buy. Make sure a camcorder fits comfortably in your hand and has controls that are easy to reach.

Related CR report: November 2002
Ratings: page 216
Reliability: page 331

CAMERAS, DIGITAL

Digital photography allows you to be more involved in the creation of the print than film photography. That's a plus or a minus, depending upon your point of view.

Digital cameras, which employ reusable memory cards instead of film, give you far more creative control than film cameras can. With a digital camera, you can transfer shots to your computer, then crop, adjust color and contrast, and add textures and other special effects. Final results can be made into cards or even T-shirts, or sent via e-mail, all using the software that usually comes with the camera. You can make prints on a color inkjet printer, drop off the memory card at one of a growing number of photofinishers, or upload the file to a photo-sharing web site for storage, viewing, or reprinting.

Digital cameras share many features with digital camcorders. They also share some features with film cameras, such as focus and flash options. Some camcorders can be used to take still pictures, but a typical camcorder's resolution is no match for a good still camera's.

> **WHAT'S AVAILABLE**

The leading brands are Kodak, Nikon, Olympus, and Sony; other brands come from consumer-electronics, computer-imaging, and traditional camera and film companies.

Digital cameras are typically categorized by how many pixels, or picture elements, the image sensor contains. A 1-megapixel camera has 1 million such elements. The more pixels, the sharper the image can be. A 1-megapixel model makes sharp 5x7-inch prints and very good 8x10s; 2- and 3-megapixel models can make excellent 8x10s and pleasing 11x14s. There are also 4-, 5-, and 6-megapixel models, which are well suited for making larger prints or for maintaining sharpness if you want to use only a portion of the original image.

Price range: 1-megapixel models, $150 to $250; 2-megapixel, $200 to $600; 3-megapixel, $350 to $800; 4-megapixel and up, $400 to $1,000 or more.

> **KEY FEATURES**

Most digital cameras are highly automated, with features such as **automatic exposure control** (which manages the shutter speed, aperture, or both according to available light) and **autofocus.**

Instead of film, digital cameras typically record their shots onto **flash-memory cards.** CompactFlash and SmartMedia, which come in capacities of 8 to 512 megabytes, are the most widely used. Once quite expensive, such cards have tumbled in price—a 64-megabyte card can now cost less than $50. A few cameras store shots on a MemoryStick or an SD card. A few newer cameras use 3¼-inch CD-R or CD-RW discs.

To save images, you transfer them to a computer, typically by connecting the camera to the computer's USB or serial port or inserting the memory card into a special reader. Some printers can take memory cards and make prints without putting the images on a computer first. **Image-handling software** such as Adobe PhotoDeluxe, MGI PhotoSuite, Microsoft Picture It, and Ulead PhotoImpact lets you size, touch up, and crop digital images using your computer. Most digital cameras work with Windows or Macintosh machines.

The **file format** commonly used for photos is the highly compressed JPEG. (It's also used for photos on the Internet.) Some cameras can save photos in uncompressed TIFF format, but this setting yields enormous files.

Digital cameras typically have both an **optical viewfinder** and a small color **LCD viewer.** LCD viewers are very accurate in framing what you get—better than most of the optical viewfinders, but they gobble up battery power and can be hard to see in bright sunlight. You can also view shots you've already taken on the LCD. Many digital cameras provide a video output, so you can view your pictures on a TV set.

Certain cameras let you record an **audio clip** with a picture. But these clips devour storage space. Some allow you to record limited video, but the frame rate is slow and the resolution poor.

A **zoom lens** provides flexibility in framing shots and closes the distance between you and your subject—ideal if you want to quickly switch to a close shot. A 3x zoom is comparable to a 35-to-105-mm lens on a film camera; a 2x zoom, to a 35-to-70-mm lens. **Optical zooms** are superior to **digital zooms,** which magnify the center of the frame without actually increasing picture detail, resulting in a somewhat coarser view.

Sensors in digital cameras are typically about as light-sensitive as ISO 100 film, though some let you increase that setting. (At ISO 100, you'll likely need to use a flash indoors and in low outdoor light.) A camera's **flash range** tells you how far from the camera the flash will provide proper exposure: If the subject is out of range, you'll know to close the distance. But digital cameras tolerate some underexposure before the image suffers noticeably.

Red-eye reduction shines a light toward your subject just before the main flash. (A camera whose flash unit is farther from the lens reduces the risk of red eye. Computer editing may also correct red eye.) With **automatic flash** mode, the camera fires the flash whenever the light entering the camera registers as insufficient.

➤ HOW TO CHOOSE

Performance differences. In CONSUMER REPORTS' most recent tests, image colors looked fine. Digital cameras did much better with fluorescent lighting than regular film processing labs have done. (Fluorescent lighting can give film photos a greenish cast.) Tests have also shown that a higher pixel count alone doesn't necessarily produce better picture quality.

The image-handling software provided with a digital camera is generally easy to use. The results are usually pleasing—or readily altered further if you are not satisfied. The software does have its limits, though. It can't fix an out-of-focus image, for example.

Recommendations. A 2-megapixel model is likely to offer you the best overall value: good quality at a relatively moderate price. Look for a camera with a 3x optical zoom lens and good image-handling software.

A 1-megapixel model is fine for small snapshots you e-mail to friends, but it's not the best choice for 8x10 enlargements.

A 3-megapixel camera provides some breathing room: files large enough for enlargements, yet not so gargantuan than you'll have difficulty saving, storing, or e-mailing them.

The current high-end consumer cameras —those in the 4- to 6-megapixel range, are for people with plenty of cash and who need a camera verging on professional-grade for special uses.

When comparing cameras, be sure you compare the so-called native pixel count. Some cameras employ software that lets them share pixels and raise the apparent pixel count.

Try before you buy. Quite a few digital cameras offer a shallow grip or no grip. Some LCD viewers are awkwardly situated and could easily be soiled with nose or thumbprints. If you wear glasses, you might look for a camera viewfinder with a diopter adjustment that may allow you to see the image without your glasses while using the camera.

The image-handling software provided with a digital camera is generally easy to use. The results are usually pleasing—or readily altered further if you are not satisfied. The software does have its limits, though. It can't fix an out-of-focus image, for example.

Related CR report: November 2002
Ratings: page 221

CAMERAS, FILM

A point-and-shoot camera doesn't require elaborate setup before the shot. Single-lens reflex models offer maximum versatility and can also be easy to use.

A film camera remains a good choice if you want point-and-shoot simplicity and good quality for relatively low cost. The same goes for anyone who wants color prints without a lot of fuss and isn't especially concerned about ordering reprints or editing photos.

If you want more control over your pictures after you've shot them—editing, publishing, or e-mailing—consider digital cameras, which are winning converts with increasing capability and easier use without an increase in price.

But you need not necessarily go digital for some of a digital camera's benefits: When you drop off a roll for processing, you can order digital storage along with your prints. Other options include scanning negatives or prints using a computer and scanner.

> **WHAT'S AVAILABLE**
Major camera companies include Canon, Fuji, Kodak, Minolta, Nikon, Olympus, and Pentax. Most make point-and-shoot cameras in both 35mm and APS (advanced photo system) formats. Many of those companies also make single-lens reflex (SLR) models.

Cameras these days, no matter the format, are highly automated. Flashes are built into practically all point-and-shoot models and some SLR models. Low-priced film cameras are fixed-focus, like an old-fashioned box camera. Features that raise the price include autofocus, automatic exposure control, automatic film winding, and a zoom lens.

Compact 35mm cameras. Small, light, and inexpensive, these cameras are capable of producing exceptional photos. They're adequate for travel scenes and group shots. More expensive models include a zoom lens and many automated features. Some can shoot in panoramic mode, giving a 3½x10-inch or 4x11½-inch photo. The lens does not actually cover a wider angle in this mode; the panoramic shape is achieved by cropping off the top and bottom of the image. Price range: $5 to $12 for single-use cameras; $20 and up for fixed-focus models; $50 and up for automatic, nonzoom cameras; and $70 and up for a model with a zoom.

APS cameras. These models use film that you never see out of its cartridge, and an accompanying magnetic coating can store such information as processing instructions and the date of the snapshot. Since APS film is smaller than 35mm film, these cameras tend to be smaller and lighter still. The format allows great flexibility—you can switch from regular to wide (semipanoramic) to panoramic in midroll. Film handling is easy. One-hour processing for this format is less widely available, however, and the cost is generally more for film and processing. Price range for APS models: same as the price range for compact 35mm.

35mm SLRs. Bulkier than point-and-shoot models, SLR cameras with interchangeable lenses let you see what the camera sees. Unlike a point-and-shoot, an SLR lets you compose a shot precisely, without the uncertainty of capturing content not shown in the viewfinder. Such exactitude gives a great deal of artistic control, and the generally high quality optics deliver the best image quality. SLRs are typically sold without a lens or are bundled with a zoom lens. Price range: $200 and up for the camera body, $100 and up for a moderate-range zoom lens.

> **KEY FEATURES**

A **zoom lens,** magnifying your subject two or three times or so, is available on many point-and-shoot models. The 35mm zoom lenses range from about 38 mm (fairly wide angle) to about 105 mm (a moderate telephoto). APS zoom ranges are comparable. Pricing is typically determined by the complexity of the lens design. You'll pay more for a "faster" lens, such as a 100-mm zoom that opens to f/3.5 to allow more light in than another 100-mm lens with an f/4.5 maximum aperture.

Most cameras automate exposure partially or fully. **Aperture** governs how wide the camera should open the lens when you take a picture. Using identical-speed film and the same shutter speed, the wider the aperture a lens can manage, the better your odds of taking good pictures indoors without a flash (and the more the lens likely costs). **Shutter speed** governs how long the aperture stays open during a shot. Fast shutter speed (1/1,000 to 1/8,000 of a second or so) lets you shoot fast-moving subjects.

Auto exposure regulates the shutter speed and aperture to get a properly exposed photo, whether in bright light or low light. An **exposure-compensation feature** prevents underexposure when the background is bright or overexposure when the background is unusually dark compared with the subject. SLRs can often set the speed or aperture automatically, after the user has manually set the other setting as needed for a particular shot (if you set the aperture, it sets the shutter speed; if you set the speed, it sets the aperture). These and more advanced compact models may offer several preset exposure modes that suit various situations.

Autofocus frees you from having to focus the camera to ensure crisp pictures; low-end cameras typically cover preset ranges, permitting quick shots but dispensing with the more precise focusing of higher-priced models. **Multi-area autofocus** reduces the risk of focusing on the background in a scene by accident. **Focus lock** lets you freeze the focus onto who or what appears in the center of the viewfinder, helpful for when you'd like to focus on a subject and then shift the camera's aim. Compact film cameras typically use an infrared beam to focus. **In-the-viewfinder signals** in many models let you know when the subject is too close to be in focus or when it's out of flash range.

Motorized film handling automatically advances the film and rewinds it at the end of the roll. With a 35mm camera, you drop the film in, pull out the leader, and close the camera; with APS, you merely drop the film in. **Midroll change,** a feature found in some APS cameras, lets you reload partially exposed rolls of film—useful if you often switch between high- and low-speed film.

Flashes cover various distances, from 4 or 5 feet to 10 feet or more. The smartest ones work with the zoom lens to broaden or narrow the beam. **Flash on demand** lets you fill in harsh shadows in bright, sunlit portraits. "Red eye" occurs when a flash reflects off people's and animals' retinas; **red-eye reduction** typically uses a light before the main flash to constrict the subject's pupils. (Flashes that are farther from the lens reduce red eye to begin with.)

Some cameras are **weatherproof,** handy if you take the camera to the beach or boating. Certain models also offer options such as a **wireless remote shutter release** or the ability to imprint photos with the date taken.

> **HOW TO CHOOSE**

Performance differences. Whether they take 35mm or the newer APS film, conventional film cameras have attained a fairly high level of quality. CONSUMER REPORTS regular tests of autofocus zoom-lens cameras shows that the lens quality is high. As a result, nearly all can produce very pleasing snapshots—sharp, properly focused, with little distortion or other drawbacks. But, of course, the cameras don't perform identically. While SLR cameras show you exactly what will appear on film, viewfinders of even the best point-and-shoot cameras show about 90 percent of the area that actually appears on film. With some, you see only about two-thirds of what's on film, so the prints may contain unwanted, distracting detail around the edges.

Also, don't expect too much from the built-in flash that is standard on point-and-shoot cameras. External-flash units, such as the detachable ones available for some compacts and most SLRs, provide more light for your subject than the built-in flashes.

Recommendations. Spending more gets you more features and often better optics. Nevertheless, you can expect a fairly high level of quality from 35mm point-and-shoot models, even from a very low-priced camera. CONSUMER REPORTS tests over the years have shown that nearly all cameras in this class can produce very good, sometimes excellent snapshots.

Despite their smaller negative size, APS cameras often produce prints as clear as those of 35mm cameras, particularly if they aren't enlarged greatly, and they offer the versatility of switching from normal to wide-angle to panoramic shots from one frame to the next within a roll. For the very best in versatility and image quality, however, 35mm SLR models remain the best, if bulkier, choice—however more complex and expensive they are.

Related CR report: November 2001

CD PLAYERS

The familiar console CD player is rapidly being replaced by more capable devices.

Delivering superb performance at an affordable price, the CD is the music medium of the moment, having turned vinyl LPs into niche products for audiophiles and music collectors. But regular console CD players are losing ground to DVD players, which can play CDs along with DVDs, and to units that can record as well as play CDs.

Niche models are still thriving. Jukebox models can hold hundreds of discs. Portable players are now incorporating MP3 capabilities.

➤ **WHAT'S AVAILABLE**

Sony dominates the CD-player category, making nearly one in three CD players sold. Other big sellers are Pioneer and Technics.

Console models. Single-disc models have virtually disappeared. Multiple-disc changers, typically holding five or six discs, can play hours of music nonstop. A magazine changer uses a slide-in cartridge the size of a small, thick book. Cartridges double as convenient disc storage boxes. Carousel changers are easier to load and unload than the magazine type. (Most let you change waiting discs without interrupting the music.) They've taken over the market. Price range: $100 to $250.

Megachangers. Also known as CD jukeboxes, these typically store 100 to 400 discs. Marketed as a way to manage and store an entire music collection, most models let you segment a collection by music genre, composer, artist, and so forth. The unit flashes album titles as you hunt through the discs. Inputting all the necessary data can be a tedious task (made easier on models that connect to a computer keyboard). But it's worth the effort, because you can then set a jukebox to shuffle and play random selections all night or play discs only from your genre choice. To fit all those CDs, megachangers can be quite large. In fact, some may not fit the typical stereo rack. And all models aren't equally efficient: Some are inconvenient to load, or noisy and slow in selecting CDs. Price range: $170 to $450.

Portable players. Small, sporty, and single-disc, these have simple controls. A growing number of models also play CDs you record yourself, using both the CD-R and CD-RW formats and digital file formats such as MP3. Early portables often skipped or had poor-quality headphones. Today's players skip less, and many have good headphones that will convey decent sound. But some still have mediocre headphones; you'll enjoy better listening if you replace them.

Battery life is improving, but it varies considerably from model to model: In CONSUMER REPORTS latest tests, batteries typically lasted 16 to 30 hours but went as high as 40 hours. Some models come with an AC adapter, and some have a built-in battery charger. Most portable players can be connected to other audio gear and in that case many will play music as well as any home unit. Price range: $30 to $200.

➤ **KEY FEATURES**

Console models come with more features than portables. Their controls should be easy to see in dim light. A **calendar display** shows a block of numbers indicating the tracks on the active disc and highlighting the current track. As play continues, previous track numbers disappear—you can quickly see how many selections are left. A **numeric keypad** on the remote gets you to a particular track more quickly than pressing Up or Down buttons.

A **remote control** is convenient and now nearly standard equipment. Buttons should be grouped by function or color-coded and should be visible in dim light. Most CD remotes operate the player only. Some changers and jukeboxes have a handy **single-play drawer** or slot so you can play a single disc without disturbing any already loaded. **Cataloging** capability offers various ways to keep track of the many CDs stored inside a jukebox, such as categorizing by genre.

Memory features that make track selection easy include **delete track,** which allows you to skip specified tracks but otherwise play a disc from start to finish, and **favorite track** program memory, which lets you mark your preferences. **Music sampling** (also called track scan) plays a few seconds of each selection. Most models can be programmed to play tracks in sequence, to shuffle play (look for non-repeat shuffle), or to repeat a track. A **volume-limiter switch** lets you hear softer passages without having other sounds at ear-splitting levels.

People who do a lot of taping will appreciate **auto edit** (also called time fit for recording): You enter the cassette's recording time, and the CD player lays out the disc's tracks, usually in sequence, to fill both sides of your tape. With **comprehensive time display,** you check time elapsed and time remaining for the current track and for the entire disc. **Running-time total** lets you total the time of tracks to be recorded to fit the maximum on a tape. **Music-peak finder** scans for the loudest passage in a track you're going to record, allowing you to adjust the tape deck's recording level correctly and quickly. **Fade out/fade in** performs the audio equivalent of a movie fade for less abrupt starts and endings. **Auto spacing** inserts a few seconds of silence between tracks.

With a **synchronizing jack,** you can connect a cable to a tape deck of the same brand so you can run both machines simultaneously. Those recording digitally to a MiniDisc recorder or a digital tape deck need a **digital output jack** to attach a fiber-optic or coaxial cable.

Portable features focus on sound-quality enhancement and power management. Most portables have a **bass-boost control** to compensate for the thin bass of poorer headphones. Some have a **digital signal processor** (DSP), which electronically simulates the ambience of concert-hall music.

Most portables have a **liquid crystal display** (LCD) showing which track is playing and a **battery-level indicator** that warns of low batteries. (The best indicators show a shrinking scale to reflect power remaining.) An **AC adapter** runs the player on house current and enables some players to charge rechargeable cells. Rechargeable batteries may cost extra.

Colorful "sports" models tend to be pricier than the rest of the pack and differ in a few other respects: Their lid is secured with a **latch** and sealed with a **rubber gasket,** and they have **rubberized plugs** covering jacks for an AC adapter and headphones. The latch keeps the lid closed so successfully that some sports models are a bit hard to open. The gasket and plugs help resist sand, dirt, and moisture, though you'll need to wipe off a player that's dusty or wet before you open it. Keep in mind that these players are **water-resistant,** not waterproof—the difference between a splash and total immersion.

A car kit, standard with some portables, consists of an **adapter** that powers the unit through a car's cigarette lighter and a **cassette adapter** that pipes the player's sound through the car's tape player and speakers. (You can also buy aftermarket kits at electronics or auto-supply stores.) Some adapters. CONSUMER REPORTS tests showed, add noise to the sound or otherwise compromised performance. A **line-out jack** is a better choice than the headphone jack for connecting a portable to a component receiver or other gear.

➤ HOW TO CHOOSE

Performance differences. Many CD players can produce excellent sound—accurate tonal balance and free of coloration or distortion. However, not all CD players are equally convenient to use.

Better home units have an uncluttered front-panel display with clearly labeled main buttons grouped together by function. They also include features that make it easy to produce tapes from CDs. For portable players, skip-free performance depends on a good buffer, a memory feature that scans the disc, continuously storing upcoming music (typically from 10 to 45 seconds, sometimes more) so the player won't cause audio dropouts. CONSUMER REPORTS tests also found that good shock absorption of the lower assembly that records the disc is also important. Some models skipped with just a mild jouncing, others only when jolted hard. Battery life in recent tests varied from 5 to 40 hours of continuous play.

Headphones differ in comfort and performance. Comfort is very subjective, depending on the individual. Headphones tested by CONSUMER REPORTS ranged from decent to mediocre. For some models, at least, you can improve sound by buying replacement headphones. A decent set

---

DVD-AUDIO AND SACD

Two new audio formats

DVD-Audio and Super Audio CD (SACD) are formats that encode music into up to six channels, promising fuller, richer sound than from stereo CDs. Relatively few players can handle these formats. You should have six full-range speakers for optimal sound.

Both formats include interesting extras. SACD discs include song/artist identification that shows up on some players, and have the potential for graphics or video. Some SACD discs have a CD layer that allows them to deliver stereo sound on a plain CD player or a DVD player.

DVD-A music discs can include video, such as still pictures, slide shows, and short full-motion clips. DVD-A players have a video output that connects to a TV set. Releases often include a Dolby Digital 5.1 or DTS version of the program for playback on conventional DVD players–backward compatibility for users who intend to, but haven't yet, invested in a DVD-A player.

In recent CONSUMER REPORTS tests, sound quality was subtly better than what you'd hear on a standard CD or DVD player, but you'd need a superb audio system to appreciate the difference.

DVD players with DVD-A support start at about $300. SACD-compatible DVD players start at about $300. A few models can play both formats. Few discs currently come in these formats, and it's not clear how widespread they will be.

costs about $10 to $30.

Recommendations. If you're looking to play CDs in a home-theater setup, consider getting a DVD player instead of a CD player. Some are nearly as cheap as CD players are now. They've become less expensive. The price of CD player/recorders has also dropped enough to make them a reasonable alternative, with the premium for the extra functionality perhaps $100.

If you want to play only CDs, a multidisc changer will save you from having to swap discs in and out. Shoppers for portable players should weigh battery life heavily if they're frequent listeners or pay particular attention to antiskip performance if they're active users.

Related CR report: September 2002
Ratings: page 225

CD PLAYER/ RECORDERS

These devices make it easy to "burn" the music you want onto CDs. Because it's all digital, copies show no loss of quality.

Audio CD player/recorders let you make your own recordings and play back prerecorded material. They still cost more than CD players without recording capability, but prices are dropping. They sell as standalone units and as components of some minisystems.

There's another way to make your own music CDs: Record them using a computer. CD drives that burn CDs are now standard on many computers and can be as adept as component CD player/recorders, often doing it faster.

Both CD player/recorders and computer CD burners let you copy entire discs or dub selected tracks to create your own CD compilations. There's no quality lost in high-speed CD-to-CD dubbing. Recording speeds usually are real-time or 4x, which records in one-quarter of that time. (Computer CD burners can be as fast as 16x.) With either approach, you can record to CD-Rs (discs you can record on only once) or to CD-RWs (rewritable discs that can be erased and rerecorded). CD-Rs play on almost any CD player, whereas CD-RWs generally play only on new disc players that are configured to accept them. Note that some older DVD players have problems reading CD-R and CD-RW discs.

➤ **WHAT'S AVAILABLE**
Audio CD player/recorders come from audio-component companies such as Denon, Harmon-Kardon, JVC, Philips, and Pioneer.

Dual-tray and changer models. One tray is for play/record, another for play. Price range: $300 to $800.

Changer models. These hold multiple discs, usually three for play and the fourth for play/record. Price range for dual-tray and changer models: $300 to $800.

➤ **KEY FEATURES**
Programming. The computer approach makes compiling "mix" discs pretty easy. Once a blank CD is inserted into a computer CD drive, the accompanying software displays a track list and allows you to "drag" the desired tracks into the lower panel. As you insert successive CDs, you can see the **playlist** for your CD-to-be and even change the order of the tracks, combine two or more tracks or files into one, or split a track or file into two or more. With CD recorders, you program your selections from up to three discs installed in the changer; the steps will be familiar to anyone

who has programmed a CD changer. Most units give you a **running total** of the accumulated time of the tracks as you are programming them.

With both the computer option and a CD player/recorder, you must program selections from each disc in succession.

Defining tracks on the CD onto which you're recording is accomplished with varying degrees of flexibility. How many track numbers a given player/recorder can add per disc, for example, differs from one model to another; additionally, assigning track numbers when you're recording from cassettes may be automatic or manual. (Such tracks are inserted automatically when recording from CDs.)

Text labeling lets you type in short text passages such as artist and song names, a much easier procedure with a computer keyboard than with a console's remote control.

> ### ▓ TECH TIP
> **Blank discs for use in computers can't be used in CD players/recorders. Look for the words "for digital audio recorders" on the package. Discs for music cost more than ones for computers. The price includes a surcharge to cover royalties that the music industry believes should be paid to musicians.**

The number of delete-track modes grants you flexibility, whether you need to delete one track or the entire disc. One-track, Multitrack, and All-disc are three common modes.

An audio CD player/recorder typically has three playback modes: Program is used to play tracks in a specific order; Repeat plays a track again; and Random Play (or Shuffle) plays tracks randomly.

Connection types can affect what external sources you're able to use to make a CD. A digital input jack may be optical or coaxial. An analog input jack lets you record your tapes and LPs. A **microphone**

input offers a low-cost way for home musicians to make digital recordings of their performances. A **record-level control** helps you control loudness while recording digitally from analog sources—a problem you don't face when recording from digital sources. An **input selector,** included on some models, makes for faster connections than going through a menu process.

➤ HOW TO CHOOSE

Performance differences. Either method of burning a CD, using an audio CD player/recorder or a computer, makes a recording that's audibly (even electronically) indistinguishable from the original CD.

Audio CD player/recorders excel in versatility; you can record from CDs, LPs, cassettes, and even TV or radio sound (anything, in fact, that you can connect to a sound system's receiver). This method is the clear standout for recording LPs, since connecting a turntable to a computer requires additional equipment.

The computer method has its own strengths. Because it affords a connection to the Internet, the computer option lets you burn downloaded MP3-encoded files onto CDs. A computer offers more setup choices when you're assembling your own CD from several prerecorded discs. And when you're recording from analog sources, the computer's burning software often includes sound processing that will reduce the snap and crackle of a vinyl LP or the tape hiss of a cassette tape.

Recommendations. The relatively low cost of making high-quality CDs makes CD recording a good alternative to making cassette tapes. If you're buying a CD player/recorder, first consider a changer model; its multidisc magazine or carousel will make it easy to record compilation CDs or to play uninterrupted music.

The computer-based CD-recording option allows you to record music from both CDs and the Internet. If you don't already have a CD-burning drive in your computer, you can buy it and the necessary software for about $160 to $250. If you're buying a new computer, you'll find that a CD-RW drive is standard equipment on many models. We'd expect any CD-burner drive to perform competently.

Related CR report: November 2000

DVD PLAYERS

These play high-quality video and also play CDs. Prices are surprisingly low.

As the fastest-growing consumer-electronics product in history—more than 13 million units were sold in 2001 alone—DVD players offer picture and sound quality that clearly surpasses what you'll get with a VCR. DVDs are CD-size discs that can contain a complete two-hour-plus movie with a six-channel Dolby Digital or DTS soundtrack, plus extra material such as multiple languages, interviews, additional camera angles for chosen scenes, behind-the-scenes documentaries, and even entire replays of the movie with commentary by the director.

DVD players also play standard audio CDs. Prices on multidisc models are low enough for a DVD player to serve as a practical stand-in for a CD player. There is a catch if you record your own CDs: Some models may still have problems reading the CD-R and CD-RW discs that you record yourself.

The DVD player is still a product in transition. New capabilities include being able to play DVD-Audio or Super Audio CD (SACD), two competing high-resolution audio formats designed to offer two- to six-channel sound. Coming are rea-

sonably priced DVD recorders. For recording your favorite TV programs, VCRs or digital video recorders are the way to go for now.

➤ WHAT'S AVAILABLE

Apex, Panasonic, Sony, and Toshiba are among the biggest-selling brands. DVD players are rapidly changing as manufacturers seek to differentiate their products and come up with a winning combination of features. You can choose from a console or portable model. Some consoles offer built-in karaoke features, MP3 and Windows Media playback, or the ability to play video games.

Single-disc consoles. Console models can be connected directly to your TV for viewing movies or routed through your receiver to play movies and audio CDs on your home-entertainment system. More low-end models include all the video-output jacks you might want. Price range: less than $100 to more than $800.

Multidisc consoles. Like CD changers, these players accommodate two to five discs. DVD jukeboxes that hold up to 300 discs are also available. Price range: $200 to $1,000.

Progressive scan. Some DVD players are so-called progressive scan models. This provides HD-ready TVs with a sharper, more stable image by letting the set draw 480 consecutive lines of the image 60 times per second. (On a conventional TV, typically every other line is redrawn at that rate.) You can use them with a conventional TV, but you'll see the added benefit only with a set that supports 480p, such as a high-definition or HD-ready set. Price range: $200 to $300.

Portables. These DVD players generally come with small but crisp widescreen-format LCD screens and batteries that claim to provide three hours or more of playback. Some low-priced models don't come with screens; they're intended for users who plan connections only to TVs. You pay extra for the portability either way. Price range: $200 to $1,000.

➤ **KEY FEATURES**

DVD-based movies often come in various formats. **Aspect-ratio control** sometimes lets you choose between the 4:3 viewing format of conventional TVs (4 inches wide for every 3 inches high) and the 16:9 of newer, wide-screen sets. Portable DVD players with screens are generally in wide-screen format.

A DVD player gives you all sorts of control over the picture—control you may never have known you needed. **Picture zoom** lets you zoom in on a specific frame. **Reverse frame-by-frame** gives you backward incremental movement in addition to the **forward frame-by-frame** and **slow motion** that most players provide.

Black-level adjustment brings out the detail in dark parts of the screen image. If you've ever wanted to see certain action scenes from different angles, **multiangle capability** gives you that opportunity. Note that this feature and some others work only with certain discs.

Navigation around a DVD is easy. Unlike a VHS tape, DVDs are sectioned for easy navigation. **Chapter preview** lets you scan the opening seconds of each section or chapter until you find what you want. **Go-to by time** lets you enter how many hours and minutes into the disc you'd like to skip to. **Marker functions** allow easy indexing of specific sections.

A **composite connection** can produce a very good picture, but there will be some

---

TWO-IN-ONE PRODUCTS

VCR/DVD combo players

DVD players are the hot electronics product, gaining favor for playing movies, though VCRs are still the device of choice for recording TV programming. Some consumers are trying to hedge their bets–and save space–by buying combination VCR/DVD players.

Combo players have many pluses. They measure only slightly larger than a VCR alone. Like separate units, they let you play a DVD or CD while recording something on videotape. Most allow you to copy DVD content onto tape, but only if the DVD has not been copy-protected (so forget about most movies). With combo units, there's only one device to connect to your TV. Some will work with the cable/antenna input that may be the only choice on older sets, but if you have a newer TV and don't mind making multiple connections, you can get better video by connecting the VCR and DVD to the TV's S-video, composite video, or

component video inputs.

There are downsides to a hybrid device, however. Combination units may be less likely to have various features, such as VCR Plus, a feature that can simplify programmed recording, or the ability to see a gallery of still shots from a DVD's chapters. The combo units we recently tested didn't match stand-alone VCRs for picture quality, although the DVD picture quality was fine. If either component breaks you may lose both, because they share some common circuitry.

If CONSUMER REPORTS' experience is any indication, you get more for your money buying separate devices. A $70 VCR and a $100 DVD player could give you more features than a combo unit costing $200 to $300. Still, if compact size and easy connections are your top priorities, a VCR/DVD player combo may be just the ticket.

loss of detail and some color artifacts such as adjacent colors bleeding into each other. An **S-video output** can improve picture quality. It keeps the black-and-white and the color signals separated, producing more picture detail and fewer color defects than standard composite video.

Component video, the best connection you can get on a DVD player (but possibly lacking on the lowest-end models), improves on S-video by splitting the color signal, resulting in a wider range of color. If you use a DVD player attached with an S-video or component connection, don't be surprised if you have to adjust the TV-picture setup when you switch to a picture coming from a VCR or a cable box that uses a radio-frequency connection or composite connection.

One selling point of DVD is the ability to enjoy movies with **multichannel surround sound.** To reap the full benefits of the audio that's encoded into DVD titles, you'll need a Dolby Digital receiver and six speakers, counting a subwoofer. **Dolby Digital decoding built-in** refers to circuitry that lets a DVD player decode the six-channel audio encoded into DVD discs; without the built-in circuitry, you'd need to have the decoder built into the receiver or use a separate decoder box to take advantage of six-channel audio. (A Dolby Digital receiver will decode an older format, Dolby Pro Logic, as well.) Players also may support **Digital Theater System (DTS) decoding** for titles using that six-channel encoding format. When you're watching DVD-based movies, **dynamic audio-range control** helps keep explosions and other noisy sound effects from seeming too loud.

DVD players also provide features such as **multilingual support,** which lets you choose dialogue or subtitles in different languages for a given movie. **Parental con-**trol** lets parents "lock out" films by their rating code.

> **HOW TO CHOOSE**

Performance differences. In CONSUMER REPORTS tests, most DVD players delivered excellent picture quality, all but eliminating noise, jitter, and other aberrations typical of pictures from a VCR. They also offered CD-quality sound and, depending on the program material, multichannel capability. Some models may be more convenient to use than others. Remote controls vary considerably, so it's worth checking them out before making a purchase.

Recommendations. A DVD player offers better picture quality for movies than a VCR—and more and more movies are being sold or rented in the DVD format. Provided you have the receiver and speakers to back it up, the sound is also superior to that of a VCR.

You'll need a VCR or a DVR to record, however. Even a low-end DVD player will provide excellent video and audio. A single-disc model is cheaper, and it should do the job if you watch mostly movies. A multidisc console makes more sense if you also plan to play music CDs.

> **TECH TIP**
> If you're connecting a DVD player to an older TV with only an antenna input, you'll need to add a special converter to convert the DVD player's composite video and audio output signal to an RF output signal.

If your audio/video setup includes a receiver with built-in Dolby Digital and DTS decoding, you don't need to pay the premium to get these decoders on your DVD player. Such models tend to be among the more expensive. Even a low-end player will allow you to enjoy six-channel surround sound, assuming you have the required speakers.

If you plan to buy a digital TV, it may be

worthwhile paying a little bit extra to get a progressive-scan DVD player. It will work with your conventional TV now and allow you to take advantage of the superior video quality when you get your digital set.
Related CR report: December 2002

DIGITAL VIDEO RECORDERS

DVRs outdo VCRs in many ways, but you'll still need a VCR to archive recordings.

Digital video recorders (DVRs) combine the easy navigation of a DVD player with the recording capability of a VCR and the convenience of a program guide. These set-top receivers have hard drives much like those in computers, generally with space for 20 to 60 hours of programming, although capacities can go as high as 320 hours. Some DVRs are integrated into devices such as satellite-TV receivers or digital TV decoders. Depending on which provider and plan you choose, you usually pay for the service as well as the equipment—either a one-time activation charge or a monthly fee on top of your current cable or satellite-TV bill.

Because they can record and play at the same time, DVRs allow you to pause (and rewind or fast-forward) the current show you're watching, picking up where you left off. Should you pause a one-hour show for 10 or 15 minutes at the beginning, you can resume watching it, skip past all the commercials, and catch up to the actual live broadcast by the end of the show. Dual-tuner models can record two programs at once, even as you're watching a third recorded program.

A DVR does not replace your usual programming source. You must still get broadcasts via cable, satellite service, or antenna. Program guides are downloaded via your phone line, generally late at night to avoid tying up the line. These guides are customized according to which broadcast channels are available in your area and which cable or satellite service you subscribe to.

➤ **WHAT'S AVAILABLE**
Most DVRs resemble VCRs in size and shape but don't have a slot for a tape or disc. (The internal hard drive is not removable.) They connect to your television like a cable or satellite receiver, using composite, S-video, or RF antenna outputs to match the input of your set.

There are only two service providers, TiVo and ReplayTV. Hardware prices depend mostly on how many hours of programming you can store; service charges vary. The DVRs intended for use with one provider will not work with the other.

TiVo, the older of the two companies, has offered service since late 1999. You can buy the equipment directly from TiVo, from AT&T Broadband, or from Hughes or Sony under their brand names. Price range: $300 to $400. Service requires a paid subscription of $13 per month or $250 for the life of the DVR (transferable if you sell it). You can also get a DirectTV satellite receiver that incorporates TiVo capability. Price range: about $400, but often discounted; TiVo service charges (with the purchase of a satellite receiver, $10 a month or a one-time fee of $250) still apply.

Recently acquired by SonicBlue, ReplayTV offers some models bundled with lifetime service included in the equipment price. Newer models don't include service in the purchase price but carry a one-time activation fee of $250. In either case, you must buy equipment directly from the company. Price: $450 to $1,800. Some ReplayTV models let you distribute programs to other ReplayTV owners via the Internet. ABC, CBS, and NBC and their parent companies have filed suit against SonicBlue, citing copyright concerns.

> ## KEY FEATURES

A recorder's **hard-drive capacity** varies in actual usage. Like digital cameras, DVRs record at **different compression settings** and thus different quality levels. For the best image quality, you have to record programming at the DVR's lowest level of compression. To get the maximum capacity advertised, you have to use the highest level of compression, which gives the lowest quality. For example, a model that advertises a 30-hour maximum capacity will fit only about 9 hours at its best-quality setting.

The **program guide** is an interactive list of the programs that can be recorded by the DVR for the next 7 to 10 days. You can use it to select the show currently being broadcast to watch or record—or you can search it by title, artist, or show type for programs you want to record automatically in the future. **Custom channels,** available with some models, are individualized groupings of programs according to your preferences; the feature allows you to set up your own "channel" for something like crime dramas, or appearances by William Shatner, whether on "Star Trek," a talk show, or any other programming. A DVR can also record a specified show every time it runs.

A **remote control** is standard. Common features include **instant replay, fast-forward, rewind,** and **pause** of a live program. The newest ReplayTV models allow users to **stream video** to other ReplayTV units in the home using an Ethernet port.

> ## HOW TO CHOOSE

Performance differences. At the highest-quality settings, the picture quality of DVRs in recent CONSUMER REPORTS tests fell below that of most DVD players and was on a par with that of high-quality VCRs; at the lowest-quality setting, picture quality matched run-of-the-mill VHS VCRs standard play (SP), at their best recording speed. Audio quality is a notch below CD quality.

Ultimately, the DVR's picture quality, like the VCR's, depends on the quality of the signal coming in via your cable or satellite provider. A noisy or mediocre signal will produce mediocre digital recordings.

Recommendations. TiVo and ReplayTV represent an intriguing technology, but the market is still developing. No one can say whether the technology will prove compelling enough for these products and services to build the broad customer base they need to succeed.

That said, your own viewing habits can provide the best indication of whether a DVR is worth your consideration. Avid TV watchers are prime candidates, as are those who seldom watch TV at prime time but want to see prime-time programming, those who hate sitting through commercials.

If satellite dishes are an option, consider a dish receiver that includes a DVR. Keep in mind that you'll have to pay a separate fee for the DVR service. Satellite DVRs work only with satellite programming and won't record from cable or an antenna.

Today's DVR can't replace a VCR, which you'll need if you want to make a permanent copy of what you record. Consider a DVR as a companion product, not a replacement, for your VCR.

Related CR report: December 2002

HOME THEATER IN A BOX

No time to mix and match speakers and receiver? All-in-one systems can minimize the hassle, although some make it tough to hook up other components.

Good speakers and the other components of a home theater cost less than ever. But selecting all those components can be time-consuming, and connecting them is a challenge even for audiophiles.

You can save some hassle by buying an all-in-one product that combines a receiver with a six-speaker set. And unless your needs are demanding, you compromise little on quality.

A "home theater in a box" combines, in a single package, all you need for the guts of a home theater: a receiver that can decode digital-audio soundtracks and a set of six compact, matched speakers—three front, two surround, and a subwoofer. You'll also get all the cables and wiring you need, labeled and color-coded for easy setup. Usually the presumption is that you already own a TV and a VCR or DVD player, although some systems come with a separate DVD player or have one built into the receiver.

➤ WHAT'S AVAILABLE

Sony, Kenwood, Pioneer, and Yamaha account for more than half of sales, with Sony commanding almost a third of the market. The cheapest models probably don't include a DVD player. Expect to pay about $300 for a basic system, $500 to $750 for a system capable of handling digital signals and a powered subwoofer. Systems aimed at audiophiles can cost $2,000 or more.

➤ KEY FEATURES

The receivers in home-theater-in-a-box systems tend to be on the simple side. They usually include both Dolby Digital and

---

PERFECT FIT

What makes a room good for sound?

The more unsymmetrical the room, the better. A square room can produce peaks and valleys in the sound level at various places around the room. A rectangular room gives a bigger "sweet spot" of sound without introducing acoustic effects. An ideal room would have no two walls the same. From an acoustical point of view, it's especially bad if one dimension of the room is the same or an exact multiple of another, such as a 12x16 foot room with an 8-foot ceiling. A 12x15 room with an 8-foot ceiling would be a good size for a home theater featuring a 36-inch TV set. For a home theater with a larger set, an ideal room would be something like 13x23 feet, with a 10-foot ceiling.

Fortunately, when a room is loaded up with furniture and other items, some of these acoustic difficulties are diminished.

A big, fat overstuffed sofa or a pair of reclining chairs not only provides comfortable seating, it will help enhance the sound in your room. So will other "cozy" items, such as pillows, curtains, wall hangings, and carpeting or area rugs. Such items absorb soundwaves and keep sound from being overly harsh. Anything that breaks up the flat surfaces of a room—wooden blinds, tables, painting, books in bookcases—also helps diffuse sound. But be careful not to overpad the room, or the sound within will be dull and lifeless.

DTS decoders. **Controls** should be easy to use. Look for a front panel with displays and controls grouped by function and labeled clearly. **Onscreen display** lets you control the receiver via a TV screen.

Switched AC outlets let you plug in other components and turn on the whole system with one button. Some receivers offer **sleep,** which turn the receiver on or off at a preset time. The included receivers also offer about 20 or more presets you can use for AM and FM stations.

Remote controls are most useful when they have clear labels and different-shaped and color-coded buttons grouped by function. A universal remote can control devices made by the same manufacturer or by others.

To get the best picture quality, look for **component video outputs** on the receiver that can connect to relatively high-end TVs; not many receivers have these outputs. Instead, most have the next-best output, **S-video,** which is better than composite-video or RF (antenna) connections.

Look also for **S-video inputs,** which let you connect an external DVD player, digital camcorder, or certain cable or satellite boxes. Any player you might want to connect will need the same digital-audio connections, either optical or coaxial, as those of the included receiver. And if you want to make occasional connections at the front—perhaps for a camcorder or an MP3 player—you'll need **front-panel inputs**.

Home-theater-in-a-box receivers that do not decode digital audio may have **5.1 inputs;** these accept input from the decoder in a a DVD player or other components with multichannel audio signals.

DSP (for **digital signal processor**) modes use a computer chip to duplicate the sound measurements of, say, a concert hall. Each mode represents a different listening environment. A **bass-boost** switch amplifies the deepest sounds. You are less likely to find stand-alone receiver controls such as a graphic equalizer.

A **subwoofer** may be powered or unpowered. Either type will do the job, but a powered subwoofer requires fewer wires, provides more control over bass, and lets a powered receiver drive the other speakers.

Models with an **integrated DVD player** typically have fewer features than do stand-alone DVD players. Features to expect are **track programmability** (more useful for playing CDs than DVDs), **track repeat,** and **disc repeat.** If you want a more fully featured player, a stand-alone DVD player may be the wiser choice.

➤ HOW TO CHOOSE

Performance differences. In recent tests, CONSUMER REPORTS found that performance doesn't always depend on price. The receivers of these systems generally had very good FM tuners and adequate power, plus they did a fine job of switching signals. But performance fell short

of component systems, and in terms of features, the boxed systems were a notch below component receivers, particularly in how easy their remote controls and onscreen menus were to use.

Recommendations. Home theaters in a box offer convenience and decent sound, better than you'd get from a typical minisystem with home-theater capability. The trade-off for that convenience is that you'll generally have to settle for less than the best in receiver and speaker technology.

Related CR report: November 2002
Ratings: page 252

MINISYSTEMS

These all-in-one sound systems offer decent sound in an economical, convenient package.

A minisystem can be just the ticket if you're cramped for space or don't have the time or inclination to search out individual components and set them up. Minisystems typically include a receiver, an AM/FM tuner, a CD changer, and a dual-cassette tape deck in a bookshelf-size box with two separate speakers. The sound on the better models is quite good, but even the best won't match the sound quality you can get from a component-based system. Still, a minisystem costs considerably less than the $1,000 or so you'd pay for a full complement of decent components, so it can be a good value for many listeners.

➤ **WHAT'S AVAILABLE**

Aiwa is the dominant brand. Other top-selling brands include Panasonic, Philips, RCA, Sharp, and Sony.

Three-quarters of the models sold are two-channel stereo systems. You'll also find surround-sound systems that come with multichannel decoders like Dolby Digital on the receiver. Such systems complement the usual two speakers with additional speakers for center- and surround-channel sound.

Models with a DVD player or CD player/recorder instead of a playback-only CD changer are becoming more common. Some systems eliminate the tape deck for maximum compactness.

Most minisystems integrate everything but the speakers into a console that's more or less a 12-inch cube with a black or silver chassis and blinking displays. More compact minisystems, or microsystems, are as narrow as 6½ inches—considerably smaller than a 17-inch standard-size component.

Price range: $120 to $500. Lower-priced minisystems may have limited power and anemic bass. Buying one of the more expensive models may get you more amplifier power, CD recording capability, Dolby B noise reduction, or more speakers.

➤ **KEY FEATURES**

Minisystems have some of the same features of full-sized components. But controls are more integrated, and displays are often more vivid, even hyperactive.

Minisystems vary in how much power their **amplifiers** deliver to the speakers—from 15 to 70 watts per channel. In recent tests, CONSUMER REPORTS found that all the systems tested, regardless of claimed wattage, produced enough sound to fill the typical office, dorm room, or bedroom, but would probably strain in a large room or noisy party. Also, power ratings in minisystem ads are calculated in so many different ways that the claims are of little use when you're comparing between brands.

Among worthwhile CD-player features, **play exchange** lets you change the CDs that are not being played without interrupting the one being played. **Direct track access** lets you go straight to a specific track. A display of the **time remaining** on either the track or the disc is useful when you're taping off a CD. **Music peak finder** sets the recording level for the highest sound level on the disc, and **digital output** lets you record onto a CD or MiniDisc using a separate recorder. Some models can play CD-R or CD-RW discs you've recorded yourself.

Some models have **dual-cassette tape decks;** such players are becoming less important and somewhat less common, given the predominance of CDs. If you are a tape listener, though, one feature CONSUMER REPORTS considers important for basic tape use is **auto reverse,** so you don't have to flip the tape over to play the second side. **An auto tape counter** helps find a particular location on a tape. **High-speed dubbing** doubles the speed when you're copying from one tape onto another, though with some loss of quality. If you're likely to play the tapes on a stereo or component system, look for the ability to record and play **Type II tapes** and for **Dolby B Noise Reduction,** which reduces background hiss.

Full-logic controls are soft-touch electronic buttons on the body of the device. The remote control may group two or more functions on one button, sometimes confusingly, although remotes for the latest models have improved. Some features are only accessible with the remote, which can be a problem if you lose track of it. A few models have a **microphone input jack,** along with **karaoke capability.**

A **subwoofer output** lets you connect a separately powered subwoofer, helpful for maximizing the lowest tones from a movie's surround-sound encoding. (This is not the same thing as a "built-in powered subwoofer," which is a speaker component.) Instead of bass and treble tone controls, some models provide a three- or five-band **equalizer,** which gives you slightly more control over the full audio spectrum and is a bit easier to use.

Some models have only **tone settings** such as Pop, Jazz, and Classical, which automatically determine the bass/treble mix, often overboosting the bass in the process.

A **clock** lets you program the system to turn on at a predetermined time; an accompanying **timer** lets you make timed recordings. Some systems permit you to set the cassette deck to record from the radio, just as you time-shift with a VCR.

➤ HOW TO CHOOSE
Performance differences. Overall sound quality varies, largely depending on the quality of the speakers. Models in the last round of testing by CONSUMER REPORTS were judged anywhere from fair to very good for sound quality. Most systems had adequate power for their speakers, although a few distorted the sound when played at very high volumes.

The FM tuners on most minisystems are fine, CONSUMER REPORTS has found. The AM tuners are mediocre, but that's true of component receivers, too. The CD players' sound quality is typically excellent across the board. Tape deck performance was adequate for playing and recording cassettes, according to the most recent CONSUMER REPORTS tests.

Recommendations. By bundling all the major audio functions in one package, a minisystem can save you the trouble of choosing separate components—and several hundred dollars in the bargain. While these units would disappoint a very demanding listener, the quality of the better minisystems is surprisingly good considering the price. Don't expect top sound quality much below $200, however.

Take along a few familiar CD recordings to play when you go to the store. If you expect to play tapes much, consider trying out a few cassettes as well. Adjust the tone controls to see if you like the sound. Check out the controls and the appearance, which can be anything from sedate to high-tech. Ask about return or exchange policies in case the sound of the minisystem isn't to your liking when you get it home.

Related CR report: November 2001

MP3 PLAYERS

They usually store at least a CD's worth of music files. You'll have to take the time to load them, and legal controversy still surrounds some usage.

MP3 encoding is currently the predominant means of compressing music files for digitizing music. Many of those files are transferred from computers to handheld MP3 players. Despite copyright-infringement lawsuits by the music and movie industries, free music-sharing web sites carry on. The sites let users download music files for transfer to MP3 players or burning onto CDs. The music industry has responded with subscription-based services that allow you to stream or download music and play it on your computer. (One service, Pressplay, allows a few songs to be burned each month.)

You can also load these small devices with music "ripped" from CDs, creating your own custom play lists and giving you new ways to manage your music library.

Many MP3 players look like portable radios, headphones and all. Others resemble large pens or watches. MP3 playback has been incorporated into some digital cameras and even cell phones, as well as some CD players and Sony's MiniDisc player.

Music can be encoded digitally in a number of formats; MP3 is the best known. The abbreviation stands for Moving Pictures Expert Group Layer 3, a file format that can compress music to one-tenth to one-twelfth the space it would ordinarily take.

Other encoding schemes include Windows Media Audio (WMA) and Adaptive Transform Acoustic Coding (ATRAC), a proprietary format used by Sony products.

➤ **WHAT'S AVAILABLE**

More than 30 brands of MP3 players are on the market. Sony and SonicBlue, which makes the Rio line, are the biggest brands, followed by RCA, Samsung, Creative Labs, and other, smaller brands. Some hybrid models incorporate CD-player functionality and PDA-like features.

Players come in all sizes and shapes. Many are quite small. A player with 64 megabytes (MB) of memory holds about an hour of music recorded at CD-quality setting. A player with 128 MB holds twice that. The MP3 standard also lets you save music at lower sampling rates; this may diminish quality but increases the amount of music you can store. High-capacity versions (sometimes called "jukeboxes") are larger, similar in size to a portable CD player and store the music on a hard drive. These currently store as much as 20 gigabytes (GB), equivalent to more than 300 hours of music.

Many devices offer the option to add more memory via card slots, or "backpacks" on the unit. Players typically come with some combination of internal and/or external memory such as CompactFlash, MultiMedia Card, or Smart Media. Some models use MagicGate (an encrypted-audio version of Sony's existing MemoryStick media), or SecureDigital. Additional memory can cost anywhere from $10 to more than $150, depending on what's compatible with your player.

All players are battery-powered and have headphone outputs, along with a means of connecting to a computer for file transfer. Price range: $90 to $300 for regular players; $300 and up for high-capacity players.

➤ **IMPORTANT FEATURES**

MP3 players come with **software** for interfacing with a computer, using a Universal Serial Bus (USB) or less often, the faster

FireWire connection. Most support Windows and many support Macs; more manufacturers are working toward Mac compatibility. Apple's iPod is now compatible with Windows. The computer-to-player interface consists of software drivers that let the computer and player communicate, along with a software application for transferring files to the player's memory. Some players appear as hard drives on your computer for easy drag-and-drop transfer of files. Many players are bundled with a more fully featured software application, such as MusicMatch or Real Jukebox, that helps you keep track of your MP3 files, manage playlists, and record songs from audio CDs.

On many players, the **firmware**—the player's built-in operating instructions—can be upgraded so the player does not become obsolete. Upgrades can add or enhance features, fix bugs, and add support for other formats and operating systems. (Check the manufacturer's web site for such upgrades.) Most upgrades these days are to eliminate bugs.

LCD screens on most players show such information as track number, song title, and memory used. Volume, track forward/reverse, and pause-play controls are standard. Most have play modes such as Repeat All and Random. A **customizable equalizer (EQ) setting** gives you the most control over the sound, but some units have just a simple bass boost control. Many also have presets for various music types (rock, classical, and so forth), along with viewable song lists.

Standard players generally use one or two AA or AAA batteries, either alkaline or rechargeable. Most high-capacity models use four AA rechargeable batteries. Either alkaline or rechargeable batteries are preferable to nonremovable batteries; when these no longer hold a charge, the player must be professionally serviced. A **battery-life in-**dicator on most models helps keep track of how much power is left.

A number of players incorporate an **FM radio tuner.** Some MP3 players have features more commonly found on a personal digital assistant (PDA), such as **voice recording** and **data file storage capability.** (PDAs that run the newest version of the Pocket PC operating system from Microsoft, and some Sony PDA models, can play MP3-encoded files. Handspring's Visor clones of Palm PDAs

> ■ **TECH TIP**
> **Figure on roughly one minute of music per megabyte to save MP3 files at the CD-quality level.**

have an expansion slot to which you can attach an MP3 player.) Certain models can be used to transfer data files between computers, sometimes via the external memory card.

➤ HOW TO CHOOSE

Performance differences. In recent CONSUMER REPORTS tests, the processing necessary to turn music into an MP3 file led to very slight degradation of the audio signal on most models, evidenced by noise or a muffling in some frequency ranges. Poor sound quality was more likely to be caused by mediocre or poor headphones bundled with the player. These can be replaced, so the problem can be remedied easily and cheaply.

CONSUMER REPORTS tests found that the players will run between 5 and 24 hours before their batteries give out—a wide range. Most play 8 hours or more. Manufacturers' specifications are useful guides to battery life.

Getting started can be tricky with some devices. When we connected some tested models to a computer, the PC often didn't recognize the player, and we had to resort to trial and error. Upgrading firmware also proved time-consuming. MP3 players use one of two methods for upgrading; one method, which executes the upgrade file on the PC while the player is still attached, can cause permanent damage to the player if there's even a slight interruption during execution.

Recommendations. Memory size counts. For people who like to have lots of music in a small package, we recommend a standard MP3 player that has some memory built in (often 64 MB, but ranging from 32 to 128) yet allows expansion via external memory cards. A 64-MB card usually costs $35 to $70. If capacity is more important than the smaller size, a high-capacity model would be a better choice. The 20 GB of storage on the most capacious models provides enough space to archive and organize a sizable library of music. Some let you record from an audio system onto the player without a computer. If you want to minimize the odds that your player will fall behind the technology curve, look for a player with upgradable firmware that can accommodate newer encoding schemes or variations of MP3 compression. The more additional formats a model can play—such as WMA or ATRAC—the more flexibility you have in downloading and transferring music files now and in the future.

Before you buy, make sure the player is compatible with your Windows or Mac computer (including the version of the operating system your computer uses) and that your computer has the USB or FireWire connection the player requires. (Apple's iPod supports FireWire.) Also, look for LCD displays and controls that are easy to read and controls that can be worked with one hand, as you would with other handheld devices.

Related CR report: May 2002

RECEIVERS

For a home-theater surround-sound system, look for a receiver that can decode Dolby Digital and DTS soundtracks.

The receiver is the brain of an audio/video system, providing AM and FM tuners, amplifiers, surround-sound, and switching capabilities. Receivers have connections for various audio components (CD player, cassette deck, turntable, multiple speakers), and most also handle video sources (TV, DVD player, VCR, satellite system).

Even as receivers accumulate new audio-switching capabilities, features that were common when receivers were the center of audio systems—tape monitors and phono inputs, for instance—are disappearing. Manufacturers say they must eliminate those less-used features to add others.

➤ WHAT'S AVAILABLE

Sony is by far the biggest-selling brand. Other top-selling brands include Denon, JVC, Kenwood, Onkyo, Panasonic, Pioneer, RCA, and Yamaha. Most models now are "digital," designed for the six-channel surround sound formats encoded in most DVDs and some TV fare. Here are the types you'll see, from least to most expensive:

Stereo. Basic receivers accept the analog stereo signals from a tape deck, CD player, or turntable. These receivers provide two channels that power a pair of stereo speakers. For a simple music setup, add a cassette deck or a CD player. For rudimentary home theater, add a TV and VCR. Power typically runs 50 to 100 watts per channel. Price range: $125 to $250.

Dolby Pro Logic. Dolby Pro Logic is the fading analog home-theater surround-sound standard. Receivers that support it can take three front channels and one surround channel from your TV or hi-fi VCR and output them to five speakers: three in front, and one or two in back. Most receivers supporting the Dolby Pro Logic standard are "digital-ready," which means they have the capability to send six channels of predecoded sound to the speakers. "Ready" means you must use a DVD player with a built-in digital decoder. (You won't be able to decode other digital audio sources such as satellite TV.) Power for Dolby Pro Logic models is typically 60 to 100 watts per channel. Price range: $150 to $250.

Dolby Digital. Now representing the prevailing digital surround-sound standard, Dolby Digital receivers have a built-in decoder for true six-channel audio capability: front left and right, front center, two rear with discrete wide-band signals, and a powered subwoofer for bass effects.

Dolby Digital is also the sound format for most DVD, high-definition TV (HDTV), digital cable TV, and some satellite TV broadcast systems. To take advantage of this capability, also called Dolby AC-3, you'll need speakers that can reproduce full-spectrum sound well. Receivers with digital decoding capability can also accept a signal that has been "digitized," or sampled, at a given rate per second and converted to digital form. Price range for Dolby Digital: $200 to $500 or more.

DTS. Receivers that add Digital Theater Systems (DTS) capability support an additional, less common, form of digital surround sound that is used in some movie tracks. Price range: $250 to $1,000 and up.

THX-certified. The high-end receivers that meet this quality standard include full support for Dolby Pro Logic, Dolby Digital, and DTS. THX Select is the standard for components designed for small and average-size rooms; THX Ultra is for

larger rooms. Price range: $800 to $2,500 and up.

➤ **KEY FEATURES**

Controls should be easy to use. Look for a front panel with displays and controls clearly labeled and grouped by function. **Onscreen display** lets you control the receiver via a TV screen, a squint-free alternative to the receiver's LED or LCD. **Switched AC outlets** (expect one or two) let you plug in other components and turn the whole system on and off with one button.

> ▓ **TECH TIP**
> Home-theater equipment can help you make the best of an imperfect listening space. Receivers, for instance, have equalizers that can help make up for deficiencies in a room's shape.

Remote controls are most useful when they have clear labels and buttons that light up, come in different shapes, and are color-coded, easy to access, and grouped by function—a goal that is seldom achieved in receiver remotes. A **learning remote** can receive programming data for other devices via their remote's infrared signal; on some remotes, the necessary codes on other manufacturers' devices are built-in.

Input/output jacks matter more on a receiver than on perhaps any other component of your home theater. Clear labeling, color coding, and logical groupings of the many jacks on the rear panel can help avert setup glitches such as reversed speaker polarities and mixed-up inputs and outputs. Input jacks situated on the front panel make for easy connections to camcorders, video games, MP3 players, digital cameras, MiniDisc players, and PDAs.

A stereo receiver will give you a few audio inputs and no video jacks. Digital-ready receivers with Dolby Pro Logic will have 5.1 inputs; these accept input from a DVD player with its own built-in Dolby Digital decoder, an outboard decoder, or other components with multichannel analog signals.

S-video and **component video jacks** allow you to route signals from DVD players and other high-quality video sources through the receiver to the TV.

Tone controls adjust bass and treble. A **graphic equalizer** breaks the sound spectrum into three or more sections, giving you slightly more control over the full audio spectrum. Instead of tone controls, some receivers come with tone styles such as Jazz, Classical, or Rock, each accentuating a different frequency pattern; you can often craft your own styles, too. But tone controls work best for correcting room acoustics and satisfying listening preferences, not enhancing a musical genre.

DSP (**digital signal processor**) modes use a computer chip to duplicate the sound characteristics of a concert hall and other listening environments. A **bass-boost** switch amplifies the deepest sounds, and midnight mode reduces loud sounds and amplifies quiet ones in music or soundtracks. Sometimes called "one touch," a **settings memory** lets you store settings for each source to minimize differences in volume, tone, and other settings when switching between sources. A similar feature, **loudness memory,** is limited to volume settings alone.

Tape monitor lets you either listen to one source as you record a second on a tape deck or listen to the recording as it's being made. **Automatic radio tuning** includes such features as seek (automatic searching for the next listenable station) and 20 to 40 presets to call up your favorite stations.

To catch stations too weak for the seek mode, most receivers also have a **manual stepping** knob or buttons, best in one-channel increments. But most models

creep in half- or quarter-steps, meaning unnecessary button tapping to find the frequency you want. **Direct tuning** of frequencies lets you tune a radio station by entering its frequency on a keypad.

➤ HOW TO CHOOSE

Performance differences. The most recent CONSUMER REPORTS tests of receivers show that you needn't spend more than $250 to $300 to get a fine performer. (THX models, however, begin at $800.) Most models we have tested have been very good at amplifying and in tuning FM stations, but only fair or good for AM stations. Ease of use was often somewhat disappointing.

Recommendations. Don't buy more receiver than you need. The size of the room you're using, how loudly you play music, and the impedance of the speakers you'll use all determine how much power is appropriate. Generally, 50 watts or more per channel should be fine for a typical system in a typical 12x20 foot room. Then it's a question of features and usability.

Look for clear labeling, color coding, and logical groupings of the jacks on the receiver's rear panel. Make sure the model you're considering has all the connection types you need. Check for how well the receiver impedance matches your speakers.

To compare receivers at the store, have the salesperson feed the same CD or DVD soundtrack to the receivers, adjust each receiver's volume to be equally loud, and select between each receiver's speaker output using the same set of speakers. Compare two receivers at a time. Stop the CD and listen for background hiss. Explore the layout of the front panel and remote control to see how easy they will be to use.

Related CR report: November 2002
Ratings: page 292

SATELLITE TV

First, can a dish be mounted with a clear view of the satellite? Then choose the system: DirecTV or Dish Network. After that, pick the hardware.

Frustration with cable companies has fueled the growth of satellite-TV broadcast systems. Some 18 million homes sport a saucer-shape dish antenna. In a recent survey of satellite- and cable-TV subscribers, CONSUMER REPORTS found that satellite-TV subscribers were more satisfied overall than their cable-TV counterparts.

Once renowned for offering hundreds of channels with the notable exception of local stations, the two satellite providers—DirecTV (also called DSS) and EchoStar's Dish Network—now provide local service in more than 40 cities and outlying areas, with more programming imminent. That's the result of a 1999 federal law that allowed satellite companies to offer so-called local-into-local service. In January 2002, the FCC ruled that if a satellite company offered one local channel, then it had to carry all local channels in the markets where local service was offered.

People in an "unserved" household—those living in rural areas where an acceptable TV signal cannot be received via a common rooftop antenna—can pick up local stations (regional affiliates of major networks) from a satellite provider. According to the FCC, you should be able to confirm your status through the satellite provider from which you're getting your setup.

For much of the country, however, cable remains the only way to receive all local programming. Since satellite providers have limited spectrum for broadcasting additional channels, the number of markets where they can offer local service is limited. This is a major reason these companies are requesting a merger.

> ➤ **WHAT'S AVAILABLE**

DirecTV (also called DSS) and EchoStar's Dish Network offer comparable programming fare, including a choice of up to 400 to 500 channels. DirecTV is stronger in sports, while Dish Network holds the advantage in foreign-language programming. In addition to television, both providers carry 30 to 40 commercial-free music services in many genres.

Basic service, with a 100-channel package, is about $32 per month. Local-channel service adds about $5 per month. Expanded programming, with 100 to 150 channels, is about $45 and adds music and some specialty channels. Premium channels such as HBO and Showtime are $6 to $10 each, sometimes less if you take two or more. Pay-per-view is usually $4 per movie. Sports packages available on DirecTV run $139 to $169 per season. Limited high-definition programming is available from both providers and requires special equipment, including a TV capable of displaying HDTV images.

The dish and receiver will work with only one of the providers' signals. These components come with various extras, including receivers that double as digital VCRs or digital video recorders (DVRs).

Typically, the dish and receiver are sold together. Hughes, RCA, and Sony are among the companies that offer DirecTV equipment; JVC and EchoStar offer Dish Network equipment.

Satellite dishes are typically 18 or 24 inches. The larger dishes offer increased programming options, such as more channels, pay-per-view movies, HDTV reception, and international programming. Sometimes a second 18-inch dish may be required to receive some of those services.

Receivers accept the signal from the dish, decode it, and transmit it to your TV. If you want to be able to watch different programs on different TVs at once, you'll need one receiver for each TV. To facilitate this, you need a dish with multiple low-noise block converters (LNB). Extra receivers cost about $100 each and add about $5 apiece to the monthly bill. Alternatively, the receiver's RF-output jack or an inexpensive splitter may be used to send the same channel to multiple TVs.

For pay-per-view ordering and other provider contact, satellite-TV receivers must be connected to a telephone line. Typically, you can use your existing line.

Price range for a dish-receiver package: $150 to over $800. Price range for single LNB dishes: $30 to $50 for one receiver, $40 to $60 for dual LNB for two receivers, and $150 to $250 for multiple receivers. Frequent promotions offer lower prices.

➤ **KEY FEATURES**

On the receiver, the number and type of **audio and video output jacks** make a difference in the quality of your picture and in what equipment you can connect. The lowest-quality connection is radio-frequency, which is the typical antenna-type connector. Better is a **composite video output;** better still are **S-video outputs,** provided your TV is appropriately equipped to accept these connections, which can take advantage of the higher visual resolution of the digital video source.

An **onscreen signal-strength meter** lets you monitor how well the satellite signal is coming in. Satellite receivers with **Dolby Digital audio** capability have optical or coaxial output for a direct digital connection to a Dolby Digital audio receiver.

Some remote controls accompanying the receiver are infrared, like TV or VCR remotes, and may also control a VCR.

CABLE VS. SATELLITE

The digital cable alternative

If you're a cable-TV subscriber, the odds are your cable company is trying to sell you on digital cable. A supplement to your regular (analog) service, it provides 50 or more additional channels that promise a superior picture and sound.

Assuming you can receive digital cable (at least 60 percent of cable customers can), upgrading the service is as simple as placing a phone call and arranging for installation of a new cable box. Opting for satellite service, on the other hand, demands determining if you home offers an unobstructed view of the satellite itself and then choosing between DirecTV and EchoStar's Dish Network.

Satellite TV still has the advantage in terms of number and diversity of channels. And in a recent CONSUMER REPORTS survey, satellite scored higher than digital cable in terms of picture and quality. The reason may be that satellite delivers all channels digitally, while most digital-cable services are hybrids that deliver additional DTV channels and premium and pay-per-view service in digital, and the remainder in analog.

Buying digital cable probably won't improve the analog channels you see now. The survey also gave cable companies marks among the lowest of any service providers that CONSUMER REPORTS regularly evaluates.

Check with your cable provider regarding availability of digital cable. If it isn't yet available, you might ask when it will be. Don't depend on the promised date; over the years, cable companies have been unreliable in their predictions of upgraded service.

Others use a radio-frequency signal, which can pass through walls, allowing the receiver to be placed in an unobtrusive, central location and controlled from anywhere in the house.

Remotes typically include a **program-description button,** which activates an onscreen program-description banner. The **program guide** helps you sort through the hundreds of channels. **Program guide with picture** lets you continue to watch one program while you scan the onscreen channel guide for another. Some receivers have a **keyword search,** allowing you to search with just a full or partial name of a program or performer.

> **HOW TO CHOOSE**

Performance differences. The differences between the two satellite providers are subtle. The best DirecTV setups are a little easier to use, with slightly better remotes, than EchoStar equipment. But the EchoStar/Dish Network system did offer a slightly better overall picture for New York network affiliates in the most recent CONSUMER REPORTS tests. When viewing pictures from both satellite providers in September 2001, we saw some subtle picture defects. Minor visual impairments, mostly in fast-moving scenes (the most bandwidth-hungry screen content), may be caused by expanded channel offerings at the expense of bandwidth.

Recommendations. Find out the program offerings in your area, including whether digital cable is available (or when it will be) and if local channels are available. Choose the service, then the hardware. You need a clear view of the southern horizon and a place to mount the dish. Satellite dealers and installers will come out to assess your location. If you decide to switch providers, you'll need to pay for everything all over again.

Related CR report: November 2001

SPEAKERS

Speakers can make or break your audio or video setup. Try to listen to them in a store before buying. If you can splurge on only part of your system, splurge here.

The best array of audio or video components will let you down if matched with poor-quality speakers. Good speakers need not bust your budget, though it's easy to spend a lot. For a home-theater system, you can start with two or three speakers and add others as your budget allows. Size is no indication of quality.

> **WHAT'S AVAILABLE**

Among the hundreds of speaker brands available, the major names include Bose, Infinity, JBL, Pioneer, Polk, RCA, Sony, and Yamaha. Speakers are sold through mass merchandisers, audio-video stores, "boutique" retailers, and online—where shipping can add up to $100 to the bill, since big speakers can be fairly heavy.

Speakers are sold as pairs or sets for traditional stereo setups, and singly or in sets of three to six for equipping a home theater. The front (or main) speakers supply stereo effect and carry most of the sound to the listener's ears. The center (or center channel) speaker chiefly delivers dialogue and is usually placed on top of or beneath the TV in a home-theater setup.

Dialogue demands a full-range, high-quality speaker. A subwoofer carries the lowest tones. Price range: $400 to more than $1,000.

Bookshelf speakers. These are among the smallest, but at 12 to 18 inches tall, many are still too large to fit on a shelf, their name notwithstanding. A pair of bookshelf speakers can serve as the sole speakers in a stereo system or as the front or rear duo in a home-theater setup. One can serve as the center-channel unit, provided it's magnetically shielded so it won't interfere with the TV. Small speakers like these have made strides in their ability to handle deep bass without buzzing or distortion. Any bass-handling limitations would be less of a concern in a multispeaker system that uses a subwoofer for the deep bass. Price range: $200 to more than $600.

> ■ TECH TIP
> Buy regular lamp cord instead of special speaker wire. It costs less and usually works just fine unless you have low-impedance speakers and the cable run is over 30 feet.

Floor-standing speakers. Typically about 3 to 4 feet tall, these large speakers are can also serve as the sole speakers in a stereo system or as the front pair in a home-theater system. Their big cabinets have the potential to do more justice to deep bass than smaller speakers, but we believe many listeners would be satisfied with smaller speakers that scored well for bass handling. Even if floor models do a bit better, their size and cost may steer buyers toward smaller, cheaper bookshelf models. Price range: $400 to more than $1,000.

Center-channel speaker. In a multichannel setup, the center-channel speaker sits on or below the TV and primarily handles dialog. Its range doesn't have to be as full as the front pair's, but its sound should be similar so all three blend well. Dedicated center-channel speakers are short and wide (6 inches high by 20 inches wide, for instance) so they perch neatly atop a TV. Price range: $100 to $300.

Rear-surround speakers. Rear speakers in a multichannel setup carry mostly background sound such as crowd noise. Newer multichannel formats such as Dolby Digital, DTS (Digital Theater Systems), DVD-Audio, and SACD make fuller use of these speakers than earlier formats. You'll get the best blend if the rear pair sounds similar to the front pair. Rear speakers tend to be small and light (often 5 to 10 inches high and 3 to 6 pounds), so they can be wall mounted or placed on a shelf. They're often called satellites. Price range: $100 to $350.

Three-piece sets. Designed to be used as stand-alone systems or integrated with other speakers, they have two satellites for midrange and higher tones and a subwoofer for bass. Price range: $300 to $800.

Six-piece sets. These systems have four satellites (used for the front and rear pairs), one center-channel speaker, and a subwoofer. Six-piece sets save you the trouble of matching the distinctive sounds of six speakers. That can be a daunting task at home, and even more of a challenge amidst the din of a store that doesn't have a decent listening room. Price range: $400 to more than $1,000.

Other shapes and sizes. A "power-tower" is a tower speaker, usually priced above $1,000, with a side-firing, powered subwoofer in its base. Flat-panel speakers save space and are priced at $500 and up per pair.

➤ **KEY FEATURES**

Lovers of loud sound should pay attention to a speaker's **measured impedance,** which affects how well the speaker and receiver get along. **Power range** refers to the familiar advertised watts per channel. The **wattage** within a matched pair, say front or rear, should be identical. Also, the power range should exceed the watts per channel supplied by your receiver or amplifier. Speakers sold to be near a TV set typically have magnetic shielding so they won't distort the picture with their core magnets.

➤ HOW TO CHOOSE

Performance differences. What distinguishes the best for the rest is the accuracy with which they reproduce the original signals fed to them. Most models we've tested have been capable of reasonable accuracy. Some models, however, require adjustments to a receiver's tone controls to compensate for the speaker's shortcomings. Making those adjustments is usually a minor, one-time inconvenience.

No speaker is perfect. Every speaker that CONSUMER REPORTS has tested alters music to some degree, overemphasizing some sounds and underemphasizing others. Some speakers "roll off" entirely at extremes of bass and treble, meaning they can't reproduce some low or high sounds at all. Some speakers buzz, distort, or otherwise complain when playing low notes at window-rattling volume.

Recommendations. Look for the size and configuration that fit your listening space. Models of equal accuracy will sound different, so try to audition before you buy, using a familiar piece of music. Especially demanding: music with wide dynamics and frequencies, such as classical symphonies, and simple music, such as a solo piano performance.

Listen to the music soft and loud, for clarity and lack of harshness in the high range and a lack of boominess in the low. Start in the best position, in an equilateral triangle with the speakers, and move off-center until you find the angle at which the high frequencies become muffled. The farther you can go, the better. Sharpen your judging skills by first comparing each store's top performer with its low-priced entry-level model.

To keep a balanced system, buy left and right speakers in pairs. The center-channel speaker should be matched to the front speakers; if it's very close to the TV, it should be magnetically shielded.

Related CR report: November 2002
Ratings: page 301

TV SETS

Conventional TVs, projection sets, digital TVs, flat screens—you have more (and better) viewing choices than before, at ever-lower prices.

Because the transition to digital broadcasts is proceeding slowly, any analog TV you buy now will serve you well for many years. Even when digital programming becomes widespread, the TV you buy now can do the job with the addition of a converter. CONSUMER REPORTS tests show that there are plenty of fine TVs to choose from, including some real bargains. You can find a very good 27-inch model for around $450, a 32-inch for about $600, and a 36-inch set for $750.

Sets capable of carrying high-definition TV (HDTV) cost considerably more—$1,100 or more. If your antenna or cable connection provides a good, strong signal, an HD-ready set has a noticeably improved picture compared with an analog set. An HD-ready set will show an even better picture when connected to a progressive-scan DVD player. These sets can display the much higher-resolution HD image, but only with the addition of a digital-TV receiver set-top box.

True HDTVs come with a built-in digital-TV receiver, for $1,500 and up. The availability of high-definition programming is still limited. Like an HD-ready set, an HDTV will let you enjoy superior video when hooked up to a progressive-scan

DVD player or when watching standard TV fare.

> **WHAT'S AVAILABLE**

Panasonic, RCA, Sony, and Toshiba are among the biggest-selling brands of TVs measuring 27 inches and larger. Other brands include JVC, Philips, Samsung, Sanyo, Sharp, and Zenith.

Small sets. Sets with a 13-inch screen are usually equipped with monophonic sound and few features. Higher-end models may offer a few more features, such as extra inputs. Price range: $90 to $300.

Sets with a 19- or 20-inch screen are also pretty basic. Most lack high-end picture refinements such as a comb filter (which can increase visual detail). Models with stereo sound usually have extra inputs for a VCR or a DVD player. Price range: $140 to $450.

Midsized sets. A 27-inch screen, once thought large, is now the norm. Sets with a 25-inch screen (difficult to tell in size from a 27-incher) are their economy-minded cousins; together the two are the biggest-selling sizes. Sets with a 27-inch screen frequently offer many features, including picture-in-picture (PIP), an S-video input jack, simulated surround-sound effects, a universal remote control, and, usually, a comb filter. These 27-inch models are among the best values for TVs, and the respectable sound quality found on some 27-inch sets can make them all many people need. What's more, they fit in most entertainment-center cabinets. Price range: $300 to $1,000. Sets with the new "flat" TV screens are at the high end of the price range.

Large sets. A 32-inch screen represents the entry level for big-screen TV; these sets often offer two-tuner PIP, universal remotes, simulated surround sound, and plenty of input jacks. The largest direct-view sets (with 36-inch screens) are feature-rich but can weigh more than 200 pounds; they might be too wide and too high for conventional component shelv-

---

RATINGS HISTORY

Which TV brands rate the best?

A new study by CONSUMER REPORTS analyzing six years of TV test results shows that some brands consistently outperform others. The two with the best results: Sony and Toshiba, whose models rated Very Good or Excellent about 80 percent of the time. The study covers more than 200 conventional, direct-view, cathode-ray-tube sets rated in CONSUMER REPORTS from February 1997 to March 2002. Sets ranged from 19-inch to 36-inch models.

Other brands with good track records include JVC, Samsung, and Hitachi. Models from those brands were rated Very Good or Excellent about 60 percent of the time. (Hitachi has since stopped making direct-view TVs.)

By contrast, fewer than 5 percent of the sets from GE rated that high. Nor have GE models, a "value brand" generally sold through mass merchandisers, fared well in CONSUMER REPORTS studies of product reliability.

CONSUMER REPORTS tests more than 40 different TV models each year, choosing popular models from leading brands as well as models whose technical innovations make them interesting.

The TV Ratings analysis looked at overall trends and took into account changes in technology, which has led steadily to the production of better and better TV sets. In the past six years, no set has been rated less than Good. No brand was always rated Excellent. Still, some brands clearly had a more consistent record than others.

ing, including entertainment-center cabinets. Price doesn't predict quality, CONSUMER REPORTS tests have found. Price range: $400 to $2,700.

Projection analog sets. Measuring 42 to 73 inches diagonally, these sets typically don't match the picture quality of a conventional picture tube. The image appears dimmer as your viewing position angles away from the center of the screen. Projection sets have plenty of features, such as two-tuner PIP and custom settings. But readers have reported that parts can be hard to get and repairers hard to find. Price range: $1,000 to more than $4,000.

HD-ready sets. These digital sets can display higher-resolution images, even from analog signals such as a good cable connection or a DVD player. They display superior images when paired with an HD source. They're available both as projection sets and direct-view sets. Picture size comes in one of two shapes, expressed as the width-to-height ratio: the conventional squarish 4:3 and the wider 16:9, which is shaped more like a movie-theater screen. An HD-ready set requires a separate digital-TV receiver ($650 and up) to display high-definition material. One advantage to a separate tuner is that it's possible to upgrade the receiver alone should technology advance in the future. Price range for HD-ready sets: $1,100 to more than $10,000.

HDTV sets. Also referred to as true high-definition sets, they come with a built-in digital TV receiver. Most of them are projection sets with the 16:9 picture size. Price range: $1,500 to more than $10,000.

➤ **KEY FEATURES**

Flat tubes, a departure from the decades-old curved TV tubes, reduce off-angle reflections and glare, but they do not necessarily improve picture quality. A **comb**

filter, found on most sets, minimizes minor color flaws at edges within the image and increases picture clarity. An **auto color control** can be set to automatically adjust color balance to make flesh tones look natural. **Color "warmth" adjustment,** or **adjustable color temperature,** lets you shade the picture toward the blue ("cooler," better for images with outdoor light) or red ("warmer," preferred for flesh tones and interiors) range.

Picture-in-picture (PIP) shows two channels at once, one on a small picture inserted in the full-screen image. Unless the set has two-tuner PIP, watching two channels typically requires extra connections using the tuner in a VCR or cable box. This can be complicated to set up and use.

All sets over 13 inches have **closed captioning,** but some also have closed captioning when muted, which automatically displays the dialogue on screen while the sound is muted. **Video-noise reduction** lowers the picture-degrading "noise" from poor reception but at the expense of detail.

Stereo sound is virtually universal on sets 27 inches or larger, but you'll generally discern little stereo separation from a set's built-in speakers. For a better stereo effect, route the signals to a sound system. A few larger TV sets have an **audio amplifier** that can power regular (unpowered) speakers connected to the set's audio output jacks, eliminating the need for a receiver. **Ambience sound** is often termed "surround sound" or the like, but this is not true surround like that from a multispeaker Dolby Digital or Pro Logic home-theater system; rather, it's accomplished through special audio processing. Some people find the wider "soundstage" pleasing; others find it distracting. Side-firing speakers can enhance the stereo effect, but not as much as external speakers, and their sound can be muffled in some

TV cabinets. **Automatic volume control** compensates for the jarring volume jumps that often accompany commercials or changes in channel.

Virtually all TV sets come with a **remote control** to change channels and adjust sound volume and picture. A **universal remote** will control all or most of your video (and some audio) devices once you program it by entering codes. Some sets have a **"smart" remote,** so you don't have to enter a code for each device. (Aftermarket universal remotes typically cost $10 to $40.) Active-channel scan automatically detects and memorizes active channels, eliminating the need to scan manually.

Last-channel recall lets you jump to the previously viewed channel. With **channel labeling,** you enter channels' names (ESPN, CNN, AMC) so you'll know where you are as you change channels. Some models offer an **Extended Data Services (XDS) decoder,** which briefly displays channel and programming information on the show that you're watching (if the station transmits that information). **Guide Plus,** which several manufacturers offer on their sets, displays program listings. The set receives program information when it's off but still in "standby."

Some features are important to specific users: **Separate audio program** (SAP) lets you receive a second soundtrack, typically in another language. Multilingual menus are also common. **Parental controls** include the V-chip, which blocks specific shows based on their content rating; for access, you must enter a code. A TV with **channel block-out** will block specific channels and may also prevent use of the audio/video input jacks to which video games are connected.

Cable/antenna, or **radio frequency** inputs are the most basic; the next step up is **composite video.** An **S-video input jack** lets you take advantage of the superior picture quality from a satellite-dish system, a DVD player, or a digital camcorder. **Component video input** offers even better quality but is useful only with equipment that comes with component outputs, such as some DVD players.

Two or more **audio/video input jacks** are useful if you need to connect more than a single video source; for a camcorder or video game, **front-mounted jacks** are easiest. Most sets of 27 inches or larger have at least two video jacks and one audio input jack, which together allow one external signal source (a VCR, for example) to be connected in a way that generally provides better picture and sound than you would get using the set's antenna jack. Audio output jacks, essential for a home-theater setup, let you direct a stereo TV's audio signal to a receiver or self-powered speakers. A headphone jack lets you watch (and listen) without disturbing others.

Sets that are **1080i/720p capable** refer to those that can display digital signals in the two high-definition specifications, termed 1080i and 720p. True HDTV sets have a built-in HDTV tuner, although the technical details remain subject to change. High-definition programming is not yet widely available, but you can watch regular TV programming on these sets. **VGA/SVGA input** lets your TV accept signals from a computer's graphics card.

➤ HOW TO CHOOSE

Performance differences. Most of the TV sets CONSUMER REPORTS has tested do at least a good job. Some of the biggest differences show up in the sound quality, which won't matter if you're outputting the audio to the external speakers of a sound system. Price doesn't track with performance.

Recommendations. Before you start shopping, decide whether you want to stick with a direct-view set or go with a big-screen projection set, and whether you want a conventional analog TV or one that can handle high-definition signals—either an HD-ready model or an HDTV set with an integrated tuner.

Size is another key consideration. For a fine picture plus many useful features, a 27-inch model may be the best deal. Prices continue to drop for 32-inch sets; some may go for as little as $400. Spend more and you get PIP, flat tubes, and better sound-enhancing features. A 35- or 36-inch set has about 20 percent more screen—at a price roughly 50 percent higher than a 32-incher.

Also consider how your TV will fit in with the other components of your home theater. If you plan to output sound to external speakers, you'll want audio output jacks. Similarly, plan for the future. DVD players, digital camcorders, and other devices require one or more S-video jacks; for DVD players, a component video input is better. Check with your cable-service provider regarding availability of digital cable service.

Be sure to measure a set before buying it, and make sure you have appropriate furniture—some 36-inch TVs may not fit in an entertainment center's cubbyhole. Given the size and weight of these sets, you may want to look into delivery and setup.

Related CR report: December 2002
Reliability: pages 337, 338

VCRS

They don't match DVD quality, but VCRs are still the most versatile and inexpensive way to play, record, and keep video.

Today's VCRs are more of a bargain than ever. Hi-fi models, which cost $155 to $290

when we tested them in November 1998, now have list prices as low as $80 and may sell for as little as $50.

➤ WHAT'S AVAILABLE

Panasonic, RCA, Emerson, and Sony are among the biggest-selling brands. Most low-end VCRs are standard VHS models, but models starting at about $200 typically can record higher-resolution S-VHS format tapes as well.

Monophonic models, starting at about $50, record sound adequately for playback through a small TV speaker, but hi-fi VCRs cost little more and offer sound of near-CD quality. They are much better for larger TVs with stereo sound or for connection to a receiver. Hi-fi models can also play surround-sound movies if used with an audio receiver that decodes surround-sound information. Dual-deck models let you copy tapes easily. There are also a few digital VCRs recording digital satellite–TV content. Price range: hi-fi, $80 to $250; dual-deck, $200 to $350; digital, $800 and up.

➤ KEY FEATURES

Hi-fi models record **high-fidelity sound,** a desirable feature for a home-theater setup. **S-VHS** (for Super VHS) records more information onto a tape for better picture detail. S-VHS requires special tapes, but a relatively new variation, **S-VHS ET,** uses standard VHS tape.

Cable/satellite-box control, also referred to as C3 (for "cable-channel changer"), lets the VCR change the channel anytime you tape a program. **VCR Plus,** now quite common, lets you set up the VCR to tape a program simply by punching in a code number from your local TV listings. Two variations, **VCR Plus Gold** and **VCR Plus Silver,** allow you to bypass the hassle of channel mapping by entering your ZIP code when prompted; the Gold version goes one better by including C3.

Memory backup saves programming information should the VCR temporarily lose power; depending on the VCR, you may have a few minutes or less before the program settings are gone.

Editing features include **shuttle and jog controls,** which let you scan large segments or move forward or backward one frame at a time to find the exact spot you want. **Audio dub,** a higher-end feature, lets you add music or narration to existing recordings. A **flying erase head** lets you insert segments without noticeable video glitches.

Many features aim to save you time. There are various "skip" features. **Automatic commercial advance** lets the VCR bypass all commercials during playback by fast-forwarding past such cues as fades-to-black and changes in sound level. **Movie advance** lets you fly over previews at the beginning of a rented tape. **One-button skip** lets you fast-forward 30 seconds or a minute with each button press. And there are different kinds of search: A **go-to search** skips to a section according to the time on the counter. A zero search finds the place on the tape where the counter was set to zero. An **index search** forwards the tape to a specific index point set by the machine each time you begin a recording.

An **onscreen menu** uses the TV to display your setup and programming choices. **Front-mounted audio/video input jacks** let you easily connect a camcorder, a video game, or another VCR. **Plug and play** eases setup; you connect the VCR to the cable system or an antenna, then plug it in. It reads signals from broadcasters to automatically program the channels and the clock. The latter feature is also known as **auto clock set.**

Some VCRs can automatically switch from SP to EP speed, a feature called **auto speed-switching,** to extend recording time

and help ensure you don't miss a climactic scene because you ran out of tape.

A **universal remote** lets you control other devices along with your VCR; if the kids misplace it, a **remote locator** will page the remote, causing it to beep from its hiding place. **Child lock** disables the VCR's controls to keep programming from being changed.

➤ HOW TO CHOOSE

Performance differences. Because DVD players have redefined excellence in picture quality for inexpensive video gear, none of the VCRs that CONSUMER REPORTS has tested could produce what we now consider an excellent picture. Still, most models have performed very well; the best VCRs in our last tests were as good as any we'd tested in the past. And the best picture you can get from a VCR is almost as good as what you'd get from a typical DVD player.

Recommendations. For basic recording of movies and TV shows, VCRs offer great value, with even inexpensive models now offering hi-fi sound and some level of VCR Plus programming. If you have an S-VHS-C, Hi-8, or digital camcorder, you'll want a VCR that supports S-VHS to view the improved video quality.

If you're hooking a VCR into a home-theater system that includes a DVD player, note that built-in encryption contained in many DVD discs typically won't let you copy DVD movies onto videotape. Such copying is a copyright violation in most cases.

While most VCRs come with four or more heads, more heads do not necessarily translate into better performance. For the best assurance of quality before you buy, try to get a side-by-side demonstration of the models you're considering.

Related CR report: December 2002
Reliability: page 340

KITCHEN & LAUNDRY

What's New in Kitchen & Laundry Products

Today's appliances are smarter, more capable, and more energy efficient than yesterday's. New technologies and tightened government energy standards have sparked the change. A bonus is that today's appliances, large and small, are likely to be more stylish than the appliances you currently own. Here's a rundown on current trends:

Added intelligence. Everything from dishwashers to mixers has been embellished with electronic sensors, controls, and monitors. "Smart" products are supposed to minimize the guesswork of knowing when the clothes are dry, the food is cooked, the dishes are washed, or the toast is browned. This technology can use water and energy more efficiently, as with a washer that automatically fills to the water level the load requires; and a refrigerator that defrosts only as necessary rather than at set intervals.

But such advances are only the first wave. Ready to debut: microwave ovens that scan bar codes on packaged-food labels and automatically set the precise cooking time and power level; Internet-connected refrigerators that scan labels and automatically reorder provisions when you're running low; and self-diagnosing appliances that can convey information to a repair center by computer, allowing a technician to make a preliminary diagnosis before a service call. Whether these products will truly fill a consumer need—or merely serve a manufacturer's need to spark sales—remains to be seen.

Faster cooking. Consumers seem to want food cooked ever faster, or at least manufacturers say they do. Titans such as General Electric, Maytag, and Whirlpool have introduced appliances that claim to reduce cooking times by as much as 60 percent over conventional means by combining various methods—microwave, convection, and halogen or quartz light bulbs. Such hybrid devices may offer another advantage: no preheating. The perceived desire for speed has even fueled a resurgence in a category from another era—pressure cookers—in more consumer-friendly and safer designs.

Improved efficiency. Over the next several years, the U.S. Department of Energy is mandating that new washing machines be 35 percent more efficient. Based on recent CONSUMER REPORTS tests, most top-loading models now on the market won't pass muster, so expect innovative designs in the future. Perhaps in anticipation of DOE regulations, manufacturers have introduced more front-loading machines, inherently more frugal because they tumble clothes through water instead of submerging them, as a top-loader does. Front-loaders consume about two-thirds less water than most top-loaders, though newly designed top-loaders are narrowing the gap. Refrigerators, which typically devour more electricity than any other kitchen appliance, are now required to be less gluttonous. In general, side-by-side units are less space- and energy-efficient than either top- or bottom-freezer models. Over the long run, a pricier model with a low annual energy cost may be less expensive than a cheaper model that uses more electricity.

Easier cleaning. More products are designed with flat, seamless surfaces, fewer buttons, and touchpad controls, making them easier to clean. Smoothtop electric continue to rise in popularity. And manufacturers are offering a new stainless-steel look-alike finish known as VCM that hides the smudges and fingerprints that seem to multiply on stainless steel.

Gas ranges are cleaning up their act, too, as companies such as GE unveil gas smoothtops: Burners and grates sit atop a solid-glass surface, eliminating pesky nooks, crannies, and dripbowls—although you do have to use a special cleansing cream. Nearly all refrigerators now feature movable, glass shelves bound by a lip to retain spills.

Sleeker styling. Just about every major appliance maker now offers stylish kitchen appliances with curved doors, sleek-looking hardware and controls, and a flashy logo or nameplate. Such equipment can cost twice as much as mainstream products, but it may come with plenty of extra features to go with the high styling to help justify the price tag.

Some dishwashers relocate controls from the front panel to the top lip of the door, where they're out of sight. With a front panel that matches kitchen cabinets, this design can help the dishwasher

blend in with its surroundings.

Color choices are proliferating as well. Stainless steel debuted in "professional" and "semi-pro" high-end models. And brushed aluminum finishes are now widely available in mass-marketed products, along with the traditional white and black. Biscuit, bisque, or linen are replacing almond. If you prefer a splashier color for your appliance—such as cobalt blue or hunter green—look to premium brands such as Jenn-Air, KitchenAid, or Viking.

Family-friendly features. Manufacturers are using child lockouts to keep curious fingers out of potentially hazardous places. Some microwave ovens let you punch in a code to prevent accidental activation. A lockout button disables the knobs on a gas range or keeps the dishwasher from shutting down midcycle if little Andy starts poking at the keypad. Such niceties are still relatively new and not yet found on many products.

More power. Sales of powerful commercial-style, stainless-steel ranges—with four or more high-output burners rated at maximum outputs of 15,000 British thermal units per hour, or Btu/hr.—continue to rise. More typical upscale stoves come with an assortment of burners with maximum outputs from 5,000 to 14,000 Btu/hr. Microwaves continue to get more powerful, too, with 1,300 watts the benchmark, up from around 800 a few years ago.

More shopping options. Frigidaire, GE, Maytag, Sears, and Whirlpool sell almost three-fourths of all major appliances. In some categories, Sears alone sells more than some of its biggest competitors combined, and the company is trying to strengthen its position by selling white goods online. But the competitive landscape is changing. Deep-discount warehouse membership clubs such as Costco have expanded their selection of refriger-

Who makes what?

Despite all the nameplates, only a handful of companies actually make refrigerators, ranges, washers, dryers, and dishwashers. They typically sell products under their own brand and also produce specific models for other manufacturers. From our laboratory inspections, we know, for example, that GE's front-loading washer comes off Frigidaire's assembly line. Sears's Kenmore brand, the biggest name in appliances, isn't made by Sears at all. Kenmore products are made entirely by others, the identities of which change from time to time. Here's a rundown of the key players and the familiar names they sell, listed alphabetically:

Frigidaire The company, owned by Sweden's Electrolux, also makes Gibson, Kelvinator, and Tappan appliances. The Frigidaire line is typically higher priced, especially in the tony Frigidaire Gallery and Gallery Professional series. Tappan is a significant force in gas ranges. Kelvinator and Gibson are harder to find, and the products sold under those names are generally less expensive with fewer features.

General Electric One of the two biggest U.S. appliance makers (along with Whirlpool), GE is particularly strong in the cooking categories. The GE name is considered a midrange brand; GE Profile and GE Profile Performance are geared toward more affluent consumers. GE Monogram, focusing on high style and a commercial look with both freestanding and built-in products, competes with boutique names like Thermador (owned by Bosch) and Viking and is distributed separately. Hotpoint is GE's value brand.

Kenmore The nation's biggest source of major appliances, Sears has its store-brand Kenmore models made to order by companies such as Whirlpool, long a manufacturer of many Kenmore laundry machines. Kenmore washing machines and dryers are also made by Frigidaire. Kenmore Elite is Sears's high-end brand of kitchen and laundry products.

Maytag The company that made its name in washers and dryers cultivates a premium image, with many of its products bearing the flagship name. Maytag Neptune is a line of premium laundry machines. Performa is the company's low-priced line. Jenn-Air, best known for modular cooktops and ranges, is Maytag's upscale kitchen brand. Admiral and Magic Chef are budget brands. Maytag purchased Amana in 2001. The company will continue to market appliances under the Amana brand name. (Amana had been the fifth-largest appliance maker, and was known mostly for its refrigerators.)

Whirlpool Also strongly positioned in the laundry room, the nation's other major appliance maker sells products under its corporate name in a wide variety of prices. Whirlpool Gold products are a notch up from the mainstream Whirlpool line; KitchenAid is the company's upscale brand; Roper is the bargain brand.

European and boutique brands Small on market share but often leaders in design and styling, brands such as Asko, Bosch, and Miele were among the first to showcase water-efficient engineering and clean-looking controls for dishwashers and washing machines. Viking is the leading manufacturer of pro-style kitchen appliances and outdoor grills. Sub-Zero is gaining market share with products sold under its own name and the Wolf brand. KitchenAid sells pro-style appliances under the KitchenAid Architect moniker. Other makers of pro-style ranges include DCS, Dacor, and Dynasty.

ators, ranges, and the like. Home Depot and Lowe's, the nation's biggest home-center chains, have publicly announced they want to dethrone Sears as the leading appliance marketer. While the Internet has become a popular way to buy books and get travel deals, it's not much of a factor in the appliance category. Still, e-commerce experts predict online appliance sales could reach $2 billion by 2004—about 6 percent of sales.

Brand battles in small appliances. Coffeemakers, toasters, and blenders rule the countertop, with consumers buying more of them every year than any other countertop appliance. Three brands account for nearly three-quarters of small-appliance sales: Black & Decker, Hamilton Beach/Proctor-Silex, and Sunbeam/Oster.

Major mass retailers, where most of the products are sold, are trying to grab an even larger share of the business by gaining exclusive rights to established national brands. Hamilton Beach/Proctor-Silex, for example, makes products under the GE name (via a licensing agreement) for sale at Wal-Mart. Philips markets a line under its own name through Target. Black & Decker has partnered with chains such as Kmart. Sears sells small appliances under its Kenmore name.

BREADMAKERS

Machines costing $50 or less can turn out white bread and raisin bread that is comparable in texture, color, and taste to loaves kneaded by hand and baked in an oven.

Breadmakers allow virtually anyone to bake bread with just minutes of effort and few skills beyond the ability to measure ingredients and push buttons. What's more, they produce bread that is better than respectable in quality. And they allow you to control what goes into your bread, which might appeal to people with food allergies or gluten intolerance.

➤ WHAT'S AVAILABLE

There are fewer brands today than there were 10 years ago, when this product was introduced. Salton, owner of the Breadman and, Toastmaster, and Welbilt brands, dominates the market. Salton also makes Kenmore (Sears), Williams-Sonoma, and Wal-Mart's Magic Chef breadmakers. They are everywhere from specialty kitchen shops to Wal-Mart.

An increasing number of machines have a rectangular bread pan, which produces a more traditional-looking loaf than did the tall, squarish pans common in the past. Most machines produce one 2-pound traditional-shaped loaf, which typically measures about 7x5 inches and yields about 13 inch-thick slices. One brand, Welbilt, makes two 1-pound loaves. Price range: $40 to $200.

➤ KEY FEATURES

With a typical machine, you place the ingredients in the **pan,** insert the pan in the machine, close the cover, and push buttons to select the right cycle. A **paddle** fitted on a shaft in the pan's base mixes the ingredients and kneads the dough, stopping at **programmed times** to allow for rising before kneading again. An **electric heating coil** in the machine's base then bakes the bread. The time required for each step depends on the type of bread. For example, whole-wheat dough needs more time to rise and bake than white, because it's heavier.

The typical breadmaker has **cycles** for basic white, whole-wheat, sweet, or fruit-and-nut bread, plus "dough" (to be used when you want to shape the dough by hand and bake it in the oven). Most machines have specialty cycles for, say, French bread and pizza dough. On their regular white-bread cycle, breadmakers can take as long as 3½ hours.

Most machines have one or two **rapid cycles,** which increase heat during mixing to prepare loaves in as little as an hour. Recipes for rapid bread often call for more yeast than recipes for regular bread.

Convenience features let you bake without constantly having to supervise the machine. A **delay-start timer,** available on most machines, lets you postpone when your bread is done—typically 13 hours from the time you press the button. A **temperature-warning signal** lets you know when the kitchen temperature isn't optimal for yeast growth. An **add-in signal** tells you when to add fruit, nuts, or other extras so they don't get chopped during kneading. Crust control adjusts baking time so you get the crust color of your choice. A **keep-warm/cool-down function** keeps the bread from getting soggy for at least an hour if you're not there to take it out right away. **Power-outage protection** ensures that when the electricity comes back on after a power outage, the breadmaker will pick up where it left off. Some machines can withstand an hour-long outage; others, an outage of only a few seconds.

➤ HOW TO CHOOSE

Performance differences. Very good bread is symmetrical and evenly baked, with an interior that's somewhat soft, moist, and airy and a crust that's crisp but not too thick or hard. All the breadmakers that CONSUMER REPORTS tested made very good white bread on their regular (not rapid) cycle (at a cost of about 90 cents per loaf). They also made very good raisin bread. Testing found differences, however, in the quality of whole-wheat bread. CONSUMER REPORTS also found that most machines produced short, dense loaves when set on the rapid cycle.

Recommendations. If you're looking for a breadmaker that will turn out very good white or raisin bread, opt for the least expensive model. The largest selection can be found in mass-marketing outlets and discount stores. Don't base your decision on the availability or speed of a rapid cycle; you're likely to be disappointed in the results.

Consider your counter space. Breadmakers typically require a lot of it. Most are 12 to 13 inches high and 10 to 11 inches deep, but they vary in width from 10 inches to 19 inches.

Should you need to replace a bread pan or dough blade after the warranty expires, it might make more sense to buy a new machine. We found that replacing those parts could cost up to 65 percent of the original purchase price.

Related CR report: November 2001

COFFEEMAKERS

You don't need to spend a lot to get a machine that makes good coffee. But you may want to spend a bit more for a model with convenience features and styling that appeals.

The profusion of Starbucks and other specialty coffee shops appears to be driving demand for a new generation of coffeemakers that seek to replicate the coffeehouse experience at home. Customized brewing, water filtration, and thermal carafes are a few of the features manufacturers are hoping will encourage consumers to trade up. Truth is, virtually any model can make a good cup as long as you use decent beans. With coffeemakers, the critical choices come down to ease of use and, perhaps, styling.

➤ WHAT'S AVAILABLE

Manual-drip systems, coffee presses, and percolators are available, but consumers buy more automatic-drip coffeemakers than any other small kitchen appliance: 17 million per year. Mr. Coffee and Hamilton Beach/Proctor-Silex are the two largest brands, along with well-known names such as Black & Decker, Braun, Krups, Melitta, and Proctor Silex.

Coffeemakers come in sizes from single-cup models to machines capable of brewing up to 12 cups at a time. Ten- and 12-cup units account for more than 80 percent of the market, although manufacturers are trying to expand sales by pushing fully featured 4-cup models.

Models range from bare-bones coffeemakers with a single switch to start the brewing and a plain metal hotplate to those with programmable starting and stopping, a water filter, frothing capability, and a thermal carafe. Most consumers opt for plainer models. Black and white remain the standard colors for coffeemakers, but some brands are adapting other hues. Price range: $15 to more than $90.

➤ KEY FEATURES

The easiest models to load with coffee have a **removable filter** basket; baskets that sit inside a pullout drawer are messy. **Paper filters**—usually "cupcake" or cone-shaped —absorb oil and keep sediment from creeping through. Models with a **permanent mesh filter** need to be cleaned after each use, but can save you money over time. Neither type of filter detracted from coffee flavor in CONSUMER REPORTS tests. The simplest way to pour water is into a **reservoir** that has a big flip-top lid with

lines that mark the number of cups in large, clearly visible numbers. Some reservoirs are removable, so you can fill up at the sink, and dishwasher safe. **Transparent fill tubes** with **cup markings** let you check the water level while pouring.

A **thermal carafe** helps retain flavor and aroma longer than a glass pot on a hotplate. Other niceties: a **small-batch setting** to adjust brew time when you make fewer than 5 cups; **temperature and brew-strength controls;** and **a drip-stop feature** that lets you pour a cup before the whole pot's done. A **programmable timer** lets you add ground coffee and water the night before, so you can wake up to a freshly brewed pot in the morning. A **clock-timer** automatically turns off the hotplate at a specified or programmed time after brewing. New models frequently have a more **compact footprint, and flat electronic-touchpad controls.** Some high-end models feature a **built-in bean grinder.** A built-in **water filter** may cut chlorine and, sometimes, mineral buildup. (But a filter can harbor bacteria if you don't regularly change it.)

➤ HOW TO CHOOSE

Performance differences. In CONSUMER REPORTS tests, just about any drip coffeemaker made good-tasting coffee. The differences among machines mostly pertain to convenience. Some models have hard-to-clean nooks and crannies or unclear markings; some easily show stains. Some programmable models were much tougher to set than others. Brewing time for a full pot took from 9 to 11 minutes; models designated as "restaurant" type— which always keeps a full reservoir of hot water at the ready—brewed 8 cups in less than 4 minutes.

Recommendations. If all you want is a good cup of java, there are plenty of coffeemakers from which to choose, starting at around $15. A few dollars more buys a machine that's easier to fill with water and carafes that are easier to pour. At higher prices, you get luxuries such as programmability, sculptural style, and extras such as a drip stop or grinder.

Related CR report: December 2002

DISHWASHERS

Models selling for $300 to $500 can excel at washing dishes, but they may not measure up to costlier models in quietness, water or energy usage, or features.

Spend $300 to $500, and you'll get a dishwasher that cleans a dirty load without prerinsing but is a little noisy. To get the best of everything—cleaning prowess plus the quietest operation, convenience features, water and energy efficiency, and designer styling—you'll have to spend $800 or more.

A dirt sensor, once a premium feature, has made its way down to lower-priced models. That's not necessarily a plus. Machines with dirt sensors have been less energy efficient in CONSUMER REPORTS tests than the federal government's Energy-Guide stickers and Energy Star designations suggest. That's because these stickers and Energy Star designations for dishwashers are calculated using completely clean loads. When washing very heavily soiled loads, these models can use much more hot water and thus energy.

> **WHAT'S AVAILABLE**

GE, Maytag, and Whirlpool make most dishwashers and sell them under flagship and associated brands, including Sears Kenmore. Whirlpool makes the high-end

KitchenAid and the cheaper Roper; Maytag, the high-end Jenn-Air and the low-end Magic Chef; and GE, the upscale GE Monogram and the value-priced Hotpoint. Kenmore dishwashers are made by Whirlpool, CONSUMER REPORTS has determined in recent tests. Asko, Bosch, and Miele are high-end European brands.

Most models fit into a 24-inch-wide space under the kitchen countertop, attached to a hot-water pipe, a drain, and an electrical line. Compact models require less width. Portable models in a finished cabinet can be rolled over to the sink and connected to the faucet. A "dishwasher in a drawer" design from Fisher & Paykel, a New Zealand-based company, has two stacked compartments that can be used simultaneously or individually. Price range: domestic brands, $250 to $1,200; foreign-made brands, $700 to $1,400.

> **KEY FEATURES**

Most models offer a choice of at least three **wash cycles**—Light, Normal, and Heavy—which should be enough for the typical dishwashing jobs in most households. **Light** is a shorter cycle that uses less water than the others and may be suitable for most dishes. **Rinse/Hold** lets you rinse dirty dishes before using the dishwasher on a full cycle. Other cycles offered in many models—none of which we consider crucial—include **Pot Scrubber, Soak/ Scrub,** and **China/Crystal.** Dishwashers often distribute water from multiple places, or "levels," in the machine. Dishwashers also typically offer a choice of drying with or without heat.

Some models use two **filters** to keep wash water free of food: a coarse outer filter for large bits and a fine inner filter for smaller particles. In most such models, a spray arm cleans residue from the coarse filter during the rinse cycle, and a food-disposal grinder cuts up large food particles. These tend to be rather noisy. Some of the more expensive models have a filter that you must pull out and clean manually; these are quieter than those with grinders.

Dirt sensors in "smart" dishwashers determine how dirty the dishes are and provide the appropriate amount of water. Some brands use **pressure sensors** that respond to the actual soil removed from the dishes. Other brands use **turbidity sensors** that work by measuring the amount of light that passes from the sender to the receiver in the sensor.

A **sanitizing wash or rinse** option that raises the water temperature above the typical 140°F doesn't necessarily mean improved cleaning. Routine use could cost a small amount more a year in electricity. Remember that as soon as you touch a dish while taking it out of the dishwasher, it's no longer sanitized.

Better **soundproofing** is a step-up feature in many lines. You'll also pay more for **electronic touchpad** controls, some of them "hidden" in the top lip of the door. Less expensive models have mechanical controls, usually operated by a dial and push buttons. Touchpads are easier to clean. **Dials** indicate progress through a cycle. Some electronic models digitally display time left in the wash cycle. Others merely show a "clean" signal.

Some models with mechanical controls require you to set both dial and push buttons to the desired setting for the correct combination of water quantity and temperature. A **delayed-start** control lets you run the washer at night, when utility rates may be lower. Some models offer **child-safety features,** such as a door and controls that can lock.

Most models hold cups and glasses on top, plates on the bottom, and silverware in a basket. Features that enhance flexibility include **adjustable and removable tines,** which flatten areas to accept bigger dishes, pots, and pans; **slots for silverware** that prevent "nesting"; **removable racks,** which enable loading and unloading outside the dishwasher; **stemware holders,** which steady wine glasses; fold-down shelves, which stack cups in a double-tiered arrangement; and **adjustable and terraced racks,** for tall items.

> ▓ **SHOP SMART**
> Bring along your favorite oversized plate or glass to make sure it fits in the dishwasher you're thinking about buying. Otherwise, you may face years of washing it by hand.

Stainless-steel tubs may last virtually forever, whereas plastic ones can discolor or crack. But most plastic tubs have a warranty of 20 years—much longer than most people keep a dishwasher. In our tests, stainless-steel-lined models had a slightly shorter drying time but didn't wash any better.

➤ HOW TO CHOOSE

Performance differences. Most dishwashers tested by CONSUMER REPORTS have done an excellent or very good job, with little or no spotting or redepositing of food. Manufacturers typically make a few different wash systems, with different "levels" and filters. Avoid the lowest-priced models—those without a filtering system. They tend to redeposit tiny bits of food. Otherwise, according to our tests, the main differences are in water and energy use and noise level. The quietest models are so unobtrusive you might barely hear them. Cycle times in recent tests varied from about 75 to 135 minutes. Several machines that did an excellent job at washing dishes had cycle times of about 90 minutes or less.

A dishwasher uses some electricity to run its motor as well as its drying heater or fan. But about 80 percent of the energy is used to heat water, both in the home's water heater and in the machine. Long-term water efficiency differences can noticeably affect the cost. Models in recent tests used between 5 and 11 gallons in a normal cycle. The annual cost of operation might range from about $25 to $67 with a gas water heater or $30 to $86 with an electric water heater.

Recommendations. The best-performing dishwashers aren't always the most expensive ones, but high-priced models offer styling and soundproofing that appeal to some buyers. Foreign brands are often more energy efficient and quieter, but they're also pricier. Some have spray arms that may hamper loading large dishes and filters that require periodic manual cleaning. You can get fine performance at a low price if you don't insist on the quietest operation and the most flexible loading; for $500 or a bit more, you can get less noise and more features. Compare prices of delivery and installation. Expect to pay about $100; removing your old dishwasher may cost an extra $25 to $50.

Related CR report: May 2002
Ratings: page 238
Reliability: page 333

DRYERS

It's hard to find a clothes dryer that can't, at the very least, dry clothes. The more sophisticated models do the job with greater finesse.

Dryers are relatively simple. Their major distinctions are how they're programmed to shut off once the load is dry (thermostat or moisture sensor) and how they heat the air (gas or electric). Both affect how much you'll pay to buy and run your machine.

CONSUMER REPORTS has found that machines with a moisture sensor tend to recognize when laundry is dry more quickly than machines that use a traditional thermostat. Since they shut themselves off sooner, they use less energy. Sensors are now offered on many models, including some relatively low-cost ones. In our most recent tests, some $400 models had sensors.

Gas dryers typically cost more than electric ones but are cheaper to operate.

➤ WHAT'S AVAILABLE
The top four brands—GE, Maytag, Kenmore (Sears), and Whirlpool—account for about 80 percent of dryer sales. Other brands include Amana (owned by Maytag), Frigidaire (owned by Electrolux), Hotpoint (made by GE), and KitchenAid and Roper (both made by Whirlpool). You may also run across smaller brands such as Crosley, Gibson, and White-Westinghouse, all of which are made by the larger brands. Asko, Bosch, and Miele are European niche brands.

Full-sized models. These dryers generally measure between 27 and 29 inches in width—the critical dimension for fitting into cabinetry and closets. Front-mounted controls on some let you stack the dryer atop a front-loading washer. Full-sized models vary in drum capacity from about 5 to 7½ cubic feet. The larger the drum, the more easily a dryer can handle bulky items. Price range: electric, $200 to $800; gas, $250 to $850. Buying one of the more expensive models may get you more capacity and a few extra conveniences such as electronic controls and a drying rack.

Space-saving models. Compacts, exclusively electric, are typically 24 inches wide, with a drum capacity roughly half that of full-sized models—about 3½ cubic feet. Aside from their smaller capacity, they perform much like full-sized machines.

They can be stacked atop a companion washer, but shorter users may have difficulty reaching the dryer controls or the inside of the drum. Some dryers operate on 120 volts, others on 240. Price range: $380 to more than $1,400.

Another space-saving option is a laundry center, which combines a washer and dryer in a single unit. Laundry centers come with gas or electric dryers. Those can be full-sized (27 inches wide) or compact (24 inches wide). The dryer in a laundry center typically has a somewhat smaller capacity than a full-sized dryer. Models with electric dryers require a dedicated 240-volt power source. Price range: $700 to $1,900.

➤ KEY FEATURES
Full-sized dryers often have two or three **auto-dry cycles,** which shut off the unit when the clothes reach desired dryness. Each cycle might have a **More Dry** setting, to dry clothes completely, and a **Less Dry** setting, to leave clothes damp and ready for ironing. Manufacturers have refined the way dryers shut themselves off. As clothes tumble past a **moisture sensor,** electrical contacts in the drum sample their conductivity for surface dampness and relay signals to electronic controls. Dryers with a **thermostat,** by contrast, measure moisture indirectly by taking the temperature of exhaust air from the drum (the temperature rises as moisture evaporates). Moisture-sensor models are more accurate, sparing your laundry unnecessary drying—and sparing you energy bills that are needlessly high.

Most dryers have a separate temperature control to use a lower heat for delicate fabrics, among other things. A **cool-down feature,** such as Press Care or Finish Guard, helps to prevent wrinkling when you don't remove clothes immediately.

Some models continue to tumble without heat; others cycle on and off. An **express dry cycle** is meant for drying small loads at high heat in less than a half hour. Large loads will take longer. **Touchpad electronic controls** found in higher-end models tend to be more versatile and convenient than mechanical dials and buttons—once you figure them out. Maytag recently introduced a computer screen with a progression of menus that enable you to program specific settings for recall at any time.

A **top-mounted lint filter** may be somewhat easier to clean than one inside the drum. Some models have a **warning light** that signals when the lint filter is blocked. It's important to clean the lint filter regularly to minimize any fire hazard. It's also advisable to use metal ducting (either rigid or flexible) rather than plastic or flexible foil, which can create a fire hazard by trapping lint.

Most full-sized models have a **drum light,** making it easy for you to spot stray items. You may be able to raise or lower the volume of an **end-of-cycle signal** or shut it off. A **rack** included with many machines attaches inside the drum and keeps sneakers or other bulky items from tumbling. Models with **doors that drop down** in front may fit better against a wall, but **side-opening doors** may make it easier to access the inside of the drum.

➤ HOW TO CHOOSE
Performance differences. CONSUMER REPORTS has found that nearly all machines dry ordinary laundry loads well. Models with a moisture sensor don't overdry as much as models using a thermostat, saving a little energy as well as sparing fabric wear and tear. If the dryer will go near the kitchen or a bedroom, pay attention to the noise level. Some models are quiet, but

others are loud enough to drown out normal conversation. Virtually all dryers can accommodate the load from a typical washer, so capacity isn't an issue unless you want to dry bulky items such as comforters.

Recommendations. It's worthwhile to spend the $30 to $50 extra for a moisture-sensor model. More efficient drying will eventually pay for the extra cost. Buy a gas dryer if you can. Although priced about $50 more than an electric model, a gas dryer usually costs about 25 cents less per load to operate, making up the price difference in a year or two of typical use. The extra hardware of a gas dryer, however, often makes it more expensive to repair.

Related CR report: July 2002
Ratings: page 245
Reliability: page 333

FREEZERS

Chest freezers cost the least to buy and run, but self-defrost uprights are the winners for convenience.

If you buy box loads of burgers at a warehouse club or like to keep a few weeks' worth of dinner fixings on hand, the 4- to 6-cubic-foot freezer compartments in most refrigerators may seem positively lilliputian. A separate freezer might be a good investment.

➤ **WHAT'S AVAILABLE**

Two companies make most freezers sold in the U.S.: Frigidaire, which makes models sold under the Frigidaire, GE, and Kenmore labels; and W.C. Wood, which makes models sold under its own name as well as Amana, Danby, Magic Chef, Maytag, and Whirlpool. There are two types of freezer: chests, which are essentially horizontal

boxes with a door that opens upward; and uprights, which come in self-defrost and manual-defrost versions and resemble a single-door refrigerator.

Chests. These freezers vary most in capacity, ranging from 4 to 25 cubic feet. Aside from a hanging basket or two, chests are wide open, letting you put in even large, bulky items; nearly all the claimed cubic-foot space is usable. The design makes chests more energy efficient and cheaper to operate than uprights. Cooling coils are built into all four walls, so no fan is required to circulate the cold air. Because the door opens from the top, virtually no cold air escapes when the door is opened. But a chest's open design makes it hard to organize the contents. Finding something can require bending and, often, moving around piles of frozen goods. If you're short, it can be difficult to extricate an item buried at the bottom (assuming you can remember that it's stashed there). A chest also takes up more floor space than an upright: A 15-cubic-foot model is about 4 feet wide by 2½ feet deep; a comparable upright is just as deep but only 2 to 2½ feet wide.

Defrosting a chest can be a hassle, especially if it's fully loaded or has a thick coating of ice. All chests are manual-defrost, meaning you have to unload the food, store it somewhere at 0°F until the ice encrusting the walls has melted, remove the water that accumulates at the drain, then put back the food. Price range: $140 to $400.

Self-defrost uprights. These models (sometimes called frost-free) have from 11 to 25 cubic feet of space. Like a refrigerator, they have shelves in the main compartment and on the door; some have pullout bins. That lets you organize and access contents but reduces usable space by about 20 percent. Interior shelves can be removed or adjusted to fit large items. When you open the door of an upright, cold air spills out from the bottom, while warm, humid air sneaks in at the top. That makes the freezer work harder and use more energy to stay cold, and temperatures may fluctuate a bit. Self-defrost models compensate by using a fan to circulate cold air from the cooling coils, which are in the back wall.

Self-defrosting, which involves heaters that turn on periodically to remove excess ice buildup, eliminates a tedious, messy chore but uses extra energy—a self-defrost model costs about $20 a year more to run than a similar-sized chest. For many people, the convenience might be worth the extra cost. Self-defrosting models are also a bit noisier than other types—an issue only if they're located near a living area rather than in the basement or garage. While freezers of old weren't recommended for use in areas that got very hot or cold, current models should work fine within a wide ambient temperature range—typically 32° to 110°F. Price range: $350 to $750.

Manual-defrost uprights. These freezers have a capacity of 5 to 25 cubic feet, of which some 15 percent isn't usable. They cost less to buy and run than self-defrost models but aren't as economical as chests. Unlike their self-defrost counterparts, these uprights don't have a fan to circulate cold air, which can result in uneven temperatures. Defrosting is quite a chore. The metal shelves in the main space are filled with coolant, so scraping ice from them is risky: You can damage the shelves and cause the coolant to leak. What's more, ice tends to cling to the wires on the shelves, so defrosting can take up to 24 hours. Because the shelves contain coolant, they can't be adjusted or removed (as they can be on self-defrost models) to hold large items. Price range: $160 to $600.

▶ KEY FEATURES

While freezers have fewer features than some other major appliances, there are several features worth looking for. **Interior lighting** makes it easier to find things, especially in dimly lit areas. A **power-on light,** indicating that the freezer has power, is helpful. A **temperature alarm** lets you know when the freezer is too warm inside, such as after a prolonged power outage. (If you lose power, don't open the freezer door; food should remain frozen for about 24 to 48 hours.) A **quick-freeze** feature brings the freezer to its coldest setting faster by making it run continuously instead of cycling on and off. A **flash-defrost** feature on manual-defrost models can speed defrosting by circulating hot gas from the compressor through the cooling tubes.

▶ HOW TO CHOOSE

Performance differences. CONSUMER REPORTS has found that most models of a type are similar in terms of performance, efficiency, and convenience. The usable capacity of chest freezers is generally the same as the labeled capacity; the capacity of some manual-defrost and self-defrost uprights is somewhat less than what is labeled. Operating a new 15-cubic-foot freezer costs $30 to $55 a year at typical electric rates, depending on the type. That's in the same ballpark as a new refrigerator's annual energy cost.

Recommendations. A chest freezer gives you the most space, with room for bulky items, and the best performance for the lowest purchase price and operating cost. But you'll have to defrost it periodically. For freedom from defrosting and ease of access, go with a self-defrost upright. It will cost a little more to buy and operate than a chest, but the convenience may be worth it. We don't see a compelling reason to buy a

manual-defrost upright when comparable self-defrosting units perform better and cost about the same. Manual models, however, do offer more usable space for the money than self-defrost models.
Related CR report: August 2002
Ratings: page 250

IRONS

Many new irons are bigger, more colorful, more feature-laden, and more expensive. But you can get a fine performer for $25 or so.

Many businesspeople are hanging up their business suits and dresses in favor of casual attire, often made of washable fabrics such as cotton. That means fewer trips to the dry cleaner and more time spent pressing machine-washed garments so they look presentable. If you're in the market for an iron, you've got plenty of choices, ranging from budget models to fancy irons with features galore.

➤ **WHAT'S AVAILABLE**
GE, Kenmore, and Toastmaster have started selling irons, joining familiar names such as Black & Decker and Proctor-Silex, which together account for more than half of all iron sales. More consumers are springing for a higher-priced iron than in years past, but three out of four still spend less than $40. Budget-priced doesn't necessarily mean bare-bones, however.

Features such as automatic shutoff, burst of steam, and self-clean are now standard on most $25 to $40 models. Irons priced at $40 and up tend to be larger, with innovations such as vertical steaming, antidrip steam vents, and even anticalcium systems designed to prevent mineral buildup.

Price range: $10 for plain vanilla to $150 for top of the line models.

➤ **KEY FEATURES**
Many new irons release more steam than earlier models. Most produce the best steaming during the first 10 minutes of use and then gradually taper off as the water is used up. You can usually adjust the amount of steam or turn it off, but models with **automatic steam** produce more steam at higher temperatures. A few won't allow you to use steam at low settings, since the water doesn't get hot enough and simply drips out. An **antidrip feature,** usually on higher-priced models, is designed to prevent leaks when using steam at lower settings.

Burst of steam, available on most new irons, lets you push a button for an extra blast to tame stubborn wrinkles. If steam isn't enough for something such as a wrinkled linen napkin, dampen it using the **spray function,** available on virtually all irons today. On some models, burst of steam can be used for vertical steaming to remove wrinkles from hanging items.

An iron should have an easy-to-see **fabric guide** with a list of settings for common fabrics. A temperature control that's clearly marked and easily accessible, preferably on the front of the handle, is a plus. Most irons have an indicator light to show that the power is on; a few also indicate when the iron reaches or exceeds the set temperature.

Automatic shutoff has become standard on most irons, but a few still lack this must-have feature. Some irons shut off only when they're left motionless in a horizontal or vertical position. Those with three-way shutoff also lose power when tipped on their side. Shutoff times vary from 30 seconds to 60 minutes.

Water reservoirs in general are getting larger. Some are a small, vertical tube; others are a large chamber that spans the saddle area under the handle. Transparent chambers, some brightly colored, make it easy to see the water level.

A growing number of irons have a **hinged or sliding cover** on the water-fill hole. The idea is to prevent leaking, but it doesn't always work. Also, the cover may get in the way or can be awkward to open and close. Most convenient is a **removable tank**. Some irons come with a handy plastic **fill cup**. Almost all new irons can use tap water, unless the water is very hard. An **anticalcium system,** usually on more expensive irons, is designed to reduce calcium deposits.

Most models now offer a **self-cleaning feature** to flush deposits from vents, but it's not always effective with prolonged use of very hard water. The burst of steam feature also cleans vents to some extent.

Many models have a nonstick **soleplate**. Some more expensive irons have a stainless-steel soleplate, while some budget irons have an aluminum one. We didn't find any difference in glide among the various types of soleplate when ironing with steam. Nonstick soleplates are generally easier to keep clean, but they may be scratched by something such as a zipper, and a scratch could create drag over time. You should clean the soleplate occasionally to remove residue, especially if you use starch, following the manufacturer's directions.

The **power cord** on many irons pivots down or to the sides during use, which keeps it out of the way. A retractable cord can be convenient, but be careful so that it doesn't whip when retracted. Cordless irons eliminate fumbling with the cord but must be reheated on the base for 90 seconds or so every couple of minutes, which can be time-consuming.

Weight is more critical to comfort than performance. Managing a heavy iron can be an arm workout you might prefer to have at the gym. Some handles might be too thick for smaller hands; others provide too little clearance for larger hands.

➤ **HOW TO CHOOSE**

Performance differences. Many of the irons on the market will do a fine job of removing wrinkles from clothing. The most significant differences come in ease of use. Some controls are easier to see and use, for example. For everyday pressing, a $20 or $25 iron should have the performance and basic features to do the job. Models selling for $10 or $15 are less likely to satisfy. A $30 to $50 model will generally have more bells and whistles but won't necessarily offer better performance. A price more than that is likely to get you the most (and the newest) features but may not result in better ironing.

> **▓ TECH TIP**
> Don't set your iron for steam if you're ironing at a low temperature. If there's not enough heat to turn the water into steam, you may get streaks of water on your clothing.

Recommendations. Features differ from model to model, so determine what is important to you—and be sure to include automatic shutoff on your must-have list. Try handling an iron that's on display in a store to see if its size and shape feel right to you.

Related CR report: August 2002

KITCHEN KNIVES

Knives that you must regularly sharpen generally cut the best. But some that never need sharpening do a good job—and cost less.

You need not be a master chef to appreciate a fine kitchen knife. While high-quality tools won't magically impart the talent to butterfly a leg of lamb or carve radish rosettes, they can help you work more precisely and with less effort. But if you can't tell crudités from canapés—or even if cooking is a still a new adventure for you—less expensive cutlery may do you just fine.

> ## WHAT'S AVAILABLE

Ekco, Farberware, and Regent Sheffield-Oxo are among the less expensive brands. High-end brands include Henckels, and Wüsthof, KitchenAid, Cuisinart, Calphalon, and Emerilware. Starter sets of kitchen knives typically sell for about 25 percent less than the same knives sold individually. Storage blocks and sharpening steels are generally extra. There are often seven or nine pieces in a set that includes a storage block, a sharpening steel, and the following four basic knives: but a set of three or four should suffice for most people.

Chef's knife. Perhaps the most versatile, it's used for chopping, dicing, slicing, and mincing, often with a rocking motion. The blade is wide for extra heft. Typical blade length: 8 to 14 inches.

Slicing knife. The thin, flexible blade of this knife is especially appropriate for carving beef, poultry, and pork. Typical blade length: 8 to 10 inches.

Utility knife. Probably second to the chef's knife in usefulness, it's good for similar but smaller cutting tasks. The blade is narrower than that of a chef's knife. Typical blade length: 5 to 6 inches.

Paring knife. Handy for peeling, coring, paring, cleaning (shrimp, say), and slicing. It's also good for creating garnishes and fine work. Like a utility knife, it has a thin blade, but it's even shorter. Typical blade length: 3 to 4 inches. Price range for sets: $10 to $200 or more.

> ## KEY FEATURES

Most expensive knives are forged from stain-resistant and rust-resistant **high-carbon steel.** Forged blades are created by pounding a steel slab into shape with a mechanical hammer that exerts tons of force. They demand regular honing, but the payoff is a razor-sharp edge.

Many cheaper kitchen knives, and a few expensive ones, are stamped from a single sheet of steel, creating a relatively thin, light blade. Some require regular honing; some don't.

Knives are typically available with three types of blades: fine-edged blades that require sharpening; fine-edged that don't require sharpening; and serrated blades, with teeth along part or all of the stamped with a toothed edge, which don't require sharpening. Serrated knives are especially good at cutting through bread and tomatoes.

Most knives have a **hard-plastic handles.** Restaurants favor plastic for sanitary reasons and because it stands up to hot water and soaking in the dishwasher. **Bare-wood handles** may be vulnerable, although a waterproof coating can helps wood handles it resist moisture. Traditionalists tend to favor **riveted handles,** but our tests uncovered no drawbacks to molded handles.

A **sharpening steel**, used to keep a fine-edged knife in top shape, is a good addition to your kitchen.

HOW TO CHOOSE

Performance differences. Knives that need routine sharpening generally cost more but do perform best, according to CONSUMER REPORTS tests. While stamping can produce a top-notch blade, stamped knives generally don't perform as well as forged ones. Blades that don't require sharpening typically cut unexceptionally, but they're usually cheaper and require little upkeep.

Recommendations. You generally get

what you pay for. But there are some decent sets for $50 or less. When shopping, hold a knife in your hand. It should feel balanced, neither too heavy nor too light. Check to ensure that the handle is attached securely, without gaps that can trap food residue.

CONSUMER REPORTS advises that kitchen knives be hand-washed, since dishwasher detergent can pit the blades.

Related CR report: December 2002

MICROWAVE OVENS

You'll see larger capacities, added power, sensors that detect doneness, and stylish designs. Countertop models have dropped in price.

Microwave ovens, which built their reputation on speed, are also showing some smarts. Many models automatically shut off when a sensor determines that the food is cooked or sufficiently heated. Such sensors are also used to automate an array of cooking chores, with buttons labeled for frozen entrées, baked potatoes, popcorn, and other items. Design touches include softer edges for less boxy styling, stainless steel, and for a few, translucent finishes.

➤ WHAT'S AVAILABLE
Sharp leads the countertop microwave-oven market with almost 25 percent of sales, followed by GE, Panasonic, Emerson, Samsung, and Kenmore. GE sells the most over-the-range models.

Microwaves come in a variety of sizes, from compact to large. Most ovens sit on the countertop, but a growing number sold, about 25 percent, are mounted over the range. Manufacturers are working to boost capacity without taking up more counter space by moving controls to the door and using recessed turntables and smaller electronic components. They also tend to tally every cubic inch, including corner spaces where food on the turntable can't rotate, to gauge capacity.

CONSUMER REPORTS has found that the diameter of the turntable is a more realistic measurement, and bases the calculation of usable capacity on that. Microwave ovens also vary in the power of the **magnetron**, which generates the microwaves. Midsized and large ovens are rated at 900 to 1,300 watts, compact ovens at 600 to 800 watts. A higher wattage may heat food more quickly, but differences of 100 watts are probably inconsequential.

Price range: countertop models, $80 to $200; over-the-range, $300 to $500; convection countertop or over-the-range, $330 to $600.

➤ KEY FEATURES
A **turntable** rotates the food so it will heat more uniformly, but the center of the dish still tends to be cooler than the rest. Most turntables are removable for cleaning. With some models, you can turn off the rotation when, say, you're using a dish too large to rotate. But results won't be as good.

You'll also tend to find similarities in the controls from model to model. A **numeric keypad** is used to set cooking times and power levels. Most ovens have **short-cut keys** for particular foods, reheating, or defrosting; some start immediately when you hit the shortcut key, and others require you to enter the food quantity or weight. Some models have an **automatic popcorn feature** that makes popcorn at the press of a button.

Pressing a **1-minute** or **30-second key** runs the oven at full power or extends the current cooking time. Microwaves typically have **several power levels**, though six are more than adequate.

Most automatic sensors are **moisture sensors**, which gauge the steam that food emits when heated and use that information to determine when the food is cooked. An alternative is an **infrared sensor**, which detects a food's surface temperature to determine doneness. CONSUMER REPORTS believes that the small premium you pay for a sensor is worth it. A few ovens have a **crisper pan** for frying eggs or crisping pizza, since microwave cooking leaves food hot but not browned or crispy. A relatively new category known as **speed cookers** use a combination of heating technologies to cook food quickly and make it crisp or browned.

Over-the-range ovens have at least **two vent-fan speeds**; often, the fan turns on whenever heat is sensed from the range below. Exhaust can go outside or into the kitchen. If you want the oven to vent inside, you'll need a charcoal filter (sometimes included). An over-the-range microwave, however, doesn't tend to handle ventilation as well as a hood-and-blower ventilation system.

➤ HOW TO CHOOSE

Performance differences. CONSUMER REPORTS has found that most microwave ovens are very good or excellent overall. Most are easy to use and competent at heating and defrosting, their main tasks. We found a few ovens that left large icy chunks while defrosting ground beef, however.

Be skeptical about special technologies that claim to improve cooking evenness. All but a few microwave ovens heated a baking dish full of cold mashed potatoes to a fairly uniform temperature in CONSUMER REPORTS tests.

Recommendations. Look for the size that best fits your kitchen. A large or midsized countertop model is a good choice

for many households. Compact models, though less expensive, typically have lower power ratings and don't heat as fast. Your kitchen layout may dictate an over-the-range microwave, which ventilates itself and the range. These models cost about twice as much as large countertop models, however, and are heavy, possibly taking two people to install. Properly installing an over-the-range model may also require an electrician.

Related CR reports: January 2002
Ratings: page 268
Reliability: page 335

MIXING APPLIANCES

You need to choose the right machine for the way you prepare foods. You may need more than one machine.

Which food-prep appliance best suits your style and the foods you prepare? Blenders usually excel at mixing icy drinks. Stick-shaped immersion blenders are handy mostly for stirring powdered drinks. Food processors are versatile machines that can chop, slice, shred, and puree many different foods. Mini-choppers are good for small jobs such as mincing garlic. Hand mixers can handle light chores such as whipping cream or mixing cake batter. And powerful stand mixers are ideal for committed cooks who make bread and cookies from scratch.

➤ WHAT'S AVAILABLE

Blenders. Rugged construction and increased power are driving blender sales. Ice-crushing ability is the key attribute consumers look for in a blender, manufacturers say. But appearance counts as well, since consumers are more likely to store the appliance on the countertop than in the cupboard. As a result, you'll see more colors and metallic finishes. Hamilton Beach and Sunbeam account for more than 60 percent of countertop blender sales. Other makers include Cuisinart, KitchenAid, Krups, Vita-Mix, and Waring, a product pioneer. Braun controls the handheld segment of the market. Price range: $20 up to $400 for high-end machines.

Immersion blenders—stick-shaped handheld devices with a swirling blade on the bottom—are on a power trip, with models juiced up to 200 watts or more. With these devices, though, power does seem to make a difference. An immersion blender in the 100-watt range didn't have the energy to mince onions in CONSUMER REPORTS tests. These blenders, popular for stirring soups and pureeing and chopping vegetables, are increasingly paired with **accessories** such as beaters, whisks, and attachments to clean baby bottles.

Food processors. With food processors, the trend is toward multifunction capability, with one piece doing the job of two appliances. Cuisinart's Smart Power Duet comes with an interchangeable food-processor container and glass blender jar and blade. Either attachment fits on the motorized base. Another design trend is a mini-bowl insert that fits inside the main container for smaller tasks. Newer designs tend to be sleeker, with rounded rather than squared-off corners.

Among food processors, the dominant brands are Cuisinart and Hamilton Beach. Black & Decker is the foremost name in mini-choppers, most of which sell for less than $20, with more powerful, fully featured models costing considerably more. Price range: $20 to $250

Hand mixers. As with blenders, the big push in mixers is for more power, good for handling heavy dough. Stand mixers come in varieties from heavy-duty (offering the most power and the largest mixing bowls) to light-service machines that are essentially detachable hand mixers resting on a stand. Models typically vary in power, from about 200 to 525 watts. Sales of light-duty, convenient hand mixers have held their own in recent years.

Black & Decker, Hamilton Beach, and Sunbeam are the predominate brands among hand mixers. KitchenAid owns half the stand-mixer market; Sunbeam is the next best-selling brand. The majority of stand mixers sell for more than $100, some up to several times as much. Price range: $10 to $100 and up.

> **KEY FEATURES**
With blenders. Three to 16 **speeds** are the norm; power ratings are from 330 to 525 watts. Manufacturers claim that higher wattage translates into better performance, but in recent CONSUMER REPORTS tests, lower-wattage models often outperformed beefier ones, turning out icy drinks faster and leaving them smoother in consistency. Three well-differentiated speeds are adequate; a dozen or more closely spaced ones are overkill.

Containers are glass, plastic, or stainless steel, and come in sizes from about a quart to a half-gallon. A glass container is heavier and more stable. In tests, the blenders with glass jugs tended to perform better because they didn't shake. Glass is also easier to keep clean. Plastic may scratch and is likely to absorb the smell of whatever is inside. A stainless-steel container makes it difficult to know whether the mixture is the right consistency.

A wide mouth makes loading food and washing easier; big and easy-to-read markings help you measure more accurately. A **pulse setting** lets you fine-tune blending time. A **power boost** offers a momentary burst of higher speed, useful for demanding jobs such as pulverizing ice. **Touchpad controls** are easy to wipe clean. A **blade** that's permanently attached to the container (typical of the Warings) is harder to clean than a removable blade.

With food processors. All have a clear-plastic **mixing bowl** and lid, an S-shaped metal **chopping blade** (and sometimes a duller version for kneading dough), and a plastic **food pusher** to prod food through the feed tube. Some tubes are wider than others, so you don't have to cut up vegetables—such as potatoes—to fit the opening. One speed is the norm, plus a pulse setting to precisely control processing. Bowl capacity ranges from around 1 cup to 14 cups (dry). Also standard on full-size processors: a **shredding/slicing disk.** Some also come with a **juicer attachment.** Touchpad controls are becoming more commonplace, too. Mini-choppers may look like little food processors, but they're for small jobs only, like chopping a clove of garlic or an onion half.

With mixers. Just about any hand mixer is good for nontaxing exercises such as beating egg whites, mashing potatoes, or whipping cream. The **slow-start feature** on some mixers prevents ingredients from spattering when you start the mixer, though it's no big deal to manually step through the three or so speeds. An indentation on the underside of the motor housing allows the mixer to sit on the edge of a bowl without taking the beaters out of the batter.

Stand mixers have one or two different-size **bowls**, a **beater** or two, and a **dough hook.** Some mixers offer options such as **splash guards** to prevent flour from spewing out of the bowl, plus **attachments** to make pasta, grind meat, and stuff sausage. Stand mixers generally have 5 to 16 speeds; CONSUMER REPORTS thinks three well-spaced settings is enough. You should be able to lock a mixer's power head in the Up position so it won't crash into the bowl when the beaters are weighed down with dough and, conversely, in the Down spot to keep the beaters from kicking back in stiff dough.

➤ HOW TO CHOOSE

Performance differences. With blenders, power, performance, and price don't always go hand in hand. Recent CONSUMER REPORTS tests revealed modestly powered, inexpensive blenders that turned out smooth-as-silk mixtures, while some bigger and fancier ones left food pulpy or lumpy. Most food processors we've tested can shred cheese, purée baby food, and slice tough, fibrous produce such as ginger and celery without missing a beat. Kneading dough takes power, and large models handled the job with aplomb. Smaller machines force you to split the dough into batches, and, even after doing so, some labored while performing the task.

Heavy-duty stand mixers can tackle tough baking tasks such as kneading large quantities of dense dough. In tests, light-duty, less powerful models strained and overheated under a heavy load.

Recommendations. Choose the right machine for your cooking tasks. Blenders excel at puréeing soup, crushing ice, grating hard cheese, and making fruit smoothies.

A food processor is better at grating cheddar cheese and chopping meat, vegetables, and nuts.

A processor can also slice and shred. Neither machine can match a mixer's prowess at mashing potatoes or whipping cream to a light velvety consistency. For those kinds of tasks, you can buy a perfectly adequate hand mixer for as little as $10.

A midsized processor is probably the best choice for basic tasks. Bigger models are geared to cooking enthusiasts who want to create picture-perfect salads and knead large quantities of pasta dough. Mini-choppers save space but aren't too versatile.

Not everyone needs a stand mixer. But if you're a dedicated baker, a stand mixer is useful and convenient. It will weigh more than 20 pounds or so, however; keep that in mind if you're planning to store the mixer in a cabinet.

Spending more will typically get you touchpad controls, sculpted styling, extra speeds and power, and perhaps colors to match your kitchen's decor. You'll pay more for a blender with a thermal, copper, or stainless-steel jar than a plastic or glass one; a food processor with a bigger container; and a more powerful, capacious mixer.

POTS & PANS

Nonstick pots and pans are easy to clean. Uncoated cookware is often more durable. Your best bet might be some of each.

Is boiling water the extent of your kitchen prowess or do you routinely take on much more challenging tasks? Could you work in the kitchen of a five-star restaurant or are you a culinary klutz? How you answer those questions is a good gauge of the price range for the cookware you need.

A basic set of seven to 10 pieces, typically one or two pots, a skillet, a stockpot, and lids, can be had for $50. At the other end of the spectrum is a set of stylish and sturdy commercial-style cookware for as much as $600. And there are lots of good choices in between.

➤ **WHAT'S AVAILABLE**
Farberware, Mirro/Wearever, Revere, and

T-Fal are the most widely sold brands. Commercial-style brands include All-Clad and Calphalon. TV's celebrity chef Emeril Lagasse is mixing it up in the cookware market with Emerilware (made by All-Clad). Other recent entrants in the cookware field include the appliance maker KitchenAid and the knife maker Henckels.

Choices abound: aluminum, stainless steel, copper, cast iron, tempered glass, or porcelain on carbon steel; nonstick, porcelain-coated, or uncoated; lightweight or heavy-duty commercial-style; handles of metal, plastic, or wood.

Commercial-style cookware is typically made of aluminum or stainless steel. Cooking enthusiasts will appreciate that these sturdy pots and pans are built to conduct heat evenly up the sides and that their riveted metal handles can be put to hard use. A stovetop grill pan often has raised ridges that sear meat and vegetables. Basic sets of cookware can be supplemented with individual pieces from what is known as open stock. Price range: $50 or less for a low-end set; $50 to $100 for midlevel; $200 and up for high-end or commercial-style.

➤ **KEY FEATURES**
The most versatile materials for pots and pans are the most common ones: aluminum and stainless steel. **Aluminum,** when it's sufficiently heavy-gauge, heats quickly and evenly. Thin-gauge aluminum, besides heating unevenly, is prone to denting and warping. **Anodized aluminum and aluminum** are excellent heat conductors and are relatively lightweight. Matte, dark-gray, anodized aluminum is durable but easily stained and not dishwasher-safe. **Enamel-coated aluminum,** typically found in low-end lines, can easily chip.

Stainless steel goes in the dishwasher, but it conducts and retains heat poorly.

It's usually layered over aluminum or comes with a copper or aluminum core on the bottom.

Copper heats and cools quickly, ideal when temperature control is important. It's good for, say, making caramel sauce. Provided that it's kept polished, copper looks great hanging on a kitchen wall. Because copper reacts with acidic foods such as tomatoes, it's usually lined with stainless steel or tin, which may blister and wear out over time. Solid-copper cookware, thin-gauge or heavy-gauge, is expensive.

You might want some **cast-iron** or **tempered-glass** pieces. Cast iron is slow to heat and cool, but it handles high temperatures well and it's great for stews or Cajunstyle blackening. Tempered glass breaks easily and cooks unevenly on the stove, but it can go from the freezer to the oven, broiler, or microwave—and to the table.

Most Americans opt for **nonstick** pots and pans to reduce the need for elbow grease when cleaning up. The first nonstick coatings, introduced on cookware more than 30 years ago, were thin and easily scratched. Nonsticks have greatly improved but still shouldn't be used with metal utensils or very high heat. To improve durability, some manufacturers use a thicker nonstick coating or create a gritty or textured surface before applying a nonstick finish. Many nonstick pots and pans aren't meant for the dishwasher, but they are easy to wash by hand.

There are some advantages to **uncoated**

> ▨ **SHOP SMART**
> A branded nonstick coating is not necessarily a good predictor of durability. CONSUMER REPORTS has found that some unbranded nonstick coatings do as well as or better than branded.

cookware. It's dishwasher-safe, it can handle metal utensils, and it's good for browning. It's also better when you want a little food to stick—say, when you want particles of meat left behind in a pan after sautéing so you can make a flavorful pan sauce. **Porcelain coatings** are easy to maintain and tough (although they can be chipped).

Handles are typically made from tubular stainless steel, cast stainless steel, heat-resistant plastic, or wood. **Solid metal handles** can be unwieldy but are sturdy. Solid or **hollow metal handles** can get hot but may be able to go from stovetop to broiler without damage. **Lightweight plastic handles** won't get as hot but can't go in ovens above 350°F, plus they can break. **Wooden handles** stay cool but don't go in the oven or dishwasher and may deteriorate over time. Handles are either welded, screwed, or riveted onto cookware. **Riveted handles** are the strongest. Some sets have removable handles that are used with different pieces, but they may fit with some pieces better than others.

Cookware with a specific shape simplifies certain cooking tasks. A skillet with **flared sides** aids sautéing or flipping omelets. **Straight sides** are better for frying. **Flat bottoms** work well on an electric range, especially a smoothtop.

➤ HOW TO CHOOSE

Performance differences. Most people now opt for nonstick, which requires little or no oil and cleans easily. But uncoated cookware is better for browning and can stand up to metal utensils better. Commercial-style sets are sturdy, but they're relatively heavy and their metal handles get hot. "Hand-weigh" pieces as you shop, and imagine how they will feel when full. You might be more comfortable using lightweight pots and pans with comfortable plastic handles that stay better insulated from the heat. Cast iron and copper are great for making certain dishes, but they may not be practical as a basic set.

Recommendations. Choose a set with pots and pans that best match your cooking needs and style. Over time, you can supplement your set by buying from open stock. Some people prefer individual pieces in different styles—a nonstick frying pan, say, and an uncoated stockpot.

Related CR report: December 2002

RANGES, COOKTOPS, AND WALL OVENS

Choices can be confusing, but you don't have to spend top dollar for impressive performance with high-end touches.

If you're in the market for a stove, you must first decide whether you want a freestanding range (with oven included) or a separate cooktop and wall oven. A cooktop/wall oven combo may offer you more flexibility with your kitchen design, although ranges can be less expensive. You'll also need to decide on gas, electricity, or both. Gas, of course, is only possible if you have access to a gas hookup.

Electric ranges now include traditional coil and newer smoothtop models, in which a sheet of ceramic glass covers the heating elements. Both types of cooktop elements offer quick heating and the ability to maintain low heat levels.

Gas ranges use burners, which don't heat as quickly as electric elements. Even high-powered burners tend to heat more slowly than the fastest electric coil elements, sometimes because the heavy cast-iron grates slow the process by absorbing

heat. But you can see how high or low you are adjusting the flame, and you can instantly shut off the burners. Many high-end gas stoves are "professional-style" models with beefy knobs, heavy cast-iron grates, stainless-steel construction, and four or more high-powered burners. These high-heat behemoths can cost thousands, and typically require a special range hood and blower system. They may also need special shielding and a reinforced floor.

You'll also find more and more shared characteristics between electric and gas ranges. For example, some gas models have electric warming zones, and a growing number of high-end gas ranges pair gas cooktop burners with an electric oven.

> **WHAT'S AVAILABLE**

GE and Whirlpool are the leading makers of ranges, cooktops, and wall ovens. Other major brands include Kenmore (Sears), Amana, Frigidaire, Maytag, Jenn-Air, and KitchenAid. Mainstream brands have established high-end offshoots, such as Kenmore Elite, GE Profile, and Whirlpool Gold. High-end, pro-style brands include Bosch, Dacor, DCS, GE Monogram, Thermador, Viking, and Wolf.

Freestanding range. These ranges can fit in the middle of a kitchen counter or at the end. Widths are usually 20 to 40 inches, although most are 30 inches wide. They typically have controls on the backguard. Slide-in models eliminate the backsplash and side panels to blend into the countertop, while drop-ins rest atop toe-kick-level cabinetry and typically lack a storage drawer. Ovens can be self-cleaning or manual-clean, although most mainstream ranges and a growing number of pro-style models now include a self-cleaning feature. Price range: $400 to $1,500.

Pro-style range. Bulkier than freestanding ranges, these can be anywhere from 30 to 60 inches wide. Larger ones include six or eight burners, a grill or griddle, and a double oven. Many have a convection feature, and some have an infrared gas broiler. But you usually don't get sealed burners, which keep crumbs from falling beneath the cooktop, or a storage drawer. Price range: $2,500 to $8,000.

Cooktop. You can install a cooktop on a kitchen island or anywhere else where counter space allows. As with freestanding ranges, cooktops can be electric coil, electric smoothtop, or gas. Paired with a wall oven, a cooktop adds flexibility, since it can be located separately. Most cooktops are 30 inches wide and are made of porcelain-coated steel or ceramic glass, with four elements or burners. Some are 36 or 48 inches wide and have space for an extra burner. Modular cooktops let you mix and match parts—removing burners and adding a grill, say—although you'll pay more for that added flexibility. Preconfigured cooktops are less expensive. Price ranges: electric cooktop, $200 to $1,200; gas cooktop, $300 to $1,750.

Wall oven. These can be electric or gas, self-cleaning or manual, with or without a convection setting. Width is typically 24, 27, or 30 inches. Best of all, you can eliminate bending by installing it at waist or eye level, although you can also nest it under a countertop. Price range: $400 to more than $3,500 for double-oven models. The convection option typically adds $400 to the price.

➤ KEY FEATURES

On all ranges. Look for easy-cleaning features such as a **glass or porcelain backguard,** instead of a painted one; **seamless corners and edges**, especially where the cooktop joins the backguard; and a **raised edge** around the cooktop to contain spills.

On electric ranges and cooktops.

Consider where the **controls** are located. Slide-in ranges have the dials to the front panel, while freestanding models have them on the backguard. Some models locate controls to the left and right, with oven controls in between, giving you a quick sense of which control operates which element. But controls clustered in the center stay visible when tall pots sit on rear heating elements.

On most electric cooktops, controls take up room on the surface. Some models have electronic touchpads, however, allowing the entire cooktop to be flush with the counter.

Coil elements, the most common and least expensive electric option, are easy to replace if they break. On an electric range with coil elements, look for a **prop-up top** for easier cleaning, and **deep drip pans** made of porcelain to better contain spills and ease cleaning.

Spending an extra $200 will buy you a **smoothtop** model; most use radiant heat, though halogen is a niche segment. Halogen elements redden immediately when turned on, while radiant elements take about six seconds. Some smoothtops have **expandable elements**, which allow you to switch between a large, high-power element and a small, low-power element contained within it. Some smoothtops also include a **low-wattage element** for warming plates or keeping just-cooked food at the optimal temperature. Some have an elongated "bridge" element that spans two burners—a nicety for accommodating rectangular or odd-shaped cookware. And many have at least one **hot-surface light**—a key safety feature, since the surface can remain hot long after the elements have been turned off. The safest setup includes a dedicated "hot" light for each element.

Most electric ranges and cooktops have

one large, **higher-wattage burner** in front and one in back. An **expanded simmer range** in some electric models lets you fine-tune the simmer setting on one burner for, say, melting chocolate or keeping a sauce from getting too hot.

On gas ranges and cooktops. Most gas ranges have four burners in three sizes, measured in British thermal units per hour (Btu/hr.): one or two medium-power burners (about 9,000 Btu/hr.), a small burner(about 5,000 Btu/hr.), and one or two large ones (about 12,500 Btu/hr.). We recommend a model with one or more 12,000 Btu/hr. burners for quick cooktop heating. On a few models, the burners **automatically reignite.**

For easier cleaning, look for **sealed burners** and removable **burner pans** and **caps.** Gas ranges typically have **knob controls**; the best give you 180 degrees or more of adjusting room. Try to avoid knobs that have adjacent "off" and "low" settings and that rotate no more than 90 degrees between High and Low.

Spending more on a gas stove or cooktop gets you **heavier grates** made of porcelain-coated cast iron, a low-power **simmer burner** with an extra-low setting for delicate sauces, an easy-to-clean **ceramic surface**, and **stainless-steel accents.**

On pro-style ranges. These models have six or more **brass or cast-iron burners**, all of which offer very high output (usually about 15,000 Btu/hr.). The burners are usually nonsealed, with hard-to-clean crevices, though sealed burners are appearing on some models. **Large knobs** are another typical pro-style feature, as are **continuous grates** designed for heavy-duty use. The latter, however, can be unwieldy to remove for cleaning.

On ovens. Electric ovens used to have an edge over gas ovens in roominess, but recently CONSUMER REPORTS has found roomy ovens among both types. Note, though, that an oven's usable capacity may be less than what manufacturers claim, because they don't take protruding broiler elements and other features into account.

A **self-cleaning cycle** uses high heat to burn off spills and splatters. Most ranges have it, although many pro-style gas models still don't. An **automatic door lock**, found on most self-cleaning models, is activated during the cycle, then unlocks when the oven has cooled. Also useful is a **self-cleaning countdown** display, which shows the time is left in the cycle.

> ■ **SHOP SMART**
> A mainstream-brand freestanding range typically costs less than buying a cooktop and wall oven separately. A pro-style freestanding range typically costs more than a pro-style cooktop and wall oven bought separately.

Higher-priced ranges and wall ovens often include a **convection mode,** which uses a fan and, sometimes, an electric element to circulate heated air. CONSUMER REPORTS tests have shown that the convection mode shaved cooking time for a large roast and baked large cookie batches more evenly because of the circulating air. But the fan can take up valuable oven space. A few electric ovens have a low-power **microwave feature** that works with bake and broil elements to speed cooking time further. Another cooking technology, found in the GE Advantium over-the-range oven, uses a **halogen heating bulb** as well as microwaves.

A **variable-broil** feature in some electric ovens offers adjustable settings for foods such as fish or thick steaks that need slower or faster cooking. Ovens with **12-hour shutoff** turn off automatically if you leave the oven on for that long. But most models allow you to disable this feature. A **child lockout** allows you to disable oven controls for safety.

Manufacturers are also updating oven controls across the price spectrum. **Electronic touchpad controls** are a high-end feature now showing up in a growing number of lower-priced ranges. A **digital display** makes it easier to set the precise temperature and keep track of it. A **cook time/delay start** lets you set a time for the oven to start and stop cooking; remember, however, that you shouldn't leave most foods in a cold oven very long. An **automatic oven light** typically comes on when the door opens, although some ovens have a switch-operated light. A **temperature probe,** to be inserted into meat or poultry, indicates when you've obtained a precise internal temperature.

Oven windows come in various sizes. Those without a decorative grid usually offer the clearest view, although some cooks may welcome the grid to hide pots, pans, and other cooking utensils typically stored inside the oven.

➤ **HOW TO CHOOSE**

Performance differences. Almost every range, cooktop, or oven we've tested cooks well. Differences are in the details. An electric range may boil a pot of water a bit more quickly than a gas range, while a gas model can sometimes be adjusted with more precision. CONSUMER REPORTS tests have also shown that the powerful burners on some pro-style gas ranges may not simmer some foods without scorching them. Among electric ranges, smoothtops are displacing coil-tops, but they aren't necessarily better or more reliable. A smoothtop's glass surface eases cleaning, but you need to wipe up sugary spills immediately to avoid pitting the surface.

Be aware that the doors and windows of some ovens can become fairly hot during self-cleaning, while others are left with a permanent residue.

Recommendations. Decide on the type you want, then consider the features, price, and brand reliability. Cabinetry, floor plan, and whether you have access to a gas hookup will also factor into your decision. A freestanding range generally offers the best value; a very basic electric or gas range costs $400 or less. Smoothtop electric ranges cost a few hundred dollars more than those with coil elements. Spending more than $1,000 buys lots of extras, including electronic controls and pro-style touches such as stainless-steel trim. Pro-style ranges cost thousands. In wall ovens, the convection feature adds hundreds of dollars to the price.

Related CR report: August 2002
Ratings: pages 235, 285, 288, 321
Reliabilty: pages 335, 336

REFRIGERATORS

Top-freezer and bottom-freezer refrigerators generally give you more usable space for your money than comparable side-by-sides. And they cost less to run.

If you're shopping for a refrigerator, you are probably considering models that are fancier than your current one. The trend is toward spacious fridges with flexible, more efficiently used storage space. Useful features such as spill-proof, slide-out glass shelves and temperature-controlled compartments, once only in expensive refrigerators, are now practically standard in midpriced models. Stainless-steel doors are a stylish but costly extra. Built-in refrigerators appeal to people who want to customize their kitchens, but they're expensive. Some brands offer less expensive, built-in-style models.

Replacing an aging refrigerator may reduce your electric bill, since refrigerators are more energy efficient now than they were a decade ago. The DOE toughened its rules in the early 1990s and imposed even stricter requirements in July 2001 for this appliance, which is the top electricity user in the house.

➤ WHAT'S AVAILABLE

Frigidaire, GE, Kenmore (Sears), and Whirlpool account for almost 60 percent of top-freezer refrigerator sales. For side-by-side models, these brands and Amana account for more than 80 percent of sales. Brands offering bottom-freezer models include Amana, GE, Kenmore, and KitchenAid. Mainstream manufacturers have launched high-end sub-brands such as GE Profile and Kenmore Elite. Two brands that specialize in built-in refrigerators, Sub-Zero and Viking, have been joined in that market by Amana, GE, and KitchenAid. Only a handful of companies actually manufacture refrigerators. The same or very similar models may be sold under several brands.

Top-freezer models. Accounting for half of all refrigerators sold, models of this type are generally less expensive to buy and run —and more space- and energy-efficient— than comparably sized side-by-side models. Width ranges from about 24 to 36 inches. Nominal labeled capacity ranges from about 10 to almost 26 cubic feet. (CONSUMER REPORTS' measurements show that a refrigerator's usable capacity is typically about 25 percent less than its nominal capacity.) Price range: typically $600 to $800, but can exceed $1,300 depending on size and features.

Side-by-side models. This type puts part of both the main compartment and the freezer at eye level, where it's easy to reach. The narrow doors are handy in tight kitchens. High, narrow compartments make finding stray items easy in front (harder in the back), but they may not hold a sheet cake or a large turkey. Compared with top- and bottom-freezer models, a higher proportion of capacity goes to freezer space. Side-by-sides are typically large—30 to 36 inches wide, with nominal capacity of 19 to 30 cubic feet. They're more expensive than similar-sized top-freezer models and less space- and energy-efficient. Price range: typically $1,000 to $1,600 but can exceed $2,150.

Bottom-freezer models. A small but fast-growing part of the market, these put frequently used items such as milk and cheese at eye level. Fairly wide refrigerator shelves provide easy access. You must bend to locate items in the freezer, even with a pull-out basket. Bottom-freezers are a bit pricier than top-freezer models and offer a bit less capacity for their external dimensions. Price range: usually $800 to $1,000, but can exceed $2,100.

Built-in models. These are generally side-by-side models, though some bottom-freezers are available. Built-ins show their commercial heritage, often with fewer standard amenities and less soundproofing than less expensive "home" models. Usually about 25 inches front to back, they fit flush with cabinets and counters. Their compressor is on top, making them about a foot taller than regular refrigerators. Some can accept front panels that match the kitchen's decor. Price range: $4,000 and up.

Built-in-style models. Sometimes called cabinet-depth models, these free standing refrigerators stick out only a few inches beyond standard cabinets. Price range: typically $1,700 to $2,200.

> **KEY FEATURES**

Interiors are ever more flexible. **Adjustable door bins** and shelves can be moved to fit tall items. Some shelves can be cranked up and down without removing the contents. Some **split shelves** can be adjusted to different heights independently. To provide clearance, the front half of some shelves slides under the rear portion, or one side folds up. **Sliding brackets** on door shelves secure bottles and jars.

IA few models have a **wine rack** that stores bottles horizontally. **Glass shelves** are easier to clean than wire racks. Most glass shelves have a **raised rim** to keep spills from dripping over. Some shelves slide out. Pullout shelves or bins in the freezer give easier access; some bottom freezers have a sliding drawer.

A **temperature-controlled drawer** can be set to be several degrees cooler than the rest of the interior, useful for storing meat or fish; some models maintained meatkeeper temperatures more precisely than others in CONSUMER REPORTS tests.

Crisper drawers have controls to maintain humidity. Our tests have shown that in general, temperature-controlled drawers work better than plain drawers; results for humidity controls were less clear-cut. **See-through drawers** let you tell at a glance what's inside. **Curved doors** give the refrigerator a distinctive profile and retro look. Many manufacturers have at least one curved-door model in their lineups.

Step-up features include a variety of finishes and colors. Every major manufacturer has a **stainless-steel** model that typically costs significantly more than one with a standard **textured finish.** Another alternative is a smooth, **glass-like finish.** New color choices are emerging: biscuit, bisque, or linen instead of almond. Several lines include black models, and Kitchen-Aid has a cobalt-blue finish that matches its small appliances.

Most models have an **icemaker** in the freezer (or the option of installing one yourself). Typically producing three or four pounds of ice per day, an icemaker reduces freezer space by about a cubic foot. The ice bin is generally located below the icemaker, but some new models place it on the inside of the freezer door, providing a bit more usable volume in the compartment itself. Some models can make more ice in less time.

A through-the-door **ice and water dispenser** is common in side-by-side refrigerators; a **child lockout button** in some models disables it. An icemaker adds $70 to $100 to the price of a refrigerator; an in-door water dispenser adds about $100. Some top-freezer models offer a water dispenser in the refrigerator.

With many models, the icemaker and water dispenser include a **water filter,** designed to reduce lead, chlorine, and other impurities—a capability you may or may not need. An icemaker or water dispenser will work without a filter. You can also have a filter installed in the tubing that supplies water to the refrigerator.

An unusual premium feature is a **refreshment center,** a small, fold-out door in the main door that gives access to bottles in a chiller.

Once a refrigerator's controls are set, there should be little need to adjust temperature. Still, accessible controls are an added convenience. Digital controls and displays have replaced temperature-setting dials on a few side-by-sides.

Top- and bottom-freezer refrigerators have **reversible hinges** so they can open to either side. The doors on side-by-side models require the least amount of front clearance space.

> **HOW TO CHOOSE**

Performance differences. Most refrigerators, even the least expensive, keep things cold very well. Many models are pretty quiet, too; some are very quiet. Energy efficiency, configurations, and convenience features vary considerably. Less expensive models usually lack niceties such as simple-to-use crispers and chillers or easily arranged shelves.

Energy efficiency can vary significantly, according to CONSUMER REPORTS tests. A highly efficient model that costs more than an inefficient model may be a better buy in the long run. Since a refrigerator can account for up to one-fifth of a household's annual electricity costs, the savings can be substantial. Models made as of July 2001 are required to meet efficiency standards up to 30 percent more stringent than those before. By 2003, new models must be made without hydrochlorofluorocarbons, which can harm the earth's ozone layer (though less so than chlorofluorocarbons, which are not used in current models).

Recommendations. Top-freezer models give you the most refrigerator for the money. But personal preference or kitchen layout may point toward another type. Once you choose which kind of refrigerator suits your needs, assess models for convenience features and accessible, flexible storage.

Before going shopping, take measurements not only of the space the refrigerator is to fit in but of your doorways and hallways. If you need to place your new fridge with the door opening against your kitchen's side wall, look for a model with a door hinge that lets it open flat against the wall.

Related CR report: August 2002
Ratings: page 295
Reliability: pages 336, 337

SEWING MACHINES

Sewing is easier than ever. Mechanical machines under $200 have many features. Spend more for an electronic model, and you get more convenience and hundreds of stitches.

New, electronic sewing machines are almost like robots. They can recommend the proper presser foot, divine the right thread tension and stitch length, size and sew a buttonhole, and automatically cut the thread. Combination embroidery/sewing machines, introduced about eight years ago, combine those features with superior sewing and the ability to produce professional-quality embroidery.

> **WHAT'S AVAILABLE**

Singer, Brother, and Kenmore sell about 70 percent of all units. Brands such as Bernina and Husqvarna Viking are gaining as the market shifts to more expensive, feature-laden machines.

Mechanical models. They require you to manipulate most controls by hand, generally cost less electronic or sewing/embroidery models, and handle the basics—repairs, hems, simple clothing, and crafts projects. They're what most people who buy sewing machines choose. Price range: less than $500.

Electronic machines. These shift many tedious sewing jobs from your hands to computer chips. The typical unit offers touchpad controls, a light-emitting diode (LED) screen, a wealth of presser feet for challenges such as pleats and topstitching, and numerous decorative stitches. Price range: $300 to $1,200.

Sewing/embroidery units. These combine the talents of a stand-alone embroidery machine with a sewing machine. The machine holds a hoop under its needle and moves the hoop in four directions as the needle sews. You push a start button, watch, and periodically change thread colors. Embroidery machines require a link to a home computer to access all their capabilities, including embroidering original designs. Price range: $1,000 to more than $6,000.

> **KEY FEATURES**

Among the most convenient features is an **automatic buttonholer** that sews in one step instead of making you continually manipulate selector dials or the fabric itself.

Setting up the machine is made easier by several innovations. A needle threader, for instance, reduces eyestrain and frustration. A **top-load bobbin,** available on both mechanical and electronic models, lets you drop the bobbin directly into the machine without fiddling; most top-load bobbins have a **window** so you can check when the bobbin's empty.

A **bobbin thread lift** function on some electronic models brings the bobbin thread to the sewing surface so you don't have to insert your fingers under the presser foot. Some electronic machines have an **"adviser"** program on their LED screens; it can recommend the stitch and presser foot to use, and it gives other handy advice.

A number of features help you avoid mistakes. A **feed-dog adjustment** lets you drop the toothy mechanism (which moves the fabric along) below the sewing surface so you can do freehand work or keep from damaging sheer fabrics. On some electronic models, **automatic tension adjustment** for the upper thread helps avoid loopy stitches and annoying "birds' nests" that can jam the machine or bend the needle.

An **adjustable presser foot** allows you to regulate how tightly the machine holds fabric while sewing; it prevents puckering in fine fabrics and ensures that knits don't stretch out of shape.

Among the features that will be especially helpful for some people are **speed control,** which lets you determine sewing speed with a button instead of with the foot pedal. It can be useful when teaching a child to sew. A **stop/start switch,** auxiliary to the power switch, lets you bypass the foot pedal to control sewing and can be a boon to people with limited foot mobility.

> **HOW TO CHOOSE**

Performance differences. Most electronic machines sew very well and offer a great variety of features, stitches, and presser feet. In CONSUMER REPORTS tests, most excelled in ease of use. Sewing/embroidery machines had the best sewing ability. Their plethora of convenience features make them, as a group, extremely easy to use. It's possible to find very good performance from some mechanical models. Most of them are easy to use, but they offer fewer convenience features and stitches than do the other types of machine.

Recommendations. Before buying a sewing machine, assess your skills and needs. Consider, too, how you might use the machine later, when your skills improve. Typically, people keep a sewing machine at least 10 years.

If you know you'll never embroider, buy an electronic or mechanical model with as many features as you can afford. A mechanical model will do for basic hemming, clothing repairs, and one or two yearly projects. If your current projects or your ambitions include more numerous and complicated projects, you'll probably be more satisfied in the long run with an electronic model. If there's a chance you might want to try embroidery, such a machine may be a wise investment. You'll also benefit from superior sewing capabilities.

You'd do well to wait for sales. Sears and Wal-Mart have larger selections of lower-priced models than other retailers. Specialty and fabric stores tend to sell more expensive brands but may offer training classes and an in-house repair shop—both a plus. Some independent dealers will accept a trade-in of your old model. Internet-based dealers offer good prices, but the warranties may be invalid if the dealer isn't authorized, and service may be very difficult to arrange.

When shopping, try the machine out with an experienced salesperson; ideally, take lessons after you buy.

If you buy a used or reconditioned machine, ask the retailer for a warranty; manufacturers' warranties are usually not transferable.

Related CR report: November 2001

TOASTING APPLIANCES

Some people like the straightforwardness of a toaster. Others prefer an appliance that toasts, bakes, and more. Either way, you can get good performance without spending a lot.

Piggybacking on the popularity of bagels, toaster pastries, and frozen, ready-to-heat omelets, manufacturers are redesigning the basic toaster for improved counter appeal and cachet.

New developments in toaster design include rounded sides; seamless housing; nonstick slots; a dedicated setting for bagels, in which only a single side of the bread is browned; and a cancel mode to interrupt the toast cycle. Black & Decker is introducing a model with clear glass sides that lets you watch the toasting operation. Extra-wide and long-slot models are becoming increasingly popular, too.

A big change in the product is the move toward "smart" toasters with microchips and heat sensors that promise perfect doneness and supposedly adjust heat output so the first batch is identical to the last (they don't always deliver). Some models incorporate a light-emitting-diode (LED) indicator to show the darkness selection and to count down the time remaining in a particular cycle.

But you needn't buy a $100 or $200 toaster to do a masterful job browning bread. For $20 or less, you can buy a competent product that will make decent toast, two slices at a time, with all the basics: a darkness control to adjust doneness, a push-down lever to raise or lower the bread, and cool-touch housing to keep you from burning your fingers.

With increased demand for multifunction appliances—and the space savings that result from having one machine that can do the work of two—many people opt for a hybrid appliance that not only can toast four or more slices of bread but can also bake muffins, heat frozen entrées, or broil a small batch of burgers or a small chicken.

> **WHAT'S AVAILABLE**

Toastmaster invented the pop-up toaster back in the 1920s and now shares shelf space with other venerable brands of toasters and toaster ovens such as Black & Decker, Hamilton Beach and Sunbeam, plus players such as Cuisinart, DeLonghi, Kenmore (Sears), KitchenAid, Krups, Rival, T-fal, and West Bend. Dualit makes old-fashioned, commercial-style, heavy-gauge stainless-steel toasters. Toasters come in a variety of exterior finishes such as chrome and brushed metal.

Of the 12 million toasters sold annually,

two-slice models outsell four-slicers 4 to 1. Nearly three-quarters of toaster ovens sold are equipped with a broiler function. Most toaster ovens are countertop models, though a few under-the-cabinet models are sold. Price range: Toasters, $20 to $380; toaster ovens, $40 and up.

➤ KEY FEATURES

For all the bells and whistles, a simple **dial** or **lever** to set for darkness is sufficient. **Electronic controls** regulate shadings and settings with a touchpad instead. A **pop-up control** lets you eject a slice early if you think it's done. A **toast boost,** or manual lift, lets you raise smaller items such as bagel halves above the slots so there's no need to fish around with a fork, a potentially dangerous exercise if you don't pull out the plug.

Another safety note: Underwriters Laboratory now requires that toasters shut off at the end of the toasting cycle even if a piece of bread jams in the carriage.

There are models that offer an astounding (and unnecessary) 63 time and temperature toasting options. One of the more curious entries comes from West Bend, with its unorthodox Slide Thru toaster. You insert the bread in the slot and remove it through a door at the base. The door doubles as a "dressing table" for spreading butter or jam.

Recent toaster-oven innovations include a **liner** that can be removed for cleaning, and various ways to speed up the cooking process, including use of a **convection fan** or **infrared heat.** A **removable crumb tray** facilitates cleaning. **Nonstick slots** also make it easy to remove baked-on goop left by toaster pastries. More and more models incorporate a control that automatically defrosts and then toasts in a single step. With toaster ovens, **a removable cooking cavity** eases cleaning.

➤ HOW TO CHOOSE

Performance differences. Most toasters make respectable toast. But few models, including those with microchips and heat sensors, toast to perfection. In CONSUMER REPORTS tests, problems included toast that came out darker on one side than the other and successive batches that were inconsistently browned. As in the past, toaster ovens as a group were not as good as their plainer cousins at making toast, although their ability to bake and broil makes them more versatile.

Recommendations. If all you want is toast, a $20 toaster will do the job fine. Toaster ovens offer versatility so you needn't, for example, heat up your big oven to warm leftovers or use the stove to melt a grilled-cheese sandwich. Elegant styling and a sleek design can carry a high price tag, but may offer little else.

Related CR report: December 2001
Ratings: page 313

WASHING MACHINES

Almost all machines do a fine job washing. Top-loaders are usually less expensive, but front-loaders cost less to operate because they use less water and energy.

Until recently, about the only place you were likely to see a front-loading washing machine was in a coin laundry. But in the past few years this type of washer, which you load the same way you would a clothes dryer, has gained in popularity. Today about 10 percent of newly purchased washing machines are front-loaders, up from less than 5 percent several years ago.

Virtually any washing machine will get your clothing clean. Front-loaders do the job using less water, including hot water, and thus less energy than most top-loaders. Two top-loading designs—one from Sears Kenmore and Whirlpool, the other from Fisher & Paykel—work somewhat like front-loaders. They fill partially with water and spray clothes with a concentrated detergent solution. In CONSUMER REPORTS tests, they outscored other top-loaders in water and energy efficiency.

Within the next few years, top-loading washing machines should become more energy efficient. In 2004 and 2007, the Department of Energy will phase in stricter standards regarding energy and hot-water use and water extraction. Front-loaders already meet the new, tougher standards.

➤ **WHAT'S AVAILABLE**

GE, Kenmore (Sears), Maytag, and Whirlpool account for about 80 percent of the washing machines sold in the U.S. Smaller brands such as Amana, Frigidaire, Roper, and Hotpoint are also available. Asko, Bosch, and Miele are key European brands. Fisher-Paykel is imported from New Zealand.

Top-loaders. Most top-loaders fill the tub with enough water to cover the clothing, then agitate it. Because they need room to move the laundry around to ensure thorough cleaning, these machines have a smaller load capacity than front-loaders—generally about 12 to 16 pounds. The Calypso models from Kenmore and Whirlpool are unusual in that they have a "wash plate," rather than an agitator to move clothes around. That enables them to hold 18-pound loads and makes them gentler on clothing.

It's easier to load laundry and to add items midcycle to a top-loader. They're also noisier than front-loaders. Top-loaders are generally 27 to 29 inches wide. Price range: $250 to $1,300.

Front-loaders. Front-loaders get clothes clean by tumbling them into water. Clothes are lifted to the top of the tub, then dropped into the water below. The design makes front-loaders gentler on clothing and more adept at handling unbalanced loads. They can typically handle 12 to 20 pounds of laundry. Front-loading washers require front-loader detergent, which produces less suds than detergent for top-loaders. Like top-loaders, they're typically 27 to 29 inches wide. Price range: $600 to $1,500.

Space-saving options. Compact models are typically 24 inches wide or less and wash 8 to 12 pounds of laundry. A compact front-loader can be stacked with a compact dryer. (Many full-sized front-loaders can also be stacked with a matching dryer.) Some compact models can be stored in a closet and rolled out to be hooked up to the kitchen sink. Price range: $450 to $2,000.

Washer-dryer laundry centers combine a washer and dryer in one unit, with the dryer located above the washer. These can be full-sized (27 inches wide) or compact (24 inches wide). Capacity is about 12 to 14 pounds. Performance is generally comparable to that of full-sized machines. Price range: $700 to $1,900.

> **■ SHOP SMART**
> **Until recently, there were two scales for the DOE's Yellow EnergyGuide Stickers: one for top-loaders, and one for the generally more efficient front-loaders. Now both types are presented on the same scale.**

➤ **KEY FEATURES**

A porcelain-coated steel **inner tub** can rust if the porcelain is chipped. Stainless-steel or plastic tubs won't rust. A porcelain top/lid resists scratching better than a painted one.

High-end models often have **touchpad**

controls; others have traditional **dials.** Controls should be legible, easy to push or turn, and logically arranged. A plus: **lights or signals** that indicate cycle. On some top-loaders, an **automatic lock** during the spin cycle keeps children from opening the lid. Front-loaders lock at the beginning of a cycle but usually can be opened by interrupting the cycle, although some doors remain shut briefly after the machine stops.

Front-loaders automatically set wash speed according to the **fabric cycle** selected, and some also automatically set the spin speed. Top-loaders typically provide **wash/spin speed combinations,** such as Regular, Permanent Press, and Delicate (or Gentle). A few models also allow an **extra rinse** or **extended spin.**

Front-loaders and some top-loaders set water levels automatically, ensuring efficient use of water. Some top-loaders can be set for four or more levels; three or four are probably as many as you'd need.

Most machines establish wash and rinse temperatures by mixing hot and cold water in preset proportions. For incoming cold water that is especially cold, an **automatic temperature control** adjusts the flow for the correct temperature. A **time-delay feature** lets you program the washer to start at a later time—when your utility rates are low, for example. **Detergent and fabric softener dispensers** automatically release powder or liquid. **Bleach dispensers** can prevent spattering. Some machines offer a **hand-washing cycle.**

➤ **HOW TO CHOOSE**
Performance differences. All washing machines get clothes clean. In CONSUMER REPORTS tests, differences in washing ability tended to be slight. Differences in water and energy efficiency and in noisiness were greater. Front-loaders have the edge on all counts.

The water efficiency of any washing machine rises with larger loads, but, overall, front-loaders use far less water per pound of laundry and excel in energy efficiency. Washing six loads of laundry per week, the most water-efficient front-loaders can save almost 6,000 gallons of water a year. Using electricity to heat the water, and using an electric dryer, the most energy-efficient front-loaders can save you about $60 worth of electrical energy a year compared with the least efficient top-loader. (Costs are based on 2002 national average utility prices; differences would narrow with a gas water heater, gas dryer, full loads, or carefully set water levels.) Front-loaders are generally quieter than top-loaders except when draining or spinning, and they are usually gentler on your laundry.

Recommendations. Top-loaders generally cost less than front-loaders and do a fine job. Best values: midpriced top-loaders with few features, which you can usually find for less than $500. Features such as extra wash/spin options or an automatic detergent dispenser may add to convenience but don't necessarily improve performance.

While front-loaders are usually more expensive to buy, they can cost significantly less to operate, especially in areas where water or energy rates are very high. In general, though, the savings are not likely to make up the price difference over a washer's typical life span.

Buying one of the more expensive top-loading or front-loading models can get you larger capacity and features that give you more flexibility, such as programming frequently used settings.

Related CR report: July 2002
Ratings: page 323
Reliability: page 340

HOME & YARD

What's New in Home & Yard Equipment

nnovations are making home and yard gear easier and safer to use, as well as friendlier to the environment. Some of the changes have been prompted by tougher state and federal environmental regulations. That means buying a new piece of equipment, rather than nursing along an old one, may be a good move. Here are trends you'll see this year:

"Greener" products. Stricter Department of Energy (DOE) rules have made today's room air conditioners more efficient. New government rules for emissions by lawn mowers and other gasoline-powered yard tools are designed to reduce emissions from gasoline-powered lawn and garden equipment by hundreds of thousands of tons per year. Emissions aren't the only type of pollutant—towns and cities have also been enacting laws designed to quiet gasoline-powered leaf blowers. Manufacturers are equipping a growing number of cordless drills and other tools with nickel-metal hydride batteries that can be safely thrown away with ordinary refuse. "Green" and "healthy" claims turn up in ads for vacuum cleaners, some of which have a high-efficiency particulate-air (HEPA) filter, designed to trap dust and allergens sucked up by vacuuming. But CONSUMER REPORTS tests have shown that many models—even those without a HEPA filter—can keep the air as free of potentially irritating particles.

Friendlier, safer controls. Many room air conditioners now have touchpad controls instead of traditional mechanical dials. Advances in battery technology also allow the latest cordless drills to run longer and more powerfully and recharge more quickly and easily than models made a few years ago.

Out in the yard, clutchless hydrostatic transmissions on a growing number of ride-on mowers and tractors make mowing go more smoothly. All of these machines stop the engine and blade when the operator leaves the seat. Even the least expensive push and self-propelled power mowers stop the blade when you release the safety handle. Some higher-priced models stop the blade but not the engine, eliminating the need to restart the mower.

More capability—and more luxury. Some lawn and garden tractors can power extra-cost accessories that allow you plow and tow, as well as throw snow. Many models have become the backyard equivalent of sport-utility vehicles with their large engines and ever-wider cutting swaths. You'll also find a growing number of "zero-turn-radius" mowers and tractors that can turn 360 degrees in one spot to better maneuver around obstacles.

Built-in gas barbecue grills with stainless-steel finishes now rival multi-thousand-dollar, professional-style kitchen ranges in size and price. You'll also find stainless-steel stand-alone grills priced at $1,000 and beyond, though increasingly, you can get grills with a thousand-dollar look for about $500.

More shopping options. Home and yard products are sold over the Internet through sites such as Amazon.com, Homedepot.com, Lowes.com, and Sears.com. Such online sites can be useful, especially as research tools, but there's still a lot to be said for the local hardware store or home center. You can't beat holding a cordless drill, hefting a vacuum, or rolling a mower to see if it feels right in your hands.

Large chains such as Sears and Wal-Mart usually have the best selection of lower-priced brands. Home centers such as Home Depot and Lowe's offer a mix of low-priced, midpriced, and upscale brands. Local hardware stores and other independent dealers tend to carry mid-priced and upscale brands. Such stores often offer service that mass merchandisers and home centers don't provide.

AIR CONDITIONERS

Individual room air conditioners are a relatively inexpensive alternative to central-air systems for cooling one or two rooms.

Refined features distinguish many of today's room air conditioners. Vague settings such as Warmer or Cooler are giving way to relatively precise electronic controls and digital temperature readouts.

New models are considerably more energy efficient than those made a decade ago. A yellow EnergyGuide tag lists each new unit's energy-efficiency rating (EER)—its capacity in British thermal units per hour (Btu/hr.) divided by power consumption in watts. EERs for models now on the market range from about 9.7 to 12. A model with an EER of 10 should use about 20 percent less energy than one whose EER is 8, other factors being equal.

Window air conditioners made as of October 1, 2000, and rated at less than 8,000 Btu/hr. are required to have at least a 9.7 EER. That's a big change from the old EER requirements of 8 for units under 6,000 Btu/hr. and 8.5 for units between 6,000 and 7,999 Btu/hr. Units rated between 8,000 and 13,999 Btu/hr. must have an EER of at least 9.8.

➤ WHAT'S AVAILABLE

Fedders, General Electric, Sears Kenmore, and Whirlpool are leading brands of room air conditioners. Together they account for more than half the units sold. Room air conditioners come in different sizes, with cooling capacities ranging from 5,000 Btu/hr. to as high as 33,000 Btu/hr. About half of room air conditioners found in stores range from 5,000 to 8,999 Btu/hr. The size you need depends on the size of the room to be cooled. Price range: $120 to more than $600, depending mostly on cooling capacity.

➤ KEY FEATURES

An air conditioner's exterior-facing portion contains a compressor, fan, and condenser, while the part that faces a home's interior contains a fan and an evaporator. But you'll find several different configurations depending on your needs. Most room models are designed to fit double-hung windows, though some are built for casement and slider windows and others for in-wall installation.

Most models now have **adjustable**

vertical and horizontal louvers to direct airflow. Many offer a fresh-air intake or exhaust setting for ventilation, although this feature moves a relatively small amount of air. An energy-saver setting on some units stops the fan when the compressor cycles off.

Electronic controls and digital temperature readouts are becoming common. A timer allows you to program the air conditioner to switch on (say, half an hour before you get home) or off at a given time. More and more models also include a remote control. Some models install with a slide-out chassis—an outer cabinet that anchors in the window, into which you slide the unit.

➤ HOW TO CHOOSE
Performance differences. Most models CONSUMER REPORTS has tested do a very good job at cooling, with the better models keeping the temperature more even than the rest. However, we found wide variations in quietness, along with significant differences in how well models direct airflow to the left or right with their louvers. Most units restart after a brownout. But some electronically controlled models must be restarted manually and reprogrammed after a power interruption.

Recommendations. Determine the right size air conditioner for the space you're cooling. An air conditioner with more cooling capacity than you need may not dehumidify properly because its compressor may cycle off too often. Check the unit's EER on the yellow EnergyGuide tag to find the most efficient model.

A typical room air conditioner can weigh anywhere from 40 to 100 pounds, making installation a two-person job. Once the air conditioner is in, maintain it by cleaning its air filter every few weeks; some units have an indicator that tells you when it's time to clean or change the filter.
Related CR report: July 2002

BARBECUE GRILLS

Many people are choosing models that do more than just grill. Go high-end, and you can pay as much as you would for a pro-style kitchen range.

A $15 charcoal hibachi is all it takes to give burgers that outdoorsy barbecue taste. But a gas or an electric grill offers more flexible controls and spares you the hassle of starting the fire and getting rid of the ashes when you're done. Many have extras such as a warming rack for rolls or an accessory burner for, say, boiling corn on the cob. Those looking for a backyard status symbol will find models that cost thousands of dollars and include stainless-steel exteriors and grates, porcelain-coated steel and aluminum lids, several separately controlled burners, utensil holders, and other perks. You'll also find more modest grills that can serve up flavor and convenience for $200 or so.

➤ WHAT'S AVAILABLE
Char-Broil, Kenmore (Sears), Sunbeam, and Weber account for more than 80 percent of gas-grill sales. Char-Broil and Sunbeam are mass-market brands, with Char-Broil selling both gas and electric models. Weber is a high-end brand that also markets its classic dome-top charcoal grills. Sears covers the entire spectrum, with Kenmore and its upscale Kenmore Elite line.

Gas. These grills are easy to start, warm up quickly, and usually cook predictably, giving meat a full, browned flavor. Step-up features include shelves and side burners. Better models offer added sturdiness and more even cooking. Price range: about

$100 to more than $2,000.

Electric. You can start them easily, and they offer precise temperature control and allow you to grill with nonstick cookware. On the downside, electrics generally take a bit longer than gas models to warm up and grill. Price range: about $100 to $300.

Charcoal. They provide an intense, smoky flavor prized by many. But they don't always light easily. They also burn less cleanly than gas, their heat is harder to regulate, and cleanup can be messy—all major reasons why charcoal models are no longer the top-selling type. Price range: usually $100 or less.

➤ KEY FEATURES

Most cooking grates are made of porcelain-coated steel or the somewhat sturdier porcelain-coated cast iron, bare cast iron, or stainless steel. A porcelain-coated grate is rustproof and easy to clean, but it can eventually chip. Bare cast iron is sturdy and sears beautifully, but you have to season it with cooking oil to fend off rust. The best of both worlds: stainless steel, which is sturdy, heats quickly, and resists rust without a porcelain coating. We've also found that cooking grates with wide, closely spaced bars tend to provide better searing than grates with thin, round rods, which may allow more food to fall to the bottom of the grill.

Both gas and electric grills are mounted on a **cart**, usually of painted steel tubing assembled with nuts and bolts. Higher-priced grills have welded joints, and a few have carts made of stainless steel. Carts with two wheels and two feet must be lifted at one end to move; better are two large wheels and two casters or four casters, which make moving easier. Wheels with a full axle are better than those bolted to the frame, which over time can bend.

Gas and electric grills generally have one or more **shelves**, which flip up from the front or side or are fixed on the side. Shelves are usually made of plastic, though some are made of wood or stainless steel, which are more durable. Some grills also have **interior racks** for keeping food warm without further cooking. Another plus for gas or electric grills is a **lid** and **firebox** made of stainless-steel or porcelain-coated-steel, which are more durable than the usual painted aluminum.

Still other features can help your next gas grill start more easily, cook more evenly, and last longer. An example is the **igniter**, which works via a knob or a push button. Knobs emit two or three sparks per turn, while push buttons emit a single spark per push. Better are **battery-powered electronic igniters**, which produce continuous sparks as long as the button is held down. Also look for **lighting holes** on the side of or beneath the grill, which are handy if the igniter fails.

Most gas grills have steel burners, though some are stainless-steel, cast-iron or cast-brass. Those premium burners typically last longer and carry longer warranties of 10 years or more. Most grills have two burners, or one with two independent halves. A few have three or four, which can add cooking flexibility. A **side burner**, which resembles a gas-stove burner and has its own heat control, is handy for cooking vegetables or sauce without leaving the grill. Other step-up features include an **electric rotisserie,** a **smoker drawer**, a **wok**, a **griddle pan,** a **steamer pan**, and a **nonstick grill basket**.

Most gas grills also use a **cooking medium**—a metal plate or metal bars, ceramic or charcoal-like briquettes, or lava rocks—between the burner and grates to distribute heat and vaporize juices, flavoring the food. CONSUMER REPORTS tests have shown that no one type is better at ensuring even heating. But grills with nothing between the burner and cooking surface typically cook less evenly.

Gas grills typically include a **propane tank,** sometimes with a **fuel gauge;** buying a tank separately costs about $25. Some tanks can be converted to run on natural gas or come in a natural-gas version. Tanks usually sit next to or on the base of the grill and attach to its gas line with a handwheel.

All tanks must now comply with upgraded National Fire Protection Association standards for **overfilling protection.** Noncompliant tanks have a circular or five-lobed valve and aren't refillable, although they can be retrofitted with a three-lobed valve or swapped for a new tank at a hardware store or other refilling capacity.

> **HOW TO CHOOSE**

Performance differences. Most grills, gas or electric, do a good job at grilling hotly and evenly. Salespeople might say that more Btus (British thermal units) mean faster warm-up, but that's not always true.

Assembling a gas or an electric grill can take anywhere from 30 minutes to 3 hours; some stores include assembly and delivery in the price, while others charge for that service. Some minor safety problems have turned up in CONSUMER REPORTS tests. Typically they involved handles, knobs, or thermometers that got too hot to handle without pot holders.

Recommendations. Consider how often you cook outdoors and how many people you typically feed. While price and performance don't track precisely, our tests have shown that some midpriced gas grills ($275 or less) are particularly good values. Gas models priced at $350 to $575 have more features—grates with wide bars, ample warming shelves, stainless-steel burners and grates, electronic igniters, longer warranties, and sturdier carts.

Spending thousands of dollars gets you many or all of those features plus more burners and mostly stainless-steel construction, but few consumers spend that much on a grill. An electric grill is a good option for places where gas grills aren't allowed. Charcoal grills cost the least overall, but they require the most work.

Related CR report: June 2002

Ratings: page 213

CHAIN SAWS

They're still noisy, but many of the latest are safer and cleaner. Gasoline-powered saws still outpower electrics, although plug-in models can be fine for light-duty use.

Chain saws are inherently dangerous and noisy, though modern designs attempt to improve usabiltity on both counts. Nearly all chain saws now have multiple shields aimed at minimizing "kickback," which occurs when the saw snaps up and back toward the operator.

Electric models are quieter than gasoline-powered ones. Gasoline-powered saws are cleaning up their act as tougher federal standards reduce allowable emissions for these two-stroke, handheld machines.

> **WHAT'S AVAILABLE**

You'll find gasoline- and electric-powered chain saws at home centers, discount stores, and lawn and garden dealers. Major brands include Craftsman (Sears), Homelite, Husqvarna, Poulan, Remington, and Stihl. Gas-powered saws use a small two-stroke engine that requires a mixture a gasoline and oil. Nearly all electric saws plug into an outlet and run off an electric motor. A few rechargeable, battery-powered chain saws are available, but they tend to be underpowered for most jobs.

As with most outdoor tools, gas-powered chain saws tend to offer the most power and mobility. But plug-in electrics compensate somewhat with lighter weight, less noise, and trigger starting. They also emit no exhaust, don't need engine tuneups, and typically cost less. Price range: gas, $100 to $300; electrics, less than $100 for most.

➤ **KEY FEATURES**

Chain saws are typically marketed by the size of the **bar** (the metal extension that supports the chain—usually between 14 and 20 inches long) as well as the **engine or motor** (measured in cubic centimeters for gas saws, amps for electrics). Usually, the larger the saw, the more you'll pay, though smaller models with high-end names such as Husqvarna and Stihl can cost more than larger ones from Craftsman, Homelite, and other lower-priced brands.

Other features are aimed mainly at safety and convenience. Major kickback-reducing devices include a **reduced-kickback chain** with added guard links to keep the cutters from taking too large a bite, along with a narrow-tipped, **reduced-kickback bar** that limits the contact area where kickback occurs.

All saws also have a **chain catcher**—an extension under the guide bar that keeps a broken chain from flying rearward. Some saws have a **chain brake,** which stops the chain almost instantly when activated, or a **bar-tip guard,** which prevents kickback by covering the bar's tip, or "nose."

Other safety features for most saws include a **trigger lockout switch** that must be pressed for the throttle trigger to operate and, for gas saws, **shielded muffler** designed to prevent burns from accidental contact. Also a plus is a **case** or **sheath** that covers the saw or guide bar and chain, to protect you from the sharp cutters while the saw is stored or carried.

Common labor-saving features include an **automatic chain oiler**, which eliminates the need to periodically push a plunger to lubricate the chain and bar, and metal **bucking spikes**, which act as a pivot point when cutting larger logs. Some saws have a **chain-adjuster screw** mounted accessibly on the side of the bar, and a few Stihl models feature a **tools-free adjuster** that lets you loosen or tighten the chain by turning a wheel.

Visible bar oil and fuel levels are also convenient, as is a wide rear handle that eases gas-saw starts by allowing room for the toe of a boot to secure the saw on the ground. Also look for **anti-vibration bushings or springs** between the handles and the engine, bar, and chain, along with a combined **choke/on-off switch** that activates a gas saw's ignition while closing off air to its carburetor for easier starting.

➤ **HOW TO CHOOSE**

Performance differences. Tests by CONSUMER REPORTS have confirmed that gas saws cut faster than electrics and more saws have important safety features. But they still must be used with care. Even quieter electric saws remain noisy enough for us to recommend ear protection.

Recommendations. Buy a gasoline-powered saw if you need go-anywhere mobility. The best electrics, which cost less than $100, are fine for small branches and other light-duty cutting. In either case, you'll find a light saw (less than 14 pounds for gas models, less than 10 pounds for electrics) easier to use for longer periods. Unless you're felling large trees, a 14- or 16-inch bar should be more than adequate.

Related CR report: May 2001
Ratings: page 228

CIRCULAR SAWS

Circular saws are a mainstay for cutting two-by-fours, plywood, and the like.

A circular saw is an essential tool for any but the most rudimentary workshop. Most models run on an electric motor. A few models are battery powered.

WHAT'S AVAILABLE

Black & Decker, Craftsman (Sears), DeWalt, Makita, Milwaukee, Porter-Cable, and Skil brands account for most of the circular saws sold.

Corded models. These models run on an electric motor that can range from 10 to 15 amps. The higher the amps, the more power you can expect. Most models are oriented so the motor is perpendicular to the blade. Another type uses a "worm drive" design in which the motor is parallel to the blade. That design gives a saw a lot of power, but at the expense of speed. Prices range: $40 to $140 for electric saws; $200 to $480 for battery-powered saws.

Battery-powered models. These use 18- or 24-volt motors. They're more expensive than corded models. Price range: $140 to $160.

➤ KEY FEATURES

Every saw has a big main **handle**, which incorporates the **on/off switch**, and a stubby auxiliary handle. Some saws include an interlock you have to press before on/off switch will work. This adds a level of safety, but can make the saw awkward to use.

Inexpensive saws have a stamped-steel base and thin housing; pricier models use thick, rugged material that stands up to hard use. A blade with two dozen large teeth cuts fast but can splinter the wood; a blade with 40 or more teeth gives a cleaner cut. The thinner the blade, the faster the cut and the less wasted wood.

Bevel adjustment is used to change the angle of the cut from 0 to 45 degrees. The **depth adjustment** changes the blade's cutting depth. A circular saw works best when the teeth just clear the bottom of the wood. The notch in the base plate that is in line with the saw blade is the **cutting guide**, which helps you follow the cutting line you've drawn on the wood.

A **blade-lock button** keeps the blade from turning when you change blades. The **dust chute** directs the sawdust away so you can see what you're doing.

➤ HOW TO CHOOSE

Performance differences. Seconds count if you have a lot of wood to cut. Speed also affects safety; you're more likely to push a slow saw, dulling the blade quickly and overheating the motor, or making the saw jam or kick back. Typically, slower saws come with a steel blade while carbide blades are on the fastest models. Most corded saws have adequate torque for any typical home-workshop job. Battery-powered saws are much weaker. A weak saw could strain when used on thick hardwood or for other tough work.

Design points that can make a saw easy to use include a visible cutting guide, a blade that's simple to change and to adjust for depth and angle, good balance, a comfortable handle, and a handy on/off switch. How well the saw is constructed impacts its potential for a long, trouble-free life. It should have durable bearings, motor brushes that are accessible for servicing or replacement, a heavy-duty base, and rugged blade-depth and cutting-angle adjustments.

Recommendations. Judging from CONSUMER REPORTS tests, you can get a fine saw for as little as $60. For $120 to $160, you can get an excellent model.

A battery-powered saw lacks the might for tough jobs but might do for occasional light work.

Whichever you buy, if it comes with a steel blade, replace it with a carbide one. Be sure to match the number of teeth with the material you want to cut; a blade for plywood, say, has more teeth than one for rough cutting.

All the saws are loud enough when cutting to warrant hearing protection. All kick up a lot of chips and dust, so safety glasses or goggles are a must. You may also want to wear a dust mask, especially when cutting pressure-treated lumber.

Related CR report: August 2002
Ratings: page 232

CORDLESS DRILLS

Many of the latest models are powerful enough to handle construction and repair chores formerly reserved for corded models. But the price of that power is often added weight.

Higher-voltage battery packs allow today's cordless drills to run longer and more powerfully per charge. Much of the credit goes to their high-capacity nickel-cadmium (nicad) batteries, which hold charges longer than before. Nicads must be recycled, however, since the cadmium is toxic and can leach out of landfills to contaminate groundwater if disposed of improperly. Incineration can release the substance into the air and pose an even greater hazard. Some cordless drills have nickel-metal-hydride (NiMH) batteries, which don't contain cadmium and can be thrown away with the rest of your trash. Manufacturers claim that NiMH batteries provide extra running time, although CONSUMER REPORTS testing showed no significant improvement.

> **WHAT'S AVAILABLE**

Black & Decker and Craftsman (Sears) account for more than half of all sales. Along with Ryobi and Skil, both brands are aimed primarily at do-it-yourselfers. Bosch, Craftsman Professional, DeWalt, Hitachi, Makita, Milwaukee, and Porter-Cable offer mostly professional-grade drills with heavier-duty components.

Cordless drills come in several sizes, based on battery voltage. In general, the higher the voltage, the greater the drilling power. The most potent models pack 18 to 24 volts, while the smallest, 7.2- and 9.6-volt models are usually limited to light-duty use. In between lie the 12- and 14.4-volt drills that often provide the best balance of high performance and low weight. Prices tend to track with voltage and features. Price range: 7.2- and 9.6-volt, $30 to $100; 12- and 14.4-volt, $75 to $200; 18- and 24-volt, $125 to $300. Sometimes, you'll also find a flashlight or a cordless saw bundled with a drill and sold as a kit.

> ■ **TECH TIP**
> Dispose of spent batteries in a battery-recycling bin at participating retailers such as RadioShack and Wal-Mart. To find a bin near you, call 800-8-BATTERY.

> **KEY FEATURES**

Most cordless drills 12 volts and higher have **two speed ranges**: low for driving screws and high for drilling. Low speed provides much more torque, or turning power, than the high-speed setting, which is useful for driving long screws and boring large-diameter holes. Many drills have a **variable speed trigger**, which can make starting a hole easier, and an **adjustable** clutch used to lower maximum torque; that can help you avoid driving a screw too far into soft wallboard or mangling the heads or threads once the screw is in.

Most drills have a ⅜-inch chuck (the attachment that holds the drill bit), though high-voltage, professional-grade models have a ½-inch chuck. In either case, most drills have replaced the little key needed to loosen and tighten the chuck with a tools-free adjuster. Most of today's models are also reversible, letting you easily remove a screw or back a drill bit out of a hole.

Still other features make some drills easier to use than others. Some models have a T-handle in the center of the motor housing, which provides better balance than a pistol grip on the back, although a pistol grip lets you slide your hand up in line with the bit to better apply pressure. Models with two batteries allow you to use one while the other is charging, while a smart charger—found with many models—charges the battery in an hour or less, rather than three hours or more. Some smart chargers indicate when the battery is too hot to charge, when charging is completed, and even when batteries are defective. And many chargers switch into a maintenance or "trickle-charge" mode after the battery is fully charged.

A few Milwaukee models have a reversible battery you can position so that it extends to the front or rear of the handle to improve the drill's balance or get into tight spots. An electric brake stops some drills instantly when you release the trigger—a handy feature that helps you avoid damaging the work piece and allows you to resume drilling or driving without waiting. Some models also include a built-in bubble level, while attachments allow others to drive screws and spin sanders, grinders, and wire brushes.

➤ **HOW TO CHOOSE**

Performance differences. New cordless drills are more capable than you might expect. The most powerful cordless drill CONSUMER REPORTS tested outperformed a powerful plug-in model. While higher voltage equals greater power, it also tends to mean added weight. That can make a drill tiring to hold for any length of time, especially overhead.

Recommendations. If you're a contractor or serious do-it-yourselfer, you may appreciate and need the extra power and endurance of an 18- or 24-volt model. But a good 12- or 14.4-volt cordless drill should meet most homeowners' needs. Drills in this range have plenty of torque for driving screws and adequate power for drilling holes.

For occasional light jobs, you'll welcome the lower weight of a 9.6-volt cordless drill, especially when working above shoulder level. Be aware, however, that the less expensive models often have longer battery-recharge times of anywhere from 3 to 16 hours. And no matter what drill you're considering, hold it above your shoulders to be sure it isn't too heavy for you.

Related CR report: November 2000
Ratings: page 242

HEDGE TRIMMERS

A good electric trimmer is all most people need to keep greenery shapely. Gasoline- or battery-powered models free you from a cord, but you pay for that convenience.

A gas or electric hedge trimmer can be a useful addition to your tool shed if your property includes lots of shrubs. Both types of trimmers can save you some of the physical effort hand clippers require, since an engine or motor—rather than elbow grease—powers their oscillating blades. But using any powered hedge trimmer can still be hard work, since you're holding these devices in midair, often with arms out, for extended periods. That can make a trimmer's weight, balance, and vibration as important as its cutting power.

> ➤ **WHAT'S AVAILABLE**

Black & Decker makes electric-powered models and sells more than half of all hedge trimmers. Craftsman (Sears) is Black & Decker's largest competitor, and sells electric plug-in and battery-powered trimmers as well as gas-powered models. Other brands include Echo, Homelite, Husqvarna, Little Wonder, Stihl, Ryobi, Toro, and Weed Eater.

Electric corded hedge trimmers. Most homeowners prefer plug-in electric trimmers for several reasons. They're relatively light and quiet, start with the push of a button, produce no exhaust emissions, and require little maintenance. The best can also perform comparably to gasoline-powered models—provided you're within 100 feet of a power outlet. Price range: about $30 to $100.

Gasoline-powered hedge trimmers. Commercial landscapers favor gas-powered models for their power and mobility. Indeed, a gas-powered, long-reach trimmer can provide access to remote spots a corded electric can't reach. But their two-stroke engines entail the fuel-mixing, pull-starting, maintenance, and exhaust emissions of other gas-powered, handheld yard tools. Gas trimmers can also be expensive. Price range: about $120 to $450.

Electric battery-powered hedge trimmers. Cordless trimmers combine the mobility of gas models with the convenience, clean running, and easy mainte-

nance of plug-in electrics, courtesy of an onboard battery. On the downside, battery-powered trimmers offer relatively little cutting power, along with litle running time before their battery must be recharged. They can also cost as much as some gas-powered models. Price range: about $80 to $120.

> ➤ **KEY FEATURES**

A hedge trimmer's **blades** comprise two flat metal plates with tooth-lined edges. **Blade length** typically ranges from 13 to 30 inches, although most are between 16 and 24 inches long. **Blade gap**—the distance between teeth—is also important, since it helps determine how large a branch the trimmer can cut. In general, the wider the gap, the larger the branch a trimmer can handle and the easier it is to push through a hedge. Gasoline-powered, professional-grade trimmers have blade gaps of 1 inch or more, while homeowner-grade models typically have ⅜- to ¾-inch gaps—narrow enough to help keep fingers safely out.

Still other factors make some blades more effective than others. **Double-sided blades** allow cutting in both directions, letting you stand in one position longer than you can with **single-sided blades**, which cut in one direction only. Pricier trimmers also tend to use **dual-action blades**, where both the top and bottom blade plates move back and forth, reducing vibration compared with **single-action blades**, where only the top blade moves.

Handle designs also vary. Trimmers with a **wrap-around front handle** let you keep your hands in a comfortable position as you pivot the trimmer to cut vertically or at odd angles. Safety features include **tooth extensions**, which are designed to prevent thighs and other body parts from contacting the blade teeth. Some tooth extensions are part of the blades and move with them; we think separate, **stationary tooth extensions** provide better protection. Trimmers also have a **front-handle shield** designed to prevent your forward hand from touching the blade.

➤ HOW TO CHOOSE

Performance differences. Any powered hedge trimmer should be up to light-duty tidying. The best can cut branches just shy of ⅝ inches in diameter, while dense ¼-inch-thick branches were enough to stop battery-powered trimmers CONSUMER REPORTS tested.

Recommendations. Begin by deciding which type of trimmer matches the trimming you do. Electric corded models are relatively quiet and inexpensive. They also deliver the best combination of cutting power, maneuverability, and ease—provided your trimming chores are within range of a power outlet. Battery-powered trimmers offer cord-free convenience, but their lack of cutting power and limited run time between charges make them best suited to touch ups and other light-duty work. In either case, look for an Underwriters Laboratories (UL) seal, which requires trimmers to have crucial safety features. Gasoline-powered models are for heavier-duty trimming beyond the range of a cord. Wear hearing protection when using gas-powered trimmers. And make sure you wear protective work gloves, safety glasses or goggles, and nonskid shoes when using any powered trimmer. Also be sure to work with care and do your trimming on firm footing or on a steady ladder. Don't try to work beyond your reach. And if you're using an electric trimmer, make sure the cord trails away from the blades.

Related CR report: May 2000

LAWN MOWERS AND TRACTORS

Practically any mower will cut your grass. But you can get better results with less effort by choosing a machine based on lawn size, your mowing preferences—and your budget.

Mowing options range anywhere from $100 manual-reel mowers to tractors that can cost $4,000 and beyond. Manual-reel and electric walk-behind mowers are appropriate for people with small yards, while gasoline-powered walk-behind mowers are fine for most lawns up to about half an acre. Those with lawns larger than that will appreciate the ease and speed of a riding mower or a lawn tractor.

Gasoline-powered mowers produce a disproportionate amount of air pollution compared with cars. Federal regulations aimed at reducing smog-producing lawn-mower emissions by 390,000 tons annually are being phased in over the next several years.

➤ WHAT'S AVAILABLE

Manual-reel mowers are still made by a few companies, while major electric-mower brands include Black & Decker and Craftsman (Sears). Craftsman is also the largest-selling brand of gasoline-powered walk-behind mowers, riding mowers, and lawn tractors. Other less expensive, mass-market brands for gas-powered mowers and tractors include Murray, Scotts, Stanley, Yard Machines, and Yard-Man. Pricier brands traditionally sold at outdoor power-equipment dealers include Ariens, Cub Cadet, Honda, Husqvarna, John Deere, Lawn Boy, Snapper, and Toro, although models from several of these brands are now available at large retailers.

Which type is best for your lawn? Here's what to think about for each:

Manual-reel mowers. Pushing these simple mowers turns a series of curved blades that spin with the wheels. Reel mowers are quiet, inexpensive, and non-polluting. They're also relatively safe to operate and require little maintenance other than periodic blade adjustment and sharpening. On the downside, our tests have shown that most can't cut grass higher than 1½ inches or trim closer than 3 inches around obstacles. Cutting swaths just 14 to 18 inches wide are also a drawback. Consider them for small, flat lawns a quarter acre or less. Price range: $100 to about $250.

Electric mowers. These push-type walk-behind mowers use an electric motor to drive a rotating blade. Both corded and cordless versions start with the push of a button, produce no exhaust emissions, and, like reel mowers, require little maintenance aside from sharpening. Most offer a grass catcher at the side or rear, and many can mulch—a process where clippings are recut until they're small enough to hide unobtrusively within the lawn. But electrics tend to be less powerful than gas mowers and less adept at tackling tall or thick grass and weeds. What's more, their narrow, 18-to-19-inch swaths take a smaller bite than most gas-powered mowers.

Both corded and cordless electrics have other significant drawbacks. Corded mowers limit your mowing to within a 100 feet of a power outlet—the typical maximum for extension cords. Cordless versions, while more versatile, weigh up to 30 pounds more than corded models and typically mow just one-quarter to one-third acre before their sealed lead-acid batteries need recharging. That makes both types of electrics suitable mainly for small, flat lawns a quarter acre or less.

Price range: corded, $125 to $250; cordless, $300 to $400.

Gasoline-powered walk-behind mowers. These include push as well as self-propelled models with driven wheels. Most have a 3.5- to 6.5-hp, four-stroke engine and a cutting swath 20 to 22 inches wide, allowing them to do more work with each pass and handle long or thick grass and weeds. All can mow as long as there's fuel in the tank. But gas mowers are relatively noisy and require regular maintenance.

Most gas mowers provide three cutting modes: bagging, which gathers clippings in a removable catcher; side-discharging, which dispenses clippings onto the lawn; and mulching, which cuts and recuts clippings until they're small enough to nestle and decompose in the lawn. Consider a push-type model for lawns up to one-half acre and for trimming larger lawns, a self-propelled model for larger or hilly lawns. Price range: push-type, $100 to more than $400; self-propelled, $250 to $900.

Riding mowers and tractors. These are suitable for lawns one-half acre or larger. Riding mowers have their engines in back and tend to be smaller, simpler, and easier to maneuver than tractors. While their 28-to-33-inch mowing swath is larger than a walk-behind mower's, it's far smaller than the 38 to 48 inches offered by lawn tractors and the 60 inches available with some larger garden tractors. Lawn and garden tractors have larger engines mounted in front for better weight distribution. Both can also accept attachments that allow them to plow and tow a cart as well as clear snow, while garden tractors accept soil-tilling equipment. Lawn tractors have become far more popular than garden tractors, although even these usually can't mulch or bag without accessories; figure on another $25 to $150 for a mulching kit and $200 to $450 for a bagging system.

Zero-turn-radius riders and tractors are also gaining ground in the marketplace. With most, you steer by pushing or pulling control levers, each controlling a driven rear wheel, although John Deere has introduced a zero-turn lawn tractor that uses a conventional steering wheel. You get added maneuverability in tight spots and around obstacles—but pay a premium. Price range: riding mowers, $700 to $2,000; lawn tractors, $800 to $3,500; garden tractors, $2,000 to $6,000; zero-turning-radius mowers, $3,000 to $7,000.

➤ KEY FEATURES

For electric mowers. A **sliding clip** helps ease turns with corded mowers by allowing the cord to move from side to side. Some have a **flip-over handle** you move from one end of the mower to the other as you reverse direction, say, at the end of a row.

For gas-powered mowers. Some more expensive models have a blade-brake clutch system that stops the blade but allows the engine to keep running when you release the handlebar safety bail. This is more convenient than the usual **engine-kill system**, which stops the engine and blade and requires you to restart the engine. A **four-stroke engine**, which burns gasoline alone, runs more cleanly than a **two-stroke engine**, which runs on a mixture of oil and gasoline. An **overhead-valve** four-stroke engine tends to pollute even less than traditional **side-valve** four-stroke engines.

With most gas mowers, you press a small rubber bulb called a **primer** to supply extra fuel for cold starting. Those with a **choke** ease the cold-start process. **Electric starters** are easier to use than a **recoil starter**, though they typically add $50 to $100 to the price. Most mowers with recoil starters are easier to start than they once were, however. Some models from

MTD-made Cub Cadet, White, and Yard-Man now have a spring-powered **self-starter**, which uses energy generated as the engine is shut off to provide push-button starts without a battery or outlet. CONSUMER REPORTS tests have found the device effective, provided you don't attempt starts in thick grass.

Some self-propelled mowers have just **one speed**, usually about 2½ mph; others have **several speeds** or a **continuous range**, typically from 1 to 3½ mph. Driven mowers also include **front-drive** and **rear-drive** models. Front-drive mowers tend to be easier to maneuver and turn, although rear-wheel-drive models tend to have better traction on hills and better steering control. Mowers with **swivel front wheels** offer the most maneuverability by allowing easy 180-degree turns. But on many, each front caster-like wheel must be removed to adjust cutting height.

Most decks are steel, although some mowers offer **aluminum** or **plastic** decks, which are rustproof; plastic also resists dents and cracks. Even many lower-priced mowers now have **tools-free cutting-height adjusters**, which raise and lower the deck with one or two levers. Most models also allow you to change mowing modes without tools, although a few still require wrenches and, sometimes, a blade change. Some models use a **side-bagging deck design**, where a side-exit chute routes clippings into a side-mounted bag or out onto the lawn—or is blocked with a plate or plug for mulching.

Mowers with a **rear-bagging deck** tend to cost more, but their rear-mounted bag holds more than side bags and eases maneuvering by hanging beneath the handlebar, rather than out to the side. The rearward opening is fitted with a chute for side-discharging or a plug for mulching. Some **"hybrid" rear-baggers** have a discharge port for clippings on the side of the deck as well as one for the bag in back.

For riding mowers and tractors. Most are gear-driven and require a lever and combination brake/clutch to change speed. Some gear-drive models use foot pedals with a pulley that allows continuously variable speed changes without the usual shift points. Spending more will buy you a model with a clutchless **hydrostatic drive**, which allows even more convenient continuously variable speed changes. Most models have a **translucent fuel tank**, making it easy to check fuel level. Some have a **fuel gauge**. Still others allow you to remove the collection bags without flipping the seat forward.

➤ HOW TO CHOOSE

Performance differences. Nearly all push and self-propelled gas mowers now handle mulching, bagging, and side-discharging. In tests, CONSUMER REPORTS found that most did at least a good job at mulching, the fastest and easiest way to dispose of clippings. All but the best mulchers in CONSUMER REPORTS tests left a few visible clippings on the lawn, while the worst left enough clippings to require raking. Even the best mulchers won't work well if the grass is too tall or wet, however. Tests also found that a mower's horsepower rating tends to have little bearing on mowing performance. Rear-bagging mowers, whether gas or electric, tended to perform better than side-baggers. Electric models did a decent job at mulching, bagging, and side-discharging. But they struggled with tall grass or weeds, and they take a relatively narrow bite with each pass.

Virtually all riding mowers and tractors can also handle all three mowing modes. In tests, most did a thorough job of vacuuming up clippings when bagging, although some clogged before their bags

were full. The best held more than twice as many clippings as the best push mowers.

Recommendations. Balance the size of your yard with how much you want to spend. Gas-powered push and self-propelled mowers are appropriate for many lawns. Electric mowers offer cleaner, quieter running and easy maintenance—but they're limited by a cord or, for cordless models, relatively little mowing time between charges. Homeowners with small lawns can also consider a manual-reel mower. Just be sure that your lawn isn't too thick and that you don't skip a week.

If you decide to ride, you'll probably want a lawn tractor unless your lawn has lots of tight areas and obstacles. Then the smaller size of a riding mower is an advantage. You can also opt for a zero-turn mower or tractor, which combines a wide deck with 360-degree turning.

Related CR report: June 2002
Ratings: pages 257, 260, 264
Reliability: page 334

PAINT

A few hundred dollars worth of paint can improve the looks of your home, protect it, and possibly boost its value.

Painting can be an arduous task, especially if there is a lot of preparation to do. And professional painters don't come cheap. High-quality paint can make a paint job last longer.

Interior paint should be washable and stain- and fade-resistant. Exterior paint (or stain) should hold its own against sun, rain, dirt, and mildew, and should resist cracking. Polymers in interior paint are relatively hard so they can hold up when scrubbed. In exterior paint, polymers are more flexible so the paint doesn't crack as the surface expands and contracts. Both interior and exterior paint should brush on easily and cover the surface thoroughly.

You'll also see kitchen and bath paints and garage-floor paints, as well a waterproofing coating for use on basement walls. These latter coatings come in two forms: premixed liquids (water or oil based) and powders that must be mixed with water or, in some cases, a special bonding agent.

Some people are sensitive to the fumes given off by wet latex paints. If you or a family member experiences headaches, nausea, or dizziness associated with the chemicals in paint, you can use a product labeled as having low levels of volatile organic compounds (VOCs) or none at all. Note that low-odor isn't the same as low-VOC or no-VOC. The fumes from relatively high levels of VOCs can be masked to make a low-odor paint. If you or someone in your family is bothered by paint fumes, a low-odor paint may not help. VOCs evaporate as the paint dries and can react with sunlight and pollutants in the air to produce ozone. Federal regulations limit the level of VOCs in indoor and outdoor paint. Some areas of the country, such as Southern California, require an even lower level.

➤ WHAT'S AVAILABLE

Major brands include Behr (sold at Home Depot), Benjamin Moore, Dutch Boy, Glidden, Sherwin-Williams, and Valspar (sold at Lowe's). Ace, Sears, and True Value sell various brands including their own. You'll also see designer names such as Martha Stewart and Ralph Lauren, as well as many brands of paint sold regionally. Sico is sold in Canada.

Interior paints have several classifica-tions. Wall paints can be used in just about any room. Glossier trim enamels are often used for windowsills, woodwork, and the like. Kitchen and bath paints are usually fairly glossy (sometimes very glossy) and are formulated to hold up to water and scrubbing and to release stains. Some paints contain mildewcide, useful in high-humidity areas. You can buy a mildewcide and add it to any paint, but we don't recommend its use because it is toxic and may not be compatible with the paint you choose.

Latex paint. This is relatively easy to use, and the popular choice for indoor and outdoor jobs. It dries fast with minimal odor, brushes on with few drips and sags, and cleans up with water. It also remains flexible and breathable, allowing pent-up humidity to escape. Because exterior latex paint can be applied to a damp surface, you can use it the day after it rains. But don't use latex paint outdoors when rain is forecast. A brisk shower can wash it off. Price range: $10 to $35 per gallon.

Oil-based (alkyd) paint. This paint is useful as a stain-blocking primer, although latex and shellac-based stain-blocking primers are available. Oil-based paint has largely disappeared, partly because today's tighter solvent-emission laws rule against their relatively high levels of VOCs. Price range: $15 to $35 per gallon.

➤ KEY FEATURES

Paint typically comes in a variety of sheens—**flat, low luster,** and **semigloss.** The degree of glossiness can be different from one manufacturer to another. Flat paint keeps reflections to a minimum and hides surface imperfections. It is usually harder to clean and picks up more dirt than glossier formulas. Semigloss is easier to clean than flat, but it may be too shiny for larger surfaces. And some semigloss paints can remain sticky after the surface has dried, making them risky for trims and shelving. A low-luster finish—often called eggshell or satin—is the middle ground. It is easy to clean and reflects less light.

A **custom color** of paint is created by mixing a colorant with a tint base. Most brands come in several tint bases, including medium and pastel, to provide a full range of colors. The **tint base** largely determines toughness, resistance to dirt and stains, and ability to withstand scrubbing. The **colorant** determines how much the paint will fade, particularly with exterior paint and interior paint in a sunny room. Whites and browns tend not to fade (but whites can yellow); reds and blues fade somewhat; bright greens and yellows fade a lot. In a mixture of pigments, as the greens and yellows fade, other colors begin to stand out.

➤ **HOW TO CHOOSE**

Performance differences. CONSUMER REPORTS tests have shown that few paints, especially whites, hide in one coat. All of the paints we tested did better with two coats. Most interior paints hold up well when scrubbed with a sponge and powdered cleanser. Nearly all low-luster paints do well when stains are cleaned away with a sponge and spray cleaner. Flat paints hold stains more tenaciously and are harder to clean. CONSUMER REPORTS has found that interior paint brands including Dutch Boy, Martha Stewart, Olympic, Pittsburgh, Sears, and Sherwin-Williams fade more than most.

The biggest difference we've found between regular paints and low-VOC paints is their drying time. Low-VOC paints dry very fast. You have to work quickly to avoid marks from overlapping roller strokes as well as brush marks around trim, and brushes and rollers may be harder to clean after applying a low-VOC paint. Tests of exterior paint in which the paints are exposed for up to five years, have revealed significant differences in durability. Most paints still looked almost new after a year. But after two years of exposure, some started to show the effects of weathering. (Testing conditions are somewhat accelerated. Each year of testing corresponds to between two and four years of real-life exposure.)

Among waterproofing coatings, recent tests found the premixed formulations easier to use than the powdered varieties, some of which thickened to a nearly unspreadable consistency after a relatively short time. And water-based paints make for an easier cleanup.

Recommendations. Most manufacturers offer three levels of quality—essentially, good, better, and best. Decades of CONSUMER REPORTS tests have clearly shown that it makes sense to look first at top-of-the-line paints.

Paint manufacturers estimate that a gallon of paint should cover 400 to 450 square feet. That's a good rule to follow when calculating how much paint you will need. Consider, too, the effect of the surface—the rougher, the more paint or stain it will take and the less square footage you'll get per gallon. Porous surfaces require a primer/sealer before painting. Some waterproofing coatings must be applied to a dry wall, hence it wouldn't be a good choice for a perpetually damp surface. Whether you buy paint from an independent paint retailer, a company store such as Sherwin-Williams, a home center, or a mass merchandiser such as Wal-Mart, be sure to ask about discounts or deals on high-quantity purchases (10 to 15 percent is common).

Related CR report: July 2002

POWER BLOWERS

Gasoline-powered models are cleaner and less noisy; electric models are quieter still, and more powerful than before.

These miniature wind machines take some of the effort out of sweeping and gathering fallen leaves and other small yard and driveway debris. Many can also vacuum and shred what they pick up. But practically all still make enough noise to be obtrusive. Indeed, some localities have ordinances restricting or forbidding their use.

➤ **WHAT'S AVAILABLE**

Mainstream brands include Black & Decker, Homelite, Craftsman (Sears), Toro, and Weed Eater. Pricier brands of gas-powered blowers include Echo, Husqvarna, John Deere, and Stihl. As with other outdoor power tools, gas and electric blowers each have their pros and cons. You'll also find variations among gas-powered models. Here are your choices:

Electric handheld blowers. Designed for one-handed maneuvering, these are light (about 7 pounds or less). They are also relatively quiet, produce no exhaust emissions, and many can vacuum and shred. Some perform as well as handheld gas-powered models, although their mobility is limited by their power cord. Price range: $30 to $100.

Gas handheld blowers. These perform similarly to the best electrics, but can venture as far as their fuel tank takes them. Tougher regulations have reduced allowable emissions for gas blowers as they have for other tools, while manufacturers have quieted these machines in response to new noise ordinances. Most models are still loud enough to warrant hearing protec-

tion, however. Other drawbacks include added weight (most weigh 7 to 12 pounds) and the fuel-and-oil mixing that is required by the two-stroke engines most models use. A few models, notably from Ryobi, have four-stroke engines that burn gasoline only. Price range: $75 to $225.

Gasoline backpack blowers. At 15 to 28 pounds, these are heavier than handheld blowers. But the payoff with most is added power and ease of use for extended periods, since your shoulders support their weight. Backpack blowers don't vacuum, however, and hearing protection is recommended. They can also be expensive. Price range: $200 to $500.

Gasoline rolling blowers. These offer enough oomph to sweep sizable areas quickly. All use four-stroke engines that require no fuel mixing. But these machines are large, heavy, and require pushing. They also cost the most and tend to be hard to maneuver, which can make it difficult to precisely direct leaves and other yard waste. And because they're noisier than gas lawn mowers, count on using hearing protection. Price range: $500 to $700.

➤ **KEY FEATURES**

Look for an **easy-to-use on/off switch** on electric blowers, a **variable throttle** you can preset on electric and gasoline-powered models, and a **convenient choke** on gas-powered units. Blowers that excel at cleaning usually have **round-nozzle blower tubes; oblong** and **rectangular nozzles** are better for moving leaves. A **control stalk** attached to the blower tube of a backpack model improves handling, while an **auxiliary handle** on the engine or motor housing of a handheld unit eases use— provided the handle is comfortable. Other useful features in gas-powered models include a **wide fuel fill** and a **translucent fuel tank**, which shows the level inside.

➤ **HOW TO CHOOSE**

Performance differences. In CONSUMER REPORTS tests, the strongest blowers could push leaves into piles 20 inches high, while the weakest had trouble building 12-inch piles. The best electric blowers are on a par with most gasoline-powered models and tend to be lighter and easier to handle. Backpack blowers, while heavy, tend to be easiest to use for extended periods, since the blower tube is all you hold in your hands.

Recommendations. Begin by matching the blower to your property. The smaller the leaf-clearing job, the less blowing power you'll need. You can also get by with less power if you'll be clearing mostly hard surfaces such as a driveway—jobs for which relatively quiet, light, and inexpensive handheld electric machines may suffice. Models that vacuum can be handy for sucking leaves out from corners and beneath shrubs. Whichever power blower you're considering, find out about any local noise restrictions before buying.

Related CR report: September 2001
Ratings: page 279

STRING TRIMMERS

An electric model can do a good job for many trimming tasks. For strong all-around performance, you'll need a gasoline-powered trimmer.

A string trimmer can pick up where a lawn mower leaves off. It provides the finishing touches, slicing through tufts of grass around trees and flowerbeds, straightening uneven edges along a driveway, and trimming stretches of lawn your mower or tractor can't reach. Gasoline-powered models can also whisk away tall grass and weeds. And all string trimmers can venture into rock-strewn areas that would destroy a mower's metal blades, thanks to their flexible plastic lines. Some, however, are less capable and convenient at those tasks.

➤ **WHAT'S AVAILABLE**

Black & Decker, Craftsman (Sears), Homelite, Ryobi, Toro, and Weed Eater are the major mainstream brands, with Weed Eater selling the most. Leading high-end brands include Echo, Husqvarna, and Stihl. You'll also find several kinds of trimmers. Here's how to determine which will work best for your needs.

Gasoline-powered trimmers. These are better than electrics at cutting heavy weeds and brush, and are often better at edging, where you turn them so that their spinning lines cut vertically along a walk or garden border. They also go anywhere and cut relatively large swaths up to 18 inches wide. Some accept a metal blade (usually an option) that can cut branches up to about ¾-inch thick. On the downside, gas trimmers can be heavy, weighing from about 10 to 16 pounds. Most have a two-stroke engine that requires a mixture of gas and oil, tends to pollute more than the four-stroke engines, and entails pull-starting and regular maintenance. Price range: less than $100 to more than $300. Most models, however, cost from $100 to $200.

Electric corded trimmers. These are least expensive and lightest; many weigh only about 5 pounds. Some work nearly as well as gas trimmers for most trimming, and all are quieter and easier to start and stop than gas trimmers; you simply pull a trigger, rather than pull a rope. But their power cord limits their range to about 100 feet from an outlet. Many models have the motor at the bottom of the shaft, rather than at the top, making them harder to handle. And even the most powerful models are unlikely to tackle the tall grass and weeds that the best gas-powered trimmers can tackle. Price range: $25 to $75.

Electric battery-powered trimmers. Cordless trimmers combine the free range of gas trimmers with the convenience of corded electrics: less noise, easy starting and stopping, no fueling, and no exhaust emissions. But they're weak at cutting and run only about 15 to 30 minutes before their onboard battery needs recharging, which can take a day. They also tend to be pricey and heavy for their size (about 10 pounds), and models with the motor at the bottom of the shaft can be even harder to handle than lighter corded versions. Price range: $70 to $100.

> **KEY FEATURES**

All trimmers have a **shaft** that connects the engine or motor and controls to the **trimmer head** where the plastic lines revolve. **Curved-shaft trimmers** are the most common, and can be easier to handle when trimming up close. **Straight-shaft trimmers** tend to be better for reaching beneath bushes and other shrubs. On models without a clutch, the string is always spinning while the engine is running—an inconvenience. Some models have a **split shaft** that comes apart so that you can replace the trimmer head with a leaf blower, edging blade, or other yard tool, though CONSUMER REPORTS has found that some of these attachments aren't very effective.

Most gas-powered trimmers have **two cutting lines**, while many electrics use just one, which provides less cutting with each

revolution. Most gas and electric trimmers have a **bump-feed line advance** that feeds out more line when you bump the trimmer head on the ground; a blade on the safety shield cuts it to the right length. **Auto-feed systems** add convenience by automatically feeding out new line as they sense a change in the centrifugal force exerted by a shortened line. But some auto-feed systems don't work very well and may compromise cutting performance. In either case, replacing the line usually involves removing and rethreading the empty spool. With some trimmers, you simply pull off the old spool and push on a new one.

Most gasoline models use **two-stroke engines**, which burn lubricating oil with the gasoline. Federal law requires manufacturers to slash exhaust emissions for new gas-powered trimmers by 70 percent by 2005, while California has required that emissions reduction since 2000. Some trimmers use inherently cleaner **four-stroke engines**, but these tend to weigh and cost more. Corded and battery models typically use a **1.8- to 5-amp motor**.

To start most gas trimmers, you set a **choke** and push a **primer bulb**, then pull a rope. On most, a **centrifugal clutch** allows the engine to idle without spinning the line—safer and more convenient than models where the line continues to turn. Electric-trimmer lines don't spin until you press the switch.

Some models make edging more convenient with a **rotating head, shaft, or handle** that makes the trimmer head easier to move to the vertical position. Heavier-duty models often offer a **shoulder harness** that can ease handling and reduce fatigue. Other convenient features include **easy-to-reach and easy-to-adjust switches, comfortable handles,** and—on gas models—a **translucent fuel tank.**

> ### ■ TECH TIP
> A trimmer's string can give you a painful sting even through clothing, draw blood on bare skin, and also fling dirt and debris. When you're trimming, wear gloves, long pants, sturdy shoes, safety glasses, and, with a gas trimmer, ear protection.

> **HOW TO CHOOSE**

Performance differences. Almost any machine can trim a small, well-maintained lawn. Some corded electric trimmers and all the battery-powered models in the most recent CONSUMER REPORTS tests proved weak. As a rule with electric trimmers, the higher the amperage, the better they cut. Slicing through tall grass and weeds generally requires a gasoline-powered trimmer, although our tests have shown no correlation between engine size and performance with these units.

Recommendations. Look for a trimmer that fits your physique, allowing you to work without stooping and maintain good balance so that your arms don't tire before the work is done. For competent performance on a range of trimming and edging tasks, you'll probably prefer a gas-powered model. For smaller spaces and lighter-duty trimming, consider a corded electric trimmer. Look for one with the motor on top of the shaft for better balance and easier handling. Consider a cordless electric model only for the lightest of trimming chores.

Related CR report: May 2002
Ratings: page 306

VACUUM CLEANERS

Fancy features don't necessarily make a better upright or canister vac. You'll find lots of competent models at a reasonable price.

Which type of vacuum to buy used to be a no-brainer. Uprights were clearly better for carpets, while canisters were the obvious choice for bare floors. That distinction is being blurred somewhat as more upright models clean floors without scattering dust and more canisters do a very good job with carpeting. You'll also see a growing number of features like dirt sensors and bagless dirt bins as manufacturers attempt to boost performance. Some of those features, however, may contribute more to price than function. Other, more essential features may not be found on the least-expensive models.

> **WHAT'S AVAILABLE**

Hoover, the oldest and largest vacuum manufacturer, is a midpriced brand with about 70 different models. Many of those models are similar, with minor differences in features; the "variety" is mostly in the marketing. And some are made exclusively for a single retail chain. Eureka has been a low-priced brand, while Dirt Devil (made by Royal Appliance) sells uprights and canisters as well as stick brooms and hand vacuums. Kenmore (Sears) accounts for about 25 percent of all canister vacuums sold in the U.S. Brands such as Miele, Panasonic, Samsung, Sanyo, Sharp, and Simplicity are more likely to be sold at specialty stores. Upscale Electrolux and Oreck vacs are sold in their own stores and by direct mail, while Kirby models are sold door-to-door.

Better uprights and canisters clean carpet very well. Uprights can also do an excellent job on bare floors, thanks in part to an on/off switch for the brush. When cleaning with tools, the brush switch can help protect the user from injury, the power cord from damage, and furnishings from undue wear. Uprights also tend to be less expensive and easier to store than canister models. A top-of-the-line upright might have a wider cleaning path, be self-propelled, and have a HEPA filter, dirt sensor, and full-bag indicator. Price range: $50 to $1,300.

Canister vacuums tend to do well on floors because they allow you to turn off the brush or use a specialized tool to avoid scattering dirt. Most are quieter than uprights and more adept at cleaning on stairs and in hard-to-reach areas. Price range: $100 to $900.

Stick vacs and hand vacs—corded or cordless—lack the power of a full-sized vacuum cleaner, but they can be handy for small, quick jobs. Price range: $20 to $75.

➤ KEY FEATURES

Typical attachments include **crevice** and **upholstery tools**. You'll also appreciate **extension wands** for reaching high places. The canisters we test have a **detachable power nozzle** that cleans carpet more thoroughly than a simple suction nozzle, and most machines have a cord of 20 to 30 feet long. While most upright vacuums require you to manually wrap the cord for storage, canisters typically have a **retractable cord** that rewinds with a tug or push of a button.

> ■ **TECH TIP**
> A regular vacuum has no tolerance for wetness and should never be used outdoors. Even moisture from a recently shampooed rug can damage the motor.

A **full-bag alert** can be handy, since an overstuffed bag impairs a vacuum's ability to clean. Lately, many uprights have adopted a **bagless** configuration with a see-through dirt bin that replaces the usual bag. But as we've found, emptying these bins can raise enough dust to concern even those without allergies.

Another worthwhile feature is **manual pile-height adjustment**, which can improve cleaning by letting you match the vacuum's height to the carpet pile more effectively than you can with machines that adjust automatically. Also look for **suction control**. Found on most canisters and some uprights, it allows you to reduce airflow for drapes and other delicate fabrics. You'll also find more uprights with a **self-propelled feature** to make pushing easy, though that can also make them heavier and harder to carry up or down the stairs.

Some models have a **dirt sensor** that triggers a light indicator according to the concentration of dirt particles in the machine's air stream. But the sensor signals only that the vacuum is no longer picking up dirt—not whether there's dirt left in your rug. Some are so sensitive that you keep vacuuming longer, working harder and gaining little in cleanliness.

Fine particles may pass through a vacuum's bag or filter and escape into the air through the exhaust. Many models claim **microfiltration** capabilities, using a bag with smaller pores or a second, electrostatic filter in addition to the standard motor filter. Some have a **HEPA filter**, which may benefit someone with asthma. But many models without a HEPA filter performed as well in CONSUMER REPORTS emissions tests, since the amount of dust emitted depends as much on the design of the entire machine as on its filter.

A vacuum's design can also affect how long it lasts. With some uprights, for example, dirt sucked into the vac passes through the blower fan before entering the bag—a potential problem, since most fans are plastic and vulnerable to damage from hard objects. Better systems filter dirt through the bag before it reaches the fan; while hard objects can lodge in the motorized brush, they're unlikely to break the fan.

Like bagless uprights, stick vacs and hand vacs typically have messy dirt-collection bins. Some have a **revolving brush**, which may help remove surface debris from a carpet. Stick vacs can hang on a hook or, if they're cordless, a wall-mounted charger base.

➤ **HOW TO CHOOSE**

Performance differences. Virtually all recently tested uprights and canisters did at least a good job overall. Bagless vacs filtered dust as well as bag-equipped models overall, but emptying their bins released enough dust to make wearing a mask a consideration. We have found stick vacs less impressive, with few excelling at all types of cleaning. Overall, hand vacs do a better job along wall edges than stick vacs by coming closer to the moldings and angling into nooks and crannies.

We've also found that high-end features such as dirt sensors don't necessarily improve performance. And ignore claims about amps and suction. Amps are a measure of running current, not cleaning power, while suction alone doesn't determine a vacuum's ability to lift dirt from carpeting. Some vacuums are extremely expensive—anywhere from $800 to $1,500 and more. CONSUMER REPORTS tests have shown that high-priced brands such as Electrolux, Filter Queen, Kirby, Miele, and Rainbow perform well, but so do many models that cost $200 to $300. We've also found that many of the least expensive uprights sacrifice key features as well as performance.

Recommendations. Begin by deciding whether you prefer an upright or a canister. Then choose a model that performs and has the right features for your kind of cleaning. Those with varied cleaning needs may want to consider a vacuum-cleaner arsenal—an upright for carpets, a compact canister when tool use is important, and a hand vac or stick vac for quick touch-ups around the kitchen and family room.

Related CR report: February 2002
Ratings: page 316
Reliability: page 339

WET/DRY VACUUMS

Aimed at sawdust, wood chips, and spills, these machines are to regular vacs what pickup trucks are to sedans.

Wet/dry vacuums are meant for life's meaner tasks. Their place is typically in the workshop or garage, where their multigallon capacities and appetite for rough stuff make them right at home. Lately, manufacturers have been plugging their smallest portable models for kitchen duty: draining a clogged sink, sucking up soda spills, or picking up broken glass. Other capabilities can include use as a handheld blower for outdoor debris or as a pump. Wet/dry vacs of any size make poor housemates, however. Even the quietest are as loud as the noisiest household versions. And while their high-pitched whine is more annoying than dangerous, some are loud enough to make ear protection advisable. Still another concern is the fine dust these machines tend to spew into the air—a potential problem if you have allergies. But a high-efficiency cartridge filter significantly reduces those emissions and is available for many models.

➤ **WHAT'S AVAILABLE**

Craftsman (Sears) and Shop-Vac account for three out of every four wet/dry vacs sold. Ridgid—sold mostly at Home Depot—and Genie are a distant third and fourth among leading brands. Ridgid and Craftsman models are made by the same manufacturer, Emerson Electric.

Wet/dry vacuums have claimed canister capacities ranging from 6 to 20 gallons for full-sized units and 1 to 2 gallons for compacts. Most units can fill about three-quarters of their canister with water before the float, an internal part designed to prevent overfilling and spilling, seals off the flow.

Claimed peak motor power ranges from 1 hp for the smallest portables to more than 6 hp for the largest. The numbers denote peak horsepower, rather than actual output while in use, however. Larger models with more powerful motors tend to pick up debris or liquid faster, according to CONSUMER REPORTS tests. But some smaller units outperform larger ones.

Use claims of canister capacity and peak motor power as a guide for comparing models within a brand or size group—not as an absolute. Price range: compact, $30 to $70; full-size, $40 to $250.

> **KEY FEATURES**

A wet/dry vacuum's **hose** usually comes in one of two diameters: 1¼ inches or 2½ inches. Models with a wider hose tend to pick up liquids and larger dry debris more quickly. A **hose lock**, found in some models, secures the hose to the canister better than a simple press-on fit, which can release as you pull the hose.

Most models come with accessories. A **squeegee nozzle**—essentially a wide floor nozzle with a rubber insert—helps slurp up liquid spills more quickly and thoroughly. Other nozzles include a **utility nozzle** for solid objects and a **dirt** and a **crevice nozzle** for corners. Some nozzles include a **brush insert** for improved dry pickup. A **built-in caddie** allows the vacuum to hold all of these accessories conveniently, though some models provide other onboard storage.

The two basic types of **filters** include **cartridge** and **two-piece paper/foam**. Cartridge filters tend to be easier to service and can stay in during wet vacuuming; with a two-piece filter, you must remove the paper element for wet cleanup. A **high-efficiency cartridge filter** (about $20 to $30) reduces the fine dust spewed into the air. While it

also reduces suction slightly, allergy sufferers should find the sacrifice worthwhile.

Other notable features include **large carrying handles** molded into the sides of the canister, which help you move the vacuum securely over ledges and up stairs. An **assist handle** mounted at or near the top of the unit also makes jockeying these machine easier. Some models have **power cords** as short as 6 feet; look for one at least 15 feet long to avoid the safety risk of using an extension cord in standing water. A **drain spout** found in some models lets you simply open a drain, rather than lift and tilt the machine, while long **extension wands** reduce stooping.

> **HOW TO CHOOSE**

Performance differences. A wet/dry vacuum's ability tend to track with its size. Compact models proved relatively wimpy in CONSUMER REPORTS tests, though they're fine for small areas and pint-sized spills. While all units we've seen pick up small wood shavings, chips, and sawdust, those with a wider hose suck up lighter dry and wet debris faster and often more thoroughly. Heavier dry waste tends to be a problem for all sizes, however.

Recommendations. Match the size of the vac with your needs. For example, models that hold 10 to 15 gallons can provide a good balance of size, power, and maneuverability. A large canister is handy for large spills. A large vac is harder to maneuver and store, however, while a small one must be emptied more often.

Maintenance includes cleaning the filter —typically about a five-minute job that involves removing it and brushing it clean (for paper elements) or washing it (for foam elements). An extra filter (about $15) you can quickly swap for a dirty one can come in handy, though changing filters is a messy task.

HOME OFFICE

What's New in Home-Office Gear

Computer gear has become easier to use and more elegant-looking. It has also become more fun. Added to the traditional word-processing, accounting, and presentation functions are capabilities that let you listen to online music, edit home movies downloaded from a camcorder, create your own CDs and DVDs, play games, and pursue hobbies from genealogy to collecting baseball cards.

Meanwhile, computers and telephones are merging, in the form of cell phones that can access the Internet and personal digital assistants that can act as phones. Other trends affecting computers, phones, and related products:

Faster, cheaper, better products. Processors, which serve as the brains of a computer, have reached clock speeds of nearly 3 gigahertz, or 3 billion cycles per second. That's nearly 1,000 times the speed of the earliest personal computers. Laser and photo-quality color inkjet printers are fast and cheaper every month. Scanners for photos and text are also inexpensive and produce excellent results. PDAs with a color screen now cost what you would have paid for a black-and-white model just last year.

Telephone answering machines have pretty much disappeared as a stand-alone product, as faster, cheaper computer chips have allowed the function to be inexpensively added to cordless and corded phones.

Smaller products. Desktop computer manufacturers have developed interesting alternatives to the familiar beige box. Apple's iMac, for example, puts an entire computer into a small hemisphere from which sprouts a stalk holding the svelte flat-panel display. Such displays are becoming the norm for all desktop systems, as they have continue to drop in price. Computer users on the go can take advantage of laptop models that are as thin as a couple of magazines. Cell phones are tiny, easily fitting into a pocket.

More ways to buy. Nearly all major computer manufacturers sell their wares directly, through the web, telephone orders, and factory stores. They offer financing programs that let you make monthly payments, as well as leasing programs for home-based businesses. Retail venues include computer superstores such as CompUSA and PC Warehouse, electronics superstores like Best Buy and Circuit City, home-office superstores such as Office Depot and Staples, and warehouse clubs like Costco and Sam's Club. At some stores, you can custom-design your own computer at an interactive kiosk. According to the most recent CONSUMER REPORTS survey, you're likely to better satisfied if you buy directly from the manufacturer than if you buy through a retail store.

The new sell in cellular. Digital models, with analog backup for the few places you might need it, are the norm. New models sport Internet-savvy features like e-mail and web access, plus the ability to send short text messages to other phones. And providers of cell-phone service are changing the way callers pay. People who make a lot of calls can use flat-rate plans that provide an allotment of minutes for a fixed charge. Families with several phones can use family plans to pool their allotted minutes. Night and weekend calls are often free, and plans with wide—even nationwide—calling areas reduce roaming charges for travelers.

Online access speeds up. More people can obtain high-speed Internet access. Broadband options that let you speed up your web connection include a cable modem, available through a cable television provider; digital subscriber line (DSL), available through an Internet service provider in conjunction with either a phone company or a third party; or two-way satellite via a rooftop dish.

More home computers get networked. More and more homes have two or more computers. For all users to take advantage of the broadband connection, as well as sharing accessory devices like printers or scanners, you need to hook the computers together into a network. Fortunately, the hardware to do that is simpler and more available.

CELL PHONES

Complex pricing schemes and incompatible technologies can make it hard to find the right calling plan and handset. Fortunately, it doesn't have to be difficult.

More than 150 million people now own a cell phone. If current trends hold, one in five cell-phone users will switch carriers this year, seeking better service or lower rates, or both. A cell phone is undeniably convenient, often essential, and has forever changed the way people keep in touch with one another. Because a cell phone offers so many clear benefits, people appear to be willing to forgive a lot. But you need not make sacrifices. If you choose wisely you can get reliable service that's easy to understand.

To use cellular service, you'll need both a phone and a service provider. But all cell phones won't work with all service providers. It's best to select a service provider and calling plan first, then choose a phone that the provider offers. If you buy the phone first, you may have to use a provider that offers mediocre service where you live or that doesn't offer the best rates for your calling pattern.

➤ **WHAT'S AVAILABLE: SERVICE**
With a cell phone, you pay for all the time you're connected—both for calls you make and for calls you receive. With a conventional wired phone ("landline" service, to cellular devotees), you pay only for calls you make. Landline service is fairly straightforward, divided into local (or, sometimes,

local and regional) and long-distance charges. Cellular service is more complex. If you're making a call from outside your home calling area, you may pay a roaming charge in addition to the basic per-minute cost of the call, to compensate another cellular company for handling your call. And whether in the home area or across the country, you may also pay a long-distance charge. Most big service providers offer plans with hundreds, even thousands, of airtime minutes each month for a flat fee. However, not all cellular minutes are created equal. In many plans, the big bucket of

> ■ **TECH TIP**
> **Many states prohibit drivers from using hand-held cell phones, so use a hands-free kit if you absolutely must talk and drive at the same time. Better still, pull off the road to make the call that can't wait.**

minutes touted in the headline is divided into minutes you can use anytime and minutes good only on nights and weekends; when you exceed your allotment, you pay 30 to 60 cents per minute for additional calling time. Most calling plans also entail a one- or two-year commitment to the carrier, with cancellation fees of $100 or more if you want to switch before the time is up. The basic types of calling plans are:

Local. These cover the smallest geographic area—as the name implies, just the central metropolitan or rural area where you live. As a rule, calls outside the local area are subject to roaming or long-distance charges. Local plans tend to offer the smallest bucket of minutes. Local plans are best suited for people who rarely leave town.

Regional. These cover a larger area—typically, all or part of several states. There's no roaming or long-distance for calls within the region. Some plans treat every call as a local call, so you never pay

long-distance charges; roaming fees could still apply. Minutes offered range from medium- to large-sized buckets. These plans are best-suited for people who do some traveling, but in a well-defined area.

National. These plans treat all 50 states as a local calling area. There are no roaming or long-distance fees. However, the basic per-month charge tends to be highest for national plans or they offer less minutes than a comparable regional plan. Most national plans offer large buckets of minutes, but with fairly high per-minute charges if you exceed the basic allotment. These plans are well suited for people with a far-flung network of friends and family, and for those who do lots of traveling across the U.S.

Family. These plans let you put as many as four separate phones on one plan, sharing the bucket of minutes, whether local, regional, or national, for a combined monthly fee that may be far lower than you'd pay for separate service for each phone. In some family plans, calls among family members are always free. Otherwise, roaming and long-distance charges apply.

Prepaid. The antithesis of the big-bucket plans, prepaid service means you buy only the calling time you think you'll need. Once you select a phone and opt for a prepaid plan, you pay for a certain number of minutes, which you generally must use within two months. When you need more minutes, you buy more. There's no long-term commitment. A prepaid plan is well suited for people who truly want a cell phone only for emergencies and occasional use, not as a virtual substitute for the regular phone. But you must keep renewing the minutes—whether you use them or not—or your phone will be disconnected.

The leading national service providers

include AT&T Wireless, Cingular, Nextel, Sprint PCS, Verizon, and VoiceStream. In addition to those big six, there are dozens of smaller regional and local providers. Each provider uses one of four distinct digital formats—none of which are compatible with one another.

Digital phones operate in the cellular band, the personal communications services (PCS) band, or the enhanced specialized mobile radio (ESMR) band. There are four incompatible digital formats: Code Division Multiple Access (CDMA), Global System for Mobile Communications (GSM), Integrated Digital Enhanced Network (iDEN), and Time Division Multiple Access (TDMA). CDMA and TDMA are the dominant digital formats in the U.S.

GSM, the de facto standard around the world, is used in the U.S. by VoiceStream and some regional carriers. Cingular and AT&T plan to migrate to GSM service as well. The iDEN format, developed by Motorola, is used by Nextel and a few others.

All carriers operating in the cellular band are also required to support the analog format, AMPS. It's the closest thing to a standard in the U.S. Because AMPS is the only analog format, it's easy for carriers to make and break roaming agreements with cellular carriers. You don't need new phones, just new programming to get existing phones to search for a different analog network.

➤ WHAT'S AVAILABLE: HARDWARE

The leading cell-phone brands include Audiovox, Kyocera, Motorola, Nokia, Samsung, and Sony Ericsson. LG, Panasonic, and Sharp also offer cell phones. Newer handsets are thinner and lighter than older models, with a large array of features on even the least expensive models. Voice-activated dialing, one-key redial, and a large

memory for storing names and numbers are just a few of the common features. Prices range from $0 (with rebates equaling the initial price of the phone) up to $300 or more. Handspring, Nokia, and Kyocera are among the companies selling a phone/PDA combination. Cost: $150 and up.

There are several types of digital phones:

Tri-mode. The most versatile, these can handle calls in the CDMA or TDMA formats in both the cellular and PCS bands. They can default to analog in the cellular band.

Dual-mode. These use either the CDMA or TDMA digital format and default to analog if the phone can't detect a digital signal.

Dual-mode, dual-band. Primarily used by Sprint, these operate in the PCS band and use the CDMA format. If they can't detect a compatible PCS signal, they default to cellular analog.

Single-mode, single-band. These use the CDMA, TDMA, or GSM format in the PCS band, or the iDEN format in the ESMR band. If they can't detect a compatible carrier, they don't work.

➤ KEY FEATURES

Cell-phone makers and service providers are beginning to offer so-called **3G service**. At this point, 3G is the frosting, not the cake. Its main benefit at present: providing business users with a higher data-transfer rate for retrieving e-mail. It's still more important to find the right service and calling plan.

Among basic cell-phone features, look for an **LCD screen** that is readable in both low- and direct-light conditions. The **keypad** should be clearly marked and easy to use. **Programmable speed dial** allows you to store the names and numbers of the people you most frequently call. **Single-key last-number redial** is useful for dropped calls or when you're having trouble connecting. Some providers offer **caller ID, voice mail,** and short **messaging,** often for an extra charge.

Some handsets let you choose a **vibrating alert** or a light to let you know about an incoming call, useful when you're in a meeting or at the movies. An **any-key answer** feature lets you answer the phone by pressing any key rather than the Talk or Send key. Many folding phones answer the call when you open the mouthpiece flap.

The **battery** offered with the phone you buy won't necessarily give you the best service—and it's not your only option. There are usually several choices of battery size, each offering different amounts of talk time and standby time.

Some phones come with a base that can accommodate an extra battery that can be kept charged while the handset is in use; that way you don't lose any time waiting for a recharge, which can take 6 to 24 hours in some "trickle" chargers. An **automobile adapter** lets you power the phone by plugging it into your car's cigarette lighter.

Some models include a **hands-free kit,** which works like a speakerphone, but more offer a free headset. Such capability is increasingly demanded by law by more and more states for drivers using cell phones.

Phones vary widely in terms of keypad design, readability of screen displays, the ease of using the function menu, and how simple it is to perform such basic tasks as one-button redial and storing frequently called numbers for speed-dialing later. It's important to handle a phone in the store before you buy, to be sure its design and your fingers are well matched.

➤ HOW TO CHOOSE

Performance differences. Today's cellular phones use digital technology. Carriers have long touted digital as offering high-quality sound and longer battery life. CONSUMER REPORTS tests have found essentially no difference in the quality of the voice between older analog phones and digital technology. Digital does deliver improved battery life. All phones in the digital mode that we've seen are able to remain in standby mode for at least 24 hours without recharging.

To assess service differences, study the carriers' service area maps closely. Also ask friends and business associates who travel in the same areas that you do which provider offers the best service. Dead zones and fringe areas, where coverage isn't available, can make a plan worthless if that's where you want to use your phone.

Recommendations. Choose a service provider and calling plan first. What you pay to use the phone will cost far more than the phone itself. If you're switching providers, check two to three months' bills to gauge not only how minutes of calling time you actually use per month, but how many of those minutes are at night and on weekends. Select a new plan accordingly. If you're buying a cell phone for the first time, make your best guess about usage, but be prepared to switch to a different bucket of minutes after a month or two, once you know your cellular habits. You can gather wireless prices by visiting web sites such as *www.getconnected.com* and *www.telebright.com.* Telebright makes both a cellular and long-distance selector available to subscribers of our web site, ConsumerReports.org.

Before you commit to a plan, make sure you have a trial period that lets you test the network and cancel the service without penalty if it doesn't deliver reliable signals in places where you make calls.

All cell phones must be able to dial 911 for emergencies, even older cell phones for which the service contract has lapsed.

But the more sophisticated E911 service that the federal government has mandated for cell phones, which allows emergency-service workers to pinpoint the location of a cellular caller, won't be fully operational until 2005 at the earliest. So it's important to be able to give officials an exact location when calling for emergency aid from a cell phone.

Related CR reports: February 2002

CELL-PHONE ALTERNATIVES

A cell phone isn't the only way to stay in touch with people who are nearby. Here's a rundown of widely used, economical alternatives.

Even though cell-phone sales remain strong, and cell phones are one of the best ways to reach people when you're traveling, there are alternatives that work at shorter range—and, more important, without needing an often expensive monthly service plan.

➤ WHAT'S AVAILABLE

Two-way radios are the leading cell-phone alternatives. There are two types: family radio service (FRS) models, which transmit with enough power to cover about two miles in an open field, and general mobile radio service (GMRS) models, which transmit at higher power and can cover five miles under ideal conditions. Neither type carries activation or service fees, but GMRS radios require a $75, five-year license from the Federal Communications Commission. Two-way radios don't rely on transmission towers, so they can operate in remote locations. Leading brands include Motorola, Cobra, Uniden, and

Audiovox. Price range: from $40 or $50 to as much as $200 per pair.

Pagers also make a good alternative to a cell phone, although they are less widely used than they were a few years ago. The newest pagers let a caller send full text messages—not just a phone number or a few numbers of code (1-4-3 equals "I love you" in pagerspeak). Pagers can be one-way (receive only) or two-way (send and receive via a tiny keyboard). The pager itself can cost $50 to $150. Monthly service ranges from $10 to $60, depending on the volume of messages you exchange.

Text-messaging services provide pager-like functions through a cell phone. Many new phones and some older ones can perform this function. Text messaging lets you exchange messages of up to 160 characters with other cell phones or Internet e-mail addresses. Some phones receive only these messages, properly called Short Message Service, or SMS. Others let you enter messages via the phone's keypad, which is tedious. Typical SMS charges are 10 cents per message sent or a few dollars a month for 100 messages. You get the service through your cellular provider.

➤ KEY FEATURES

For two-way radios: **22 channels with subcodes.** This effectively expands the number of channels you can communicate on to more than 500. Any two-way radio can communicate with any other brand as long as both are tuned to the same channel and subcode. A side-mounted **talk button** is easier to use than one on the front. **Button lock** prevents important controls from accidentally being pressed when you carry the radio. **Vibrate alert** signals an incoming call without disturbing those around you. **Transmitter cutoff** stops transmissions when you've held the talk button for longer than a minute, to conserve battery power. **Auto squelch** automatically quiets background noise when no signal is present. **Batteries** that can recharge in the radio are also handy (however, some radios use only disposable batteries). A **low-battery indicator** helps you monitor battery usage. Pagers have no important features to speak of.

➤ HOW TO CHOOSE
Performance differences. You can expect a two-way radio to perform as expected in the open or in a vast interior space such as a shopping mall. But reception may suffer downtown or in the suburbs. Pagers also communicate reliably, although those with minuscule keyboards tend to be hard to use, and service may be hard to get. With SMS messaging, most providers now let you send messages to—and receive messages from—phones connected to other providers. But SMS may only work when you are in your home area.

Recommendations. All the cell-phone alternatives have their uses. The type you choose will depend on how you need to stay in touch. If a brief text message will suffice, then a pager or SMS service is what you want. If messages must arrive reliably, look into pager service. SMS is best when time isn't critical and you're in your home. If you need to have a conversation, then choose a two-way radio.
Related CR report: July 2002

DESKTOP COMPUTERS

Even the least expensive desktop machines deliver impressive performance. The quality of technical support may be a deciding factor.

The desktop computer has reached a level of acceptance accorded the TV set or refrigerator—just another appliance you use every day. Replacement sales—not first-time purchases—now drive the computer market. Prices continue to drop. Fully loaded desktop systems selling for less than $1,000, a novelty a few years ago, are now common, even among established brands.

➤ WHAT'S AVAILABLE
There are dozens of companies vying to put a new desktop in your home. Dell, Gateway, Hewlett-Packard (which merged with Compaq in 2002), IBM, and Sony all make Windows machines. Another contender, eMachines, has emerged as a player over the past few years with a series of budget-priced Windows systems. Apple is the sole maker of Macintosh models. Small mail-order and store brands cater to budget-minded buyers. Price range: $500 to $2,500. (The monitor is often extra.)

➤ KEY FEATURES
The **processor** houses the "brains" of a computer. Its clock speed, measured in megahertz (MHz), determines how fast the chip can process information. In general, the higher the clock speed, the faster the computer. But not always. In our tests, a computer with a 1.4-GHz chip outperformed a machine driven by a 2-GHz chip. Manufacturers of Windows machines generally use 1.2- to 2.5-GHz processors with one of the following names: Intel's Pentium 4 or Celeron or AMD's Athlon XP or Duron. Celeron and Duron are lower-priced processors that are equal to higher-priced chips in many respects. Apple's Macintosh machines use 700-MHz to 1-GHz PowerPC G4 processors, which are manufactured by Motorola. Apple has maintained that the system architecture of G4 PowerPC chips allows them to be as fast as or faster than Pentium 4s with higher clock speeds.

All name-brand computers sold today have at least 128 megabytes (MB) of RAM, or **random access memory,** the memory that the computer uses while in operation. **Video RAM,** also measured in megabytes, is secondary RAM essential for smooth video imaging and game play. The **hard drive** is your computer's long-term data storage system. Given the disk-space requirements of today's multimedia games and video files, bigger is better. You'll find hard drives ranging in size from 20 to 120 gigabytes (GB).

A **CD-ROM drive** has been standard on most desktops for a number of years. Fast replacing it is **CD-RW** (CD-rewritable), which lets you create backup files or make music compilations. **DVD-ROM** brings full-length movies or action-packed multimedia games with full-motion video to the desktop. It complements the CD-RW drive on higher-end systems, allowing you to copy CDs directly between the two. A DVD drive will also play CD-ROMs.

The newest in this family is the **DVD-writer,** which lets you transfer home-video footage to a DVD disc. There are three competing, incompatible formats: DVD-RW, DVD+RW, and DVD-RAM.

The **diskette drive** is where 3.5-inch diskettes are inserted, allowing you to read or store data. Apple Macintoshes don't have one built in. The traditional capacity of a 3.5-inch diskette is 1.4 MB, too small for many purposes today, so many people use a CD-RW as a large "diskette" drive to transport files.

The computer's **cathode ray tube** (CRT) or flat-panel **liquid crystal display** (LCD) monitor contains the screen and displays the images sent from the **graphics board**—internal circuitry that processes the images. **Monitors** come in sizes (measured diagonally) ranging from 15 inches to 21 inches and larger. Seventeen-inch monitors are the most common. Apple's iMac comes with a built-in monitor. For more on monitors, see page 126.

The critical components of a desktop computer are usually housed in a case called a **tower.** A **minitower** is the typical configuration. More expensive machines have a **midtower,** which has extra room for upgrades. A **microtower** is a space-saving alternative that is usually less expensive. The Apple iMac has no tower; everything but the keyboard and mouse is built into a small case that supports the monitor. Apple's Power Mac line of computers has a tower.

A **mouse,** a small device that fits in your hand and has a "tail" of wire that connects to the computer, moves the cursor (the pointer on the screen) via a rolling ball on the underside of the mouse. Alternatives include a mouse that replaces the ball with a light sensor; a trackball, which is rolled with the fingers or palm in the direction the user wants the cursor to go; a pad, which lets you move the cursor by sliding a finger; and a joystick, used to play computer games.

All computers come with a **standard keyboard,** although you can also buy one separately. Many keyboards have **CD (or DVD) controls** to pause playback, change tracks, and so on. Many also have keys to facilitate getting online, starting a search, or retrieving e-mail.

Multimedia computers for home use feature a **high-fidelity sound system** that can play music from CDs or downloaded music files, synthesized music, game sounds, and DVD-movie soundtracks. **Speaker systems** with a subwoofer have deeper, more powerful bass. Some PCs come with a **microphone** for recording, or one can be added.

You can expect a new computer to include a modem rated for 56 kilobits per second (kbps). This **speed rating** refers to how quickly information travels to your modem from the Internet, although the speed is limited by federal rules to 53 kbps. In actual practice, however, the speed rarely exceeds 50 kbps. Faster ways to connect to the Internet include cable modem, DSL (digital subscriber line), and satellite.

Parallel and serial ports are the traditional connection sites for printers and scanners. **USB (Universal Serial Bus) ports,** seen on all new computers, are designed to replace parallel and serial ports. **FireWire or IEEE 1394 ports** are used to capture video from digital camcorders and other electronic equipment. An Ethernet, Phoneline, or wireless **network** lets you link several computers in the household to share files, a printer, or an Internet connection. An **S-video output jack** lets you run video cables from the computer to a TV, which allows you to use the computer's DVD drive and view a movie on a TV instead of on the computer monitor.

> ➤ **HOW TO CHOOSE**

Performance differences. Judged on performance alone in CONSUMER REPORTS tests, most desktop computers are closely matched and extremely good overall. But there are differences in connectivity, expandability, the design of the keyboard and controls, and the sound of the loudspeakers. Surveys of users have found differences in reliability (frequency of repair), and survey respondents report that some manufacturers are better than others at providing support to consumers with problems.

Recommendations. You'll have to decide between Windows and Macintosh. Windows has the advantage for its sheer number of compatible software applications and peripheral devices. Macintosh

has the edge for its ease of setup and use. Then decide on power, speed, and features that suit your work—or play.

Related CR reports: December 2002
Reliability: page 332

LAPTOP COMPUTERS

A long-time companion at school or on the road, the laptop is proving its mettle as a replacement or backup for a home's desktop computer.

Even as the pace of desktop computer sales slows, laptops are selling at an ever-increasing rate. It's not hard to understand why. Laptops now belong in the same league as desktop computers, thanks to brighter and larger displays, faster processors, and more efficient batteries. The thinnest laptops are only an inch or so thick and weigh only 3 to 5 pounds. To get these light, sleek models, you'll have to pay a premium and sacrifice some functionality.

A laptop makes an attractive choice as a replacement computer or the household's second machine. Laptops are already fixtures in classrooms and boardrooms. An advantage for a laptop is the growing availability of high-speed wireless Internet access at airports, schools, and hotels.

> ➤ **WHAT'S AVAILABLE**

Dell, Gateway, Hewlett-Packard (which merged with Compaq in 2002), IBM, Sony, and Toshiba are the leading Windows laptop brands. Apple alone makes Macs. Laptops come in various configurations:

All-in-one. These machines can do just about everything a desktop can. Sometimes called "three-spindle" machines because the hard drive, diskette drive, and CD-RW or DVD-ROM drive reside onboard, these models also have a full complement of jacks, connectors, and expansion slots for PC cards. But they're the biggest and heaviest, measuring 1¾ inches thick and weighing 7 to 8 pounds. The keyboard is full-size, and the screen measures 14 to 15 inches diagonally. Some models can hold a second battery for increased running time, and others can shed drives to reduce size and weight. With a docking station, you can easily turn an all-in-one model into a desktop stand-in.

So-called reduced-legacy laptops from brands including Apple and IBM are similar to all-in-ones but lack a diskette drive. ("Legacy" refers to components, including the diskette drive, whose use dates back to the earliest desktop computers.) With reduced-legacy laptops, you can use a CD writer or a network for transferring files. Price range for all-in-ones: $1,000 to $2,500.

Modular. These "two-spindle" units come with a hard drive and space for either a diskette drive, CD-RW, combo CD-RW/DVD-ROM drive, or second battery. They're considerably slimmer than all-in-one models—about 1 to 1½ inches thick—and weigh 5 to 6 pounds. Drives can easily be swapped or left out to reduce weight, but some people find it inconvenient to swap drives regularly.

A modular model is easier to travel with than an all-in-one, provided you don't need to use all three drives at once. Other features of a modular laptop, including the keyboard and screen, are generally identical to those in an all-in-one. Some have smaller screens (12 or 13 inches). Price range: $1,200 to $2,500.

Slim-and-light. Especially good for traveling, these models measure about 1 inch thick and weigh 3 to 4 pounds. The case contains the hard drive and a smallish battery. The CD-ROM drive and the diskette drive are external, tethered to the laptop when need be. A port expander—a strip with jacks and connectors for printer, monitor, mouse, and the like—is also connected via cable. The screen may be only about 12 inches diagonally, and the keyboard may be small and somewhat hard to use. Price range: $1,800 to $2,500.

➤ KEY FEATURES

Laptops generally have a 1- to 1.8-gigahertz **processor** and a 20- to 40-gigabyte **hard drive.** Expect even faster processors and more capacious hard drives in the near future. Most models have 256 megabytes (MB) **of random access memory** (RAM) and can be upgraded to 512 MB or more. Most of today's laptops use a rechargeable **lithium-ion battery.** In our tests, lithium-ion batteries provided about three hours of continuous use when running office applications. (Laptops go into sleep mode when used intermittently, extending the time between charges.) You can extend battery life somewhat by dimming the display as you work and by removing PC cards when they aren't needed. Playing a DVD movie devours battery power.

A laptop's **keyboard** can be quite different from that of a desktop computer. The keys themselves may be full-sized (generally only slim-and-light models pare them down), but they may not feel as solid. Some laptops have extra buttons to expedite your access to e-mail or a web browser.

A 12- to 15-inch **display,** measured diagonally, should suit many people. A 15-inch display is the biggest practical size; a few larger, heavier models have 16-inch displays. With liquid crystal display (LCD) monitors, the display size represents the actual viewing area you get. (By contrast, the viewing area is smaller than the measured display with traditional cathode ray tube monitors.) A resolution of 1,280 x 1,024 pixels (picture elements) is better for fine detail than 1,024 x 768, but may shrink screen objects.

A thin-film transistor (TFT) active-matrix screen provides bright, crisp images. Most laptops use a small **touch-sensitive pad** in place of a mouse—you drag your finger across the pad to move the cursor. You can also program the pad to respond to a "tap" as a "click," or to scroll as you sweep your index finger along the pad's right edge. An alternative pointing system, less preferred by our testers, uses a pencil-eraser-size joy stick in the middle of the keyboard.

Laptops typically include two **PC-card slots** for expansion. You might add a **wireless network card** or a **digital-camera memory card reader,** for example. Many laptops offer a connection for a **docking station,** a $100 or $200 base that makes it easy to connect an external monitor, keyboard, mouse, printer, or phone line. Most laptops let you attach these devices anyway, without the docking station. At least one **USB port,** for easy hookup of, say, a printer, digital camera, or scanner, is standard. A **wired network (Ethernet) port** is common. Some models have a **FireWire port** for digital video transfer.

Laptops typically come with far less software than desktop computers, although almost all are bundled with a basic home-office suite (such as Microsoft Works) and a personal-finance package. The small speakers built into laptops often sound tinny, with little bass. Headphones or external speakers deliver much better sound.

➤ HOW TO CHOOSE

Performance differences. In CONSUMER REPORTS tests, most laptop computers have performed solidly in many ways. But manufacturers still have to build trade-offs into these small packages. Bigger and heavier models pack almost all the computing muscle of their desktop cousins, while slimmer and lighter ones sacrifice drive space for easy portability.

Aside from size and weight, a major factor distinguishing laptops is battery performance. Some models run longer on a charge and have better power management than others.

Recommendations. Consider buying a little more laptop than you think you need, since upgrading a notebook can be difficult or impossible. While desktop computers often use interchangeable, off-the-shelf components, a laptop's parts are typically proprietary. Adding more RAM might be relatively easy, but installing a larger hard drive or upgrading a video card might be out of the question.

Related CR report: March 2002

MONITORS

A roomier screen—or more space on your desktop—is now within reach.

Call it the incredible shrinking workspace. Over the past few years, bulky monitors have all but overrun the tops of desks. Their screens, filled nearly to overflowing with icons, web pages, and digital photos, haven't fared much better. It has become clear that computer users need more real estate—on both their screens and their desks.

If a larger screen is a must, a 19-inch cathode ray tube (CRT) may be the answer. Prices have fallen so much in the past couple of years that you can find plenty in the $250-to-$500 range. If desk space is a priority, a flat-panel monitor with a thin liquid crystal display (LCD), similar to the display that comes with a laptop, can now be had for as little as $400 for the 15-inch size. To get the best of both worlds, you can buy a 17- or 18-inch flat-panel LCD monitor in the $650 to $1,000 range.

Desktop computers and monitors are often sold as a package, though some people buying a new desktop decide to hold on to their old monitor and others choose to buy a new monitor for their existing PC. When buying a desktop from a direct seller such as Dell or Gateway, you choose from a selection that includes basic monitors and higher-end versions.

➤ WHAT'S AVAILABLE

Apple, Dell, Gateway, Hewlett-Packard (which merged with Compaq in 2002), IBM, and Sony all market their own brands of monitors for their PCs. In addition, you'll find monitors sold separately from brands such as CTX, Mitsubishi, NEC, Philips, Samsung, ViewSonic, and eMachines. Many brands of monitor are manufactured on an outsource basis.

CRTs. Most desktop monitors sold today are CRTs, typically ranging from 17 to 21 inches. Some CRTs have flattened, squared-off screens (not to be confused with flat-panel LCD screens) that reduce glare. The nominal image size—the screen size touted in ads—is generally based on the diagonal measurement of the picture tube, usually an inch larger than the viewable image size (VIS)—the image you see. Thus a 17-inch CRT has a 16-inch VIS. As a result of a class-action suit, an ad must also display a CRT's VIS, but to find it, you may have to squint at the fine print.

The bigger a CRT, the more room it takes up on your desk, but "short-depth" models shave an inch or more off the depth, which otherwise roughly matches the nominal screen size.

A 17-inch monitor, the most popular choice these days, has almost one-third more viewable area than the 15-inch ver-

sion now vanishing from the market. The larger size is especially useful when you're surfing the Internet, playing video games, watching DVD movies, editing photos, or working in several windows. Price range: $150 to $450.

If you regularly work with graphics or sprawling spreadsheets, consider a 19-inch monitor. Its viewable area is one-fourth larger than a 17-inch screen's. A short-depth 19-inch model doesn't take up much more desktop space than a standard 17-inch. Price range for 19-inch: $250 to $550.

Aimed at graphics professionals, 20- and 21-inch models provide ample viewing area but gobble up desktop space. Price range: $500 to $800.

Flat-panel LCDs. These monitors, which operate with analog or digital input or both, use a liquid-crystal display instead of a TV-style picture tube and take up much less desktop space than CRTs. For desktop use, they typically measure 15 inches diagonally and just a few inches deep and weigh 10 pounds or less, compared with 40 pounds for a 17-inch CRT and 50 pounds for a 19-inch CRT. LCDs with screens 17 inches or larger are available, but they are still somewhat pricey. Unlike with a CRT, the nominal and viewable image sizes of a flat-panel LCD are the same.

Flat-panel displays deliver a very clear image, but they have some inherent quirks. Their range of color is a bit more narrow that that of CRT monitors. And you have to view a flat-panel screen straight on; the picture loses contrast as you move off-center, except those models with a wider viewing angle. Fine lines may appear grainy. In analog mode, you have to tweak the controls to get the best picture.

Price range: 15-inch, $400 to $600. 17- and 18-inch, $650 to $1,000 and up.

➤ KEY FEATURES

A monitor's **resolution** refers to the number of picture elements, or pixels, that make up an image. More pixels mean finer details. Most monitors can display several resolutions, generally ranging from 640x480 to 1,600x1,200, depending on the monitor and graphics card. Many 15-inch flat-panel displays, however, have noticeable image degradation—images look smeared and less pleasing—when set at a resolution other than 1,024x768 pixels. The higher the resolution, the smaller the text and images, so more content fits on the screen. Bigger CRT screens can handle higher resolutions and display more information.

Dot pitch, measured in millimeters, refers to the spacing between a CRT's pixels. All else being equal, a smaller dot pitch produces a more detailed image, though that's no guarantee of an excellent picture. In general, avoid models with a dot pitch higher than 0.28 mm.

A CRT requires a high **refresh rate** (the number of times per second the image is redrawn on the screen) to avoid annoying image flicker. In general, you'll be more comfortable with a 17-inch monitor set at a refresh rate of at least 75 hertz (Hz) at the resolution you want. With a 19-inch monitor, you may need an 85-Hz rate to avoid eyestrain, especially at higher resolutions. While the refresh rate of a flat panel display is 60 or 75-Hz, its native resolution is 1,024x768, unless otherwise specified. Refresh rate isn't an issue with flat-panel displays.

Monitors have controls for **brightness** and **contrast.** Most of them also have controls for **color balance** (usually called color temperature), **distortion,** and such. Buttons activate onscreen controls and menus.

Bigger CRTs use a considerable amount of juice: about 100 watts for a typical 19-inch model, more than 80 watts for a 17-incher, and about 20 watts for a 15-inch flat-panel LCD, for example. Most monitors have a **sleep mode** that uses less than 3 watts when the computer is on but not in use.

CRTs can be designed with either a **shadow mask** or an **aperture grille,** and each has a distinctive look. A shadow mask, a perforated metal sheet, directs the beam emitted by electron guns arranged in a triangle so colors are composed of little dots of red, green, and blue. An aperture grille is a shadow mask in a CRT with the electron guns arranged in a horizontal row, which results in colors that are made up of little lines. View both types to see which you prefer.

Plug and play capability makes adding a new monitor to an existing computer relatively easy.

Some monitors include a **microphone,** integrated or separate **speakers,** or **composite video inputs** for viewing the output of a VCR or camcorder.

➤ HOW TO CHOOSE

Performance differences. All 17-inch and 19-inch CRT monitors CONSUMER REPORTS has recently tested have at least very good display quality. Visibility differs, however. CRTs with flattened, squared-off screens may pick up fewer reflections, though not necessarily resulting in better display quality. Some CRTs have control buttons that are poorly labeled or onscreen controls that are difficult to use. Tilting is difficult with some models.

Most of the flat-panel LCDs we have tested have excellent display quality. Advantages over CRTs include compactness and lower power consumption.

Recommendations. Buy the right size for your task and work space. You may decide that the slim profile and power savings of a flat-panel monitor make the premium you'll pay worthwhile.

Try to view a monitor before buying it. At the store, look at a page of text to be sure both center and edges are bright and clear. Open up a picture file to see whether the colors look natural and clear. Compare monitors side-by-side, if possible, with the same image displayed on each screen. Buying through mail-order or the Internet won't let you see firsthand. If you aren't planning to buy from a bricks-and-mortar store, see if a friend or co-worker has the model you're considering or try to see it in a store. Wherever you buy, it's wise to get a 30-day money-back guarantee.

Once you've bought a monitor, think about where you'll place it. You should sit 18 to 30 inches away, with the top line of text just below eye level. Good lighting and correct placement of the keyboard and mouse are also critical.

Related CR report: September 2002
Ratings: page 273

MULTIFUNCTION DEVICES

With a multifunction device, you get a printer, scanner, copier, and sometimes a fax machine in a single small unit, often for less than $500.

A multifunction device offers compactness, versatility, and affordability. You get a printer, scanner, copier, and fax machine all in one. That's great if you need all that compatibility and you're pressed for space. But a basic printer and a separate fax machine may be all you need, for about $400. Multifunction devices have improved greatly over the past few years, so even a workhorse home office that produces a substantial amount of printed material will be satisfied with their print quality.

➤ WHAT'S AVAILABLE

The main types are inkjet and laser. Inkjet models can print and copy in color. Laser units print and copy in black-and-white only, but some can scan in color. Most multifunction devices support both Windows and Macintosh computers, but models usually don't have a serial port, which means that not all work with Macintosh computers manufactured before mid-1998. Most major printer manufacturers are also in the multifunction business. The key brands in this category are Brother, Canon, Hewlett-Packard, and Lexmark. Price range: $200 to $600.

➤ KEY FEATURES

The **resolution** at the default setting is usually 2,400 by 1,200 dots per inch (dpi) and all are TWAIN-compliant (TWAIN refers to an interface between image-processing software and a scanner or digital camera). As with printers, maximum printer resolution, or maximum dpi, is often used as a selling point. But a model with a high maximum printer resolution does not necessarily produce the highest quality output. Note that not all multifunction devices can reduce or enlarge images.

All multifunction devices can fax in black and white, but some can also **fax in color** to other color-capable devices. Multifunction devices with **sheet-fed scanners** can't scan or copy material such as books. Most current models have **flatbed scanners.** After scanning, text must be "read" by an optical-character-recognition (OCR) program before it's edited on the computer. Images can be used immediately by a graphics program that either comes with the scanner or that you can buy separately.

➤ **HOW TO CHOOSE**

Performance differences. CONSUMER REPORTS tests have shown that the print quality of multifunction devices usually matches that of a printer-only model that uses the same ink cartridges or toner and that has the same resolution options.

Recommendations. If you're outfitting a home office from scratch and space is scarce, a multifunction device can be a good choice. If you do choose to count on one machine to do everything, you will sacrifice some future flexibility. You can't upgrade just one function in a multifunction device. And if a major part breaks down, the entire machine will be out of service. A separate fax machine and printer may make more sense.

Also consider how the machine will be used. If you scan and print mostly color photos or graphics, look for an inkjet model. But if you only plan to print, or copy black-and-white text or graphics, a laser multifunction device is the more appropriate choice.

Related CR report: September 2002

PDAS

Besides keeping track of phone numbers, appointments, and things to do, many personal digital assistants can now deliver wireless access to the web and manage your e-mail.

Personal digital assistants store thousands of phone numbers, appointments, to-do chores, and notes. All models can exchange, or synchronize, information with a full-sized computer. To do that, you place the PDA on a cradle, or docking station, and press a button. The cradle connects directly to your desktop computer with a cable. For models that run on rechargeable batteries, the cradle doubles as the charger. Infrared technology can let you synchronize with a computer without wires or a cradle.

Most PDAs can be made to work with both Windows and Macintosh computers, either out of the box, with an inexpensive adapter, or with third-party software. Most provide access to an abbreviated form of the Internet, most often with the addition of separately purchased accessories such as a modem. Some PDAs can record your voice, play videos, display digital photos, or hold maps, city guides, or a novel.

➤ **WHAT'S AVAILABLE**

There are now nearly two dozen models on the market. Most are the now-familiar tablet with a stylus and squarish display screen, a design pioneered by Palm Inc. several years ago. Today the main choices are PDAs using the Palm operating system (Handera, Handspring, Palm, and Sony) and PocketPC devices from Audiovox, Casio, and Hewlett-Packard that use a stripped-down version of Microsoft Windows. A few PDAs use a proprietary operating system.

Handspring, Kyocera, Nokia, and Samsung offer units that combine a cell phone and PDA.

Palm OS systems. Equipped with software to link with Windows and Macintosh computers, Palm units and their clones are small and simple to operate. You use a stylus to enter data on these units by tapping on an onscreen keyboard or writing in a shorthand known as Graffiti. Or you can download keyed data from your computer. Most can synchronize with a variety of e-mail software and include their own basic personal information management (PIM) application.

Models with a backlit monochrome display are easy to read under normal lighting conditions and very easy on batteries. CONSUMER REPORTS tests have shown that monochrome models can operate continuously with the backlight off for at least 24 hours, equivalent to seven weeks of use at a half hour per day. Models with a color display use a rechargeable lithium-ion battery that must be recharged after just a few hours in continuous use. When the battery can no longer be recharged, you need to have a dealer or the manufacturer remove and replace it.

While Palm OS-based units are easy to use, navigation between different programs is cumbersome because of the "single-tasking" nature of the operating system.

New Palm-OS models have expansion slots that let you add memory or attach separately purchased accessories. All Palm-based PDAs can be enhanced by adding third-party software applications—the more free memory in a model, the more software that can be accommodated. There is a large body of Palm OS-compatible freeware, shareware, and commercial software available for download at such sites as *www.palmgear.com*. Many Palm models come with Documents to Go, word-processing and spreadsheet software similar to that used in Pocket PCs.

Price range: $130 to $500.

Pocket PC systems. These resemble Palm-based models, but they are more like a miniature computer. They have a processor with far more horsepower and come with familiar applications such as a word processor and a spreadsheet. Included is a scaled-down version of Internet Explorer, plus voice-recording and some financial functions. An application that plays MP3 music files, as well as Microsoft Reader, an e-book application, is also standard.

As you might expect, all the application software included in a Pocket PC integrates well into the Windows computer environment. You need to purchase third-party software to use a Mac. And you'll need Microsoft Office programs such as Word, Excel, and Outlook to exchange data with a PDA.

Most have a color display that livens up the interface but also drains their rechargeable lithium-ion batteries quickly. As with some Palm-based PDAs, the battery of most Pocket PCs must be removed and replaced by a dealer when it can no longer be recharged.

> **TECH TIP**
> Test ease of use while shopping for a PDA. Far too many people invest in one only to find its keypad, stylus, or shorthand are hard for them to use.

Price range: $200 to $500.

➤ KEY FEATURES

Whichever operating system your PDA uses, you'll need to install programs in your main computer to enable the PDA to synchronize with it. Most such software lets you swap data with leading personal-information-manager programs such as Lotus Organizer or Microsoft Outlook; some do not.

Most PDAs have the tools for basic tasks: a **calendar** to keep track of your appointments, **contact software** for addresses and phone numbers, **notes/tasks** for reminders and to-do lists, and a **calculator.** A **memo function** allows you to make quick notes to yourself. Other capabilities include **word-processing, spreadsheet, database, and money-management functions. A voice recorder,** which includes a built-in microphone and speaker, works like a tape recorder.

A PDA's **processor** is the system's brain. In general, the higher the processing speed of this chip, the faster the unit will execute tasks—and the more expensive the unit will be. But higher-speed processors require more battery power and may deplete batteries quickly. Processing speeds are 16 to 200 megahertz.

Models typically have 8 to 64 megabytes of user memory. Even the smallest amount in that range should be more than enough for most people.

Many Palm OS PDAs run on AA batteries. These are the easiest to maintain. Many newer PDAs (both Palm and Pocket PC-based) use rechargeable lithium-ion batteries. In some models, the batteries are sealed inside the case and can only be replaced by the manufacturer. There are PDAs with removable rechargeable batteries, which are obviously more convenient.

A **backlight** for the display, which illuminates the characters, is standard. With monochrome screens, you need the backlight when using the PDA in the dark. The backlight is always used with color screens. In general, the degree of web accessibility for PDAs is not yet equal to what you can get from your desktop or laptop computer. Some applications can browse specially designed pages known as "clipped web pages." Other applications (such as Avant-go) allow you to download text-based information from a desktop computer.

➤ **HOW TO CHOOSE**

Performance differences. For basic functions, CONSUMER REPORTS tests have shown that Pocket PCs are generally easier to use than Palm OS models. Navigation between programs is easier than with the Palms because you can run several programs simultaneously. Onscreen keyboards leave most of the display visible.

Palm-based units, which tend to be the least expensive, offer simple operation, compact size, an easy-to-use interface, a wide range of features, and expandability. All can work with Macintosh computers. Pocket PCs are easier to use for basic functions, and have built in multimedia capability. Their biggest drawback is price and short battery life. They work only with Microsoft applications, such as Word, Excel, and Outlook.

Recommendations. If you expect to put fairly basic demands on a PDA, choose one of the low-priced Palm-based units with 8 MB of memory. On the other hand, if you already have a Palm-based PDA and find it needs more memory, choose a unit with 16 MB of memory. And if you need a PDA for wireless e-mail access, choose the Palm i705.

If you want a computer (a Windows computer, that is) in your pocket and regularly run Microsoft applications or want multimedia capability, choose a Pocket PC.

Related CR report: June 2002
Ratings: page 275

PRINTERS

New, inexpensive inkjets print color superbly and faster than ever. Laser printers excel at printing black-and-white text.

Inkjet printers are now the standard home-computer accompaniment. They do an excellent job with color—turning out color photos nearly indistinguishable from photographic prints, along with banners, stickers, transparencies, T-shirt transfers, and greeting cards. Some even turn out excellent black-and-white text. With some very good models selling for less than $200, the vast majority of printers sold for home use are inkjets.

Laser printers still have their place in home offices. If you print reams of black-

and-white text documents, you probably need the speed, quality, and low per-copy cost of a laser printer.

Printers use a computer's microprocessor and memory to process data. The latest models are so fast partly because computers themselves have become more powerful and contain much more memory than before.

Unlike the computers they serve, most home printers can't be upgraded except for adding memory to laser printers. Most people usually get faster or more detailed output by buying a new printer.

➤ WHAT'S AVAILABLE

The printer market is dominated by a handful of well-established brands. Hewlett-Packard is the market leader. Other brands are Brother, Canon, Epson, Lexmark, and Samsung.

The type of computer a printer can serve depends on its ports. A Universal Serial Bus (USB) port lets a printer connect to Windows or Macintosh computers. Some models have a parallel port, which lets the printer work with older Windows computers. Many printers lack a serial port, which means they won't work with older Macintosh computers.

Inkjet printers. Inkjets use droplets of ink to form letters and graphics. Most inkjet printers use two cartridges to supply the droplets. One holds cyan (greenish-blue), magenta, and yellow inks, the other black. Both cartridges are used for full-color work, the black one alone for plain text. Some low-priced inkjets take either a black or a color cartridge, but not both at the same time; they're usually sold without the black cartridge and use all three colors to print—expensively—"black." For photos, some inkjets also have additional cartridges that contain lighter shades of some inks. But CONSUMER REPORTS tests

have shown that the three basic colors can produce excellent photos.

Most inkjets print at two to four pages per minute (ppm) for black-and-white text, but are much slower for color photos, taking 4 to 18 minutes to print a single 8x10. The cost of printing a black-and-white page with an inkjet varies considerably from model to model–3 to 11 cents. The cost of printing a color photo can range from 70 cents to $1.40. Price range: $50 to $400.

Laser printers. These work much like plain-paper copiers, forming images by transferring toner (powdered ink) to paper passing over an electrically charged drum. The process yields sharp black-and-white text and graphics. Laser printers usually outrun inkjets, cranking out black-and-white text at a rate of five to eight ppm. Black-and-white laser printers generally cost about as much as high-end inkjets, but they're cheaper to operate. Color laser printers are also available. Laser cartridges, about $100, often contain both the toner and the drum and can print thousands of black-and-white pages, for a per-page cost of 2 to 3 cents. Price range: black-and-white, $200 to $500; color, $1,200 and up.

KEY FEATURES

Printers differ in the fineness of detail they can produce. **Resolution,** expressed in dots per inch (dpi), is often touted as the main measure of print quality. But other factors count too, such as the way dot patterns are formed by software instructions from the printer driver. Maximum printer resolution is often touted as a selling point. But a high maximum printer resolution is not necessarily synonymous with quality. At their default settings—where they're usually expected to run—inkjets currently on the market typically have a resolution between 600x600 dpi and 4,800x1,200 dpi. Lasers for home use typically offer 600 or 1,200 dpi. Printing photos on special paper at a higher dpi setting can produce smoother shading of colors.

Most inkjet printers include an **ink monitor** to warn you when you're running low. Generic ink cartridges and refill kits can cut costs, but think twice before using them. Usually a printer's warranty won't cover repairs if an off-brand cartridge damages the printer.

For **double-sided printing,** you can have printers print the odd-numbered pages of a document first, then flip those pages over to print the even-numbered pages on a second pass through the printer. A few printers can automatically print on both sides, but doing so slows down printing considerably.

➤ HOW TO CHOOSE

Performance differences. When it comes to producing graphics and photos, many inkjets do an excellent job. The best in CONSUMER REPORTS tests print graphics that are crisp, clean, and vibrant-looking. Photos rival the output of a photofinishing lab, with smooth gradations and deep blacks. The worst inkjets turn out graphics that are dull, grainy, or banded. Photos may suffer from overinked dark areas, textures that make skin seem pebbled and grainy, or dull colors.

In recent tests, laser printers had the advantage when it came to producing excellent-quality black-and-white text, though more than half of the dual-cartridge inkjets we tested rivaled them. Page for page, laser models are cheaper to operate.

In tests, printing results were sometimes better for one side of the paper than the other. Some brands of paper indicate on the package which side to use.

Recommendations. An inkjet printer is the more versatile choice, and the only inexpensive one for both color and black-and-white output. If you plan on printing color graphics and photos, then a dual-cartridge inkjet printer is the way to go. A single-cartridge inkjet might be inexpensive to purchase, but it will be more costly to use and usually delivers inferior results. Buy a laser printer if you need to turn out a large amount of high-quality black-and-white text.

If the printer and the computer allow it, connect the printer to a USB port for easy setup. If you have to use the parallel port, use an IEEE 1284-compliant printer cable.

Related CR report: September 2002
Ratings: page 283

SCANNERS

A scanner is a simple, cheap way to digitize images for printing out, manipulating on your computer, or sending in e-mail.

You don't need a digital camera to take advantage of the computer's ability to edit photos. Images captured on film can be digitized by the photo processor and delivered on a CD or via the web. But if you do more than a modest amount of film photography, having a processor digitize your photos, at $5 to $10 per roll, can become expensive quickly, and means you pay for digitizing outtakes as well as winners. A more cost-effective way to digitize select photographs is with a scanner, which can capture the image of nearly anything placed on its glass surface—even those old photos you've tucked away in a family album or a shoebox.

Most scanners basically work the same way. As with photocopiers, a bar housing a light source and an array of sensors pass beneath a plate of glass on which the document lies facedown (or, in the case of a sheet-fed model, is passed over). The scanner transmits data from the sensor to the host computer, which runs driver software that works in coordination with the hardware to scan at certain settings. Once the image is in the computer, software bundled with the scanner (or purchased separately) lets you crop, resize, or otherwise edit it to suit your needs. From there, you can print the image, attach it to e-mail, or post it on the web.

➤ WHAT'S AVAILABLE

A number of scanners come from companies that made their names in scanning technology, including Microtek and Visioneer. Other brands include computer makers and photo specialists such as Canon, Epson, Hewlett-Packard, and Nikon.

What type of scanner you should consider—flatbed, sheet-fed, or film—depends largely on how you will use it. If you're short on space, consider a multifunction device (see page 129).

Flatbed scanners. More than 90 percent of the scanners on the market are flatbeds. They work well for text, graphics, photos, and anything else that is flat, including a kindergartner's latest drawing. Flatbeds include optical character recognition (OCR) software, which can convert words on a printed page into a word-processing file in your computer. Some stores may throw in a flatbed scanner for free, or for a few dollars extra, when you buy a desktop computer.

A key spec for a scanner is its maximum optical resolution, measured in dots per inch (dpi). You'll pay more for greater resolution. Price ranges: 600 by 1,200 dpi, under $100; models with greater resolution, $100 to $500.

Sheet-fed models. Sheet-fed models can automatically scan a stack of loose pages, but they sometimes damage pages that pass through their innards. And they can't scan anything much thicker than a sheet of paper. This type is often used in multifunction devices, which can also print, send, and receive faxes. Sheet-fed scanners also use OCR software. Price range: $150 to $600.

Film scanners. Serious photographers may want a film-only scanner that scans directly from an original slide or negative. These offer a higher maximum resolution than you get from an ordinary flatbed or sheet-fed model. Some can accept small prints as well. Price range: $400 to $800.

➤ KEY FEATURES

While the quality of images a scanner produces depends in part on the software included with the scanner, there are several hardware features to consider.

You start scanning by running **driver software** that comes with the scanner or by pressing a **preprogrammed button** on the scanner itself. Models with buttons automate routine tasks to let you operate your scanner as you would other office equipment; on some models, you can customize their functions. Any of these tasks can also be performed through the scanner's software without using buttons. A copy/print button initiates a scan and sends a command to print the results on your printer, effectively making the two devices substitute as a copier. Other button functions found on some models include scan to a file, scan to a fax modem, scan to e-mail, scan to web, scan to OCR, cancel scan, power save, start scanner software, and power on/off.

You can also start the driver software from within an application, such as a word processor, that adheres to an industry standard known as TWAIN. A scanner's driver software allows you to preview a scan on-screen and crop it or adjust contrast and brightness. Once you're satisfied with the edited image, you can perform a final scan and pass the image to a running program or save it on your computer. You can make more extensive changes to an image with specialized image-editing software. And to scan text from a book or letter into a word-processing file in your computer, you run OCR software.

Many documents combine text with graphic elements, such as photographs and drawings. A handy software feature called **multiple-scan mode,** found on many scanners, lets you break such hybrids down into different sections that can be processed separately in a single scan. You can designate, for example, that the sections of a magazine article that are pure text go to the OCR software independently of the article's graphic elements. Other scanners would require a separate scan for each section of the document.

➤ HOW TO CHOOSE

Performance differences. In recent tests of flatbed scanners, CONSUMER REPORTS used the scanner software provided by the manufacturer to print scanned photos on a high-resolution inkjet printer at 150, 300, 600, and (when possible) 1,200 dpi. There was little improvement in the quality of scanned color and black-and-white photographs above 300 dpi. For the flatbed scanners tested, the manufacturer's recommended scan ranges were 150 to 300 dpi for photos, text, and line art, and 72 to 96 dpi for e-mail, web sites, and onscreen viewing. Taking the time and trouble to do high-resolution scans is worse than unnecessary. It results in scans that take two to four times longer and creates files that are much larger.

Another specification is color depth, a measure of the number of colors the scanner is able to recognize. This is expressed as the number of data bits (ones or zeroes) that are associated with each pixel of a scanned image. Recently tested models scanned with at least 36-bit depth (some have a 42-bit depth), but their software usually reduced the output images to 24-bit depth. Even 24-bit equates to more colors than the human eye can distinguish, so there's certainly no point in paying extra for 42-bit depth.

The OCR software that came with our test models did a nearly error-free job of converting a typewritten memo. The scanners made more errors processing a page from CONSUMER REPORTS magazine, but few enough that our testers were able to fix them with minimal effort.

Images produced with film-scanning adapters that come with some flat-bed scanners aren't really worth the effort, according to our tests. The adapters weren't very effective at flattening the film and had no focus adjustment to control the distance between the scan head and the film. The resulting images were usually slightly fuzzy. Worse, the images were off in color or contrast. Some even looked grainy. If you need to scan film or slides frequently, it's generally worth buying a dedicated film scanner. Matching the original version of a color photo is the most demanding of a scanner's functions. You'll sometimes need to use image-editing software to get a printed version that's faithful to the original.

Recommendations. For most home users, a flatbed scanner offers the best combination of versatility, performance, and price. Most consumers don't need a high-resolution scanner with considerably more than 300 dpi. Look instead for features and conveniences you can use, such as photo-editing software or one-button functions. If your older Windows PC does not have a USB port, make sure the scanner you're buying can be connected to a parallel port.

Related CR report: September 2001

TELEPHONES

Cordless phones with better range and expanded features are ringing in four out of five U.S. households. But very good corded phones still have the edge in voice quality and privacy.

Shoppers are snapping up cordless phones at a furious rate—more than 40 million per year. Falling prices have helped fuel the explosion. No-frills models now sell for just $20 or $30, so more people can afford to buy a cordless phone, or, in some cases, two or three. Those who already own a cordless phone might be tempted to add another one or upgrade to a newer, better model.

The corded phone, however, hasn't become obsolete. A very good one retains the edge in terms of voice quality and, usually, protection from eavesdropping. And no matter how many telephones in a home, there should be at least one corded phone, so you have a working phone in the event of a power outage. All but a few cordless phones require house current.

Cordless phones

If you have a cordless phone and it's several years old, it's probably a 49-megahertz (MHz) analog model. Newer phones use higher frequencies, either 900-MHz or 2.4 gigahertz (GHz), in analog or digital versions. Poised to enter the market are 5.8-GHz phones. The higher-frequency phones

we've seen aren't inherently better at sending or receiving calls, nor do they offer better voice quality or appreciably longer range. Yet manufacturers persist in introducing higher-frequency phones, selling their capabilities rather the way Detroit once sold horsepower in new cars.

Digital technology offers less interference and improved security from eavesdroppers. Step-up features include two lines (good for home businesses), multiple handsets, built-in answering machines, caller ID, and hands-free speakerphones. At 5 to 10 ounces, cordless handsets are generally heavier than corded-phone handsets.

> **INTERACTIVE**
> **Americans spend billions on directory assistance. These six web-based services give you listings for free:**
> • www.anywho.com
> • www.infospace.com
> • www.infousa.com
> • www.switchboard.com
> • www.whowhere.com
> • www.555-1212.com

➤ WHAT'S AVAILABLE

A few brands—AT&T, Bell South, General Electric, Panasonic, Uniden, and VTech—account for more than 70 percent of the market. VTech owns the AT&T Consumer Products Division and now makes phones under the AT&T brand as well as its own name.

A main distinction between cordless phones is how they transmit their signals. The major types are:

900-MHz analog. These phones offer enough range to let you chat anywhere in your house and yard, or even a little beyond. But they're not very secure if there is no voice-scrambling capability; anyone with a scanner can listen in. They're also more likely than digital models to suffer occasional static and interference from other devices. Price range: $20 to $100.

900-MHz digital. These models offer

about the same range as 900-MHz analog phones, but with better security. Price range: $50 to $150.

900-MHz digital spread spectrum (DSS). With these models, a call is distributed across several frequencies, providing still tighter security. The range is slightly better than that of other 900-MHz models. Price range: $60 to $200.

2.4-GHz analog or DSS. The analog phones have pros and cons similar to those of 900-MHz analog phones. Some digitals claim better voice quality, longer range, or less interference; CONSUMER REPORTS tests haven't supported those claims. Indeed, some DSS phones, both 2.4-GHz and 900-MHz, use such a wide swath of the spectrum even in standby mode that they may interfere with baby monitors and other devices operating in the same frequency band. It's not a good idea to have a 2.4-GHz analog phone in the kitchen, where the microwave oven could create interference.

Some 2.4-GHz DSS phones support multiple handsets, so you can have several handsets around the house, each charging in a base, without the need for extra phone jacks. Price range: $30 to $230 (for multiple-handset systems).

KEY FEATURES

Most cordless phones have a **jack** for a headset, plus a **belt clip**, allowing hands-free conversation.

About a third of the cordless phones sold include an **answering machine**, nearly always a digital unit that works without tape. Useful answerer features include message recording time of 15 to 20 minutes; **separate mailboxes** where callers can direct messages for separate family members; and **advanced playback controls** for fast playback, rewind, and skip forward or back.

Caller ID displays the name and number of a caller and the date and time of the call if you use your phone company's caller ID service. If you have caller ID

MESSAGE CENTERS

Answering machines

Answering machines come as stand-alone devices ($20 to $80) and as part of a phone/answerer combo unit ($40 to $250). The main advantage to a combo unit–less clutter–has to be weighed against the loss of one part of the combo if the other goes bad. Both types use memory chips, similar to those found in computers, to store the greeting and messages. They are quieter and less likely to break down than the first cassette answering machines, since they have fewer moving parts, and they let you skip or delete messages more quickly.

AT&T is the biggest-selling brand of stand-alone answerers. Other major brands include Casio, GE, RadioShack, and Southwestern Bell.

Features you'll want include ample recording time, separate mailboxes, and advanced playback controls, all described in the report on cordless phones on page 137. Other useful features: a time and date stamp, which records the day and time when messages come in; skipping and deleting, which allow you to pick and choose the messages you want to listen to or save; a digital readout that indicates the number of messages received; a display or audible message that lets you know when you have new messages; remote access that lets you listen to messages on your answering machine from a touchtone phone anywhere; and caller ID, with some versions able to recognize a number and play a specific greeting or announce a caller's name (talking caller ID).

with call waiting, the phone will display data on a second caller when you're already on the phone.

Some models include a **speakerphone,** which lets you make hands-free calls from the base. **Two-way intercom** allows for conversation between the handset and the speakerphone. For multihandset models, **handset-to-handset talk,** also called handset-to-handset intercom, allows conversation between handsets. **Conferencing** allows multiple-party conversation that includes outside callers.

A **secondary keypad** on the base can be handy for navigating menu-driven systems because you don't have to take the handset away from your ear to punch the keys.

A phone with **two lines** is useful for subscribing to online services or separating a business and home number. Some phones have **two ringers,** each with a distinctive pitch, to let you know which line is ringing. A two-line phone can receive calls for two numbers. Some have an **auxiliary jack data port** to plug in a fax, modem, or other phone device.

On most models, the handset rings, and many phones have a second ringer in the base. An **LCD screen** on the handset or base can provide useful information such as the phone number dialed, battery strength, or how long you've been connected.

All cordless phones have a **handset-locator button** to help you find the handset when it is hiding under a sofa cushion.

Cordless-phone **batteries** may be rechargeable nickel-cadmium (NiCd) or nickel-metal hydride (NiMH). Some models may provide a compartment in the base for charging a spare handset battery and, on some, can be used as the base power backup in the event of a power outage. Keep a corded phone somewhere in your home; it will work in a power outage because it draws its power from the phone system, not the household wiring.

HOW TO CHOOSE

Performance differences. Most new cordless phones have very good voice quality, CONSUMER REPORTS tests show. Some are excellent, approaching the voice quality of the best corded phones. Size and shape vary considerably, as do features.

In our latest tests, fully charged nickel-cadmium or nickel-metal hydride batteries handled anywhere from 4 to about 13 hours of continuous conversation before they needed recharging. Most manufacturers claim that a new battery will last at least a week in standby mode.

Some phones offer better surge protection than others against damage from lightning or faulty wiring.

Recommendations. A 900-MHz phone should suit most users. Analog models, apt to be less expensive than digital, are fine for many people. However, these phones may soon disappear from the market, replaced by higher-frequency hardware. We don't think 2.4-GHz phones offer enough added functionality to be worth their higher cost. But it won't be long before these phones are considered entry-level.

To ensure voice-transmission security, look for wording in ads and packaging such as "digital phone," "digital spread spectrum," or "phone with voice scrambling." Just because the word "digital" is used, however, doesn't mean the company is promising a secure transmission. Phones that aren't secure might have packaging with wording such as "phone with digital security code," "phone with all-digital answerer," or "spread-spectrum technology."

Before you buy, hold the handset to your head to see if it feels comfortable. The handset of a cordless phone should fit the contours of your face. The earpiece should have rounded edges and a recessed center that fits nicely over the middle of your ear. Also, check the buttons and controls to make sure they're reasonably sized and readable.

If possible, see what the LCD display looks like as well. You might also want to determine how easy it is to use the functions, especially for models with an answering machine.

Corded phones

Today's basic phone is sleeker and more versatile than its boxy predecessor. For $10, you can now buy a phone with such features as volume control and speed-dialing for 10 or more numbers. For $50 or more, you get a console with speakerphone or two-line capability, sometimes both. Every home should have at least one corded phone, if only for emergencies. You can't always rely on a cell phone because circuits fill up quickly in emergencies or the signal may not reach your house. A cordless phone may not work if you lose electrical power. Because a corded phone draws its power from the phone network, it will operate even in a blackout.

➤ **WHAT'S AVAILABLE**

AT&T (currently made by VTech) and GE are the dominant brands. When shopping, you'll find these types:

Console models. These are updated versions of the traditional Bell desk phone. Price range: $15 to more than $100.

Trim-style models. These spacesavers have push buttons on the handset, and the base is about half as wide as a console model's. Price range: $10 to $30.

Phones with answerers. Combo units can sometimes be less expensive than buying a phone and an answerer separately. Price range: $50 to $150.

➤ **KEY FEATURES**

Corded phones tend to be less feature-laden than cordless ones. Even some less expensive phones have a **volume control** on the receiver, handy if the voice at the other end of the line starts to fade.

It's practically standard for any phone to have **last-number redial** and **speed dialing.** Features such as a **speakerphone, two-line capability,** or **caller ID** add to the price.

Trim-style phones, with a keypad on the handset, can be hard to use if you need to listen and punch buttons at the same time, which you might have to do when navigating an unfamiliar voice-mail or automated-banking menu.

➤ **HOW TO CHOOSE**

Performance differences. Most corded phones perform quite capably, conveying voices intelligibly under normal conditions, according to CONSUMER REPORTS tests. The variations in sound quality that we have found are likely to matter only in very noisy environments.

Recommendations. Since good quality is pretty much a given, your main considerations should be features and price. Before you buy, make sure the handset is comfortable to hold in your hand and to your ear. Look for a good-sized, clearly labeled keypad, especially if your eyesight isn't good.

Related CR report: November 2002
Ratings: page 309

AUTOS

What's New in Autos for 2003

For 2003, the emphasis in new-vehicle design continues to be on versatility. There about 30 new or redesigned 2003 (and even some early-2004) models. Most are sport-utility vehicles or wagonlike "crossover" vehicles. Automakers are focusing on developing vehicles that provide passenger- and cargo-carrying flexibility, often accompanied by the option of four- or all-wheel drive for better capability in adverse weather.

In addition, 2003 brings several new or redesigned sedans and sports cars, a new gasoline/electric hybrid, and the first car-based pickup in 16 years.

Best-selling models. Despite the influx of many new models, the top sellers have remained consistent for several years. The best-selling vehicles overall in the U.S. are still pickups—the Ford F-Series and Chevrolet Silverado—with each outselling the top passenger cars by almost a two-to-one margin. The popularity of pickups is fueled by both commercial demand and by the increasing use of trucks for private transportation. Both the Ford and Chevy have scored reasonably well in our testing, but only the Silverado is recommended by CONSUMER REPORTS. The Ford has a poor IIHS offset-crash-test result.

Among cars, the Toyota Camry and Honda Accord are again the overall top sellers, with the Honda Civic and Ford Focus topping the list for smaller cars. The Camry and Civic are among the highest-rated models for their respective categories; both are recommended. The Accord has received a major redesign for 2003. The outgoing model was recommended, but CONSUMER REPORTS has not yet fully tested the new version. The Focus was rated highest in its category in CR testing, but below-average reliability has kept it from the recommended list.

Among SUVs, traditional truck-based models still sell the best, including the mid-sized Ford Explorer, Chevrolet TrailBlazer, and Jeep Grand Cherokee, and the full-sized Chevrolet Tahoe. All four have scored reasonably well in CR testing, but only the Tahoe has been reliable enough for the vehicle to be recommended.

Buying trends. In 2001, for the first time, light trucks (SUVs, pickups, and minivans) outsold cars by a slim margin. Sedans as a category offer the most choice of models, with about 95 available.

The average transaction price of a new vehicle (including domestic and imports) is around $26,000. Lower residual values caused by zero-percent financing and other aggressive sales programs over the last year have caused leasing to become less popular than in past years. About 30 percent of all new-car transactions are leases.

Used cars continue to sell strongly. In 2001, 42.6 million used cars were sold in the U.S., about 2½ times the number of new vehicles. More buyers are turning to certified used cars, which are intended to take some of the perceived risk out of the process. Factory-certified vehicles are ones that have been screened, inspected, and refurbished, and carry some kind of warranty coverage. In 2001, dealers sold about 670,000 certified used cars, a 46 percent increase from the 460,000 sold in 2000.

The Internet remains a popular source of automotive information. About half of the households that are purchasing new vehicles use it during the buying process. Only about 2 percent percent actually bought the vehicle online.

The new-vehicle scene. In any given year, most models—roughly 80 to 90 percent—receive no or only minor changes over the previous year's versions. In 2003, there are about 20 truly new models on the market. About 15 models have been discontinued. The rest of the 2003 models are basically the same as last year, with perhaps freshened styling, some new features, a revised powertrain, or a new trim line.

"Crossover" vehicles: hot category. This is the fastest-growing segment. According to WardsAuto.com, a web site that analyzes the auto industry, in the first six months of 2002 sales for crossovers were up 21 percent (compared with the same months in the previous year) during a period in which almost every other category was down. Crossover vehicles are SUVs based on a car platform and tall wagons that blend cargo-carrying versatility with a comfortable carlike driving experience. In contrast to traditional SUVs, which are based on truck platforms, car-based SUVs typically provide better ride and handling

and a lower stance for easier access and better handling, at the expense of some off-road capability. All of CR's top-rated SUVs are car-based models. For 2003, there are nine new models in this segment.

The midsized Honda Pilot is an especially noteworthy model. It's basically Honda's version of the very good Acura MDX. In a recent CONSUMER REPORTS test, it narrowly outranked the Toyota Highlander as the top-rated recommended SUV. It's the CR top pick among SUVs.

The Nissan Murano, based on the Altima sedan, is also new this year. Several vehicles are now offering a type of automatic transmission called a continuously variable transmission (CVT), which is designed for better performance and economy. The Murano is the first to offer one with a seven-speed manual-shift mode for a sportier feel and better shift control.

> ■ **SHOP SMART**
> Every issue of Consumer Reports has road tests of selected vehicles. The annual auto issue in April provides the latest Ratings and survey results. For all models, you can find updates year-round at *ConsumerReports.org*

The Mitsubishi Outlander, a smaller car-based SUV, is based on the mediocre Mitsubishi Lancer sedan and resembles a Subaru Forester in its dimensions. The squarish and quirky four-passenger Element, which shares many drivetrain and suspension components with Honda's CR-V, is designed to hold lots of gear or cargo. There's no pillar between the front and rear doors, which are forged at the rear, so opening both creates a wide entry space for loading gear or for access to the rear seat. There's also a fold-away rear seat that opens up floor space for cargo.

The Volvo XC90 and the Chrysler Pacifica, due as an early 2004-model release, are new seven-passenger crossover SUVs that are very wagonlike. Both will offer side-curtain air bags that are designed to protect passengers in all three rows of seats. The XC90 also includes a second-row seat in which the middle section can slide forward separately so that a child can be positioned closer to front-seated parents. The Pacifica will offer a power liftgate for easier loading.

Porsche and Volkswagen have teamed up to develop two SUVs, the 2003 Porsche Cayenne and the 2004 Volkswagen Touareg. Both are based on the same platform.

Traditional SUVs: Less trucklike. Several new models among traditional truck-based SUVs are adaptations of current models sold under different nameplates. The Lincoln Aviator is basically an AWD version of the Ford Explorer. Isuzu's seven-passenger Ascender, which replaces the Trooper, is a rebadged version of the extended-length Chevrolet TrailBlazer EXT/GMC Envoy XL. The new Lexus GX470 is a higher-priced version of the redesigned Toyota 4Runner. The Hummer H2, designed to resemble the original military vehicle, is based on GM's Yukon/Tahoe/Suburban platform.

Major redesigns in this category include the Ford Expedition, Lincoln Navigator, and Land Rover Range Rover. The Expedition and Navigator include a fully independent suspension that improves handling, a lower step-in height, and an optional power-operated fold-into-the-floor third-row seat. Like the Volvo XC90, they also offer a second-row seat with a center section that can slide forward individually. The Range Rover now offers a smooth, powerful BMW-built V8.

Korean manufacturer Kia has added a not-so-small truck-based SUV called the Sorento to compete among small SUVs.

There are still safety and fuel-economy concerns with taller and larger SUVs, but automakers have made significant strides in reducing those concerns with lighter, better-handling models and the greater availability of stability-control systems.

Cars: New life for old models. Relatively few completely new car models are being introduced for 2003. Following on the heels of the Camry redesign for 2002, the Honda Accord has been redesigned for 2003. Based on our initial driving experience, it is more comfortable, quieter, nimbler, and quicker than the previous model. Therefore, the new version should compete well with the top-rated family sedans. Sedan and coupe versions have different rear styling, and antilock brakes are standard on all models. The new Accord also offers a four-cylinder engine so clean it meets California's stringent Super Ultra Low Emissions Vehicle (SULEV) standards.

The similarly sized Mazda 626 is being replaced by a model simply called the Mazda 6, which will be available in sedan, wagon, and four-door hatchback versions. Mazda is touting the 6 as a sportier model than the pedestrian 626. A redesigned Nissan Maxima is being released next spring as an early-2004 model.

There are few notable new small cars for 2003. Saturn's 12-year-old S-series has been replaced by the new Ion. Available as a sedan or coupe, the Ion is expected to offer an optional CVT and, on the coupe, a pair of small, rear-hinged doors that provide easier access to the rear seat. Removable roof rails and interior trim pieces will allow buyers to customize the vehicle's appearance.

Among higher-priced models, Volkswagen's Passat W8, introduced in mid-2002, is a slightly quicker, eight-cylinder version of a GLX V6 4Motion model, for $5,000 more. In contrast to the typical "V" configuration of V8 engines, the W8 uses an innovative design that allows the engine to be shorter in length and better able to fit in smaller cars.

The Saab 9-3 is being redesigned as a sedan after having retained the same basic hatchback design for eight years. It's based on GM's new global platform, which will be the basis for many future GM sedans. Handling is improved as well as some controls. A notch up in price is the redesigned Mercedes-Benz E-Class. A sedan will appear first, followed by a wagon version next year. The CLK-coupe version of the C-Class is also redesigned.

The only new sedan nameplates for 2003 are Infiniti's new, sporty-looking G35, available as a sedan or coupe, and the midline M45, which is positioned between the G35 and the top-of-the-line Q45.

The coupe category, a relatively small segment of the market, has a lot of activity this year. The Nissan 350Z sports car revives the company's Z line after a seven-year hiatus. The rear-wheel-drive 350Z is based on the same platform as the Infiniti G35. The Mazda RX-8 brings back Mazda's rotary engine (last used in the RX-7 two-seater sports car, which was withdrawn from the U.S. market in 1995). The RX-8 has a small rear seat and, like the Ion, two small rear-hinged rear doors. Chrysler is expected to release the Crossfire as an early 2004 model. This stylish coupe will use drivetrain, suspension, and braking components from the Mercedes-Benz SLK.

Other automakers are pumping up the performance of existing models to help revive slow sellers. Mercury released the Marauder, a higher-performance version of its large Grand Marquis cruiser. Meanwhile, with sales of the once red-hot Chrysler PT Cruiser having cooled, DaimlerChrysler is adding a 215-hp turbocharged model called the PT Cruiser Turbo. This should give the retro car some much-needed power.

Pickups: more versatile. In a recent test of the Chevrolet Avalanche, CONSUMER REPORTS applauded the versatility of GM's removable partition between the cabin and cargo bed and the solidity of the truck's one-piece body (designs shared by the Avalanche's twin, the Cadillac Escalade EXT). Those concepts have been incorporated into the new Subaru Baja crew cab. The four-passenger AWD Baja, based on the Legacy wagon, is the first car-based pickup since the company discontinued its small two-seat Brat in 1987. The Baja's opening hatch, called a "Switchback" door, allows longer items to extend into the cabin. Like GM's design, it requires folding down the rear seat, which effectively converts the vehicle into a two-seater. The Baja is also the only pickup to offer four-wheel independent suspension, which typically provides better ride and handling.

Redesigns of the Ford F-150 and Chevrolet S-10 and a new full-sized pickup from Nissan are expected to go on sale in 2003 as 2004 models.

Features & options

Equipping a vehicle with only the options you want can often be a juggling act. If you want a car quickly, you may have to settle for what's on the dealer's lot. Special ordering a car could take weeks.

Many options can be selected individually, but often certain items are only available as part of an option package, with a name like "convenience group" or "preferred equipment package." If you want most or all of the package's components, than such as package can save you money over buying the items separately. On the other hand, sometimes you can't get an option you want without buying ones you don't care for.

CONSUMER REPORTS sorts out this complicated

situation in its New Car Price Report (call 800-269-1139 or go to *www.Consumer Reports.org*). The report includes a complete list of options and option packages for a particular model, with both invoice and retail prices. It also includes CR's equipment recommendations.

➤ **UPGRADES TO CONSIDER**

Audio. Many standard audio systems provide good sound and some form of theft protection. Higher-level systems typically improve audio quality and convenience. Many systems now come with CD players standard, but you can often upgrade to a multidisc CD changer. The trend these days is for CD changers to be mounted in the dash or center console, which is much more convenient than changers mounted in the trunk, as they used to be.

Comfort and convenience. From leather upholstery to heated seats, sunroofs, navigation systems, and roof racks, the list of small and large conveniences can seem almost endless and maybe irresistible. Be careful, though, because the tally can add up quickly.

If the vehicle has power door locks, then a key-fob remote control is a handy addition. It lets you unlock the vehicle's doors and, often, turn on interior lights from a distance. That's both a convenience and a security consideration.

Engine. If price and fuel economy are more important to you than performance, a vehicle's base engine is likely to be fine. Many models allow you to upgrade to a more powerful engine. That usually gets you quicker acceleration, better hill-climbing, and quieter operation. Often the model with the larger engine comes with higher quality tires that contribute to better cornering and braking. Larger engines sometimes also boost towing capacity. The trade-off is usually worse fuel economy.

Four-wheel and all-wheel drive. Both maximize traction (as does traction control; see page 147). Although the terms are often used interchangeably, 4WD systems are generally heavier-duty and equipped with low-range gearing for serious off-road or hazardous-terrain travel. Part-time 4WD systems, the type found on most pickups and less expensive SUVs, should not be used on dry pavement. Full-time 4WD systems are more versatile. All-wheel drive, which usually uses smaller and lighter components, lacks the low-range setting and is intended for all-weather and light off-road travel.

Two-wheel drive is enough for most people, especially if the vehicle is front-wheel drive. Modern rear-drive cars (these days, most are luxury and high-performance models) can provide decent traction in slippery conditions if they're equipped with electronic traction-control and stability-control systems.

Transmission. A manual transmission can provide an edge in fuel economy and performance over an automatic, and some prefer the greater control and sporty feel that a stick shift provides. But automatic transmissions have become much smoother and more responsive and are far more popular, particularly among drivers who have to deal with a lot of traffic congestion.

Tires and wheels. The only parts of a car that actually touch the road, tires can make a big difference in handling, braking, and ride comfort. Most vehicles offer an upgrade to higher-performance tires, either as a stand-alone option or as part of an option package or trim line. Such tires improve handling and braking, although they tend to ride more firmly and noisily, and can wear faster. Whatever tires you choose, keeping them inflated to the right pressure optimizes a vehicle's driving dynamics and maximizes the tread life.

➤ KEY SAFETY FEATURES

Every year, new safety features and technology show up to help drivers avoid an accident or help protect passengers during a collision. Systems that were available only on luxury cars just a few years ago are now common among all price ranges, sometimes mandated by law. Seatbelts remain the most important safety feature. Here's a rundown of other important ones.

Antilock brakes (ABS). Antilock brakes prevent the wheels from locking up during an emergency stop. Locked-up wheels can cause a sideways skid and also impede your steering control. ABS can not only help you stop faster or shorter, particularly on slippery surfaces, but it also helps keep the vehicle heading straight. And, it allows the driver to retain steering control while braking, so you can steer around an obstacle if necessary. CONSUMER REPORTS strongly recommends ABS when available.

Brake assist. This is an adjunct to ABS, pioneered by Mercedes-Benz. By sensing the speed or force with which the brake pedal is depressed, it determines if the driver wants to make an emergency stop. If so, it applies greater pressure on the pedal even if the driver is too tentative in pressing the pedal. It's now available on some Audi, Lexus, Mercedes, Nissan, Toyota, and other vehicles.

Traction control. This system limits wheel spin during acceleration. It's particularly useful when starting from a standstill in wet or icy conditions. It can serve as a less expensive (though less effective) alternative to all- or four-wheel drive, particularly in rear-wheel-drive cars.

Stability control. This electronic system keeps a vehicle on its intended path in slippery conditions. It selectively brakes one or more wheels if it detects that the vehicle is on the verge of a slide or skid during cornering. On many luxury vehicles and some SUVs, CONSUMER REPORTS strongly recommends stability control when available.

Front air bags. All new vehicles come with front air bags. Dual-stage deployment is the latest enhancement. With this design, the bags may not inflate or may inflate with reduced force in a low-level collision. In a higher-speed collision, the bags inflate with full force. Another enhancement on more and more models: occupant-sensing systems that tailor the air bags to fit certain conditions, such as when a small person or no person is inhabiting the passenger seat.

Side air bags. Side air bags for the front seats are now common. Some automakers offer side air bags for the rear seats too. Some models provide occupant-sensing systems for side bags. The system in Honda and Acura models deactivates the side bags if a front passenger is leaning too close to the door, to prevent possible air-bag injury.

Head-protection bags. Many models now provide some type of head-protection air bag, often in conjunction with a side air-bag system. The most common are side-curtain air bags, which cover both front and rear side windows to prevent occupants from hitting their head on the glass or roof pillars, to help shield them from debris, and to prevent someone from being ejected through the window.

Belt pretensioners and force limiters. These features help seatbelts do their job more effectively. Pretensioners, for instance, can work in conjunction with the front air bags. In a frontal crash, pretensioners retract the seatbelts slightly, removing slack. Force limiters then relax the seatbelt tension slightly, paying the belt back out following the initial impact. That can help prevent chest and internal injuries caused by the belt.

Rollover-detection system. This new system is now available on the Ford

Explorer and Expedition, Mercury Mountaineer, and Lincoln Aviator and Navigator, Volvo XC90, Lexus LX470, and Toyota Land Cruiser. If sensors determine that the vehicle has leaned beyond a certain angle, indicating that a rollover is imminent, they automatically trigger the side-curtain air bags to help prevent occupants from being injured or ejected.

Child-seat attachments. All new vehicles now must have anchors for top-tether attachments and a universal lower mounting system, called LATCH (for Lower Anchors and Tethers for Children), that uses anchors in the crease between the car's rear-seat backrest and lower cushion.

Smart buying or leasing

To get the vehicle you want at the best price do your homework. Think about what you need and like and then follow these steps:

➤ STEP 1: NARROW YOUR CHOICES

CONSUMER REPORTS information is a good place to start. Check out the overall Ratings of models that CONSUMER REPORTS has recently tested, page 170. Beginning on page 152 are overviews for nearly all the 2003 and some 2004 models, including predictions on how reliable the model is likely to be. Models that CR recommends are highlighted. The Frequency-of-Repair charts that begin on page 180 detail the reliability histories for more than 200 vehicles.

➤ STEP 2: RESEARCH THE DETAILS

Once you have a short list of cars, gather key details on features, prices, safety equipment, and insurance options. Many sources—both in print and online—offer basic information and specifications. The automaker's own brochures and web sites can be useful for learning about the various features available and how the vehicles come equipped. You'll find automaker web addresses in the Brand Locator beginning on page 341.

➤ STEP 3: BUY OR LEASE?

With the average new vehicle now selling for almost $26,000, not many people plunk down cash and drive away. Most people finance the transaction either through a loan or lease the vehicle. How you use the car should determine which is best for you.

Leasing generally makes sense only if:

• You don't exceed the annual mileage allowance—typically 12,000 to 15,000 miles per year. Extra miles usually cost 15 to 25 cents each.

• You don't terminate the lease early. You risk thousands of dollars in penalties if you do.

• You keep your vehicle in very good shape. "Excess wear and tear" charges at lease end can run several hundred to a thousand dollars or more.

• You prefer to trade your vehicle in every two or three years. If you keep a car longer, you're probably better off buying it from the start. If you'll keep the car more than five years, it usually makes more sense to buy.

➤ STEP 4: NAIL DOWN THE PRICE

Once you're fairly certain of the car you want and how you want to pay for it, get a benchmark price for bargaining. The amount of the monthly loan or lease payment hinges on your ability to negotiate the lowest possible price for the vehicle.

Finding the sticker price is easy. It's on the car window and available at many web sites. But you also want to find the invoice price that dealers pay the manufacturer. You can get that information from various printed guides as well as from many web sites.

But dealers get various discounts and incentives that effectively lower their wholesale price below the official invoice price. Knowing about them can help you establish an even better place to start your price negotiations. To help you get to the true bottom price, CONSUMER REPORTS provides the CR Wholesale Price. It takes the dealer's invoice price and figures in any rebates or other direct-to-dealer discounts in effect. The CR Wholesale Price is provided as part of the Consumer Reports New Car Price Service (call 800-269-1139 or go to *www.ConsumerReports.org*).

Typically, models in ample supply sell for 4 to 8 percent over the CR Wholesale Price. Slow-selling models may sell for less than invoice. High-demand vehicles sell for prices closer to the sticker. Most domestic models, even those newly introduced, often sell at a discount right away.

➤ STEP 5: SHOP FOR FINANCING

Check online services, local banks, and your credit union for the best rates. Most automakers have finance arms, such as Ford Motor Credit for Ford products or GMAC for General Motors vehicles. They often offer very favorable financing terms, but don't be drawn into a great deal on a car you don't really want.

Here are some tips:

• Examine the terms. The most attractive rates, like zero-percent financing, often have limitations. They apply only to short-term loans, or only to people with faultless credit histories, or to cars that aren't selling well.

• Know what's really discounted. Make sure that the "great low rate" is available on the car after you bargain down the price. If it applies only to a car selling for full price, then it may not be such a bargain.

• Avoid needless extras. Pass up extras like credit-life and disability insurance, an extended warranty, rustproofing, paint sealant, and so on.

➤ STEP 6: TAKE SOME TEST DRIVES

This important step lets you see how the car fits you. Seat comfort, visibility, roominess, and the ergonomics of the controls can make a big difference in how happy you'll be with a vehicle over the long term.

Test drive the trim line you're considering, since comfort and performance features can change from one trim level to another. Take your time. Get a feel for the ride and noise level by driving the vehicle over different types of roads.

Make sure that the driving position and view out is comfortable, and that the driver's seat accommodates everyone who will be driving the vehicle. The controls should be easy to use and the safety belt should be comfortable. Check the ease of getting in and out of the rear seat, and the roominess of the trunk.

➤ STEP 7: NEGOTIATE SMARTLY

If you can, visit three or four dealers to see how the cars in stock are typically equipped and to gauge which dealers might be willing to accept a smaller profit margin. Then follow this gameplan:

Keep the deal simple. Negotiate the price of the new car or of your trade-in first, but don't do both deals at once. It's simplest to negotiate the price of the new vehicle first, and treat it as if it were a straight-out cash deal. When it's concluded, then discuss the possibility of leasing or the price of the trade-in. Make it clear from the outset you're serious about buying soon but won't sign a contract on the spot. Tell the salesperson you are shopping different dealers and whichever offers the lowest price will get your business.

Don't bid against yourself. Bargain up from the lowest figure a little at a time.

Once you've made an offer, say nothing until you receive a counteroffer.

Be prepared to walk. Avoid pinning your hopes on one dealer or one car. There will always be other good deals on other good cars.

Tips on handling the trade-in. Negotiate a trade-in separately from the purchase or lease deal. You're apt to get the best price for your old car if you can sell it privately, but that's too much trouble for some.

Clean the old car as thoroughly as you can, and consider fixing small dings or other items. Such measures, though largely cosmetic, can improve the resale value substantially. To learn what your old car should net as a trade-in, try shopping it around at local dealers' used-car department. That will establish a rock-bottom price. Then check local classified-ad publications and Internet used-car sites to see what dealers and private parties are asking for cars like yours. That establishes the high end of the range. Your trade-in price is apt to be somewhere in the middle between those extremes.

Special tips for leasing. Proceed with the leasing deal only after you receive a firm price quote for the car. Make sure that the purchase price is the figure used to calculate the lease terms. Other items you can negotiate include the annual mileage limit, the down payment, and the purchase-option price.

• Be sure the value of any trade-in is deducted from the "capitalized cost" or selling price, on which the monthly figure is calculated. To figure out what you're really paying in interest, ask the dealer for the "money factor," a four- or five-digit decimal. Multiply that by 2,400 to get an approximate annual interest-rate percentage. For example, a "money factor" of .00375 is about equivalent to a 9 percent annual interest rate (.00375 x 2,400 = 9).

• In a typical lease calculation, your monthly payment consists of depreciation, a "lease fee," and applicable taxes. The lease fee is the money factor multiplied by the sum of the capitalized cost and the residual value. Since residual value is already part of the capitalized cost it may look like it's being counted twice. It isn't. The money factor takes it into account.

Try to avoid a lease that extends past the vehicle's basic warranty. Otherwise you might be saddled with expensive repairs on a vehicle you don't own.

If you might buy the car at lease-end, find out the purchase-option fee and pay it up front. And if you think you'll exceed the annual mileage allowance, buy extra miles up front, too. It's much cheaper that way.

Buying a used car

You can find the best auto value by buying a late-model used car. With a used car, the original owner, not you, pays for the steepest part of the depreciation.

Manufacturer-certified used cars are late-model used cars sold by franchised dealers. They're advertised as being carefully selected, inspected against a long factory checklist, then reconditioned to ensure top-notch condition. They generally come with manufacturer's warranty lasting three months to a year or more.

Cars from used-car dealers are usually a notch down in price from those available at new-car dealers, but also a notch down in quality and after-sale care.

You might be able to get the lowest price by buying from a private owner, but you may have little recourse if the car turns out to have problems.

➤ **KEY RESEARCH**
If buying from a new-car dealer who sells the same make, ask that the car's vehicle

identification number (VIN) be run through the dealer's computer and get a printout of any completed warranty repairs. The dealer can also check the status of any federal recalls and service bulletins.

Inspect any used car carefully, top to bottom and inside and out, in broad daylight. The car's overall condition should jibe with its odometer reading. Signs of high mileage include excessive wear on the pedals or brand-new pedal pads; a new set of tires or more than one brand; a well-worn ignition key; a worn or sagging driver's seat; frayed carpeting; and a sagging driver's door.

When you find a good prospect, take it to a mechanic for a thorough inspection—well worth the $60 to $100 cost. If you're an American Automobile Association member, consider using a AAA-sanctioned garage.

CONSUMER REPORTS can also help. The Best and Worst Used Cars lists that start on page 000 help you avoid a problem-prone model. In addition, the reliability histories (beginning on page 000) give you more detailed information about each vehicle's problem areas. For help in determining prices, see the section on trade-ins on page 150 or call the Consumer Reports Used Car Price Service at 800-422-1079.

ONLINE RESEARCH

Using the web to shop for a car

You can find specs, pictures, and prices online. You can find out what car testers such as CONSUMER REPORTS and others have to say, and what sort of financing is available. You can check insurance rates, bank rates, lease deals, and look at your own credit report. It's getting easier to separate good sites from bad ones. Still, you should treat web-generated information with caution. When it comes to a car, nothing beats seeing it in person.

If you want to buy or lease a car, various services can get the ball rolling for you by quoting a price (either their set price or one from a participating dealership). Or they can handle the entire deal, from arranging financing to delivery of the car.

With a buying site, you are cued to fill out a detailed questionnaire about the car or cars you are looking for. The service then quotes a price (sometimes instantly, sometimes within hours or days), and searches for a dealer who has the car.

Some buying sites essentially put you in touch with a local dealer who has agreed to sell a car at a specified price. But when you visit the dealer you may or may not be pressured to buy more equipment, extended warranties, or other extras. Other buying sites arrange a final, out-the-door price, and you go to a dealer only to write a check and pick up the car.

Used-car buying sites essentially work like extensive classified-ad publications. After you enter the model in which you're interested, they typically list all vehicles that are available within a specified price and distance from your home. You can use them to find a car, or just to get a handle on the going prices, whether you are in the market to sell or buy.

PREVIEWS OF THE 2003 MODELS

This rundown of all the major 2003 models can start you on your search for a new car. You'll find a capsule summary of each model, as well as the CONSUMER REPORTS prediction of how reliable the vehicle will be, and how much it's likely to depreciate in value. Model descriptions in this book are based on recent road tests that pertain to this year's models.

Models with a ✔ are recommended by CONSUMER REPORTS. These are models that performed well in CONSUMER REPORTS testing, have average or better reliability according to our annual survey, and have not performed poorly in a crash test.

Entries include, where available, the date of the last road test for that model published in CONSUMER REPORTS magazine. These road-test reports are also available to subscribers of our web site, *(www.ConsumerReports.org)*.

The 2003 cars, trucks, SUUs & minivans

Predicted reliability is a judgment based on our annual reliability survey data. New or recently redesigned models are marked "New." **Depreciation** predicts how well a new model will keep its value, based on the difference between the original sticker price of a 2000 model and its current resale value. The average depreciation for all vehicles was 43 percent. As a group, full-sized pickup trucks have the lowest depreciation rate. Sporty cars also tend to hold value. Large luxury cars, on the other hand, have a relatively high depreciation rate. Throughout, ✔ indicates a model is recommended by CONSUMER REPORTS; NA means data not available.

			Better ⟵ ⊜ ⊜ ○ ⊖ ● ⟶ Worse
Model	**Predicted reliability**	**Depreciation**	**Comments**
Acura CL	⊜	NA	This coupe is a two-door version of the Acura TL. The ride is compliant and the handling competent, but the CL doesn't feel all that sporty, even in the higher-performance Type-S trim level.
✔ Acura MDX	⊜	NA	The MDX is a well-designed car-based SUV that can hold seven passengers. Ride and handling are competent. The interior is flexible, with a third-row seat that folds flat into the cargo floor. **Last road test: July 2001**
✔ Acura RL	⊜	○	Acura's flagship sedan is quiet, spacious, and impeccably finished, but a bit bland. It handles securely and delivers a smooth, quiet ride. Although comfortable and competent, the RL lacks the superb performance found in its competitors, the BMW 5-Series and the Mercedes-Benz E-Class. **Last road test: Nov. 2000**

Model	Predicted reliability	Depre- ciation	Comments
✔ **Acura RSX**	○	NA	With its hatchback design, this small coupe offers some versatility. In the sportier Type-S variant, handling is capable, but the ride is noisy and choppy. **Last road test: Dec. 2001**
✔ **Acura TL**	⊖	⊖	This upscale midsized sedan is based on the previous-generation Honda Accord. A sprightly and quiet V6, sound handling, a fairly comfortable ride, and excellent reliability make it a sensible, competitively priced choice. **Last road test: Mar. 2002**
Audi A4	◒	NA	The A4 handles nimbly and accelerates well, though the ride at low speeds is a bit too firm. The interior is polished and luxurious —comfortable in front, meager in the rear. All-wheel drive is available; a continuously variable transmission is available on front-drive models. **Last road test: Mar. 2002**
Audi A6/Allroad	◒	○	Audi's refined midsized sedan has a supple ride and handles responsively. The Allroad variant is a good-performing (if pricey) wagon with an adjustable height suspension for moderate off-road use. The 2.7T variant is quick but a bit hesitant off the line. **Last road test: Nov. 2001**
Audi A8	NA	○	A full-sized all-wheel-drive luxury car that competes with the BMW 7-Series, Mercedes S-Class, and Lexus LS430. It doesn't ride as well as those, but AWD is unusual in the class. Expect a redesign in summer '03.
Audi TT	●	⊖	This stylish two-seater is available in both convertible and coupe versions. A nicely detailed interior and available all-wheel drive offset a character that is less sporty than a Porsche Boxster's. The ride is stiff and the engine noisy. **Last road test: June 2002**
BMW 3-Series	◒	⊖	The 3-Series models are an ideal blend of comfort, luxury, sportiness, and safety. They are quiet and refined, yet quick and agile. Wagon and all-wheel-drive xi versions are also available. Reliability has deteriorated. **Last road test: May 2001**
✔ **BMW 5-Series**	○	⊖	These superbly designed rear-wheel-drive luxury sports sedans embody pure precision and nimble, responsive handling. The ride is supple and quiet, with extremely comfortable, supportive seats. Powertrains are smooth and punchy. The 530i is the highest-scoring car CR has tested. **Last road test: Nov. 2001**
BMW 7-Series	NA	NA	BMW's flagship sedan, quick, quiet, and agile, is loaded with features that include an innovative but complicated control system ("iDrive") and several safety advances.
BMW X5	●	⊖	This SUV drives like a capable sports sedan. The Six performs well, though the V8s are quicker. Handling and braking are top notch, but the ride is a bit choppy and cargo space is modest. **Last road test: June 2000**
BMW Z4	NEW	NA	The Z4 replaces the Z3 as BMW's "affordable" roadster. Engines are carried over from the Z3. A more sophisticated rear suspension promises better handling.
Buick Century	⊖	●	The Century feels like an old car. The ride is quiet and soft, at least at low speeds, but bumpy roads easily upset its composure. The front bench seat is roomy, but the soft seats offer little support.

Model	Predicted reliability	Depre- ciation	Comments
✔ Buick LeSabre	○	◒	The big LeSabre has a roomy interior and a quiet ride. Handling is secure, especially with the Touring suspension, which also makes the ride more settled. The seats are unsupportive. **Last road test: Feb. 2000**
Buick Park Avenue	◒	●	Buick's top-of-the-line sedan rides and handles relatively well. Acceleration is effortless in the supercharged Ultra. The interior is roomy and quiet, and the seats are fairly comfortable.
Buick Regal	◓	◒	This car rides well at low speeds, although handling is a bit cumbersome. Its V6 accelerates adequately and the cabin is quiet. The seats are soft and grow less comfortable on long rides.
Buick Rendezvous	◒	NA	This minivan-based SUV features independent suspension, optional all-wheel drive, and room for seven. The ride is OK, and handling is secure. Good points are offset by so-so acceleration and a cheap-feeling interior. **Last road test: Oct. 2001**
Cadillac CTS	NEW	NA	This capable rear-wheel-drive sedan replaces the Catera. Its ride is firm and controlled, handling is nimble, and acceleration is smooth though not overly powerful.
Cadillac DeVille	◒	◒	This big, plush freeway cruiser handles well for such a large car. It offers plenty of power and a very comfortable ride. Well-thought-out details festoon the interior. **Last road test: Nov. 2000**
Cadillac Escalade	●	NA	Essentially a Chevrolet Tahoe, this SUV has a powerful engine and a smooth-shifting transmission. Though the interior is spacious, it's not very flexible and the third seat is uncomfortable.
Cadillac Escalade EXT	NA	NA	This crew-cab pickup is essentially a higher-priced version of the Chevrolet Avalanche. The interior is an uneasy mix of stylish Cadillac and cheap Chevy truck.
Cadillac Seville	●	●	The Seville has a sophisticated V8, but lacks the dynamic prowess of most of its European and Japanese competitors. Ride and handling are just OK, and the rear seat is tight.
Chevrolet Astro	●	◒	The rear-wheel-drive Astro is seriously outclassed by all modern minivan designs. Handling is ponderous, and the ride is uncomfortable. However, it can haul lots of cargo or tow a heavy trailer. AWD is optional.
✔ Chevrolet Avalanche	○	NA	Essentially a crew-cab pickup version of the Suburban, this truck has an innovative "midgate" that allows long items to extend into the rear-passenger compartment. The ride is comfortable. **Last road test: Sep. 2002**
Chevrolet Blazer	●	●	This dated SUV offers adequate cargo space and a tolerable ride. Emergency handling is subpar. Its replacement, the vastly superior TrailBlazer, has made this model mostly a rental-fleet filler.
Chevrolet Cavalier	○	◒	An outdated design for basic transportation. Rough roads make the body bounce. The front seats are uncomfortable, the rear seat low and cramped. **Last road test: Feb. 2001**
Chevrolet Corvette	●	◓	The Corvette comes as a coupe or convertible. You get muscular V8 performance and commendable handling finesse. The tires grip tenaciously. But taking the convertible top down is a nuisance. **Last road test: June 2002**

Model	Predicted reliability	Depre-ciation	Comments
✓ Chevrolet Impala	○	◒	The Impala is a roomy sedan. Ride and handling are sound, and the powertrain is smooth. The rear seat is uncomfortable, and some controls are not well located. **Last road test: May 2000**
✓ Chevrolet Malibu	○	●	Positioned as a lower-priced alternative to a Honda Accord or Toyota Camry, the Malibu is less refined than either. It handles soundly, and the ride is tolerable if a bit jiggly. The interior is roomy but feels cheaply finished. **Last road test: June 2001**
Chevrolet Monte Carlo	○	○	A coupe version of the Impala, the Monte Carlo accelerates well, but road noise is pronounced and rear access is a chore. Overall, it offers an underwhelming driving experience.
Chevrolet S-10	●	○	This compact pickup and its sibling, the GMC Sonoma, ride stiffly and handle clumsily. The cabin is quiet, but the seats are uncomfortable. The V6 accelerates well. **Last road test: Aug. 2001**
✓ Chevrolet Silverado 1500	○	⊖	The Silverado, a full-sized pickup, drives fairly nicely. The optional four-wheel drive is a selectable full-time system. The extended-cab version has a handy but expensive four-wheel-steer option for easier maneuverability. **Last road test: Nov. 1999**
✓ Chevrolet Suburban	○	⊜	One of the largest SUVs, the Suburban can seat eight people with luggage and tow a heavy trailer. It's quiet, comfortable, and handles fairly well. The GMC Yukon XL is virtually identical. **Last road test: June 2000**
✓ Chevrolet Tahoe	○	○	This SUV is similar to the Suburban, but with less cargo room. Eight can ride, but the tight third seat is best for kids. It (and the similar GMC Yukon) boast an impressive towing capability. **Last road test: Nov. 2002**
Chevrolet Tracker	○	◒	This compact SUV uses the old truck-based, body-on-frame design. It's slow, noisy, and crude. Built by Suzuki, it's the same as the Suzuki Vitara.
Chevrolet TrailBlazer	●	NA	This SUV is quiet and spacious, with a comfortable ride and a spirited inline six-cylinder engine. Handling is a bit ponderous and can be tricky at the limit. A longer EXT model with a third seat was introduced late in 2002. **Last road test: Sep. 2001**
Chevrolet Venture	◒	◒	This well-designed minivan has a responsive powertrain and comfortable seating. Subpar reliability and a poor offset-crash test keep it out of contention. **Last road test: Jan. 2001**
✓ Chrysler 300M	○	○	The 300M sedan is a roomier, upscale sibling of the Dodge Intrepid and Chrysler Concorde. The ride is stiff, and the cabin admits too much noise, but handling is nimble. The front seats are soft and unsupportive. **Last road test: Oct. 1999**
✓ Chrysler Concorde	⊜	●	This large sedan handles fairly nimbly and has a supple ride, although both available engines lack refinement. Road noise is constant, and access is a chore.
Chrysler Crossfire	NEW	NA	The Crossfire is a small, sporty, rear-wheel drive, two-seat coupe that uses powertrain, suspension, and braking components from the Mercedes SLK roadster.

Model	Predicted reliability	Depreciation	Comments
Chrysler Pacifica	NEW	NA	The Pacifica is a new entry to the tall, all-wheel-drive wagon brigade. It goes on sale in March. Access should be easy and a third row of seats folds down when not needed. It will share many components with the 300M.
✓ Chrysler PT Cruiser	⊖	NA	The retro-styled PT Cruiser is a tall front-drive wagon. It offers a versatile interior and secure handling, but with the automatic, acceleration is languid. A quicker, turbocharged version is new for 2003. **Last road test: Oct. 2000**
Chrysler Sebring	○	NA	The Sebring is available in sedan, coupe, and convertible forms. The coupe is derived from the mediocre Mitsubishi Eclipse. The sedan has a quick V6 but it's not agile or smooth-riding. **Last road test: June 2001**
Chrysler Town & Country	◒	◓	This minivan is a higher-priced version of the Dodge Grand Caravan. It's quiet inside and offers a flexible interior and dual power side doors. Engines are lackluster and reliability has deteriorated. AWD is optional. **Last road test: Jan. 2001**
Chrysler Voyager	●	NA	Aimed at budget buyers, this is a short-wheelbase version of the Town & Country and is similar to the Dodge Caravan. It rides quietly and offers good interior flexibility.
Dodge Caravan/ Grand Caravan	◒	◒	The Caravan rides quietly and competently, though engines are lackluster. The flexible interior includes a removable split third-row seat, but it doesn't stow into the floor. The Caravan is available in short or long ("Grand") versions. **Last road test: Jan. 2001**
Dodge Dakota	○	○	The Dakota handles a little less clumsily than most pickups, though the ride is jarring and the V6 and V8s all guzzle gas. The brakes are marginal. A spacious four-door crew-cab is available. Performed poorly in an offset-crash test. **Last road test: Aug. 2001**
Dodge Durango	◒	○	This uninspired SUV offers three rows of seats, although the third row is pretty tight. The front seats are uncomfortable, and the ride is stiff and choppy. Two V8 engines are available; the 4.7 is the better choice. **Last road test: Sep. 2001**
✔ Dodge Intrepid	○	●	This large and stylish car delivers so-so performance overall. Handling is fairly nimble, and the ride is OK. Both available V6 engines are noisy. **Last road test: Feb. 2002**
Dodge Neon	◒	●	This small sedan handles securely, brakes well, and has a relatively roomy interior. But the ride is stiff and uncomfortable and the cabin noisy. The four-speed automatic is not responsive enough. **Last road test: Sep. 2001**
Dodge Ram 1500	●	NA	This pickup was redesigned for 2002 but still falls short of the competition. The handling and powertrain are improved, but the ride is jittery and the cabin noisy. **Last road test: Sep. 2002**
Dodge Stratus	○	NA	The Stratus, available as a sedan or coupe, feels a bit rough and underdeveloped. The sedan offers quick acceleration with the V6, but ride and handling fall short. The cabin is noisy and hard to get in and out of. **Last road test: June 2001**

Model	Predicted reliability	Depreciation	Comments
Ford Crown Victoria	⊖	⊖	A big, quiet, comfortable-riding sedan, the Crown Victoria handles ponderously despite recent improvements. Braking and emergency handling are fairly good. Rear leg room is skimpier than you might expect.
Ford Escape	⊖	NA	The Escape and its cousin, the Mazda Tribute, are small, car-based SUVs with good interior space and fairly nimble handling, but a stiff and noisy ride. The V6 is lively. Some interior appointments look and feel cheap. **Last road test: Mar. 2001**
Ford Excursion	○	○	Designed to be the largest SUV on the road, the Excursion is a clumsy, fuel-guzzling behemoth with a noisy engine, an uncomfortable ride, and marginal brakes. It will cease production at the end of 2003. **Last road test: June 2000**
Ford Expedition	NEW	NA	Redesigned for 2003, this large SUV has a well-designed interior with flexible seating and a roomy fold-down split third seat. Ride and handling are commendable, but the available engines are slow and thirsty. **Last road test: Nov. 2002**
Ford Explorer	●	NA	Redesigned and much improved for 2002, the spacious Explorer rides fairly comfortably and quietly and handles securely. A third-row seat adds versatility. Advanced safety gear is another plus. **Last road test: Sep. 2001**
Ford Explorer Sport Trac	⊖	NA	This crew-cab truck is based on the previous-generation Ford Explorer and features a short pickup bed and five-person cabin. The ride is stiff and choppy, but handling is secure and relatively responsive. **Last road test: Aug. 2001**
Ford F-150	⊖	○	The F-150 feels like an old design, with ride and cabin quietness not up to the level of Toyota or Chevy trucks. The crew-cab version is roomy but has a high step-up. It did poorly in an offset-crash test. **Last road test: Sep. 2002**
Ford Focus	●	○	The small Focus sedan tested very well—it's agile, spacious, and fun to drive—but reliability has been well below average. It is also available in wagon and hatchback models. The SVT version holds its own among sports cars. **Last road test: Aug. 2002**
Ford Mustang	⊖	○	This old-fashioned rear-drive muscle car got its last upgrade for 1999. Ride, handling, and braking are OK, but the car doesn't feel very sporty. The V8 is the engine of choice.
Ford Ranger	⊖	⊖	The Ranger and similar Mazda B-Series stand out as all-around competent pickup trucks. Handling is not too clumsy, although the ride is stiff and choppy. The "Super Cab" models offer ample storage space as well as four doors.
✔ Ford Taurus	○	●	This is a roomy sedan or wagon. Ride handling and braking are sound but unimpressive. Choose the uplevel V6. Adjustable pedals could be handy for short drivers. **Last road test: May 2000**
Ford Thunderbird	NA	NA	The T-bird is a retro-revival two-seater that handles well but is more of a cruiser than a sports car. Headroom is tight. The soft top is power operated; a removable hard top is also available. **Last road test: June 2002**

Model	Predicted reliability	Depreciation	Comments
Ford Windstar	●	●	This minivan rides smoothly and offers strong acceleration and acceptable handling. A low floor eases access. It's not quite as spacious as GM's and Chrysler's minivans nor as refined as the Honda Odyssey and Toyota Sienna. **Last road test: Jan. 2001**
GMC Envoy	●	NA	This midsized SUV, twin of the Chevrolet TrailBlazer, is quiet and spacious, with a comfortable ride and a spirited inline-Six. Handling is a bit ponderous and can be tricky at the limit. A longer EXT model has a third seat. **Last road test: Sep. 2001**
GMC Safari	●	◒	This outdated rear-wheel-drive minivan can haul lots of cargo or tow a heavy trailer. All-wheel drive is optional. It handles ponderously and feels very much like a truck.
✔ **GMC Sierra 1500**	○	◓	This full-sized pickup drives fairly nicely and offers selectable full-time 4WD. The Denali version has a handy four-wheel-steer option for easier maneuverability. Extended-cab versions have a usable rear seat. **Last road test: Nov. 1999**
GMC Sonoma	◒	◒	Like its sibling, the Chevy S-10, this compact pickup rides stiffly and lacks agility, but it's more comfortable and responsive than the Japanese competitors. The cabin is quiet, and the 4.3-liter V6 accelerates well. **Last road test: Aug. 2001**
✔ **GMC Yukon**	○	◓	This SUV is similar to the Chevy Suburban, but with less cargo room. Eight can ride, but those in the third seat will be very uncomfortable. It (and the similar Chevrolet Tahoe) boast an impressive towing capability. **Last road test: Nov. 2002**
✔ **GMC Yukon XL**	○	○	Formerly called the GMC Suburban, this is one of the largest SUVs offered. It can accommodate eight people and tow a heavy trailer. It's quiet and comfortable, and handles relatively well. **Last road test: June 2000**
Honda Accord	NEW	NA	Redesigned for '03, the Accord comes with more powerful engines, standard antilock brakes, and steering that adjusts for height and reach. Handling is improved and the ride is more comfortable and quieter.
✔ **Honda Civic**	◓	◓	One of the best small sedans, the Civic handles well and gets good fuel economy, though its ride is a bit nervous. The interior is well finished, and controls are excellent. The hybrid gets excellent fuel economy. **Last road test: Dec. 2002**
✔ **Honda CR-V**	◓	◓	The CR-V is responsive and fairly fuel efficient for an SUV. It rides comfortably and has a roomy rear seat. With the RAV4 and Forester, it's one of the best small SUVs available. **Last road test: May 2002**
Honda Element	NEW	NA	This small, boxy SUV is based on Honda's very good CR-V. The rear doors are hinged at the rear and there's no roof pillar between front and rear doors, so opening the side doors creates a huge loading port. The two rear seats fold away to create a big cargo area.
Honda Insight	NA	◓	This lightweight two-seat hybrid has a three-cylinder engine and a 13-hp electric motor that assists the gas engine. Handling is secure but not nimble. A stiff, uncomfortable ride, lack of storage space, and intrusive interior noise are major trade-offs for the car's excellent fuel economy. **Last road test: Dec. 2000**

Model	Predicted reliability	Depre- ciation	Comments
✔ Honda Odyssey	⊖	⊖	The Odyssey is our top-rated minivan. It has a sprightly V6, dual sliding rear doors, an optional navigation system, and a fold-down third row. It handles well and has a steady, supple ride. **Last road test: Jan. 2001**
✔ Honda Pilot	⊖	NA	The Pilot is a well-designed car-based SUV that can hold eight people. Ride and handling are competent. The interior is flexible, with a third-row seat that folds flat into the cargo floor. **Last road test: Nov. 2002**
✔ Honda S2000	⊖	⊖	The S2000 is a pure sports car that delivers impressive accelera-tion, handling, and braking. But it's noisy and hard riding, and feels a bit ordinary in normal driving. **Last road test: Aug. 2000**
Hummer H2	NEW	NA	GM's Hummer H2 is based on the Chevy Tahoe/Suburban and has much more usable interior space than the grossly impractical original Hummer. It offers very good off-road ability, but visibility is compromised and at $50,000, it's no bargain.
Hyundai Accent	○	⊜	The Accent offers basic transportation. The ride is choppy but relatively quiet, and its 1.6-liter Four accelerates adequately. Antilock brakes are not available. It comes as either a sedan or a hatchback.
Hyundai Elantra	○	NA	The Elantra, spacious for a small sedan, rides well and handles securely, making it competitive with other good small sedans. Seats are firm and supportive. Models with the optional antilock brakes are hard to find. **Last road test: Feb. 2001**
✔ Hyundai Santa Fe	⊖	NA	This car-based SUV has a supple, quiet ride and handles secure-ly, if not nimbly. Acceleration and fuel economy are not impres-sive. A steeply raked windshield makes the cockpit feel a bit confining. **Last road test: Mar. 2001**
✔ Hyundai Sonata	⊖	⊜	The midsized Sonata offers good power, comfort, convenience, and a long warranty. Handling is clumsy but secure. **Last road test: June 2001**
Hyundai Tiburon	NEW	NA	The GT V6 version of this sporty coupe delivers quick accelera-tion, but handling is not so agile. The ride is stiff. Even medium-tall drivers will have to duck under the low roof. **Last road test: Oct. 2002**
Hyundai XG350	○	NA	This quiet, roomy sedan, a little larger than the Sonata, comes with lots of standard features. Handling is short on agility, and the ride floats a bit at highway speeds.
Infiniti FX45	NEW	NA	The new FX45 is a luxury-class SUV introduced as an early 2004 model. Resembling a tall hatchback, it's a car-based five-seater with all-wheel drive, a powerful V8, and not much interior space.
Infiniti G35	NEW	NA	This rear-wheel-drive car is Infiniti's new entry-level model. Available as a sedan or coupe, it aims to compete with the BMW 3-Series. The powertrain is very smooth, but its handling is not as agile as that of a BMW.
✔ Infiniti I35	○	○	The I35 is essentially a Nissan Maxima with a price premium and a plusher interior. The ride is unexceptional. Handling is secure but not inspiring. **Last road test: Mar. 2002**

Model	Predicted reliability	Depre- ciation	Comments
Infiniti M45	NEW	NA	The new-for-2003 M45 is powered by the same smooth, powerful V8 that's used in the Q45. It offers many luxury appointments but has a relatively cramped interior.
Infiniti Q45	NA	◖	Nissan's flagship sedan competes against the Lexus LS430. The engine is smooth and quiet. But ride and handling aren't all that impressive.
Infiniti QX4	◔	○	The QX4 is Infiniti's version of the Nissan Pathfinder, with more luxury features. It has a strong 240-hp V6, but cargo space and payload are modest.
Isuzu Ascender	NEW	NA	This midsized seven-passenger SUV is essentially a rebadged Chevy Trailblazer EXT. Expect a quiet and spacious interior with a comfortable ride and a spirited inline six-cylinder engine but sometimes-ponderous handling.
Isuzu Axiom	NA	NA	Beneath its modernistic countenance, the Axiom is a traditional body-on-frame SUV that borrows heavily from the Trooper and Rodeo. Pluses include a potent 3.5-liter V6 and selectable full-time 4WD.
Isuzu Rodeo/ Rodeo Sport	◖	○	This truck-based SUV offers a smooth, powerful V6 but a busy and jittery ride. Handling is sluggish. The seats are well shaped but too low. The Rodeo Sport, previously known as the Amigo, is a two-door version available with either a soft or a hard top.
Jaguar S-Type	●	○	The S-Type shares a platform with the Lincoln LS. The V8 is strong and smooth, the V6 much less so. The interior is a bit cramped, and the trunk is small. The overall experience is more run-of-the-mill than luxurious. **Last road test: Nov. 2001**
Jaguar X-Type	●	NA	Based on the European Ford Mondeo, this entry-level Jag comes with standard all-wheel drive and a choice of two V6 engines. It targets the BMW 3-Series and Audi A4 but lacks their interior quality, refinement, and driving enjoyment. **Last road test: Mar. 2002**
Jaguar XJ8	NA	○	This venerable luxury sedan provides a ride that is one of the best in the world. Accommodations are relatively tight, however. A complete redesign is due in June 2003.
Jeep Grand Cherokee	●	◖	Cramped and rough riding by today's standards, the Grand Cherokee is showing its age. Handling is imprecise, and the standard Six is noisy. The 4.7 V8 is a better choice. Accommodations are tight with an uncomfortable rear seat. **Last road test: Sep. 2001**
✔ **Jeep Liberty**	○	NA	The Liberty, despite its independent front suspension and modern rack-and-pinion steering setup, is not nearly as agile and comfortable as, say, a Honda CR-V. The ride is jittery, the cockpit is narrow, and access is awkward. Off-road ability is impressive, though. **Last road test: May 2002**
Jeep Wrangler	●	◓	The Wrangler is the smallest and crudest Jeep. The ride is hard and noisy, handling is primitive, and the driving position is unpleasant. Nevertheless, it remains popular wth off-road enthusiasts.
Kia Optima	NA	NA	This midsized sedan is essentially a Hyundai Sonata with more-conservative styling. The interior is fairly spacious and quiet, and the V6 powertrain reasonably refined.

Model	Predicted reliability	Depre- ciation	Comments
Kia Rio	NA	NA	The Rio is one of the lowest-priced cars sold in the U.S. Expect to get what you pay for. It's based on the dreadful Ford Aspire, which was made for Ford by Kia in the mid-1990s.
Kia Sedona	○	NA	The Sedona is the first Korean minivan to be sold in the U.S. It's relatively refined, but not very nimble or quick.
Kia Sorento	NEW	NA	Larger than the outdated Sportage, this body-on-frame SUV competes with the car-based Honda CR-V and Hyundai Santa Fe. It's similar in size and concept to the Nissan Xterra.
Kia Spectra	NA	NA	Available as a sedan or hatchback, the Spectra trails the competition in just about every way. It suffers from a noisy cabin, a poor ride, an unrefined powertrain, and clumsy handling.
Land Rover Discovery	NA	○	The Discovery is designed primarily for off-road use, which compromises its on-road dynamics. The steering is imprecise, and the ride is stiff and choppy. Controls are not intuitive.
Land Rover Freelander	NA	NA	The Freelander offers full-time AWD and fully independent suspension. Ride and handling are commendable and it's quite capable off-road. But it's noisy, thirsty, and not very quick. Its controls are confusing. **Last road test: May 2002**
Land Rover Range Rover	NEW	NA	Redesigned for 2003, this Range Rover was developed under the former corporate parent BMW. It delivers improved performance, comfort, and refinement, with interior details comparable to those found in similarly priced luxury sedans.
✓ **Lexus ES300**	⊖	⊖	The ES300 is a quiet, comfortable, easy-going car with a nicely trimmed interior. The V6 is smooth and powerful. Handling though, is not its forte. **Last road test: Mar. 2002**
✓ **Lexus GS300/GS430**	⊖	⊖	These sedans are sportier and less expensive than Lexus's LS430 flagship. Ride and handling are competent but unexceptional for this class. Seating is comfortable, but the rear is tight for three.
Lexus GX470	NEW	NA	The new-for-2003 GX470 is a Lexus version of the redesigned Toyota 4Runner. It shares a powertrain and many of the LX470's luxury appointments, and offers a third seat.
✓ **Lexus IS300**	⊖	NA	This rear-drive sedan has a smooth, powerful inline Six and handles and brakes very capably. But the trunk is small and the rear seat tight. A hatchback version is called the SportCross. **Last road test: May 2001**
Lexus LS430	⊖	○	Lexus's flagship is one of the world's finest luxury sedans. The engine and transmission are extremely smooth, and the ride is smooth, supple, and quiet.
Lexus LX470	NA	○	This luxury SUV, based on the Toyota Land Cruiser, features a height-adjustable suspension and a well-equipped interior. Like the Cruiser, it has a smooth engine and transmission, full-time 4WD, and a comfortable, quiet ride.
✓ **Lexus RX300**	⊖	⊖	A car-based SUV, the RX300 is easy and pleasant to drive. Handling is secure with the standard stability control but unremarkable. The ride is comfortable and quiet. Unlike the Acura MDX, however, it has no third seat. **Last road test: July 2001**

Model	Predicted reliability	Depre-ciation	Comments
Lexus SC430	○	NA	This convertible features an electrically operated hard top. Power comes from the potent and refined V8 used in the GS and LS sedans. Handling, though, isn't as sporty as some of its competitors.
Lincoln Aviator	NEW	NA	The Aviator is a Lincoln version of the Ford Explorer and Mercury Mountaineer. It has a modern, powerful V8, many luxury features, and styling reflective of the Lincoln Navigator.
Lincoln LS	●	○	The LS is a capable rear-drive sedan with a smooth powertrain, agile handling, and a firm, comfortable ride. The optional V8 is far more muscular than the V6. Cabin storage is sparse and road noise is pronounced for this class. **Last road test: Oct. 1999**
Lincoln Navigator	NEW	NA	Redesigned for 2003, the Navigator has a flexible interior and a fully independent suspension that provides much-improved ride and handling. It's basically the same as the Ford Expedition, but with different styling and more luxury features.
✓ Lincoln Town Car	○	●	The Town Car is the last of the domestic rear-wheel-drive luxury cruisers. The ride is smooth, and handling is OK. The front seats are soft but poorly shaped. The rear seats three with ease, and the trunk is very large.
Mazda 6	NEW	NA	The Mazda 6 replaces the 626. It competes against the likes of the Honda Accord and Toyota Camry and comes with a Mazda 4-cylinder or Ford 3.0-liter V6. Hatchback and wagon versions will debut later.
Mazda B-Series	◐	◐	This is a compact Ford Ranger pickup with a Mazda nameplate. Handling is not that clumsy for a truck, but the ride is stiff and jiggly. The 4.0-liter SOHC V6 is a welcome option. The rear seats in the extended-cab version are tight.
✓ Mazda MPV	⊖	○	The MPV minivan is smaller and narrower than most competitors but has some clever interior details, such as a fold-flat third-row seat. It rides fairly well and handles securely. **Last road test: Mar. 2000**
✓ Mazda MX-5 Miata	⊖	○	Zesty performance, nimble handling, and precise steering make this a fun if noisy car to drive. The interior, though, is cramped for tall people. **Last road test: Aug. 1998**
✓ Mazda Protegé	⊖	○	This small sedan has fallen behind its main competitors, the Honda Civic and Toyota Corolla. Handling is secure, but the ride is stiff, choppy, and noisy. The Protegé5 is a small wagon version. **Last road test: July 2002**
Mazda RX-8	NEW	NA	The new RX-8 revives the rotary-engine Mazda sports cars made famous by the RX-7. The new coupe is nominally a four-seater, with access to the rear seats aided by rear-hinged rear doors.
Mazda Tribute	◐	NA	The car-based Tribute is a cousin of the Ford Escape. The Tribute is slightly nimbler but has a stiffer ride. It offers good interior space and a powerful V6, but too much wind and road noise penetrates the cabin. **Last road test: Mar. 2001**

Model	Predicted reliability	Depre-ciation	Comments
Mercedes-Benz C-Class	●	⊖	The C-Class is Mercedes' entry level series, with sedan, coupe, and wagon versions available. These models offer quick acceleration, a quiet, comfortable ride, and agile, secure handling. The seats are exceptionally comfortable and supportive, but the rear is tight. **Last road test: May 2001**
Mercedes-Benz CLK	NEW	NA	Redesigned for 2003, the CLK accelerates quickly and handles well. It rides comfortably. Rear seating is reasonably hospitable for a coupe. The convertible version is still the old model.
Mercedes-Benz E-Class	NEW	NA	Redesigned for 2003. The outgoing version combined spirited acceleration with acceptable fuel economy, and precise handling with a luxurious ride. The seats and driving position were first class. The 2003 version should be similar.
Mercedes-Benz M-Class	●	⊖	This SUV is relatively civilized on the road and fairly capable off-road. Both the V6 and V8 engines are smooth and powerful. The cabin is spacious, and the seats are comfortable. **Last road test: June 2000**
Mercedes-Benz S-Class	●	⊖	The S-Class sedans and their CL coupe cousins are among the world's most expensive luxury cars. Both are loaded with state-of-the-art convenience and safety equipment. They're comfortable and quiet, with handling capabilities belying their size.
Mercedes-Benz SLK	◒	⊖	This two-seat convertible has an electrically retractable hardtop, which makes this car feel almost as solid as a fixed-roof coupe. The SLK's chief liability is its steering, which lacks precision and feedback, and makes the driving experience not as sporty as some might expect. **Last road test: June 2002**
Mercury Grand Marquis	◒	◒	A big, quiet, comfortable-riding sedan, the Grand Marquis handles well for a car this large. Braking and emergency handling are fairly good. Rear leg room is skimpier than you might expect.
Mercury Mountaineer	●	NA	The much-improved Mountaineer has an independent suspension, an optional third-row seat, and up-to-date safety gear. In contrast with its twin, the Ford Explorer, the Mountaineer comes only with AWD, with no low range.
✔ **Mercury Sable**	○	●	A twin of the Ford Taurus, this roomy sedan is showing its age. The ride is firm and well controlled. The front seat is available as a bench seat. The rear seat can hold three adults comfortably, but access is difficult. The Sable is also available as a wagon with a rear-facing third row seat. **Last road test: May 2000**
Mini Cooper	NA	NA	The diminutive Mini, from BMW, blends much of the old model's rakish charm with modern levels of creature comforts. Handling is extremely agile, but the ride is choppy. Even tall people will find the cockpit adequately roomy, but the rear is very tight. **Last road test: Oct. 2002**
Mitsubishi Diamante	NA	◒	This mid-luxury sedan is nice enough, but doesn't measure up to key competitors. Its strongest assets are a lively engine and a nifty sound system, but ride, handling, and interior room are all unimpressive. **Last road test: Oct. 1999**

Model	Predicted reliability	Depreciation	Comments
✔ **Mitsubishi Eclipse**	○	○	A powerful engine in the GT version is this coupe's major appeal. The cockpit is cramped. Handling and braking are nothing special, and the ride is stiff and busy. **Last road test: Aug. 2000**
✔ **Mitsubishi Galant**	○	◑	This sedan's high points include smooth V6 power and a competitive price. Handling is fairly nimble, and the ride is fairly comfortable. The front seats aren't very comfortable, and the rear is cramped. **Last road test: July 2000**
Mitsubishi Lancer	NA	NA	This small sedan falls short of the competition–and offers no price advantage. Handling is clumsy, the ride unsettled, and the interior noisy. **Last road test: July 2002**
Mitsubishi Montero	NA	NA	We rated the 2001 Montero Limited Not Acceptable after it exhibited repeated tip-ups in our avoidance maneuver test. The 2003 model gets a stability-controlled system.
Mitsubishi Montero Sport	○	●	The Montero Sport is very trucklike. Common road bumps deliver stiff, rubbery kicks, and even the highway ride is jittery. Handling is rather cumbersome, and access is awkward.
Mitsubishi Outlander	NEW	NA	Think of the Outlander as Mitsubishi's answer to the Subaru Forester: a practical, small car-based SUV with well-thought-out interior packaging with either front- or all-wheel drive.
Nissan 350Z	NEW	NA	The new 350Z revives Nissan's famous Z line of sports cars. It's a two-seater hatchback coupe sharing underpinnings and a smooth-revving 3.5-liter V6 with the Infiniti G35.
✔ **Nissan Altima**	○	NA	The new Altima is a roomy sedan with a strong four-cylinder or V6 engine and secure handling, But the ride is only so-so, and interior fit and finish includes many plastic surfaces that look and feel cheap. **Last road test: Jan. 2002**
Nissan Frontier	○	◑	This compact pickup is fairly crude. An optional supercharged V6 adds some oomph but whines annoyingly. Handling is cumbersome and the ride awful. **Last road test: Aug. 2001**
✔ **Nissan Maxima**	◕	○	The Maxima is a good family sedan, with an outstanding engine, a roomy and quiet interior, and good fit and finish. Handling is secure, although the ride is a bit stiff. A redesigned version is due in spring 2003. **Last road test: May 2000**
Nissan Murano	NEW	NA	The Murano is a car-based SUV derived from the Altima sedan. A smooth V6 links to a continuously variable transmission with seven "manual" shift points for more shift control. The rear seat is cramped and cargo space is limited.
✔ **Nissan Pathfinder**	◕	○	This midsized SUV has a tolerable ride and handles securely. Cargo space is modest. A powerful V6 and outstanding reliability are pluses. Four-wheel drive is part-time on all trim lines but the LE . **Last road test: Sep. 2001**
✔ **Nissan Sentra**	○	○	This is a solid small sedan with a refined powertrain, decent handling, and a well-designed interior. But ride comfort, braking, and rear-seat room fall short. **Last road test: Sep. 2000**

Model	Predicted reliability	Depre- ciation	Comments
Nissan Xterra	○	⊖	The Xterra has all the advantages and flaws of a truck-based SUV: good cargo space, towing capacity, and off-road capability, but also clumsy handling, an uncomfortable ride, leisurely acceleration, and poor fuel economy. Stability control has been added for 2003. **Last road test: Oct. 2000**
Oldsmobile Alero	⊖	●	A cousin of the Pontiac Grand Am, the Alero is Olds' entry-level sedan and coupe. Handling is secure and fairly agile in V6 models. The ride is a bit jittery. The interior is cheap, and rear head room is tight. 2003 is this model's last year. **Last road test: June 2001**
Oldsmobile Aurora	⊖	NA	Built on the same platform as the Buick LeSabre and Pontiac Bonneville. the Aurora is quiet, roomy, and comfortable. Handling is sound, helped out by electronic stability control. **Last road test: Nov. 2000**
Oldsmobile Bravada	●	NA	The Bravada is similar to the Chevrolet TrailBlazer and the GMC Envoy. It's quiet and spacious, with a comfortable ride and a spirited inline six-cylinder engine. Handling is ponderous, though, and the brakes are unimpressive. After the 2003 model year, the Bravada will essentially be rebadged as the Buick Rainier.
Oldsmobile Silhouette	⊖	⊖	This well-designed minivan, like its cousin, the Chevy Venture, has a responsive powertrain and comfortable seating. Subpar reliability and poor performance in an offset crash test keep it out of contention. **Last road test: Jan. 2001**
Pontiac Aztek	○	NA	This minivan-derived SUV includes some innovative interior touches and lots of neat little storage nooks. The rear seat is too low, though, and the rear gate is a nuisance. AWD is available.
Pontiac Bonneville	○	⊖	Pontiac's flagship sedan offers lots of gadgets and frills. The SE has a supple, well-controlled ride. Handling is taut, though not sporty. **Last road test: Feb. 2000**
Pontiac Grand Am	⊖	●	Pontiac's best-selling model has little to recommend it. The Grand Am's handling is adequate but not agile and its ride is unremarkable. Wind noise is quite pronounced. The cabin offers plenty of headroom, but the front seats are soft and unsupportive. **Last road test: Jan. 1999**
Pontiac Grand Prix	○	●	With its heavy steering, stiff suspension, and busy, overly firm ride, the Grand Prix tries—mostly unsuccessfully—to be sporty. Handling is forgiving and secure, but the car isn't particularly agile. Flimsy and cheap-looking plastic trim give the interior a low-rent feel. **Last road test: Feb. 2002**
Pontiac Montana	⊖	⊖	This minivan is competitive in most ways, but its subpar reliability and poor offset-crash-test performance keep it out of contention. The third-row seat folds flat into the cargo floor, a handy design. All-wheel drive is optional. **Last road test: Jan. 2001**
Pontiac Sunfire	○	●	The Sunfire, cousin of the Chevy Cavalier, is basic transportation only—crude and outdated. The ride is noisy and hard. Seats are uncomfortable, and interior fit and finish are subpar. For 2003 it's available as a coupe only.

Model	Predicted reliability	Depreciation	Comments
✔ **Pontiac Vibe**	⊖	NA	The Vibe, twin of the Toyota Matrix, is a roomy small wagon that's easy to get people and cargo in and out of. Handling and ride are OK, but the engine is noisy and the driving position is not ideal. All-wheel drive is optional. **Last road test: Aug. 2002**
✔ **Porsche Boxster**	⊖	⊖	This roadster is everything a sports car should be. With front and rear storage compartments, it's almost practical. Handling and braking are superb, and the ride is firm but not punishing. Lowering the top is very easy. A glass rear window arrives for 2003. **Last road test: June 2002**
Porsche Cayenne	NEW	NA	The Cayenne, Porsche's first SUV, was codeveloped with the upcoming 2004 Volkswagen Touareg. It's a midsized car-based design with all-wheel drive and a high-end pricetag. It comes with a choice of two Porsche V8 engines.
Saab 9-3	NEW	NA	The 9-3 gets its first redesign since 1994, this time as a sedan, not a hatchback. The new turbo engine is less hesitant than in the predecessor. Handling is improved. Some controls are friendlier.
✔ **Saab 9-5**	⊖	○	The 9-5 is competent and pleasant to drive, with a firm, compliant ride. Front seats are comfortable, and the rear is relatively roomy. The wagon is well designed but has no third-seat option.
Saturn Ion	NEW	NA	The Ion replaces Saturn's long-running S-Series. Roomier and with a more refined engine, it's still a fairly plain small sedan. The coupe version has rear-hinged back doors for easier access.
Saturn L-Series	⊖	⊖	The midsized L-Series tries to compete with the VW Passat, Toyota Camry, and Honda Accord. The strong V6 and automatic work very well. Handling is competent and secure, but not nimble, and the ride is a bit stiff and noisy. **Last road test: Jan. 2000**
✔ **Saturn VUE**	○	NA	The VUE's handling is carlike and secure, but the steering is too light at low speeds and the AWD system is slow to respond. Interior fit and finish are subpar, the front seats lack support, and the rear bench is too low. **Last road test: May 2002**
Subaru Baja	NEW	NA	This four-passenger, four-door pickup is essentially a Subaru Outback with no rear roof section. A fold-down hatch between the cabin and cargo bed allows longer items to extend into the cabin.
✔ **Subaru Forester**	⊖	⊖	One of the best small SUVs, the car-based Forester has a roomy cargo area and a controlled, compliant ride. Handling is relatively responsive and acceleration adequate. The rear seat is a bit cramped. **Last road test: Oct. 2000**
✔ **Subaru Impreza**	○	⊖	The small Impreza delivers agile handling and a supple, controlled ride. The line includes an Outback Sport, a wagon, and the sporty turbo-powered WRX, available as sedan or wagon. **Last road test: July 2002**
✔ **Subaru Legacy/ Outback**	⊖	○	The all-wheel-drive Legacy feels almost as agile as a sports sedan. The ride is firm but supple. It's also available in wagon models, including the Outback, which is a reasonable alternative to a car-based SUV. **Last road test: Mar. 2000**

Model	Predicted reliability	Depreciation	Comments
Suzuki Aerio	NA	NA	The Aerio replaces the unimpressive Esteem as Suzuki's only non-SUV offering in the U.S. It features a tall roofline designed to increase head room and improve outward visibility. It's available in sedan and four-door wagon/hatchback versions.
✔ **Suzuki Vitara/XL-7**	○	◗	These small, truck-based SUVs are hampered by a crude, unresponsive automatic transmission and a stiff ride. Handling is vague but secure. The driver's seat lacks support, and the cockpit feels narrow. The extended-length XL-7 has a small, cramped third-row seat. **Last road test: May 2002**
Toyota 4Runner	NEW	NA	The 4Runner, redesigned for 2003, is much roomier. It's still a conventional body-on-frame design. At first only a V8 will be offered, with a new V6 coming later in the model year.
✔ **Toyota Avalon**	◕	○	The Avalon is an upscale Camry with an extra-roomy rear seat and trunk. It features interior ambience similar to that of a Lexus, a powerful V6, and a quiet cabin. The seats are large and comfortable. **Last road test: Feb. 2000**
✔ **Toyota Camry**	○	NA	The Camry remains an excellent sedan—quiet, refined, secure. Both the Four and V6 are smooth and responsive. Cabin controls are logical, with plenty of storage. Lack of front-seat thigh support and a telescoping wheel makes finding a comfortable driving postion difficult for some. **Last road test: Jan. 2002**
✔ **Toyota Camry Solara**	◕	○	The Solara is a sportier two-door version of the previous-generation Camry. The ride is well controlled, handling is fairly nimble, and the cabin is hushed. A convertible is available.
✔ **Toyota Celica**	◕	◕	The Celica is a fun-to-drive sporty coupe that handles nimbly. The ride is pretty good for a sporty car. The budget-minded may prefer the plain GT, which is isn't as quick or agile as the high-revving GT-S, but is about $4,500 cheaper. **Last road test: Aug. 2000**
✔ **Toyota Corolla**	◕	NA	The Corolla, redesigned for 2003, is a very good small car, now much roomier and with a higher-quality interior. It handles and rides better than the previous version. The standard four-cylinder engine delivers both responsive performance and excellent fuel economy. **Last road test: July 2002**
✔ **Toyota Echo**	◕	◕	The Echo is a surprisingly roomy small runabout. The driving position is fairly high, and it's easy to get in and out. The 1.5-liter 108-hp engine provides excellent fuel economy. **Last road test: Dec. 2000**
✔ **Toyota Highlander**	◕	NA	This Camry-derived all-wheel-drive SUV is roomy, quiet, comfortable, and well designed. It offers a responsive four-cylinder engine or a punchy V6. One of our top-rated SUVs, it scored slightly better than the similar, more expensive Lexus RX300. **Last road test: Oct. 2001**
✔ **Toyota Land Cruiser**	◕	◕	This big, expensive SUV sports a smooth, quiet 4.7-liter V8 and rides smoothly and quietly. The interior offers lots of room and a third seat. Permanent 4WD is standard. Stability control, also standard, makes handling more secure. **Last road test: Mar. 2001**

Model	Predicted reliability	Depre-ciation	Comments
✔ Toyota Matrix	⊖	NA	A twin of the Pontiac Vibe, the Matrix is a roomy small wagon that's easy to get people and cargo in and out of. Handling and ride are OK, but the engine is noisy and the driving position is not ideal. AWD is optional. **Last road test: Aug. 2002**
✔ Toyota MR2 Spyder	⊜	⊜	Think of this sporty mid-engine convertible as a small Porsche Boxster at a Mazda Miata price. It offers impressive steering and acceleration, precise shifting, and excellent brakes, but luggage space is close to zero. **Last road test: Aug. 2000**
✔ Toyota Prius	⊜	NA	The Prius managed 41 mpg in our tests, thanks to its gas-electric hybrid powerplant. It seats five and provides adequate acceleration, secure handling, and a comfortable ride, making it a good choice as a small, economy car. **Last road test: Dec. 2000**
✔ Toyota RAV4	⊖	⊜	The RAV4 is one of our top-rated small SUVs. It has a flexible interior layout, easy access, nimble handling, and excellent brakes. There's still no V6, but the four-cylinder engine accelerates adequately. **Last road test: Mar. 2001**
✔ Toyota Sequoia	⊜	NA	The full-sized Sequoia competes against the Ford Expedition and Chevrolet Tahoe. It's roomier than the Land Cruiser, but rides stiffly and handles clumsily though securely with the standard stability control. It boasts a V8 powertrain and a third-row seat. Side-curtain air bags are optional. **Last road test: Nov. 2002**
✔ Toyota Sienna	⊜	⊜	One of our higher-rated minivans, the Sienna rides quietly and smoothly. Front- and middle-row seats are comfortable. The third-row seat is a bit cramped. Stability control is optional. A redesigned 2004 model is due in spring 2003. **Last road test: Jan. 2001**
✔ Toyota Tacoma	⊖	⊜	The compact, utilitarian Tacoma pickup is a super off-roader but rides uncomfortably and handles ponderously. Acceleration is adequate with the V6. The seats are low and flat, making for an uncomfortable driving position. **Last road test: Aug. 2001**
✔ Toyota Tundra	⊜	⊜	The Tundra is a high-rated full-sized pickup. The V8 is smooth and powerful, the cabin is quiet, and the ride is pleasant. The rear seat in extended-cab versions is very cramped. **Last road test: Nov. 1999**
Volkswagen EuroVan	NA	◖	The EuroVan is so large it can hardly be considered a minivan. It lacks the interior flexibility of most modern minivans, but offers a dedicated Camper version.
Volkswagen Golf	●	⊖	The Golf's responsive but noisy 2.0-liter Four and easy-shifting manual perform well together. You can also get a smooth, powerful V6, a 1.8-liter turbo Four, or a diesel engine. The ride is supple. The front seats offer good, firm support, but the rear is cramped. **Last road test: Dec. 2000**
Volkswagen Jetta	◖	⊖	The Jetta shares underpinnings with the Golf and boasts many thoughtful details, a comfortable ride, and responsive handling. The front seats are supportive; the rear is cramped. The standard 2.0-liter Four is noisy, the diesel is economical but slow and noisy. **Last road test: Dec. 2002**

Model	Predicted reliability	Depre-ciation	Comments
Volkswagen New Beetle	◒	⊖	The modern, well-equipped New Beetle rides and handles well. The front seats are supportive, but the rear is cramped. A 180-hp Turbo S model is quick but not very sporty. **Last road test: Oct. 2002**
✓ **Volkswagen Passat**	○	⊖	Our top-rated family sedan is roomy and comfortable. The Passat handles precisely and delivers a firm yet supple ride. The interior appointments have a high-quality feel. All-wheel drive is available in V6 sedans and wagons and is standard on the eight-cylinder W8 version. **Last road test: Jan. 2002**
Volkswagen Touareg	NEW	NA	Codeveloped with the Porsche Cayenne, the Touareg is a midsized car-based SUV. With low-range gearing and advanced electronics, it promises better off-road capability than most car-based models. It comes with a V6, but no third seat.
Volvo C70	NA	○	A convertible based on the old Volvo S70 sedan, the C70's handling is capable but not sporty, and the brakes work well. The coupe version has been discontinued and this is the last year for the convertible.
Volvo S40/V40	◒	○	The S40 sedan and V40 wagon are cramped and a bit noisy. Handling is secure and the brakes are excellent, but the ride is stiff. The engine is responsive, and the wagon offers optional built-in booster seats. **Last road test: Jan. 2000**
✓ **Volvo S60**	○	NA	The S60 tries to compete with the BMW 3-Series, but it's not as sporty or comfortable. It comes with a plethora of advanced safety gear, and an all-wheel-drive version is available. More horsepower has been added to AWD models for 2003. **Last road test: May 2001**
Volvo S80	●	○	Volvo's front-drive flagship performs well in its class. It's roomy, quiet, and comfortable. The base engine is a smooth straight six-cylinder engine; the turbocharged T6 version offers effortless acceleration. **Last road test: Oct. 1999**
✓ **Volvo V70/ XC70**	○	○	The V70 is a spacious, comfortable wagon, and very quick in T5 trim. The XC70 Cross Country model is an SUV alternative that rides and handles more roughly than the V70. Horsepower was increased in AWD models for 2003. **Last road test: July 2001**
Volvo XC90	NEW	NA	This new seven-seater is Volvo's first real SUV. It's a unibody vehicle based on the S80 sedan and powered by either an inline five- or six-cylinder engine, both turbocharged. Expect the latest in safety gear.

RATINGS OF THE 2003 MODELS

Which cars are best? This section can give you a head start in answering that question. Included here are overall Ratings on 154 vehicles from CONSUMER REPORTS extensive testing program. Though most tests were conducted on 2002 or slightly earlier models, results still apply since cars typically change little from year to year.

Recommended models are indicated with a (✔). They performed competently in our tests; our survey data indicate they should have at least average reliability; and they have not performed poorly in any crash tests. Twins and triplets (similar models sold under different nameplates) are grouped together in the chart below and marked with (■) symbols when only one version has been tested. **Overall mpg** is based on our tests in a range of mixed highway and city driving conditions.

Listed within type, in order of performance

Make and model	Overall score P F G VG E	Overall mpg	Tested model
SMALL SEDANS			
Ford Focus		24	ZTS 2.0 Four; auto 4
✔ Honda Civic		29	EX 1.7 Four; auto 4
✔ Honda Civic		36	Hybrid 1.3 Four; CVT
✔ Toyota Prius		41	1.5 Four; CVT
Volkswagen Jetta		32	GLS 1.9 Four turbodiesel; auto 4
✔ Toyota Corolla		29	LE 1.8 Four; auto 4
Hyundai Elantra		25	GLS 2.0 Four; auto 4
✔ Subaru Impreza		22	2.5 RS 2.5 Four; auto 4
✔ Mazda Protegé		26	LX 2.0 Four; auto 4
✔ Nissan Sentra		26	GXE 1.8 Four; auto 4
Dodge Neon		23	ES 2.0 Four; auto 3
Mitsubishi Lancer		26	LS 2.0 Four; auto 4
Chevrolet Cavalier		23	LS 2.4 Four; auto 4
FUEL-EFFICIENT CARS			
Volkswagen Golf		41	GLS 1.9 Four turbodiesel; man 5
✔ Honda Civic		36	Hybrid 1.3 Four; CVT
✔ Toyota Prius		41	1.5 Four; CVT
Volkswagen Jetta		32	GLS 1.9 Four turbodiesel; auto 4
✔ Toyota Echo		38	1.5 Four; man 5
Honda Insight		51	1.0 Three; man 5

Make and model	Overall score (P F G VG E)	Overall mpg	Tested model
FAMILY SEDANS			
✔ Volkswagen Passat		22	GLS 2.8 V6; auto 5
✔ Toyota Camry		20	XLE 3.0 V6; auto 4
✔ Volkswagen Passat		23	GLS 1.8 Four turbo; auto 5
✔ Toyota Camry		24	LE 2.4 Four; auto 4
✔ Nissan Maxima		21	GXE 3.0 V6; auto 4
✔ Nissan Altima		20	SE 3.5 V6; auto 4
✔ Nissan Altima		22	S 2.5 Four; auto 4
Volvo S40		22	1.9 Four turbo; auto 4
✔ Subaru Legacy		22	L 2.5 Four; auto 4
✔ Hyundai Sonata		21	GLS 2.5 V6; auto 4
✔ Mitsubishi Galant		22	ES 3.0 V6; auto 4
✔ Chevrolet Malibu		22	LS 3.1 V6; auto 4
✔ Chevrolet Impala		20	LS 3.8 V6; auto 4
✔ ▪ Ford Taurus		21	SE 3.0 V6; auto 4
✔ ▪ Mercury Sable		21	Ford Taurus SE 3.0 V6; auto 4
Oldsmobile Alero		20	GL 3.4 V6; auto 4
✔ Dodge Intrepid		19	ES 3.5 V6; auto 4
▪ Chrysler Sebring		21	LX 2.7 V6; auto 4
▪ Dodge Stratus		21	Chrysler Sebring LX 2.7 V6; auto 4
Saturn L-Series		23	LS1 2.2 Four; auto 4
Pontiac Grand Am		23	SE 2.4 Four; auto 4
Pontiac Grand Prix		19	GT 3.8 V6; auto 4
UPSCALE SEDANS			
BMW 3-Series		22	330i 3.0 Six; auto 5
✔ Lexus IS300		21	3.0 Six; auto 5
Mercedes-Benz C-Class		21	C320 3.2 V6; auto 5
✔ Lexus ES300		21	3.0 V6; auto 5
Lincoln LS		23	3.0 V6; auto 5
Audi A4		20	Quattro 3.0 V6; auto 5
✔ Acura TL		22	Type-S 3.2 V6; auto 5
Oldsmobile Aurora		19	4.0 V8; auto 4
✔ Infiniti I35		20	3.5 V6; auto 4
Jaguar X-Type		19	3.0 V6; auto 5
✔ Volvo S60		21	2.4T 2.4 Five turbo; auto 5
✔ Chrysler 300M		21	3.5 V6; auto 4
Mitsubishi Diamante		20	3.5 V6; auto 4

Make and model	Overall score	Overall mpg	Tested model
	P F G VG E		
⮞ **LARGE SEDANS**			
✔ Toyota Avalon		21	XLS 3.0 V6; auto 4
Pontiac Bonneville		20	SE 3.8 V6; auto 4
✔ Buick LeSabre		20	Limited 3.8 V6; auto 4
⮞ **LUXURY SEDANS**			
✔ BMW 5-Series		19	530i 3.0 Six; auto 5
Audi A6		18	2.7T 2.7 V6 turbo; auto 5
Cadillac DeVille		19	DHS 4.6 V8; auto 4
✔ Acura RL		21	3.5 V6; auto 4
Volvo S80		21	Base 2.9 Six; auto 4
Jaguar S-Type		20	3.0 V6; auto 5
⮞ **SPORTY CARS**			
Ford Focus		24	SVT 2.0 Four; man 6
✔ Subaru Impreza		21	WRX 2.0 Four turbo; man 5
✔ Toyota Celica		28	GT-S 1.8 Four; man 6
Mini Cooper		31	Base 1.6 Four; man 5
Volkswagen New Beetle		25	Turbo S 1.8 Four turbo; man 6
✔ Honda Civic		26	Si 2.0 Four; man 5
✔ Acura RSX		26	Type-S 2.0 Four; man 6
Hyundai Tiburon		21	GT 2.7 V6; man 6
✔ Mitsubishi Eclipse		24	GT 3.0 V6; man 5
⮞ **ROADSTERS**			
✔ Honda S2000		27	2.0 Four; man 6
Chevrolet Corvette		21	Base conv. 5.7 V8; man 6
✔ Porsche Boxster		22	Base 2.7 Six; man 5
✔ Toyota MR2		31	1.8 Four; man 5
Mercedes-Benz SLK		23	SLK320 3.2 V6; man 6
Audi TT		22	Conv. AWD 1.8 Four turbo; man 6
✔ Mazda MX-5 Miata		27	1.8 Four; man 5
Ford Thunderbird		17	Premium 3.9 V8; auto 5
⮞ **MINIVANS**			
✔ Honda Odyssey		19	EX 3.5 V6; auto 4
✔ Toyota Sienna		18	LE 3.0 V6; auto 4
▪ Chrysler Town & Country		17	Dodge Grand Caravan Sport 3.3 V6; auto 4
▪ Dodge Grand Caravan		17	Sport 3.3 V6; auto 4
✔ Mazda MPV		18	LX 2.5 V6; auto 4
▪ Chevrolet Venture		19	LS 3.4 V6; auto 4
▪ Oldsmobile Silhouette		19	Chevrolet Venture LS 3.4 V6; auto 4

Make and model	Overall score	Overall mpg	Tested model
	P F G VG E		
⊳ **MINIVANS** *continued*			
▪ Pontiac Montana		19	Chevrolet Venture LS 3.4 V6; auto 4
Ford Windstar		17	SE Sport 3.8 V6; auto 4
⊳ **WAGONS & FOUR-DOOR HATCHBACKS**			
✓ Volkswagen Passat		18	GLX 4Motion 2.8 V6; auto 5
✓ Volkswagen Passat		21	GLS 1.8 Four turbo; auto 5
Audi Allroad		16	2.7 V6 turbo; auto 5
Ford Focus Wagon		23	SE 2.0 Four; auto 4
Volkswagen Jetta Wagon		23	GLS 1.8 Four turbo; auto 5
✓ Subaru Legacy Outback		20	H6 VDC 3.0 Six; auto 4
✓ Subaru Legacy Outback		20	Limited 2.5 Four; auto 4
✓ Volvo V70		18	XC 2.4 Five turbo; auto 5
✓ Toyota Matrix		24	XR AWD 1.8 Four; auto 4
✓ Pontiac Vibe		26	Base 1.8 Four; auto 4
Ford Focus Hatchback		24	ZX5 2.0 Four; auto 4
Volvo V40		21	1.9 Four turbo; auto 4
✓ Chrysler PT Cruiser		18	Limited 2.4 Four; auto 4
✓ Mazda Protegé5		25	2.0 Four; auto 4
Saturn L-Series		21	LW2 3.0 V6; auto 4
✓ Subaru Impreza Outback		22	Sport 2.5 Four; auto 4
⊳ **SMALL SPORT-UTILITY VEHICLES**			
✓ Toyota RAV4		22	2.0 Four; auto 4
✓ Subaru Forester		20	S 2.5 Four; auto 4
✓ ▪ Pontiac Vibe		24	Toyota Matrix XR AWD 1.6 Four; auto 4
✓ ▪ Toyota Matrix		24	XR AWD 1.6 Four; auto 4
✓ Honda CR-V		21	EX 2.4 Four; auto 4
✓ Hyundai Santa Fe		18	GLS 2.7 V6; auto 4
Ford Escape		17	XLT 3.0 V6; auto 4
Mazda Tribute		17	LX 3.0 V6; auto 4
✓ Saturn VUE		18	3.0 V6; auto 5
Land Rover Freelander		17	SE 2.5 V6; auto 5
✓ Suzuki XL-7		17	Touring 2.7 V6; auto 4
✓ Jeep Liberty		15	Sport 3.7 V6, auto 4
Nissan Xterra		15	SE 3.3 V6; auto 4

Make and model	Overall score	Overall mpg	Tested model
	P F G VG E		

⮞ SPORT-UTILITY VEHICLES

Make and model	Overall score	Overall mpg	Tested model
Audi Allroad		16	2.7 V6 turbo; auto 5
BMW X5		15	4.4i V8; auto 5
✔ Honda Pilot		19	EX 3.5 V6; auto 5
✔ Toyota Highlander		18	Limited 3.0 V6; auto 4
✔ Acura MDX		18	3.5 V6; auto 5
✔ Lexus RX300		19	3.0 V6; auto 4
✔ Subaru Legacy Outback		20	H6 VDC 3.0 Six; auto 4
✔ Volvo V70		18	XC 2.4 Five turbo; auto 5
✔ Toyota Land Cruiser		14	4.7 V8; auto 4
Mercedes-Benz M-Class		15	ML430 4.3 V8; auto 5
✔ Toyota Sequoia		15	Limited 4.7 V8; auto 4
✔ ▪ Chevrolet Suburban		13	LT 5.3 V8; auto 4
✔ ▪ GMC Yukon XL		13	Chevrolet Suburban LT 5.3 V8; auto 4
Ford Explorer		16	XLT 4.0 V6; auto 5
Ford Expedition		12	Eddie Bauer 5.4 V8; auto 4
✔ Nissan Pathfinder		16	LE 3.5 V6; auto 4
Buick Rendezvous		16	CXL 3.4 V6; auto 4
✔ ▪ Chevrolet Tahoe		13	LT 5.3 V8; auto 4
✔ ▪ GMC Yukon		13	Chevrolet Tahoe LT 5.3 V8; auto 4
▪ Chevrolet TrailBlazer		15	GMC Envoy SLE 4.2 Six; auto 4
▪ GMC Envoy		15	SLE 4.2 Six; auto 4
Dodge Durango		13	SLT Plus 4.7 V8; auto 4
Jeep Grand Cherokee		16	Laredo 4.0 Six; auto 4
Ford Excursion		10	XLT 6.8 V10; auto 4

⮞ COMPACT PICKUP TRUCKS - CREW CAB V6 4WD

Make and model	Overall score	Overall mpg	Tested model
Ford Explorer Sport Trac		15	4.0 V6; auto 5
Dodge Dakota Quad Cab		13	SLT Plus 4.7 V8; auto 4
✔ Toyota Tacoma Double Cab		16	TRD 3.4 V6; auto 4
▪ Chevrolet S-10 Crew Cab		15	LS 4.3 V6; auto 4
▪ GMC Sonoma Crew Cab		15	Chevrolet S-10 LS 4.3 V6; auto 4
Nissan Frontier Crew Cab		14	SC 3.3 V6 supercharged; auto 4

⮞ LARGE PICKUP TRUCKS - V8 4WD

Make and model	Overall score	Overall mpg	Tested model
✔ Chevrolet Avalanche 1500		13	5.3 V8; auto 4
✔ Toyota Tundra extended		15	SR5 4.7 V8; auto 4
✔ ▪ Chevrolet Silverado 1500 ext.		15	LS 5.3 V8; auto 4
✔ ▪ GMC Sierra 1500 extended		15	Chevrolet Silverado LS 5.3 V8; auto 4
Ford F-150 Supercrew		14	XLT 5.4 V8; auto 4
Dodge Ram 1500 Quad cab		12	SLT 4.7 V8; auto 4

THE BEST AND WORST USED CARS

The good news, if you're thinking of buying a used car, is that cars in general are much more reliable than they used to be. The better news: CONSUMER REPORTS reliability surveys can help you limit the used-car risk even further with information about what has actually happened to hundreds of thousands of real-world vehicles.

Every year, CR conducts an extensive survey of car owners, asking them about serious problems that have cropped up in the past 12 months. The survey generates more than half a million responses, which together paint a detailed picture of how cars up to eight years old are holding up.

Vehicles with consistently high reliability year after year that have also done well in CONSUMER REPORTS performance tests are named "CR Good Bets." Most have Japanese nameplates. That's because Japanese cars, whether they're assembled in this country or overseas, have the most consistent records of above-average reliability.

The list of "Reliable used cars by price," on the following two pages, highlights all the cars in the survey that racked up better-than-average reliability scores. They may or may not have done especially well in performance tests. We also list the less reliable models starting on page 178.

The best used cars

You can increase your odds of getting a reliable used car by choosing one of the models listed below.

Acura Integra
Acura RL
Acura TL
BMW 3-Series
Ford Escort
Geo/Chevrolet Prizm
Honda Accord
Honda Civic
Honda CR-V
Honda Odyssey
Infiniti G20
Infiniti I30
Isuzu Oasis
Lexus ES300

Lexus GS300/GS400
Lexus LS400
Lexus RX300
Lincoln Town Car
Mazda Millenia
Mazda MX-5 Miata
Mazda Protegé
Mercury Tracer
Nissan Altima
Nissan Maxima
Nissan Pathfinder
Nissan Sentra
Saab 9-5
Saturn S-Series

Subaru Forester
Subaru Impreza
Subaru Legacy
Toyota 4Runner
Toyota Avalon
Toyota Camry
Toyota Camry Solara
Toyota Celica
Toyota Corolla
Toyota RAV4
Toyota Sienna
Toyota Tacoma

➤ CR GOOD BETS

These models have performed well in CONSUMER REPORTS road tests and have proved to be better than average in overall reliability for the model years 1994 to 2001. Models are listed alphabetically. Some are twins, essentially similar models sold under different nameplates. We've included only the models for which we have sufficient data for at least three model years. Problems with the engine, cooling system, transmission, and driveline are weighted more heavily than other problems in calculating the overall reliability scores for both the best- and worst-car lists.

Reliable used cars by price

These models have shown above-average reliability for the years indicated. Within a price range, models are listed alphabetically by make. Prices are what you'd pay for a typically equipped car with average mileage.

LESS THAN $8,000

FORD Escort '97-99
• Ranger 2WD '94-96
GEO Prizm '94-97
• Tracker '94-96
HONDA Civic '94-95
MAZDA B-Series 2WD '94-95
• MX-5 Miata '94 • Protegé '96-97
MERCURY Tracer '97-98
NISSAN Altima '94 • Pickup '94 • Sentra '96
SUBARU Impreza '94-95
• Legacy '94
SUZUKI Sidekick '94-96
TOYOTA Corolla '94-95
• Tercel '94-96

$8,000-$10,000

ACURA Integra '94
BUICK Century '97
CHEVROLET Lumina '98
• Prizm '98
DODGE Stratus V6 '98
FORD Crown Victoria '95-96
• Ranger 2WD '98
HONDA Accord '94 • Civic '96
INFINITI G20 '94-95
MAZDA B-Series 2WD '96
• MX-5 Miata '95-96
• Protegé '98
MERCURY Grand Marquis '95
• Tracer '99
NISSAN Altima '96-97
• Maxima '94-95 • Pickup

'95-96 • Sentra '97-98
SATURN S-Series '98
SUBARU Impreza '96
• Legacy '95
TOYOTA Camry '94
• Celica '94 • Corolla '96-98
• Pickup '94-95 • T100 '94
• Tercel '97

$10,000-$12,000

ACURA Integra '95-96
BUICK Century '98
CHEVROLET Prizm '99-00
CHRYSLER Cirrus V6 '98
FORD Crown Victoria '97
• F-150 2WD '95
HONDA Accord '95 • Civic '97-98 • Prelude '94-95
INFINITI G20 '96 • J30 '94-95
LINCOLN Town Car '94
MAZDA B-Series 2WD '98
• MX-5 Miata '97 • Protegé '99-00
MERCURY Grand Marquis '96
NISSAN Altima '98 • Maxima '96 • Pathfinder '94-95
• Pickup '97 • Sentra '99
PLYMOUTH Breeze '00
SATURN S-Series '99-00
SUBARU Impreza '97-98
TOYOTA Avalon '95 • Camry '95-96 • Celica '95 • Corolla '99-00 • Echo '00 • Previa '94 • RAV4 '96 • Tacoma '95
VOLVO 940 '94

$12,000-$14,000

ACURA Integra '97
BUICK Century '99-00
CHEVROLET Prizm '01
FORD Crown Victoria '98
• F-150 2WD '98
HONDA Accord '96
• Civic '99 • Odyssey '95
• Prelude '97
INFINITI I30 '96 • Q45 '94
ISUZU Oasis '96
LEXUS ES300 '94
LINCOLN Town Car '95
MAZDA 626 '99 • Millenia '96
• Protegé '01
MERCURY Grand Marquis '97
NISSAN Altima '99 • Frontier '98-99 • Maxima '97
• Sentra '00
SATURN S-Series '01
SUBARU Impreza '99
TOYOTA 4Runner '94-95
• Avalon '96 • Camry '97
• Celica '96 • Corolla '01
• Echo '01 • Previa '95
• RAV4 '97 • T100 '95-96
• Tacoma '96-97
VOLVO 940 '95

$14,000-$16,000

ACURA CL '97 • Integra '98
• Legend '94 • TL '96
BMW 3-Series '94
CHRYSLER Cirrus '00

DODGE Stratus '00

FORD F-150 2WD '99

HONDA Accord '97-98
• Civic '00 • CR-V '97
• Odyssey '96

INFINITI I30 '97 • J30 '97
• Q45 '95

ISUZU Oasis '97

LEXUS ES300 '95

LINCOLN Town Car '96

MAZDA 626 '00

MERCURY Grand Marquis '98

NISSAN Altima '00
• Frontier '00 • Maxima '98
• Pathfinder '96

SUBARU Impreza '00-01
• Legacy '97

TOYOTA Avalon '97 • Camry
'98 • Celica '97 • Previa '96
• RAV4 '98-99 • T100 '97
• Tacoma '98

$16,000–$20,000

ACURA CL '98 • Integra
'99-00 • Legend '95 • RL '96
• TL '97

BMW 3-Series '95

BUICK Century '01 • Regal '00

CHEVROLET Impala '01
• Monte Carlo '00

CHRYSLER PT Cruiser '01

FORD Crown Victoria '99
• F-150 2WD '00

HONDA Accord '99-00 • CR-V
'98-00 • Odyssey '97-98
• Prelude '98

INFINITI G20 '99 • I30 '98

ISUZU Oasis '98

LEXUS ES300 '96 • GS300 '94
• LS400 '94 • SC300/400 '94

LINCOLN Continental '98

• Town Car '97

MAZDA Millenia '97-98
• MPV '00 • MX-5 Miata
'99-00

MERCURY Grand Marquis '99

NISSAN Maxima '99-00
• Pathfinder '97-98

SUBARU Forester '98-00
• Legacy '98-00

TOYOTA 4Runner '96-97
• Avalon '98-99 • Camry
'99-00 • Camry Solara '99-00
• Celica '99-01 • Previa '97
• RAV4 '00 • Sienna '98
• T100 '98 • Tacoma '99-01
• Tundra '00

$20,000–$25,000

ACURA CL '99 • RL '97-98 •
TL '98-99

BMW 3-Series '96-98

HONDA Accord '01 • CR-V '01
• Prelude '99-00

INFINITI G20 '00 • I30 '99
• Q45 '97 • QX4 '97-99

LEXUS ES300 '97-98
• GS300 '95 • LS400 '95
• SC300/SC400 '95

LINCOLN Continental '99
• Town Car '98

MAZDA Millenia '99-00
• MX-5 Miata '01

MERCEDES-BENZ C-Class
'96 • E-Class '95

NISSAN Maxima '01
• Pathfinder '99 • Xterra '00

SUBARU Forester '01
• Legacy '01

TOYOTA 4Runner '98-99
• Avalon '00 • Camry '01
• Camry Solara '01
• Prius '01 • Sienna '99-00
• Tundra '01

VOLKSWAGEN Passat 1.8T
'00-01

$25,000–$30,000

ACURA CL '01 • RL '99
• TL '00-01

BMW 3-Series '99

HONDA Odyssey '01

INFINITI I30 '00-01 • Q45 '98
• QX4 '00

LEXUS ES300 '99-00 • LS400
'96 • SC300/SC400 '96

LINCOLN Continental '00

MERCEDES-BENZ E-Class
'96

NISSAN Pathfinder '00-01

SAAB 9-3 '00

TOYOTA 4Runner '00-01
• Avalon '01 • Highlander '01
• Sienna '01

$30,000 AND UP

ACURA MDX '01 • RL '00

BMW 5-Series '99, '01
• Z3 '00

HONDA S2000 '00-01

INFINITI Q45 '99 • QX4 '01

LEXUS ES300 '01
• GS300/400/430 '98-01
• LS400/430 '97-01
• RX300 '99-01

LINCOLN Town Car '01

MERCEDES-BENZ C-Class
'00 • E-Class '99-00

SAAB 9-5 '00-01

TOYOTA Land Cruiser '99-00
• Sequoia '01

The worst used cars

Some cars have a bad year, while others trail the pack consistently. The vehicles on these lists have had more problems than average. Buying one could be asking for trouble.

Cadillac Catera	Dodge Durango	Jeep Grand Cherokee
Chevrolet Astro	Dodge Grand Caravan ('94-97)	Mercedes-Benz M-Class
Chevrolet Blazer	Dodge Intrepid	Oldsmobile Bravada
Chevrolet Camaro	Dodge Neon	Oldsmobile Cutlass
Chevrolet Malibu	Dodge Ram 1500 4WD	Plymouth Grand Voyager ('94-97)
Chevrolet S-10 V6 4WD	Ford Windstar	Plymouth Neon
Chevrolet Silverado 1500 4WD	GMC Jimmy	Pontiac Firebird
Chrysler New Yorker, LHS	GMC S-15 Sonoma V6 4WD	Pontiac Grand Am
Chrysler Town & Country ('94-97)	GMC Safari	Volkswagen New Beetle
Dodge Dakota 4WD	GMC Sierra 1500 4WD	Volvo S70/V70 AWD
		Volvo S80

➤ RELIABILITY RISKS

The models on this list have been consistently risky buys. They have exhibited multiple years of much worse than average overall reliability for the model years 1994 to 2001. Some are twins or triplets, essentially similar models sold under different nameplates. Models are listed alphabetically.

Used cars to avoid by make and year

Models on this list have shown below-average reliability for the model years indicated.
Listed alphabetically by make, model, and year.

AUDI A4 V6 '97-98
- **A6** '98-01 • **TT** '01

BMW X5 '01

BUICK Park Avenue '97
- **Riviera** '95
- **Roadmaster** '96

CADILLAC Catera '97-99
- **DeVille** '96-97, '00 • **Seville** '94, '96-98, '00-01

CHEVROLET Astro '95-01
- **Blazer** '94-01 • **C1500** '97, '99 • **Camaro** '95-01
- **Caprice** '95-96 • **Cavalier** '94-96, '99 • **Corsica, Beretta** '96 • **Corvette** '99-00
- **Express Van** '96-00
- **K1500** '96, '98-99 • **Lumina APV** '95-96 • **Malibu** '97-01
- **Monte Carlo** '96

- **S-10 4** '95-96, '98-00
- **S-10 V6 2WD** '96, '98, '01
- **S-10 V6 4WD** '94-00
- **Silverado 1500** '99-00
- **Sportvan** '95 • **Suburban** '95-00 • **Tahoe** '96-00
- **Tracker** '99-00 • **Venture (reg.)** '97 • **Venture (ext.)** '98 • **Venture** '99-01

CHRYSLER 300M '99
- **Cirrus** '95-96 • **Concorde** '94-97 • **LeBaron Convertible** '94-95 • **New Yorker, LHS** '94-97 • **Sebring Convertible** '96-97 • **Town & Country 2WD** '94-97 • **Town & Country 4WD** '94, '97, '99-01

DODGE Caravan '94-96
- **Caravan 4 cyl.** '97-98

- **Dakota 2WD** '96, '98-00
- **Dakota 4WD** '95, '97-01
- **Durango** '98-99, '01 • **Grand Caravan V6 2WD** '94-97
- **Grand Caravan V6 4WD** '94, '97, '99-01 • **Intrepid** '94-99, '01 • **Neon** '95-00 • **Ram 1500 V8 2WD** '97 • **Ram 1500 V8 4WD** '94, '96-01
- **Ram Van/Wagon 1500** '96-00 • **Shadow** '94
- **Stratus** '95-96 • **Stratus 4 cyl.** '97

EAGLE Vision '94-96

FORD Aerostar '94 • **Club Wagon/Van 150** '94-98, '00
- **Contour 4 cyl.** '95
- **Contour V6** '95-98
- **Crown Victoria** '01

- **Escape V6** '01
- **Excursion** '00
- **Expedition 4WD** '99, '01
- **Explorer 2WD** '98-00
- **Explorer 4WD** '94, '97-99
- **Explorer Sport Trac** '01
- **F150 4WD** '94 • **Focus** '00-01 • **Mustang** '95-96, '00
- **Probe** '94-95 • **Ranger 4WD** '97, '99-00 • **Ranger** '01
- **Taurus** '94-95 • **Tempo** '94
- **Thunderbird** '94
- **Windstar** '95-96, '98-01

GMC Jimmy '94-01 • **S-15 Sonoma 4 cyl.** '95-96, '98-00
- **S-15 Sonoma V6 2WD** '96, '98, '01 • **S-15 Sonoma V6 4WD** '94-00 • **Safari** '95-01
- **Savana Van** '96-00 • **Sierra Classic 1500 2WD** '97, '99
- **Sierra Classic 1500 4WD** '96, '98-99 • **Sierra 1500** '99-00 • **Suburban** '95-99
- **Yukon** '96-00 • **Yukon XL** '00

HONDA Passport '96-98, '00

HYUNDAI Elantra '01
- **Santa Fe** '01 • **Sonata** '00

ISUZU Rodeo V6 '96-98, '00

JAGUAR S-Type '00 • **XJ8** '98

JEEP Cherokee '94, '97-00
- **Grand Cherokee** '94-00
- **Wrangler** '95, '97-98, '01

LINCOLN Continental '94
- **LS** '00 • **Mark VIII** '95, '98
- **Navigator** '99

MAZDA 626 '94 • **B-Series 4WD** '97, '99-00 • **B-Series** '01 • **Tribute V6** '01

MERCEDES-BENZ CLK '00
- **M-Class** '98-01
- **S-Class** '00

MERCURY Cougar '94, '99-00
- **Grand Marquis** '01
- **Mountaineer 2WD** '98-00
- **Mountaineer 4WD** '97-99
- **Mystique 4 cyl.** '95
- **Mystique V6** '95-98 • **Sable** '94-95 • **Topaz** '94

MITSUBISHI Galant '99, '01

NISSAN Frontier 2WD '01

OLDSMOBILE Alero '99, '01
- **Aurora** '95, '98, '01
- **Bravada** '94, '96-00
- **Cutlass** '97-99 • **Cutlass Supreme** '94, '96 • **88** '95, '97
- **Intrigue** '99, '01

- **Silhouette** '99-01
- **Silhouette (ext.)** '98
- **Silhouette (reg.)** '95-97

PLYMOUTH Breeze '96-97
- **Grand Voyager** '94-97
- **Neon** '95-00 • **Sundance** '94 • **Voyager** '94-96
- **Voyager 4-cyl.** '97-98

PONTIAC Bonneville '95, '97-98, '01 • **Firebird** '95-01 • **Grand Am** '94-99, '01 • **Grand Prix** '96-97 • **Sunbird** '94
- **Sunfire** '95-96, '99 • **Trans Sport (reg.)** '95-97 • **Trans Sport/ Montana (ext.)** '98
- **Montana** '99-01

PORSCHE Boxster '98-00

SATURN L-Series '00

SUZUKI Vitara '99-00

VOLKSWAGEN Jetta 4-cyl. '95-97, '99-00 • **New Beetle** '98-00 • **Passat 4 cyl.** '98
- **Passat V6** '95-98

VOLVO S40/V40 '00
- **S70/V70** '98 • **S70/V70 AWD** '99-00 • **S80** '99-00
- **S90/V90** '98 • **V70/Cross Country** '01

AUTO RELIABILITY

For any car shopper, whether you're buying new or used, reliability is one of the key considerations. To gauge reliability, CONSUMER REPORTS asks readers every year to tell us about any serious problems they've experienced in the last year with the cars they own. That survey information enables us to predict the reliability of new cars and to zero in on trouble spots found in older cars, trucks, minivans, and SUVs. See the previews on page 152 for the results as they apply to new models. The histories here can help you shop for a used car.

The most common complaints across all model years continue to involve the electrical system, body hardware, and body integrity (squeaks and rattles). Problems with engine, cooling, and fuel have ceased to be big worries in recent years. Rust problems have almost vanished, and complaints about the driveline, exhaust system, and the paint and trim have fallen significantly.

How to use the CR Reliability Histories

➤ ZERO IN ON A SPECIFIC MODEL

Find the make, model, and year for the vehicle you're interested in. For an overall idea of how its reliability stacks up, check the Reliability Verdict. Models with a ✔ Reliability Verdict have proved more trouble-

free than the average. They're the same models you'll find on the list of "Reliable Used Cars" list on page 176.

➤ WHAT'S THE TROUBLE?

Use the specific trouble-spot scores to determine whether the vehicle you're interested in is likely to have problems that you need to check out. What's covered in each score is explained at the right.

➤ COMPARE TO THE AVERAGE

Use the chart for "The Average Model" at right as a benchmark to determine if the problems with the model and year you're considering are unusually extensive or are just related to normal aging.

Every model experiences troubles as it ages. "The Average Model" shows the overall average for all models for each model year. To see if the car you're considering might be unusually troublesome in some area, compare its score with the average here. If you look up the 1995 Dodge Intrepid, for instance, you'll see that it gets a ● for transmission problems—more than its share, even for a car that old. In general, for most trouble spots, a score of ● or ◒ reflects too many problems, regardless of how old the car is. On newer models, even a score of ○ or ◓ warrants caution. Have those components carefully checked before you buy.

➤ WHY A CAR MIGHT GET NO CHECK

Sometimes a vehicle (especially a 2001 model) with mostly high scores in the 14 trouble spots gets a below-average Reliability Verdict. That's because even

---

Reliability Verdict

✔ = better than average overall reliability
✔ = average overall reliability
no check = worse than average overall reliability

though it had few problems, it was still worse than the average model for that year. The 2001 Oldsmobile Intrigue, for instance, scored ⊖ in seven categories and ⊖ in seven others. Two of the areas in which it was worse than average were cooling and transmission, which are weighted more heavily. The result: worse-than-average overall reliability. By contrast, the Honda Accord got ⊖ in all but one category. It earned a ✓ for better-than-average reliability.

What the trouble spots include

Scores for the individual trouble spots represent the percentage of respondents to CR's 2001 survey who reported problems occurring in the 12 months from April 1, 2000 through March 31, 2001 that they deemed serious on account of cost, failure, compromised safety, or downtime.

ENGINE Pistons, rings, valves, block, heads, bearings, camshafts, gaskets, supercharger, turbocharger, cam belts and chains, oil pump.

COOLING Radiator, heater core, water pump, thermostat, hoses, intercooler, and plumbing.

FUEL Fuel injection, computer and sensors, fuel pump, tank, emission controls, check-engine light.

IGNITION Spark plugs, coil, distributor, electronic ignition, sensors and modules, timing.

TRANSMISSION Transaxle, gear selector and linkage, coolers and lines. (We no longer provide separate data for manual transmissions, since survey responses in this area are few.)

ELECTRICAL Starter, alternator, battery, horn, gauges, lights, wiring, and wiper motor.

AIR CONDITIONING Compressor, condenser, evaporator, expansion valves, hoses, fans, electronics.

SUSPENSION Steering linkage, power-steering gear, pump, coolers and lines, alignment and balance, springs and torsion bars, ball joints, bushings, shocks and struts, electronic or air suspension.

BRAKES Hydraulic system, linings, rotors and drums, power boost, antilock brake system, parking brake and linkage.

EXHAUST Manifold, muffler, catalytic converter, pipes.

POWER EQUIPMENT Electronically operated accessories such as mirrors, sunroof, windows, door locks and seats, cruise control, audio system, navigational system.

PAINT/TRIM/RUST Fading, discoloring, chalking, peeling, cracking paint; loose trim or moldings; rust.

BODY INTEGRITY Seals, weather stripping, air and water leaks, wind noise, rattles and squeaks.

BODY HARDWARE Manual mirrors, sunroof, window, door, and seat mechanisms; locks; safety belts; loose interior trim; glass defects.

RELIABILITY HISTORY

TROUBLE SPOTS	The Average Model							
	94	95	96	97	98	99	00	01
Engine	⊖	⊖	⊖	⊖	⊖	⊖	⊖	⊖
Cooling	⊖	⊖	⊖	⊖	⊖	⊖	⊖	⊖
Fuel	⊖	⊖	⊖	⊖	⊖	◔	⊖	⊖
Ignition	⊖	⊖	⊖	⊖	⊖	⊖	⊖	⊖
Transmission	○	○	⊖	⊖	⊖	⊖	⊖	⊖
Electrical	◑	◑	◑	◑	○	○	○	⊖
Air conditioning	◑	○	○	⊖	⊖	⊖	⊖	⊖
Suspension	○	○	○	⊖	⊖	⊖	⊖	⊖
Brakes	◑	◑	○	○	○	○	⊖	⊖
Exhaust	⊖	⊖	⊖	⊖	⊖	⊖	⊖	⊖
Power equipment	◑	○	○	○	○	○	⊖	⊖
Paint/trim/rust	○	○	⊖	⊖	⊖	⊖	⊖	○
Body integrity	○	○	○	○	○	○	○	○
Body hardware	○	○	○	○	○	○	○	⊖
RELIABILITY VERDICT	✓	✓	✓	✓	✓	✓	✓	✓

Key to trouble spots
- ⊖ 2.0% or less
- ⊖ 2.0% to 5.0%
- ○ 5.0% to 9.3%
- ◑ 9.3% to 14.8%
- ● More than 14.8%

Acura CL / Acura Integra / Acura Legend, RL / Acura MDX

TROUBLE SPOTS	Acura CL (94 95 96 97 98 99 00 01)	Acura Integra (94 95 96 97 98 99 00 01)	Acura Legend, RL (94 95 96 97 98 99 00 01)	Acura MDX (94 95 96 97 98 99 00 01)
Engine				
Cooling				
Fuel				
Ignition				
Transmission				
Electrical				
A/C				
Suspension				
Brakes				
Exhaust				
Power equipment				
Paint/trim/rust				
Integrity				
Hardware				
RELIABILITY VERDICT				

Acura MDX columns 94–00: Insufficient data

Acura TL / Audi A4 4 cyl. / Audi A4 V6 / Audi A6

TROUBLE SPOTS	Acura TL (94 95 96 97 98 99 00 01)	Audi A4 4 cyl. (94 95 96 97 98 99 00 01)	Audi A4 V6 (94 95 96 97 98 99 00 01)	Audi A6 (94 95 96 97 98 99 00 01)
Engine				
Cooling				
Fuel				
Ignition				
Transmission				
Electrical				
A/C				
Suspension				
Brakes				
Exhaust				
Power equipment				
Paint/trim/rust				
Integrity				
Hardware				
RELIABILITY VERDICT				

Audi A6 columns 94–96: Insufficient data

Top section

TROUBLE SPOTS	Audi TT (94–01)	BMW 3-Series (94–01)	BMW 5-Series (94–01)	BMW X5 (94–01)
Engine	Insufficient data			Insufficient data
Cooling	Insufficient data			Insufficient data
Fuel	Insufficient data			Insufficient data
Ignition	Insufficient data			Insufficient data
Transmission	Insufficient data			Insufficient data
Electrical	Insufficient data			Insufficient data
A/C	Insufficient data			Insufficient data
Suspension	Insufficient data			Insufficient data
Brakes	Insufficient data			Insufficient data
Exhaust	Insufficient data			Insufficient data
Power equipment	Insufficient data			Insufficient data
Paint/trim/rust	Insufficient data			Insufficient data
Integrity	Insufficient data			Insufficient data
Hardware	Insufficient data			Insufficient data
RELIABILITY VERDICT				

Bottom section

TROUBLE SPOTS	BMW Z3 (94–01)	Buick Century (94–01)	Buick LeSabre (94–01)	Buick Park Avenue (94–01)
Engine	Insufficient data			
Cooling	Insufficient data			
Fuel	Insufficient data			
Ignition	Insufficient data			
Transmission	Insufficient data			
Electrical	Insufficient data			
A/C	Insufficient data			
Suspension	Insufficient data			
Brakes	Insufficient data			
Exhaust	Insufficient data			
Power equipment	Insufficient data			
Paint/trim/rust	Insufficient data			
Integrity	Insufficient data			
Hardware	Insufficient data			
RELIABILITY VERDICT				

TROUBLE SPOTS

Trouble Spot	Buick Regal 94	95	96	97	98	99	00	01	Buick Roadmaster 94	95	96	Cadillac Catera 97	98	99	00	01	Cadillac DeVille 94	95	96	97	98	99	00	01
Engine	○	●	⊖	⊖	⊖	⊖	⊖	⊖	○	⊖	○	●	○	⊖	⊖		⊖	○	○	⊖	⊖	⊖	⊖	⊖
Cooling	○	●	●	○	⊖	⊖	⊖	⊖	⊖	○	●	●	●	⊖	⊖		○	○	⊖	⊖	⊖	⊖	⊖	⊖
Fuel	⊖	⊖	⊖	⊖	⊖	⊖	⊖	⊖	⊖	⊖	○	○	⊖	⊖	⊖		○	●	●	○	○	⊖	⊖	⊖
Ignition	⊖	⊖	⊖	⊖	⊖	⊖	⊖	⊖	○	⊖	⊖	⊖	○	⊖	⊖		⊖	⊖	⊖	⊖	⊖	⊖	⊖	⊖
Transmission	⊖	○	⊖	⊖	⊖	⊖	⊖	⊖	⊖	⊖	⊖	○	○	⊖	⊖		○	○	⊖	⊖	⊖	⊖	⊖	⊖
Electrical	●	●	○	○	○	○	○	⊖	⊖	⊖	⊖	●	●	⊖	○		●	●	●	●	●	●	●	⊖
A/C	○	⊖	⊖	⊖	⊖	⊖	⊖	⊖	○	○	⊖	⊖	○	○	⊖		⊖	○	⊖	⊖	⊖	⊖	⊖	⊖
Suspension	⊖	⊖	⊖	⊖	⊖	⊖	⊖	⊖	○	○	○	⊖	●	○	⊖		○	⊖	⊖	⊖	⊖	⊖	⊖	⊖
Brakes	●	●	⊖	○	⊖	⊖	⊖	⊖	○	○	○	○	⊖	⊖	⊖		●	⊖	⊖	⊖	⊖	⊖	⊖	○
Exhaust	⊖	⊖	⊖	⊖	⊖	⊖	⊖	⊖	⊖	⊖	⊖	⊖	⊖	⊖	⊖		⊖	⊖	⊖	⊖	⊖	⊖	⊖	⊖
Power equipment	●	○	○	⊖	⊖	⊖	⊖	⊖	⊖	○	○	●	●	⊖	⊖		⊖	●	⊖	⊖	⊖	⊖	⊖	⊖
Paint/trim/rust	○	⊖	○	○	⊖	⊖	⊖	⊖	●	○	○	⊖	⊖	⊖	⊖		○	○	○	○	⊖	⊖	○	⊖
Integrity	⊖	○	○	⊖	⊖	○	○	⊖	○	○	⊖	○	○	○	⊖		○	⊖	○	○	⊖	○	⊖	⊖
Hardware	⊖	○	○	⊖	⊖	○	○	⊖	○	○	⊖	⊖	○	○	○		○	○	○	⊖	⊖	○	⊖	⊖
RELIABILITY VERDICT	✓	✓	✓	✓	✓	✓	✓	✓	✓		✓					✓	✓	✓			✓	✓		✓

Cadillac Catera: Insufficient data

TROUBLE SPOTS

Trouble Spot	Cadillac Seville 94	95	96	97	98	99	00	01	Chevrolet Astro 94	95	96	97	98	99	00	01	Chevrolet Blazer, S-10 Blazer 94	95	96	97	98	99	00	01	Chevrolet C1500, Silverado 2WD 94	95	96	97	98	99	00	01
Engine	⊖	●	⊖	○	⊖	⊖	⊖		○	⊖	⊖	⊖	⊖	⊖	⊖		○	○	○	○	○	⊖	⊖	⊖	⊖	⊖	⊖	○	⊖	⊖	⊖	⊖
Cooling	⊖	○	⊖	○	○	○	⊖		○	○	⊖	⊖	⊖	⊖	⊖		●	⊖	●	○	⊖	⊖	⊖	⊖	○	○	⊖	⊖	⊖	⊖	⊖	⊖
Fuel	○	●	⊖	○	⊖	⊖	○		⊖	○	○	⊖	⊖	⊖	⊖		●	●	●	⊖	⊖	⊖	⊖	⊖	⊖	⊖	●	○	⊖	⊖	⊖	⊖
Ignition	⊖	⊖	⊖	⊖	⊖	○			⊖	⊖	⊖	⊖	⊖	⊖	⊖		○	○	⊖	⊖	⊖	⊖	⊖	⊖	⊖	⊖	○	⊖	⊖	⊖	⊖	⊖
Transmission	○	○	○	⊖	⊖	⊖	○		⊖	⊖	○	⊖	⊖	⊖	○		○	○	○	○	⊖	⊖	⊖	⊖	⊖	○	⊖	⊖	⊖	⊖	⊖	⊖
Electrical	●	●	●	●	⊖	○	⊖		●	●	●	●	●	○	○		●	●	●	●	⊖	○	⊖	⊖	●	●	●	●	⊖	⊖	○	○
A/C	⊖	⊖	⊖	●	○	○	⊖		●	●	●	⊖	●	⊖	○		○	○	○	⊖	⊖	○	○	⊖	⊖	⊖	⊖	⊖	⊖	⊖	⊖	⊖
Suspension	⊖	⊖	⊖	⊖	⊖	⊖	⊖		●	●	⊖	⊖	●	⊖	○		○	○	○	⊖	⊖	⊖	⊖	⊖	○	○	⊖	⊖	⊖	⊖	⊖	⊖
Brakes	●	●	○	⊖	○	⊖	⊖		●	●	●	●	⊖	⊖	⊖		●	●	●	⊖	⊖	⊖	⊖	⊖	⊖	⊖	⊖	⊖	⊖	⊖	⊖	⊖
Exhaust	⊖	⊖	⊖	⊖	⊖	⊖	⊖		●	○	⊖	⊖	⊖	⊖	⊖		⊖	⊖	⊖	⊖	⊖	⊖	⊖	⊖	○	⊖	⊖	⊖	⊖	⊖	⊖	⊖
Power equipment	●	○	●	⊖	⊖	⊖	○		⊖	⊖	●	●	●	●	○		⊖	⊖	⊖	○	⊖	⊖	⊖	⊖	○	○	⊖	⊖	⊖	⊖	⊖	⊖
Paint/trim/rust	⊖	⊖	⊖	⊖	⊖	⊖	⊖		○	⊖	⊖	⊖	⊖	⊖	○		●	○	⊖	⊖	⊖	⊖	⊖	⊖	○	○	⊖	⊖	⊖	⊖	⊖	⊖
Integrity	⊖	○	○	⊖	○	○	○		○	⊖	⊖	⊖	⊖	⊖	●		●	●	⊖	●	●	○	○	⊖	⊖	○	⊖	⊖	⊖	●	⊖	⊖
Hardware	⊖	○	⊖	⊖	⊖	○	○		○	⊖	●	●	⊖	○	○		⊖	⊖	○	⊖	⊖	○	○	○	○	⊖	○	⊖	⊖	●	⊖	⊖
RELIABILITY VERDICT	✓			✓					✓																✓	✓	✓		✓			✓

Cadillac Seville: Insufficient data. Chevrolet Astro: Insufficient data.

Chevrolet Camaro / Chevrolet Caprice / TROUBLE SPOTS / Chevrolet Cavalier / Chevrolet Corsica, Beretta

TROUBLE SPOTS	Camaro 94 95 96 97 98 99 00 01	Caprice 94 95 96	Cavalier 94 95 96 97 98 99 00 01	Corsica, Beretta 94 95 96 97 98 99 00 01
Engine	○○○●○⊖⊖⊖	⊖○○	⊖●●○○⊖⊖⊖	○⊖⊖
Cooling	○○○○⊖⊖⊖⊖	●●◐	●⊖⊖○○⊖⊖⊖	○⊖⊖
Fuel	⊖○○●○⊖⊖⊖	○○○	○⊖⊖○⊖⊖⊖⊖	○○⊖
Ignition	○○○●○⊖⊖⊖	○○○	⊖⊖⊖○⊖⊖⊖⊖	⊖○○
Transmission	○○○○○⊖⊖⊖	○○○	○○○○⊖⊖⊖⊖	○○○
Electrical	●●●◐●●○⊖	●●●	●●●○○⊖⊖⊖	●●●
A/C	○◐⊖⊖○⊖⊖⊖	○○○	●○⊖○○⊖⊖⊖	○○⊖
Suspension	⊖⊖⊖⊖⊖⊖⊖⊖	⊖○⊖	⊖○⊖○⊖⊖⊖⊖	○○○
Brakes	●●○○○⊖⊖⊖	⊖○⊖	●○⊖⊖⊖⊖⊖⊖	●●●
Exhaust	⊖⊖○⊖⊖⊖⊖⊖	○○⊖	○⊖⊖⊖⊖⊖⊖⊖	⊖⊖⊖
Power equipment	○●●◐○○○⊖	○○⊖	○○○○○⊖⊖⊖	○○○
Paint/trim/rust	⊖○○⊖⊖⊖⊖⊖	○○⊖	●⊖○⊖○⊖⊖⊖	○○○
Integrity	○◐○●○●○○	○○◐	◐◐◐○⊖○⊖⊖	●○◐
Hardware	⊖⊖○⊖○○⊖⊖	○○◐	⊖⊖○○○⊖⊖⊖	○○○
RELIABILITY VERDICT	✓	✓	✓✓ ✓✓	✓✓

Chevrolet Corvette / Chevrolet Express Van / TROUBLE SPOTS / Chevrolet Impala / Chevrolet K1500, Silverado 4WD

TROUBLE SPOTS	Corvette 94 95 96 97 98 99 00 01	Express Van 94 95 96 97 98 99 00 01	Impala 94 95 96 97 98 99 00 01	K1500, Silverado 4WD 94 95 96 97 98 99 00 01
Engine	⊖⊖⊖	⊖○○⊖	⊖⊖	○○⊖⊖⊖⊖⊖⊖
Cooling	⊖⊖⊖	○○⊖⊖	⊖⊖	⊖⊖⊖⊖⊖⊖⊖⊖
Fuel	○⊖⊖	●○⊖○	⊖⊖	○⊖⊖○⊖⊖⊖⊖
Ignition	⊖⊖⊖	⊖⊖⊖⊖	⊖⊖	○⊖⊖⊖⊖⊖⊖⊖
Transmission	○⊖⊖	●○○⊖	⊖⊖	⊖⊖⊖⊖⊖⊖⊖⊖
Electrical	◐●○⊖	●○○○	⊖⊖	○○○⊖○○⊖⊖
A/C	⊖⊖⊖	○○○⊖	⊖⊖	○○○○⊖⊖⊖⊖
Suspension	○○⊖	○○○○	⊖⊖	○○○○○○⊖⊖
Brakes	⊖⊖⊖	⊖●●⊖	⊖⊖	○●●●●○○⊖
Exhaust	⊖⊖⊖	⊖⊖⊖⊖	⊖⊖	○⊖⊖⊖⊖⊖⊖⊖
Power equipment	○●○	●●○○	⊖⊖	⊖⊖⊖⊖⊖○○⊖
Paint/trim/rust	⊖⊖⊖	○○○⊖	⊖⊖	⊖⊖⊖⊖⊖⊖⊖⊖
Integrity	○○◐⊖	◐●●○	⊖⊖	○○○○○●●⊖
Hardware	○○○⊖	●●●○	⊖⊖	○○◐○○○●⊖
RELIABILITY VERDICT	✓ ✓		✓✓	✓✓ ✓ ✓

Insufficient data noted for several early-year columns.

Chevrolet Lumina / Chevrolet Lumina, Venture (reg.) / Chevrolet Malibu / Chevrolet Monte Carlo

TROUBLE SPOTS	Chevrolet Lumina (94–01)	Chevrolet Lumina, Venture (reg.) (94–01)	Chevrolet Malibu (94–01)	Chevrolet Monte Carlo (94–01)
Engine				
Cooling				
Fuel				
Ignition				
Transmission				
Electrical				
A/C				
Suspension				
Brakes				
Exhaust				
Power equipment				
Paint/trim/rust				
Integrity				
Hardware				
RELIABILITY VERDICT				

Chevrolet Lumina: Insufficient data (00, 01)
Chevrolet Lumina, Venture (reg.): Insufficient data (00, 01)
Chevrolet Malibu: (94, 95, 96 insufficient)
Chevrolet Monte Carlo: Insufficient data (97, 99, 00, 01)

Chevrolet S-10 4 cyl. / Chevrolet S-10 V6 2WD / Chevrolet S-10 V6 4WD / Chevrolet Suburban

TROUBLE SPOTS	Chevrolet S-10 4 cyl. (94–01)	Chevrolet S-10 V6 2WD (94–01)	Chevrolet S-10 V6 4WD (94–01)	Chevrolet Suburban (94–01)
Engine				
Cooling				
Fuel				
Ignition				
Transmission				
Electrical				
A/C				
Suspension				
Brakes				
Exhaust				
Power equipment				
Paint/trim/rust				
Integrity				
Hardware				
RELIABILITY VERDICT				

Chevrolet S-10 4 cyl.: Insufficient data (01)
Chevrolet S-10 V6 4WD: Insufficient data (96, 97, 98, 99)

Top section

TROUBLE SPOTS	Chevrolet Tahoe								Chevrolet Venture (ext.)								Chevrolet/Geo Prizm								Chevrolet/Geo Tracker							
	94	95	96	97	98	99	00	01	94	95	96	97	98	99	00	01	94	95	96	97	98	99	00	01	94	95	96	97	98	99	00	01
Engine																																
Cooling																																
Fuel																																
Ignition																																
Transmission																																
Electrical																																
A/C																																
Suspension																																
Brakes																																
Exhaust																																
Power equipment																																
Paint/trim/rust																																
Integrity																																
Hardware																																
RELIABILITY VERDICT	✓					✓						✓					✓	✓	✓	✓	✓	✓	✓	✓	✓	✓	✓					

Note: "Insufficient data" is marked for early years of Chevrolet Tahoe (94), Chevrolet Venture (94–96), and Chevrolet/Geo Tracker (98–00).

Bottom section

TROUBLE SPOTS	Chrysler 300M								Chrysler Cirrus V6								Chrysler Concorde								Chrysler New Yorker, LHS							
	94	95	96	97	98	99	00	01	94	95	96	97	98	99	00	01	94	95	96	97	98	99	00	01	94	95	96	97	98	99	00	01
Engine																																
Cooling																																
Fuel																																
Ignition																																
Transmission																																
Electrical																																
A/C																																
Suspension																																
Brakes																																
Exhaust																																
Power equipment																																
Paint/trim/rust																																
Integrity																																
Hardware																																
RELIABILITY VERDICT						✓	✓					✓	✓	✓	✓						✓	✓	✓							✓	✓	

Note: "Insufficient data" is marked for Chrysler Concorde (01) and Chrysler New Yorker, LHS (00–01).

TROUBLE SPOTS

Top section

	Chrysler PT Cruiser	Chrysler Sebring convertible	Chrysler Sebring V6	Chrysler Town & Country 2WD
	94 95 96 97 98 99 00 01	94 95 96 97 98 99 00 01	94 95 96 97 98 99 00 01	94 95 96 97 98 99 00 01
Engine				
Cooling				
Fuel				
Ignition				
Transmission				
Electrical				
A/C				
Suspension				
Brakes				
Exhaust				
Power equipment				
Paint/trim/rust				
Integrity				
Hardware				
RELIABILITY VERDICT				

Chrysler Sebring V6: Insufficient data for 94 95 96 97 99 00

Bottom section

	Chrysler Town & Country AWD	Chrysler/Plymouth Voyager V6	Dodge Caravan 4 cyl.	Dodge Caravan V6
	94 95 96 97 98 99 00 01	94 95 96 97 98 99 00 01	94 95 96 97 98 99 00 01	94 95 96 97 98 99 00 01
Engine				
Cooling				
Fuel				
Ignition				
Transmission				
Electrical				
A/C				
Suspension				
Brakes				
Exhaust				
Power equipment				
Paint/trim/rust				
Integrity				
Hardware				
RELIABILITY VERDICT				

Chrysler Town & Country AWD: Insufficient data for 94 95 96
Dodge Caravan V6: Insufficient data

TROUBLE SPOTS

Vehicle	94 95 96 97 98 99 00 01
Dodge Dakota 2WD	
Dodge Dakota 4WD	
Dodge Durango	
Dodge Grand Caravan V6 2WD	

Trouble spots (rows for all vehicles above):
- Engine
- Cooling
- Fuel
- Ignition
- Transmission
- Electrical
- A/C
- Suspension
- Brakes
- Exhaust
- Power equipment
- Paint/trim/rust
- Integrity
- Hardware
- RELIABILITY VERDICT

Dodge Dakota 4WD 96 column: Insufficient data

TROUBLE SPOTS

Vehicle	94 95 96 97 98 99 00 01
Dodge Grand Caravan V6 AWD	
Dodge Intrepid	
Dodge Ram 1500 2WD	
Dodge Ram 1500 4WD	

Trouble spots (rows for all vehicles above):
- Engine
- Cooling
- Fuel
- Ignition
- Transmission
- Electrical
- A/C
- Suspension
- Brakes
- Exhaust
- Power equipment
- Paint/trim/rust
- Integrity
- Hardware
- RELIABILITY VERDICT

Dodge Grand Caravan V6 AWD 95–96 columns: Insufficient data
Dodge Ram 1500 4WD 94–95 columns: Insufficient data

Dodge Ram Van/Wagon 1500 · Dodge Stratus 4 cyl. · Dodge Stratus V6 · Dodge/Plymouth Neon

TROUBLE SPOTS	Dodge Ram Van/Wagon 1500 94 95 96 97 98 99 00 01	Dodge Stratus 4 cyl. 94 95 96 97 98 99 00 01	Dodge Stratus V6 94 95 96 97 98 99 00 01	Dodge/Plymouth Neon 94 95 96 97 98 99 00 01
Engine	○ ◐ ○ — Insufficient data —	Insufficient data — ● ● ◐ ◐ ◐	◐ ○ ◐ ◐ ◐ ◐ ◐	● ● ● ◐ ◐ ◐ ◐
Cooling	○ ○ ○	○ ◐ ◐ ◐ ◐	○ ◐ ◐ ◐ ○ ◐ ◐	◐ ◐ ○ ○ ◐ ◐
Fuel	◐ ○ ○	○ ◐ ◐ ◐ ◐	○ ◐ ◐ ◐ ○ ◐ ◐	◐ ◐ ○ ○ ○ ◐
Ignition	◐ ○ ○	◐ ○ ◐ ◐ ◐	○ ◐ ◐ ◐ ◐ ◐ ◐	○ ◐ ○ ○ ○ ◐
Transmission	◐ ● ●	◐ ○ ◐ ○ ◐	◐ ○ ○ ○ ◐ ◐ ◐	○ ◐ ○ ○ ○ ◐
Electrical	◐ ◐ ○	◐ ◐ ◐ ○ ◐	◐ ○ ○ ◐ ◐ ◐ ○	○ ◐ ○ ○ ○ ◐
A/C	○ ○ ○	◐ ○ ◐ ○ ◐	● ○ ◐ ◐ ◐ ◐ ◐	◐ ○ ○ ○ ○ ◐
Suspension	○ ○ ○	○ ◐ ◐ ◐ ○	○ ○ ○ ◐ ◐ ◐ ◐	○ ○ ○ ○ ◐ ◐
Brakes	● ◐ ◐	◐ ◐ ◐ ◐ ◐	● ● ◐ ◐ ○ ◐ ◐	● ● ◐ ○ ○ ◐
Exhaust	◐ ◐ ◐	◐ ◐ ◐ ◐ ◐	◐ ○ ◐ ◐ ○ ◐ ◐	◐ ○ ◐ ◐ ◐ ◐
Power equipment	◐ ○ ○	◐ ○ ◐ ◐ ○	◐ ○ ○ ○ ◐ ◐ ◐	○ ○ ○ ◐ ○ ◐
Paint/trim/rust	● ◐ ◐	◐ ○ ◐ ◐ ○	◐ ○ ◐ ◐ ◐ ◐ ◐	● ○ ◐ ◐ ◐ ◐
Integrity	◐ ● ●	◐ ◐ ○ ○ ○	◐ ◐ ○ ◐ ◐ ◐ ◐	● ● ● ◐ ○
Hardware	◐ ◐ ●	○ ○ ◐ ◐ ○	◐ ○ ◐ ○ ○ ◐ ◐	○ ◐ ○ ◐ ○ ◐
RELIABILITY VERDICT	✔ ✔	✔ ✔ ✔	✔ ✔ ✔ ✔ ✔	

Ford Aerostar · Ford Club Wagon, Van 150 · Ford Contour 4 cyl. · Ford Contour V6

TROUBLE SPOTS	Ford Aerostar 94 95 96 97 98 99 00 01	Ford Club Wagon, Van 150 94 95 96 97 98 99 00 01	Ford Contour 4 cyl. 94 95 96 97 98 99 00 01	Ford Contour V6 94 95 96 97 98 99 00 01
Engine	○ ◐ ◐	○ ○ ◐ ◐ ◐ ◐	◐ ○ ◐ ◐ ◐	○ ◐ ○ ◐ ◐ ◐
Cooling	● ○ ◐ ○	● ● ○ ○ ◐ ◐	◐ ○ ○ ◐ ○	○ ○ ◐ ○ ◐
Fuel	○ ◐ ○	○ ◐ ○ ○ ◐ ◐	○ ◐ ○ ◐ ◐	● ● ◐ ○ ◐
Ignition	○ ◐ ◐	◐ ○ ○ ◐ ◐ ◐	○ ◐ ◐ ◐ ◐	○ ◐ ◐ ◐ ◐
Transmission	○ ○ ◐	◐ ○ ○ ◐ ◐ ◐	○ ○ ◐ ◐ ◐	○ ○ ◐ ◐ ◐
Electrical	● ○ ○	● ○ ○ ◐ ○ ◐	● ● ◐ ◐ ◐	● ● ◐ ◐ ◐
A/C	○ ○ ◐	◐ ● ● ○ ◐ ◐	○ ○ ◐ ○ ○	○ ○ ◐ ○ ○
Suspension	◐ ○ ◐	◐ ◐ ◐ ◐ ○ ◐	◐ ○ ○ ◐ ○	◐ ○ ○ ○ ○
Brakes	● ● ●	● ● ● ● ◐ ◐	◐ ◐ ○ ○ ○	● ● ● ◐ ○
Exhaust	◐ ◐ ◐	◐ ◐ ◐ ◐ ◐ ◐	◐ ◐ ◐ ◐ ◐	◐ ○ ◐ ◐ ◐
Power equipment	◐ ○ ◐	◐ ○ ○ ○ ◐ ◐	○ ○ ◐ ◐ ◐	◐ ○ ◐ ◐ ◐
Paint/trim/rust	○ ○ ◐	○ ○ ◐ ◐ ◐ ◐	◐ ◐ ◐ ◐ ◐	◐ ○ ◐ ◐ ◐
Integrity	● ◐ ◐ ○	○ ○ ◐ ◐ ◐ ○	◐ ◐ ○ ○ ○	◐ ○ ◐ ◐ ◐
Hardware	● ◐ ◐ ○	○ ◐ ◐ ◐ ◐ ○	◐ ◐ ○ ○ ○	◐ ◐ ○ ○ ○
RELIABILITY VERDICT	✔ ✔ ✔	✔	✔ ✔ ✔ ✔	✔ ✔

(Ford Club Wagon, Van 150 column marked "Insufficient data" for later years)

TROUBLE SPOTS

	Ford Crown Victoria	Ford Escape V6 2WD	Ford Escape V6 4WD	Ford Escort
	94 95 96 97 98 99 00 01	94 95 96 97 98 99 00 01	94 95 96 97 98 99 00 01	94 95 96 97 98 99 00 01
Engine				
Cooling				
Fuel				
Ignition				
Transmission				
Electrical				
A/C				
Suspension				
Brakes				
Exhaust				
Power equipment				
Paint/trim/rust				
Integrity				
Hardware				
RELIABILITY VERDICT	✔ ✔ ✔ ✔ ✔ ✔ ✔			✔ ✔ ✔ ✔ ✔ ✔ ✔

Ford Escort 00–01: Insufficient data

TROUBLE SPOTS

	Ford Excursion	Ford Expedition 4WD	Ford Explorer 2WD	Ford Explorer 4WD
	94 95 96 97 98 99 00 01	94 95 96 97 98 99 00 01	94 95 96 97 98 99 00 01	94 95 96 97 98 99 00 01
Engine				
Cooling				
Fuel				
Ignition				
Transmission				
Electrical				
A/C				
Suspension				
Brakes				
Exhaust				
Power equipment				
Paint/trim/rust				
Integrity				
Hardware				
RELIABILITY VERDICT		✔ ✔ ✔	✔ ✔ ✔ ✔ ✔	✔ ✔ ✔ ✔

Ford Excursion 94–99: Insufficient data

Top section

TROUBLE SPOTS	Ford Explorer Sport Trac 2WD	Ford Explorer Sport Trac 4WD	Ford F-150 2WD	Ford F-150 4WD
(years)	94 95 96 97 98 99 00 01	94 95 96 97 98 99 00 01	94 95 96 97 98 99 00 01	94 95 96 97 98 99 00 01
Engine				
Cooling				
Fuel				
Ignition				
Transmission				
Electrical				
A/C				
Suspension				
Brakes				
Exhaust				
Power equipment				
Paint/trim/rust				
Integrity				
Hardware				
RELIABILITY VERDICT			✓ ✓ ✓ ✓ ✓ ✓ ✓ ✓	✓ ✓ ✓ ✓ ✓ ✓ ✓

Bottom section

TROUBLE SPOTS	Ford Focus	Ford Mustang	Ford Ranger 2WD	Ford Ranger 4WD
(years)	94 95 96 97 98 99 00 01	94 95 96 97 98 99 00 01	94 95 96 97 98 99 00 01	94 95 96 97 98 99 00 01
Engine				
Cooling				
Fuel				
Ignition				
Transmission				
Electrical		Insufficient data		
A/C				
Suspension				
Brakes				
Exhaust				
Power equipment				
Paint/trim/rust				
Integrity				
Hardware				
RELIABILITY VERDICT		✓ ✓ ✓ ✓	✓ ✓ ✓ ✓ ✓ ✓ ✓ ✓	✓ ✓ ✓ ✓

Top section

Ford Taurus								Ford Thunderbird								TROUBLE SPOTS	Ford Windstar								GMC Jimmy, S-15 Jimmy							
94	95	96	97	98	99	00	01	94	95	96	97	98	99	00	01		94	95	96	97	98	99	00	01	94	95	96	97	98	99	00	01
																Engine																
																Cooling																
																Fuel																
																Ignition																
																Transmission																
																Electrical																
																A/C																
																Suspension																
																Brakes																
																Exhaust																
																Power equipment																
																Paint/trim/rust																
																Integrity																
																Hardware																
		✓	✓	✓	✓	✓	✓			✓	✓	✓				RELIABILITY VERDICT					✓											

Bottom section

GMC Safari								GMC Savana Van								TROUBLE SPOTS	GMC Sierra 1500 2WD								GMC Sierra 1500 4WD							
94	95	96	97	98	99	00	01	94	95	96	97	98	99	00	01		94	95	96	97	98	99	00	01	94	95	96	97	98	99	00	01
						Insufficient data		Insufficient data						Insufficient data		Engine																
																Cooling																
																Fuel																
																Ignition																
																Transmission																
																Electrical																
																A/C																
																Suspension																
																Brakes																
																Exhaust																
																Power equipment																
																Paint/trim/rust																
																Integrity																
																Hardware																
✓																RELIABILITY VERDICT	✓	✓	✓		✓			✓	✓		✓		✓			✓

TROUBLE SPOTS

	GMC Sonoma V6 2WD								GMC Sonoma V6 4WD								GMC Suburban, Yukon XL								GMC Yukon							
	94	95	96	97	98	99	00	01	94	95	96	97	98	99	00	01	94	95	96	97	98	99	00	01	94	95	96	97	98	99	00	01
Engine																																
Cooling																																
Fuel																																
Ignition																																
Transmission																																
Electrical																																
A/C																																
Suspension																																
Brakes																																
Exhaust																																
Power equipment																																
Paint/trim/rust																																
Integrity																																
Hardware																																

GMC Sonoma V6 4WD: "Insufficient data" for 96, 97, 98, 99, 00, 01.
GMC Yukon: "Insufficient data" for years shown.

RELIABILITY VERDICT

TROUBLE SPOTS

	Honda Accord								Honda Civic								Honda CR-V								Honda Odyssey							
	94	95	96	97	98	99	00	01	94	95	96	97	98	99	00	01	94	95	96	97	98	99	00	01	94	95	96	97	98	99	00	01
Engine																																
Cooling																																
Fuel																																
Ignition																																
Transmission																																
Electrical																																
A/C																																
Suspension																																
Brakes																																
Exhaust																																
Power equipment																																
Paint/trim/rust																																
Integrity																																
Hardware																																

RELIABILITY VERDICT

Honda Passport V6 · Honda Prelude · Honda S2000 · Hyundai Elantra

Trouble Spots	| Honda Passport V6 (94–01)	| Honda Prelude (94–01)	| Honda S2000 (94–01)	| Hyundai Elantra (94–01)
Engine	○ · · · ○ ⊖ ⊖ ·	· · ⊖ ⊖ · ·	⊖	○ ⊖
Cooling	⊖ · · ⊖ ⊖ ⊖ ·	· · ⊖ ⊖ · ·	⊖	○ ⊖
Fuel	○ · · ◐ ⊖ ⊖ ·	· · ⊖ ⊖ · ·	⊖	○ ○
Ignition	○ · · ⊖ ⊖ ⊖ ·	· · ⊖ ⊖ · ·	⊖	○ ⊖
Transmission	⊖ · · ⊖ ⊖ ⊖ ·	· · ⊖ ⊖ · ·	⊖	○ ⊖
Electrical	● · · ○ ○ ○ ·	· · ⊖ ○ · ·	⊖	○ ○
A/C	○ · · ● ○ ○ ·	· · ○ ○ · ·	⊖	○ ○
Suspension	○ · · ● ○ ○ ·	· · ⊖ ○ · ·	⊖	○ ○
Brakes	○ · · ● ○ ○ ·	· · ⊖ ○ · ·	⊖	○ ○
Exhaust	⊖ · · ⊖ ⊖ ⊖ ·	· · ⊖ ⊖ · ·	⊖	⊖ ⊖
Power equipment	● · · ⊖ ⊖ ⊖ ·	· · ⊖ ⊖ · ·	⊖	⊖ ⊖
Paint/trim/rust	○ · · ⊖ ⊖ ⊖ ·	· · ⊖ ⊖ · ·	⊖	⊖ ⊖
Integrity	● · · ● ○ ○ ·	· · ⊖ ⊖ · ·	⊖	⊖ ⊖
Hardware	○ · · ○ ○ ○ ·	· · ⊖ ⊖ · ·	○	⊖ ⊖
RELIABILITY VERDICT	✓ · · · ✓ · ·	· · ✓ ✓ · ·	✓	✓

Honda Passport V6, Honda Prelude, Honda S2000 and Hyundai Elantra columns marked "Insufficient data" for years without symbols.

Hyundai Santa Fe · Hyundai Sonata · Infiniti G20 · Infiniti I30

Trouble Spots	| Hyundai Santa Fe (94–01)	| Hyundai Sonata (94–01)	| Infiniti G20 (94–01)	| Infiniti I30 (94–01)
Engine	⊖ (01)	⊖ (01)	⊖ ⊖ ⊖ · · ⊖ ·	· · ⊖ ⊖ ⊖ ⊖ ⊖
Cooling	⊖ (01)	⊖ (01)	⊖ ⊖ ⊖ · · ⊖ ·	· · ⊖ ⊖ ⊖ ⊖ ⊖
Fuel	⊖ (01)	○ (01)	⊖ ⊖ ⊖ · · ⊖ ·	· · ⊖ ⊖ ⊖ ⊖ ⊖
Ignition	⊖ (01)	○ (01)	⊖ ⊖ ⊖ · · ⊖ ·	· · ⊖ ⊖ ⊖ ⊖ ⊖
Transmission	⊖ (01)	○ (01)	⊖ ⊖ ⊖ · · ⊖ ·	· · ⊖ ⊖ ⊖ ⊖ ⊖
Electrical	⊖ (01)	○ (01)	○ ○ ○ · · ⊖ ·	· · ○ ○ ○ ⊖ ⊖
A/C	⊖ (01)	○ (01)	○ ○ ⊖ · · ⊖ ·	· · ⊖ ⊖ ⊖ ⊖ ⊖
Suspension	⊖ (01)	○ (01)	○ ○ ○ · · ⊖ ·	· · ⊖ ⊖ ⊖ ○ ⊖
Brakes	⊖ (01)	⊖ (01)	○ ○ ⊖ · · ⊖ ·	· · ⊖ ⊖ ⊖ ○ ⊖
Exhaust	⊖ (01)	⊖ (01)	⊖ ⊖ ⊖ · · ⊖ ·	· · ⊖ ⊖ ⊖ ⊖ ⊖
Power equipment	⊖ (01)	○ (01)	○ ⊖ ○ · · ⊖ ·	· · ⊖ ⊖ ⊖ ⊖ ⊖
Paint/trim/rust	⊖ (01)	⊖ (01)	○ ⊖ ⊖ · · ○ ·	· · ⊖ ⊖ ⊖ ⊖ ⊖
Integrity	⊖ (01)	⊖ (01)	⊖ ⊖ ⊖ · · ⊖ ·	· · ⊖ ⊖ ○ ⊖ ⊖
Hardware	⊖ (01)	⊖ (01)	○ ⊖ ⊖ · · ⊖ ·	· · ⊖ ⊖ ⊖ ⊖ ⊖
RELIABILITY VERDICT			✓ ✓ ✓ · · ✓ ·	· · ✓ ✓ ✓ ✓ ✓ ✓

Hyundai Santa Fe, Hyundai Sonata and inner Infiniti columns marked "Insufficient data" for years without symbols.

TROUBLE SPOTS

Infiniti QX4								TROUBLE SPOTS	Isuzu Oasis								Isuzu Rodeo V6								Isuzu Trooper							
94	95	96	97	98	99	00	01		94	95	96	97	98	99	00	01	94	95	96	97	98	99	00	01	94	95	96	97	98	99	00	01
							⊖	Engine			○	⊖	⊖					○			⊖	⊖	⊖	⊖		⊖			⊖	⊖		
							⊖	Cooling			⊖	⊖	⊖					⊖			⊖	⊖	⊖			⊖			⊖	⊖		
							⊖	Fuel			⊖	⊖	⊖					○			⊖	⊖	⊖	⊖		⊖			⊖	⊖		
							⊖	Ignition			⊖	⊖	⊖					○			⊖	⊖	⊖			⊖			⊖	⊖		
							⊖	Transmission			⊖	⊖	○					⊖			⊖	⊖				○			⊖	⊖		
	Insufficient data	Insufficient data	Insufficient data	Insufficient data			⊖	Electrical	Insufficient data		⊖	⊖	⊖	Insufficient data				●	Insufficient data	Insufficient data	⊖	⊖	⊖	⊖	Insufficient data	○	Insufficient data	Insufficient data	Insufficient data	Insufficient data	Insufficient data	Insufficient data
							⊖	A/C			⊖	⊖	⊖					○			○	○	○			⊖			⊖	⊖		
							⊖	Suspension			⊖	⊖	⊖					⊖			⊖	⊖	○	○		○			⊖	⊖		
							⊖	Brakes			○	○	○					⊖			○	○	○	⊖		○			⊖	⊖		
							⊖	Exhaust			⊖	⊖	⊖					⊖			○	○	○			○			⊖	⊖		
							⊖	Power equipment			○	⊖	⊖					●			⊖	⊖	⊖	⊖		⊖			⊖	⊖		
							⊖	Paint/trim/rust			⊖	⊖	⊖					⊖			⊖	⊖	⊖			⊖			⊖	⊖		
							⊖	Integrity			⊖	⊖	⊖					●			●	○	○			○			⊖	⊖		
							⊖	Hardware			⊖	⊖	⊖					⊖			○	○	○			⊖			⊖	⊖		
							✓	RELIABILITY VERDICT			✓	✓	✓					✓			✓					✓			✓	✓		

Jaguar S-Type								TROUBLE SPOTS	Jeep Cherokee								Jeep Grand Cherokee 4WD								Jeep Wrangler							
94	95	96	97	98	99	00	01		94	95	96	97	98	99	00	01	94	95	96	97	98	99	00	01	94	95	96	97	98	99	00	01
						⊖	⊖	Engine	○	⊖	⊖	⊖	⊖	⊖	⊖	⊖	○	○	○	⊖	⊖	⊖	⊖	⊖				⊖	⊖	⊖	⊖	
						⊖	⊖	Cooling	○	●	⊖	⊖	⊖	⊖	⊖	⊖	⊖	⊖	⊖	⊖	⊖	⊖	⊖	⊖				○	⊖	⊖	⊖	
						⊖	⊖	Fuel	○	⊖	○	⊖	⊖	⊖	⊖	⊖	○	○	○	⊖	○	⊖	⊖	⊖				⊖	⊖	⊖	⊖	
						⊖	⊖	Ignition	○	○	○	○	⊖	⊖	⊖	⊖	⊖	○	○	⊖	○	⊖	⊖	⊖				⊖	⊖	⊖	⊖	
						⊖	⊖	Transmission	○	○	○	○	⊖	○	⊖	⊖	●	●	⊖	⊖	○	○	⊖	⊖				○	○	○	⊖	
						○	⊖	Electrical	○	○	○	○	○	○	○	⊖	●	●	⊖	⊖	○	○	⊖	⊖	Insufficient data	Insufficient data		⊖	●	⊖	⊖	Insufficient data
						⊖	⊖	A/C	○	○	○	○	⊖	⊖	⊖	⊖	○	○	○	○	○	○	⊖	⊖				⊖	⊖	⊖	⊖	
						⊖	⊖	Suspension	○	○	○	○	○	⊖	⊖	⊖	○	○	○	○	○	○	⊖	⊖				⊖	⊖	⊖	⊖	
						⊖	⊖	Brakes	●	⊖	●	●	●	●	⊖	○	●	●	●	●	●	●	●	⊖				⊖	⊖	⊖	⊖	
						⊖	⊖	Exhaust	○	○	⊖	⊖	⊖	⊖	⊖	⊖	○	○	⊖	⊖	⊖	⊖	⊖	⊖				○	⊖	⊖	⊖	
						○	⊖	Power equipment	○	⊖	○	○	⊖	⊖	○	○	⊖	⊖	⊖	⊖	⊖	●	⊖	⊖				⊖	⊖	⊖	⊖	
						⊖	⊖	Paint/trim/rust	●	○	○	○	⊖	⊖	⊖	⊖	○	⊖	⊖	⊖	⊖	⊖	⊖	⊖				○	⊖	○	⊖	
						○	⊖	Integrity	●	●	●	○	○	○	○	○	○	○	⊖	○	○	⊖	⊖	⊖				●	●	⊖	○	
						⊖	⊖	Hardware	○	○	○	○	○	○	○	⊖	○	○	○	○	○	○	○	⊖				○	⊖	⊖	○	
							✓	RELIABILITY VERDICT		✓	✓					✓								✓					✓	✓		

Lexus (1994–2001)

TROUBLE SPOTS	Lexus ES300								Lexus GS300/GS400,GS430								Lexus IS300								Lexus LS400, LS430							
	94	95	96	97	98	99	00	01	94	95	96	97	98	99	00	01	94	95	96	97	98	99	00	01	94	95	96	97	98	99	00	01
Engine	○	⊖	⊖	⊖	⊖	⊖	⊖	⊖					⊖	⊖	⊖	⊖								⊖	⊖	⊖	⊖	⊖	⊖	⊖	⊖	⊖
Cooling	⊖	⊖	⊖	⊖	⊖	⊖	⊖	⊖					⊖	⊖	⊖	⊖								⊖	⊖	⊖	⊖	⊖	⊖	⊖	⊖	⊖
Fuel	⊖	⊖	⊖	⊖	⊖	⊖	⊖	⊖					⊖	⊖	⊖	⊖								⊖	⊖	⊖	⊖	⊖	⊖	⊖	⊖	⊖
Ignition	⊖	⊖	⊖	⊖	⊖	⊖	⊖	⊖					⊖	⊖	⊖	⊖								⊖	⊖	⊖	⊖	⊖	⊖	⊖	⊖	⊖
Transmission	⊖	⊖	⊖	⊖	⊖	⊖	⊖	⊖					⊖	⊖	⊖	⊖								⊖	⊖	⊖	⊖	⊖	⊖	⊖	⊖	⊖
Electrical	⊖	○	⊖	⊖	⊖	○	⊖	⊖	_Insufficient data_	_Insufficient data_	_Insufficient data_	_Insufficient data_	○	⊖	⊖	⊖								⊖	○	●	○	⊖	⊖	⊖	⊖	⊖
A/C	○	○	⊖	⊖	⊖	⊖	⊖	⊖					○	⊖	⊖	⊖								⊖	○	○	○	⊖	⊖	⊖	⊖	⊖
Suspension	○	○	⊖	⊖	⊖	⊖	⊖	⊖					○	⊖	⊖	⊖								⊖	○	○	○	○	⊖	⊖	⊖	⊖
Brakes	○	⊖	⊖	⊖	⊖	⊖	⊖	⊖					⊖	⊖	⊖	⊖								⊖	○	○	⊖	⊖	○	⊖	⊖	⊖
Exhaust	⊖	⊖	⊖	⊖	⊖	⊖	⊖	⊖					⊖	⊖	⊖	⊖								⊖	⊖	⊖	⊖	⊖	⊖	⊖	⊖	⊖
Power equipment	○	○	⊖	⊖	⊖	⊖	⊖	⊖					○	⊖	⊖	⊖								⊖	○	○	○	⊖	⊖	⊖	⊖	⊖
Paint/trim/rust	⊖	○	⊖	⊖	⊖	⊖	⊖	⊖					⊖	⊖	⊖	⊖								⊖	⊖	⊖	⊖	⊖	⊖	⊖	⊖	⊖
Integrity	○	⊖	⊖	⊖	⊖	⊖	⊖	⊖					○	⊖	⊖	⊖								⊖	⊖	⊖	⊖	⊖	⊖	⊖	⊖	⊖
Hardware	⊖	⊖	⊖	⊖	⊖	⊖	⊖	⊖					⊖	⊖	⊖	⊖								⊖	⊖	⊖	⊖	⊖	⊖	⊖	⊖	⊖
RELIABILITY VERDICT	✓	✓	✓	✓	✓	✓	✓	✓					✓	✓	✓	✓								✓	✓	✓	✓	✓	✓	✓	✓	✓

Lexus / Lincoln (1994–2001)

TROUBLE SPOTS	Lexus RX300								Lincoln Continental								Lincoln LS								Lincoln Mark VIII							
	94	95	96	97	98	99	00	01	94	95	96	97	98	99	00	01	94	95	96	97	98	99	00	01	94	95	96	97	98	99	00	01
Engine						⊖	⊖	⊖	●	⊖	⊖	⊖	⊖	⊖	⊖	⊖							⊖	⊖	○				⊖	⊖		
Cooling						⊖	⊖	⊖	●	⊖	⊖	⊖	⊖	⊖	⊖	⊖							⊖	⊖	○				⊖	⊖		
Fuel						⊖	⊖	⊖	○	⊖	⊖	⊖	⊖	⊖	⊖	⊖							⊖	⊖	⊖				○	○		
Ignition						⊖	⊖	⊖	○	⊖	⊖	⊖	⊖	⊖	⊖	⊖							⊖	⊖	⊖				○	○		
Transmission						⊖	⊖	⊖	○	⊖	⊖	⊖	⊖	⊖	⊖	⊖							⊖	⊖	●				○	○		
Electrical						⊖	⊖	⊖	○	◑	●	○	○	⊖	⊖	⊖							⊖	⊖	●	_Insufficient data_	_Insufficient data_	●	●	○		
A/C						⊖	⊖	⊖	○	○	○	○	○	⊖	⊖	⊖							⊖	⊖	○			◑	⊖	○		
Suspension						⊖	⊖	⊖	●	●	●	●	●	⊖	⊖	⊖							⊖	⊖	●			⊖	⊖		
Brakes						⊖	⊖	⊖	⊖	○	○	○	○	○	○	⊖							⊖	⊖	⊖			⊖	○	○		
Exhaust						⊖	⊖	⊖	⊖	⊖	⊖	⊖	⊖	⊖	⊖	⊖							⊖	⊖	⊖			⊖	⊖		
Power equipment						⊖	⊖	⊖	●	●	◑	⊖	⊖	○	○	○							○	○	⊖			⊖	●	●		
Paint/trim/rust						⊖	⊖	⊖	○	⊖	⊖	⊖	○	○	⊖	⊖							⊖	⊖	⊖			⊖	⊖		
Integrity						⊖	⊖	⊖	◑	◑	◑	○	○	⊖	⊖	⊖							○	⊖	○			⊖	○		
Hardware						⊖	⊖	⊖	●	●	●	○	○	⊖	⊖	⊖							○	⊖	○			○	⊖		
RELIABILITY VERDICT						✓	✓	✓		✓	✓	✓	✓	✓	✓	✓								✓	✓			✓				

Lincoln Navigator / Lincoln Town Car / Mazda 626 / Mazda B-Series 4WD

TROUBLE SPOTS	Lincoln Navigator (94–01)	Lincoln Town Car (94–01)	Mazda 626 (94–01)	Mazda B-Series 4WD (94–01)
Engine				
Cooling				
Fuel				
Ignition				
Transmission				
Electrical				
A/C				
Suspension				
Brakes				
Exhaust				
Power equipment				
Paint/trim/rust				
Integrity				
Hardware				
RELIABILITY VERDICT				

(Lincoln Navigator: years 94–97 Insufficient data)
(Mazda 626: years 99–01 Insufficient data)

Mazda Millenia / Mazda MPV / Mazda MX-5 Miata / Mazda Protege

TROUBLE SPOTS	Mazda Millenia (94–01)	Mazda MPV (94–01)	Mazda MX-5 Miata (94–01)	Mazda Protege (94–01)
Engine				
Cooling				
Fuel				
Ignition				
Transmission				
Electrical				
A/C				
Suspension				
Brakes				
Exhaust				
Power equipment				
Paint/trim/rust				
Integrity				
Hardware				
RELIABILITY VERDICT				

(Insufficient data noted for various years across Mazda Millenia, Mazda MPV, and Mazda MX-5 Miata)

Top section

TROUBLE SPOTS	Mazda Tribute V6 2WD 94 95 96 97 98 99 00 01	Mazda Tribute V6 4WD 94 95 96 97 98 99 00 01	Mercedes-Benz C-Class 94 95 96 97 98 99 00 01	Mercedes-Benz CLK 94 95 96 97 98 99 00 01
Engine				
Cooling				
Fuel				
Ignition				
Transmission				
Electrical				
A/C				
Suspension				
Brakes				
Exhaust				
Power equipment				
Paint/trim/rust				
Integrity				
Hardware				
RELIABILITY VERDICT			✓ ✓ ✓ ✓ ✓ ✓ ✓ ✓	✓

Mercedes-Benz CLK: Insufficient data

Bottom section

TROUBLE SPOTS	Mercedes-Benz E-Class 94 95 96 97 98 99 00 01	Mercedes-Benz M-Class 94 95 96 97 98 99 00 01	Mercedes-Benz SLK 94 95 96 97 98 99 00 01	Mercury Cougar 94 95 96 97 98 99 00 01
Engine				
Cooling				
Fuel				
Ignition				
Transmission				
Electrical				
A/C				
Suspension				
Brakes				
Exhaust				
Power equipment				
Paint/trim/rust				
Integrity				
Hardware				
RELIABILITY VERDICT	✓ ✓ ✓ ✓ ✓ ✓ ✓ ✓		✓ ✓	✓ ✓ ✓

Mercedes-Benz SLK: Insufficient data
Mercury Cougar: Insufficient data

Mercury Grand Marquis / Mercury Mountaineer 4WD / Mercury Mystique V6 / Mercury Sable

TROUBLE SPOTS	Mercury Grand Marquis (94 95 96 97 98 99 00 01)	Mercury Mountaineer 4WD (94 95 96 97 98 99 00 01)	Mercury Mystique V6 (94 95 96 97 98 99 00 01)	Mercury Sable (94 95 96 97 98 99 00 01)
Engine				
Cooling				
Fuel				
Ignition				
Transmission				
Electrical				
A/C				
Suspension				
Brakes				
Exhaust				
Power equipment				
Paint/trim/rust				
Integrity				
Hardware				
RELIABILITY VERDICT	✔ ✔ ✔ ✔ ✔ ✔ ✔	✔ ✔	✔ ✔	✔ ✔ ✔ ✔ ✔ ✔

Mercury Tracer / Mercury Villager / Mitsubishi Eclipse / Mitsubishi Galant

TROUBLE SPOTS	Mercury Tracer (94 95 96 97 98 99 00 01)	Mercury Villager (94 95 96 97 98 99 00 01)	Mitsubishi Eclipse (94 95 96 97 98 99 00 01)	Mitsubishi Galant (94 95 96 97 98 99 00 01)
Engine			Insufficient data	
Cooling				
Fuel				
Ignition				
Transmission				
Electrical				
A/C	Insufficient data			Insufficient data
Suspension				
Brakes				
Exhaust				
Power equipment				
Paint/trim/rust				
Integrity				
Hardware				
RELIABILITY VERDICT	✔ ✔ ✔ ✔ ✔	✔ ✔ ✔ ✔ ✔ ✔ ✔	✔ ✔	✔ ✔ ✔

Top section

TROUBLE SPOTS	Mitsubishi Montero Sport 94 95 96 97 98 99 00 01	Nissan Altima 94 95 96 97 98 99 00 01	Nissan Frontier, Pickup 2WD 94 95 96 97 98 99 00 01	Nissan Maxima 94 95 96 97 98 99 00 01
Engine	Insufficient data (94–99) ⊖⊖	○○⊖⊖⊖⊖⊖⊖	⊖⊖⊖⊖⊖ ⊖⊖	⊖⊖⊖⊖⊖⊖⊖⊖
Cooling	⊖	⊖⊖⊖⊖⊖⊖⊖⊖	⊖⊖⊖⊖⊖ ⊖⊖	⊖⊖⊖⊖⊖⊖⊖⊖
Fuel	⊖	⊖○○⊖⊖⊖⊖⊖	⊖⊖○○⊖ ⊖⊖	○○⊖⊖⊖⊖⊖⊖
Ignition	⊖	⊖○⊖⊖⊖⊖⊖⊖	⊖⊖⊖⊖⊖ ⊖⊖	⊖⊖⊖⊖⊖⊖⊖⊖
Transmission	⊖	⊖⊖⊖○⊖⊖⊖⊖	⊖⊖⊖⊖ ⊖ ⊖⊖	⊖⊖⊖⊖⊖⊖⊖⊖
Electrical	⊖	⊖●●○○⊖⊖⊖	⊖⊖⊖⊖⊖ ⊖⊖	⊖○○○⊖⊖⊖⊖
A/C	⊖	○○⊖⊖⊖⊖⊖⊖	⊖⊖⊖⊖⊖ ⊖⊖	○⊖⊖⊖⊖⊖⊖⊖
Suspension	⊖	○○○⊖⊖⊖⊖⊖	○⊖⊖⊖⊖ ⊖⊖	○⊖⊖⊖⊖⊖⊖⊖
Brakes	⊖	○○○○○⊖⊖⊖	⊖⊖⊖⊖⊖ ⊖⊖	●○○○⊖⊖⊖⊖
Exhaust	⊖	○○⊖⊖○⊖⊖⊖	○⊖⊖⊖⊖ ⊖⊖	○⊖⊖⊖⊖⊖⊖⊖
Power equipment	⊖	⊖⊖⊖○⊖⊖⊖⊖	⊖⊖⊖⊖⊖ ⊖⊖	●⊖⊖⊖⊖⊖⊖⊖
Paint/trim/rust	⊖	○○⊖⊖⊖⊖⊖⊖	⊖⊖⊖⊖⊖ ⊖⊖	○⊖⊖⊖⊖⊖⊖⊖
Integrity	⊖	○○○⊖○●○○⊖	⊖⊖⊖⊖⊖ ⊖⊖	○⊖⊖⊖⊖⊖⊖⊖
Hardware	⊖	○○○⊖⊖⊖⊖⊖	⊖⊖⊖⊖⊖ ○⊖	○⊖⊖⊖⊖⊖⊖⊖
RELIABILITY VERDICT	✓	✓✓✓✓✓✓✓✓	✓✓✓✓✓ ✓✓	✓✓✓✓✓✓✓✓

Bottom section

TROUBLE SPOTS	Nissan Pathfinder 94 95 96 97 98 99 00 01	Nissan Quest 94 95 96 97 98 99 00 01	Nissan Sentra 94 95 96 97 98 99 00 01	Nissan Xterra 94 95 96 97 98 99 00 01
Engine	⊖⊖⊖⊖⊖⊖⊖⊖	○○⊖⊖⊖⊖⊖⊖	○○⊖⊖⊖⊖⊖⊖	⊖⊖
Cooling	⊖⊖⊖⊖⊖⊖⊖⊖	○○⊖⊖⊖⊖⊖⊖	○⊖⊖⊖⊖⊖⊖⊖	⊖⊖
Fuel	⊖⊖○○○⊖⊖⊖	●●⊖○○⊖⊖⊖	○⊖○○⊖⊖⊖⊖	⊖⊖
Ignition	⊖⊖⊖⊖⊖⊖⊖⊖	⊖⊖⊖⊖⊖⊖⊖⊖	⊖⊖⊖⊖⊖⊖⊖⊖	⊖⊖
Transmission	⊖⊖⊖⊖⊖⊖⊖⊖	⊖⊖⊖⊖⊖⊖⊖⊖	⊖⊖⊖⊖⊖⊖⊖⊖	⊖⊖
Electrical	○⊖⊖⊖⊖⊖⊖⊖	●●●⊖○○○⊖	●●●○○⊖⊖⊖	⊖⊖
A/C	⊖⊖⊖⊖⊖⊖⊖⊖	⊖○○○⊖⊖⊖⊖	○⊖⊖⊖○⊖⊖⊖	⊖⊖
Suspension	⊖⊖○○⊖⊖⊖⊖	○⊖○○○○⊖⊖	○⊖⊖⊖○⊖⊖⊖	⊖⊖
Brakes	○○⊖⊖⊖⊖⊖⊖	⊖⊖○○○⊖○⊖	⊖○⊖⊖⊖⊖⊖⊖	⊖⊖
Exhaust	○○●⊖⊖⊖⊖⊖	○⊖○○○⊖⊖⊖	⊖⊖⊖⊖⊖⊖⊖⊖	⊖⊖
Power equipment	○○⊖⊖⊖⊖⊖⊖	⊖●⊖●●○○○	○⊖⊖⊖⊖⊖⊖⊖	⊖⊖
Paint/trim/rust	○⊖⊖⊖⊖⊖⊖⊖	○⊖○○⊖○⊖○	⊖⊖⊖⊖⊖⊖⊖⊖	⊖⊖
Integrity	●○⊖⊖⊖⊖⊖⊖	⊖⊖⊖○⊖⊖⊖○	●○○○○○○⊖	○○
Hardware	○⊖⊖⊖⊖⊖⊖⊖	⊖●⊖⊖⊖⊖⊖○	○○○○○○⊖⊖	⊖⊖
RELIABILITY VERDICT	✓✓✓✓✓✓✓✓	✓✓✓✓✓✓✓✓	✓✓✓✓✓✓✓✓	✓✓

Note: Nissan Quest column marked "Insufficient data" (vertical). Mitsubishi Montero Sport columns 94–99 marked "Insufficient data".

Oldsmobile 88

TROUBLE SPOTS	94	95	96	97	98	99	00	01
Engine								
Cooling								
Fuel								
Ignition								
Transmission								
Electrical								
A/C								
Suspension								
Brakes								
Exhaust								
Power equipment								
Paint/trim/rust								
Integrity								
Hardware								
RELIABILITY VERDICT	✓	✓		✓	✓			

Oldsmobile Alero

TROUBLE SPOTS	94	95	96	97	98	99	00	01
Engine								
Cooling								
Fuel								
Ignition								
Transmission								
Electrical								
A/C								
Suspension								
Brakes								
Exhaust								
Power equipment								
Paint/trim/rust								
Integrity								
Hardware								
RELIABILITY VERDICT						✓		

Oldsmobile Aurora

TROUBLE SPOTS	94	95	96	97	98	99	00	01
Engine								
Cooling								
Fuel								
Ignition								
Transmission								
Electrical								
A/C								
Suspension								
Brakes								
Exhaust								
Power equipment								
Paint/trim/rust								
Integrity								
Hardware								
RELIABILITY VERDICT		✓		✓				

Insufficient data (96, 00, 01)

Oldsmobile Bravada

TROUBLE SPOTS	94	95	96	97	98	99	00	01
Engine								
Cooling								
Fuel								
Ignition								
Transmission								
Electrical								
A/C								
Suspension								
Brakes								
Exhaust								
Power equipment								
Paint/trim/rust								
Integrity								
Hardware								
RELIABILITY VERDICT								

Insufficient data (94, 95, 96, 00, 01)

Oldsmobile Cutlass

TROUBLE SPOTS	94	95	96	97	98	99	00	01
Engine								
Cooling								
Fuel								
Ignition								
Transmission								
Electrical								
A/C								
Suspension								
Brakes								
Exhaust								
Power equipment								
Paint/trim/rust								
Integrity								
Hardware								
RELIABILITY VERDICT								

Oldsmobile Cutlass Ciera

TROUBLE SPOTS	94	95	96	97	98	99	00	01
Engine								
Cooling								
Fuel								
Ignition								
Transmission								
Electrical								
A/C								
Suspension								
Brakes								
Exhaust								
Power equipment								
Paint/trim/rust								
Integrity								
Hardware								
RELIABILITY VERDICT	✓	✓	✓					

Oldsmobile Cutlass Supreme

TROUBLE SPOTS	94	95	96	97	98	99	00	01
Engine								
Cooling								
Fuel								
Ignition								
Transmission								
Electrical								
A/C								
Suspension								
Brakes								
Exhaust								
Power equipment								
Paint/trim/rust								
Integrity								
Hardware								
RELIABILITY VERDICT		✓	✓					

Oldsmobile Intrigue

TROUBLE SPOTS	94	95	96	97	98	99	00	01
Engine								
Cooling								
Fuel								
Ignition								
Transmission								
Electrical								
A/C								
Suspension								
Brakes								
Exhaust								
Power equipment								
Paint/trim/rust								
Integrity								
Hardware								
RELIABILITY VERDICT					✓	✓		

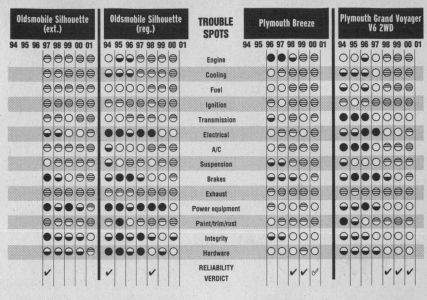

TROUBLE SPOTS	Oldsmobile Silhouette (ext.) 94 95 96 97 98 99 00 01	Oldsmobile Silhouette (reg.) 94 95 96 97 98 99 00 01	Plymouth Breeze 94 95 96 97 98 99 00 01	Plymouth Grand Voyager V6 2WD 94 95 96 97 98 99 00 01
Engine				
Cooling				
Fuel				
Ignition				
Transmission				
Electrical				
A/C				
Suspension				
Brakes				
Exhaust				
Power equipment				
Paint/trim/rust				
Integrity				
Hardware				
RELIABILITY VERDICT				

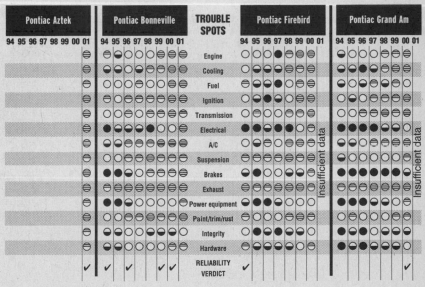

TROUBLE SPOTS	Pontiac Aztek 94 95 96 97 98 99 00 01	Pontiac Bonneville 94 95 96 97 98 99 00 01	Pontiac Firebird 94 95 96 97 98 99 00 01	Pontiac Grand Am 94 95 96 97 98 99 00 01
Engine				
Cooling				
Fuel				
Ignition				
Transmission				
Electrical				
A/C				
Suspension				
Brakes				
Exhaust				
Power equipment				
Paint/trim/rust				
Integrity				
Hardware				
RELIABILITY VERDICT				

Insufficient data (Pontiac Firebird)

Insufficient data (Pontiac Grand Am)

Top Section

Pontiac Grand Prix	Pontiac Montana (ext.)	TROUBLE SPOTS	Pontiac Sunbird, Sunfire	Porsche Boxster
94 95 96 97 98 99 00 01	94 95 96 97 98 99 00 01		94 95 96 97 98 99 00 01	94 95 96 97 98 99 00 01
		Engine		
		Cooling		
		Fuel		
		Ignition		
		Transmission		
		Electrical		
		A/C		
		Suspension		*Insufficient data*
		Brakes		
		Exhaust		
		Power equipment		
		Paint/trim/rust		
		Integrity		
		Hardware		
✔ ✔ ✔ ✔ ✔ ✔	✔	RELIABILITY VERDICT	✔ ✔ ✔ ✔	

Bottom Section

Saab 9-5	Saab 900, 9-3	TROUBLE SPOTS	Saturn L-Series	Saturn S-Series
94 95 96 97 98 99 00 01	94 95 96 97 98 99 00 01		94 95 96 97 98 99 00 01	94 95 96 97 98 99 00 01
		Engine		
		Cooling		
		Fuel		
		Ignition		
		Transmission		
	Insufficient data	Electrical		
		A/C		
		Suspension		
		Brakes		
		Exhaust		
		Power equipment		
		Paint/trim/rust		
		Integrity		
		Hardware		
✔ ✔ ✔	✔ ✔ ✔ ✔ ✔ ✔	RELIABILITY VERDICT	✔	✔ ✔ ✔ ✔ ✔ ✔ ✔ ✔

Top section

Subaru Forester								Subaru Impreza								TROUBLE SPOTS	Subaru Legacy/Outback								Suzuki Sidekick, Vitara							
94	95	96	97	98	99	00	01	94	95	96	97	98	99	00	01		94	95	96	97	98	99	00	01	94	95	96	97	98	99	00	01
				⊖	⊖	⊖	⊖		○	⊖	○	⊖	⊖	⊖	⊖	Engine	○	○	⊖	●	○	⊖	⊖	⊖	⊖	⊖	○			⊖	⊖	
				⊖	⊖	⊖	⊖		⊖	⊖	⊖	⊖	⊖	⊖	⊖	Cooling	○	⊖	⊖	⊖	⊖	⊖	⊖	⊖	⊖	⊖	⊖			⊖	⊖	
				⊖	⊖	○	⊖		○	⊖	⊖	⊖	⊖	⊖	⊖	Fuel	○	⊖	⊖	⊖	⊖	⊖	○	⊖	⊖	⊖	○			⊖	⊖	
				⊖	⊖	⊖	⊖		⊖	⊖	⊖	⊖	⊖	⊖	⊖	Ignition	⊖	⊖	⊖	⊖	⊖	⊖	⊖	⊖	⊖	○	○			⊖	⊖	
				⊖	⊖	⊖	⊖		⊖	⊖	⊖	○	⊖	⊖	⊖	Transmission	⊖	⊖	⊖	⊖	⊖	⊖	⊖	⊖	⊖	⊖	⊖			○	⊖	
				⊖	⊖	⊖	⊖		○	⊖	⊖	○	⊖	⊖	⊖	Electrical	○	⊖	⊖	●	⊖	⊖	⊖	⊖	○	○	○			⊖	⊖	
				⊖	⊖	⊖	⊖		⊖	⊖	⊖	⊖	⊖	⊖	⊖	A/C	⊖	⊖	⊖	⊖	⊖	⊖	⊖	⊖	○	●	⊖			⊖	○	
				⊖	⊖	⊖	⊖		⊖	⊖	⊖	⊖	⊖	⊖	⊖	Suspension	⊖	⊖	⊖	⊖	⊖	⊖	⊖	⊖	⊖	⊖	⊖			⊖	⊖	
				○	⊖	⊖	⊖		○	○	○	○	○	⊖	⊖	Brakes	○	○	○	○	⊖	⊖	⊖	⊖	○	○	○			⊖	⊖	
				⊖	⊖	⊖	⊖		⊖	⊖	⊖	⊖	⊖	⊖	⊖	Exhaust	⊖	⊖	⊖	⊖	⊖	⊖	⊖	⊖	⊖	⊖	⊖			⊖	⊖	
				⊖	⊖	⊖	⊖		⊖	⊖	⊖	⊖	⊖	⊖	○	Power equipment	⊖	⊖	⊖	⊖	⊖	⊖	⊖	⊖	⊖	⊖	⊖			⊖	○	
				⊖	⊖	⊖	⊖		○	⊖	⊖	⊖	⊖	⊖	⊖	Paint/trim/rust	⊖	⊖	⊖	⊖	⊖	⊖	⊖	⊖						○	○	
				⊖	⊖	⊖	⊖		⊖	○	⊖	○	○	○	⊖	Integrity	⊖	⊖	⊖	⊖	⊖	⊖	⊖	⊖	⊖	○	⊖			●	○	
				⊖	⊖	⊖	⊖		⊖	⊖	⊖	○	○	⊖	⊖	Hardware	⊖	⊖	⊖	⊖	⊖	⊖	⊖	⊖	⊖	⊖	○			○	○	
				✓	✓	✓	✓		✓	✓	✓	✓	✓	✓	✓	RELIABILITY VERDICT	✓	✓	✔	✓	✓	✓	✓	✓	✓	✓	✓					

Subaru Forester: Insufficient data for 1994–1997.
Suzuki Sidekick, Vitara: Insufficient data for 1997, 1998, 1999.

Bottom section

Toyota 4Runner								Toyota Avalon								TROUBLE SPOTS	Toyota Camry								Toyota Camry Solara							
94	95	96	97	98	99	00	01	94	95	96	97	98	99	00	01		94	95	96	97	98	99	00	01	94	95	96	97	98	99	00	01
○	○	○	⊖	⊖	⊖	⊖	⊖		⊖	⊖	⊖	⊖	⊖	⊖	⊖	Engine	○	⊖	⊖	⊖	⊖	⊖	⊖	⊖						⊖	⊖	⊖
○	○	○	⊖	⊖	⊖	⊖	⊖		⊖	⊖	⊖	⊖	⊖	⊖	⊖	Cooling	⊖	⊖	⊖	⊖	⊖	⊖	⊖	⊖						⊖	⊖	⊖
⊖	⊖	⊖	⊖	⊖	⊖	⊖	⊖		⊖	⊖	⊖	⊖	⊖	⊖	⊖	Fuel	⊖	⊖	⊖	⊖	⊖	⊖	⊖	⊖						⊖	⊖	⊖
⊖	⊖	⊖	⊖	⊖	⊖	⊖	⊖		⊖	⊖	⊖	⊖	⊖	⊖	⊖	Ignition	⊖	⊖	⊖	⊖	⊖	⊖	⊖	⊖						⊖	⊖	⊖
⊖	⊖	⊖	⊖	⊖	⊖	⊖	⊖		⊖	⊖	⊖	⊖	⊖	⊖	⊖	Transmission	⊖	⊖	⊖	⊖	⊖	⊖	⊖	⊖						⊖	⊖	⊖
○	○	⊖	⊖	⊖	⊖	⊖	⊖		○	⊖	⊖	⊖	⊖	⊖	⊖	Electrical	○	○	⊖	⊖	⊖	⊖	⊖	⊖						⊖	⊖	⊖
⊖	○	⊖	⊖	⊖	⊖	⊖	⊖		⊖	⊖	⊖	○	⊖	⊖	⊖	A/C	⊖	⊖	⊖	⊖	⊖	⊖	⊖	⊖						⊖	⊖	⊖
○	○	⊖	⊖	⊖	⊖	⊖	⊖		○	⊖	●	⊖	⊖	⊖	⊖	Suspension	○	⊖	⊖	⊖	⊖	⊖	⊖	⊖						⊖	⊖	⊖
○	○	○	⊖	○	⊖	⊖	⊖		○	⊖	⊖	⊖	⊖	⊖	⊖	Brakes	○	○	○	⊖	⊖	⊖	⊖	⊖						⊖	⊖	⊖
⊖	⊖	⊖	⊖	⊖	⊖	⊖	⊖		⊖	⊖	⊖	⊖	⊖	⊖	⊖	Exhaust	⊖	⊖	⊖	⊖	⊖	⊖	⊖	⊖						⊖	⊖	⊖
○	○	⊖	⊖	⊖	⊖	⊖	⊖		○	○	⊖	⊖	⊖	⊖	⊖	Power equipment	○	○	○	⊖	⊖	⊖	⊖	⊖						⊖	⊖	⊖
○	⊖	⊖	⊖	⊖	⊖	⊖	⊖		⊖	⊖	⊖	⊖	⊖	⊖	⊖	Paint/trim/rust	⊖	⊖	⊖	⊖	⊖	⊖	⊖	⊖						⊖	⊖	⊖
○	⊖	⊖	⊖	⊖	⊖	⊖	⊖		○	●	○	○	○	○	⊖	Integrity	⊖	⊖	⊖	⊖	⊖	⊖	⊖	⊖						○	⊖	⊖
○	○	⊖	⊖	⊖	⊖	⊖	⊖		⊖	⊖	⊖	⊖	⊖	⊖	⊖	Hardware	○	⊖	⊖	⊖	⊖	⊖	⊖	⊖						⊖	⊖	⊖
✓	✓	✓	✓	✓	✓	✓	✓		✓	✓	✓	✓	✓	✓	✓	RELIABILITY VERDICT	✓	✓	✓	✓	✓	✓	✓	✓						✓	✓	✓

Toyota Celica / Toyota Corolla / Toyota Echo / Toyota Highlander

Trouble Spots	Celica 94	95	96	97	98	99	00	01	Corolla 94	95	96	97	98	99	00	01	Echo 94	95	96	97	98	99	00	01	Highlander 94	95	96	97	98	99	00	01
Engine	⊖	⊖					⊖	⊖	⊖	⊖	⊖	⊖	⊖	⊖	⊖	⊖							⊖	⊖								⊖
Cooling	⊖	⊖					⊖	⊖	⊖	⊖	⊖	⊖	⊖	⊖	⊖	⊖							⊖	⊖								⊖
Fuel	⊖	⊖					⊖	⊖	⊖	⊖	⊖	⊖	⊖	⊖	⊖	⊖							⊖	⊖								⊖
Ignition	⊖	⊖					⊖	⊖	⊖	⊖	⊖	⊖	⊖	⊖	⊖	⊖							⊖	⊖								⊖
Transmission	⊖	⊖					⊖	⊖	⊖	⊖	⊖	⊖	⊖	⊖	⊖	⊖							⊖	⊖								⊖
Electrical	○	○					⊖	⊖	●	●	○	⊖	⊖	⊖	⊖	⊖							⊖	⊖								⊖
A/C	⊖	⊖					⊖	⊖	⊖	⊖	⊖	⊖	⊖	⊖	⊖	⊖							⊖	⊖								⊖
Suspension	⊖	⊖					⊖	⊖	⊖	⊖	⊖	⊖	⊖	⊖	⊖	⊖							⊖	⊖								⊖
Brakes	⊖	○					⊖	⊖	○	○	⊖	⊖	⊖	⊖	⊖	⊖							⊖	⊖								⊖
Exhaust	⊖	⊖					⊖	⊖	⊖	⊖	⊖	⊖	⊖	⊖	⊖	⊖							⊖	⊖								⊖
Power equipment	○	○					⊖	⊖	○	⊖	⊖	⊖	⊖	⊖	⊖	⊖							⊖	⊖								⊖
Paint/trim/rust	○	⊖					⊖	⊖	⊖	⊖	⊖	⊖	⊖	⊖	⊖	⊖							⊖	⊖								⊖
Integrity	○	⊖					○	⊖	⊖	⊖	⊖	⊖	⊖	⊖	⊖	⊖							⊖	⊖								⊖
Hardware	⊖	○					⊖	⊖	○	○	⊖	⊖	⊖	⊖	⊖	⊖							⊖	⊖								⊖
RELIABILITY VERDICT	✓	✓					✓	✓	✓	✓	✓	✓	✓	✓	✓	✓							✓	✓								✓

Celica columns 96–99: Insufficient data. Echo columns 94–99: Insufficient data.

Toyota Land Cruiser / Toyota Prius / Toyota RAV4 / Toyota Sequoia

Trouble Spots	Land Cruiser 94	95	96	97	98	99	00	01	Prius 94	95	96	97	98	99	00	01	RAV4 94	95	96	97	98	99	00	01	Sequoia 94	95	96	97	98	99	00	01
Engine						⊖	⊖	⊖								⊖			⊖	⊖	⊖	⊖	⊖	⊖								⊖
Cooling						⊖	⊖	⊖								⊖			⊖	⊖	⊖	⊖	⊖	⊖								⊖
Fuel						⊖	⊖	⊖								⊖			⊖	⊖	⊖	⊖	⊖	⊖								⊖
Ignition						⊖	⊖									⊖			⊖	⊖	⊖	⊖	⊖	⊖								⊖
Transmission						⊖	⊖									⊖			⊖	⊖	⊖	⊖	⊖	⊖								⊖
Electrical						⊖	⊖									⊖			⊖	⊖	⊖	⊖	⊖	⊖								⊖
A/C						⊖	⊖									⊖			⊖	⊖	⊖	⊖	⊖	⊖								⊖
Suspension						⊖	⊖									⊖			⊖	⊖	⊖	⊖	⊖	⊖								⊖
Brakes						⊖	⊖									⊖			○	○	○	⊖	⊖	⊖								⊖
Exhaust						⊖	⊖									⊖			⊖	⊖	⊖	⊖	⊖	⊖								⊖
Power equipment						○	⊖									⊖			⊖	⊖	○	⊖	⊖	⊖								⊖
Paint/trim/rust						⊖	⊖									⊖			⊖	⊖	⊖	⊖	⊖	⊖								⊖
Integrity						○	⊖									⊖			○	⊖	⊖	⊖	⊖	○								⊖
Hardware						⊖	⊖									⊖			⊖	⊖	⊖	⊖	⊖	⊖								⊖
RELIABILITY VERDICT						✓	✓									✓			✓	✓	✓	✓	✓	✓								✓

Land Cruiser columns 94–98, 01: Insufficient data.

Top section

Toyota Sienna								Toyota T100								TROUBLE SPOTS	Toyota Tacoma 2WD								Toyota Tacoma 4WD							
94	95	96	97	98	99	00	01	94	95	96	97	98	99	00	01		94	95	96	97	98	99	00	01	94	95	96	97	98	99	00	01
				◐	◐	◐	◐	○	○	◐	◐	◐				Engine	◐	◐	◐	◐	◐	◐	◐	◐	◐	○	◐	◐	◐	◐	◐	◐
				◐	◐	◐	◐	◐	◐	◐	◐	◐				Cooling	◐	◐	◐	◐	◐	◐	◐	◐	◐	◐	◐	◐	◐	◐	◐	◐
				◐	◐	◐	◐	◐	◐	◐	◐	◐				Fuel	◐	◐	◐	◐	◐	◐	◐	◐	◐	◐	○	◐	◐	◐	◐	◐
				◐	◐	◐	◐	○	◐	◐	◐	◐				Ignition	◐	◐	◐	◐	◐	◐	◐	◐	◐	◐	◐	◐	◐	◐	◐	◐
				◐	◐	◐	◐	○	◐	◐	◐	◐				Transmission	◐	◐	◐	◐	◐	◐	◐	◐	◐	◐	◐	◐	◐	◐	◐	◐
				◐	◐	◐	◐	◐	◐	◐	◐	◐				Electrical	○	○	◐	◐	◐	◐	◐	◐	○	◐	◐	◐	◐	◐	◐	◐
				◐	◐	◐	◐	◐	◐	◐	◐	◐				A/C	○	○	◐	◐	◐	◐	◐	◐	◐	◐	◐	◐	◐	◐	◐	◐
				◐	◐	◐	◐	○	◐	◐	◐	◐				Suspension	○	○	◐	◐	◐	◐	◐	◐	◐	◐	◐	◐	◐	◐	◐	◐
				◐	◐	◐	◐	◐	◐	○	◐	◐				Brakes	○	○	◐	○	◐	◐	◐	◐	◐	◐	◐	◐	◐	◐	◐	◐
				◐	◐	◐	◐	◐	◐	◐	◐	◐				Exhaust	○	○	◐	◐	◐	◐	◐	◐	◐	◐	◐	◐	◐	◐	◐	◐
				○	○	◐	◐	◐	◐	◐	◐	◐				Power equipment	◐	◐	◐	◐	◐	◐	◐	◐	◐	◐	◐	◐	◐	◐	◐	◐
				◐	◐	◐	◐	◐	◐	◐	◐	◐				Paint/trim/rust	◐	◐	◐	◐	◐	◐	◐	◐	◐	◐	◐	◐	◐	◐	◐	◐
				○	○	○	◐	◐	◐	○	◐	◐				Integrity	◐	○	◐	◐	◐	◐	◐	◐	◐	◐	◐	◐	◐	◐	◐	◐
				●	○	○	◐	○	○	○	○	○				Hardware	◐	○	○	◐	◐	◐	◐	◐	○	◐	◐	◐	◐	◐	◐	◐
				✓	✓	✓	✓	✓	✓	✓	✓	✓				RELIABILITY VERDICT	✓	✓	✓	✓	✓	✓	✓	✓	✓	✓	✓	✓	✓	✓	✓	✓

Bottom section

Toyota Tundra 2WD								Toyota Tundra 4WD								TROUBLE SPOTS	Volkswagen Golf 4 cyl.								Volkswagen Jetta 4 cyl.							
94	95	96	97	98	99	00	01	94	95	96	97	98	99	00	01		94	95	96	97	98	99	00	01	94	95	96	97	98	99	00	01
						◐	◐							◐	◐	Engine						◐	◐	◐	○	◐	◐	◐	◐	◐	◐	◐
						◐	◐							◐	◐	Cooling						◐	◐	◐	◐	◐	◐	◐	◐	◐	◐	◐
						◐	◐							◐	◐	Fuel						◐	○	◐	◐	○	○	◐	◐	◐	◐	○
						◐	◐							◐	◐	Ignition						○	◐	◐	◐	◐	◐	◐	◐	◐	◐	◐
						◐	◐							◐	◐	Transmission						◐	◐	◐	◐	◐	◐	◐	◐	◐	◐	◐
						◐	◐							◐	◐	Electrical						○	◐	◐	●	●	●	●	●	●	◐	●
						◐	◐							◐	◐	A/C						◐	◐	◐	●	◐	◐	◐	◐	◐	◐	◐
						◐	◐							◐	◐	Suspension						◐	◐	◐	◐	◐	◐	◐	◐	◐	◐	◐
						○	◐							○	◐	Brakes						◐	◐	◐	○	◐	○	◐	◐	◐	◐	◐
						◐	◐							◐	◐	Exhaust						◐	◐	◐	◐	◐	◐	◐	◐	◐	◐	◐
						◐	◐							◐	◐	Power equipment						○	○	◐	●	●	●	●	●	●	○	◐
						◐	◐							◐	◐	Paint/trim/rust						○	◐	◐	◐	●	◐	◐	◐	◐	◐	◐
						◐	◐							◐	◐	Integrity						○	○	◐	○	◐	◐	◐	◐	○	◐	◐
						◐	◐							◐	◐	Hardware						○	◐	◐	●	●	●	○	○	○	◐	◐
						✓	✓							✓	✓	RELIABILITY VERDICT						✓	✓	✓	✓			✓			✓	

Volkswagen Golf 4 cyl. — Insufficient data for years 94, 95, 96, 97, 98.

Volkswagen New Beetle

TROUBLE SPOTS	94	95	96	97	98	99	00	01
Engine					○	⊖	⊖	⊖
Cooling					○	⊖	⊖	⊖
Fuel					○	○	⊖	⊖
Ignition					⊖	⊖	⊖	⊖
Transmission					⊖	⊖	⊖	⊖
Electrical					●	●	○	⊖
A/C					○	⊖	⊖	⊖
Suspension					○	⊖	⊖	⊖
Brakes					⊖	⊖	⊖	⊖
Exhaust					⊖	⊖	⊖	⊖
Power equipment					●	●	○	⊖
Paint/trim/rust					⊖	⊖	⊖	⊖
Integrity					○	○	⊖	⊖
Hardware					●	●	○	⊖
RELIABILITY VERDICT								✓

Volkswagen Passat 4 cyl.

TROUBLE SPOTS	94	95	96	97	98	99	00	01
Engine	*Insufficient data*	*Insufficient data*	*Insufficient data*	*Insufficient data*	○	⊖	⊖	⊖
Cooling					⊖	⊖	⊖	⊖
Fuel					⊖	⊖	⊖	⊖
Ignition					⊖	⊖	⊖	⊖
Transmission					⊖	⊖	⊖	⊖
Electrical					○	⊖	⊖	⊖
A/C					⊖	⊖	⊖	⊖
Suspension					⊖	⊖	⊖	⊖
Brakes					⊖	⊖	⊖	⊖
Exhaust					⊖	⊖	⊖	⊖
Power equipment					●	○	○	⊖
Paint/trim/rust					⊖	⊖	⊖	⊖
Integrity					○	○	○	⊖
Hardware					○	○	○	⊖
RELIABILITY VERDICT						✓	✓	✓

Volkswagen Passat V6

TROUBLE SPOTS	94	95	96	97	98	99	00	01
Engine			○	⊖	*Insufficient data*	⊖	⊖	⊖
Cooling			○	⊖		⊖	⊖	⊖
Fuel			●	○		○	○	⊖
Ignition			○	○		⊖	⊖	⊖
Transmission			○	○		⊖	⊖	⊖
Electrical			●	●		○	○	⊖
A/C			○	⊖		○	○	⊖
Suspension			⊖	⊖		⊖	⊖	⊖
Brakes			⊖	⊖		⊖	⊖	⊖
Exhaust			⊖	⊖		⊖	⊖	⊖
Power equipment			●	●		○	○	⊖
Paint/trim/rust			⊖	⊖		⊖	⊖	⊖
Integrity			○	○		⊖	⊖	⊖
Hardware			●	●		○	⊖	⊖
RELIABILITY VERDICT						✓	✓	✓

Volvo 850, S70/V70 FWD

TROUBLE SPOTS	94	95	96	97	98	99	00	01
Engine	○	⊖	⊖	⊖	⊖	⊖	⊖	⊖
Cooling	○	⊖	⊖	⊖	⊖	⊖	⊖	⊖
Fuel	○	○	○	○	○	○	○	⊖
Ignition	○	○	○	⊖	⊖	⊖	⊖	⊖
Transmission	○	○	○	○	⊖	⊖	⊖	⊖
Electrical	○	○	⊖	⊖	⊖	⊖	⊖	⊖
A/C	●	●	○	○	⊖	⊖	⊖	⊖
Suspension	⊖	⊖	○	⊖	⊖	⊖	⊖	⊖
Brakes	○	⊖	⊖	⊖	⊖	⊖	⊖	⊖
Exhaust	⊖	⊖	⊖	⊖	⊖	⊖	⊖	⊖
Power equipment	⊖	○	○	○	○	○	○	○
Paint/trim/rust	⊖	○	○	○	○	○	⊖	⊖
Integrity	○	○	○	○	○	○	⊖	⊖
Hardware	⊖	○	○	○	○	—	○	⊖
RELIABILITY VERDICT	✓	✓	✓	✓		✓	✓	

Volvo 960, S90/V90

TROUBLE SPOTS	94	95	96	97	98	99	00	01
Engine	*Insufficient data*	○	○	⊖	⊖			
Cooling		●	○	○	⊖			
Fuel		⊖	○	⊖	⊖			
Ignition		⊖	⊖	⊖	⊖			
Transmission		⊖	⊖	⊖	⊖			
Electrical		●	●	○	⊖			
A/C		⊖	⊖	⊖	⊖			
Suspension		●	●	●	○			
Brakes		⊖	⊖	⊖	⊖			
Exhaust		⊖	⊖	⊖	⊖			
Power equipment		●	○	○	●			
Paint/trim/rust		○	○	⊖	⊖			
Integrity		⊖	○	⊖	○			
Hardware		●	○	○	○			
RELIABILITY VERDICT		✓	✓	✓				

Volvo S40/V40

TROUBLE SPOTS	94	95	96	97	98	99	00	01
Engine							⊖	⊖
Cooling							⊖	⊖
Fuel							○	⊖
Ignition							⊖	⊖
Transmission							⊖	⊖
Electrical							○	⊖
A/C							⊖	⊖
Suspension							⊖	⊖
Brakes							○	⊖
Exhaust							⊖	⊖
Power equipment							○	⊖
Paint/trim/rust							⊖	⊖
Integrity							○	⊖
Hardware							○	⊖
RELIABILITY VERDICT							✓	

Volvo S70/V70 AWD

TROUBLE SPOTS	94	95	96	97	98	99	00	01
Engine					○	⊖	⊖	⊖
Cooling					⊖	⊖	⊖	⊖
Fuel					○	○	⊖	○
Ignition					⊖	⊖	⊖	⊖
Transmission					⊖	⊖	⊖	⊖
Electrical					●	●	●	○
A/C					○	○	⊖	⊖
Suspension					○	○	⊖	⊖
Brakes					●	○	⊖	⊖
Exhaust					⊖	⊖	⊖	⊖
Power equipment					○	○	⊖	⊖
Paint/trim/rust					⊖	⊖	⊖	⊖
Integrity					○	⊖	⊖	⊖
Hardware					⊖	○	○	⊖
RELIABILITY VERDICT								

Volvo S80

TROUBLE SPOTS	94	95	96	97	98	99	00	01
Engine						⊖	⊖	⊖
Cooling						⊖	⊖	⊖
Fuel						○	⊖	⊖
Ignition						⊖	⊖	⊖
Transmission						⊖	⊖	⊖
Electrical						●	○	⊖
A/C						○	○	⊖
Suspension						●	○	⊖
Brakes						○	⊖	⊖
Exhaust						⊖	⊖	⊖
Power equipment						●	○	○
Paint/trim/rust						⊖	⊖	⊖
Integrity						○	⊖	○
Hardware						●	⊖	⊖
RELIABILITY VERDICT								✓

STATEMENT OF OWNERSHIP, MANAGEMENT, AND CIRCULATION
(Required by 39 U.S.C. 3685)

1. Publication Title: Consumer Reports. 2. Publication No: 0010-7174. 3. Filing Date: October 4, 2002. 4. Issue Frequency: Monthly, except two issues in December. 5. No. of Issues Published Annually: 13. 6. Annual Subscription Price: $26.00. 7. Complete Mailing Address of Known Office of Publication: 101 Truman Avenue, Yonkers, New York 10703-1057. 8. Complete Mailing Address of Headquarters or General Business Office of Publisher: 101 Truman Avenue, Yonkers, New York 10703-1057. 9. Full Names and Complete Mailing Addresses of Publisher, Editor, and Managing Editor. Publisher: Consumers Union of United States, Inc., 101 Truman Avenue, Yonkers, New York 10703-1057. President: James A. Guest; Editor: Margot Slade; Executive Editor: Eileen Denver. 10. Owner: (If the publication is published by a nonprofit organization, its name and address must be stated.) Full Name: Consumers Union of United States, Inc., a non-profit organization. Complete Mailing Address: 101 Truman Avenue, Yonkers, New York 10703-1057. 11. Known Bondholders, Mortgagees, and Other Security Holders Owning or Holding 1 Percent or More of Total Amount of Bonds, Mortgages, or Other Securities. If none, so state: None. 12. For Completion by Nonprofit Organizations Authorized to Mail at Special Rates: The purpose, function, and nonprofit status of this organization and the exempt status for federal income tax purposes has not changed during preceding 12 months.

15. Extent and Nature of Circulation:

	Average no. copies each issue during past 12 mo.	Actual no. copies of single issue published nearest to filing date
A. Total no. of copies (net press run)	4,348,984	4,311,190
B. Paid and/or requested circulation		
1. Sales through dealers, carriers, street vendors, counter sales (not mailed)	92,742	74,755
2. Paid or requested mail subscriptions (include advertisers' proof copies/exchange copies)	4,006,243	4,037,846
C. Total paid and/or requested circulation (sum of 15b(1) and 15b(2))	4,098,984	4,112,601
D. Free distribution by mail (samples, complimentary, and other free)	19,891	21,968
E. Free distribution outside the mail	15,759	14,457
F. Total free distribution (sum of 15d and 15e)	35,650	36,425
G. Total distribution (sum of 15c and 15f)	4,134,634	4,149,026
H. Copies not distributed		
1. Office use, leftovers, spoiled	65,119	8,889
2. Return from news agents	149,795	153,275
I. TOTAL (sum of 15g, 15h(1) and 15h(2)	4,348,984	4,311,190
J. Percent paid and/or requested circulation	99.14%	99.12%,

17. I certify that the statements made by me above are correct and complete.

Louis J. Milani, Senior Director, Business Affairs & Strategic Marketing

REFERENCE

PRODUCT RATINGS

How to use the ratings

First, read the general buying advice article for the product you're interested in. The page numbers for these reports are noted on each Ratings page. The Overall Ratings chart gives the big picture in performance. Notes on features and performance for individual models are listed under "Recommendations & notes." In addition, you'll find "features at a glance" tables for some products. You can use the key numbers to move easily between the charts and the other information.

CONSUMER REPORTS checked the availability for most products especially for this book. Some tested models may no longer be available. Models similar to the tested models, when they exist, are listed in "Recommendations & notes." Such models differ in features, not essential performance, according to manufacturers.

Barbecue grills

Shop Smart Most grills tested were very good or even excellent in our tests. The Weber Summit 450, $2,200, and the Broilmaster P3, $840, performed superbly and offer the style and durability of stainless steel. But the Weber Genesis Silver-B, $450—a **CR Best Buy**—did almost as well and has premium features for less. Superb performance helps the Weber Genesis Silver-A, $350—another **CR Best Buy**—stand out among less expensive grills. Two more **CR Best Buys** that cost even less: the Char-Broil Big Easy 4638247, $250, and Sunbeam Grillmaster BG6522RPB, $200. Key features for these models are listed in the table on page 215. See the product guide for an explanation of the features.

Excellent	Very good	Good	Fair	Poor
⊖	⊖	○	⊖	●

Overall Ratings In performance order

KEY NO.	BRAND & MODEL	PRICE	OVERALL SCORE	EVENNESS	GRILLING	FEATURES AND CONVENIENCE
			0 P F G VG E 100			
1	**Weber** Summit 450 26[1]101	$2,200		⊖	⊖	⊖
2	**Broilmaster** P3[BL]	840		⊖	⊖	⊖
3	**Coleman** 4000 HG49810S	500		⊖	⊖	⊖
4	**Weber** Genesis Silver-B 228[1]001 **A CR Best Buy**	450		⊖	⊖	⊖
5	**Ducane** 1605SHLPE [1]	800		⊖	⊖	⊖
6	**Char-Broil** Commercial Series 4632215 [1]	500		⊖	⊖	⊖
7	**Jenn-Air** JLG7130ADS	1,500		⊖	⊖	⊖
8	**Weber** Genesis Silver-A 227[1]001 **A CR Best Buy**	350		⊖	⊖	⊖
9	**Ducane** 1305SHLPE [1]	700		⊖	⊖	⊖
10	**Ducane** 1504SHLPE [1]	600		⊖	⊖	⊖
11	**Ducane** 804SHLP [1]	550		⊖	⊖	⊖
12	**Kenmore** (Sears) 15227 [1]	550		⊖	⊖	⊖
13	**Char-Broil** Big Easy 4638247 **A CR Best Buy**	250		⊖	⊖	○
14	**Sunbeam** Grillmaster BG6522RPB **A CR Best Buy**	200		⊖	⊖	○
15	**Great Outdoors Grill Company** 6000	300		⊖	⊖	⊖
16	**Kenmore** (Sears) 15221 [1]	300		⊖	⊖	⊖
17	**Sunbeam** Grillmaster BG4622YPB-S	260		⊖	⊖	⊖
18	**Holland** Tradition BH421SG4 [1]	650		⊖	○	○
19	**Fiesta** Advantis 3000 EZT34545	170		⊖	○	○
20	**Fiesta** Advantis 1000 EZH30030	120		⊖	⊖	⊖
21	**Char-Broil** 4637115	140		⊖	○	⊖

[1] Price does not include tank ($25 to $30).
See report, page 94. Based on tests published in Consumer Reports in June 2002, with updated prices and availability.

The tests behind the Ratings

Overall score is based on a gas grill's performance, features, and convenience. We tested **evenness** of heating at high and low settings using temperature sensors, then combined the performance scores. Results were verified by searing 15 burgers on the worst and best grills' high setting for 1½ minutes. **Grilling** measures the ability to cook chicken and fish on the low setting. **Features and convenience** evaluates construction and materials, accessory burners and shelves, rack space, and ease of use. **Price** is approximate retail. For similar models, empty brackets indicate a color code.

Recommendations & notes

All grills: Are mounted on patio carts. Have side shelves. **Most grills:** Have a thermometer on the lid. Have a warming rack. Have warranties ranging from 25 years to life for the castings, 3 to 5 years for the burners, 1 or 2 years for other parts. Have a 370- to 425-square-inch cooking area and 300 to 500 square inches of shelf space. Require significant assembly. Have dual burner controls. Use a steel rack full of ceramic or charcoal-like briquettes, or steel triangles or plates, to distribute heat. Have a rotary or push-button igniter, porcelain-coated wire cooking grates and warming rack, a side burner, and four casters. Have spider protectors on the gas-line venturi tubes.

1 ▷ **WEBER** Summit 450 26[1]101 **Superb performance-but you pay for it.** The most shelf space of tested models. Less assembly than most. Wider than most. Knobs and removable thermometer got hot.

2 ▷ **BROILMASTER** P3[BL] **A premium grill at a premium price.** Lots of shelf space.

3 ▷ **COLEMAN** 4000 HG49810S **Excellent for entertaining large groups.** Extra-large cooking area. Lots of shelf space. Less assembly than most. Discontinued, but similar LG40811E is available.

4 ▷ **WEBER** Genesis Silver-B 228[1]001 **A CR Best Buy Excellent overall.** Lots of shelf space. Removable thermometer got hot. Similar: 228[ ]411, 228[ ]398.

5 ▷ **DUCANE** 1605SHLPE **Very good, but lower-**

priced models performed as well. Extra-large cooking area. Lit-burner indicator. Less assembly than most. No thermometer. Inner handle got hot during use.

6 ▷ **CHAR-BROIL** Commercial Series **4632215 Very good, with lots of shelf space.** Extra-large cooking area. Griddle. No spider protector. Similar: 4632210.

7 ▷ **JENN-AIR** JLG7130ADS **Lots of style and shelf space.** Mostly stainless-steel construction. Extra-large cooking area. Less assembly than most. No thermometer. No warming radio. Handle got hot during use. Similar: Dynasty DBQ-30F.

8 ▷ **WEBER** Genesis Silver-A 227[1]001 **A CR Best Buy Similar in appearance to #4, but narrower.** Less cooking area than most. Removable thermometer got hot. Similar: 227[ ]411, 227[ ]398

9 ▷ **DUCANE** 1305SHLPE **Very good.** Lit-burner indicator. Less assembly than most. Inner handle got hot during use. No thermometer.

10 ▷ **DUCANE** 1504SHLPE **Less assembly than most.** Lit-burner indicator. Less shelf space than most. No spider protector. No thermometer. Inner handle got hot.

11 ▷ **DUCANE** 804SHLP **Similar in appearance to #10, but smaller and only one burner.** Less cooking area than most. Must use match to light grill. Discontinued, but similar

Recommendations & notes

1005SHLPE with igniter and spider protector is available.

12> **KENMORE** (Sears) 15227 **More shelf space than most but less warming-rack space.** No spider protector. Smoker tray. Infrared rotisserie burner. Warranty shorter than most.

13> **CHAR-BROIL** Big Easy 4638247 **A CR Best Buy Very good performer.** Flared up more than others. Has griddle. Cart less sturdy than others. Less assembly than most. No thermometer.

14> **SUNBEAM** Grillmaster BG6522RPB **A CR Best Buy More warming-rack space than others, but less shelf space.** Handle got hot during use. No thermometer. No spider protector. Similar: WG6522RPB.

15> **GREAT OUTDOORS GRILL COMPANY** 6000 **Very good.** Less assembly than most. No thermometer. Smaller cooking area than most.

16> **KENMORE** (Sears) 15221 **Very good.** More shelf space than most, but smaller cooking area and less warming-rack space. No spider protector. Warranty shorter than most. Similar: 15223.

17> **SUNBEAM** Grillmaster BG4622YPB-S **Very good.** More warming-rack space than others, but less shelf space. Less assembly than most. No thermometer. No spider protector.

18> **HOLLAND** Tradition BH421SG4 **Can steam and smoke as well as grill.** Smaller cooking area than most. Only one temperature setting. Smoker-drawer knob got hot. No warming rack. Similar: Heritage BH421SG5.

19> **FIESTA** Advantis 3000 EZT34545 **Very good, but smaller cooking area than most and less shelf space.** Cart judged less sturdy than others. No thermometer. Similar: EZA34545.

20> **FIESTA** Advantis 1000 EZH30030 **Good.** Smaller cooking area than most. Flared up more than others. Cart judged less sturdy than others. No thermometer. Similar: EZH30030.

21> **CHAR-BROIL** 4637115 **There are better choices.** Tools-free assembly. Smaller cooking area than most. No heat-transfer medium. Cart judged less sturdy than others. Discontinued, but similar 4637133 is available.

FEATURES AT A GLANCE BARBECUE GRILLS

Tested products (keyed to the Ratings) Key no. Brand	Long warranty	Burners		Grates		Fuel gauge	Electronic ignitor
		3 or 4	Side	Porcelain-cast iron	Stainless		
1> Weber		•			•	•	
2> Broilmaster	•			•			•
3> Coleman		•			•	•	•
4> Weber	•	•				•	
5> Ducane	•			•			
6> Char-Broil	•	•	•	•			•
7> Jenn-Air	•			•			
8> Weber	•						
9> Ducane	•						
10> Ducane	•						
11> Ducane	•						
12> Kenmore		•	•	•			
13> Char-Broil		•	•				
14> Sunbeam				•			
15> Great Outdoors Grill Company	•						
16> Kenmore		•					•
17> Sunbeam				•			•
18> Holland	•				•		
19> Fiesta		•					
20> Fiesta							
21> Char-Broil							

Camcorders

Shop Smart Digital camcorders generally capture high-quality images and very good sound. They're easy to use and come with lots of features. If you want to try video editing or downloading to the web, invest in a digital model. The Sony DCR-TRV25, $900, Sony DCR-TRV240, $1,600, and Canon ZR45MC, $700, are worthy choices. Most analog models were rated good and cost hundreds of dollars less than digital models. Picture quality, though generally a notch below digital, is still perfectly fine. Consider the Hi8 Sony CCD-TRV608, $400, or the CCD-TRV308, $350.

KEY NO.	BRAND AND MODEL	PRICE	FORMAT	OVERALL SCORE	PICTURE QUALITY	EASE OF USE	IMAGE STABILIZER	WEIGHT (LBS)
	DIGITAL MODELS							
1	**Sony** DCR-TRV25	$900	MiniDV		⊖	⊖	⊖	1.6
2	**Sony** DCR-PC120BT	2,000	MiniDV		⊖	○	⊖	1.5
3	**Panasonic** PV-DV402	800	MiniDV		⊖	⊖	●	1.4
4	**Panasonic** PV-DC152	800	MiniDV		⊖	○	◐	1.2
5	**Sony** DCR-TRV240	600	D8		⊖	○	○	2.1
6	**Sony** DCR-TRV140	500	D8		⊖	⊖	●	2.2
7	**Canon** ZR45MC	700	MiniDV		⊖	⊖	○	1.4
8	**JVC** GR-DVL920U	900	MiniDV		⊖	○	◐	1.5
9	**Canon** Optura 100MC	1,500	MiniDV		⊖	○	○	1.7
10	**Panasonic** PV-DV52	500	MiniDV		⊖	○	●	1.4
11	**Panasonic** PV-DV102	600	MiniDV		⊖	○	●	1.4
12	**JVC** GR-DVL120U	500	MiniDV		⊖	○	◐	1.5
13	**Sony** DCR-IP7BT	1,700	MicroMV		⊖	◐	●	0.8
14	**Hitachi** DZ-MV200A	900	8cm DVD-RAM, 8cm DVD-R		○	○	⊖	1.8
15	**JVC** GR-DVM76U	750	MiniDV		○	○	◐	1.2
16	**Samsung** SC-D80	475	MiniDV		○	⊖	○	1.4
17	**Sharp** VL-NZ50U	500	MiniDV		○	○	●	1.2

Overall Ratings   In performance order

Excellent ⊖   Very good ○   Good ○   Fair ◐   Poor ●

OVERALL SCORE: 0   P   F   G   VG   E   100

Overall Ratings, cont.

			Excellent	Very good	Good	Fair	Poor
			⊖	⊖	○	◑	●

KEY NO.	BRAND AND MODEL	PRICE	FORMAT	OVERALL SCORE	PICTURE QUALITY	EASE OF USE	IMAGE STABILIZER	WEIGHT (LBS)
				0 100 P F G VG E				
	ANALOG MODELS							
18	**Sony** CCD-TRV608	$400	Hi8		○	⊖	○	2.2
19	**Sony** CCD-TRV308	350	Hi8		⊖	⊖	●	2.2
20	**JVC** GR-SXM240U	300	SVHS-C		○	◑	○	2.4
21	**Sony** CCD-TRV108	300	Hi8		○	⊖	NA	2.1
22	**Samsung** SC-L700	270	Hi8		○	⊖	NA	2.0
23	**Panasonic** PV-L352	280	VHS-C		◑	○	◑	2.6
24	**Sharp** VL-AD260U	360	Hi8		○	○	◑	2.0
25	**Canon** ES75	230	Hi8		◑	○	NA	1.9
26	**Sharp** VL-AH131U	280	Hi8		◑	○	NA	1.9

See report, page 20. Based on tests published in Consumer Reports in November 2002.

The tests behind the Ratings

Format lists the recording format used. **Overall score** mainly reflects SP picture quality and ease of use. **Picture quality** is based on the judgments of trained panelists, who viewed still images shot at standard (SP) tape speed. **Ease of use** takes into account ergonomics, weight, how accurately the viewfinders framed the scene being shot, and measurements of the LCD's contrast. **Image stabilizer** scores reflect how well the circuitry worked, for models that have it. "NA" in a column means the camcorder lacks it. **Weight** is our measurement. **Price** is the approximate retail.

Recommendations & notes

Models listed as similar should offer performance comparable to the tested model's, although features may differ.

Most of these camcorders have: Rechargeable battery pack. AC adapter/battery charger. A/V cable. Playpack adapter (VHS-C and S-VHS-C models only). Ability to load tape, plug in power, or change battery when mounted on tripod. 10x optical zoom. 2.5-inch color LCD viewer. Selection of built-in autoexposure programs. Audio and video fade. Backlight compensation. High-speed manual shutter. Image stabilizer. LCD viewer. Brightness control. Manual aperture, shutter speed, focus, and white balance controls. Quick review. S-video output jack (not on VHS-C). Tape counter. **Most digital camcorders also have:** FireWire or iLink connection, digital still feature.

Optical zoom is as stated by the manufacturer. Audio frequency response, when recording with the built-in microphone, was very good and relatively noise-free for most camcorders. Most camcorders with LP/EP mode yielded same picture quality as in SP mode. In dim lighting, most camcorders yielded a tolerable picture quality.

DIGITAL MODELS

1 **SONY** DCR-TRV25 **Feature-laden, with the least audio noise among tested models.** Includes medium-resolution digital still. Similar DCR-TRV27 has a large LCD. Can't load tape if mounted on tripod.

2 **SONY** DCR-PC120BT **Excellent image stabilization in a feature-laden model, but poor**

Recommendations & notes

performance in low light. Includes Bluetooth wireless interface and novel communications capability to send video clips, stills, or e-mail over the Internet without a computer. Includes medium-resolution still feature. Can't load tape if mounted on tripod. Similar DCR-TRV27 has a large LCD.

3 > PANASONIC PV-DV402 **Excellent in performance in good lighting, but poor image stabilization and zoom is noisy.** Barely adequate in low light, but very good if built-in light and manual controls are used. Includes a very large LCD viewer (3.5 in.) and medium-resolution digital-still feature. Similar PVDV-202 has typical 2.5 in. LCD. CCD and battery warranties on the short side (6 mo. and 10 days, respectively).

4 > PANASONIC PV-DC152 **Very good overall and lightweight, but LCD viewer hard to see in bright light.** Short warranties for image sensor and battery (6 mo. and 10 days, respectively). Poor picture quality in low light but using manual controls helps. Lacks digital-still feature (similar PV-DC252 has it).

5 > SONY DCR-TRV240 **Moderately priced and very good overall, with a 25x zoom that's among the longest.** Can play back analog tapes in Hi8 and 8mm formats. But LCD viewer hard to see in bright light. No manual white balance. Can't load tape if mounted on tripod. Lacks digital-still feature (similar DCR-TRV340 has it).

6 > SONY DCR-TRV140 **Very good, with 20x zoom.** Good in low light, and easy to use overall, but poor image stabilization and noisy audio. Cannot play back analog tapes. Lacks digital-still feature, manual white balance.

7 > CANON ZR45MC **Lightweight, with no major flaws.** Very good and easy to use, with large

FEATURES AT A GLANCE CAMCORDERS

Tested products (keyed to the Ratings) Key Brand no.	LCD viewer size, in.	Battery life, min.	Full auto switch	Quick review	Video light	A/V input	Microphone jack
CONVENTIONAL DIGITAL MODELS							
1 > Sony	2.5	145/115		•		•	•
2 > Sony	2.5	130/110		•		•	•
3 > Panasonic	3.5	N.S.	•	•			
4 > Panasonic	2.5	130/95		•			
5 > Sony	2.5	100/80		•		•	•
6 > Sony	2.5	110/85	•	•			
7 > Canon	2.5	90/75	•	•		•	•
8 > JVC	3.5	70/55	•		•	•	
9 > Canon	2.5	120/100	•	•		•	•
10 > Panasonic	2.5	N.S.	•	•			
11 > Panasonic	2.5	NA	•	•			
12 > JVC	2.5	75/60	•				
13 > Sony	2.5	80/65		•	•		
14 > Hitachi	2.5	115-130/100-115				•	•
15 > JVC	2.5	65/50	•				
16 > Samsung	2.5	120/90	•	•			
17 > Sharp	3.0	-/90	•				
ANALOG MODELS							
18 > Sony	3.0	165/100		•	•		
19 > Sony	2.5	165/120		•	•		
20 > JVC	2.5	95/80	•	•	•		
21 > Sony	2.5	165/120		•	•		
22 > Samsung	2.5	130/90	•	•	•		
23 > Panasonic	2.5	70/55			•		
24 > Sharp	3.5	-/90		•			
25 > Canon	–	150/-	•	•	•		
26 > Panasonic	3	120/90			•		

Recommendations & notes

controls, 18x zoom, good low-light performance (on manual setting), and flutter-free audio. ZR45MC and similar ZR50MC have low-resolution digital still. ZR40 lacks digital still. Tape-head warranty on the short side (3 mo.). Can't load tape if mounted on tripod. No backlight compensation switch.

8▷ **JVC** GR-DVL920U **Very good overall. Poor in low light but becomes good if video light and manual settings are used.** This and similar DVL820U have large LCD viewer (3.5 in.), but it's hard to view in bright light. DVL725U has 2.5 in. LCD. Has medium-resolution digital-still feature. Battery life is under one hour. No quick review. Short warranties for image sensor and battery (3 mo.).

9▷ **CANON** Optura 100MC **Very good overall, with medium-resolution digital-still feature.** Includes features advanced users might want (microphone jack, hot shoe, A/V input), which bring up the price. Tape-head warranty on the short side (3 mo.). Poor low-light picture quality, but using its low-light program helps. Can't load tape if mounted on tripod. No backlight compensation switch.

10▷ **PANASONIC** PV-DV52 Similar to the PV-DV102 but without the digital-still camera feature.

11▷ **PANASONIC** PV-DV102 **Very good overall, and good in low light if built-in light and manual settings used.** Includes medium-resolution digital-still feature. But image stabilizer is poor, and its zoom is noisy. Short warranties for image sensor and battery (6 mo. and 10 days, respectively). LCD viewer hard to view in bright light. No S-video jack.

12▷ **JVC** GR-DVL120U **Low-light performance improves if manual settings are used.** Short warranty on image sensor and battery. No audio fade. Can't load tape if mounted on

tripod. Similar GR-DVL520U and GR-DVL720U have medium-resolution digital still. GR-DVL720U has a large LCD viewer. Has 16x zoom. Similar models have video light, 10x zoom.

13▷ **SONY** DCR-IP7BT **Good overall and very compact, but with cumbersome menu system and uses new recording format (MicroMV tape).** Includes Bluetooth wireless interface and novel communications capability to send video clips, stills, or e-mail over the Internet without a computer. Poor low-light performance and image stabilizer. Can't load tape if mounted on tripod.

14▷ **HITACHI** DZ-MV200A **Records directly onto disks.** You can navigate a disk randomly via thumbnail previews. No backlight-compensation switch. Fair picture quality in standard mode.

15▷ **JVC** GR-DVM76U **There are better digital choices.** Short warranty on image sensor and battery.

16▷ **SAMSUNG** SC-D80 **There are better digital choices.** Can't load tape if mounted on tripod. SC-D86 adds digital still.

17▷ **SHARP** VL-NZ50U **Lacks an eyepiece, quick review, and S-video jack.** Good overall, with a larger 3-inch LCD viewer but otherwise few frills. Poor image stabilizer. Zoom is noisy. High-speed manual shutter. Battery warranty on the short side (1 mo.). Lacks digital-still feature (similars VL-NZ100U and VL-NZ150U have it).

ANALOG MODELS

18▷ **SONY** CCD-TRV608 **Good, very easy to use, with 20x zoom and a larger 3-inch LCD viewer.** Good in low light. Picture quality drops a notch at LP speed. No manual white balance.

Recommendations & notes

19 **SONY** CCD-TRV308 **Good, very easy to use, with 20x zoom.** Good in low light. This model offers poorer image stabilization, but better picture at SP speed than on the CCD-TRV608. No manual white balance.

20 **JVC** GR-SXM240U **A good, basic unit with 16x zoom and good low-light performance.** VHS playback on a VCR is a plus, but has inferior audio. LCD viewer hard to see in bright light, and camcorder not as easy to use as many. Short warranties for image sensor and battery (3 mo.). Similar SXM340U has 2.5 in. LCD; SXM740U has 3.5 in. LCD.

21 **SONY** CCD-TRV108 **A good and basic camcorder with 20x zoom.** Lack of image stabilizer and video light help hold the price. Picture quality drops a notch at LP speed. No manual white balance.

22 **SAMSUNG** SC-L700 **Good, basic, easy to use, and very inexpensive as camcorders go, with a 22x zoom.** No image stabilization, slow recording speed, or manual aperture control.

23 **PANASONIC** PV-L352 **Good overall, with 20x zoom.** VHS playback on a VCR is a plus, but background noise and flutter mar audio quality, and battery life is under one hour. Eyepiece not too accurate at framing scenes. Short warranties for image sensor and battery (6 mo. and 10 days, respectively). No quick review, tape counter, manual aperture, or white balance controls. Similar: PV-L4S2, PV-L552, PV-L652.

24 **SHARP** VL-AD260U **There are better choices.** No slow speed, eyepiece, S-video jack. Short battery warranty.

25 **CANON** ES75 **There are better choices.** No slow speed, LCD viewer, image stabilizer. Short warranty on image sensor.

26 **SHARP** VL-AH131U **Has 16x zoom, but lacks an eyepiece and S-video jack.** Has a hard-to-use menu and no image stabilizer or slow recording speed. Fair performance overall, and battery warranty on the short side (1 mo.).

Cameras-digital

Shop Smart   Paying more gets you more pixels, but not always improved results. The 2-megapixel Kodak EasyShare DX3600 Zoom and Nikon Coolpix 2500, each $300, produced images that rivaled higher-megapixel models'. Consider a 3- to 5-megapixel camera for greater latitude in cropping and enlarging. The 5-megapixel, 5x-zoom Sony DSC-F707 gives both, but at the steep price of $1,000. The Olympus Camedia C-3040 Zoom and D-40 Zoom, each $600, offer excellent image quality and a compact design for less money.

			Excellent ⊖	Very good ⊖	Good ○	Fair ⊖	Poor ●

Overall Ratings   In performance order

KEY NO.	BRAND & MODEL	PRICE	OVERALL SCORE	PRINT QUALITY	MEGA-PIXELS	FLASH RANGE (FT.)	BATTERY LIFE (SHOTS)	NEXT-SHOT DELAY (SEC.)
			0 P F G VG E 100					
3- TO 5-MEGAPIXEL CAMERAS								
1	**Sony** DSC-F707	$1,000		⊖	5	15	240	2
2	**Canon** PowerShot G2	800		⊖	4	15	600	3
3	**Olympus** Camedia C-3040 Zoom	600		⊖	3.3	18	320	3
4	**Olympus** Camedia D-40 Zoom	600		⊖	4.1	10	50	4
5	**Fujifilm** FinePix F601 Z	550		⊖	3	15	250	2
6	**Sony** Cyber-shot DSC-S75	500		⊖	3.3	10	300	3
7	**HP** PhotoSmart 812	500		⊖	4.1	9	80	4
8	**Kodak** EasyShare DX4900	400		⊖	4	10	95	2
9	**Olympus** Camedia E-10	1,200		⊖	4.1	21	50	2
10	**Canon** Powershot S40	550		⊖	4.1	16	320	3
11	**Casio** QV-4000	650		⊖	4.1	11	440	4
12	**Kyocera** Finecam S4	580		⊖	4	7	90	5
13	**Panasonic** Lumix DMC-LC5	700		⊖	3.9	15	240	5
14	**Sony** Cyber-shot DSC-P71	400		⊖	3.3	12	100	4
15	**Sony** CD Mavica MVC-CD400	700		⊖	4.1	16	190	5
16	**Minolta** Dimage S404	500		⊖	4.1	7	70	5
17	**Toshiba** PDR-3310	470		⊖	3.3	8	90	4
18	**Kyocera** Finecam S3	600		⊖	3.3	8	75	11

Overall Ratings, cont.

Excellent	◓
Very good	◒
Good	○
Fair	◑
Poor	●

KEY NO.	BRAND & MODEL	PRICE	OVERALL SCORE	PRINT QUALITY	MEGA-PIXELS	FLASH RANGE (FT.)	BATTERY LIFE (SHOTS)	NEXT-SHOT DELAY (SEC.)
			P F G VG E					
2-MEGAPIXEL CAMERAS								
19	**Kodak** EasyShare DX3600 Zoom	$300		◒	2.2	10	360	3
20	**Canon** PowerShot A40	300		◒	2	14	800	2
21	**Nikon** Coolpix 2500	300		◒	2	10	140	3
22	**Olympus** Camedia C-700 Ultra Zoom	500		◒	2.1	18	70	3
23	**Kodak** EasyShare DX3500	230		◒	2.2	6	420	2
24	**Olympus** Camedia D-380	200		◒	2.1	8	1050	3
25	**Minolta** Dimage X	400		◒	2	10	240	4
26	**Pentax** Optio 230	250		◒	2.1	16	30	5
27	**Panasonic** Lumix DMC-LC20	300		○	2.1	8	30	5

See report, page 23. Based on tests published in Consumer Reports in November 2002.

The tests behind the Ratings

Overall score is based on picture quality and convenience. **Print quality** reflects judgments by trained viewers of glossy 5x7-inch photos made on a high-quality inkjet. **Megapixels** is how many million elements the image sensor has. **Weight,** indicated in the Recommendations and notes, includes battery and memory card or disk. **Flash range** is the maximum claimed range for a well-lighted photo. **Battery life** is the number of high-resolution photos taken on a fresh set of alkaline cells or the included battery pack; half the shots used flash, and the zoom lens was racked in and out. **Next-shot delay** is the time a camera needed to be ready for the next photo. **Price** is approximate retail.

Recommendations & notes

Most have: Optical viewfinder, LCD viewer. Autofocus, autoexposure, multiple flash modes, and exposure-compensation settings. Self-timer and tripod socket. Software for Windows and Mac OS. Ability to connect to a computer through a USB (universal serial bus) port. One-year warranty on parts and labor.

3- TO 5-MEGAPIXELS

1 > **SONY** DSC-F707 **Very good, but expensive.** Uses camcorder-type battery (included). Infrared-sensitive mode. Secure grip. Electronic viewfinder, tiltable body. 25 oz.

2 > **CANON** PowerShot G2 **Very good, with pro-style features.** Uses camcorder-type battery (included). Swing out LCD display. Displays histogram in preview mode. Secure grip. Hot shoe. 18 oz.

Recommendations & notes

3> **OLYMPUS** Camedia C-3040 Zoom **Very good, with secure grip.** Battery life approx. 3,500 shots using lithium batteries. Complicated menus. Can record audio and movie clips. 14 oz.

4> **OLYMPUS** Camedia D-40 Zoom **Very good and small, with only shallow grip.** Battery life approx. 700 shots using lithium batteries. 8 oz.

5> **FUJIFILM** FinePix F601 Z **Good, and allows you to crop images in camera.** 10 oz.

6> **SONY** Cyber-shot DSC-S75 **Very good, and uses camcorder-type battery (included).** Secure grip. Can record audio and movie clips. 16 oz.

7> **HP** PhotoSmart 812 **Very good, with direct printing to HP printers.** 9 oz

8> **KODAK** EasyShare DX4900 **Very good.** Supplied AA batteries gave fair results. Battery life approx. 590 shots using lithium batteries. Optional camera docking cradle for easy picture transfer. 10 oz.

9> **OLYMPUS** Camedia E-10 **Very good, with secure grip.** Battery life is about 540 shots using lithium batteries. Very accurate SLR viewfinder. 40 oz.

10> **CANON** Powershot S40 **Very good, and allows direct printing to Canon printer.** 11 oz.

11> **CASIO** QV-4000 **Very good, and displays histogram in record mode.** External flash socket. Secure grip. 17 oz.

12> **KYOCERA** Finecam S4 **Very good, and allows you to crop images in camera.** 6 oz.

13> **PANASONIC** Lumix DMC-LC5 **Very good, with secure grip.** Hot shoe. 16 oz.

FEATURES AT A GLANCE DIGITAL CAMERAS

Tested products (keyed to the Ratings) Key Brand & model no.	Memory	Zoom lens	Manual controls	AA batteries	Charger	AC adapter	Eyeglasses
3- TO 5-MEGAPIXEL CAMERAS							
1> Sony DSC-F707	MS	5x	•		•	•	•
2> Canon PowerShot G2	CF	3x	•		•	•	•
3> Olympus Camedia C-3040 Zoom	SM	3x	•	•			
4> Olympus Camedia D-40 Zoom	SM	2.8x	•	•			
5> Fujifilm FinePix F601 Z	SM	3x			•	•	•
6> Sony Cyber-shot DSC-S75	MS	3x	•		•		
7> HP PhotoSmart 812	SD	3x			•	•	
8> Kodak EasyShare DX4900	CF	2x		•			
9> Olympus Camedia E-10	CF, SM	4x	•	•		•	
10> Canon PowerShot S40	CF	3x	•		•		
11> Casio QV-4000	CF	3x	•		•	•	
12> Kyocera Finecam S4	SD	3x	•	•		•	
13> Panasonic Lumix DMC-LC5	SD	3x	•		•		
14> Sony Cyber-shot DSC-P71	MS	3x	•	•	•	•	
15> Sony CD Mavica MVC-CD400	CD-R/RW	3x	•		•		
16> Minolta Dimage S404	CF	4x	•	•			
17> Toshiba PDR-3310	SD	3x	•		•	•	
18> Kyocera Finecam S3	SD	2x	•		•	•	
2-MEGAPIXEL CAMERAS							
19> Kodak EasyShare DX3600 Zoom	CF	2x	•	•			
20> Canon PowerShot A40	CF	3x	•	•			
21> Nikon Coolpix 2500	CF	3x		•		•	
22> Olympus Camedia C-700 Ultra Zoom	SM	10x	•	•			•
23> Kodak EasyShare DX3500	CF	–		•			
24> Olympus Camedia D-380	SM	–		•			
25> Minolta Dimage X	SD	3x		•		•	
26> Pentax Optio 230	CF	3x	•				
27> Panasonic Lumix DMC-LC20	SD	3x	•	•			

Recommendations & notes

14> **SONY** Cyber-shot DSC-P71 **Very good, and allows you to crop images in camera.** 10 oz.

15> **SONY** CD Mavica MVC-CD400 **Very good, with holographic illuminator for low-light autofocus.** Hot shoe. 23 oz.

16> **MINOLTA** Dimage S404 **Very good, and displays histogram in playback mode.** Secure grip. 16 oz.

17> **TOSHIBA** PDR-3310 **Very good, and allows you to crop images in camera.** 7 oz.

18> **KYOCERA** Finecam S3 **Very good, but no grip or port for connecting camera to computer.** Uses camcorder-type battery (included). Can record movie clips. 7 oz.

2-MEGAPIXELS

19> **KODAK** EasyShare DX3600 Zoom **Very good. Images rival higher megapixel models, but shallow grip**. Can record audio and movie clips. 9 oz.

20> **CANON** PowerShot A40 **Very good, with direct printing to Canon printer.** 12 oz.

21> **NIKON** Coolpix 2500 **Very good.** Images rival higher megapixel models, but no viewfinder. Swivel lens. 7 oz.

22> **OLYMPUS** Camedia C-700 Ultra Zoom **Very good.** Battery life approx. 500 shots using lithium batteries. Electronic viewfinder. 14 oz.

23> **KODAK** EasyShare DX3500 Very good, but no zoom. **Shallow grip.** 10 oz.

24> **OLYMPUS** Camedia D-380 **Very good, and allows you to resize images in camera.** 9 oz.

25> **MINOLTA** Dimage X **Very good, but no grip.** Lens shoots though prism, zoom is internal. 6 oz.

26> **PENTAX** Optio 230 **Very good.** Battery life approx. 300 shots using lithium batteries. Swing-out LCD for self portrait. 8 oz.

27> **PANASONIC** Lumix DMC-LC20 **Good.** 10 oz.

CD players–portable

Shop Smart   Whether you want a conventional CD player or an MP3-capable model, you can find one that offers very good or excellent sound quality. Any of the top five conventional CD players would be a fine choice. The Panasonic SL-CT490, $60, scored highest for bump immunity and would be a good choice for joggers. If you want maximum music from one device, get a CD player that can also play MP3 music you've recorded onto CDs. The Sony D-CJ01, $130, combines excellent sound quality, good bump immunity, and long battery life. Key features for these models are listed on page 227. See the product guide for an explanation of the features.

						Excellent ⊜	Very good ⊖ Good ○ Fair ◖ Poor ●	

Overall Ratings   In performance order

KEY NO.	BRAND & MODEL	PRICE	OVERALL SCORE	SOUND QUALITY	BUMP IMMUNITY	BATTERY LIFE CD	BATTERY LIFE MP3	EASE OF USE
			P F G VG E					
CONVENTIONAL PLAYERS								
1	Panasonic SL-CT490	$60		⊜	⊖	40 hr.	-	⊖
2	Panasonic SL-SX390	55		⊜	○	36	-	⊖
3	Philips AX5011	50		⊜	○	21	-	⊖
4	Sony D-E350	50		⊜	◖	30	-	⊖
5	Philips AZT9240	70		⊜	○	20	-	⊖
6	RCA RP-2420	42		◖	◖	19	-	⊖
7	RCA RP-2430	60		◖	◖	16	-	⊖
MP3-CAPABLE PLAYERS								
8	Sony D-CJ01	130		⊜	○	30	23 hr.	⊖
9	Philips EXP503/17	180		⊜	◖	17	15	⊖
10	Panasonic SL-MP50	100		⊜	○	29	11	⊖
11	Philips EXP203	100		⊜	◖	7	11	⊖
12	SonicBlue Rio Volt SP90	100		⊖	◖	6	15	⊖
13	SonicBlue Rio Volt SP250	180		○	○	5	13	⊖
14	RCA RP-2415	120		○	◖	6	8	○
15	Samsung MCD-SM60	80		◖	○	17	15	⊖

See report, page 28. Based on tests published in Consumer Reports in September 2002.

The tests behind the Ratings

Overall score is based primarily on sound quality, bump immunity, battery life, and ease of use. **Sound quality** indicated tonal accuracy as measured by automated equipment, and distortion and background noise as judged by trained listeners using very good reference headphones. Unless noted, scores represent playback in all available modes (standard CDs with the memory buffer on or at maximum with the buffer off, and, where applicable, MP3 files with and without the buffer). **Bump immunity** reflects how well a player with its buffer on resisted skipping when jolted (results shown are for standard CDs; results for MP3 discs are comparable unless noted). **Battery life** reflects play time using fresh alkaline batteries. **Ease of use** is our judgment of the main function buttons and the liquid-crystal display (LCD) panel. **Price** is approximate retail.

Recommendations & notes

Models listed as similar should offer performance comparable to the tested model's, although features may differ.

CONVENTIONAL PLAYERS

1> **PANASONIC** SL-CT490 **Excellent choice, especially for jogging.** Lightweight and sleeker than most, with exceptional battery life.Similar: SL-CT495J.

2> **PANASONIC** SL-SX390 **Very good, with long battery life and remote control.** Similar: SL-SX392C.

3> **PHILIPS** AX5011 **Very good overall.** Similar: AX5012, AX5013, AX5014, AX5015, AX5018.

4> **SONY** D-E350 **Very good, but skipped more than others in active use.** 3-mo. labor warranty. Similar: D-E330, D-E356CK, D-EQ550.

5> **PHILIPS** AZT9240 **Very good.** Has AM/FM tuner.

6> **RCA** RP-2420 **Fair.** Decreased treble. Headphones only fair. Lacks battery-level indicator. Similar: RP-2421.

7> **RCA** RP-2430 **Fair.** Decreased treble. Has FM tuner. Headphones only fair.

MP3-CAPABLE PLAYERS

8> **SONY** D-CJ01**Excellent and sleeker than most, with long battery life.** Good choice for jogging. Very good bump immunity with MP3. 3-mo. labor warranty.

9> **PHILIPS** EXP503/17 **Very good overall.** Standard CDs skipped more than others in active use; very good bump immunity with MP3.

10> **PANASONIC** SL-MP50 **Very good, with long battery life with standard CDs.** But no support for MP3 ID3 tags. Fair bump immunity with MP3.

11> **PHILIPS** EXP203 **Very good, but no support for MP3 ID3 tags.** Standard CDs skipped more than others in active use; good bump immunity with MP3. Similar: EXP201, EXP301, EXP303.

12> **SONICBLUE** Rio Volt SP90 **Good, and low-priced for an MP3-capable unit.** Excellent sound with MP3 and standard CDs with buffer off, but CD sound poor with buffer on. Standard CDs skipped more than others in active use; good bump immunity with MP3. Headphones only fair. Also plays WMA files.

Recommendations & notes

13 > **SONICBLUE** Rio Volt SP250 **Good.** Excellent sound with MP3 and very good with standard CDs with buffer off, but CD sound poor with buffer on. Has FM tuner. Headphones only fair. Also plays WMA files.

14 > **RCA** RP-2415 **There are better choices.** Very good sound with MP3 and standard CDs with buffer off, but CD sound poor with buffer on. Bulkier and heavier than most. Headphones only fair.

15 > **SAMSUNG** MCD-SM60 **There are better choices.** 3-mo. labor warranty.

FEATURES AT A GLANCE CD PLAYERS

Tested products (keyed to the Ratings) Key Brand & model no.	AC adapter	Built-in charger	Car kit	Remote control
CONVENTIONAL PLAYERS				
1 > **Panasonic** SL-CT490		•		•
2 > **Panasonic** SL-SX390				•
3 > **Philips** AX5011				
4 > **Sony** D-E350				
5 > **Philips** AZT9240				
6 > **RCA** RP-2420				
7 > **RCA** RP-7430				
MP3-CAPABLE PLAYERS				
8 > **Sony** D-CJ01	•	•		
9 > **Philips** EXP503/17	•		•	
10 > **Panasonic** SL-MP50		•	•	
11 > **Philips** EXP203			•	
12 > **SonicBlue** Rio Volt SP90				
13 > **SonicBlue** Rio Volt SP250	•	•		•
14 > **RCA** RP-2415	•	•	•	
15 > **Samsung** MCD-SM60		•		

Chain saws

Shop Smart Gasoline-powered saws offer greater mobility and better cutting performance than their electric counterparts. If you're willing to pay a premium for the fastest cutting, consider the Stihl 025 C, $300, or the Husqvarna 345, $270. But several models priced much lower were also rated excellent. They're all **CR Best Buys:** Stihl 018 C, Craftsman Gray Chassis 35046, Craftsman Green Chassis 35048, Poulan Pro 295, Husqvarna 136. The Stihl is among the lightest gas models available. For lighter-duty sawing, consider an electric. This type costs and weighs less than gas saws and starts with the squeeze of a trigger. The Craftsman Green Chassis 34106 and Poulan Handyman Plus ES300, $90 each, are competent and easy to use. Key features for all these models are listed in the table on page tk. See the product guide for an explanation of features.

Overall Ratings — In performance order

Excellent ⊖ Very good ⊖ Good ○ Fair ⊖ Poor ●

KEY NO.	BRAND & MODEL	PRICE	WEIGHT (LB.)	OVERALL SCORE	CUTTING SPEED	HANDLING	SAFETY	EASE OF USE	EASE OF SERVICE
				0 P F G VG E 100					
	GASOLINE MODELS								
1	**Stihl** 025 C	$300	13.5		⊖	⊖	⊖	⊖	○
2	**Echo** CS-4400	390	15.0		●	⊖	⊖	⊖	⊖
3	**Husqvarna** 345	270	14.0		⊖	⊖	⊖	⊖	⊖
4	**Husqvarna** 350	300	14.5		⊖	⊖	⊖	⊖	⊖
5	**Stihl** 018 C A CR Best Buy	200	11.0		⊖	⊖	⊖	⊖	●
6	**Stihl** 021	230	12.5		⊖	⊖	⊖	⊖	○
7	**Craftsman** (Sears) Gray Chassis 35046 A CR Best Buy	150	13.5		⊖	⊖	⊖	⊖	○
8	**Craftsman** (Sears) Green Chassis 35048 A CR Best Buy	180	14.0		⊖	⊖	⊖	⊖	○
9	**Poulan Pro** 295 A CR Best Buy	200	14.5		⊖	⊖	⊖	⊖	⊖
10	**Husqvarna** 136 A CR Best Buy	180	12.5		⊖	⊖	⊖	⊖	⊖
11	**Solo** 636	280	11.5		⊖	⊖	⊖	○	●
12	**Poulan Pro** 260	160	14.0		⊖	○	⊖	⊖	○
13	**Poulan** Wood Master 2550	200	13.5		⊖	○	⊖	⊖	○
14	**Poulan** Woodsman 2150	130	13.0		⊖	⊖	⊖	⊖	⊖

Overall Ratings, cont.

Ratings legend: Excellent ◖ | Very good ◑ | Good ○ | Fair ◐ | Poor ●

KEY NO.	BRAND & MODEL	PRICE	WEIGHT (LB.)	OVERALL SCORE	CUTTING SPEED	HANDLING	SAFETY	EASE OF USE	EASE OF SERVICE
15	**Poulan** Wild Thing 2375	$140	13.5		Very good	Good	Fair	Very good	Fair
16	**Poulan** Wood Shark 1950	110	13.0		Very good	Very good	Fair	Very good	Fair
17	**Homelite** Ranger	140	13.0		Good	Fair	Very good	Good	Fair
ELECTRIC MODELS									
18	**Craftsman** (Sears) Green Chassis 34106	90	11.0		Very good	Very good	Good	Very good	Very good
19	**Poulan** Handyman Plus ES300	90	10.5		Good	Very good	Fair	Very good	Fair
20	**Remington** 100089-05	60	7.0		Good	Fair	Good	Good	Poor
21	**Craftsman** (Sears) Black Chassis 34114	70	8.0		Fair	Fair	Good	Good	Poor
22	**Remington** 075762J	40	7.0		Fair	Fair	Good	Good	Poor
23	**Remington** Limb N' Trim 099178H	40	5.5		Poor	Fair	Good	Good	Poor

See report, page 96. Based on tests published in Consumer Reports in May 2001, with updated prices and availability.

The tests behind the Ratings

Overall score is based on cutting speed, handling, safety, convenience, ease of service, and noise. **Cutting speed** denotes how quickly a saw cut through a maple beam with a 10-inch-square cross section. **Handling** reflects lack of vibration and ease of vertical and horizontal sawing, balance, weight, and handle comfort. **Safety** denotes resistance to kickback, protection from muffler contact, and safety equipment. **Ease of use** denotes ease of adjusting chain tension and, for gas saws, securing when starting. **Ease of service** denotes how easy it is to add and check bar oil and refuel gas models. **Price** is the estimated average, based on a national survey. The Recommendations and notes includes cubic centimeters (cc) of engine displacement for gas models and motor amperage for electrics, based on manufacturer specifications, as well as bar length.

Recommendations & notes

Models listed as similar should offer performance comparable to the tested models, although features may differ.

Most chain saws: Are claimed to conform to an American National Standards Institute (ANSI) safety standard (for gas saws) or an Underwriters Laboratory standard (for electrics), which includes a measurement of kickback intensity. Showed relatively mild kickback intensity in our tests. Have labels claiming compliance with at least EPA/CARB Tier I emissions requirements. (EPA/CARB Tier II began appearing in 2002.) Registered between 90 and 106 dBA at the operator's ear. Have a one-year warranty against defects in material and workmanship.

Most gas saws have: Adequate room to place

Recommendations & notes

the toe of a boot in the rear handle to secure the saw during pull-starting. An ignition switch that can be reached easily for quickly shutting off the engine or motor.

GASOLINE MODELS

1 STIHL 025 C **Fast, with easy vertical and horizontal cuts.** Tools-free chain adjustment. Foot room in rear handle tight. Kickback greater than most, but acceptable. 45 cc/16 in.

2 ECHO CS-4400 **Easy vertical and horizontal cuts.** Kickback moderate without tip guard. Hard-to-use ignition switch. 43.6 cc/16 in.

3 HUSQVARNA 345 **Fast and impressive.** Inconvenient choke location. Kickback greater than most, but acceptable. 45 cc/16 in.

4 HUSQVARNA 350 **Impressive overall.** Kickback greater than most, but acceptable. Inconvenient choke location. 50 cc/18 in.

5 STIHL 018 C **A CR Best Buy Lightweight.** Tools-free service access. Foot room in rear handle tight. Kickback moderate. Hard-to-use ignition switch. 31.8 cc/14 in. Similar: 018 C with catalyst.

6 STIHL 021 **Lightweight, with easy vertical and horizontal cuts.** Tools-free chain adjustment. Kickback moderate. 35.2 cc/16 in.

7 CRAFTSMAN (Sears) Gray Chassis 35046 **A CR Best Buy Strong performance at a low price.** Extra-large filler caps. 36 cc/16 in.

8 CRAFTSMAN (Sears) Green Chassis 35048 **A CR Best Buy Strong performance at a low price.** Extra-large filler caps. Inconvenient choke location. 42 cc/18 in.

9 POULAN PRO 295 **A CR Best Buy Competent, and more convenient than most.** Kickback moderate. 46 cc/20 in.

10 HUSQVARNA 136 **A CR Best Buy A light, impressive saw at a low price.** Hard-to-use ignition switch. 36 cc/14 in.

FEATURES AT A GLANCE CHAIN SAWS

Tested products (keyed to the Ratings) Key Brand no.	Chain brake	Reduced-kickback bar	Case or sheath	Effective bucking spikes	Choke/on-off switch	Easy chain adjuster	Anti-vibration	Visible bar-oil level	Filler-cap retainers
GASOLINE MODELS									
1 Stihl	•		•	•	•	•	•		•
2 Echo	•			•			•		•
3 Husqvarna	•		•	•	•	•	•		•
4 Husqvarna	•		•	•	•	•	•		•
5 Stihl	•	•	•	•	•			•	•
6 Stihl	•		•	•	•		•		
7 Craftsman	•	•	•		•	•			•
8 Craftsman	•	•	•			•	•		•
9 Poulan Pro	•						•		•
10 Husqvarna	•	•	•				•	•	
11 Solo	•	•	•	•					
12 Poulan Pro	•	•							
13 Poulan		•	•						
14 Poulan		•			•				
15 Poulan		•	•						
16 Poulan		•	•						
17 Homelite	•								•
ELECTRIC MODELS									
18 Craftsman		•	•		•	•	•		
19 Poulan		•	•		•		•		
20 Remington		•	•		•		•		
21 Craftsman		•	•		•		•		
22 Remington		•	•		•		•		
23 Remington		•	•		•		•		

Recommendations & notes

11 ▷ **SOLO** 636 **Less convenient than most.** Foot room tight in rear handle. Bar-oil and fuel caps hard to grasp. Kickback moderate. No ANSI label. 36.3 cc/16 in.

12 ▷ **POULAN PRO** 260 **Competent overall.** Extra-large filler caps. Inconvenient choke location. 42 cc/18 in.

13 ▷ **POULAN** Wood Master 2550 **Competent overall.** Extra-large filler caps. Hard-to-use ignition switch. Inconvenient choke location. 42 cc/18 in.

14 ▷ **POULAN** Woodsman 2150 **Competent and low-priced.** Extra-large filler caps. Hard-to-use ignition switch. 36 cc/16 in.

15 ▷ **POULAN** Wild Thing 2375 **Competent and low-priced.** Extra-large filler caps. Lots of vibration. Hard-to-use ignition switch. 42 cc/18 in.

16 ▷ **POULAN** Wood Shark 1950 **Competent and low-priced, but few features.** Extra-large filler caps. Hard-to-use ignition switch. 36 cc/14 in.

17 ▷ **HOMELITE** Ranger **Low-priced, but less convenient than most.** Lots of vibration. Uncomfortable front handle. Foot room tight in rear handle. Inconvenient choke location. Kickback moderate without tip guard. 33 cc/16 in.

ELECTRIC MODELS

18 ▷ **CRAFTSMAN** (Sears) Green Chassis 34106 **More convenient than most, though motor makes horizontal sawing awkward.** Kickback moderate. 12 amp/16 in. Discontinued; replaced by 34116, $80. 12 amp/16 in.

19 ▷ **POULAN** Handyman Plus ES300 **More convenient than most, though motor makes horizontal sawing awkward.** Kickback moderate. 12 amp/16 in.

20 ▷ **REMINGTON** 100089-05 **Less convenient than most.** Lacks wraparound top handle. Kickback moderate. Hard-to-use trigger lockout. Small bar-oil filler. 11.5 amp/16 in.

21 ▷ **CRAFTSMAN** (Sears) Black Chassis 34114 **Less convenient than most.** Lacks wraparound top handle. Hard-to-use trigger lockout. Small bar-oil filler. Kickback moderate. 10.5 amp/14 in.

22 ▷ **REMINGTON** 075762J **Less convenient than most.** Lacks wraparound top handle. Hard-to-use trigger lockout. Small bar-oil filler. Kickback moderate. 11.5 amp/14 in.

23 ▷ **REMINGTON** Limb N' Trim 099178H **Less convenient than most.** Lacks wraparound top handle. Kickback moderate. Hard-to-use trigger lockout. Small bar-oil filler. 8 amp/14 in. Similar: 34125.

Circular saws

Shop Smart If you're a serious do-it-yourselfer, look for a top-rated circular saw, which can cost $120 to $160. But you can get a fine saw for as little as $60 for occasional use. Two **CR Best Buys** represent an excellent combination of performance and good price: the Makita 5740NB, $90, and the Craftsman 10842, $80. Among lower-priced saws, consider the Skil 5275-05 Classic, $60, and the Craftsman 10840, $50. Battery-powered saws such as the DeWalt DW939K, $260, lack the power for tough jobs but might do for occasional light work. For heavy-duty use, consider a top-rated model. The Milwaukee 6390-21, $140, and the Porter-Cable 347K, $120, scored high in all our tests. They're solidly constructed and very easy to use. The worm-drive DeWalt DW378GK, $155, outperformed the others in its class, but was noticeably slower than the best of the regular saws.

Overall Ratings	In performance order		Excellent ⊖	Very good ⊖	Good ○	Fair ◑	Poor ●		
KEY NO	**BRAND & MODEL**	**PRICE**	**OVERALL SCORE** P F G VG E	**CUTTING SPEED**	**POWER**	**EASE OF USE**	**CONSTRUCTION**	**WEIGHT (LB.)**	**AMPS** 1
	REGULAR SAWS								
1	**Milwaukee** 6390-21	$140		⊖	⊖	⊖	⊖	11	15
2	**Porter-Cable** 347K	120		⊖	⊖	⊖	⊖	10½	13
3	**DeWalt** DW369CSK	140		⊖	⊖	⊖	⊖	11	15
4	**DeWalt** DW364K	160		⊖	⊖	⊖	⊖	12½	15
5	**Makita** 5740NB **A CR Best Buy**	90		⊖	○	⊖	⊖	8½	10.5
6	**Hitachi** C7SBK	110		⊖	⊖	⊖	⊖	10½	13
7	**Makita** 5007NBK	130		⊖	⊖	○	⊖	11	13
8	**Craftsman** (Sears) 10842 **A CR Best Buy**	80		⊖	⊖	⊖	⊖	11	13
9	**Craftsman** (Sears) Professional 27108	100		⊖	⊖	⊖	⊖	11	15
10	**Ryobi** CSB130K	80		⊖	⊖	⊖	⊖	11	13
11	**Bosch** 1658K	110		⊖	⊖	○	⊖	11	13
12	**Skil** 5275-05 Classic	60		⊖	○	○	○	11	12
13	**Craftsman** (Sears) 10840	50		⊖	⊖	○	○	10	11
14	**Craftsman** (Sears) 10841	60		⊖	⊖	○	○	10½	12
15	**Skil** 5150	45		⊖	⊖	○	○	10	10
16	**Skil** 5155K Legend	50		○	○	○	○	10	11
17	**Black & Decker** CS1000	40		○	⊖	○	○	11	11
18	**Black & Decker** CS1010K	50		○	⊖	○	○	11	12

Overall Ratings, cont.

Excellent ⊖ Very good ⊖ Good ○ Fair ◑ Poor ●

KEY NO	BRAND & MODEL	PRICE	OVERALL SCORE	CUTTING SPEED	POWER	EASE OF USE	CONSTRUCTION	WEIGHT (LB.)	AMPS ①
			P F G VG E						
BATTERY-POWERED SAWS									
19	DeWalt DW939K	$260		⊖	●	○	○	8½	18
20	Craftsman (Sears) Professional 27119	200		○	●	⊖	○	10	18
21	Makita BSS730SHK	480		○	●	○	⊖	9½	24
22	Bosch 1659K	300		○	●	○	○	9	18
WORM-DRIVE SAWS									
23	DeWalt DW378GK	155		⊖	⊖	⊖	⊖	13	15
24	Skil HD77	160		◑	⊖	○	⊖	16	13
25	Craftsman (Sears) Professional 2761	140		◑	⊖	○		16	13

① For battery-powered saws, figure is in volts.

See report, page 98. Based on tests published in Consumer Reports in August 2002.

The tests behind the Ratings

Overall score is based mainly on cutting speed, power, and ease of use. **Cutting speed** is how fast each saw crosscut and ripped a series of 2x12 pine and a 24-inch sheet of ¾-inch-thick hardboard; the best were up to four times as fast as the slowest. **Power,** measured with a dynamometer, indicates how well a saw can handle thick or hard wood. **Ease of use** shows how easy it was to use the cutting guide, adjust depth and bevel, and change blades, as well as our judgment of the saw's balance and handle comfort. **Construction** includes our assessment of bearings, access to motor brushes, and ruggedness of the base, housing, and adjustments. **Weight** is to the nearest half-pound with blade and, for cordless models, battery. **Price** is approximate retail.

Recommendations & notes

All models have: Blade guard that retracts when you push the saw forward. Cutting depth adjustable to at least 3½ inches. Cutting angle adjustable to 45 degrees. **Most have:** Carbide 7¼-inch blade. Blade lock to make blade changes easier. One-year warranty.

REGULAR SAWS

1 MILWAUKEE 6390-21 **Excellent.** Adjustable handle. Heavy-duty base.

2 PORTER-CABLE 347K **Excellent.** Heavy-duty base. Blade-wrench storage. Extra-long cord.

Left-handed version readily available.

3 DEWALT DW369CSK **Excellent.** Blade brake. Heavy-duty base. Earlier version of saw was subject of safety recall.

4 DEWALT DW364K **Excellent.** Blade brake. Heavy-duty base.

5 MAKITA 5740NB **A CR Best Buy Excellent.** Heavy-duty base. Safety interlock button. Attached wrench for blade change. Newest version has different front handle.

Recommendations & notes

6 ▷ **HITACHI** C7SBK **Excellent.** Heavy-duty base. Small front handle. Additional backside cutting-line guide adds accuracy.

7 ▷ **MAKITA** 5007NBK **Excellent.** Heavy-duty base. Sharp bevel-angle guide can contact fingers on front handle.

8 ▷ **CRAFTSMAN** (Sears) 10842 **A CR Best Buy Excellent.** Blade-wrench storage.

9 ▷ **CRAFTSMAN** (Sears) Professional 27108 **Very good.** Heavy-duty base. Extra-long cord. Padded switch.

10 ▷ **RYOBI** CSB130K **Very good.** Extra-long cord. Plastic cover over blade improves cutting line of sight. Blade-wrench storage. Can be hard to maintain pressure on switch, so it can slide into "off" position. Earlier version of saw was subject of safety recall.

11 ▷ **BOSCH** 1658K **Very good.** Blade-wrench storage.

12 ▷ **SKIL** 5275-05 Classic **Good.** Safety interlock button, but it's awkward to use. Blade-wrench storage. Short cord. No blade lock. 2-yr. warranty.

13 ▷ **CRAFTSMAN** (Sears) 10840 **Good.** Not supplied with carbide blade. Short cord. No blade lock. Blade-wrench storage.

14 ▷ **CRAFTSMAN** (Sears) 10841 **Good.** Not supplied with carbide blade. Short cord. Blade-wrench storage.

15 ▷ **SKIL** 5150 **Good.** Safety interlock button, but it's awkward to use. Blade-wrench storage. Not supplied with carbide blade. Short cord. No blade lock. 2-yr. warranty.

16 ▷ **SKIL** 5155K Legend **Good.** Safety interlock button, but it's awkward to use. Blade-

wrench storage. Not supplied with carbide blade. Short cord. No blade lock. 2-yr. warranty.

17 ▷ **BLACK & DECKER** CS1000 **Good.** Not supplied with carbide blade or blade lock. Short cord. Base less substantial. Blade-wrench storage. 2-yr. warranty.

18 ▷ **BLACK & DECKER** CS1010K **Good.** Not supplied with carbide blade. Short cord. No blade lock. Base less substantial. Blade-wrench storage. 2-yr. warranty.

BATTERY-POWERED SAWS

19 ▷ **DEWALT** DW939K **Good.** Safety interlock button. Blade-wrench storage.

20 ▷ **CRAFTSMAN** (Sears) Professional 27119 **Good.** Safety interlock button. Blade-wrench storage.

21 ▷ **MAKITA** BSS730SHK **Good.** Blade brake. Heavy-duty base. Safety interlock button, but it's awkward to use. Blade-wrench storage. Bevel adjustment has fasteners front and rear.

22 ▷ **BOSCH** 1659K **Good.** Blade brake. Safety interlock button, but it's awkward to use. Blade-wrench storage.

WORM-DRIVE SAWS

23 ▷ **DEWALT** DW378GK **Excellent.** Heavy-duty base. Not double-insulated.

24 ▷ **SKIL** HD77 **Good.** Extra-long cord. Not supplied with carbide blade. Poor dust ejection. Not double-insulated.

25 ▷ **CRAFTSMAN** (Sears) Professional 2761 **Good.** Not supplied with carbide blade. Not double-insulated. Poor dust ejection.

Cooktops

Shop Smart Electric smoothtops offer quick heating and easy-to-clean glass surfaces. The top-rated Frigidaire Gallery GLEC30S8A, $500, is the lowest-priced model, and it's a **CR Best Buy.** At the other end of the price spectrum, the GE Profile JP938WC, $1,200, offers features such as touch controls, pan sensors, a timer, and a child lockout. Gas cooktops provide easily adjustable flame controls and choices ranging from basic to pro-style. Among gas models, a fine choice is the Jenn-Air CCG2523, $750, **a CR Best Buy.** You can get a stylish, stainless-steel look from the top-rated GE Monogram ZGU375NSD, but it'll cost you $1,300. The lowest-priced gas cooktop, the Frigidaire Gallery GLGC36S8A, $600, offers good performance overall.

Excellent Very good Good Fair Poor
⊖ ⊖ ○ ⊖ ●

Overall Ratings — In performance order

KEY NO	BRAND & MODEL	PRICE	OVERALL SCORE	SPEED OF HEATING	SIMMER
			0 P F G VG E 100		
30-INCH ELECTRIC SMOOTHTOPS					
1	**Frigidaire** Gallery GLEC30S8A[S] **A CR Best Buy**	$500		⊖	⊖
2	**GE** Profile JP930TC[WW]	790		⊖	⊖
3	**GE** Profile JP938WC[WW]	1,200		⊖	⊖
4	**Kenmore** (Sears) Elite 4402[2]	600		⊖	⊖
5	**Whirlpool** RCC3024K[Q]	510		⊖	⊖
6	**Maytag** CSE9000A[CE]	500		⊖	⊖
7	**Amana** AKT3040[WW]	540		⊖	⊖
8	**KitchenAid** KECC502G[WH]	650		⊖	○
36-INCH GAS COOKTOPS					
9	**GE** Monogram ZGU375NSD[SS]	1,300		⊖	⊖
10	**Jenn-Air** CCG2523[W] **A CR Best Buy**	750		⊖	⊖
11	**Dacor** SGM365[R]	1,100		⊖	⊖
12	**GE** Profile JGP962TC[WW]	1,050		⊖	⊖
13	**Kenmore** (Sears) Elite 3303[2]	750		⊖	○
14	**KitchenAid** KGCC566H[WH]	900		⊖	⊖
15	**Frigidaire** Gallery GLGC36S8A[B]	600		○	⊖
16	**Whirlpool** Gold GLT3615G[Q]	740		○	⊖
17	**Viking** VGSU161-6B[SS]	1,750		○	⊖

See report, page 79. Based on tests published in Consumer Reports in August 2002.

The tests behind the Ratings

Under **brand & model,** brackets show a tested model's color code. **Overall score** includes cooktop speed and simmer performance. **Speed of heating** is how quickly the highest powered burner or element heated 6⅓ quarts of room-temperature water to a near boil. **Simmer** shows how well the least powerful burner or element melted and held chocolate without scorching it and whether the most powerful, set to Low, held tomato sauce below a boil. **Price** is approximate retail.

Recommendations & notes

All 30-inch electric smoothtops have: Four burners. Glass cooktop. Hot surface indicator lights. **Most have:** Control-knobs. Expandable element. Limited five-year warranties on glass and burner units. "On" light and four "hot" indicator lights. No rim to contain spills. Most need: 40-amp circuit.

All 36-inch gas cooktops have: Control knobs. Sealed burners. Lift-off burner base and cap for cleaning. Burner-cap covers. **All need:** 120-volt electrical connection. **Most have:** Five burners. Propane conversion kit. Has bridge element (small heating element inside a larger one that lets you heat various-sized pots).

30-INCH ELECTRIC SMOOTHTOPS

1▷ **FRIGIDAIRE** Gallery GLEC30S8A[S] **A CR Best Buy Excellent.** Has bridge element (heated connection between elements), but no "on" light. Elements: 1@1,200, 2@1,800, 1@1,000/2,500 watts. Similar: GLEC36S8A[ ].

2▷ **GE** Profile JP930TC[WW] **Excellent.** Bridge element. Elements: 1@1,200, 2@1,800, 1@1,000/2,500 watts. Similar: JP960TC[ ].

3▷ **GE** Profile JP938WC[WW] **Excellent.** Touchpad controls. Bridge. Pan sensors. Timer. Child lockout. Warming feature on regular element. Not as hot as others with all burners on. Elements: 1@1,200, 2@1,800, 1@1,000/2,500 watts. Similar: JP968WC[ ].

4▷ **KENMORE** (Sears) Elite 4402[2] **Excellent.** Bridge element. Elements: 1@1,200, 2@1,800, 1@1,000/2,500 watts.

5▷ **WHIRLPOOL** RCC3024K[Q] **Excellent.** No expandable element. No "on" light. One "hot" light indicator. Elements: 2@1,200, 1 @1,800, 1@2,500 watts.

6▷ **MAYTAG** CSE9000A[CE] **Excellent.** No expandable element. Spill-guard rim, but seam with cooktop could trap soil. Only one "hot" light indicator. Needs only 30-amp circuit. Elements: 2@1,200, 2@2,200 watts. Warranties: 2-yr. on parts, limited 5-yr. on electronics. Similar: CSE9600A[ ].

7▷ **AMANA** AKT3040[WW] **Very good.** Install knobs to left or to right. Large element unable to simmer. Warranty: 2-yr. on parts. No 5-yr. electronics warranty. Elements: 1@1,200, 1@1,500, 1@2,000, 1@1,000/2,500 watts. Similar: AKT3020[ ], AKT3630[ ], AKT3650[ ].

8▷ **KITCHENAID** KECC502G[WH] **Very good.** Two expandable elements. But two largest elements unable to simmer. No 5-yr. burner warranty. Elements: 1@1,200, 1@1,500, 1@1,000/1,800, 1@1,000/2,500 watts.

36-INCH GAS COOKTOPS

9▷ **GE** Monogram ZGU375NSD[SS] **Excellent.** Auto reignition. Stainless–steel cooktop. "On" lights on each control knob. Wok ring. Simmer setting. Continuous, double-long, cast-iron grates. But tomato sauce stained burner. Not convertible to propane. Burners: 4@10,000, 1@14,000 Btu/hr. Similar: ZGU375LSD[SS] is propane.

Recommendations & notes

10> JENN-AIR CCG2523[W] **A CR Best Buy Very good.** Easy to clean. Auto reignition. Glass cooktop. Enamel grates. No rim for spills. Warranty: 2-yr. on parts. Burners: 1@6,500, 2@9,100, 1@10,500, 1@12,000 Btu/hr. Similar: JGC7536A[ ].

11> DACOR SGM365[R] **Very good.** Auto reignition. Enamel cooktop. Simmer plate. Continuous, double-long cast-iron grates. Tomato sauce stained burner. Burners: 1@6,000, 2@8,500, 1@12,500, 1@14,000 Btu/hr. Propane conversion kit not included. Similar: SGM304[ ].

12> GE Profile JGP962TC[WW] **Very good.** Easy to clean. Glass cooktop. Continuous, double-long enamel grates. Available wok ring. No rim for spills. Burners: 2@6,000, 1@9,100, 1@11,000, 1@12,000 Btu/hr.

13> KENMORE (Sears) Elite 3303[2] **Very good.** Easy to clean. Glass cooktop. Double-long enamel grates. Wok ring. No rim for spills. Burners: 1@5,000, 1@9,500, 1@11,000, 1@14,200 Btu/hr. One electric/radiant warming element.

14> KITCHENAID KGCC566H[WH] **Good.** Easy to clean. Glass cooktop. Continuous, double-long enamel grates. Tomato sauce stained burner. No rim for spills. Burners: 2@6,000, 1@9,100, 1@12,500, 1@14,000 Btu/hr.

15> FRIGIDAIRE Gallery GLGC36S8A[B] **Good.** Glass cooktop. Enamel grates. Cooktop has wells but no rim for spills. Burners: 2@5,000, 2@9,100, 1@13,000 Btu/hr. Similar: PLGC36S9A[ ], GLGC30S8A[ ].

16> WHIRLPOOL Gold GLT3615G[Q] **Good.** Easy to clean. Glass cooktop. Enamel grates. No rim for spills. Burners: 2@6,000, 2@9,000, 1@12,500 Btu/hr.

17> VIKING VGSU161-6B[SS] **Good.** Auto reignition. Stainless cooktop. Continuous cast-iron grates. Not as hot as others with all burners on. Scorched melted chocolate. Tomato sauce stained burner. Propane conversion kit not included. Burners: 1@6,000, 1@9,000, 3@12,000, 1@14,000 Btu/hr.

Dishwashers

Shop Smart Most dishwashers do a very good or even excellent job. The costliest are not necessarily the best performers, although high-priced models may have desirable styling and extra soundproofing. The top-rated Bosch, Asko, and Viking models cost the most—from $900 to nearly $1,400. Several washed nearly as well and cost $600 or less. The GE Triton XL GSD6600G is excellent at washing and convenient to use. At $520, it's a **CR Best Buy.** Key features for these models are listed in the table on page 98. See the product guide for an explanation of features.

Excellent	Very good	Good	Fair	Poor
⊖	⊖	○	◑	●

KEY NO.	BRAND & MODEL	PRICE	OVERALL SCORE	WASHING	ENERGY USE	NOISE	LOADING	EASE OF USE
1	**Bosch** SHV680[3]	$1,140		⊖	⊖	⊖	⊖	⊖
2	**Bosch** SHU995[2]	900		⊖	⊖	⊖	⊖	⊖
3	**Asko** D1996FI	1,250		⊖	⊖	⊖	○	○
4	**Viking** DFUD140	1,375		⊖	⊖	⊖	○	○
5	**Asko** D1716	800		⊖	⊖	⊖	○	○
6	**Kenmore** (Sears) 1563[2]	420		⊖	⊖	◑	◑	⊖
7	**Maytag** MDB9150AW[W]	920		⊖	○	⊖	⊖	⊖
8	**Miele** Novotronic G841SC Plus	900		⊖	⊖	⊖	○	○
9	**Bosch** SHU330[2]	600		⊖	⊖	⊖	○	○
10	**GE** Profile PDW7800G[WW]	620		⊖	○	○	⊖	⊖
11	**KitchenAid** KUDM01TJ[WH]	680		⊖	⊖	○	○	⊖
12	**Fisher & Paykel** DD603[W]	1,200		⊖	⊖	⊖	⊖	⊖
13	**Kenmore** (Sears) 1552[2]	350		⊖	⊖	◑	◑	⊖
14	**KitchenAid** KUDS01DJ[WH]	980		⊖	○	⊖	○	⊖
15	**KitchenAid** Superba KUDS01FK[SS]	1,200		⊖	○	⊖	⊖	⊖
16	**GE** Triton XL GSD6600G[WW] **A CR Best Buy**	520		⊖	○	⊖	⊖	⊖
17	**Frigidaire** Gallery GLDB957J[S]	400		⊖	○	○	○	⊖
18	**Maytag** MDB6650AW[W]	600		⊖	⊖	○	○	⊖
19	**Jenn-Air** JDB9910[W]	800		⊖	○	⊖	⊖	⊖
20	**Kenmore** (Sears) 1568[2]	450		⊖	○	◑	◑	⊖
21	**Kenmore** (Sears) 1576[2]	490		⊖	○	◑	○	⊖
22	**Frigidaire** Gallery GPDB998J[C]	550		⊖	○	○	○	⊖
23	**Maytag** PDB4600AW[E]	345		⊖	⊖	◑	○	⊖

Overall Ratings   In performance order

Overall Ratings, cont.

		Excellent	Very good	Good	Fair	Poor
		⊖	⊖	○	⊖	●

KEY NO.	BRAND & MODEL	PRICE	OVERALL SCORE	WASHING	ENERGY USE	NOISE	LOADING	EASE OF USE
			P F G VG E					
24	**Whirlpool** Quiet Partner II DU960PWK[B]	470		⊖	○	⊖	○	⊖
25	**Viking** Quiet Clean VUD141	1,575		○	⊖	⊖	○	⊖
26	**Frigidaire** Gallery Ultra Quiet GLDB756A[S]	350		○	⊖	○	⊖	⊖

See report, page 64. Based on tests published in Consumer Reports in May 2002, with updated prices and availability.

The tests behind the Ratings

Under **brand & model,** a bracketed letter or number is the color code. **Overall score** stresses washing but factors in noise, energy use, convenience, water use, and cycle time. **Washing** was tested using a full load of very dirty dishes, glasses, and flatware. **Energy use** is for a normal cycle. **Noise** was judged by a listening panel, aided by sound-level measurements. **Loading** reflects ability to hold extra place settings and oversized items. **Ease of use** considers convenience of controls and maintenance. **Recommendations & notes** cite long or short cycle length and high or low water use (8.5 gallons was average). Brand repair information is based on our most recent reader survey. **Price** is approximate retail.

Recommendations & notes

Models listed as similar should offer performance comparable to the tested model's, although features may differ.

All dishwashers: Are standard-sized, under-the-counter models that can wash a complete 10-piece place setting with two serving bowls and one serving platter. **Most models:** Have touchpad controls and at least three cycles (light, normal, pots-and-pans). Have rinse-and-hold, heated-water, and drain/cancel control for stopping midcycle. Have normal cycle times of 90 to 120 minutes. Have heated-dry and delay-start option. Use between 7 and 9 gallons of water during their normal cycle. Have 1-year warranty on parts and labor. Have 20-year or longer limited warranty on plastic tub and door liner.

1 **BOSCH** SHV680[3] **Excellent but expensive.** Among the quietest models tested. More loading flexibility than most, with adjustable upper rack. But heated-dry feature can't be turned off. Among the more water-efficient sensor models (about 7 gal.). Hidden controls; needs front panel (costs extra).

2 **BOSCH** SHU995[2] **Excellent; much like #1, but doesn't allow for custom door panel and has fewer wash options.**

3 **ASKO** D1996FI **Excellent but pricey.** Faster (85-min. cycle) and used less water than most (about 5 gal.). Hidden controls; needs front panel (costs extra). Full 3-yr. warranty. But has been among the more repair-prone brands. Similar: D1976[ ].

4 **VIKING** DFUD140 **Excellent but pricey.** Used less water than most (about 5.5 gal.). Hidden controls; needs front panel (costs extra).

5 **ASKO** D1716 **An excellent performer.** Efficient with energy and water (about 5.5 gal.). Full

Recommendations & notes

3-yr. warranty. Has been among the more repair-prone brands. No delay start.

6> KENMORE (Sears) 1563[2] **A good buy, but not very flexible for special loading.** Noisier than most. Similar: 1663[ ] .

7> MAYTAG MDB9150AW[W] **Feature-laden.** More flexible loading than most, with adjustable upper rack. Long cycle time (130 min.).

8> MIELE Novotronic G841SC Plus **Very good performer.** Adjustable upper rack. But heated-dry option can't be turned off. No delay start.

9> BOSCH SHU330[2] **Among the more water-efficient sensor models (about 8 gal.).** Push-button controls. No light wash cycle. Similar: SHU332[ ], SHU333[ ].

10> GE Profile PDW7800G[WW] **Feature-laden.** More flexible loading than most. But high water use (10 gal.). Similar: PDW7300G[ ], PDW7700G[ ] .

11> KITCHENAID KUDM01TJ[WH] **Fewer features than #14 and no hidden controls.** Long cycle time (130 min.). Similar: KUDM01FK[ ].

12> FISHER & PAYKEL DD603[W] **Very good but expensive.** Has two separate drawers. More flexible loading than most. Partially hidden controls. No heated-dry option. Full 2-yr. warranty.

13> KENMORE (Sears) 1552[2] **Good price, with adjustable upper rack, but not very flexible for special loading.** Dial and touchpad controls. But noisier than most. Similar: 1652[ ].

14> KITCHENAID KUDS01DJ[WH] **Feature-laden.** More flexible loading than most, with adjustable upper rack. Most controls hidden.

FEATURES AT A GLANCE DISHWASHERS

Tested products (keyed to the Ratings) Key no.	Brand	Sensor	Self-cleaning filter	Stainless-steel tub	Child safety	Flatware slots
1>	Bosch	•		•		•
2>	Bosch	•		•		•
3>	Asko			•		
4>	Viking			•		
5>	Asko			•	•	
6>	Kenmore		•		•	•
7>	Maytag	•	•	•	•	
8>	Miele			•	•	•
9>	Bosch	•		•		•
10>	GE	•	•		•	•
11>	KitchenAid		•	•	•	
12>	Fisher & Paykel			•		
13>	Kenmore		•			
14>	KitchenAid	•	•	•	•	
15>	KitchenAid	•	•	•	•	
16>	GE	•	•		•	•
17>	Frigidaire	•	•	•		
18>	Maytag		•	•	•	
19>	Jenn-Air	•	•	•	•	
20>	Kenmore	•	•		•	•
21>	Kenmore	•	•		•	•
22>	Frigidaire	•	•	•		
23>	Maytag		•			
24>	Whirlpool	•	•		•	
25>	Viking			•		
26>	Frigidaire		•			

Recommendations & notes

But long cycle time (130 min.) and high water use (about 10 gal.).

15 > **KITCHENAID** Superba KUDS01FK[SS] **Feature-laden but expensive.** Much like #14, but adds a stainless-steel door and all controls are hidden.

16 > **GE** Triton XL GSD6600G[WW] A CR Best Buy **Good price for excellent cleaning, plenty of features.** More flexible loading than most. But high water use (about 10 gal.). 10-yr. tub and door liner warranty. Similar: GSD6200G[ ].

17 > **FRIGIDAIRE** Gallery GLDB957J[S] **High water use (about 10.5 gal.).** Has been among the more repair-prone brands. Discontinued, but similar GLDB957A[ ] is available.

18 > **MAYTAG** MDB6650AW[W] **Very good, with stainless-steel tub.** Short cycle time (85 min.).

19 > **JENN-AIR** JDB9910[W] **Feature-laden.** More flexible loading than most, with adjustable upper rack. But long cycle time (130 min.). Similar: JDB8910[ ].

20 > **KENMORE** (Sears) 1568[2] **Good price for excellent cleaning.** But high water use (about 11 gal.); noisier and less flexible loading than most. Similar: 1668[ ].

21 > **KENMORE** (Sears) 1576[2] **Much like #20, but has more flexible loading.** But high water use (about 11 gal.), and noisier than most. Similar: 1676[ ].

22 > **FRIGIDAIRE** Gallery GPDB998J[C] **Many features.** Stainless-steel door. But high water use (about 11 gal.), and has been among the more repair-prone brands. Discontinued, but similar PLDB998A[ ] is available.

23 > **MAYTAG** PDB4600AW[E] **Very good but basic.** Noisier than most.

24 > **WHIRLPOOL** Quiet Partner II DU960PWK[B] **Very good performance.** Adjustable upper rack. But noisier than most. High-temp scour option disabled sensor.

25 > **VIKING** Quiet Clean VUD141 **Pricey, but has some pluses: shorter cycle time than most (75 min.), low water use (about 5.5 gal.).** Stainless-steel exterior. Dial controls. No drain/cancel button.

26 > **FRIGIDAIRE** Gallery Ultra Quiet GLDB756A[S] **Good price, basic features.** But less flexible loading than most. Manual-control push buttons and cycle dial must be synchronized. Has been among the more repair-prone brands. 10-yr. tub and door liner warranty.

Drills-cordless

Shop Smart Drills range from light-duty 9.6-volt models that start at about $55 to heavy-duty professional-grade 24-volt units that can top $300. A cordless drill's performance tracks to a large extent with its voltage, although the most powerful models tend to be heavy, expensive, and overkill for small jobs. The best 12- and 14.4-volt models should meet most people's needs. In those sizes, several models by Milwaukee, Porter-Cable, Makita, and Craftsman, all priced between $135 to $220, performed well. Consider a 9.6-volt model only if you rarely tackle heavy jobs.

Overall Ratings — In performance order

Excellent ⊖ Very good ⊖ Good ○ Fair ◓ Poor ●

KEY NO.	BRAND & MODEL	PRICE	OVERALL SCORE	WEIGHT (LBS)	EASE OF USE	EFFICIENCY	TORQUE (SCREWS)	POWER (DRILLING)	ENDUR-ANCE
24-VOLT DRILLS									
1	**Bosch** 3960K-CC	$320		6.3	⊖	⊖	⊖	⊖	⊖
2	**Craftsman** Professional 27125	260		8	⊖	⊖	⊖	⊖	⊖
18-VOLT AND 19.2 VOLT DRILLS									
3	**Milwaukee** Power Plus 0522-22	265		5.7	⊖	⊖	⊖	⊖	⊖
4	**Porter-Cable** 9884	245		5.9	⊖	⊖	⊖	⊖	⊖
5	**Craftsman** (Sears) 27127	240		6.9	⊖	⊖	⊖	⊖	⊖
6	**Craftsman** (Sears) Professional 27124	230		6.5	⊖	⊖	⊖	⊖	⊖
7	**Skil** High Performance 2892-04	200		4.6	⊖	⊖	⊖	○	○
14.4-VOLT DRILLS									
8	**Milwaukee** Power Plus 0516-20	190		5.5	⊖	⊖	⊖	○	○
9	**Porter-Cable** 9876	155		5.1	⊖	⊖	⊖	○	○
10	**MaKita** 6233DWAE	190		4.5	⊖	⊖	⊖	○	○
11	**Porter-Cable** 9877	220		5.7	⊖	⊖	⊖	⊖	○
12	**Milwaukee** Power Plus 0512-21	205		4.4	⊖	⊖	○	○	○
13	**MaKita** 6233DWBLE	180		4.5	⊖	⊖	○	○	○
14	**Craftsman** (Sears) Professional 27123	190		4.7	⊖	⊖	○	○	○
15	**Skil** Warrior 2580-04	100		3.1	○	○	●	◓	◓
12-VOLT DRILLS									
16	**Porter-Cable** 9866	135		4.5	⊖	⊖	⊖	○	○
17	**MaKita** 6213DWAE	170		4.3	⊖	⊖	○	○	◓
18	**Craftsman** (Sears) Professional 27121	160		4.5	⊖	⊖	○	◓	◓

Overall Ratings, cont.

Excellent	Very good	Good	Fair	Poor
⊜	⊖	○	◐	●

KEY NO.	BRAND & MODEL	PRICE	OVERALL SCORE	WEIGHT (LBS)	EASE OF USE	EFFICIENCY	TORQUE (SCREWS)	POWER (DRILLING)	ENDUR-ANCE
			P F G VG E						
12-VOLT DRILLS continued									
19	**Milwaukee** Power Plus 0502-26	160	▬	3.8	⊜	⊖	○	◐	◐
20	**Skil** High Performance 2492-04	120	▬	3.6	⊖	⊖	○	◐	●
21	**Skil** Warrior 2480-04	125	▬	2.9	○	○	◐	◐	◐
9.6-VOLT DRILLS									
22	**DeWalt** DW926K-2	110	▬	3.4	⊖	⊖	○	◐	◐
23	**Craftsman** (Sears) Professional 27120	120	▬	4.1	⊖	○	○	●	●
24	**Skil** Warrior 2380-02	55	▬	2.7	○	○	◐	●	●

See report, page 99. Based on tests published in Consumer Reports in May 2002, with updated prices and availability.

The tests behind the Ratings

Overall score is based mainly on ease of use, design efficiency, torque, power, and endurance. **Weight,** to the nearest tenth of a pound, is for the drill and battery pack. **Ease of use** rates the drill's balance, ease of removing and recharging its battery, and ease of tightening and changing direction of its chuck. **Efficiency** measures how much power and torque a drill delivers for its weight. **Torque** denotes twisting force, important mainly for driving screws. **Power** is how fast the drill can do its work, important mainly for drilling holes. **Endurance** is how much work the drill can do per battery charge. **Price** is the estimated average, based on a national survey.

Recommendations & notes

Models listed as similar should offer performance comparable to the tested model's, although features may differ.

All cordless drills have: A keyless chuck. Are reversible.

Most have: A ⅜-in.chuck (½-inch for 18-and 24-volt models, except as noted). Variable-speed trigger. T-handle. Two speed ranges, with a slow range of 0 to about 400 rpm and a fast range of 0 to 1,100 to 1,650 rpm (single-speed models have a range of only 0 to 550 to 850 rpm). Electric brake. Two NiCd battery packs. Smart charger. Carrying case. Variable clutch with at least 16 settings. One-year warranty.

24-VOLT DRILLS

1 ▷ **BOSCH** 3960K-CC **Surprisingly light for a heavy-duty drill, but pricey.** One-handed chuck. Auxiliary handle.

2 ▷ **CRAFTSMAN** (Sears) Professional 27125 **Capable but heavy and bulky.** One-handed chuck. Auxiliary handle. Overload protection. Bubble level.

18-VOLT AND 19.2-VOLT DRILLS

3 ▷ **MILWAUKEE** Power Plus 0522-22 **Impressive blend of performance, balance, and versatility.** Two battery-mounting positions.

Recommendations & notes

4▷ PORTER-CABLE 9884 (19.2-volt) **A very good, versatile drill.**

5▷ CRAFTSMAN (Sears) 27127 **A very good hammer drill, but bulky.** Auxiliary handle. Bubble level. Overload protector.

6▷ CRAFTSMAN (Sears) Professional 27124 **Lots of features for the price, but bulky.** One-handed chuck. Auxiliary handle. Overload protection. Bubble level.

7▷ SKIL High Performance 2892-04 **A good, relatively light drill.** One-handed chuck. Auxiliary handle. Bubble level. 2-year warranty.

14.4-VOLT DRILLS

8▷ MILWAUKEE Power Plus 0516-20 **A very good drill with excellent balance.** Two battery mounting positions. Half-inch chuck.

9▷ PORTER-CABLE 9876 **A very good drill.**

10▷ MAKITA 6233DWAE **Very good.** Easily removable brushes.

11▷ PORTER-CABLE 9877 **A very good hammer drill, but bulky.** Half-inch chuck.

12▷ MILWAUKEE Power Plus 0512-21 **A very good drill with excellent balance.** Two battery mounting positions. Half-inch chuck.

13▷ MAKITA 6233DWBLE **Easily removable brushes.** Nickel-metal-hydride (NiMH) batteries. Flashlight included.

14▷ CRAFTSMAN (Sears) Professional 27123 **Lots of features, but bulky.** One-handed

chuck. Overload protection. Bubble level.

15▷ SKIL Warrior 2580-04 **Fair performance.** 6 clutch positions. No smart charger or electric brake. One speed range. 2-year warranty.

12-VOLT DRILLS

16▷ PORTER-CABLE 9866 **A very good drill.**

17▷ MAKITA 6213DWAE **A good drill.** Easily removable brushes.

18▷ CRAFTSMAN (Sears) Professional **27121 Lots of features, but bulky.** One-handed chuck. Overload protection. Bubble level.

19▷ MILWAUKEE Power Plus 0502-26 **Excellent balance.** Two battery mounting positions. Flashlight included.

20▷ SKIL High Performance 2492-04 **A good, relatively light drill.** Bubble level. 2-year warranty.

21▷ SKIL Warrior 2480-04 **Light and low-priced, but spartan.** No smart charger or electric brake. 6 clutch positions. One speed range. 2-year warranty.

9.6-VOLT DRILLS

22▷ DEWALT DW926K-2 **A good drill with excellent balance.**

23▷ CRAFTSMAN (Sears) Professional 27120 **Fair performance and bulky.** One-handed chuck. Overload protector. Bubble level.

24▷ SKIL Warrior 2380-02 **Fair performance.** 6 clutch positions. No smart charger or electric brake. One speed range. 2-year warranty.

Dryers

Shop Smart   Virtually all of the dryers we tested did a very good or excellent job and had ample capacity and convenient controls. Choosing the right one depends on which features you want. You can get a very good dryer for around $400. The Kenmore 6280, $410, and the Whirlpool LEQ8000J, $400, are **CR Best Buys**. When you pay more, you get a dryer loaded with conveniences, such as a porcelain top and touchpad controls. Key features for these models are listed in the table. See the guide for an explanation of features.

			Excellent ⊖	Very good ⊖	Good ○	Fair ⊖	Poor ●
Overall Ratings In performance order							
KEY NO.	BRAND & MODEL	PRICE	OVERALL SCORE		DRYING	CAPACITY	NOISE
			0 P F G VG E 100				
1	**Kenmore** (Sears) Elite 6393[2]	$540			⊖	⊖	⊖
2	**Kenmore** (Sears) 6280[2] **A CR Best Buy**	410			⊖	⊖	⊖
3	**GE** Profile Performance DPSE592EA[WW]	650			⊖	⊖	⊖
4	**Maytag** Neptune MDE7500AY[W]	800			⊖	⊖	○
5	**GE** Profile DPSB519EB[WW]	520			⊖	⊖	⊖
6	**Kenmore** (Sears) Elite HE3 8282[2]	900			○	⊖	⊖
7	**Whirlpool** Duet GEW9200L[W]	800			⊖	⊖	⊖
8	**Whirlpool** LEQ8000J[Q] **A CR Best Buy**	400			⊖	⊖	⊖
9	**Whirlpool** Gold GEW9878J[O]	530			⊖	⊖	⊖
10	**Whirlpool** GEW9868K[Q]	700			⊖	⊖	⊖
11	**Kenmore** (Sears) Elite 6283[2]	430			⊖	⊖	⊖
12	**Kenmore** (Sears) Elite 6304[2]	730			⊖	⊖	⊖
13	**Kenmore** (Sears) Elite 6206[2]	770			⊖	⊖	⊖
14	**Whirlpool** Gold GEQ9858J[Q]	500			⊖	⊖	⊖
15	**Frigidaire** Gallery GLER642A[S]	400			⊖	⊖	⊖
16	**Amana** ALE866SA[W]	530			⊖	⊖	⊖
17	**GE** DPXH46EA[WW]	450			⊖	⊖	○
18	**KitchenAid** Superba KEYS850J[W]	415			⊖	⊖	⊖
19	**Fisher & Paykel** DE05	550			⊖	⊖	⊖
20	**Maytag** Atlantis MDE8600AY[W]	550			⊖	⊖	⊖
21	**Maytag** Performa PYE4500AY[W]	420			⊖	⊖	○
22	**GE** DWSR405EB[WW]	400			○	⊖	⊖
23	**Maytag** Performa L MDE3500AY[W]	480			⊖	⊖	○

See report, page 66. Based on tests published in Consumer Reports in July 2002, with updated prices and availability.

The tests behind the Ratings

In **brand & model,** the bracketed letter or number is a color code. **Overall score** is based primarily on drying performance, drum capacity, noise, and convenience. **Drying** combines performance on four types of laundry loads of different sizes and fabric mixes. **Capacity** varies from about 5.7 to 7.5 cubic feet. **Noise** reflects judgments by panelists. **Price** is approximate retail.

Recommendations & notes

Models listed as similar and gas equivalents should offer performance comparable to the tested model's, although features may differ. **Most full-sized dryers have:** A moisture sensor. A dial with two or three automatic drying cycles. Separate start and temperature controls with at least three settings. Timed-dry and air-fluff (without heat) settings of at least one hour. An end-of-cycle signal. Raised edges to contain spills. A lint filter located in the drum opening. A drum light. A door that can be reversed to open left or right. Dimensions of about 44 inches high, 27 inches wide, and 28 inches deep. A full one-year warranty.

1> **KENMORE** (Sears) Elite 6393[2] **Excellent overall.** Impressive on large loads and delicates. Similar: 6394[ ], 6395[ ]. Gas equivalent: 7393[ ], 7394[ ], 7395[ ].

2> **KENMORE** (Sears) 6280[2] **A CR Best Buy Superb drying for a good price.** But warmer than most on delicates. Fewer features than most. Similar: 6281[ ], 6282[ ]. Gas equivalent: 7280[ ], 7281[ ], 7282[ ].

3> **GE** Profile Performance DPSE592EA[WW] **Very good.** Impressive on large loads and delicates. 10-yr. warranty. Gas equivalent: DPSE592GA[ ].

4> **MAYTAG** Neptune MDE7500AY[W] **Strong performer.** Impressive on large loads and delicates. Similar: MDE5500AY[W]. Gas equivalent: MDG7500AW[ ], MDG5500AW[ ].

5> **GE** Profile DPSB519EB[WW] **Very good and feature-rich.** Impressive on large loads and delicates. Gas equivalent: DPSB519GB[ ].

6> **KENMORE** (Sears) Elite HE3 8282[2] **Very good, but pricey.** Performs better when paired with the Kenmore Elite 4292 HE3t washer. Feature-rich and exceptionally quiet. Has front window. Gas equivalent: HE3 9282[ ].

7> **WHIRLPOOL** Duet GEW9200L[W] **Much like #6.** Performs better when paired with the Whirlpool Duet HT GHW9200L washer. Exceptionally quiet. Gas equivalent: GGW9200L[ ].

8> **WHIRLPOOL** LEQ8000J[Q] **A CR Best Buy Very good performance for a good price.** But fewer features than most. Similar: LEQ9858L[ ]. Gas equivalent: LGQ8000J[ ].

9> **WHIRLPOOL** Gold GEW9878J[O] **Impressive on large loads and delicates.** Similar: GEQ9858J[ ]. Gas equivalent: GGW9878J[ ].

10> **WHIRLPOOL** GEW9868K[Q] **Solid, feature-rich performer.** Very quiet. Gas equivalent: GGW9868K[ ].

11> **KENMORE** (Sears) Elite 6283[2] **Lots of performance for the price.** Simple, basic controls. Similar: 6284[ ], 6285[ ]. Gas equivalent: 7283[ ], 7284[ ], 7285[ ].

12> **KENMORE** (Sears) Elite 6304[2] **Very good.** Lots of features. Impressive on delicates. Similar: 6305[ ], 6306[ ]. Gas equivalent: 7304[ ], 7305[ ].

Recommendations & notes

13 **KENMORE** (Sears) Elite 6206[2] **Lots of features.** Impressive on delicates. Similar: 6208[ ]. Gas equivalent: 7206[ ], 7208[ ]

14 **WHIRLPOOL** Gold GEQ9858J[Q] **A very good machine.** Gas equivalent: GGQ9858J[ ].

15 **FRIGIDAIRE** Gallery GLER642A[S] **A very good machine.** Gas equivalent: GLGR642A[ ].

16 **AMANA** ALE866SA[W] **Very good.** Stainless-steel drum. Gas equivalent: ALG866SA[ ].

17 **GE** DPXH46EA[WW] **Very good.** Impressive on large loads and delicates. Gas equivalent: DPXH46GA[ ].

18 **KITCHENAID** Superba KEYS850J[W] **Very good.** 2-yr. warranty. Similar: KEYS700J[ ], KEYS750J[ ]. Gas equivalent: KGYS850J[ ], KGYS700J[ ], KGYS750J[ ].

19 **FISHER & PAYKEL** DE05 **Very good overall.** 2-yr. warranty. Gas equivalent: DG05.

20 **MAYTAG** Atlantis MDE8600AY[W] **Very good.** Moisture monitor shows load's dryness; use to get clothes damp-dry for ironing. Similar: MDE7600AY[ ]. Gas equivalent: MDG8600AW[ ], MDG7600AW[ ].

21 **MAYTAG** Performa PYE4500AY[W] **Very good machine.** Impressive on delicates. Drum opening smaller than most. Similar: PYE4057[ ], PYE4058[ ]. Gas equivalent: PYG4500AY[ ].

22 **GE** DWSR405EB[WW] **Not as good at drying as other sensor models.** Gas equivalent: DWSR405GB[ ].

23 **MAYTAG** Performa L MDE3500AY[W] **A very good, no-frills machine.** Moisture monitor shows load's dryness; use to get clothes damp-dry for ironing. Gas equivalent: MDG3500AW[ ].

FEATURES AT A GLANCE DRYERS

Tested products. (keyed to the Ratings) Key Brand no.	End-of-cycle signal	Drying rack	Express dry	Cool-down	Porcelain top	Touchpad controls
1 Kenmore	•	•				
2 Kenmore						
3 GE			•	•	•	•
4 Maytag	•			•	•	•
5 GE	•	•	•	•		•
6 Kenmore	•	•	•	•	•	
7 Whirlpool	•	•	•	•		
8 Whirlpool				•		
9 Whirlpool	•			•		
10 Whirlpool	•	•		•	•	•
11 Kenmore	•	•				
12 Kenmore	•	•	•	•	•	
13 Kenmore	•	•	•	•	•	
14 Whirlpool	•			•		
15 Frigidaire		•		•		
16 Amana	•	•		•		
17 GE		•		•		
18 KitchenAid	•	•		•	•	
19 Fisher & Paykel		•		•		
20 Maytag		•		•	•	
21 Maytag	•			•		
22 GE		•		•		
23 Maytag					•	

Food processors & choppers

Shop Smart   If you make a lot of soups, salads, or slaws, a food processor's versatility and capacity make it a good kitchen companion. The KitchenAid KFP670, $240, was excellent—strong and quiet. Two Cuisinarts, the DLC-8S ($200) and DLC-5, ($100), were nearly as good. The smaller one, the DLC-5, is an exceptional buy. For light chores, a chopper will do. The Cuisinart DLC-2, $40, is noisy but very good at chopping and puréeing.

Overall Ratings In performance order

Excellent ⊖ Very good ⊖ Good ○ Fair ◒ Poor ●

KEY NO.	BRAND AND MODELS	APPROX. PRICE	WEIGHT (LB.)	CLAIMED BOWL SIZE (CUPS)	OVERALL SCORE	SLICING	SHREDDING	PURÉEING
1	**KitchenAid** KFP670[WH]	$240	14	11		⊖	⊖	⊖
2	**Cuisinart** DLC-8S	200	13	11		⊖	⊖	⊖
3	**Cuisinart** DLC-5	100	11	7		⊖	⊖	⊖
4	**Cuisinart** DLC2014	330	15	14		⊖	⊖	⊖
5	**KitchenAid** KFP450[WW]	125	10	7		⊖	⊖	⊖
6	**KitchenAid** KFP350[WH]	100	10	5		⊖	⊖	⊖
7	**Cuisinart** Little Pro Plus	75	7	3		⊖	⊖	⊖
8	**Black & Decker** FP1000	67	6	6		⊖	⊖	⊖
9	**Black & Decker** FP1400	40	6	8		⊖	⊖	⊖
10	**Krups** 705	125	6	8		○	⊖	⊖

Overall Ratings In performance order

Excellent ⊖ Very good ⊖ Good ○ Fair ◒ Poor ●

KEY NO	BRAND AND MODEL	APPROX. PRICE	CLAIMED CAPACITY (CUPS)	OVERALL SCORE	CHOPPING	PURÉEING
11	**Cuisinart** DLC-2	$40	2½		⊖	⊖
12	**Cuisinart** DLC-1	31	2½		⊖	⊖
13	**Black & Decker** EHC600 Ergo	28	2		⊖	◒

See report, page 74. Based on tests published in Consumer Reports in December 2000, with updated prices and availability.

The tests behind the Ratings

Overall score reflects performance across a spectrum of chores, as well as noisiness and convenience. We judged the processors' prowess at **slicing, shredding,** and **puréeing,** and whipping cream using the standard blade or any whipping attachment (all at least did a good job), mixing batter and cookie dough, and **kneading** bread dough. Using the choppers, we **chopped** onions, garlic, beef cubes, and nuts, and **puréed** peas and carrots. **Claimed bowl size** sometimes differed from actual capacity. **Price** is the estimated average, based on a national survey. In model numbers, color codes are in brackets.

Recommendations & notes

FOOD PROCESSORS

1 > **KITCHENAID** KFP670 [WH] **Excellent performer, and very quiet.** Pricey. Dough blade and egg whip work well. Good controls. Has juicer attachment. Mini bowl. Similar: KFP650[ ], 17 lb.; KFP600[ ], no juicer.

2 > **CUISINART** DLC-8S **Very good, very quiet.** Dough blade works well. Good controls. Large feed-tube assembly hard to use and clean. Similar: DFP-11 .

3 > **CUISINART** DLC-5 **Very good, very quiet, and a good buy.** Worked well in heavy-duty tasks. Good controls.

4 > **CUISINART** DLC2014 **Very good, and fairly quiet.** Pricey. Good dough blade, controls. Large feed-tube assembly hard to use and clean, must remove before lid. Bowl really 12 cups.

5 > **KITCHENAID** KFP450[WW] **Very good, very quiet.** Worked well using half recipe for heavy-duty tasks. Good controls. Juicer attachment. Minibowl. Slight leaks when puréeing.

6 > **KITCHENAID** KFP350 [WH] **Very good, very quiet; a nice price.** Worked well using half recipe for heavy-duty tasks. Good controls. Mini bowl. Slight leaks when puréeing. Simlar: KFP300[ ], no mini bowl.

7 > **CUISINART** Little Pro Plus **Very good, very quiet**. Worked well using half recipe for heavy-duty tasks. Good controls. Has juicer attachment but spins disconcertingly fast. Small bowl. Combination bowl and chute.

8 > **BLACK & DECKER** FP1000 **Good, but noisy.** Good controls. Bowl, lid easy to assemble. Labored in heavy-duty tasks. Bowl really 9 cups.

9 > **BLACK & DECKER** FP1400 **Good, cheap—but noisy.** 2 speeds. Combination bowl and chute. Labored in heavy-duty tasks. Similar: FP1300, no food chute.

10 > **KRUPS** 705 **Good overall. 2 speeds.** Dough blade, egg-whip attachment. Slight leaks when puréeing.

CHOPPERS

11 > **CUISINART** DLC-2 **Very good but noisy.** Touchpad controls easy to clean.

12 > **CUISINART** DLC-1 **Very good but noisy.** Blade was inconvenient to use.

13 > **BLACK & DECKER** EHC600 Ergo **Good overall.** Easy-to-use design, soft grip surface, housing sits on bowl.

Freezers

Shop Smart   All the chests in our Ratings performed very well. For easy access and freedom from defrosting, go with a self-defrost upright. It will cost a little more to buy and operate than a chest, but the convenience may be worth it. The Frigidaire Commercial FFU20FC6A, $650, is a very good and capacious model. Manual-defrost uprights give you more usable space for the money, but comparable self-defrosting units perform better and cost little more. For the most space, the best performance, and the lowest purchase price and operating cost, a chest freezer is your best bet. But you'll have to defrost it periodically.

Overall Ratings				Excellent ⊖	Very good ⊖	Good ○	Fair ◐	Poor ●
KEY NO	BRAND & MODEL	PRICE	OVERALL SCORE	CAPACITY (AS LABELED)	TEMP. TESTS	ENERGY EFFICIENCY	EASE OF USE	
			0 P F G VG E 100					
MANUAL-DEFROST CHESTS								
1	**Kenmore** (Sears) 1154[1]	$350		14.9 cu. ft.	⊖	⊖	◐	
2	**Whirlpool** EH150FXK[Q]	380		14.8	⊖	⊖	◐	
3	**Frigidaire** Heavy Duty Commercial FFC15C3A[W]	350		14.9	⊖	⊖	◐	
4	**Wood's** C12NAA	350		12.2	⊖	⊖	◐	
SELF-DEFROST UPRIGHTS								
5	**Frigidaire** Commercial FFU20FC6A[W]	650		20.3	⊖	○	⊖	
6	**Kenmore** (Sears) Elite 2108[2]	750		20.3	⊖	○	⊖	
7	**Kenmore** (Sears) 2142[1]	530		13.7	⊖	○	⊖	
8	**Frigidaire** Commercial FFU14FC4A[W]	420		13.7	⊖	○	⊖	
9	**Wood's** F17NAC	500		16.7	⊖	○	⊖	
10	**Whirlpool** Commercial EV200NXK[Q]	600		19.6	○	○	⊖	
MANUAL-DEFROST UPRIGHTS								
11	**Whirlpool** EV150FXK[Q]	400		15.2	○	⊖	○	
12	**Frigidaire** Heavy Duty Commercial FFU17C3A[W]	420		17.1	○	⊖	○	

See report, page 68. Based on tests published in Consumer Reports in September 2002.

The tests behind the Ratings

Overall score is based on temperature performance, energy efficiency, ease of use, and noise. **Capacity** is as labeled by the manufacturer. We found that usable space in self-defrost uprights was about 20 percent less than labeled; on manual-defrost uprights, about 15 percent was not usable; on chests, only 5 percent or less was not usable. **Temperature** performance combines results of several tests: We measured how closely the manufacturer's recommended settings matched the ideal temperature of 0° F and how well a model kept optimum temperatures in all parts of the freezer, kept temperatures constant despite changes in room temperature, and maintained set temperature even in a 110° F room. **Energy efficiency** reflects energy consumption for the usable volume (our measurement) based on the 2002 average of 8.3 cents per kilowatt-hour. **Ease of use** considers controls, lighting, defrosting, and general convenience. Noise (not shown) reflects judgments by panelists. Chests were judged good to excellent for noise; self-defrost uprights fair; and manual-defrost uprights good. All models have a lock and a full one-year warranty. **Price** is approximate retail.

Recommendations & notes

Models listed as similar should offer performance comparable to the tested model's, although features may differ.

MANUAL-DEFROST CHESTS

1> **KENMORE** (Sears) 1154[1] **Very good, quiet, and inexpensive.** Has two baskets, interior and power-on lights, and flash defrost. Discontinued, but similar 1254[ ] is available.

2> **WHIRLPOOL** EH150FXK[Q] **Very good and quiet, with three baskets.** No interior or power-on lights.

3> **FRIGIDAIRE** Heavy Duty Commercial FFC15C3A[W] **Much like Kenmore 1154 but louder.** No interior light, one basket.

4> **WOOD'S** C12NAA **Very good and especially quiet.** On the small side. No interior or power-on lights, one basket.

SELF-DEFROST UPRIGHTS

5> **FRIGIDAIRE** Commercial FFU20FC6A[W] **Very good with lots of features, including power-on light and temperature alarm.**

6> **KENMORE** (Sears) Elite 2108[2] **Much like Frigidaire FFU20FC6A, adds quick-freeze option that resets after 24 hours.** Has glass shelves that adjust more than most.

7> **KENMORE** (Sears) 2142[1] **Very good with fairly basic features.** No power-on light.

8> **FRIGIDAIRE** Commercial FFU14FC4A[W] **Much like Kenmore 2142; adds power-on light, but lacks interior light.**

9> **WOOD'S** F17NAC **Good.** Has quick-freeze setting that must be reset after 24 hours. No adjustable shelves or power-on light. Discontinued, but similar F17NAD is available.

10> **WHIRLPOOL** Commercial EV200NXK[Q] **Good, but temperature not as uniform as others.** Has quick-freeze setting that must be reset after 24 hours. No adjustable shelves or power-on light. There are better choices.

MANUAL-DEFROST UPRIGHTS

11> **WHIRLPOOL** EV150FXK[Q] **Very good, but temperature not as uniform as others.** Has quick-freeze setting that must be reset after 24 hours. No power-on light.

12> **FRIGIDAIRE** Heavy Duty Commercial FFU17C3A[W] **Good, but temperature not as uniform as others.** Has power-on light.

Home theater in a box

Shop Smart A home theater in a box, which consists of at least a receiver and six speakers, is an easy way to start a system. Make sure that the components you already own—DVD player, camcorder, and MP3 player—can connect to the system you're considering. Then look for a model that includes the features and capabilities you need. The top-rated Sony HT-DDW740 is very good, and is **a CR Best Buy** at $300. Key features for these models are listed in the table on page 253. See the product guide for an explanation of the features.

Overall Ratings	In performance order							

Excellent ⊖ Very good ⊖ Good ○ Fair ◔ Poor ●

KEY NO.	BRAND & MODEL	PRICE	OVERALL SCORE	SOUND QUALITY	EASE OF USE	FEATURES
			0 P F G VG E 100			
1	**Sony** HT-DDW740	$300		⊖	⊖	⊖
2	**Pioneer** HTD-510DV	400		⊖	○	◔
3	**Panasonic** SC-HT75	400		⊖	○	○
4	**Yamaha** YHT-500	600		⊖	○	⊖
5	**Yamaha** YHT-300	400		⊖	○	⊖
6	**Kenwood** HTB-505	500		⊖	○	◔
7	**RCA** RT-DVD1	375		⊖	○	○
8	**Sony** DAV-C450	500		⊖	○	○
9	**JBL** Cinema ProPack 600II	900		○	○	⊖

See report, page 38. Based on tests published in Consumer Reports in November 2002.

The tests behind the Ratings

Overall score is based mostly on sound quality. **Sound quality** represents the accuracy of the front speakers, subwoofer, and center-channel speaker. **Ease of use** evaluates the console controls and remote control. We also judge models for useful **features.** **Recommendations & notes** include size (height by width by depth, in inches) and weight. **Price** is approximate retail.

Recommendations & notes

All tested models have: A receiver and six speakers: front left and right, center channel, rear left and right surround, and subwoofer. Decoders for Dolby Digital audio, Dolby Pro Logic or Pro Logic II surround audio, and other digital-signal processing (DSP) modes. At least 24 radio-station presets. Headphone jack. Mute button. Wiring and setup instructions. **Most tested models:** Have DTS decoder. Can play CD-RW discs and discs with MP3 files. Can't play SACD or DVD-Audio discs.

1 **SONY** HT-DDW740 **Very good and low-priced.** No DVD player. DVD player. Front and rear surround 5.75x3.25x4.75 in., 1.7 lb. each; center channel 3.25x9.25x4.75 in., 2.1 lb.; subwoofer 13x10.75x16 in., 20 lb. Optical and

Recommendations & notes

coaxial digital-audio inputs. 2-yr. warranty.

2▷ PIONEER HTD-510DV **Excellent sound, but shy on features.** DVD player. Front 10.75x6x7 in., 4.1 lb. each; rear surround 6x4.5x4 in., 1.6 lb. each; center channel 4.75x 14.5x5 in., 3.8 lb.; subwoofer 14.25x7.5x13 in., 10.6 lb. Coaxial digital-audio input. Bass-boost switch. Can't play CDs containing MP3 files.

3▷ PANASONIC SC-HT75 **Very good.** DVD player. Can play DVD-Audio discs. Front, center channel, and rear surround 5.5x3.5x4.5 in., 1.7 lb. each; subwoofer 12.5x6.5x12 in., 8.4 lb. No digital-audio input, bass/treble adjustment, or receiver-display dimmer.

4▷ YAMAHA YHT-500 **Very good.** DVD player. Front and rear surround 8.25x4x5 in., 2.7 lb. each; center channel 4x10.75x5 in., 3.8 lb.; subwoofer 14.5x8x14.5 in., 18.7 lb. 5.1 input for external digital-audio decoder. Has S-video and component-video outputs that can be used only with included DVD player. Optical and coaxial digital-audio inputs. 2-yr. warranty. Separate tone control for headphone jack.

5▷ YAMAHA YHT-300 **Very good.** No DVD player. Front, center channel, and rear surround 6.75x 4.25x4.75 in., 1.7 lb. each; subwoofer 14.5x8x14.5 in., 18.7 lb. 5.1 input for external digital-audio decoder. Optical and coaxial digital-audio inputs. 2-yr. warranty. Separate tone control for headphone jack.

6▷ KENWOOD HTB-505 **Very good.** No DVD player. Front 15.25x7.5x8.5 in., 9 lb. each; rear surround 8.5x 5.25x5 in., 3.1 lb. each; center channel 6x14x4.5 in., 6.1 lb.; subwoofer 11x11.75x17.5 in., 31 lb. 5.1 input for external digital-audio decoder. Optical and coaxial digital-audio inputs. Bass-boost switch. Loudness control. 2-yr. warranty on receiver (1-yr. on speakers). No sleep timer.

7▷ RCA RT-DVD1 **Good.** DVD player. Can play DVD-Audio discs, but lacks standard audio input. Front, center channel, and rear surround 5.25x3.5x4.25 in., 1.1 lb. each; subwoofer 14x6.5x14 in., 10.8 lb. Optical and coaxial digital-audio inputs. No DTS decoder.

8▷ SONY DAV-C450 **Good.** DVD player. Front, center channel, and rear surround 4.5x4.5x4.5 in., 1.4 lb. each; subwoofer 14x7x14 in., 11.3 lb. Optical digital-audio input. Has S-video and component-video outputs that can be used only with included DVD player. No bass/treble adjustment or sleep timer. Can play SACD music discs but not CD-RW discs or CDs containing MP3 files.

9▷ JBL Cinema ProPack 600II **Good, and full-featured.** DVD player. Front and rear surround 4.5x3.25x3.75 in., 1.1 lb. each; center channel 3.25x7.75x3.75 in., 1.8 lb.; subwoofer 15x13x13 in., 20.1 lb. Only tested model with front-panel A/V input. Has S-video and component-video outputs that can be used only with included DVD player. 5.1 input for external digital-audio decoder. Optical and coaxial digital-audio inputs.

FEATURES AT A GLANCE HOME THEATER

Tested products (keyed to the Ratings) Key Brand & model no.	DVD player (no. of discs)	Powered subwoofer	Composite-video inputs	Composite-video outputs	S-video inputs	S-video outputs
1▷ Sony		•	3	1		
2▷ Pioneer	5					
3▷ Panasonic	5					
4▷ Yamaha	1	•	4	1		
5▷ Yamaha		•	4	1		
6▷ Kenwood		•	2	1	2	
7▷ RCA	1		2	1	1	
8▷ Sony	5					
9▷ JBL	5		3	1	3	1

Irons

Shop Smart Even the least expensive steam irons on the market today come with plenty of convenient features, such as automatic shut-off and self-cleaning capabilities. Consider the Sunbeam Breeze 4892, $37, or the Black & Decker ProFinish X714, $40. The top-rated Rowenta Professional Luxe DM-880, $98, produced an impressive amount of steam, but it's heavy and expensive. Key features for these models are listed in the table on page 256. See the product guide for an explanation of features.

				Excellent ⊖	Very good ⊖	Good ○	Fair ◒	Poor ●

KEY NO.	BRAND & MODEL	PRICE	OVERALL SCORE	STEAM RATE	FILLING EASE	WATER GAUGE
1	**Rowenta** Professional Luxe DM-880	$98		⊖	○	○
2	**Krups** Intelligent V70	100		⊖	○	○
3	**Rowenta** Powerglide 2 DM-273	57		○	○	⊖
4	**Sunbeam** Breeze 3030	37		⊖	○	⊖
5	**T-Fal** Avantis 90	60		⊖	○	◒
6	**T-Fal** UltraGlide Turbo 1664	52		○	○	◒
7	**Black & Decker** ProFinish 3030	40		⊖	◒	⊖
8	**Black & Decker** ProFinish X750	50		⊖	◒	⊖
9	**Panasonic** Cord Reel NI-760R	45		●	⊖	⊖
10	**Proctor-Silex** Clear Steam 14429	30		⊖	○	⊖
11	**Rowenta** Powerglide DE-08	53		⊖	●	○
12	**Black & Decker** ProFinish X747	50		⊖	◒	⊖
13	**Black & Decker** SteamXpress S680	30		○	⊖	●
14	**Panasonic** Cordless NI-1500Z	110		●	⊖	⊖
15	**Black & Decker** Quick 'N Easy X380	20		◒	○	◒
16	**Kenmore** (Sears) Pro Steam KSR400	45		◒	◒	⊖
17	**Proctor-Silex** Steam Excel 14410	21		○	○	◒
18	**Black & Decker** Quick 'N Easy X340	16		◒	○	◒
19	**Toastmaster** 3302	11		○	◒	○
20	**Proctor-Silex** Perfect Press 16110	16		○	◒	◒
21	**Proctor-Silex** Steam & Reach 11420	30		●	⊖	●

See report, page 70. Based on tests published in Consumer Reports in September 2001, with updated prices and availability.

The tests behind the Ratings

Overall score is based primarily on steam rate, ease of filling the reservoir, visibility of the water gauge, and setting ease. **Steam rate** reflects the amount of steam produced within the first ten minutes of ironing. **Filling ease** indicates how easy it is to fill and empty the water tank. **Water gauge** reflects how easy it is to see the water level in the gauge. In Recommendations & Notes, weight is without water, rounded to the nearest quarter pound. Price is approximate retail.

Recommendations & notes

Models listed as similar should offer performance comparable to the tested model's although features may differ.

Most irons have: Spray, burst of steam, automatic shutoff, and self-cleaning. One or two indicator lights, adjustable or variable steam control, a temperature control and fabric guide under the handle, and a large water chamber (5 to 9¼ ounces) at the saddle area. A pivoting 7½- to 10½-foot cord that wraps around the iron for storage. A one-year warranty and draws 1,100 to 1,500 watts. Except as noted, setting ease was Very Good or Good.

1 > **ROWENTA** Professional Luxe **DM-880 Outstanding steamer, but expensive and heavy.** Large tank capacity and antidrip feature. But fabric guide cluttered, cord may get in way, auto shutoff light hard to see. 3½ lb.

2 > **KRUPS** Intelligent V70 **Illuminated temperature dial, heatproof carrying case, large tank capacity.** But fabric guide cluttered, cord may get in way. Spit or leaked from fill hole occasionally. 3¼ lb. Similar: V65.

3 > **ROWENTA** Powerglide 2 DM-273 **Very good spray, temperature-ready light easy to see.** But fabric guide cluttered, leaked from soleplate at low settings. Self-cleaning only so-so. 2¾ lb. Similar: DM-253.

4 > **SUNBEAM** Breeze 3030 **Very good spray; large, clear water chamber; large tank capacity.** But leaked from soleplate at low settings, cord and steam control may get in way. 2½ lb. Similar: 3890.

5 > **T-FAL** Avantis 90 **Very good spray, anticalcium feature.** But fabric guide cluttered, water level hard to see, and cord may get in way. 3¼ lb. Similar: Avantis 100.

6 > **T-FAL** UltraGlide Turbo 1664 **Very good spray, anticalcium feature.** 2¾ lb.

7 > **BLACK & DECKER** ProFinish X714 **Fabric guide easy to read, front temperature control easy to set.** But cord may get in way and steam/spray controls awkward. Tank cover inconvenient, leaked from soleplate at low settings. 3 lb. Sold only at Wal-Mart. Similar: ProFinish X712.

8 > **BLACK & DECKER** ProFinish X750 **Similar comments to X714 (above), but did not leak at low settings.** Adds vertical steam. 3 lb.

9 > **PANASONIC** Cord Reel NI-760R **Very good spray, removable tank, and retractable cord.** But steamed lightly and self-cleaning only so-so. Handle clearance tight for large hands, no indicator for auto shutoff. 2¾ lb. Similar: Cord Reel NI-790R.

10 > **PROCTOR-SILEX** Clear Steam 14429 **Large, clear water tank.** 2-yr. warranty. But sprayed too far, steam control hard to turn. Occasionally leaked heavily from fill hole. Indicator light hard to see, handle clearance tight for large hands. 2½ lb.

11 > **ROWENTA** Powerglide DE-08 **Very good spray.** But fabric guide cluttered and cord may get in way. Tank hard to fill, no indicator for auto shutoff. 2¾ lb.

Recommendations & notes

12 ▷ **BLACK & DECKER** ProFinish X747 **Similar comments to X750, but steamed more lightly.** 3 lb. Sold only at Wal-Mart.

13 ▷ **BLACK & DECKER** SteamXpress S680 **Fabric guide easy to read, front temperature control easy to set.** But sprayed unevenly and too far, and cord may get in way. 2¼ lb. Similar: S650.

14 ▷ **PANASONIC** Cordless NI-1500Z **Cordless iron reheats in base.** Touchpad temperature control easy to set, fabric guide easy to read. Removable water tank, antidrip. Had tight handle clearance for large hands and smaller tank capacity than most. 2½ lb.

15 ▷ **BLACK & DECKER** Quick 'N Easy X380 **Fabric guide easy to read, front temperature control easy to set.** But steam/spray controls awkward, spit or leaked from fill hole occasionally. 2 lb. Similar: X360.

16 ▷ **KENMORE** (Sears) Pro Steam KSR400 **Beeps for auto shutoff.** Anticalcium, antidrip feature. Weighs more than most. 3½ lb.

17 ▷ **PROCTOR-SILEX** Steam Excel 14410 **Very good spray.** 2-yr. warranty (excluding soleplate). But fabric guide cluttered and steam control hard to turn. Leaked from soleplate at low settings. 2¼ lb.

18 ▷ **BLACK & DECKER** Quick 'N Easy X340 **Similar comments to X380 (above), but no spray, burst of steam, or auto shutoff.** 1¾ lb.

19 ▷ **TOASTMASTER** 3302 **There are better choices.** 1¾ lb.

20 ▷ **PROCTOR-SILEX** Perfect Press 16110 **There are better choices.** 2 lb. Similar: 16100.

21 ▷ **PROCTOR-SILEX** Steam & Reach 11420 **There are better choices.** 2¾ lb.

FEATURES AT A GLANCE IRONS

Tested products (keyed to the Ratings) Key no. / Brand	Auto shutoff	Self-cleaning	Spray	Burst of steam	Vertical steam	Soleplate
1 ▷ Rowenta	•	•	•	•	•	SS
2 ▷ Krups	•	•	•	•	•	SS
3 ▷ Rowenta	•	•	•	•	•	SS
4 ▷ Sunbeam	•	•	•	•	•	NS
5 ▷ T-Fal	•	•	•	•	•	EN
6 ▷ T-Fal	•	•	•	•	•	EN
7 ▷ Black & Decker	•	•	•	•		NS
8 ▷ Black & Decker	•	•	•	•	•	NS
9 ▷ Panasonic	•	•	•	•	•	NS
10 ▷ Proctor-Silex	•		•	•		NS
11 ▷ Rowenta	•	•	•	•	•	SS
12 ▷ Black & Decker	•	•	•	•	•	SS
13 ▷ Black & Decker	•	•	•	•		NS
14 ▷ Panasonic	•			•		NS
15 ▷ Black & Decker		•	•	•		NS
16 ▷ Kenmore	•		•	•		SS
17 ▷ Proctor-Silex	•		•	•		NS
18 ▷ Black & Decker		•				NS
19 ▷ Toastmaster		•				AL
20 ▷ Proctor-Silex		•	•			AL
21 ▷ Proctor-Silex	•	•	•	•		NS

Soleplate surface material: AL=Aluminum; EN=Enamel nonstick; NS=Nonstick; SS=Stainless steel

Lawn mowers–push-type

Shop Smart Push-type power mowers are good for small yards and trimming around flower beds. There are many very good choices. Choose a rear-bagging model if you bag your clippings. Consider the top-rated Yard Machines by MTD 11A-439G129, $200, and 11A-549G129, $220—both **CR Best Buys.** Side-bagging models often cost less. The Yard Machines by MTD 11C-084C062, $140, and Poulan Pro 38618, $180, are **CR Best Buys.** Electric models are lighter, quieter, and run cleaner than gas models, but keep you tethered to an outlet. The Black & Decker MM675, $200, includes a reversible handlebar to help keep the cord from tangling.

Overall Ratings In performance order

Excellent ◓ Very good ◒ Good ○ Fair ◑ Poor ●

KEY NO.	BRAND & MODEL	PRICE	OVERALL SCORE	EVENNESS	MULCH	BAG	SIDE	HANDLING	EASE OF USE
			0 P F G VG E 100						
REAR-BAGGING MODELS									
1	**Yard Machines** by MTD 11A-439G129 **A CR Best Buy**	$200		◓	◓	◓	○	◓	○
2	**Yard Machines** by MTD 11A-549G129 **A CR Best Buy**	220		◓	◓	◓	○	○	○
3	**Craftsman** (Sears) 38880	310		◓	○	○	◓	○	○
4	**Stanley** 223230x692A	260		○	○	◓	○	○	○
5	**Murray** 205310x92A	200		○	◓	○	○	○	○
6	**Craftsman** (Sears) 38875	270		○	◒	○	○	○	○
7	**Snapper** MR216015B	310		○	○	◓	◒	○	○
8	**Murray** Select 22315x8	199		◓	◒	○	◒	◒	○
SIDE-BAGGING MODELS									
9	**Yard Machines** by MTD 11C-084C062 **A CR Best Buy**	140		◓	◓	○	○	◓	○
10	**Poulan Pro** 38618 **A CR Best Buy**	180		◓	◓	○	○	◓	○
11	**Craftsman** (Sears) 38762	200		◓	◓	○	○	○	○
12	**Yard Machines** by MTD 11A-509W300 Gold	230		◓	○	○	◓	◓	○
13	**Honda** Harmony II HRS216PDA	300		◓	○	●	◓	○	○
14	**Yard-Man** by MTD 11B-106C401	280		○	○	●	◓	○	○
15	**Murray** Select 22415x8A	160		○	◒	◒	●	◓	○
16	**Murray** 22516x92	150		○	◒	●	●	○	○
SIDE-BAGGING ELECTRIC MODELS									
17	**Black & Decker** MM675	200		○	◓	○	○	◓	◓

See report, page 102. Based on tests published in Consumer Reports in June 2002.

The tests behind the Ratings

Overall score is based mainly on cutting performance, handling, and ease of use. **Evenness** shows average cutting performance for three modes. **Mulching** reflects how completely clippings are distributed over the lawn's surface. **Bagging** denotes how many clippings the bag held before it filled or the chute clogged. **Side discharge** shows how evenly clippings were dispersed in that mode. **Handling** includes ease of pushing and pulling, making U-turns, and maneuvering in tight spots. **Ease of use** includes ease of starting the engine, operating the blade-stopping controls, and adjusting the cutting height. Bag convenience and ease of changing modes are separate judgments that contribute to the overall score. **Price** is approximate retail, and includes equipment for all three mowing modes unless noted in the Recommendations & Notes.

Recommendations & notes

Most models have: A four-stroke engine with primer bulb instead of choke. An engine-kill safety system. No throttle control on handle. Stamped-steel deck. A two-year warranty on mower and engine.

REAR-BAGGING MODELS

1 ▷ YARD MACHINES by MTD 11A-439G129 **A CR Best Buy Well-rounded performance at a good price.** Easy to push. Cut height hard to adjust. Engine: 6 hp. Swath: 21 in. Not sold in CA.

2 ▷ YARD MACHINES by MTD 11A-549G129 **A CR Best Buy Well-rounded performance, and good handling for a high-wheel model.** Easy to push. Cut height hard to adjust. Engine: 6 hp. Swath: 21 in. Not sold in CA, though similar: 11A-546U724 is.

3 ▷ CRAFTSMAN (Sears) 38880 **Very good overall performance.** Good choice for side-discharging. Throttle and choke. Engine: 5.5 hp. Swath: 21 in.

4 ▷ STANLEY 223230x692A **Very good, with good handling for a high-wheel model.** Engine: 6 hp. Swath: 22 in.

5 ▷ MURRAY 205310x92 **An average performer at good price.** Good handling for a high-wheel model. Less noisy than most. Weak in tall grass. Engine: 5.5 hp. Swath: 20 in. Not sold in CA.

6 ▷ CRAFTSMAN (Sears) 38875 **Good handling for a high-wheel model.** Noisier than most. Cut height hard to adjust. Chute $30. Engine: 6.5 hp. Swath: 21 in.

7 ▷ SNAPPER MR216015B **Good.** Mediocre vacuuming. Bag inconvenient to empty. U-turns and jockeying side-to-side hard. Noisier than most. Engine: 6 hp. Swath: 21 in. Bag $65; mulch kit $36; chute $20.

8 ▷ MURRAY Select 22315x8 **Good.** Weak in tall grass. U-turns and jockeying side-to-side hard. High rear wheels. Engine: 6 hp. Swath: 22 in. Bag $43. Not sold in CA.

SIDE-BAGGING MODELS

9 ▷ YARD MACHINES by MTD 11C-084C062 **A CR Best Buy Well-rounded performer.** Easy to push. Bag inconvenient. Engine: 4 hp. Swath: 22 in. Bag $40. Not sold in CA.

10 ▷ POULAN PRO 38618 **A CR Best Buy Very good performer at a good price.** Easy to push. High rear wheels. U-turns hard. Cut height hard to adjust. Bag $40. Engine: 4 hp. Swath: 22 in. Not sold in CA.

11 ▷ CRAFTSMAN (Sears) 38762 **Fine for mulching and side-discharging.** Easy to push. U-turns hard. Cut height hard to adjust. High rear

Recommendations & notes

wheels. Bag $40. Engine: 6 hp. Swath: 22 in. Not sold in CA, though similar 38763 is. Discontinued, but may still be available.

12> **YARD MACHINES** by MTD **11A-509W300 Gold** Very good, with good handling for a high-wheel model. Easy to push. Bag inconvenient. Handle vibrates. Bag $40. Engine: 6 hp. Swath: 22 in.

13> **HONDA** Harmony II HRS216PDA **Great for side-discharging, but pricey.** Throttle and choke. Weak in tall grass. Bagging requires blade change. Engine: 5.5 hp. Swath: 21 in. Bag $45.

14> **YARD-MAN** by MTD 11B-106C401 **Competent performer.** Engine: 6 hp. Swath: 20 in. Bag $40. Not sold in CA.

15> **MURRAY** Select 22415x8A **There are better choices.** Mediocre vacuuming. Weak in tall grass. Handle vibrates. Requires blade change for mulching. Engine: 4 hp. Swath: 22 in. Mulch kit $25; bag $39. Not sold in CA.

16> **MURRAY** 22516X92 **Lackluster performer.** Mediocre vacuuming. Weak in tall grass. Noisier than most. U-turns and jockeying side-to-side hard. Mulching cover hard to remove. Engine: 4 hp. Swath: 22 in. Bag $39. Not sold in CA.

SIDE-BAGGING ELECTRIC

17> **BLACK & DECKER** MM675 **Impressive-and pricey-for an electric.** Flip-over handle eases U-turns, but cord is still an inconvenience. Plastic deck. Engine: 12 amps. Swath: 18 in. Bag $40.

Lawn mowers–self-propelled

Shop Smart   Self-propelled power mowers are good choices for larger yards. Rear-bagging models generally have more bagging capacity and maneuverability than side-baggers, though they usually cost more. All of the tested mowers cut competently. The top-rated John Deere JX75, $800, delivers carpetlike evenness and easy mode changes but it's pricey. For strong performance at a lower price, consider the Craftsman 37779, $500, or John Deere JS63C, $410. Both are **CR Best Buys.**

Overall Ratings — In performance order

Ratings key: Excellent ⊖ Very good ⊖ Good ○ Fair ◐ Poor ●

KEY NO.	BRAND & MODEL	PRICE	OVERALL SCORE	EVENNESS	MULCH	BAG	SIDE	HANDLING	EASE OF USE
	REAR-BAGGING MODELS								
1	**John Deere** JX75	$800		⊖	○	⊖	○	○	⊖
2	**Craftsman** (Sears) 37779 **A CR Best Buy**	500		⊖	○	⊖	○	⊖	⊖
3	**Honda** Harmony HRB216TXA	700		○	⊖	⊖	⊖	⊖	⊖
4	**Honda** Masters HR215K1HXA	950		⊖	⊖	⊖	○	○	○
5	**Honda** Harmony HRB216TDA	640		○	⊖	⊖	⊖	⊖	⊖
6	**John Deere** JS63C **A CR Best Buy**	410		⊖	⊖	⊖	⊖	⊖	⊖
7	**Toro** Super Recycler 20037 Personal Pace	520		⊖	⊖	⊖	⊖	○	○
8	**Yard-Man** 12A-979L401	430		●	⊖	⊖	○	○	⊖
9	**Toro** Super Recycler 20487	670		⊖	⊖	⊖	⊖	◐	⊖
10	**Craftsman** (Sears) 37765	420		⊖	⊖	⊖	○	○	⊖
11	**Ariens** LM21ST	560		○	○	⊖	⊖	○	⊖
12	**Toro** Recycler 20017	370		⊖	○	⊖	○	○	⊖
13	**Snapper** ELP21602	600		○	⊖	⊖	○	○	⊖
14	**Snapper** P216012	520		⊖	⊖	⊖	○	○	⊖
15	**Craftsman** (Sears) 37890	410		○	⊖	⊖	○	◐	⊖
16	**Craftsman** (Sears) 37834	310		○	⊖	⊖	⊖	◐	⊖
17	**Craftsman** (Sears) 37845	360		○	⊖	⊖	⊖	◐	⊖
18	**Snapper** P2167517B1	550		⊖	○	⊖	○	○	⊖
19	**Toro** Recycler 20016	320		⊖	⊖	⊖	○	○	○
20	**Troy-Bilt** 12A-466N063	300		○	⊖	⊖	○	⊖	○
21	**Lawn-Boy** Silver Series 10360	258		⊖	○	○	⊖	⊖	○

Overall Ratings, cont.

	Excellent	Very good	Good	Fair	Poor
	⊖	⊖	○	◑	●

KEY NO.	BRAND & MODEL	PRICE	OVERALL SCORE	EVENNESS	MULCH	BAG	SIDE	HANDLING	EASE OF USE
22	**Snapper** MRP216015B	400		○	○	⊖	○	○	⊖
23	**Lawn-Boy** SilverPro 10324	380		○	⊖	○	○	⊖	○
24	**Murray** 206311x92A	235		○	⊖	○	○	○	○
25	**Troy-Bilt** 12AD-466N063	350		○	○	○	○	◑	○
26	**Yard-Man** by MTD 12A569T401	400		⊖	○	○	○	◑	○
27	**Stanley** 228630x692A	300		○	○	○	○	◑	○
28	**Husqvarna** Crown Series 6522CH	400		○	⊖	◑	⊖	●	○
	SIDE-BAGGING MODELS								
29	**Honda** Harmony II HRS216K2SDA	$390		⊖	⊖	●	⊖	○	○
30	**Yard Machines** by MTD 12A-288A300 Gold	250		⊖	⊖	○	⊖	○	○
31	**Craftsman** (Sears) 37/803	270		○	○	○	⊖	◑	○

See report, page 102. Based on tests published in Consumer Reports in June 2002, with updated prices and availabilty.

The tests behind the Ratings

Overall score is based mainly on cutting performance, handling, and ease of use. **Evenness** shows average cutting performance for three modes. **Mulching** reflects how completely clippings are distributed over the lawn's surface. **Bagging** denotes how many clippings the bag held before it filled or the chute clogged. **Side discharge** shows how evenly clippings were dispersed in that mode. **Handling** includes ease of operating the drive controls, pushing and pulling, making U-turns, and maneuvering in tight spots. **Ease of use** includes ease of starting the engine, operating the blade-stopping controls, shifting speeds, and adjusting the cutting height. Bag convenience and ease of changing modes are separate judgments that contribute to the overall score. **Price** is approximate retail, and includes equipment for all three mowing modes unless noted in the Recommendations & Notes.

Recommendations & notes

Most models have: A four-stroke engine with primer bulb instead of choke. An engine-kill safety system. No throttle control on handle. Rear-wheel drive. Stamped-steel deck. A two-year warranty on mower and engine.

REAR-BAGGING MODELS

1 > **JOHN DEERE** JX75 **Excellent, with blade-brake clutch.** Easy to use, with easy bag handling. Drive starts abruptly. Throttle and choke. Aluminum deck. Engine: 6 hp. Swath: 21 in. Mulch kit $29; chute $18.

Recommendations & notes

2 > **CRAFTSMAN** (Sears) 37779 **A CR Best Buy Easy to use and moderately priced.** Blade-brake clutch. Throttle and choke. Engine: 5.5 hp. Swath: 21 in.

3 > **HONDA** Harmony HRB216TXA **Easy to use, with easy bag handling.** Blade-brake clutch. Front lifts with full bag. Throttle and choke. Plastic deck. Engine: 5.5 hp. Swath: 21 in. Chute $28.

4 > **HONDA** Masters HR215K1HXA **Easy to use, with easy bag handling, though mulching requires a blade change.** Blade-brake clutch. Throttle and choke. Aluminum deck. Engine: 5 hp. Swath: 21 in. Mulch kit $20; chute $28.

5 > **HONDA** Harmony HRB216TDA **Easy to use, with easy bag handling.** Less noisy than most. Front lifts with full bag. Throttle and choke. Plastic deck. Engine: 5.5 hp. Swath: 21 in. Chute $28.

6 > **JOHN DEERE** JS63C **A CR Best Buy Easy to use, and a good price.** But hard to jockey side to side. Bag hard to empty. Engine: 6.5 hp. Swath: 21 in. Bag: $49.

7 > **TORO** Super Recycler 20037 **Among the less repair-prone brands.** Less noisy than most. Hard to jockey side to side. Bag inconvenient to empty. 5-year mower warranty. Engine: 6.5 hp. Swath: 21 in.

8 > **YARD-MAN** 12A-979L401 **Very good, but among the more repair-prone brands.** Hard to pull. Engine: 6.5 hp. Swath: 21 in.

9 > **TORO** Super Recycler 20487 **Very good with blade-brake clutch.** Among the less repair-prone brands. Less noisy than most. U-turns and jockeying side-to-side hard. Drive control and bag emptying inconvenient. Aluminum deck. 5-year mower warranty.

Engine: 6.5 hp. Swath: 21 in. Bag $80; chute $66.

10 > **CRAFTSMAN** (Sears) 37765 **Easy to use, but hard to push and pull.** Noisier than most. Engine: 6.75 hp. Swath: 21 in.

11 > **ARIENS** LM21ST **Very good.** U-turns and jockeying side to side hard. Bag hard to empty. Tools needed to change modes. Engine: 6.5 hp. Swath: 21 in.

12 > **TORO** Recycler 20017 **Very good, and among the less repair-prone brands.** Engine: 6.5 hp. Swath: 22 in.

13 > **SNAPPER** ELP21602 **Very good, with easy bag handling, but among the more repair-prone brands.** Mulching requires blade change. Front lifts with full bag. Aluminum deck. 3-year mower warranty. Engine: 6 hp. Swath: 21 in. Mulch kit $45; chute $28. Not sold in CA.

14 > **SNAPPER** P216012 **Very good, but among the more repair-prone brands.** Clippings may discharge at operator with bag off. Mulching requires blade change. 5-year mower warranty. Engine: 6 hp. Swath: 21 in. Mulch kit $35; chute $20. Not sold in CA.

15 > **CRAFTSMAN** (Sears) 37890 **Very good.** Hard to jockey side to side, and hard to push manually. Inconvenient drive control. Engine: 7 hp. Swath: 21 in.

16 > **CRAFTSMAN** (Sears) 37834 **Deck and blade similar to #15, but different engine and chute.** Good price. Engine: 6.25 hp. Swath: 21 in. Chute: $29.

17 > **CRAFTSMAN** (Sears) 37845 **High-wheel version of #15 with different engine and chute.** U-turns hard. Engine: 6.5 hp. Swath: 21 in. Chute: $30.

Recommendations & notes

18 **SNAPPER** P2167517B1 **Very good, but among repair-prone brands.** U-turns and jockeying side to side hard. Noisier than most. Bag inconvenient to empty. Clippings may discharge at operator with bag off. Tools needed to change modes. 3-year mower warranty. Engine: 6.5 hp. Swath: 21 in. Mulch kit: $36.

19 **TORO** Recycler 20016 **Very good.** U-turns and jockeying side to side hard. Engine: 6.5 hp. Swath: 22 in.

20 **TROY-BILT** 12A-466N063 **Very good.** Bag hard to empty. Cut height hard to adjust. Engine: 6.5 hp. Swath: 21 in.

21 **LAWN-BOY** Silver Series 10360 **Good for side-discharging.** Weak in tall grass. Hard to jockey side to side. Clippings may discharge at operator with bag off. Cut height hard to adjust. Engine: 5 hp. Swath: 21 in. Bag: $69. Not sold in CA.

22 **SNAPPER** MRP216015B **Among the more repair-prone brands.** Mediocre vacuuming. U-turns hard. Clippings may discharge at operator with bag off. Bag inconvenient to empty. Mode changes require tools, mulching requires a blade change. Inconvenient shift lever. 3-year mower warranty. Engine: 6 hp. Swath: 21 in. Bag $100; chute $20. Not sold in CA.

23 **LAWN-BOY** SilverPro 10324 **Good.** Weak in tall grass. Hard to jockey side to side. Clippings may discharge at operator with bag off. Cut height hard to adjust. Two-stroke engine. Engine: 6.5 hp. Swath: 21 in. Not sold in CA.

24 **MURRAY** 206311x92A **Good.** Weak in tall grass. Inconvenient drive control. Cut height hard to adjust. Engine: 5.5 hp. Swath: 20 in. Not sold in CA.

25 **TROY-BILT** 12AD-466N063 **Good.** Hard to pull. Bag hard to empty. Cut height hard to adjust. Engine: 6.5 hp. Swath: 20 in.

26 **YARD-MAN BY MTD** 12A569T401 **Good, but among the more repair-prone brands.** Push-button starter. Hard to push and pull. U-turns, jockeying side-to-side, and bag emptying hard. Engine: 6 hp. Swath: 21 in. Not sold in CA.

27 **STANLEY** 228630x692A **There are better choices.** Engine: 6.5 hp. Swath: 22 in.

28 **HUSQVARNA** Crown Series 6522CH **There are better choices.** Engine: 6.5 hp. Swath: 22 in.

SIDE-BAGGING MODELS

29 **HONDA** Harmony II HRS216K2SDA **Capable in all modes but bagging.** Drive starts abruptly. Bagging requires blade change. Throttle and choke. Engine: 5.5 hp. Swath: 21 in. Bag $37.

30 **YARD MACHINES** by MTD 12A-288A300 Gold **Among the more repair-prone brands.** Hard to pull. Bag inconvenient. Handle vibrates. Engine: 5 hp. Swath: 22 in. Bag: $40. Not sold in CA.

31 **CRAFTSMAN** (Sears) 37803 **There are better choices.** Less noisy than most. Mediocre vacuuming. Hard to jockey side-to-side and push. Inconvenient drive control. Cut height hard to adjust. Engine: 6 hp. Swath: 22 in. Bag: $40. Not sold in CA.

Lawn tractors

Shop Smart   Models with hydrostatic drive allow you to infinitely adjust speed without shifting. The John Deere Spin-Steer SST-16, $4,300, is a hydrostatic-drive model with a zero-turn-radius, allowing the tractor to drive around trees and squeeze into tight spots. If you don't mind some extra maneuvering, consider the White Outdoor LT 1650, $1,800, **a CR Best Buy,** or the Stanley 425605x692, $1600. These hydrostatic-drive lawn tractors cut more evenly than the Deere at a fraction of the price. Gear-drive models have distinct ground-speed settings. Many we tested also performed impressively.

KEY NO.	BRAND & MODEL	PRICE	OVERALL SCORE	EVENNESS	SIDE	MULCH	BAG	HANDLING
	HYDROSTATIC-DRIVE TRACTORS							
1	**White Outdoor** LT 1650 **A CR Best Buy**	$1,800		⊖	⊖	⊖	⊖	⊖
2	**John Deere** Spin-Steer SST-16	4,300		○	⊖	○	⊖	⊖
3	**Snapper** LT160H42FBV	2,500		○	⊖	⊖	○	⊖
4	**Husqvarna** YTH1542XP	2,000		○	⊖	⊖	⊖	⊖
5	**Stanley** 425605x692	1,600		⊖	⊖	○	⊖	○
6	**Toro** Wheel Horse 16-38 HXL	2,200		○	○	⊖	○	⊖
7	**Cub Cadet** 2000 Series 2166	3,400		○	○	⊖	⊖	⊖
8	**John Deere** LT155	2,500		○	⊖	○	○	⊖
9	**Craftsman** (Sears) 27208	1,750		○	⊖	○	○	○
10	**Ariens** EZR 1742 915013	3,000		○	⊖	○	⊖	○
11	**Scotts** S1642	1,700		○	⊖	○	◔	○
12	**Yard-Man** Revolution 624G	2,900		○	⊖	○	○	◔
	GEAR-DRIVE TRACTORS							
13	**Cub Cadet** 1000 Series 1170	1,800		⊖	○	⊖	⊖	⊖
14	**Craftsman** (Sears) 27207	1,550		○	⊖	○	○	◔
15	**Yard Machines** by MTD 13AK608G062	1,300		⊖	⊖	⊖	⊖	○
16	**Murray** WideBody 40508x92	800		⊖	⊖	○	○	◔
17	**Yard Machines** by MTD 13A1608H062	1,400		○	○	⊖	○	○

See report, page 102. Based on tests published in Consumer Reports in May 2002, with updated prices and availability.

The tests behind the Ratings

Overall score is based mainly on performance, handling, ease of use, and stability. **Evenness** is how close tractors came to even, carpetlike mowing in all modes. **Side** is how evenly clippings were dispersed from the side-discharge chute. **Mulch** is how finely and evenly clippings were cut and dispersed in this mode. **Bag** denotes effective capacity of the grass-catcher bags, measured when bags were filled or when chute clogged and collection stopped. **Handling** includes clutching or drive engagement, braking, steering, and turning radius. We also evaluated ease of use, including leg room, steering-wheel/lever comfort, getting on and off, and reaching and using controls. **Price** is approximate retail and does not include bagging, mulching, or other accessories, unless noted.

Recommendations & notes

Listed under each brand and model are the engine horsepower and the cutting swath in inches. Models listed as similar should offer performancea comparable to the tested model's, although features may differ.

Most have: Single-cylinder, overhead-valve engine. Manual power takeoff (PTO) lever for blade-engagement. 2-year parts and labor warranty. No bag and mulching kits (they are extra-cost options). Performance: Most cut better on straight runs than in turns. Were easy to switch between side-discharge and bagging, but required at least a blade change for mulching. Can cut in reverse. Were reasonably stable on slopes.

HYDROSTATIC-DRIVE MODELS

1> **WHITE OUTDOOR** LT 1650 **A CR Best Buy Strong performance at a reasonable price.** Two-cylinder side-valve engine. Cruise control. No blade change needed for mulching. Clutch pedal too close. Won't cut in reverse. Mediocre vacuuming. Engine: 16.5 hp. Swath: 42 in. Bag $299. Mulch kit $55.

2> **JOHN DEERE** Spin-Steer SST-16 **Very good overall, with a steering wheel, but pricey.**

Very smooth drive engagement and steering. Reverse safety switch allows cutting in reverse. Cut-height control inconvenient to use. Less noisy than most. Engine: 16 hp. Swath: 42 in. Bag kit: $390. Mulch kit: $46.

3> **SNAPPER** LT160H42FBV **Very good.** Electric PTO. Cut more evenly when side-discharging. Mediocre vacuuming. 3-year warranty on mower. Engine: 16 hp. Swath: 42 in. Bag $260. Mulch kit $75. Discontinued, but LT160H42FBV is available.

4> **HUSQVARNA** YTH1542XP **A competent, agile tractor with premium features.** Two-cylinder engine. Electric PTO. Front bumper. Comes with two sets of blades, but mulching set works best in all modes. Fuel level hard to check. Engine: 15 hp. Swath: 42 in. Bag: $239. Mulch kit included.

5> **STANLEY** 425605x692 **Very good.** No blade change needed for mulching. PTO lever obstructs right knee. Sold only at Wal-Mart. Engine: 17.5 hp. Swath:42 in. Bag: $300. Mulch kit included.

6> **TORO** Wheel Horse 16-38 HXL **Very good.** No blade change needed for mulching. Clutch

Recommendations & notes

pedal too close. PTO hard to engage. Catcher bags inconvenient to install. Weak in tall grass. Cut more evenly when bagging. Engine: 16 hp. Swath: 38 in. Bag $329. Mulch kit included.

7> **CUB CADET** 2000 Series 2166 **Very good.** Cruise control. Electric PTO. Clutch pedal too close. Won't cut in reverse. Wide turning. Fueling and fuel-level checks hard. Mediocre vacuuming. 3-year warranty on PTO clutch, 5 years on frame driveshaft, and drivetrain. Engine: 16 hp. Swath: 42 in. Bag $329. Mulch kit included.

8> **JOHN DEERE** LT155 **Very good, but some flaws.** Mulching conversion complicated. Cut more evenly when side-discharging, less evenly when mulching. Mediocre vacuuming. Fuel-level checks hard. Engine: 15 hp. Swath: 38 in. Bag $349. Mulch kit $89.

9> **CRAFTSMAN** (Sears) 27208 **Very good, but spending a little more buys a lot more features.** Similar design to #4, but has one-cylinder engine and fewer features. No blade change needed for mulching. Engine: 17 hp. Swath: 42 in. Bag: $260. Mulch kit included.

10> **ARIENS** EZR 1742 915013 **Very good overall, but difficult mode changes.** Evenness very good in mulching mode. Switching between mulching and side-discharge or bagging requires changing blade and other parts, using tools. Limited access to engine with cover raised. Noisier than most. Engine: 17 hp. Swath: 42 in. Bag kit: $499. Mulch kit: $99.

11> **SCOTTS** S1642 **OK, but poor choice for bagging.** Mulching conversion complicated. Front wheels can rear up with full grass bags. Cut more evenly when side-discharging. Engine: 16 hp. Swath: 42 in. Bag $269. Mulch kit $78.

12> **YARD-MAN** Revolution 624G **Good, but has handling flaws.** Steering levers difficult to control precisely. Mediocre vacuuming in bagging mode. Cannot cut in reverse. Abrupt drive engagement. Parking brake hard to engage. Limited access to engine with cover raised. Engine: 17.5 hp. Swath: 42 in. Bag kit: $299. Mulch kit included.

GEAR-DRIVE MODELS

13> **CUB CADET** 1000 Series 1170 **Very good, with convenient drive system.** Cruise control. Electric PTO. Pedal-operated variable-speed drive. No blade change needed for mulching. Won't cut in reverse. Clutch pedal too close. Front wheels can rear up with full grass bags. Cut less evenly when side-discharging. Mediocre vacuuming. Engine: 17 hp. Swath: 42 in. Bag $299. Mulch kit included.

14> **CRAFTSMAN** (Sears) 27207 **Competent but basic.** Similar design to #4, but has one-cylinder engine and fewer features. No blade change needed for mulching. Engine: 17 hp. Swath: 42 in. Bag: $260. Mulch kit included.

Recommendations & notes

15▷ YARD MACHINES by MTD 13AK608G062 **Very good, with convenient drive system.** Two-cylinder side-valve engine. Pedal-operated variable-speed drive. No blade change needed for mulching. Won't cut in reverse and can run too fast in that mode. Clutch pedal too close. Front wheels can rear up with full grass bags. Cut less evenly when mulching. Mediocre vacuuming. Engine: 17hp. Swath: 42 in. Bag $279. Mulch kit $30. Discontinued, but similar 13AF608G062 is available.

16▷ MURRAY WideBody 40508x92 **Very good, but some flaws.** Side-valve engine. No blade change needed for mulching. Abrupt drive engagement and braking. Grass buckets awkward to empty. Uncomfortable steering wheel. Engine: 12.5 hp. Swath: 40 in. Bag $249. Mulch kit $30.

17▷ YARD MACHINES by MTD 13A1608H062 **Very good, with convenient drive system.** Two-cylinder side-valve engine. Pedal-operated variable-speed drive. Clutch pedal too close. Won't cut in reverse and can run too fast in that mode. Cut more evenly when mulching. Mediocre vacuuming. Engine: 20 hp. Swath: 46 in. Bag $329. Mulch kit $50. Discontinued, but similar 13B1675H062 is available.

Microwave ovens

Shop Smart Most microwave ovens tested, especially the larger sizes, did a very good job overall. If you're selecting a countertop model, buy the largest model that will comfortably fit to get more features and have more room for oversized dishes. For a larger interior, consider the moderately priced Kenmore 6128(9), a **CR Best Buy** at $100. Any of the over-the-range models would be a very good choice. Among compacts, the Goldstar MA-790 stands out for performance and at $80 is a **CR Best Buy**. Key features for these models are listed in the table on page 271. See the product guide for an explanation of features.

Overall Ratings	In performance order				Excellent ⊖ Very good ◑ Good ○ Fair ◒ Poor ●			
KEY NO.	BRAND & MODEL	PRICE	WATTAGE	CAPACITY (CU. FT.)	OVERALL SCORE	COOK EVENLY	AUTO DEFROST	EASE OF USE
COMPACT COUNTERTOP OVENS *600-800 watts, 0.5-0.9 cu. ft.*								
1	**Goldstar** MA-790[B] **A CR Best Buy**	$80	700	0.7		⊖	⊖	⊖
2	**GE** JE740[G]Y	100	700	0.7		⊖	●	⊖
3	**GE** Profile JEM31[G]A	180	800	0.9		◒	○	⊖
4	**Samsung** MW4699[S]	110	700	0.7		⊖	-	⊖
5	**Sharp** Half Pint R-120D[K]	75	600	0.5		◒	◒	◒
MIDSIZED COUNTERTOP OVENS *900-1,300 watts, 1.0-1.2 cu. ft.*								
6	**Sharp** Platinum Collection R-370E[K]	130	1,000	1.0		⊖	⊖	⊖
7	**Kenmore** 6128[9] **A CR Best Buy**	100	1,100	1.1		○	⊖	⊖
8	**Sharp** Carousel R-330E[K]	150	1,200	1.2		⊖	⊖	⊖
9	**Whirlpool** MT2115SJ[B]	130	1,100	1.1		◒	⊖	⊖
10	**GE** Profile JE1160[B]C	120	1,100	1.1		○	○	⊖
11	**Samsung** MW1255[W]A	95	1,200	1.2		⊖	○	⊖
12	**Sanyo** Super Shower Wave EM-V3405S[W]	100	1,200	1.2		⊖	◒	⊖
13	**Emerson** MW8107[W]A	80	1,000	1.1		⊖	◒	⊖
14	**Emerson** MW8102[SS]	150	1,100	1.0		⊖	⊖	○
LARGE COUNTERTOP OVENS *1,100-1,300 watts, 1.3-2.2 cu. ft.*								
15	**Goldstar** MA-1302S	160	1,150	1.3		⊖	⊖	⊖
16	**Sharp** Carousel R-420E[K]	150	1,200	1.6		⊖	⊖	⊖
17	**GE** Profile JE1860[G]B	170	1,100	1.8		○	⊖	⊖
18	**Kenmore** Elite 6158[9]	150	1,200	2.0		⊖	○	⊖
19	**GE** Profile JE1360[B]C	140	1,100	1.3		○	⊖	⊖

Overall Ratings, cont.

Excellent ◓ Very good ◓ Good ○ Fair ◒ Poor ●

KEY NO.	BRAND & MODEL	PRICE	WATTAGE	CAPACITY (CU. FT.)	OVERALL SCORE	COOK EVENLY	AUTO DEFROST	EASE OF USE
	LARGE COUNTERTOP OVENS *1,100-1,300 watts, 1.3-2.2 cu. ft.*							
20	**Goldstar** MA-2117[B]	$170	1,150	2.1		◓	◓	◓
21	**Sharp** Carousel R-530E[K]	165	1,200	2.0		◓	◓	◓
22	**Goldstar** MA-2003[W]	130	1,150	2.0		◓	○	◓
23	**Panasonic** Inverter NN-S961[B]F	160	1,300	2.2		◓	○	◓
24	**Whirlpool** MT4140SK[B]	110	1,100	1.4		○	○	◓
	OVER-THE-RANGE OVENS *900-1,100 watts, 1.4-1.9 cu. ft.*							
25	**Kenmore** Elite 6168[2]	460	1,100	1.8		○	◓	◓
26	**Whirlpool** Gold GH8155XJ[B] **A CR Best Buy**	425	1,000	1.5		◓	◓	◓
27	**Kenmore** 6065[9] **A CR Best Buy**	400	1,000	1.5		◓	◓	◓
28	**Kenmore** 6163[9]	380	1,000	1.5		◓	◓	◓
29	**KitchenAid** KHMS147H[BL]	700	1,000	1.4		○	◓	◓
30	**LG** Intellowave LMV-1915NV	550	1,000	1.9		○	○	◓
31	**Sharp** Carousel R-1750[0]	435	1,100	1.6		◓	◒	◓
32	**Goldstar** MV-1715[B]	360	1,000	1.7		○	○	◓
33	**Maytag** MMV5100AA[B]	390	1,000	1.7		○	◒	◓
34	**GE** Profile Spacemaker JVM1860[B]D	480	1,000	1.8		○	○	◓
35	**Amana** Radarange ACO1860A[B]	440	1,000	1.8		○	○	◓
36	**GE** Spacemaker JVM1650[B]B	380	1,000	1.6		○	◒	◓
37	**Sanyo** EM-S9000	300	1,000	1.5		○	◒	◓

See report, page 73. Based on tests published in Consumer Reports in January 2002, with updated prices and availability.

The tests behind the Ratings

Overall score is based largely on evenness of cooking, ability to defrost, and ease of use. Space efficiency, window view, and features are also factored in. **Wattage** and **capacity** are as claimed by the manufacturer and listed on product and/or packaging; our measurements of both were lower. Ability to **cook evenly** reflects how well a model heated a dish of cold mashed potatoes. **Auto defrost** is based on how well the automatic-defrost program defrosted 1 pound of frozen ground chuck. **Ease of use** includes our judgment of how easily each model can be set without instruction. **Price** is approximate retail. Under **brand & model,** bracketed letters and numbers refer to color of the tested model. Most are black, but some are white.

Recommendations & notes

Models listed as similar should offer performance comparable to the tested model's, although features may differ.

All models: Operate on full power unless programmed otherwise. Stop operating when door is opened. Hold a 10-inch dinner plate or one large TV dinner on the turntable. Have electronic digital display with clock, removable glass turntable with rim, screened window, left-opening door, steel housing, and automatic popcorn feature.

Most have: Child-lock feature. Interior light that goes on when oven is in use or the door opens. Reheat and automatic-defrost settings. 1-year parts-and-labor warranty; additional 4 years on magnetron, parts only.

All over-the-range models: Fit above a standard 30-inch range. Have an exterior light and a venting system with two or more settings.

Most over-the-range models: Have a rack for bi-level cooking. Come with installation hardware and instructions included.

COMPACT COUNTERTOP OVENS

1> **GOLDSTAR** MA-790[B] **A CR Best Buy Only tested compact that performed very well.** Low-priced. But has small turntable and short cord. No sensor.

2> **GE** JE740[G]Y **Decent performer, but no sensor.** Easy to use except for popcorn setting. Poor at defrosting. Similar: JE710[ ].

3> **GE** Profile JEM31[G]A **OK but high-priced, and no turntable.** To reduce power, you must press keypad multiple times. Clunky keypad entry in defrost. Didn't heat as evenly as most. Similar: JEM25[ ].

4> **SAMSUNG** MW4699[S] **Decent and easy to use, except for popcorn.** No sensor or auto defrost. No kitchen timer. No child lock.

5> **SHARP** Half Pint R-120D[K] **More style than substance.** Fair performer with plastic, iMac-style exterior. Lacks useful features, including sensor. No child lock. So-so window view.

MIDSIZED COUNTERTOP OVENS

6> **SHARP** Platinum Collection R-370E[K] **Very good and relatively quiet.** So-so window view. Similar: R-360E[ ].

7> **KENMORE** 6128[9] **A CR Best Buy Very good.**

8> **SHARP** Carousel R-330E[K] **A fine performer across the board.** Similar: R-320E[ ], R-310E[ ].

9> **WHIRLPOOL** MT2115SJ[B] **Very good, but didn't heat as evenly as most.** Similar: MT2110SJ[ ].

10> **GE** Profile JE1160[B]C **Very good performer.** But auto reheat didn't work well. Discontinued, replaced by JE1160[D].

11> **SAMSUNG** MW1255[W]A **Very good, but cumbersome keypad entry.** Auto popcorn doesn't work with small popcorn bags.

12> **SANYO** Super Shower Wave EM-V3405S[W] **Good, but no sensor.** No auto reheat. Reheat, popcorn settings take time to learn.

13> **EMERSON** MW8107[W]A **Good and low-priced.** But no auto reheat. Some settings take time to learn.

14> **EMERSON** MW8102[SS] **Good, relatively quiet.** But auto reheat didn't work well. Auto defrost, reheat settings take time to learn. Some dial controls.

LARGE COUNTERTOP OVENS

15> **GOLDSTAR** MA-1302S **Very good oven.** Excellent defrost when using its own plastic tray. Dial controls.

16> **SHARP** Carousel R-420E[K] **Very good machine.** To reduce power, you must press

FEATURES AT A GLANCE MICROWAVES

Key no.	Brand	Sensor	Detailed user prompts	Power level in display	Handle	Tone adjust	Power level recall	Built-in installation	Instant on
COMPACT COUNTERTOP OVENS									
1	Goldstar						•		
2	GE			•	•		•		•
3	GE	•	•			•	•		•
4	Samsung					•			
5	Sharp			•		•			
MIDSIZED COUNTERTOP OVENS									
6	Sharp	•	•			•	•		
7	Kenmore	•	•			•	•		
8	Sharp	•				•	•		
9	Whirlpool	•	•			•	•	•	
10	GE	•	•				•	•	•
11	Samsung						•	•	
12	Sanyo						•		
13	Emerson		•						
14	Emerson					•		•	
LARGE COUNTERTOP OVENS									
15	Goldstar	•	•				•		
16	Sharp	•	•			•	•	•	
17	GE	•	•						•
18	Kenmore	•	•	•	•	•	•	•	
LARGE COUNTERTOP OVENS *continued*									
19	GE	•	•			•	•		
20	Goldstar				•		•		•
21	Sharp	•	•			•	•	•	
22	Goldstar		•	•					
23	Panasonic	•	•	•					
24	Whirlpool					•	•	•	
OVER-THE-RANGE OVENS									
25	Kenmore	•	•	•	•	•		•	
26	Whirlpool	•	•	•	•	•		•	
27	Kenmore	•	•		•	•	•		
28	Kenmore	•	•	•			•		
29	KitchenAid	•			•	•	•		
30	LG	•	•			•	•	•	
31	Sharp	•			•	•		•	
32	Goldstar		•	•	•			•	•
33	Maytag	•	•	•				•	•
34	GE	•	•			•	•		•
35	Amana	•	•		•	•	•	•	
36	GE	•	•	•	•	•		•	•
37	Sanyo	•	•	•				•	•

Recommendations & notes

keypad multiple times. Cumbersome keypad entry in defrost. Similar: R-430E[ ].

17 **GE** Profile JE1860[G]B **Very good overall.** Many instant-on keys. Can turn off turntable for more usable capacity.

18 **KENMORE** Elite 6158[9] **Very good and fully featured.** Turntable fits 9x15-in. dish.

19 **GE** Profile JE1360[B]C **Commendable**

performance. Similar: JE1340[ ], JE1351[ ].

20 **GOLDSTAR** MA-2117[B] **Very good machine, but no sensor.**

21 **SHARP** Carousel R-530E[K] **Performed very well.** Turntable fits 9x15-in. dish.

22 **GOLDSTAR** MA-2003[W] **Very good, but no sensor.** Turntable fits 9x15-in. dish.

Recommendations & notes

23> **PANASONIC** Inverter NN-S961[B]F **Spacious.** Turntable fits 9x15-in. dish. Popcorn setting takes time to learn. Discontinued, but similar NN-T990[ ]A is available.

24> **WHIRLPOOL** MT4140SK[B] **Good and very quiet, but no sensor.** Auto defrost takes time to learn.

OVER-THE-RANGE OVENS

25> **KENMORE** Elite 6168[2] **Very good, roomy, very quiet.** 5 vent settings.

26> **WHIRLPOOL** Gold GH8155XJ[B] **A CR Best Buy Very good, feature-laden.** Very quiet. Similar: MH8150XJ[ ], GH7155XH [ ].

27> **KENMORE** 6065[9] **A CR Best Buy Performed very well, at a good price.** 5 vent settings. Auto defrost takes time to learn.

28> **KENMORE** 6163[9] **Very good, with very quiet vent.**

29> **KITCHENAID** KHMS147H[BL] **Very good.** Very quiet, with many features. Intuitive in adjusting controls for "doneness." Similar: KHMS145J[ ].

30> **LG** Intellowave LMV-1915NV **Very good and roomy, with large turntable.** Very quiet, except when vent is on. No auto popcorn setting.

31> **SHARP** Carousel R-175[0] **Very good machine.** But popcorn setting takes time to learn. The most repair-prone brand for over-the-range ovens.

32> **GOLDSTAR** MV-1715[B] **Very good.** But small turntable; no sensor. Noisy vent, even on low.

33> **MAYTAG** MMV5100AA[B] **A very good machine.** But among the more repair-prone brands for over-the-range ovens.

34> **GE** Profile Spacemaker JVM1860[B]D **Very good and relatively quiet.** But some settings take time to learn. Cookbook included.

35> **AMANA** Radarange ACO1860A[B] **A very good performer.** Similar: ACO1840A[ ].

36> **GE** Spacemaker JVM1650[B]B **Very good and relatively quiet.** But noisy vent, even on low.

37> **SANYO** EM-S9000 **Very good.** Includes temperature probe, cookbook. To reduce power, you must press keypad multiple times. Similar: EM-S8000.

Monitors

Shop Smart If you spend hours staring at a computer screen, it may be wise to pay more for a flat-panel LCD screen. In our tests, LCDs provided the clearest, sharpest images. Still, the best CRTs are very good and cost significantly less. LCD monitors deliver crisp pictures and text while saving desk space. The top 15-inch models—the Philips 150P2E and the NEC MultiSync LCD 1550X, each $550—offer flexible adjustments and easy-to-use controls. CRT monitors are an excellent value but they're big and use a lot of power.

			Excellent ⊖	Very good ⊖	Good ○	Fair ⊖	Poor ●

Overall Ratings In performance order

KEY NO.	BRAND & MODEL	PRICE	OVERALL SCORE	VIEWABLE IMAGE	DISPLAY	EASE OF USE
			P F G VG E	100		
LCD MONITORS These have a space-saving flat display like that on notebook computers.						
1	**Apple** Studio Display	$1,000	▰▰▰▰	17 in.	⊖	⊖
2	**Philips** 150P2E	550	▰▰▰▰	15	⊖	⊖
3	**IBM** T750	875	▰▰▰▰	17	⊖	⊖
4	**NEC** MultiSync LCD 1550X	550	▰▰▰▰	15	⊖	⊖
5	**Sony** SDM-S51	500	▰▰▰▰	15	⊖	⊖
6	**Gateway** FPD1810	980	▰▰▰▰	18	⊖	⊖
7	**Apple** New iMac	1,500	▰▰▰▰	15	⊖	⊖
8	**ViewSonic** VX500	500	▰▰▰▰	15	⊖	⊖
CRT MONITORS These use a bulky TV-style cathode-ray tube.						
9	**Dell** P992	430	▰▰▰▰	19	⊖	○
10	**Sony** HMD-A440	400	▰▰▰▰	19	○	⊖
11	**NEC** MultiSync FE700+	220	▰▰▰▰	17	⊖	○
12	**Sony** CPD-E240	250	▰▰▰▰	17	○	⊖
13	**IBM** G78	230	▰▰▰▰	17	○	⊖
14	**IBM** P97	550	▰▰▰▰	19	○	○
15	**Philips** 107B30	200	▰▰▰	17	○	○
16	**ViewSonic** A90f	300	▰▰▰	19	○	⊖
17	**HP** Pavilion mx90	550	▰▰▰	19	○	○

See report, page 126. Based on tests published in Consumer Reports in September 2002, with updated prices and availability.

The tests behind the Ratings

Overall score is based mainly on image clarity. Image gives a monitor's nominal image size, measured diagonally; the **viewable image** size is the same as the nominal size for LCD monitors; an inch less than the nominal size for CRTs. Our viewing panelists gauged **display** quality for text and photo. **Ease of use** covers the front-panel controls, onscreen menus, tilt adjustment, and the like. **Price** is approximate retail.

Recommendations & notes

Most monitors have: A control to restore factory settings; a three-year warranty on parts, labor, tube or backlight; multilingual menus; nondetachable video cable; setup guide; no adapter for Macintosh. **These LCD monitors have:** Factory-set resolution of 1,024x768 pixels (15-inch), 1,280x1,024 (17- and 18-inch); depth of 6½ to 9½ inches and weight of 8 to 16 pounds. **These CRT monitors have:** Maximum resolution of 1,280x1,024 pixels (17-inch), 1,600x1,200 (19-inch); depth that's roughly equal to nominal screen size; weight of 35 to 57 pounds.

LCD MONITORS

1> **APPLE** Studio Display **Excellent overall, with wide viewing angle.** But harder to tilt, and control buttons are harder to use than most. Warranty of only 90 days on parts, 1 year on labor.

2> **PHILIPS** 150P2E **Very good overall, but control buttons harder to use than most.** Detachable video cable. Display rotates from landscape to portrait. Mac adapter supplied. Similar: 150B2B, 150P2M.

3> **IBM** T750 **Very good overall, with wide viewing angle.** But control buttons harder to use than most. Detachable video cable.

4> **NEC** MultiSync LCD 1550X **Very good overall, with wide viewing angle.** Detachable video cable. Display rotates from landscape to portrait, but monitor is harder to tilt than most. 3-year warranty.

5> **SONY** SDM-S51 **Very good overall.** Detachable video cable.

6> **GATEWAY** FPD1810 **Very good overall.** Detachable video cable. Warranty of only 1 year on parts and labor.

7> **APPLE** New iMac **Very good overall, but control buttons harder to use than most.** Sold only as integral part of Apple iMac computer. Has microphone, speakers. Warranty of only 90 days on parts, 1 year on labor. Monitor supplied with computer rated on page 163.

8> **VIEWSONIC** VX500 **Very good overall, with wide viewing angle.** Has microphone, speakers, detachable video cable.

CRT MONITORS

9> **DELL** P992 **Very good overall, but harder to tilt than most.** Menu and controls harder to use than most.

10> **SONY** HMD-A440 **Very good overall, but control buttons harder to use than most.** Only 1-year warranty on parts and labor. Monitor supplied with computer rated on page 163.

11> **NEC** MultiSync FE700+ **Very good overall, but harder to tilt than most.** 3-year warranty. Similar: FE700M+.

12> **SONY** CPD-E240 **Good overall.** Similar: HMD-A240.

13> **IBM** G78 **Good overall, but control buttons harder to use than most.** Monitor supplied with computer rated on page 163.

14> **IBM** P97 **Good overall, but menu and control buttons hard to use.**

15> **PHILIPS** 107B30 **Good.**

16> **VIEWSONIC** A90f **Good.**

17> **HP** Pavilion mx90 **Good overall, but harder to tilt than most.** Has microphone. Only 1-year warranty.

PDAs

Shop Smart First decide which of the two leading PDA styles you prefer: a Palm-based unit or a Pocket PC. Palm-based models offer easy access to an address book, memo pad, appointment calendar, and to-do list. The Palm m105, $150, can be used with either a PC or a Mac. For $195, the Sony Clié PEG-S360 offers 16-MB of RAM but has a sealed battery that requires professional replacement. Pocket PCs are designed to work with Microsoft software. They also tend to cost and weigh more than Palm OS models. The HP Jornada 565, $550, tops the Pocket PC Ratings. A few PDAs such as the Casio BE-300, $200, use a proprietary operating system, which limits connectivity and available software.

Overall Ratings   In performance order

Excellent ⊖   Very good ⊖   Good ○   Fair ◒   Poor ●

KEY NO.	BRAND & MODEL	PRICE	OVERALL SCORE	EASE OF USE	BATTERY LIFE	DISPLAY	IN SYNC	CONVENIENCE
			0 P F G VG E 100					
PALM-OS MODELS								
1	**Sony** Clié PEG-S360	$195		○	⊖	⊖	⊖	◒
2	**Palm** m500	330		⊖	⊖	○	⊖	◒
3	**HandEra** 330	300		○	⊖	⊖	○	◒
4	**Kyocera** Smartphone QCP6035	450 [1]		○	⊖	○	⊖	◒
5	**Palm** m105	150		○	⊖	○	⊖	◒
6	**Handspring** Visor Edge	250		○	⊖	○	⊖	○
7	**Handspring** Visor Platinum	170		○	⊖	○	⊖	◒
8	**Palm** i705	450		○	⊖	◒	⊖	◒
9	**Palm** m505	400		⊖	⊖	○	⊖	◒
10	**Palm** m125	200		○	⊖	○	⊖	◒
11	**Handspring** Visor Pro	230		○	⊖	◒	◒	○
12	**Handspring** Visor Prism	300		○	○	○	⊖	○
13	**Sony** Clié PEG-T615C	400		○	◒	◒	⊖	◒
14	**Samsung** SPH-I300	500 [1]		○	○	◒	○	○
POCKET PC MODELS								
15	**HP** Jornada 565	550		⊖	○	○	○	◒
16	**Compaq** iPaq H3835	600		○	○	○	○	◒
17	**Compaq** iPaq H3765	500		○	◒	○	○	○
PROPRIETARY SYSTEM								
18	**Casio** BE-300	200		◒	◒	◒	◒	○

[1] Price varies depending on cellular phone plan or special offers.

See report, page 130. Based on tests published in Consumer Reports in June 2002, with updated prices and availability.

The tests behind the Ratings

Overall score is based on ease of use, battery life, display quality, synchronization with a computer, and convenience. Models with the same score are listed in alphabetical order. **Ease of use** considers ergonomic factors; navigation among tasks; and usability of phone lists, calendar, to-do list, and memo pad. **Battery life** indicates how long fully charged batteries lasted in continuous use (with the backlight mostly turned off for monochrome models): ◖ 20 hours or more; ◒ 10 to 20 hours; ○ 5 to 10 hours; ◐ fewer than 5 hours. **Display** reflects screen readability in low and normal room light and in sunlight. Monochrome and color displays were scored on a different scale. **In sync** gauges how easy it is to synchronize data (including word-processing and spreadsheet files for models that come with such software) with a computer. **Convenience** considers battery type, expansion capability, bundled software, and fit for shirt pocket. **Price** is approximate retail.

Recommendations & notes

Models listed as similar should offer performance comparable to the tested model's, although features may differ.

Except as noted, all models have: Basic personal-information-management functions (phone lists, calendar, to-do list, memo pad). Ability to transfer e-mail to and from a desktop computer. Docking station to synchronize with a computer; the station usually doubles as a charger for models with a rechargeable battery. Ability to synchronize via universal serial bus port or serial port. User manual on CD only.

PALM-OS MODELS

1▷ **SONY** Clié PEG-S360 **Very good and reasonably priced, with an excellent monochrome display.** Overall design better than most. Handy jog dial. Easily readable in sunlight. Includes picture viewer and some multimedia software. Fits easily in shirt pocket. Printed manual. But battery can't be replaced by user. Doesn't include backup program or docking station (comes with cables only). 4¼ oz.

2▷ **PALM** m500 **Very good; small, light case.** Overall design better than most. Easily readable in sunlight. Includes eBook reader, picture viewer, expense-tracker, and mobile connectivity software. LED and vibrating alarm. Fits easily in shirt pocket. But battery

can't be replaced by user. Word-processing and spreadsheet programs can't use expansion cards, and you can't enter formulas in spreadsheets. Doesn't include backup program. 4 oz.

3▷ **HANDERA** 330 **Very good for peripherals and has many features, though some aren't well integrated.** Two expansion slots. Viewable screen area larger than that of most Palm-based units. Easily readable in sunlight. Includes expense-tracker and voice-recording software. LED alarm. Uses AAA batteries. But word-processing and spreadsheet programs can't use expansion cards. 6 oz.

4▷ **KYOCERA** Smartphone QCP6035 **Very good, and one of the better choices for wireless access.** Basic organizer functions easy to use and well integrated with cell-phone functions. Easily readable in sunlight. Includes expense-tracker and voice-recording software. Printed manual. But display is small. Doesn't include backup program. 7¼ oz.

5▷ **PALM** m105 **A very good, low-cost model.** Basic organizer functions easy to use. Easily readable in bright sunlight. Includes mobile connectivity software. Uses AAA batteries. Fits easily in shirt pocket. But doesn't include backup program. 5 oz.

Recommendations & notes

6 > **HANDSPRING** Visor Edge **A very good, basic model in a slim case.** Basic organizer functions easy to use. Easily readable in sunlight. Includes expense-tracker software. Fits easily in shirt pocket. But battery can't be replaced by user. Doesn't include backup program. Expansion sleeve makes unit bulky. 4¾ oz.

7 > **HANDSPRING** Visor Platinum **A very good, basic model.** Basic organizer functions easy to use. Includes expense-tracker software. Uses AAA batteries. But doesn't include backup program. 6 oz. Discontinued, but the similar Visor Neo is available.

8 > **PALM** i705 **Very good overall, with many features in a small package.** Has built-in wireless modem and the most versatile e-mail capability of any tested PDA. Easily readable in bright sunlight. Includes picture viewer and eBook reader. LED and vibrating alarm. Fits easily in shirt pocket. Printed manual. But battery can't be replaced by user. Doesn't include backup program. 5¼ oz.

9 > **PALM** m505 **Very good; like the m500, with a color display.** Overall design better than most. Basic organizer functions easy to use. Includes eBook reader, picture viewer, expense-tracker, and mobile connectivity software. Fits easily in shirt pocket. But batteries can't be replaced by user. Word-processing and spreadsheet programs can't use expansion cards, and you can't enter formulas in spreadsheets. Doesn't include backup program. 5 oz. Discontinued, but the similar m515 is available; has 16 MB of RAM and allows you to enter formulas in spreadsheets.

10 > **PALM** m125 **A very good, low-cost model with expansion capability.** Easily readable in bright sunlight. Includes eBook reader. Uses AAA batteries. Fits easily in shirt pocket. But

doesn't include backup program. Word-processing and spreadsheet programs can't use expansion cards, and you can't enter formulas in spreadsheets. 4¾ oz.

11 > **HANDSPRING** Visor Pro **Very good overall, especially for Palm users looking to upgrade.** Easily readable in bright sunlight. Includes expense-tracker software. But battery can't be replaced by user. Doesn't include backup program. 5¾ oz.

FEATURES AT A GLANCE PDAS

Tested products (keyed to the Ratings) Key no. Brand	Memory (MB)	Replaceable battery	Color display	Display size (in.)	Expansion slot	Office software
PALM-OS MODELS						
1 > Sony	16			2.9	MS	•
2 > Palm	8			3.0	M	
3 > HandEra	8	•		3.7	M, C	•
4 > Kyocera	8	•		2.5		
5 > Palm	8	•		2.6		
6 > Handspring	8			3.1	SB	
7 > Handspring	8	•		3.1	SB	
8 > Palm	8			3.0	M	•
9 > Palm	8		•	3.0	M	•
10 > Palm	8	•		2.7	M	•
11 > Handspring	16			3.3	SB	
12 > Handspring	8		•	3.2	SB	
13 > Sony	15		•	3.0	MS	•
14 > Samsung	8	•	•	2.9		
POCKET PC MODELS						
15 > HP	32	•	•	3.5	C	•
16 > Compaq	64	•	•	3.8	M	•
17 > Compaq	64		•	3.8		
PROPRIETARY SYSTEM						
18 > Casio	16		•	3.2	C	

Recommendations & notes

12▷ HANDSPRING Visor Prism **Good overall.** Basic organizer functions easy to use. Includes expense-tracker software. But battery can't be replaced by user. Doesn't include backup program. 7 oz.

13▷ SONY Clié PEG-T615C **A good choice for Palm users looking to upgrade.** Handy jog dial. Includes picture viewer, some multimedia software. Can function as remote control. LED and vibrating alarm. Fits easily in shirt pocket. Printed manual. But battery can't be replaced by user. Thin case not as comfortable to hold as most. 5 oz.

14▷ SAMSUNG SPH-I300 **Good overall, but not the best PDA/cell-phone combo we've seen.** Includes expense-tracker and voice-recording software. Vibrating alarm. Fits easily in shirt pocket. Printed manual. But screen washes out in sunlight. Doesn't include backup program. E-mail program cumbersome. Not tested as a cell phone. 6 oz.

POCKET PC MODELS

15▷ HP Jornada 565 **Good overall, with the best design among the Pocket PCs.** User interface better than most. Basic organizer functions easy to use. Buttons more useful than most.

Includes picture viewer, eBook reader, and voice-recording software. Bundled HP applications well integrated with OS. Has handy task-switcher software. LED alarm. Printed manual. 6¼ oz. Similar: HP Jornada 568.

16▷ COMPAQ iPaq H3835 **Good overall.** User interface better than most. The only iPaq with an integrated expansion card. Includes picture viewer, eBook reader, and voice-recording software. LED alarm. But battery can't be replaced by user. 6½ oz. Similar iPaq H3850.

17▷ COMPAQ iPaq H3765 **Good, but there are better choices.** Includes picture viewer, eBook reader, voice-recording software. LED alarm. But battery can't be replaced by user and can permanently lose charge if unit is not left on charger when idle for long periods. 6¾ oz. Similar iPaq H3760.

PROPRIETARY SYSTEM

18▷ CASIO BE-300 **Fair.** Includes picture viewer, Word and Excel file viewer. But user interface worse than most. Basic organizer functions hard to use. Battery can't be replaced by user. Requires purchase of MS Outlook to synchronize with a PC. Screen washes out in sunlight. 5½ oz.

Power blowers

Shop Smart For yards that can be navigated with an extension cord, an electric blower is the best and cheapest choice. All the models tested were very good or excellent and cost $35 to $80. If you can't drag an extension cord around, consider the gasoline-powered Stihl BG45, $150. For an additional $15, you can upgrade to the BG55, which includes an accessory vacuum mode. For larger jobs that require lots of power, consider a backpack model. You'll find several excellent choices for around $400.

Overall Ratings In performance order

Excellent ⊖ Very good ⊖ Good ○ Fair ⊖ Poor ●

KEY NO.	BRAND & MODEL	PRICE	OVERALL SCORE	PERFORMANCE			NOISE	
			P F G VG E	BLOWING	HANDLING	VACUUMING	OPERATOR EAR	FROM 50 FT.
ELECTRIC HANDHELD BLOWERS								
1	**Weed Eater** 2595 Barracuda	$55	▬▬	⊖	○	⊖	○	○
2	**Ryobi** 190r	65	▬▬	○	⊖	⊖	○	⊖
3	**Black & Decker** BV 1500	70	▬▬	○	⊖	⊖	○	○
4	**Black & Decker** Leaf Hog BV2500	70	▬▬	⊖	⊖	⊖	○	⊖
5	**Ryobi** RESV1300	80	▬▬	○	○	○	⊖	⊖
6	**Ryobi** 160r	45	▬▬	⊖	⊖	NA	⊖	⊖
7	**Weed Eater** 2540 Groundskeeper	40	▬▬	○	⊖	○	○	○
8	**Weed Eater** 2510 Groundsweeper	35	▬▬	⊖	⊖	NA	○	⊖
GASOLINE HANDHELD BLOWERS								
9	**Stihl** BG45	150	▬▬	⊖	⊖	NA	○	⊖
10	**Stihl** BG55	165	▬▬	⊖	⊖	⊖	○	○
11	**Weed Eater** BV1650	110	▬▬	⊖	⊖	○	⊖	○
12	**Ryobi** RGBV3100	130	▬▬	○	⊖	○	⊖	○
13	**Craftsman** (Sears) 79720	90	▬▬	⊖	○	NA	○	⊖
14	**Weed Eater** FL 1500 Featherlite	80	▬▬	⊖	○	NA	○	⊖
15	**Ryobi** 310BVr	105	▬▬	⊖	⊖	⊖	⊖	○

Overall Ratings, cont.

				Excellent ⊖	Very good ⊖	Good ○	Fair ◐	Poor ●

KEY NO.	BRAND & MODEL	PRICE	OVERALL SCORE	PERFORMANCE			NOISE	
			0 P F G VG E 100	BLOWING	HANDLING	VACUUMING	OPERATOR EAR	FROM 50 FT.
	GASOLINE BACKPACK BLOWERS							
16	**Husqvarna** 145BT	$350		⊖	⊖	NA	●	○
17	**Makita** RBL500	425		⊖	⊖	NA	●	○
18	**Echo** PB-46LN Quiet 1	430		⊖	⊖	NA	●	⊖
19	**Solo** 470	390		⊖	○	NA	◐	○
20	**Echo** Pro Lite PB260L	300		⊖	⊖	NA	◐	⊖
21	**John Deere** BP40	420		⊖	○	NA	●	○
22	**Homelite** Backpacker UT 08017H	160		⊖	⊖	NA	●	○

See report, page 108. Based on tests published in Consumer Reports in May 2002, with updated prices and availability.

The tests behind the Ratings

Overall score includes blowing performance, handling, and, where applicable, vacuuming. **Blowing** reflects the ability to move increasingly large piles of leaves. **Handling** gauges ease of maneuvering and moving from side to side in the blower mode. **Vacuuming** denotes how quickly the machines took in a measured pile of leaves and how easily they handled in that mode. "NA" means that model isn't designed to vacuum. **Noise** is as measured at the operator's ear and from 50 feet, using a decibel meter. Models judged Excellent from 50 feet are quieter than 65 dBA. Models judged Fair or Poor at operator's ear are louder than 90 dBA; we recommend using them with ear protection. **Weight** is based on our own measurements with a full fuel tank for gas models. **Price** is approximate retail.

Recommendations & notes

Models listed as similar should offer performance comparable to the tested model's, although features may differ.

Typical features for these models: Reduce leaf volume by about 4-to-1 or 6-to-1 when vacuuming. Switch without tools. 2-yr. warranty.

Most electric models: Aren't loud enough to require the use of hearing protection. On/off switch that can be reached only by the hand not holding the blower. Two speed settings.

Most handheld gas models: Are loud enough to warrant hearing protection. Require a firm hold when starting to avoid twisting. Ignition switch that can be reached by the same hand holding the blower. Trigger throttle. Translucent fuel tank.

Most backpack models: Require the use of hearing protection. Require a firm hold when starting to avoid twisting. Ignition switch that can be reached by the hand holding the main handle. Translucent fuel tank.

Recommendations & notes

ELECTRIC HANDHELD BLOWERS

1> **WEED EATER** 2595 Barracuda **Excellent overall and most powerful electric.** Weight: 7 lb. Features: Better than most at reducing vacuumed volume. But: Control takes two hands. Similar: 695 Barracuda.

2> **RYOBI** 190r **Very good and excellent at vacuuming.** Weight: 7 lb. Features: Better than most at reducing vacuumed volume.

3> **BLACK & DECKER** BV 1500 **Very good.** Weight: 6½ lb. Features: Better than most at reducing vacuumed volume. Comfortable handle.

4> **BLACK & DECKER** Leaf Hog BV2500 **Easiest to convert to vacuuming, but unimpressive at blowing.** Weight 7 lb. Features: Excellent at vacuuming. Vacuum bag easy to remove for emptying. Quietest at 50 ft. Ergonomic molded handle. But: Only one speed.

5> **RYOBI** RESV1300 **Very good with unique design.** Weight: 9 lb. Features: Permanently mounted blower nozzle and vacuum tube; lever easily switches between the two. Vacuum bag easy to remove. But: Small bag.

6> **RYOBI** 160r **Very good, but unimpressive at blowing.** Weight: 6 lb. Only one speed. No vacuum mode.

7> **WEED EATER** 2540 Groundskeeper **Very good.** Weight: 7 lb. Optional $35 vacuum attachment.

8> **WEED EATER** 2510 Groundsweeper **Very good, but unimpressive at blowing.** Weight: 5 lb. But: Only one speed. No vacuum mode.

GASOLINE HANDHELD BLOWERS

9> **STIHL** BG45 **Best of the gas handheld models, and relatively quiet.** Weight: 10 lb. Features: Lightweight and easy to handle for a gas blower. Comfortable handle. But: No vacuum mode.

10> **STIHL** BG55 **Similar to #9, but with a vacuum mode; not as quiet.** Weight: 10 lb. Features: Strong performer in both modes, though conversion is complicated. Very good at grinding debris. Lightweight and easy to handle for a gas blower. Comfortable handle. Vacuum kit: $30.

11> **WEED EATER** BV 1650 **Very good and fairly quiet.** Weight: 11½ lb. Features: Easy to start without twisting. But: Inconvenient throttle. Small bag. Hard to tell when opaque fuel tank is full.

12> **RYOBI** RGBV3100 **An unimpressive performer.** Weight: 12½ lb. Features: A lever switches between blowing and vacuuming. But: Vacuum tube blocks view when blowing. Heavy. Throttle difficult to use.

13> **CRAFTSMAN** (Sears) 79720 **Good, but intense handle vibration.** Weight: 7½ lb. Features: Easy to start without twisting. But: Only 1-yr. warranty. Inconvenient throttle. No vacuum mode.

14> **WEED EATER** FL 1500 Featherlite **Good, but intense handle vibration.** Weight: 7½ lb. Features: Easy to start without twisting. But: Inconvenient throttle. No vacuum mode.

15> **RYOBI** 310BVr **Good, but there are better choices.** Weight: 12 lb. Features: Easy to start without twisting. But: Complicated to convert from blower to vacuum. Hard to tell when opaque fuel tank is full. Choke hard to operate.

GASOLINE BACKPACK BLOWERS

16> **HUSQVARNA** 145BT **Excellent performer.** Weight: 22 lb. Features: Comfortable handle with presettable throttle on blower tube, a convenience. Large fuel-tank opening. But: Only 1-yr. warranty. Sliding shoulder straps.

Recommendations & notes

17▷ MAKITA RBL500 **Excellent but pricey.** Weight: 24½ lb. Features: Comfortable handle with a presettable throttle on blower tube, a convenience. Straps easy to adjust. Large fuel-tank opening. Excellent ease of use. But: Only 1-yr. warranty. Models sold between March 1997 and January 2001 have been recalled because of a leaky fuel tank.

18▷ ECHO PB-46LN Quiet 1 **Excellent, but pricey.** Weight: 28½ lb. Features: Straps easy to adjust.

19▷ SOLO 470 **A capable backpack blower, but pricey.** Weight: 24 lb. Features: Convenient handle controls nozzle and throttle. Excellent at clearing small debris. Carrying handle. Shoulder straps easy to adjust in use. Large fuel-tank opening. But: Awkward hand and arm position make use tiring.

20▷ ECHO Pro Lite PB260L **Relatively inexpensive, though a bit less powerful than most backpacks.** Weight: 16 lb. Features: Carrying handle. Shoulder straps easy to adjust in use. Relatively quiet at 50 ft. Optional curved blower nozzle ($6) improves performance.

21▷ JOHN DEERE BP40 **Very good, but pricey.** Weight: 20½ lb. Features: Large fuel-tank opening. But: Short throttle arm; controls hard to reach. Sliding shoulder straps. Ease of use less than other tested models.

22▷ HOMELITE Backpacker UT 08017H **Very good, and at a reasonable price.** Weight: 15½ lb. Features: Handle on blower tube, a convenience. Excellent ease of use.

Printers

Shop Smart   You can purchase an inkjet printer with excellent text and color-photo quality for as little as $100. The two **CR Best Buys**—the Epson Stylus C60 and Canon Color Bubble Jet S300—each sell for $100. The Epson is faster for photo printing, while the Canon is very economical for printing a page of text. For printing lots of text, laser printers are still far less costly to use.

		Excellent	Very good	Good	Fair	Poor
		⊜	⊖	○	◓	●

KEY NO.	BRAND & MODEL	PRICE	OVERALL SCORE	TEXT			COLOR PHOTO			GRAPHICS QUALITY
				QUALITY	SPEED	COST	QUALITY	TIME	COST	
			0 P F G VG E 100							
	INKJET MODELS									
1	**Canon** Color Bubble Jet S520	$150		⊖	4.9 ppm	3.6¢	⊖	2 min.	$1.00	⊖
2	**Epson** Stylus C80	150		⊖	5.5	6.2	⊖	3	0.90	⊖
3	**Epson** Stylus C60 **A CR Best Buy**	100		⊖	4.5	4.8	⊖	3	0.90	⊖
4	**Lexmark** Z65 Color JetPrinter	200		⊖	6.2	10.7	⊖	8	1.90	⊖
5	**Canon** Color Bubble Jet S300 **A CR Best Buy**	100		⊖	4.6	1.9	⊖	11	0.80	⊖
6	**Lexmark** Z45 Color JetPrinter	90		⊖	4.4	5.7	⊖	12	1.40	⊖
7	**HP** DeskJet 995c	400		⊖	2.7	4.1	⊖	9	1.00	⊖
8	**Epson** Stylus Photo 785EPX	200		⊖	1.9	3.4	⊖	3	0.70	⊖
9	**Epson** Stylus Photo 890	300		⊖	1.8	3.4	⊖	3	0.70	⊖
10	**Canon** Photo Printer S820D	400		⊖	2.1	4.2	⊖	4	1.10	⊖
11	**Epson** Stylus Photo 820	100		⊖	1.8	6.5	⊖	18	1.10	⊖

See report, page 132. Based on tests published in Consumer Reports in September 2002, with updated prices and availability.

The tests behind the Ratings

Brand & model includes printers tested for previous reports. **Overall score** is based primarily on text, color-photo, and graphics quality and on text speed. **Text quality** indicates how crisply and clearly a printer produced black text in a variety of typefaces, sizes, and styles. **Text speed** is our calculation of the typical output in pages per minute (ppm) for a three-page document at the default setting. **Color-photo quality** is our assessment of a photo's appearance. **Color-photo time** is our measurement, to the nearest minute, of how long it took to produce an 8x10-inch color print at the printer's best-quality setting. Cost is for a single text page (including ink and paper, sold by the 5,000-sheet, 10-ream box) or for a single photo (ink and glossy photo paper, plus the amortized cost of the printhead based on the manufacturer's stated life). **Graphics quality** assesses color graphics—illustrations, charts, and drawings. **Price** is approximate retail.

Recommendations & notes

Models listed as similar should offer performance comparable to the tested model, although features may differ.

All models: Work with most versions of Windows and Mac OS. Have a 1-year parts-and-labor warranty. **Most models:** Have parallel and universal serial bus ports (but require a USB for Macs). Can hold 100 sheets or at least 10 envelopes in their input tray. Indicate when ink supply is low. Use water-resistant black ink. Can print banners at least 44 inches long. Have no separate envelope input. Do not include a cable.

REGULAR MODELS

1 ▷ **CANON** Color Bubble Jet S520 **Among the fastest for color photos and text.**tk

2 ▷ **EPSON** Stylus C80 **Among the fastest for text and photos.** Holds 150 sheets and 15 envelopes. But noisier than most.

3 ▷ **EPSON** Stylus C60 A CR Best Buy **Low-priced and fast.** But noisier than most.

4 ▷ **LEXMARK** Z65 Color JetPrinter **The fastest for text.** But per-page cost for text and photos the highest. Similar: Z65n

5 ▷ **CANON** Color Bubble Jet S300 A CR Best Buy **Low cost for text and photos.** Fast for text, but slow for photos.

6 ▷ **LEXMARK** Z45 Color JetPrinter **Low-priced, but relatively slow and expensive for photos (uses a special cartridge).**

7 ▷ **HP** DeskJet 995c **Very good but expensive.** Holds 150 sheets or 15 envelopes. Quiet.

8 ▷ **EPSON** Stylus Photo 785EPX **Among the slowest for text and fastest for photos.** Can print directly from PC-card adapter. But noisier than most.

9 ▷ **EPSON** Stylus Photo 890 **Low printing costs may offset high price.**

10 ▷ **CANON** Photo Printer S820D **Expensive, but among the fastest for photos.** Among the slowest for text. Can print directly from PC-card adapter. Similar:S820.

11 ▷ **EPSON** Stylus Photo 820 **Good overall, but noisier than most.** Slowest for photos and text.

Ranges–electric

Shop Smart You can purchase a very good electric range without spending a fortune. Whether you're buying a smoothtop model or one with coil elements, look for a capacious oven and more than one large, fast burner. Smoothtops, while generally more expensive than coil models, are easier to clean and provide extra counter space when not in use. Tests of smoothtop models turned up two **CR Best Buys:** the Maytag Performa PER5710BA, $565, and the Frigidaire FEF366A, $555. If smoothtop styling isn't a must, any of the four coil ranges tested would be a fine choice.

Legend: Excellent = ⊖ (red top), Very good = ⊖, Good = ○, Fair = ◖, Poor = ●

Overall Ratings — In performance order

KEY NO	BRAND & MODEL	PRICE	OVERALL SCORE	COOKTOP HIGH	COOKTOP LOW	OVEN CAPACITY	OVEN BAKE	OVEN BROIL
	SMOOTHTOP MODELS							
1	**GE** Profile JBP79WB[WW]	$850		Very good	Very good	Very good	Very good	Very good
2	**Amana** ACF4265A[W]	900		Very good	Very good	Very good	Very good	Very good
3	**GE** Profile Performance JB960WB[WW]	1,400		Very good	Very good	Very good	Very good	Very good
4	**Kenmore** (Sears) Elite 9901[2]	1,200		Very good	Very good	Very good	Very good	Very good
5	**Maytag** Accellis MER6750AA[W]	1,050		Very good	Very good	Very good	Very good	Very good
6	**Maytag** Gemini MER6769BA[W]	1,000		Very good	Very good	Very good	Very good	Very good
7	**Kenmore** (Sears) 9559[2]	750		Very good	Very good	Very good	Very good	Very good
8	**GE** Profile JSP46WD[WW]	1,250		Very good	Very good	Very good	Very good	Good
9	**Kenmore** (Sears) 9582[2]	1,050		Very good	Very good	Very good	Very good	Good
10	**Maytag** Performa PER5710BA[W] **A CR Best Buy**	565		Very good	Very good	Very good	Very good	Very good
11	**Frigidaire** FEF366A[S] **A CR Best Buy**	555		Very good	Very good	Very good	Very good	Very good
12	**Frigidaire** Gallery GLEF378A[S]	700		Very good	Very good	Very good	Very good	Very good
13	**KitchenAid** KERC500H[WH]	750		Very good	Very good	Good	Very good	Very good
14	**Maytag** MER5880BA[W]	1,200		Very good	Very good	Very good	Very good	Very good
15	**GE** Profile Performance JS966TD[WW]	1,900		Very good	Very good	Good	Good	Good
16	**Jenn-Air** JES8850AA[W]	1,600		Very good	Very good	Good	Good	Good
17	**Whirlpool** Gold GR460LXK[P]	900		Very good	Very good	Very good	Very good	Poor
	COIL MODELS							
18	**GE** JBP35BB[WH]	500		Very good	Very good	Very good	Very good	Very good
19	**Kenmore** (Sears) 9375[1]	550		Very good	Very good	Very good	Very good	Very good
20	**Hotpoint** RB757WC[WW]	400		Very good	Very good	Very good	Very good	Good
21	**Whirlpool** RF379LXK[Q] RF367LXK[ ]	550		Very good	Very good	Very good	Very good	Poor

See report, page 64. Based on tests published in Consumer Reports in August 2002.

The tests behind the Ratings

Under **brand & model,** brackets show a tested model's color code. **Overall score** includes cooktop high power and low power performance, oven capacity, baking, broiling, and self-cleaning. **Cooktop high power** is how quickly the highest powered burner or element heated 6 /3 quarts of room-temperature water to a near boil. **Low power** shows how well the least powerful burner or element melted and held chocolate without scorching it and whether the most powerful, set to Low, held tomato sauce below a boil. **Oven capacity** is usable oven space. **Bake** shows baking evenness for cakes and cookies. **Broil** shows cooking and searing evenness for a tray of burgers. **Price** is approximate retail.

Recommendations & notes

Similar models have the same burners or elements, oven, and broiler; other details may differ.

All ranges: Are 30 inches wide. Have an oven light and anti-tip hardware. **Most ranges have:** Freestanding construction. Touchpad oven controls. A cooktop rim to hold spills. A self-cleaning oven. Two or three oven racks with five positions. An oven window with a reasonably clear view. A storage drawer. A warranty of one year for parts and labor, five years for smoothtop surfaces.

SMOOTHTOP RANGES

1> GE Profile JBP79WB[WW] **Excellent.** "Hot" light for each element. Expandable element (larger or smaller element that lets you heat various-sized pots). Elements: 1@1,000/2,500, 1@2,000, 2@1,500 watts. Similar: JBP82WF[ ].

2> AMANA ACF4265A[W] **Excellent.** Warming and expandable elements. Elements: 1@1,000/2,500, 1@2,000, 1@1,500, 1@1,200 watts.

3> GE Profile Performance JB960WB[WW] **Very good.** Convection option. "Hot" light for each element. Bridge heated (connection between elements) and expandable elements. Elements: 1@1,000/2,500, 2@1,800, 1@1,500 watts. Similar: JBP95TF[ ].

4> KENMORE (Sears) Elite 9901[2] **Very good.** Convection option. "Hot" light for each element. Warming drawer and element. Bridge and expandable elements. Excelled at self-cleaning. Elements: 1@1,000/2,500, 2@1,800, 1@1,200 watts.

5> MAYTAG Accellis MER6750AA[W] **Very good.** Microwave feature. "Hot" light for each element. Expandable elements. Excelled at self-cleaning. Window view worse than most. Elements: 1@750/2,200, 1@2,200, 2@1,200 watts.

6> MAYTAG Gemini MER6769BA[W] **Very good.** Dual ovens. Excellent at self-cleaning. No storage drawer. Elements: 2@2,200, 2@1,200 watts.

7> KENMORE (Sears) 9559[2] **Very good.** Warming drawer and element. Expandable element. Elements: 1@1,000/2,500, 1@2,200, 2@1,200 watts.

8> GE Profile JSP46WD[WW] **Very good.** Slide-in design. "Hot" light for each element. Expandable element. Excelled at self-cleaning. Elements: 1@1,000/2,500, 2@2,000, 1@1,500 watts.

9> KENMORE (Sears) 9582[2] **Very good.** Warming drawer and element. "Hot" light for each element. Expandable element. Split rack. Elements: 1@1,600/2,400, 1@2,500, 2@1,500 watts.

10> MAYTAG Performa PER5710BA[W] **A CR Best Buy Very good.** Excelled at self-cleaning. Window view worse than most. Elements: 2@2,200, 2@1,200 watts. Similar: PER5702BA[ ], PER5705BA[ ].

Recommendations & notes

11> FRIGIDAIRE FEF366A[S] **A CR Best Buy Very good.** Elements: 1@2,500, 1@2,200, 2@1,200 watts.

12> FRIGIDAIRE Gallery GLEF378A[S] **Very good.** Convection option. Warming and expandable elements. Window view worse than most. Elements: 1@1,000/2,500, 1@2,200, 2@1,200 watts. Similar: FEF379A[ ].

13> KITCHENAID KERC500H[WH] **Very good.** Warming and expandable elements. "Hot" light for each element. Elements: 1@1,000/2,500, 2@1,800, 1@1,500 watts.

14> MAYTAG MER5880BA[W] **Very good.** Convection option. Warming drawer and element. Expandable element. Window view worse than most. Elements: 1@750/2,200, 1@2,200, 2@1,200 watts. Similar: MER5870BA[ ].

15> GE Profile Performance JS966TD[WW] **Very good.** Slide-in design. Convection option. Warming, expandable, and bridge elements. "Hot" light for each element. Elements: 1@1,000/2,500, 2@1,800, 1@1,500 watts.

16> JENN-AIR JES8850AA[W] **Very good.** Among the more repair-prone brands. Slide-in design. Convection option. "Hot" light for each element. Expandable element. Split rack. Excelled at self-cleaning. Elements: 1@1,700/2,700, 1@2,200, 2@1,200 watts.

17> WHIRLPOOL Gold GR460LXK[P] **Very good.** Warming and expandable elements. "Hot" light for each element. Split rack. Window view worse than most. Elements: 1@1,000/2,400, 1@1,800, 2@1,200 watts. Similar: GR465LXK[ ], GR470LXK[ ], GR475LXK[ ].

COIL MODELS

18> GE JBP35BB[WH] **Excellent.** Elements: 2@2,600, 2@1,500 watts. Similar: JBP30BB[ ], JBP48WB[ ].

19> KENMORE (Sears) 9375[1] **Very good.** Warming drawer. Elements: 2@2,600, 2@1,500 watts.

20> HOTPOINT RB757WC[WW] **Very good.** Oven dial. Window view worse than most. Elements: 2@2,600, 2@1,500 watts.

21> WHIRLPOOL RF379LXK[Q] **Very good.** Window view worse than most. Elements: 2@2,600, 2@1,500 watts. Similar: RF367LXK[ ].

Ranges–gas

Shop Smart You can buy a very good gas range for $500 to $600. When you pay more than that, you typically get more features, such as sealed burners, cast-iron grates, and a self-cleaning oven. You also pay for styling. Three GE models top the Ratings, with prices from $800 to $1,250. Hotpoint models are also made by GE. The RGB745WEA, $550, is **a CR Best Buy.** Dual-fuel ranges, which combine a gas cooktop with an electric oven, are often pro-style with stainless-steel construction. The Kenmore Elite 4683, $1,600, performed nearly as well overall as the top-scoring KitchenAid KDRP407H and costs much less.

Overall Ratings   In performance order

Excellent ⊖   Very good ⊖   Good ○   Fair ◐   Poor ●

KEY NO	BRAND & MODEL	PRICE	OVERALL SCORE	COOKTOP HIGH	COOKTOP LOW	OVEN CAPACITY	OVEN BAKE	OVEN BROIL
	GAS RANGES		0 P F G VG E 100					
1	**GE** Profile Performance JGB910WEC[WW]	$1,250	▬▬▬▬	⊖	⊖	⊖	⊖	⊖
2	**GE** Profile JGBP85WEB[WW]	950	▬▬▬▬	○	⊖	⊖	⊖	⊖
3	**GE** JGBP35WEA[WW]	800	▬▬▬▬	○	⊖	⊖	⊖	⊖
4	**Hotpoint** RGB745WEA[WW] **A CR Best Buy**	550	▬▬▬▬	⊖	⊖	⊖	⊖	⊖
5	**Magic Chef** CGR3742CD[W]	625	▬▬▬	○	⊖	⊖	⊖	○
6	**Maytag** MGR5880BD[W]	1,075	▬▬▬	○	⊖	⊖	⊖	⊖
7	**Maytag** Performa PGR5710BD[W]	565	▬▬▬	○	⊖	⊖	⊖	⊖
8	**GE** Profile Performance JGB920WEC[WW]	1,350	▬▬▬	○	○	⊖	⊖	⊖
9	**Kenmore** (Sears) 7584[2]	1,050	▬▬▬	○	⊖	○	⊖	⊖
10	**Jenn-Air** JGS8750AD[W]	1,500	▬▬▬	⊖	⊖	○	○	⊖
11	**Kenmore** (Sears) 7566[1]	700	▬▬▬	⊖	⊖	○	⊖	○
12	**Kenmore** (Sears) Elite 7901[2]	1,200	▬▬▬	○	⊖	○	⊖	○
13	**Tappan** TGF363A[W]	550	▬▬▬	○	⊖	⊖	○	○
14	**Kenmore** (Sears) 7575[1]	600	▬▬▬	○	⊖	○	⊖	○
15	**Frigidaire** Gallery GLGF377A[S]	700	▬▬▬	●	⊖	⊖	⊖	○
16	**KitchenAid** KGRT607H[BS]	1,360	▬▬▬	⊖	○	⊖	⊖	⊖
17	**Whirlpool** Gold GS460LEK[Q]	830	▬▬▬	○	⊖	⊖	○	◐
18	**Frigidaire** Gallery GLGF366A[S]	600	▬▬▬	○	⊖	⊖	⊖	○
19	**Viking** VGSC3064B[SS]	3,890	▬▬	⊖	◐	◐	○	⊖
20	**Dacor** PGR30[S]	2,650	▬▬	○	◐	○	⊖	●
21	**DCS** RGA-304[SS]	1,990	▬	○	◐	◐	⊖	○

Excellent	Very good	Good	Fair	Poor
◒	◓	○	◒	●

KEY NO	BRAND & MODEL	PRICE	OVERALL SCORE	COOKTOP		OVEN		
				HIGH	LOW	CAPACITY	BAKE	BROIL
			P F G VG E					
	DUAL-FUEL RANGES							
22	**KitchenAid** KDRP407H[SS]	3,450		○	◓	◓	◓	◓
23	**Kenmore** (Sears) Elite 4683[3]	1,600		○	◓	◒	◓	◓
24	**Jenn-Air** JDS9860AA[W]	1,900		◒	◓	○	◓	◓
25	**Dacor** ERD30S06[BK]	3,850		○	◓	◓	◓	◒
26	**Viking** VDSC305B[SS]	3,800		◓	◓	◒	○	◓
27	**GE** Monogram ZDP30N4D[SS]	3,600		○	◓	◒	◓	◓
28	**DCS** RD-304[SS]	3,500		◒	◓	◒	◓	◓

See report, page 79. Based on tests published in Consumer Reports in August 2002.

The tests behind the Ratings

Under **brand & model,** brackets show a tested model's color code. **Overall score** includes cooktop high power and low power performance, oven capacity, baking, broiling, and self-cleaning. **Cooktop high power** is how quickly the highest powered burner or element heated 6½ quarts of room-temperature water to a near boil. **Low power** shows how well the least powerful burner or element melted and held chocolate without scorching it and whether the most powerful, set to Low, held tomato sauce below a boil. **Oven capacity** is usable oven space. **Bake** shows baking evenness for cakes and cookies. **Broil** shows cooking and searing evenness for a tray of burgers. **Price** is approximate retail.

Recommendations & notes

Similar models have the same burners or elements, oven, and broiler; other details may differ. **All ranges:** Are 30 inches wide. Have an oven light and anti-tip hardware. **Most ranges have:** Freestanding construction. Touchpad oven controls. A cooktop rim to hold spills. A self-cleaning oven. Two or three oven racks with five positions. An oven window with a reasonably clear view. A storage drawer. A warranty of one year for parts and labor. Sealed burners and cast-iron grates. Can be converted to LP fuel.

GAS MODELS

1 > **GE** Profile Performance JGB910WEC[WW] **Convection option.** Warming drawer. Burners: 2@12,000, 1@9,500, 1@5,000 Btu/hr.

2 > **GE** Profile JGBP85WEB[WW] **Warming drawer.** Window view worse than most. Burners: 2@12,000, 1@9,500, 1@5,000 Btu/hr. Similar: JGBP90MEB[ ], JGBP86WEB[ ].

3 > **GE** JGBP35WEA[WW] **Window view worse than most.** Burners: 1@12,000, 2@9,500, 1@5,000 Btu/hr. Similar: JGBP79WEB[ ].

4 > **HOTPOINT** RGB745WEA[WW] **A CR Best Buy Oven dial.** Window view worse than most.

Recommendations & notes

Steel grates. Burners: 1@12,000, 2@9,500, 1@5,000 Btu/hr.

5▷ MAGIC CHEF CGR3742CD[W] Burners: 1@12,000, 3@9,200 Btu/hr.

6▷ MAYTAG MGR5880BD[W] **Among the more repair-prone gas-range brands.** Convection option. Warming drawer. Burners: 1@12,000, 2@9,200, 1@7,200 Btu/hr. Similar: MGR5870BD[ ].

7▷ MAYTAG Performa PGR5710BD[W] **Among the more repair-prone gas-range brands.** Steel grates. Window view worse than most. Burners: 1@12,000, 3@9,200 Btu/hr. Similar: PGR5705BD[ ].

8▷ GE Profile Performance JGB920WEC[WW] **Convection option.** Glass ceramic cooktop. Warming drawer and element. Burners: 2@12,000, 1@9,500, 1@5,200 Btu/hr.

9▷ KENMORE (Sears) 7584[2] **Warming drawer.** Split rack. Continuous grates. Burners: 1@13,500, 2@9,500, 1@5,000 Btu/hr.

10▷ JENN-AIR JGS8750AD[W] **Among the more repair-prone gas-range brands.** Slide-in design. Cooktop burners reignite. Continuous grates. Burners: 1@12,000, 1@10,500, 1@9,100, 1@6,500 Btu/hr.

11▷ KENMORE (Sears) 7566[1] **Warming drawer.** Burners: 1@14,200, 1@12,000, 1@9,500, 1@5,000 Btu/hr.

12▷ KENMORE (Sears) Elite 7901[2] **Convection option.** Glass ceramic cooktop. Warming drawer and element. Burners: 1@14,200, 1@12,000, 1@9,500, 1@5,000 Btu/hr.

13▷ TAPPAN TGF363A[W] Burners: 2@12,000, 1@9,500, 1@5,000 Btu/hr.

14▷ KENMORE (Sears) 7575[1] **Warming drawer.** Burners: 1@12,000, 3@9,500 Btu/hr.

15▷ FRIGIDAIRE Gallery GLGF377A[S] **Convection option.** Window view worse than most. Burners: 1@12,000, 2@9,500, 1@5,000 Btu/hr. Similar: FGF378A[ ].

16▷ KITCHENAID KGRT607H[BS] **Stainless-steel door and trim.** Convection option. Continuous grates. Burners: 1@14,000, 1@12,500, 2@6,000 Btu/hr. Similar: KGRT600H[ ].

17▷ WHIRLPOOL Gold GS460LEK[Q] **Continuous grates.** Window view worse than most. Split rack. Burners: 1@13,500, 2@9,500, 1@5,000 Btu/hr. Similar: SF387LEK[ ], GS465LEK[ ], GS470LXK[ ], GS475LXK[ ].

18▷ FRIGIDAIRE Gallery GLGF366A[S] Burners: 1@12,000, 3@9,500 Btu/hr. Similar: FGF366A[ ].

19▷ VIKING VGSC3064B[SS] **Pro-style.** Stainless-steel construction. Convection option. Unsealed burners, which reignite. Continuous grates. Oven dial. Window view worse than most. Burners: 4@15,000 Btu/hr.

20▷ DACOR PGR30[S] **Pro-style features.** Slide-in design. Stainless-steel construction. Convection option. Continuous grates. Cooktop burners reignite. Burners: 2@12,500, 2@9,500 Btu/hr.

21▷ DCS RGA-304[SS] **Pro-style.** Stainless-steel construction. Convection option. Unsealed burners. Oven dial. Four rack positions. No self-cleaning. Burners: 4@15,000 Btu/hr.

DUAL-FUEL MODELS

22▷ KITCHENAID KDRP407H[SS] **Pro-style.** Stainless-steel construction. Convection option. Continuous grates. Simmer plate. Oven dial. Burners: 4@15,000 Btu/hr.

Recommendations & notes

23▷ KENMORE (Sears) Elite 4683[3] **Stainless-steel door and trim.** Slide-in design. Glass ceramic cooktop. Convection option. Continuous grates. Warming drawer. Four rack positions. Burners: 1@14,200, 1@11,000, 1@9,500, 1@5,000 Btu/hr.

24▷ JENN-AIR JDS9860AA[W] **Slide-in design.** Convection option. Continuous grates. Grill with downdraft vent. Burners: 2@10,000, 2@8,000 (grill) Btu/hr.

25▷ DACOR ERD30SO6[BK] **Pro-style.** Stainless-steel construction. Convection option. Continuous grates. Simmer plate. Cooktop burners reignite. Excelled at self-cleaning. Burners: 4@15,000 Btu/hr.

26▷ VIKING VDSC305B[SS] **Pro-style.** Stainless-steel construction. Convection option. Continuous grates. Oven dial. Unsealed burners. Window view worse than most. Least effective at self-cleaning. Burners: 4@15,000 Btu/hr.

27▷ GE Monogram ZDP30N4D[SS] **Pro-style.** Stainless-steel construction. Convection option. Continuous grates. Unsealed burners. Oven dial. Three rack positions. Burners: 4@15,000 Btu/hr.

28▷ DCS RD-304[SS] **Pro-style.** Stainless-steel construction. Unsealed burners. Convection option. Continuous grates. Oven dial. Three rack positions. Burners: 4@15,000 Btu/hr.

Ranges and Cooktops: Newer Is Easier

More and more, ranges and cooktops are being designed with easy cleaning in mind. Touch-pad controls put an end to greasy knobs, and smoothtops do away with pesky nooks, crannies, and drip bowls. New designs also include some relatively low-tech innovations such as raised edges around cooking surfaces to keep spills off the floor. If you're outfitting your kitchen with a new stove, you'll probably be delighted with the array of labor-saving options that are now available.

Receivers

Shop Smart   Receivers are typically capable performers these days. Most of those rated offer a good selection of features. At $300, the Panasonic SA-HE100 is a **CR Best Buy**. The top performer in our tests, it's easy to use and has many useful features. It has the power to handle 4-ohm speakers—ideal if you have a very large room or if you like to play bass-heavy music. If you don't need that extra power and can settle for fewer features, consider the Panasonic SA-HE70, another very good performer priced at just $200. Key features for these models are listed in the table on page 294. See the product guide for an explanation of the features

Overall Ratings	In performance order							
						Excellent ⊖	Very good ⊖	Good ○ Fair ◒ Poor ●

KEY NO.	BRAND & MODEL	PRICE	OVERALL SCORE	PERFORMANCE	EASE OF USE	FEATURES	WATTS PER CHANNEL		
			0 100 P F G VG E				8 OHM	6 OHM	4 OHM
1	**Panasonic** SA-HE100 **A CR Best Buy**	$300	▬▬▬	⊖	⊖	⊖	85	112	45
2	**Onkyo** TX-SR600	500	▬▬▬	⊖	⊖	○	109	127	—
3	**Harman Kardon** AVR 320	650	▬▬▬	⊖	○	○	88	105	—
4	**Onkyo** TX-SR500	300	▬▬▬	⊖	○	○	92	110	—
5	**Yamaha** RX-V430	300	▬▬▬	⊖	○	○	101	115	74
6	**Harman Kardon** AVR 120	350	▬▬▬	⊖	○	○	77	88	—
7	**Panasonic** SA-HE70	200	▬▬▬	⊖	○	⊖	73	94	—
8	**Kenwood** VR-6060	500	▬▬▬	⊖	⊖	◒	128	152	—
9	**Pioneer** VSX-D811S	400	▬▬▬	○	○	○	140	157	—
10	**Pioneer** VSX-D511	200	▬▬▬	○	○	○	135	149	—
11	**RCA** STAV-3990	250	▬▬▬	○	○	○	139	152	—
12	**Sony** STR-DE685	250	▬▬▬	○	⊖	○	131	151	—
13	**JVC** RX-6020VBK	200	▬▬▬	○	⊖	◒	98	114	—
14	**Sony** STR-DE485	200	▬▬▬	○	⊖	◒	106	124	—

See report, page 44. Based on tests published in Consumer Reports in November 2002.

The tests behind the Ratings

Overall score is based on amplifier and AM/FM tuner performance, ease of use, and convenience features. **Performance** combines lack of noise and distortion in the amplifier, plus AM and FM reception. **Ease of use** reflects our judgments on the ergonomics of the front panel and remote control (including visibility and clarity of labeling); ease of operation; and, on the remote, button size and overall physical balance. Features reflects the presence or absence of convenience features. **Watts per channel** is our measure of power when the receiver is used with 8-ohm, 6-ohm, and 4-ohm speakers (a dash means the manufacturer does not recommend use with such speakers).

Recommendations & notes

All tested models: Can decode Dolby Digital and DTS soundtracks. Have a 75-ohm FM-antenna connection. Have output jack for powered subwoofer. Have Dolby Pro Logic and other DSP modes besides Dolby Surround. Have test-tone function for setting sound level. Have remote control that can operate devices of the same brand. Have display dimmer. Lack direct tuning of frequency on console. Lack function to scan preset radio stations for a few seconds.

Most tested models: Have a two-year warranty for parts and labor. Lack center-channel pre-amp out jack. Have 5.1 inputs for external decoder. Lack bass-boost switch. Lack phono input. Have sleep-timer function. Have universal remote control to operate devices from other manufacturers. Have a good AM tuner. Have Dolby Pro Logic II mode. Lack tape monitor. Have one or two switched AC outlets. Have at least 30 AM or FM station presets.

Similar models should offer performance comparable to that of the tested model, although features may differ.

1 > PANASONIC SA-HE100 **A CR Best Buy Best value among tested models.** FM tuner adjusts in full-channel increments. Troubleshooting "help" button. Tape monitor. Phono input. Lacks sleep timer. Warranty only 1 yr.

2 > ONKYO TX-SR600 **Very good performer, though pricey.** Extra back-center channel for 6.1 surround. Mediocre AM performance. Similar: TX-SR700.

3 > HARMAN KARDON AVR 320 **Very good, but**

pricey and lacking some features available in less expensive models. Extra back-center channel for 6.1 surround. Center-channel pre-amp out jacks. Similar: AVR 520.

4 > ONKYO TX-SR500 **Very good performer and very good value.**

5 > YAMAHA RX-V430 **Good value.** FM tuner adjusts in full-channel increments. Mediocre AM performance. Similar: RX-V530.

6 > HARMAN KARDON AVR 120 **Very good overall performer.** Lacks 5.1 inputs for external decoders like DVD players. Discontinued, but similar AVR 125 is available.

7 > PANASONIC SA-HE70 **Very good value.** FM tuner adjusts in full-channel increments. Tape monitor. Troubleshooting "help" button. Lacks sleep timer. Warranty only 1 yr.

8 > KENWOOD VR-6060 **Good overall, but lacking some features available in less expensive models.** Extra back-center channel for 6.1 surround. Phono input. Bass-boost switch. Mediocre AM performance. Lacks sleep timer. Similar: VR-6070.

9 > PIONEER VSX-D811S **Good.** Extra back-center channel for 6.1 surround. Can program to display station call letters. Tape monitor. Lacks sleep timer. Warranty only 1 yr. Similar: VSX-D711.

10 > PIONEER VSX-D511 **Good, basic model.** Can program to display station call letters. Lacks

Recommendations & notes

sleep timer and universal remote. Warranty only 1 yr. Similar: VSX-D411.

11▷ **RCA** STAV-3990 **Good value.** Tape monitor. Mediocre AM performance. Lacks sleep timer. Surround lacks Dolby Pro Logic II. Similar: STAV-4090.

12▷ **SONY** STR-DE685 **Good.** Can program to display station call letters. Mediocre AM performance. Similar: STR-DE885.

13▷ **JVC** RX-6020VBK **Good.** There are better choices. Mediocre FM and AM performance. Lacks universal remote and AC outlets. Similar: RX-7020VBK.

14▷ **SONY** STR-DE48 Good. **There are better choices.** Can program to display station call letters. Mediocre FM and AM performance. Lacks AC outlets. Surround lacks Dolby Pro Logic II.

FEATURES AT A GLANCE RECEIVERS

Tested models (keyed to the Ratings) Key no. Brand & model	Front-panel input	S-video inputs/outputs	Component-video inputs	Direct AM/FM tuning	Onscreen display
1▷ **Panasonic**	•	3/0	•	•	
2▷ **Onkyo**	•	5/1	•		•
3▷ **Harman Kardon**	•	5/2	•	•	•
4▷ **Onkyo**	•	4/1			
5▷ **Yamaha**	•	0/0			
6▷ **Harman Kardon**	•	5/1		•	
7▷ **Panasonic**		3/0		•	
8▷ **Kenwood**	•	5/1	•		
9▷ **Pioneer**	•	4/1	•	•	
10▷ **Pioneer**		3/1			
11▷ **RCA**	•	4/1	•	•	
12▷ **Sony**	•	3/1	•	•	
13▷ **JVC**		0/0			
14▷ **Sony**		0/0		•	

Refrigerators

Shop Smart Choose the size and style, then look for the features you want, good performance, and a brand with a good track record for reliability. Among top-freezer models, the Maytag MTB1956GE, $825, is feature-laden and convenient. Nearly as good, and quieter, is the Kenmore 7118, $750. The GE GSS25JFM, $890, **a CR Best Buy,** is a real bargain among side-by-side refrigerators. More full-featured are the side-by-side Kenmore 5255, $1,400, and the Kenmore Elite 5260, $1,700, which top the Ratings, and come with more features. Among built-in models with a freezer on the bottom, consider the GE Monogram ZIC360NM, $3,900. It scored nearly as well as the Sub-Zero, costs less, and it's quieter. Key features for these models are listed in the table on page 299. See the product guide for an explanation of the features.

Overall Ratings   In performance order

Excellent ⊖ Very good ⊖ Good ○ Fair ◑ Poor ●

KEY NO	BRAND & MODEL	PRICE	OVERALL SCORE	ENERGY COST/YR.	ENERGY EFFICIENCY	TEMP. TESTS	NOISE	EASE OF USE
			0 P F G VG E 100					
TOP-FREEZER MODELS (18-22 CU. FT.)								
1	**Maytag** MTB1956GE[W]	$825		$36	⊖	⊖	○	⊖
2	**Kenmore** (Sears) 7118[2]	750		43	⊖	⊖	⊖	○
3	**Maytag** MTB2156GE[W]	850		39	⊖	○	○	⊖
4	**Kenmore** (Sears) Elite 7120[2]	1,000		38	⊖	⊖	⊖	○
5	**Amana** ART2107B[W]	800		38	⊖	⊖	○	○
6	**GE** GTS18KCM[WW]	600		40	⊖	⊖	○	⊖
7	**Kenmore** (Sears) 7198[2]	750		35	⊖	⊖	⊖	○
8	**Frigidaire** Gallery GLHT216TA[W]	680		38	⊖	⊖	○	○
9	**Kenmore** (Sears) 7285[2]	680		40	⊖	⊖	○	○
10	**Whirlpool** Gold GR9SHKXK[Q]	940		37	⊖	⊖	○	○
11	**Frigidaire** Gallery GLRT186TA[W]	680		40	⊖	⊖	○	○
12	**GE** GTS22KCM[WW]	650		44	⊖	⊖	○	⊖
13	**Whirlpool** ET1FTTXK[Q]	800		43	⊖	⊖	○	○
14	**Whirlpool** Gold GR2SHTXK[Q]	1,050		40	⊖	⊖	○	○
15	**Frigidaire** FRT18P5A[W]	510		40	⊖	⊖	○	○
SIDE-BY-SIDE MODELS (20-28 CU. FT.)								
16	**Kenmore** (Sears) 5255[2]	$1,400		52	⊖	⊖	⊖	⊖
17	**Kenmore** (Sears) Elite 5260[2]	1,700		52	⊖	⊖	⊖	⊖
18	**Amana** ARSE66MB[B]	1,570		54	⊖	⊖	○	⊖
19	**Frigidaire** Gallery GLHS267ZA[W]	1,275		$54	⊖	⊖	○	⊖

	Excellent	Very good	Good	Fair	Poor
	⊖	⊖	○	◒	●

Overall Ratings, cont.

KEY NO	BRAND & MODEL	PRICE	OVERALL SCORE	ENERGY COST/YR.	ENERGY EFFICIENCY	TEMP. TESTS	NOISE	EASE OF USE
			0 P F G VG E 100					
SIDE-BY-SIDE MODELS (20-28 CU. FT.)								
20	**GE** Profile Arctica PSS29NGM[WW]	2,220	▬▬▬	63	○	⊖	⊖	⊖
21	**Kenmore** (Sears) 5275[2]	1,800	▬▬▬	55	⊖	⊖	⊖	⊖
22	**Kenmore** (Sears) 5225[2]	1,350	▬▬▬	50	⊖	⊖	⊖	⊖
23	**Whirlpool** Gold GC5THGXK[Q]	2,300	▬▬▬	53	○	⊖	⊖	⊖
24	**KitchenAid** Superba KSRG27FK[WH]	1,700	▬▬▬	55	⊖	○	⊖	⊖
25	**Maytag** MSD2456GE[W]	1,210	▬▬▬	52	⊖	⊖	○	⊖
26	**GE** Profile Arctica PSI23NGM[WW]	2,300	▬▬▬	57	⊖	⊖	○	⊖
27	**GE** GSS25JFM[WW] **A CR Best Buy**	890	▬▬▬	60	⊖	⊖	○	⊖
28	**Frigidaire** Gallery GLRS237ZA[W]	1,100	▬▬▬	57 ·	○	○	⊖	○
29	**Kenmore** (Sears) 5106[2]	1,200	▬▬▬	56	○	⊖	○	⊖
30	**Whirlpool** ED2FHGXK[Q]	1,020	▬▬▬	54	○	⊖	○	⊖
31	**Maytag** Plus MZD2766GE[W]	1,500	▬▬▬	55	⊖	◒	○	⊖
32	**GE** GSS20IEM[WW]	800	▬▬▬	54	○	○	○	⊖
BUILT-IN BOTTOM-FREEZER MODELS (20-21 CU. FT.)								
33	**Sub-Zero** 650/F	4,600	▬▬▬	42	⊖	⊖	○	○
34	**GE** Monogram ZIC360NM	3,900	▬▬▬	47	⊖	⊖	⊖	○
35	**KitchenAid** KBRS36FKX[ ]	4,100	▬▬▬	43	⊖	⊖	○	○
36	**Viking** DDBB363R[SS]	4,800	▬▬▬	47	⊖ ·	⊖	○	○

See report, page 82. Based on tests published in Consumer Reports in August 2002, with updated prices and availability.

The tests behind the Ratings

Under **brand & model,** brackets indicate the tested model's color code. **Overall score** gives the most weight to energy efficiency and temperature performance. **Energy cost/year** is based on 2002 national average electricity rate, 8.3 cents per kilowatt-hour. Expected annual usage is based on model's EnergyGuide sticker. **Energy efficiency** reflects consumption per EnergyGuide and model's usable volume. **Temperature tests** combines the outcome of tests run at different room temperatures, including extreme heat; they judge how closely and uniformly the maker's recommended settings match our ideal temperatures for refrigerators. **Noise** was gauged with compressors running. **Ease of use** assesses more than 100 features, including controls and ice/water dispenser. **Price** is approximate retail; includes optional icemaker on some models.

Recommendations & notes

Models listed as similar should offer performance comparable to the tested model's, although features may differ.

Most models have: Ability to keep main space at 37° F and freezer at 0° with good temperature uniformity. Very good or excellent ability to handle heavy loads on hot days. Meatkeeper that reaches good storage temperature. Ability to make more than 3½ pounds of ice daily. Spillproof glass shelves. Slide-out bins or shelves. One-year full warranty on parts and labor, five years on refrigeration system.

All side-by-sides have: Icemaker with lighted, through-the-door dispenser for ice and water; selection for cubes or crushed ice. **Most side-by-sides have:** Water filter.

Most top- and bottom-freezers have: Half shelves, for storage flexibility.

TOP-FREEZER MODELS

1 > **MAYTAG** MTB1956GE[W] **Very good performance, with features that make it more convenient than most top-freezers.** Crank-adjustable shelf. 67x30x29½ in. 18.5 cu. ft. (14.4 usable).

2 > **KENMORE** (Sears) 7118[2] **Very good performer, though short on features.** 66x32½x29½ in. 20.8 cu. ft. (16.9 usable). Similar: 7119[ ].

3 > **MAYTAG** MTB2156GE[W] **Very good overall with features that make it more convenient than most top-freezers.** Crank-adjustable shelf. 67x33x29 in. 20.7 cu. ft. (15.1 usable).

4 > **KENMORE** (Sears) Elite 7120[2] **Very good and quiet, with attractive features, but pricey.** Curved front; water dispenser with filter; speed icemaker. 66x33½x31½ in. 21.6 cu. ft. (15.8 usable).

5 > **AMANA** ART2107B[W] **A very good, basic model.** 69x30x32½ in. 20.6 cu. ft. (16.0 usable).

6 > **GE** GTS18KCM[WW] **Well priced for very good performance, with features that make it more convenient than most top-freezers.** 66½x30x30½ in. 17.9 cu. ft. (14.0 usable). Similar: GTS18KBM[ ], GTH18KBM[ ].

7 > **KENMORE** (Sears) 7198[2] **Very good and quiet, with attractive features.** Made more ice than the other top-freezers–about 4.5 lbs. per day. 66x30x31 in. 18.8 cu. ft. (14.1 usable).

8 > **FRIGIDAIRE** Gallery GLHT216TA[W] **Well priced for very good performance.** But among the more repair-prone brands of top-freezers with icemakers. 69x30x32½ in. 20.6 cu. ft. (16.4 usable). Similar: PLHT217TAC[ ].

9 > **KENMORE** (Sears) 7285[2] **Well priced for very good performance, though short on features.** 66x30x30 in. 18.1 cu. ft. (14.1 usable). Similar: 7286[ ].

10 > **WHIRLPOOL** Gold GR9SHKXK[Q] **Very good overall.** Curved, smooth-surface doors. 66x30x32 in. 18.8 cu. ft. (14.1 usable).

11 > **FRIGIDAIRE** Gallery GLRT186TA[W] **Very good overall and well priced, but among the more repair-prone brands of top-freezers with icemakers.** 66½x30x31 in. 18.3 cu. ft. (14.3 usable). Similar: GLHT186TA[ ].

12 > **GE** GTS22KCM[WW] **Well priced for very good performance, with features that make it more convenient than most top-freezers.** But manufacturer's recommended settings left fridge and freezer too cold. 67½x33x31½ in. 21.7 cu. ft. (16.5 usable). Similar: GTS22KBM[ ].

13 > **WHIRLPOOL** ET1FTTXK[Q] **A very good, basic model.** Water dispenser with filter. 66x32½x30½ in. 20.8 cu. ft. (16.5 usable).

14 > **WHIRLPOOL** Gold GR2SHTXK[Q] **Very good, with attractive features, though pricey.**

Recommendations & notes

Curved, smooth-surface doors. Water dispenser with filter. 66½x33x31½ in. 21.6 cu. ft. (15.9 usable). Similar: GR2SHKXK[ ].

15▷ FRIGIDAIRE FRT18P5A[W] **Very good overall and well priced.** No meatkeeper controls, pull-out shelves, or freezer light. Frigidaire has been among the more repair-prone brands of top-freezers with icemakers. 66½x30x30 in. 18.4 cu. ft. (14.5 usable). Similar: FRT18HP5A[ ].

SIDE-BY-SIDE MODELS

16▷ KENMORE (Sears) 5255[2] **Very good and quiet.** Excellent at making ice—more than 7 lbs. per day. Ice bin located on the freezer door for easy access and removal. 69½x36x30 in. 25.5 cu. ft. (16.0 usable). Similar: 5256[ ].

17▷ KENMORE (Sears) Elite 5260[2] **Very good overall, but pricey.** Digital temperature controls inexact when room is hot. Excellent at making ice—more than 7 lbs. per day. Ice bin located on the freezer door for easy access and removal. Curved, smooth-surface doors. 70x36x33 in. 25.6 cu. ft. (15.1 usable).

18▷ AMANA ARSE66MB[B] **Very good overall and feature-rich.** Has a temperature-controlled beverage chiller and a tall ice/water dispenser. But Amana has been among the more repair-prone side-by-side brands. 70x36x32 in. 25.6 cu. ft. (16.3 usable).

19▷ FRIGIDAIRE Gallery GLHS267ZA[W] **Very good overall and relatively inexpensive compared with similar performers.** Excellent at making ice—about 8.5 lbs. per day. But among the more repair-prone side-by-side brands. 69½x36x33½ in. 25.9 cu. ft. (17.5 usable). Similar: PLHS267ZA[ ].

20▷ GE Profile Arctica PSS29NGM[WW] **Pricey but very good, with some novel features: digital temperature controls, thaw/chill**
bin, tall ice/water dispenser. But not as energy efficient as most. 70x36x33½ in. 28.6 cu. ft. (17.3 usable).

21▷ KENMORE (Sears) 5275[2] **Pricey but very good overall and excellent at making ice— more than 7 lbs. per day.** Ice bin located on the freezer door for easy access and removal. 70x36x32½ in. 27 cu. ft. (17.0 usable). Discontinued, but similar 5276 is available.

22▷ KENMORE (Sears) 5225[2] **Very good overall. Ice bin located on the freezer door for easy access and removal.** 66½x33x30½ in. 21.9 cu. ft. (14.2 usable). Similar: 5226[ ].

23▷ WHIRLPOOL Gold GC5THGXK[Q] **Cabinet depth (requires door panels and 36-in.-wide opening).** 72x35½x27½ in. 24.5 cu. ft. (14.7 usable). Discontinued, but similar GC5THGXL[ ] is available.

24▷ KITCHENAID Superba KSRG27FK[WH] **Pricey but very good overall.** Ice bin located on the freezer door for easy access and removal. 70x36x32 in. 26.8 cu. ft. (16.8 usable). Similar: KSRD27FK[ ].

25▷ MAYTAG MSD2456GE[W] **Very good overall, but has been the most repair-prone side-by-side brand.** Crank-adjustable shelf. 69x33x32 in. 23.6 cu. ft. (13.3 usable).

26▷ GE Profile Arctica PSI23NGM[WW] **A pricey but very good counter-depth, built-in-style model with some novel features.** But not as energy efficient as most. 70½x36x27½ in. 22.6 cu. ft. (13.1 usable).

27▷ GE GSS25JFM[WW] **A CR Best Buy Well priced for very good performance and fairly large capacity.** But freezer door was a bit too warm. 70x36x31 in. 24.9 cu. ft. (16.9 usable). Similar: GSS25JEM[ ].

Recommendations & notes

28▷ **FRIGIDAIRE** Gallery GLRS237ZA[W] **Very good overall and excellent at making ice.** But among the more repair-prone brands and not as energy efficient as most. 69½x33x33 in. 22.6 cu. ft. (14.6 usable). Similar: GLHS237ZA[ ].

29▷ **KENMORE** (Sears) 5106[2] **Very good overall, but not as energy efficient as most.** 66½x33½x29 in. 20 cu. ft. (13.2 usable). Similar: 5104[ ].

30▷ **WHIRLPOOL** ED2FHGXK[Q] **Very good overall, but not as energy efficient as most.** 66½x33x31 in. 22 cu. ft. (13.3 usable).

31▷ **MAYTAG** Plus MZD2766GE[W] **Good overall and novel design holds wider items than most side-by-sides.** But warm spots throughout fridge, especially butter compartment, and has been the most repair-prone side-by-side brand. 70½x36x32 in. 26.8 cu. ft. (17.7 usable).

32▷ **GE** GSS20IEM[WW] **Good overall and well priced, but not as energy efficient as most.** Meatkeeper too warm. No spillproof shelves or water filter. 67½x32x31½ in. 19.9 cu. ft. (13.3 usable).

FEATURES AT A GLANCE REFRIGERATORS

Tested products (keyed to the Ratings) Key no. Brand	Child lock-out	Energy Star	Ice/water dispenser	Ice Bin on Door	Pullout shelves/bins	Speed Ice
TOP-FREEZER MODELS						
1▷ Maytag		•			•	
2▷ Kenmore						
3▷ Maytag		•			•	
4▷ Kenmore		•	W		•	•
5▷ Amana					•	
6▷ GE						
7▷ Kenmore		•			•	•
8▷ Frigidaire		•			•	
9▷ Kenmore						
10▷ Whirlpool		•			•	
11▷ Frigidaire					•	
12▷ GE						
13▷ Whirlpool			W			
14▷ Whirlpool		•	W		•	
15▷ Frigidaire						
SIDE-BY-SIDES						
16▷ Kenmore	•	•	•	•	•	•
17▷ Kenmore	•	•	•	•	•	•
18▷ Amana	•	•	•		•	

Tested products (keyed to the Ratings) Key no. Brand	Child lock-out	Energy Star	Ice/water dispenser	Ice Bin on Door	Pullout shelves/bins	Speed Ice
19▷ Frigidaire		•	•		•	•
20▷ GE	•		•		•	
21▷ Kenmore	•	•	•	•	•	•
22▷ Kenmore	•	•	•	•	•	•
23▷ Whirlpool	•	•	•		•	
24▷ Kitchenaid	•	•	•		•	•
25▷ Maytag	•	•	•		•	
26▷ GE	•		•		•	•
27▷ GE		•	•			
28▷ Frigidaire		•	•		•	•
29▷ Kenmore		•	•		•	
30▷ Whirlpool		•	•		•	
31▷ Maytag	•	•	•		•	
32▷ GE		•	•		•	
BUILT-INS (BOTTOM-FREEZERS)						
33▷ Sub-Zero					•	
34▷ GE					•	
35▷ KitchenAid			•		•	
36▷ Viking					•	

Recommendations & notes

BUILT-IN BOTTOM-FREEZER MODELS

33> SUB-ZERO 650/F **Very good overall and very energy efficient.** Bottom freezer opens like a drawer. Sub-Zero is among the most repair-prone brands. 2-yr. full warranty. 84x36½x25½ in. 20.6 cu. ft. (15.4 usable).

34> GE Monogram ZIC360NM **Very good overall and very quiet.** Bottom freezer opens like a drawer. 2-yr. full warranty. 84x36½x25½2 in. 20.6 cu. ft. (13.6 usable). Water filter. Similar: ZICS360NM[ ].

35> KITCHENAID KBRS36FKX[ ] **Very good overall and very energy efficient.** Bottom freezer opens like a drawer. 2-yr. full warranty. 83½x36x25½ in. 20.9 cu. ft. (14.4 usable).

36> VIKING DDBB363R[SS] **Very good, with stainless steel front.** Bottom freezer opens like a drawer. 2-yr. full warranty. 83½x36x24½ in. 20.3 cu. ft. (15.0 usable). Similar: DFBB363[ ], VCBB363[ ], DTBB363[ ].

Energy-saving tip

The condenser coil helps disperse heat and is outside the cabinet. Since it tends to collect dust, which lowers the refrigerator's efficiency and raises energy costs, it should be cleaned once or twice a year. This is especially important before the onset of summer, when high temperatures impose heavy demands on the refrigerator. The condenser is usually located behind or beneath the refrigerator, though on built-in models it is on top of the unit.

To clean the condensers on all but built-in models, turn off and unplug the refrigerator, then pull it out so you can easily reach the back. (You may have to remove the "service access" panel to reach the condenser.) Use a condenser-coil cleaning brush (available in hardware and appliance stores) to dust the condenser, then vacuum it with the crevice tool. To clean the condenser of a built-in unit, consult a professional.

Speakers

Shop Smart   Paired with today's receivers, speakers—whether bookshelf, floor-standing, or three- and six-piece systems—can easily fill a large room with loud sound. Consumer Reports tests show that some are better than others at playing loud bass without buzzing or otherwise distorting the sound. Keep in mind that most speakers perform better with a little elbow room, so a corner, crowded bookshelf, or wall-mount is unlikely to be the ideal location. Paying more for speakers won't always get you better sound, but it may get you more stylish boxes.

					Excellent	Very good	Good	Fair	Poor
					⊜	⊖	○	◒	●

Overall Ratings   In performance order

KEY NO	BRAND & MODEL	PRICE	OVERALL SCORE	ACCURACY	BASS HANDLING	IMPEDANCE (OHMS)
			P F G VG E			
	BOOKSHELF MODELS					
1	**Pioneer** S-DF3-K	$350		89	⊜	4
2	**Bose** 301 Series IV	300		89	⊜	7
3	**Cambridge Soundworks** Model Six	150		88	⊜	7
4	**BIC** America Venturi DV62si	200		90	○	7
5	**Infinity** Entra One	300		87	⊜	4
6	**B&W** DM 602 S2	550		85	⊜	5
7	**Bose** 201 Series IV	200		88	⊜	9
8	**Acoustic Research** 215PS	130		89	⊜	4
9	**Mission** MS M72	350		88	○	4
10	**Pioneer** S-DF2-K	250		87	⊜	5
11	**Sony** SS-MB300H	100		86	⊜	9
12	**PSB** Image 2B	370		84	⊜	4
13	**Pioneer** S-H252B-K	100		85	⊜	8
14	**Mission** 780	600		87	○	5
15	**Pioneer** S-DF1-K	200		85	⊜	4
16	**Bose** 141	100		86	○	6
17	**Acoustic Research** Stature S20	300		83	⊜	4
18	**Cerwin** Vega RL-16M	300		81	⊜	4
19	**Acoustic Research** Stature S10	220		80	⊜	4
20	**Acoustic Research** AR15	230		77	⊜	4
21	**Klipsch** Synergy SB-3 Monitor	450		76	⊜	4
22	**KLH** 911B	70		79	○	7

Overall Ratings, cont.

		Excellent	Very good	Good	Fair	Poor
		⊖	⊖	○	◔	●

KEY NO	BRAND & MODEL	PRICE	OVERALL SCORE	ACCURACY	BASS HANDLING	IMPEDANCE (OHMS)
			P F G VG E			
23	**Acoustic Research** AR17	$180	▬▬▬	79	◔	4
24	**Mission** MS 700	180	▬▬▬	78	◔	5
	FLOOR-STANDING MODELS					
25	**Mission** MS M73	500	▬▬▬▬	89	⊖	5
26	**Acoustic Research** Stature S40	350	▬▬▬▬	85	⊖	5
27	**Cerwin Vega** E-710	360	▬▬▬▬	84	⊖	3
28	**Yamaha** NS-A200XT	400	▬▬▬▬	83	⊖	5
	THREE-PIECE SYSTEMS					
29	**Cambridge Soundworks** Ensemble III	250	▬▬▬▬▬	94	◔	4
30	**Bose** Acoustimass 3 Series IV	300	▬▬▬▬	88	⊖	5
31	**Bose** Acoustimass 5 Series III	600	▬▬▬▬	86	⊖	6
32	**Cambridge Soundworks** New Ensemble II	300	▬▬▬	83	⊖	4

See report, page 49. Based on tests published in Consumer Reports in November 2002.

The tests behind the Ratings

Overall score is based primarily on the ability to reproduce sound accurately. For bookshelf and floor-standing speakers and for three-piece systems, it also considers the ability to play bass music loudly without distortion. We measured the **accuracy** with which a speaker reproduced test signals containing the range of frequencies appropriate to each type of speaker; 100 is the best possible score. **Bass handling** reflects the ability to play bass-heavy music loudly without buzzing or distortion. **Impedance,** measured in ohms, is an electrical characteristic you should consider when matching speakers to a receiver or amplifier. We list our measurement, which in almost all cases was lower than the manufacturer's rating (theirs was typically 8 ohms). **Price** is approximate retail for a pair of bookshelf, floor-standing, or rear-surround speakers; for one center-channel speaker; and for two satellites and a bass module in three-piece sets. **Size** is height by width by depth, in inches; **weight** is per speaker, in pounds. For three-piece systems, the size and weight shown are for satellites. Bass modules are about 14x8 inches, with depth of 13 to 19 inches; they weigh 12 to 21 pounds. **Recommendations & notes** include optimal placement and Audio Notes, a technical description of the sound profile.

Recommendations & notes

Most tested models have: A black veneer finish (some may be available in other colors). A five-year warranty. Magnetic shielding to prevent video interference when placed near a TV. No included wires.

BOOKSHELF MODELS

1 ▷ **PIONEER** S-DF3-K **Excellent.** Best placed 54 in. from side wall, 12 in. from back. Audio notes: Very smooth. 16.5x10x13 in., 18 lb.

Recommendations & notes

2▷ BOSE 301 Series IV **Excellent speakers but rather wide.** Designed for left or right position. Best placed 18 in. from side wall, 24 in. from back. May cause video interference near a TV. Audio notes: Slight emphasis in midbass. 10.75x16.5x9.5 in., 12 lb.

3▷ CAMBRIDGE SOUNDWORKS Model Six **Very good and low-priced, with long (10-yr.) warranty.** Best placed 36 in. from side wall, 6 in. from back. May cause video interference near a TV. Audio notes: Not quite as smooth as other high-accuracy models. 18.25x11.25x7.5 in., 16 lb.

4▷ BIC America Venturi DV62si **Very good.** Best placed 36 in. from side wall, 6 in. from back. Long (7-yr.) warranty. Audio notes: Smooth and accurate, but shy in deep bass, strong in treble. 14.25x9x9.25 in., 13 lb.

5▷ INFINITY Entra One **Very good.** Best placed 48 in. from side wall, 18 in. from back. Audio notes: Smooth, with good extreme treble, slight dip in midrange. 15x8.5x9.25 in., 15 lb.

6▷ B&W DM 602 S2 **Very good but expensive.** Best placed 48 in. from side wall, 18 in. from back. May cause video interference near a TV. Audio notes: Good deep bass, noticeable weakness in upper midrange. 19.25x9.25x12 in., 23 lb.

7▷ BOSE 201 Series IV **Very good and compact.** Best placed 60 in. from side wall, 12 in. from back. Designed for left or right position. May cause video interference near a TV. Audio notes: Fairly smooth overall response, but lacks deep bass, overemphasizes midbass region. 9.5x15x6.75 in., 9 lb.

8▷ ACOUSTIC RESEARCH 215PS **Very good, light, and low-priced.** Best placed 30 in. from side wall, 18 in. from back. Audio notes: Somewhat uneven overall response. Emphasizes lower midrange and de-emphasizes upper midrange. 10.25x7x6.5 in., 7 lb.

9▷ MISSION MS M72 **Very good.** Best placed 24 in. from side wall, 12 in. from back. Short (2-yr.) warranty. Audio notes: Somewhat uneven overall response, with emphasis in lower midrange, de-emphasis in upper midrange. 13.25x7.75x12 in., 15 lb.

10▷ PIONEER S-DF2-K **Very good.** Best placed 48 in. from side wall, 12 in. from back. Audio notes: Fairly smooth response. Slight emphasis in midrange region, lacks extreme treble. 14x8.25x9.25 in., 13 lb.

11▷ SONY SS-MB300H **Very good and low-priced.** Best placed 48 in. from side wall, flush with rear. Removable grille. Audio notes: Fairly even overall response except for treble region. Slight de-emphasis in upper midrange but a peak in treble, lacks extreme treble. 21x9.5x10 in., 14 lb.

12▷ PSB Image 2B **Very good.** Best placed 48 in. from side wall, 18 in. from back. 5-yr. warranty only if card mailed in; otherwise 1-yr. Audio notes: Smooth, but slopes from strong midbass to weak treble. Moderate treble boost can improve accuracy. 15.25x8x12 in., 17 lb.

13▷ PIONEER S-H252B-K **Very good and low-priced.** Best placed 48 in. from side wall, 12 in. from back. May cause video interference near a TV. Audio notes: Somewhat uneven overall, with emphasis in lower midrange, severe de-emphasis in upper midrange. 21.5x11x10 in., 15 lb.

14▷ MISSION 780 **Very good and compact, but expensive.** Best placed 30 in. from side wall, 18 in. from back. May cause video interference near a TV. Audio notes: Extended treble, slightly weak deep bass, slightly strong midbass. 11x6.5x11 in., 11 lb.

Recommendations & notes

15▷ PIONEER S-DF1-K **Very good.** Best placed 48 in. from side wall, 18 in. from back. Audio notes: Somewhat uneven overall response, with lack of deep bass and overemphasized lower midrange. 12x7x9.75 in., 10 lb.

16▷ BOSE 141 **Very good overall.** Small, light, and low-priced. Shortest bookshelf model tested. Compact, gray vinyl cabinet. Best placed 24 in. from side wall, 18 in. from back. Designed for left or right position. May cause video interference near a TV. Audio notes: Smooth, but lacks deep bass and soft treble. Slight tone-control boost in both can improve accuracy. 6x10x6.25 in., 5 lb.

17▷ ACOUSTIC RESEARCH Stature S20 **Very good.** Best placed 48 in. from side wall, 12 in. from back. Audio notes: Smooth, but mid-bass a bit strong, treble slightly soft. 14.75x8x11.25 in., 16 lb.

18▷ CERWIN VEGA RL-16M **Good choice.** Best placed 48 in. from side wall, 18 in. from back. Audio notes: Emphasized midbass, reduced midrange and treble. Moderate treble boost can improve accuracy. 14x8.5x11 in., 14 lb.

19▷ ACOUSTIC RESEARCH Stature S10 **Good.** Best placed 18 in. from side wall, 12 in. from back. Audio notes: Somewhat uneven overall response, with overemphasis across lower midrange region and significant treble roll-off. 13.25x7x10.25 in., 12 lb.

20▷ ACOUSTIC RESEARCH AR15 **Good.** Best placed 48 in. from side wall, 18 in. from back. Audio notes: Somewhat uneven overall response, with overemphasis across entire midrange region. 14.25x8.5x9 in., 16 lb.

21▷ KLIPSCH Synergy SB-3 Monitor **Good.** Best placed 36 in. from side wall, 24 in. from back. Audio notes: Emphasis on midbass, weak tre-

ble. Moderate treble boost can improve accuracy. 17x8.25x11.25 in., 18 lb.

22▷ KLH 911B **Good, lightweight speakers at a low price.** Best placed 18 in. from side wall, 12 in. from back. Short (1-yr.) warranty. Audio notes: Uneven response, with little bass, muted upper midrange, peak in treble. 11x6.5x6.75 in., 7 lb.

23▷ ACOUSTIC RESEARCH AR17 **Good, but avoid if you play bass-heavy music very loud.** Best placed 60 in. from side wall, 12 in. from back. Audio notes: Lacks deep bass and extreme treble, overemphasizes bass and lower midrange region. 13x8x8 in., 13 lb.

24▷ MISSION MS 700 **Good, but avoid if you play bass-heavy music very loud.** Short (1-yr.) warranty. Best placed 36 in. from side wall, 24 in. from back. Audio notes: Bass and lower midrange region overemphasized, with slight treble roll-off. 13.5x7.25x10 in., 11 lb.

FLOOR-STANDING MODELS

25▷ MISSION MS M73 **Very good.** Short (2-yr.) warranty. Best placed 24 in. from side wall, 12 in. from back. Audio notes: Smooth overall, but lacks deep bass, de-emphasizes upper midrange. 33.5x8x12 in., 30 lb.

26▷ ACOUSTIC RESEARCH Stature S40 **Very good.** Best placed 60 in. from side wall, 18 in. from back. Audio notes: Somewhat uneven overall, with extended bass and overemphasis in midrange. 39x7.75x13.25 in., 39 lb.

27▷ CERWIN VEGA E-710 **Very good.** Among the best choices for playing bass-heavy music very loud. May cause video interference near a TV. Best placed 42 in. from side wall, 24 in. from back. Audio notes: Smooth overall, with strong midbass. Slight treble boost can help. 31.25x12.5x12 in., 40 lb.

Recommendations & notes

28> YAMAHA NS-A200XT **Very good.** Short (2-yr.) warranty. Includes speaker wires. Best placed 48 in. from side wall, 24 in. from back. Audio notes: Somewhat uneven overall, with slight emphasis in bass, treble roll-off. 42.75x12x17.5 in., 44 lb.

THREE-PIECE SYSTEMS

29> CAMBRIDGE SOUNDWORKS Ensemble III **Excellent.** Very accurate and smooth. Black metal cabinet. Bass unit best placed 60 in. from side wall, 18 in. from back. Audio notes: Midrange de-emphasized, treble uneven. 6.5x4.25x3.5 in., 3 lb.

30> BOSE Acoustimass 3 Series IV **Excellent.** Black plastic cabinet. Includes speaker wires. Bass unit best placed 60 in. from side wall, 18 in. from back. Audio notes: Smooth, with slight reduction in treble and deep bass. 3x3.25x4 in., 1 lb.

31> BOSE Acoustimass 5 Series III **Very good.** Bass unit best placed 48 in. from side wall, 18 in. from back. Audio notes: Slight emphasis on bass, slight de-emphasis on treble. 6.25x3.25x4.25 in., 2 lb.

32> CAMBRIDGE SOUNDWORKS New Ensemble II **Very good.** Long (10-yr.) warranty. Gray plastic cabinet. Bass unit best placed 30 in. from side wall, flush with back. Audio notes: Midrange de-emphasized, treble uneven. 8.25x5.25x4.5 in., 4 lb.

String trimmers

Shop Smart   You don't have to spend a lot of money to get a capable trimmer. Consider a corded electric trimmer for smaller yards or for lighter-duty trimming. The best among those we tested is the Ryobi 132r TrimmerPlus, $70, and 105r, $60. Battery-powered models combine mobility with easy starting, but are only suitable for light trimming chores. Gasoline-powered string trimmers are your best bet for large properties or for clearing tall grass. Consider the top-performing John Deere S1400, $170—a CR Best Buy.

KEY NO.	BRAND & MODEL	PRICE	WEIGHT	OVERALL SCORE	TRIM	CUT	EDGE	HANDLING	EASE OF USE
				P F G VG E					
GASOLINE MODELS									
1	**John Deere** S1400 A CR Best Buy	$170	13 lb.		⊖	⊖	⊖	⊖	⊖
2	**Stihl** FS 55R	200	12		⊖	⊖	⊖	⊖	○
3	**Stihl** FS 45 A CR Best Buy	150	~10		⊖	⊖	⊖	⊖	⊖
4	**Stihl** FS 75	200	11		⊖	⊖	⊖	⊖	⊖
5	**Echo** GT2000	170	10		⊖	⊖	⊖	⊖	○
6	**Ryobi** 775r EZ TrimmerPlus A CR Best Buy	140	14		⊖	⊖	⊖	⊖	○
7	**Husqvarna** 325CX E-tech	200	10		⊖	⊖	⊖	⊖	⊖
8	**Stihl** FS 46	170	9		⊖	⊖	⊖	⊖	⊖
9	**Ryobi** 875r TrimmerPlus	185	13		⊖	⊖	⊖	⊖	○
10	**Echo** SRM-2100	200	11		⊖	⊖	⊖	⊖	⊖
11	**John Deere** C1200	150	11		⊖	⊖	⊖	⊖	⊖
12	**John Deere** T105C	170	9		⊖	⊖	⊖	⊖	⊖
13	**Homelite** VersaTool	110	11		⊖	⊖	⊖	⊖	○
14	**Homelite** Trim N' Edge	85	10		⊖	○	⊖	⊖	⊖
15	**Ryobi** 700r	75	11		⊖	⊖	⊖	○	⊖
16	**Weed Eater** FeatherLite 25 HO SST	95	9		⊖	○	○	○	○
17	**Weed Eater** FeatherLite Plus	85	9		⊖	○	○	⊖	⊖
18	**Craftsman** (Sears) Weedwacker 79514	100	10		⊖	○	○	⊖	○
19	**Poulan** PP031	115	12		⊖	◐	⊖	⊖	⊖
CORDED MODELS									
20	**Ryobi** 132r TrimmerPlus	70	10		⊖	○	○	○	⊖
21	**Ryobi** 105r	60	8		⊖	○	○	⊖	⊖

Overall Ratings   In performance order

Rating key: Excellent ⊖   Very good ⊖   Good ○   Fair ◐   Poor ●

Overall Ratings, cont.

Legend: Excellent ⊖ Very good ⊖ Good ○ Fair ⊖ Poor ●

KEY NO.	BRAND & MODEL	PRICE	WEIGHT	OVERALL SCORE P F G VG E	TRIM	CUT	EDGE	HANDLING	EASE OF USE
	CORDED MODELS								
22	**Black & Decker** Grass Hog GH400	$55	5	▬▬▬▬	⊖	○	○	⊖	⊖
23	**Black & Decker** Grass Hog GH500	55	5	▬▬▬▬	⊖	○	○	⊖	⊖
24	**Craftsman** (Sears) Weedwacker 74512	30	5	▬▬▬▬	⊖	○	○	○	⊖
25	**Weed Eater** YardMaster YM 600	65	8	▬▬▬▬	⊖	⊖	○	⊖	⊖
26	**Craftsman** (Sears) Weedwacker 74517	60	9	▬▬▬▬	○	○	○	⊖	⊖
27	**Weed Eater** Snap 'N Go SG14	40	5	▬▬▬	○	○	⊖	○	⊖
28	**Weed Eater** XT110	30	5	▬▬▬	○	⊖	○	○	⊖
29	**Weed Eater** Snap 'N Go SG12	30	4	▬▬▬	⊖	○	○	○	⊖
30	**Weed Eater** XT112	30	4	▬▬▬	⊖	○	⊖	○	⊖
31	**Toro** 51353	45	5	▬▬▬	○	⊖	○	○	⊖
32	**Toro** 51301	35	4	▬▬▬	○	⊖	⊖	○	⊖
33	**Toro** 51332	35	4	▬▬▬	○	⊖	⊖	○	⊖
34	**Weed Eater** ElectraLite EL 10 Type 1	20	3	▬	●	●	●	○	⊖
35	**Weed Eater** ElectraLite EL8	20	4	▬	●	⊖	●	○	⊖
36	**Black & Decker** ST1000	25	3	▬	●	●	●	○	○
	BATTERY-POWERED MODELS								
37	**Ryobi** 155r	100	10	▬▬▬	⊖	⊖	⊖	○	⊖
38	**Black & Decker** Grass Hog CST2000	105	10	▬▬	⊖	⊖	●	○	⊖

See report, page 76. Based on tests published in Consumer Reports May 2002.

The tests behind the Ratings

The **overall score** is based mainly on trimming near a wall, cutting weeds and tall grass, edging, handling, and ease of use. **Weight** is rounded to the nearest pound and includes a full spool of string but not fuel, which can add one-half pound to gas models. **Trim** indicates how quickly and neatly models cut grass. **Cut** measures cutting power in overgrown weeds. **Edge** reflects the ability to quickly trim a neat, vertical line along the lawn's border on a walkway or other hard surface. **Handling** assesses responsiveness and balance. **Ease of use** is the ease of starting the engine and feeding out more line, along with handle comfort and ease of accessing controls. **Price** is approximate retail.

Recommendations & notes

GASOLINE MODELS

1. **JOHN DEERE** S1400 **A CR Best Buy Straight shaft.** Can also power blower and other tools. Heavier than most. Adjusting front handle requires tools.

2. **STIHL** FS 55R **Straight shaft.** Adjusting front handle requires tools.

3. **STIHL** FS 45 **A CR Best Buy Curved shaft.** Better balance and less vibration than most.

4. **STIHL** FS 75 **Curved shaft.** Adjusting front handle requires tools.

5. **ECHO** GT2000 **Curved shaft.** Starting easier than most. Lighter than most. Spool change more difficult than most.

6. **RYOBI** 775r EZ TrimmerPlus **A CR Best Buy Straight shaft.** Can also power blower and other tools. Heavier than most.

7. **HUSQVARNA** 325CX E-tech **Curved shaft.** Tall grass wrapped around head.

8. **STIHL** FS 46 **Curved shaft.** Lighter than most. Rear handle more comfortable than most.

9. **RYOBI** 875r TrimmerPlus **Straight shaft.** Can power other tools. 4-stroke engine. Heavier than most. Starting harder than most.

10. **ECHO** SRM-2100 **Straight shaft.**

11. **JOHN DEERE** C1200 **Curved shaft.** Can power blower and other optional tools. Adjusting front handle requires tools.

12. **JOHN DEERE** T105C **Curved shaft.** Inconvenient choke. Lighter and better balanced than most.

13. **HOMELITE** VersaTool **Curved shaft.** Can also power blower and other tools. Head rotates for edging. Tall grass wrapped around head.

14. **HOMELITE** Trim N' Edge **Curved shaft.** Starting harder than most.

15. **RYOBI** 700r **Curved shaft.**

16. **WEED EATER** FeatherLite 25 HO SST **Straight shaft.** Lighter than most. Quick-release spool. Starting harder than most. Only one cutting line.

17. **WEED EATER** FeatherLite Plus **Curved shaft.** Lighter than most. Quick-release spool. Only one cutting line.

18. **CRAFTSMAN** (Sears) Weedwacker 79514 **Curved shaft.** Lighter than most. Starting harder than most. Discontinued, but similar 79555 available.

19. **POULAN** PP031 **Curved shaft.** Only one cutting line. 1-year warranty.

CORDED MODELS

20. **RYOBI** 132r TrimmerPlus **Curved shaft.** Dual cutting lines. Motor on top, improving balance. Can also power blower and other tools.

21. **RYOBI** 105r **Curved shaft.** Dual cutting lines. Motor on top, improving balance.

22. **BLACK & DECKER** Grass Hog GH400 **Curved shaft.** Quick-release spool. Lighter than most.

23. **BLACK & DECKER** Grass Hog GH500 **Curved shaft.** Quick-release spool. Lighter than most.

24. **CRAFTSMAN** (Sears) Weedwacker 74512 **Curved shaft.** Quick-release spool. Vibrates more than most.

25. **WEED EATER** YardMaster YM 600 **Straight shaft.** Motor on top, improving balance. Quick-release spool. No cord retainer.

26. **CRAFTSMAN** (Sears) Weedwacker 74517 **Straight shaft.** Motor on top, improving balance. No cord retainer. 1-year warranty.

27. **WEED EATER** Snap 'N Go SG14 **Curved shaft.** Lighter than most. Quick-release spool.

28. **WEED EATER** XT110 **Curved shaft.** Lighter than most. Quick-release spool.

29. **WEED EATER** Snap 'N Go SG12 **Curved shaft.** Lighter than most. Quick-release spool.

30. **WEED EATER** XT112 **Curved shaft.** Lighter than most. Quick-release spool.

31. **TORO** 51353 **Curved shaft.** Lighter than most. Quick-release spool.

32. **TORO** 51301 **Curved shaft.** Lighter than most. Quick-release spool.

33. **TORO** 51332 **Curved shaft.** Lighter than most. Quick-release spool.

34. **WEED EATER** ElectraLite EL 10 Type 1 **Curved shaft.** Lighter than most. Quick-release spool.

35. **WEED EATER** ElectraLite EL8 **Curved shaft.** Lighter than most. Quick-release spool.

36. **BLACK & DECKER** ST1000 **Curved shaft.** Lighter than most. Quick-release spool.

BATTERY-POWERED MODELS

37. **RYOBI** 155r **Straight shaft.** Awkward start safety button.

38. **BLACK & DECKER** Grass Hog CST2000 **Straight shaft.** Quick-release spool. Automatic line feed. Shield contacts ground during trimming.

Telephones—cordless

Shop Smart   Most cordless phones deliver a fairly high level of voice quality. There's no reason to shy away from a 900-MHz phone. It will work just as well as a more expensive, higher-frequency phone. The Uniden EXI 376 IIS, a **CR Best Buy** at $30, is a very good analog model. If security is an issue, consider the digital Panasonic KX-TC1703B, $50. Among two-line phones, the AT&T 9312, $80, and VTech VT2931, $100, are economical choices. If you're looking for a phone with a built-in answerer, you'll find many very good choices. The AT&T 9357, $60, performed very well overall, although it failed a surge test. Several models support additional handsets.

	Excellent	Very good	Good	Fair	Poor
	⊖	⊖	○	◓	●

Overall Ratings   In performance order

KEY NO.	BRAND & MODEL	PRICE	OVERALL SCORE	VOICE QUALITY	EASE OF USE	TALK TIME
			P F G VG E			
	PHONES					
1	**Uniden** EXI 376 HS 900-MHz analog A CR Best Buy	$30		⊖	⊖	11 hr.
2	**Panasonic** KX-TC1460W 900-MHz analog	30		⊖	○	11
3	**VTech** VT2431 2.4-GHz DSS	120		⊖	⊖	13
4	**Panasonic** KX-TC1461B 900-MHz analog	35		⊖	○	11
5	**AT&T** 9312 (2-line) 900-MHz analog	80		⊖	○	12
6	**RadioShack** ET-1122 900-MHz analog	50		⊖	○	11
7	**Uniden** TRU 346 2.4-GHz DSS	130		⊖	⊖	9
8	**AT&T** 1430 2.4-GHz analog	50		⊖	⊖	17
9	**Panasonic** KX-TC1703B 900-MHz digital	50		⊖	○	9
10	**VTech** VT20-2431 (2-line) 2.4-GHz DSS	180		⊖	⊖	8
11	**Walker** W-400 900-MHz analog	80		⊖	○	5
12	**GE** 27931GE7 2.4-GHz analog	60		⊖	○	8
13	**VTech** VT2421 2.4-GHz DSS	100		⊖	⊖	9
14	**VTech** VT2428 2.4-GHz analog	50		⊖	○	14
15	**VTech** VT2931 (2-line) 900-MHz digital	100		⊖	○	9
16	**Siemens** 4010 2.4-GHz DSS	100		⊖	⊖	11
17	**Bell South** GH9404BK 2.4-GHz analog	25		⊖	○	9
18	**Bell South** MH9915BK 900-MHz analog	40		⊖	○	9

			Excellent	Very good	Good	Fair	Poor
			⊜	⊖	○	◑	●

KEY NO.	BRAND & MODEL	PRICE	OVERALL SCORE	VOICE QUALITY	EASE OF USE	TALK TIME
			P F G VG E			
PHONES WITH ANSWERERS						
19	**Panasonic** KX-TG2593B (2-line) 2.4-GHz DSS	200		⊖	⊖	5
20	**GE** 27939GE3 2.4-GHz analog	100		⊜	⊖	8
21	**VTech** VT2461 2.4-GHz DSS	140		⊖	⊖	13
22	**Panasonic** KX-TG2680N 2.4-GHz DSS	250		⊖	○	6
23	**AT&T** 2255 2.4-GHz DSS	150		⊖	⊖	8
24	**AT&T** 9357 900-MHz analog	60		⊖	⊖	11
25	**Siemens** 4215 2.4-GHz DSS	180		⊖	⊖	10
26	**VTech** VT9152 900-MHz analog	40		⊖	○	5

Overall Ratings, cont.

See report, page 137 Based on tests published in Consumer Reports in October 2002.

The tests behind the Ratings

Overall score for phones and phone-answerers is based primarily on phone voice quality, ease of use, resistance to electrical damage, privacy, and band efficiency. Except as noted, all answerers were judged very good. **Voice quality** covers talking and listening, as evaluated by trained panelists. **Ease of use** includes handset comfort, weight, talk time, setup, controls, and labeling of keys. **Talk time** tells how long you can converse, to the nearest hour, when the handset's battery has been fully charged. **Price** is approximate retail.

Recommendations & notes

All of the phones: Have a one-year warranty, flash, handset volume control, page to locate handset, 10 or more memory-dial slots, last-number redial, and low-battery indicator. Most of the phones: Can be wall-mounted and have a headset jack.

All of the answerers: Have call screening, day/time stamp, remote access from Touch-Tone phone, selectable number of rings, repeat, and skip-to next or previous message. Prevent messages and greeting from being lost after a brief power outage. Most of the answerers: Have toll-saver mode, message-counter display, and announce-only mode.

PHONES

1 **UNIDEN** EXI 376 HS 900-MHz analog **A CR Best Buy Fine performer.** Includes headset.

2 **PANASONIC** KX-TC1460W 900-MHz analog **Fine performer, but few features.** No headset jack.

3 **VTECH** VT2431 2.4-GHz DSS **Feature-laden, with small, lightweight handset.** Phone had noticeable background noise. Can work during power outage with optional battery. Can take up to 4 handsets.

4 **PANASONIC** KX-TC1461B 900-MHz analog **Fine performer.** Twice the channels of Panasonic KX-TC1460W. Few features. No headset jack.

Recommendations & notes

5▷ AT&T 9312 (2-line) 900-MHz analog **Very good overall.** Has data port for fax or modem.

6▷ RADIOSHACK ET-1122 900-MHz analog **Fine performer.** Handset ringer can't be turned off.

7▷ UNIDEN TRU 346 2.4-GHz DSS **Fine performer.** Can't be wall-mounted. Handset ringer can't be turned off. Discontinued, buy may still be available.

8▷ AT&T 1430 2.4-GHz analog **Very good overall.** Longer talk time than most. Dual-band (2.4 GHz/900 MHz).

9▷ PANASONIC KX-TC1703B 900-MHz digital **Good value in a digital model.**

10▷ VTECH VT20-2431 (2-line) 2.4-GHz DSS **Fine performer.** Small, lightweight handset. Phone had noticeable background noise. Can work during power outage with optional battery. Data port for fax or modem. Caller ID and headset jack also on base. Can't be wall-mounted. Can take up to 8 handsets.

11▷ WALKER W-400 900-MHz analog **Very good overall.** Shorter talk time than most. Requires extra button press to activate volume setting.

12▷ GE 27931GE7 2.4-GHz analog **Fine performer.** Phone had noticeable background noise.

13▷ VTECH VT2421 2.4-GHz DSS **Many features.** Small, lightweight handset. Phone had noticeable background noise. Can take up to 4 handsets.

14▷ VTECH VT2428 2.4-GHz analog **Very good overall.** Dual-band (2.4 GHz/900 MHz).

FEATURES AT A GLANCE CORDLESS PHONES

Tested products (keyed to the Ratings) Brand	Two phone lines	Caller ID	Base speaker & keypad	Handset speaker	Base ringer	Lighted keypad	Voice-mail alert	Mailboxes	Advanced playback	Remote handset access
PHONES										
1▷ Uniden		•								
2▷ Panasonic										
3▷ VTech	•	•	•	•	•	•	•			
4▷ Panasonic										
5▷ AT&T	•		•		•					
6▷ RadioShack		•								
7▷ Uniden		•					•			
8▷ AT&T		•					•			
9▷ Panasonic		•		•			•			
10▷ VTech	•	•	•	•	•	•	•			
11▷ Walker					•	•				
12▷ GE		•				•	•			
13▷ VTech		•			•		•			
14▷ VTech		•			•		•			
15▷ VTech	•	•	•		•		•			
16▷ Siemens		•					•			
17▷ Bell South										
18▷ Bell South		•					•			
PHONES WITH ANSWERERS										
19▷ Panasonic	•	•	•		•	•		1		
20▷ GE		•	•		•	•		1		
21▷ VTech		•		•	•	•	•	3	•	
22▷ Panasonic		•	•	•	•	•		1		•
23▷ AT&T		•			•		•	3	•	
24▷ AT&T		•			•			3	•	
25▷ Siemens		•		•			•	1		
26▷ VTech					•			1	•	•

Recommendations & notes

15▷ VTECH VT2931 (2-line) 900-MHz digital **Very good overall.** Caller ID also on base. Data port for fax or modem. Only 10 channels.

16▷ SIEMENS 4010 2.4-GHz DSS **Very good overall.** Phone had noticeable background noise. Failed surge test. Can't be wall-mounted. Can take up to 4 handsets.

17▷ BELL SOUTH GH9404BK 2.4-GHz analog **There are better choices.** No base ringer. Dual-band (2.4 GHz/900 MHz).

18▷ BELL SOUTH MH9915BK 900-MHz analog **There are better choices.**

PHONES WITH ANSWERERS

19▷ PANASONIC KX-TG2593B (2-line) 2.4-GHz DSS **Fine combo.** Caller ID also on base. Shorter talk time than most. Answerer setup judged more complicated than most. Easy to accidentally erase unplayed messages.

20▷ GE 27939GE3 2.4-GHz analog **Fine combo.** Caller ID also on base. Answerer doesn't play new messages first, and lacks toll-saver and announce-only modes.

21▷ VTECH VT2461 2.4-GHz DSS **Fine combo.** Small, lightweight handset. Phone had noticeable background noise. Can work during power outage with optional battery. Can take up to 4 handsets.

22▷ PANASONIC KX-TG2680N 2.4-GHz DSS **Fine, feature-laden combo.** Small, lightweight handset. Talking caller ID. Pager-call feature. Caller ID and headset jack also on base. Answerer setup judged more complicated than most. Easy to accidentally erase unplayed messages.

23▷ AT&T 2255 2.4-GHz DSS **Fine, multiple-handset combo, but message quality not as good as other tested models.** Includes second handset with charging cradle. Phone and answerer had noticeable background noise.

24▷ AT&T 9357 900-MHz analog **Fine combo.** Answerer very easy to use. Failed surge test.

25▷ SIEMENS 4215 2.4-GHz DSS **Fine phone with good answerer, but message quality not as good as other tested models.** Small, lightweight handset. Phone and answerer had noticeable background noise. Voice-activated dialing. Talking caller ID. Handset answerer. Failed surge test. Can't be wall-mounted. Lacks headset jack. Can take up to 4 handsets.

26▷ VTECH VT9152 900-MHz analog **Fine combo.** Shorter talk time than most. Answerer lacks message-counter display. Setup judged more complicated than most.

Toasters & toaster ovens

Shop Smart If you want the best toast, choose a toaster over a toaster-oven/broiler. Just about any of the toasters CONSUMER REPORTS tested would be a fine choice. A standout for value is the GE 106641, $20, **a CR Best Buy.** A notch lower, but cheaper still is the Proctor-Silex 22475, $13. If money is no object, consider the KitchenAid KTT261. For $100, it offers very good performance and a sleek, elongated design. A toaster-oven/broiler toasts adequately but is handy for many other kitchen chores. The Cuisinart TOB-175, $205, performed best and has features such as electronic touchpad controls and convection. But it's big and expensive. The Kenmore KTES8, **a CR Best Buy** at $70, is more basic but performed well.

			Excellent ⊖	Very good ⊖	Good ○	Fair ◡	Poor ●

Overall Ratings   In performance order

KEY NO.	BRAND & MODEL	PRICE	OVERALL SCORE	COLOR RANGE	FULL BATCH	EASE OF USE
			0 100 P F G VG E			
	TOASTERS					
1	**KitchenAid** KTT261	$100		⊖	⊖	⊖
2	**Philips** HD2533	30		⊖	⊖	○
3	**GE** 106641 **A CR Best Buy**	20		⊖	○	⊖
4	**West Bend** 6220	45		○	⊖	⊖
5	**Proctor-Silex** 2247[5]	13		○	○	⊖
6	**Proctor-Silex** 2220[5]	10		○	○	⊖
7	**Proctor-Silex** 2444[5]	24		○	⊖	⊖
8	**Toastmaster** T2030[W]	20		⊖	⊖	○
9	**Proctor-Silex** 2241[5]	17		◡	○	⊖
10	**Toastmaster** T2050[W]	27		⊖	⊖	○
11	**Rival** TT9264	10		○	○	○
12	**Krups** 156	45		○	○	○
	The following two models were downrated because they didn't shut off when the carriage was jammed, as is required by a new UL standard.					
13	**Sunbeam** 6225	29		⊖	⊖	⊖
14	**Oster** 6322	55		○	○	⊖
	TOASTER-OVEN/BROILERS					
15	**Cuisinart** TOB-175	205		⊖	⊖	⊖
16	**Kenmore** (Sears) KTES8 **A CR Best Buy**	70		◡	⊖	⊖
17	**Krups** F286-45	80		◡	○	⊖
18	**Black & Decker** CTO 9000	140		◡	◡	⊖

	Excellent	Very good	Good	Fair	Poor
	⊖	⊖	○	◔	●

Overall Ratings, cont.

KEY NO.	BRAND & MODEL	PRICE	OVERALL SCORE	COLOR RANGE	FULL BATCH	EASE OF USE
			0 100 P F G VG E			
TOASTER-OVEN/BROILERS						
19	**Black & Decker** TRO 5900CT	79	▬▬▬	○	⊖	⊖
20	**Black & Decker** TRO 3000	55	▬▬▬	⊖	⊖	⊖
21	**Delonghi** XU120	53	▬▬▬	⊖	○	⊖

See report, page 87. Based on tests published in Consumer Reports in December 2001, with updated prices and availability.

The tests behind the Ratings

Overall score blends performance, ease of use, and safety. **Color range** is the ability to make toast ranging from very light to dark. **Full batch** is the ability to evenly toast full batches. **Ease of use** is based on ease of setting controls. **Overall score** also reflects ability to make one slice and successive batches, plus ease of cleaning. All models were good or very good in all three areas, except as noted. Toaster-oven/broiler scores also reflect baking and broiling ability. **Price** is approximate retail. Brackets indicate a color code.

Recommendations & notes

Models listed as similar should offer performance comparable to the tested model's, although features may differ.

All toasters: Have wide slots, with "jaws" that adjust to fit item being toasted. Except as noted all have: Two slots. White, stay-cool plastic body. Hinged crumb tray. Auto shutoff if toast gets jammed. One-year warranty.

All toaster-oven/broilers: Were rated at least good for baking and broiling. Have a removable rack. Have oven pan.

Most toaster-oven broilers have: Room for four large slices of bread. A timer. Hinged crumb tray. Metal body that gets hot in use. One-position rack. Broiler-rack insert for pan. One-year warranty.

TOASTERS

1 > **KITCHENAID** KTT261 **Highest-scoring toaster tested, but you can spend far less.** Elongated one-slot design with electronic touchpad controls and digital display. Removable crumb tray. Cord wrap.

2 > **PHILIPS** HD2533 **Very good overall; excelled at making full range of shades.** Removable crumb tray with rounded edges. Cord wrap. Audible signal when toast is done. Comes with warming rack that sits atop slots. But symbols for some settings unclear. Sold only at Target.

3 > **GE** 106641 **A CR Best Buy An outstanding value.** Fewer features than some, but very good performance. Removable crumb tray. Two-year warranty. Sold only at Wal-Mart. Similar: 106691.

4 > **WEST BEND** 6220 **Very good overall.** Toast slides down onto removable crumb tray. One elongated slot. Cord wrap. Couldn't make dark English muffins; only 90-day warranty.

5 > **PROCTOR-SILEX** 2247[5] **Very good overall and inexpensive.** Two-year warranty.

6 > **PROCTOR-SILEX** 2220[5] **Inexpensive and very basic, but very good overall.** Has plastic end panels, but sides are metal and get hot in use. Two-year warranty. Similar: 22225, 22315.

Recommendations & notes

7▷ **PROCTOR-SILEX** 2444[5] **Very good perfor-mance.** Four slots. Two-year warranty. Similar: Hamilton Beach 24505, 24507, 24508.

8▷ **TOASTMASTER** T2030[W] **Inexpensive and good overall.** Removable crumb tray.

9▷ **PROCTOR-SILEX** 2241[5] **Good overall, but only fair at making full range of shades.** Removable crumb tray. Two-year warranty. Similar: Hamilton Beach 22416.

10▷ **TOASTMASTER** T2050[W] **Good overall.** Four slots. But shade dial is mostly unmarked.

11▷ **RIVAL** TT9264 **Basic, but good overall.** Similar: TT9222-W.

12▷ **KRUPS** 156 **Good overall, though only fair at making single slice (one side of bread darker).** Cord wrap.

13▷ **SUNBEAM** 6225 **Good overall, but did not shutoff when the carriage was jammed, as is required by a new UL standard.** Removable crumb tray with rounded edges. Audible signal when toast is done. Similar: 6223, 6220.

14▷ **OSTER** 6322 **Good overall, but did not shutoff when the carriage was jammed, as is required by a new UL standard.** Electronic touchpad controls and digital display. Removable crumb tray with rounded edges. Cord wrap. Audible signal when toast is done. Two-year warranty. Similar: 6320.

TOASTER-OVEN/BROILERS

15▷ **CUISINART** TOB-175 **Very good overall and feature-laden, but big and pricey.** Convection option, electronic touchpad controls, digital display, three-position rack, removable crumb tray. Three-year warranty. Similar: TOB-165, TOB-160.

16▷ **KENMORE** (Sears) KTES8 **A CR Best Buy Very good performance and value, though fewer features than some.** Two- position rack. Removable crumb tray. Cord wrap.

17▷ **KRUPS** F286-45 **Good overall, but burned bottoms of corn muffins.** Electronic touchpad controls and digital display. Rack advances when door is opened. Cord wrap.

18▷ **BLACK & DECKER** CTO 9000 **Good overall and roomy enough for six slices of bread, but poor at toasting consecutive batches.** Oven is convection only. Shuts off when door is opened. Top of oven stays cool. Removable crumb tray. Similar: CTO8[0]00.

19▷ **BLACK & DECKER** TRO **5900CT Good overall, but poor at toasting consecutive batches.** Shuts off when door is opened. Top of oven stays cool. Removable crumb tray. Similar: TRO 6000CT, TRO 6100CT.

20▷ **BLACK & DECKER** TRO 3000 **Similar in performance to more-expensive brand-mates: Good overall, but just fair at toasting consecutive batches.** Similar: TRO3200, TRO2000, TRO2100, TRO2200.

21▷ **DELONGHI** XU120 **Good overall, though just fair at making successive batches of toast.**

Vacuum cleaners

Shop Smart There are many very good choices among uprights and canisters. These days, either type does a good job on both carpeting and bare floors. High scores for carpet and floors make the upright Kenmore Progressive 31912, $380, a top pick. Among canisters, there are several very good models for under $400. Key features for these models are listed in the table on page 319. See the product guide for an explanation of features.

Ratings key: Excellent ⊖ Very good ⊖ Good ○ Fair ◒ Poor ●

Overall Ratings — In performance order

KEY NO.	BRAND & MODEL	PRICE	OVERALL SCORE	CARPET	BARE FLOOR	TOOLS	EASE OF USE	NOISE	EMISSIONS
	UPRIGHTS								
1	**Kenmore** (Sears) Progressive with Direct Drive 31912	$380	▬▬▬	⊖	⊖	⊖	⊖	○	⊖
2	**Hoover** WindTunnel Self-Propelled Ultra U6430-900	300	▬▬▬	⊖	⊖	⊖	○	◒	⊖
3	**Eureka** Boss Smart Vac 4870	150	▬▬▬	⊖	⊖	○	○	○	⊖
4	**Panasonic** Dual Sweep MC-V7515	170	▬▬▬	⊖	⊖	⊖	○	◒	⊖
5	**Kenmore** (Sears) Progressive 32612	180	▬▬▬	⊖	⊖	⊖	○	○	⊖
6	**Hoover** WindTunnel Bagless Self-Propelled U6630-900	400	▬▬▬	⊖	⊖	⊖	○	◒	⊖
7	**Hoover** WindTunnel Bagless U5720-900	200	▬▬▬	⊖	⊖	○	○	◒	⊖
8	**Eureka** Ultra Whirlwind 4885	240	▬▬▬	⊖	⊖	⊖	○	○	⊖
9	**Bissell** ProLite 3560	300	▬▬▬	⊖	⊖	NA[1]	⊖	◒	⊖
10	**Oreck** XL21-600	700	▬▬▬	◒	⊖	NA[1]	⊖	○	⊖
11	**Bissell** Power Glide Ultra 3545-5	130	▬▬▬	⊖	⊖	◒	○	◒	⊖
12	**Dirt Devil** Vision with Sensor 89900	200	▬▬▬	⊖	⊖	⊖	○	○	⊖
13	**Hoover** Bagless U5290-900	170	▬▬▬	⊖	⊖	◒	○	●	⊖
14	**Hoover** Preferred U5061-900	80	▬▬▬	⊖	⊖	○	○	●	⊖
15	**Dirt Devil** Featherlite Plus 85550	60	▬▬▬	⊖	⊖	◒	⊖	●	⊖
16	**Bissell** Lift-Off 3554	175	▬▬▬	◒	⊖	⊖	○	○	⊖
17	**Eureka** Boss Power 7685	90	▬▬▬	⊖	⊖	◒	○	●	⊖
18	**GE** 106585	130	▬▬▬	○	⊖	○	○	○	⊖
19	**Eureka** Whirlwind Plus 4686	150	▬▬▬	○	⊖	○	○	◒	⊖
20	**Sharp** Multi-Floor EC-T5180	200	▬▬▬	○	⊖	○	○	○	●

Overall Ratings, cont.

Excellent ⊖ Very good ⊖ Good ○ Fair ⊖ Poor ●

KEY NO.	BRAND & MODEL	PRICE	OVERALL SCORE	CLEANING			EASE OF USE	NOISE	EMIS-SIONS
			0 P F G VG E 100	CARPET	BARE FLOOR	TOOLS			
21	**Dirt Devil** Swivel Glide Vision 86925	$150		○	⊖	⊖	○	⊖	⊖
22	**Eureka** The Boss Power 2270	60		⊖	⊖	○	○	○	⊖
23	**Kenmore** (Sears) Quick Clean Bagless 32720	130		⊖	⊖	○	⊖	⊖	⊖
24	**Eureka** Whirlwind 4488	120		⊖	⊖	●	○	○	⊖
25	**Bissell** Cleanview Bagless 8990	100		○	⊖	○	○	●	●
	CANISTERS								
26	**Kenmore** (Sears) Progressive 22612	380		⊖	⊖	⊖	⊖	⊖	⊖
27	**Miele** Plus S251	425		○	⊖	⊖	⊖	○	⊖
28	**Eureka** Home Cleaning System 6984	240		⊖	⊖	○	⊖	⊖	⊖
29	**Samsung** Quiet Jet VAC-9048R	300		⊖	⊖	⊖	⊖	⊖	⊖
30	**Miele** Solaris Electro Plus S514	700		○	⊖	⊖	⊖	⊖	⊖
31	**Hoover** WindTunnel Plus S3639	350		⊖	⊖	⊖	⊖	⊖	⊖
32	**Oreck** DutchTech DTX1300C	900		⊖	⊖	⊖	⊖	⊖	⊖
33	**Kenmore** (Sears) Magic Blue DX 21295	180		○	⊖	○	⊖	⊖	⊖
34	**Eureka** Oxygen 6997	700		⊖	⊖	⊖	⊖	⊖	⊖
35	**Panasonic** Dirt Sensor MC-V9635	300		○	⊖	⊖	⊖	⊖	⊖
36	**Sanyo** High Power SC-800P	325		○	⊖	⊖	⊖	⊖	⊖
37	**Hoover** PowerMAX Deluxe S3607	200		⊖	⊖	○	⊖	○	●
38	**Hoover** PowerMAX Runabout S3614	200		⊖	⊖	○	⊖	⊖	●
39	**Dirt Devil** Vision 82600	180		○	⊖	⊖	⊖	○	⊖

[1] *Comes with minicanister for tool-cleaning. Minicanister tool performance was fair for #9, poor for #10.*
See report, page 111. Based on tests published in Consumer Reports in September 2002.

The tests behind the Ratings

Overall score reflects mainly cleaning performance and ease of use. **Cleaning for carpet** denotes how much embedded talc and sand was lifted from a medium-pile carpet. **Cleaning for bare floor** shows ability to removed sand from bare floor without dispersing it. **Cleaning with tools** reflects airflow through the hose. **Ease of use** denotes how easy models were to push, pull, carry, and use beneath furniture, as well as bag or bin capacity. **Noise** reflects results using a decibel meter. **Emissions** is how much wood "flour," used to simulate dust, is released while vacuuming. **Price** is approximate retail; bag/filter prices are per unit.

Recommendations & notes

Most newly tested vacuums: Have a disposable microfiltration dust bag, upholstery and crevice tools and a brush, a flexible hose at least 5 feet long, a full bag/bin alert, a foot-controlled on/off switch, a warranty of at least one year on parts and labor. Lack suction control and manual pile-height adjustment. **Most uprights:** Have a 30- to 35-foot cord with quick-release and wrap-around storage, a blower motor protected in case of jamming, overheating, or electrical overload. Lack a retractable cord and independent on/off switch for the brush. **Most canisters:** Have a 20- to 30-foot retractable power cord, a detachable power nozzle, an independent on/off switch for the rotating brush.

UPRIGHTS

1> **KENMORE** (Sears) Progressive with Direct Drive 31912 **Very good all around.** Weight: 20 lb. Bag: $4 to $5. HEPA filter: $21. Similar: 31913.

2> **HOOVER** WindTunnel Self-Propelled Ultra U6430-900 **Excelled at cleaning, but noisy.** May not fit on some stairs. Weight: 21 lb. Bag: $2. Similar: U6432-900, U6446-900, U6435-900.

3> **EUREKA** Boss Smart Vac 4870 **Excelled at most cleaning, but hard to pull.** Weight: 21 lb. Bag: $2.33. HEPA filter: $20.

4> **PANASONIC** Dual Sweep MC-V7515 **Very good, but noisy and hard to push and pull.** More stable than most on stairs. Weight: 17 lb. Bag: $1.65. HEPA filter: $12. Similar: MC-V7521.

5> **KENMORE** (Sears) Progessive 32612 **Very good, but prone to tip with hose extended.** Weight: 18 lb. Bag: $4 to $5. HEPA filter: $21. Similar: 32613, 32212, 32213.

6> **HOOVER** WindTunnel Bagless Self-Propelled U6630-900 **Very good, but noisy, heavy, and tippy on stairs.** Weight: 24 lb. HEPA filter: $20. Similar: U6660-900, U6655-900, U6625-900.

7> **HOOVER** WindTunnel Bagless U5720-900 **Excelled at most cleaning, but noisy.** Small capacity. Weight: 21 lb. HEPA filter: $30. Similar: U5720-990, U5721-900, U5750-900, U5755-900, U5757-900.

8> **EUREKA** Ultra Whirlwind 4885 **A very good bagless vac, but small capacity.** Has window to check belt. Weight: 23 lb. HEPA filter: $20. Similar: 4880.

9> **BISSELL** ProLite 3560 **Very good, but noisy and awkward to carry.** No overload protection. Price includes minicanister with hose and tools. Minicanister tool performance was fair. Weight: 9 lb. Bag: $2.

10> **ORECK** XL21-600 **Very good. Includes minicanister with hose and tools.** Minicanister tool performance was poor. No overload protection. Filter on tested model wasn't a HEPA, despite label. Weight: 11 lb. Bag: $3.

11> **BISSELL** Power Glide Ultra 3545-5 **Very good, but tippy with hose extended.** Weight: 15 lb. Bag: $5. Filter: $3 (plain), $8 and $10 (upgrades).

12> **DIRT DEVIL** Vision with Sensor 89900 **A good bagless vac, but noisy.** No overload protection. Weight: 20 lb. HEPA filter: $25. Similar: 89800.

13> **HOOVER** Bagless U5290-900 **Good, but noisy.** Manual pile-height adjustment. No brush switch or overload protection. Inconvenient on/off switch. Cord shorter than most. Weight: 18 lb. HEPA filter: $30. Similar: U5296-900, U5298-900, U5280-940.

14> **HOOVER** Preferred U5061-900 **Good and inexpensive, but very noisy and tippy on stairs.** Hard to push and pull. Few tools. Short hose and cord. Weight: 15 lb. Bag: $2. Similar: U5064-94, U5046-930.

Recommendations & notes

15▷ **DIRT DEVIL** Featherlite Plus 85550 **Good, but noisy.** No full-bag alert, overload protection, or upholstery tool. Hose and cord shorter than most. Weight: 13 lb. Standard bag: $1. Microfilter bag: $3.30. Discontinued, but similar 85560 is available.

16▷ **BISSELL** Lift-Off 3554 **Fine for most cleaning, but not carpets.** Tippy with hose extended. Weight: 19 lb. Bag: $9. Filter: $15.

17▷ **EUREKA** Boss Power 7685 **Good and inexpensive, but very noisy.** Large capacity. Short hose and cord. Weight: 15 lb. Bag: $2.

18▷ **GE** 106585 **A good bagless vac, but small capacity and poor furniture clearance.** Sold only at Wal-Mart. Weight: 18 lb. HEPA filter: $16.

19▷ **EUREKA** Whirlwind Plus 4686 **A good bagless vac.** Tippy on stairs and with hose extended. Weight: 20 lb. HEPA filter: $20. Similar: 4684, 4680, 4689.

20▷ **SHARP** Multi-Floor EC-T5180 **Good, but high emissions.** Suction control. Independent brush on/off switch. Hose longer than most.

FEATURES AT A GLANCE VACUUMS

Key no.	Brand	Bag-equipped	Brush on/off switch	Cord retract	Easy on/off switch	Full bag/bin alert	Manual pile adjust	Suction control
	UPRIGHTS							
1	**Kenmore**	•	•		•	•	•	
2	**Hoover**	•	•		•	•	•	
3	**Eureka**	•	•					
4	**Panasonic**	•	•		•			
5	**Kenmore**	•	•		•	•	•	•
6	**Hoover**	•	•		•	•	•	
7	**Hoover**				•	•	•	
8	**Eureka**		•		•	•	•	
9	**Bissell**	•						
10	**Oreck**	•						
11	**Bissell**	•				•		
12	**Dirt Devil**		•			•	•	
13	**Hoover**					•	•	
14	**Hoover**	•				•	•	
15	**Dirt Devil**	•			•	•		
16	**Bissell**	•	•					
17	**Eureka**	•					•	
18	**GE**					•	•	
19	**Eureka**				•	•	•	

Key no.	Brand	Bag-equipped	Brush on/off switch	Cord retract	Easy on/off switch	Full bag/bin alert	Manual pile adjust	Suction control
20	**Sharp**		•		•	•		
21	**Dirt Devil**					•	•	
22	**Eureka**	•			•			
23	**Kenmore**		•		•	•		
24	**Eureka**		•		•	•		
25	**Bissell**					•	•	
	CANISTERS							
26	**Kenmore**	•	•	•	•	•	•	
27	**Miele**	•	•	•	•	•	•	
28	**Eureka**	•	•	•	•	•	•	
29	**Samsung**	•	•	•	•	•	•	
30	**Miele**	•	•	•	•	•	•	
31	**Hoover**	•	•	•	•	•	•	
32	**Oreck**	•	•	•	•	•	•	
33	**Kenmore**	•	•	•	•	•	•	
34	**Eureka**	•	•	•	•	•	•	
35	**Panasonic**	•	•	•	•	•	•	
36	**Sanyo**	•	•	•	•	•	•	
37	**Hoover**	•	•	•	•	•	•	
38	**Hoover**	•	•	•	•	•	•	
39	**Dirt Devil**		•	•	•	•	•	

Recommendations & notes

Tippy on stairs and with hose extended. Cumbersome power-head release. No upholstery tool. Weight: 17 lb. Main foam filter: $7. HEPA filter: $10.

21> **DIRT DEVIL** Swivel Glide Vision 86925 **Good, but tippy on stairs.** Weight: 14 lb. Bag: $1.

22> **EUREKA** The Boss Power 2270 **Good.** Hose longer than most. Cord shorter than most. No full-bag alert. Weight: 17 lb. Bag: $1.30. Motor filter: $2. Exhaust filter: $3. Similar: 2271.

23> **KENMORE** (Sears) Quick Clean Bagless 32720 **There are better choices.** Manual pile-height adjustment. Tippy on stairs and with hose extended. Hose and cord shorter than most. No upholstery tool. Weight: 16 lb. Tower filter: $20. Exhaust filter: $14. Similar: 32721.

24> **EUREKA** Whirlwind 4480 **There are better choices.** Tippy on stairs. Poor furniture clearance. Small capacity. Bagless. Weight: 19 lb. Filter: $20. Similar: 4489.

25> **BISSELL** Cleanview Bagless 8990 **There are better choices.** Manual pile-height adjustment. High emissions. Noisy. Tippy on stairs and with hose extended. Inconvenient on/off switch. No upholstery tool. Cord shorter than most. Weight: 16 lb. Upper-tank filter: $4. Premotor filter: $1.50. Postmotor filter: $3. Similar: 3590.

CANISTERS

26> **KENMORE** (Sears) Progressive 221612 **Very good, but noisy and heavy.** Longer hose than most. Weight: 24 lb. Bag: $4. HEPA filter: $21. Similar: 22813, 22812, 22613.

27> **MIELE** Plus S251 **Very good, and relatively quiet and compact.** Less bulky and heavy than most canisters. Suction control. Cord shorter than most. Weight: 20 lb. Bag: $2.60.

28> **EUREKA** Home Cleaning System 6984 **Very good, but Eureka canisters have been among the more trouble-prone vacuum brands.** Hose longer than most. Suction control. Manual pile-height adjustment. Cord shorter than most. Weight: 23 lb. Bag: $1.70. HEPA filter: $20. Similar: 6983.

29> **SAMSUNG** Quiet Jet VAC-9048R **Very good, and quieter than most, but hard to push.** No overload protection. Weight: 22 lb. Bag: $2. Similar: 9069G.

30> **MIELE** Solaris Electro Plus S514 **Very good, but hard to push and pull.** Short cord and hose. Price includes power nozzle. Weight: 21 lb. Filters and 5-bag set: $12.

31> **HOOVER** WindTunnel Plus S3639 **A very good, well-rounded vac.** Weight: 22 lb. Bag: $2.

32> **ORECK** DutchTech DTX 1300C **Very good, but hard to push and pull.** Quieter than most. Weight: 20 lb. Bag: $2.79. HEPA filter: $40.

33> **KENMORE** (Sears) Magic Blue DX 21295 **Very good and compact, but small capacity.** Short cord. Weight: 18 lb. Bag: $1.23.

34> **EUREKA** Oxygen 6997 **Very good, but among the more trouble-prone canister brands.** Long hose, but small capacity and short cord. Weight: 22 lb. Bag: $2. HEPA filter (washable): $30.

Wall ovens

Shop Smart   The wall ovens tested performed well and were convenient to use. The Frigidaire Gallery GLEB30S8A, though slightly smaller inside than most, is a relative bargain at $700, and it is **a CR Best Buy**. The top-rated Thermador SC301T, $1,600, is a capacious model that baked very well and broiled excellently. Any of the top seven in our Ratings are very good, though pricey choices.

Overall Ratings In performance order			Excellent ⊖	Very good ⊖	Good ○	Fair ⊖	Poor ●
KEY NO	**BRAND & MODEL**	**PRICE**	**OVERALL SCORE**			**BAKE**	**BROIL**
			0 P F G VG E	100			
	ELECTRIC CONVECTION WALL OVENS						
1	**Thermador** SC301T[W]	$1,600	▬▬▬▬			⊖	⊖
2	**Jenn-Air** JJW9530BA[W]	1,380	▬▬▬▬			⊖	⊖
3	**Dacor** PCS130[R]	1,700	▬▬▬▬			⊖	⊖
4	**GE** Profile JTP18WD[WW]	1,300	▬▬▬▬			⊖	⊖
5	**Kenmore** (Sears) Elite 4902[2]	1,450	▬▬▬▬			⊖	⊖
6	**Frigidaire** Gallery GLEB30S8A[S] **A CR Best Buy**	700	▬▬▬▬			⊖	○
7	**KitchenAid** Superba KEBC107K[WH]	1,500	▬▬▬▬			⊖	⊖
8	**Whirlpool** Gold GBS307PD[Q]	1,180	▬▬▬▬			⊖	⊖
9	**Viking** DESO100-[SS]	2,150	▬▬▬▬			○	⊖

See report, page 79. Based on tests published in Consumer Reports in August 2002.

The tests behind the Ratings

Under **brand & model,** brackets show a tested model's color code. **Overall score** includes oven capacity, baking, broiling, and self-cleaning. **Bake** shows baking evenness for cakes and cookies. **Broil** shows cooking and searing evenness for a tray of burgers. **Price** is approximate retail.

Recommendations & notes

Similar models have the same burners or elements, oven, and broiler; other details may differ.

1 ▷ THERMADOR SC301T[W] **Excellent window view.** Larger capacity than most. Two timers. No temperature probe. Similar: SC301Z[ ].

2 ▷ JENN-AIR JJW9530BA[W] **Excellent window view.** Excellent at self-cleaning, and door and window not as hot as others in this mode. Two timers. Offset shelf. Four rack positions. One oven light. Warranties: 2-yr. on parts; 5 yr. on controls, element. Discontinued, but similar nonconvection oven JJW8530CA[ ] is available.

3 ▷ DACOR PCS130[R] **Excellent window view.** Two timers. Needs 30-amp circuit. 2-yr. warranty.

4 ▷ GE Profile JTP18WD[WW] **Excellent window view.** Auto shutoff. Covered bottom element, removable floor. Rack for broiling pan. One oven light.

5 ▷ KENMORE (Sears) Elite 4902[2] **Excellent window view.** Auto shutoff. Covered bottom element, removable floor. But no temperature probe.

6 ▷ FRIGIDAIRE Gallery GLEB30S8A[S] **A CR Best Buy Smaller capacity than most.** Excellent window view. Excellent at self-cleaning. Offset shelf. Rack for broiling pan. Four rack positions. One oven light. No temperature probe. Similar: PLEB30S8A[ ], FEB30S5A[ ].

7 ▷ KITCHENAID Superba KEBC107K[WH] **Larger capacity than most.** Covered bottom element. Convection broil. Rack for broiling pan. But needs 30-amp circuit. Warranty: 5-yr. limited.

8 ▷ WHIRLPOOL Gold GBS307PD[Q] **Larger capacity than most.** Rack for broiling pan. Two rack positions. Needs 30-amp circuit. Similar: RBS305PD[ ].

9 ▷ VIKING DESO100-[SS] **Knobs for controls.** Convection-broil, defrost, convection-defrost modes. But no temperature display or probe. No child lockout. Manual light switch. Needs 40-amp circuit. Stainless steel. Least effective at self-cleaning. Warranties: 5-yr. on element; 10-yr. on rust-through. Similar: VES0105[ ].

Washing machines

Shop Smart — Most machines do a fine job of washing. Top-loaders use the most energy and water, but typically cost less. Two high-priced but excellent top-loaders are the Kenmore Elite Calypso 2206, $1,100, and the Whirlpool Calypso GVW9959K, $1,250. You can get excellent performance for less money with the Maytag Performa PAV2300A, a **CR Best Buy** at $390, but you will sacrifice some water and energy efficiency. Front-loaders are efficient and quiet, but they usually cost more. If money is no object, consider the top four models, excellent choices for $1,000 and up. Less expensive and very good alternatives: the Kenmore, Frigidaire, and GE models priced at $750 to $800. Key features for these models are listed in the table. See the product guide for an explanation of the features.

Overall Ratings   In performance order

Excellent ⊖ Very good ⊖ Good ○ Fair ◒ Poor ●

KEY NO.	BRAND & MODEL	PRICE	OVERALL SCORE	WASHING	EFFICIENCY ENERGY	EFFICIENCY WATER	CAPACITY	NOISE
			0 — 100 P F G VG E				
TOP-LOADERS								
1	**Kenmore** (Sears) Elite Calypso 2206[2]	$1,100		⊖	⊖	⊖	⊖	⊖
2	**Whirlpool** Calypso GVW9959K[Q]	1,250		⊖	⊖	⊖	⊖	⊖
3	**Fisher & Paykel** GWL10 US	700		⊖	⊖	◒	○	⊖
4	**Kenmore** (Sears) Elite Catalyst 2203[2]	920		⊖	◒	○	⊖	⊖
5	**Whirlpool** Catalyst GSX9885J[Q]	800		⊖	○	○	⊖	⊖
6	**GE** Profile WHSB9000B[WW]	600		⊖	◒	○	⊖	◒
7	**Maytag** Performa PAV2300A[WW] **A CR Best Buy**	390		⊖	○	○	⊖	○
8	**Frigidaire** Gallery GLWS1749A[S]	450		⊖	◒	◒	○	⊖
9	**Kenmore** (Sears) 2381[2]	460		⊖	◒	○	⊖	⊖
10	**Kenmore** (Sears) Elite 2303[2]	590		⊖	◒	○	⊖	⊖
11	**Maytag** Performa PAV5000A[WW]	500		⊖	◒	○	⊖	◒
12	**GE** Profile Performance WPSE7003A[WW]	800		⊖	⊖	◒	○	⊖
13	**Hotpoint** VWSR4150B[WW]	370		⊖	◒	◒	⊖	◒
14	**Amana** ALW480DA[W]	530		⊖	◒	○	⊖	◒
15	**Amana** ALW895SA[W]	650		⊖	○	○	⊖	◒
16	**GE** WWSE6260B[WW]	450		⊖	◒	○	○	◒
17	**KitchenAid** Superba KAWS850J[Q]	480		⊖	◒	○	⊖	◒
18	**Maytag** Performa LAT3500A[AE]	450		⊖	◒	○	◒	○
19	**Haier** XQJ100-96	500		⊖	◒	○	○	○

Overall Ratings, cont.

Excellent ⊖ Very good ⊖ Good ○ Fair ◑ Poor ●

KEY NO.	BRAND & MODEL	PRICE	OVERALL SCORE	WASHING	EFFICIENCY		CAPACITY	NOISE
					ENERGY	WATER		
	FRONT-LOADERS							
20	**Kenmore** (Sears) Elite 4292[2] HE3t	$1,450		⊖	⊖	⊖	⊖	⊖
21	**Whirlpool** Duet HT GHW9200L[W]	1,300		⊖	⊖	⊖	⊖	⊖
22	**Kenmore** (Sears) Elite 4282[2] HE3	1,100		⊖	⊖	⊖	⊖	⊖
23	**Whirlpool** Duet GHW9100L[Q]	1,000		⊖	⊖	⊖	⊖	⊖
24	**Maytag** Neptune MAH7500A[WW]	1,300		⊖	⊖	⊖	○	⊖
25	**Kenmore** (Sears) 4204[2]	800		⊖	⊖	⊖	⊖	⊖
26	**Frigidaire** Gallery GLTR1670A[S]	750		⊖	⊖	⊖	○	⊖
27	**GE** Profile WPXH214A[WW]	750		⊖	⊖	⊖	○	⊖

See report, page 88. Based on tests published in Consumer Reports in July 2002, with updated prices and availability.

The tests behind the Ratings

In **brand & model,** the bracketed letter or number is a color code. **Overall score** is based primarily on washing ability, efficiency, capacity, and noise; gentleness and ease of use also figure in. For **washing,** machines were loaded with 8 pounds of cotton items, run on their most aggressive cycle, and judged on soil removed from test items. **Energy efficiency** is based on electricity needed to run the washer, energy needed to heat the water for a warm wash, and amount of water extracted (since that reduces drying time). **Water efficiency** denotes how much water per pound of clothing it took to wash an 8-pound load and each model's maximum load. **Capacity** denotes how large a load each machine could wash effectively. **Noise** reflects judgments by panelists. **Price** is approximate retail.

Recommendations & notes

TOP-LOADERS

1> **KENMORE** (Sears) Elite Calypso 2206[2] **An excellent, efficient washer without usual agitator.** Especially large capacity, gentle on clothes, and quiet.

2> **WHIRLPOOL** Calypso GVW9959K[Q] **Much like #1; some minor differences.**

3> **FISHER & PAYKEL** GWL10 US **A well-equipped machine that was the most energy efficient in this category.**

4> **KENMORE** (Sears) Elite Catalyst 2203[2] **Fully featured, with numerous wash/spin speed combinations.** Similar: 2205[ ], 2204[ ].

5> **WHIRLPOOL** Catalyst GSX9885J[Q] **A very good performer with lots of features.**

6> **GE** Profile WHSB9000B[WW] **A very good performer.**

7> **MAYTAG** Performa PAV2300A[WW] **A CR Best Buy Strong performance for the price.** But fewer features than most. Similar: PAV3300A[ ].

Recommendations & notes

8 > FRIGIDAIRE Gallery GLWS1749A[S] **Good.**

9 > KENMORE (Sears) 2381[2] **Good basic machine.** Numerous wash/spin speed combinations. But only fair at handling unbalanced loads, and fewer features than most. Similar: 2383[ ], 2382[ ].

10 > KENMORE (Sears) Elite 2303[2] **Good.** Numerous wash/spin speed combinations. But fewer features than most.

11 > MAYTAG Performa PAV5000A[WW] **Numerous wash/spin speed combinations.** But only fair at handling unbalanced loads. Similar: PAV5157[ ], PAV5158[ ].

12 > GE Profile Performance WPSE7003A[WW] **A good performer.**

13 > HOTPOINT VWSR4150B[WW] **Excellent washing.** Lots of features. But less gentle than most.

14 > AMANA ALW480DA[W] **A good performer.** Similar: ALW540RA[ ], ALW432RA[ ].

15 > AMANA ALW895SA[W] **Good.** Numerous wash/spin speed combinations. But only fair capacity.

16 > GE WWSE6260B[WW] **Good.** Numerous wash/spin speed combinations. Similar: WWSE5200B[ ].

17 > KITCHENAID Superba KAWS850J[Q] **Good.** But less gentle than most.

18 > MAYTAG Performa LAT3500A[AE] **There are better choices.** Similar: LAT2300A[ ], LAT2500A[ ].

19 > HAIER XQJ100-96 **There are better choices.** Being phased out; may be hard to find in stores.

FEATURES AT A GLANCE WASHING MACHINES

Tested products (keyed to the Ratings) Key Brand No.	Auto. dispensers	Auto. temp. control	End-of-cycle signal	Porcelain top and lid	Stainless-steel tub	Touchpad controls	Two-direction dials	Cycle time (in min.)
TOP-LOADERS								
1 > Kenmore	•	•	•	•	•	•	•	70
2 > Whirlpool	•	•	•	•	•	•	•	65
3 > Fisher & Paykel		•	•		•	•		50
4 > Kenmore	•	•	•	•		•	•	50
5 > Whirlpool	•	•	•	•		•		50
6 > GE		•	•				•	45
7 > Maytag								50
8 > Frigidaire		•	•					50
9 > Kenmore								40
10 > Kenmore		•						45
11 > Maytag		•	•					50
12 > GE		•	•			•		10
13 > Hotpoint								45
14 > Amana				•			•	40
15 > Amana		•			•		•	55
16 > GE		•						45
17 > KitchenAid		•	•	•				45
18 > Maytag			•					45
19 > Haier					•			50
FRONT-LOADERS								
20 > Kenmore	•	•	•		•	•		70
21 > Whirlpool	•	•	•		•	•		60
22 > Kenmore	•	•	•		•	•		70
23 > Whirlpool	•		•		•	•	•	70
24 > Maytag	•	•	•		•	•		75
25 > Kenmore	•	•	•		•	•		60
26 > Frigidaire	•	•	•		•			60
27 > GE	•	•	•		•			55

Recommendations & notes

FRONT-LOADERS

20▷ KENMORE (Sears) Elite 4292[2] HE3t **Top performance, at a top price.** Exceptional capacity: 20 lb. Similar: 4293[ ] HE3t.

21▷ WHIRLPOOL Duet HT GHW9200L[W] **Strong performer with handy two-direction dial controls.** Exceptional capacity: 20 lb.

22▷ KENMORE (Sears) Elite 4282[2] HE3 **Excellent overall.** Exceptional capacity: 20 lb.

23▷ WHIRLPOOL Duet GHW9100L[Q] **Much like #21; some minor differences.** Exceptional capacity: 20 lb.

24▷ MAYTAG Neptune MAH7500A[WW] **Strong performer.** But Maytag front-loaders have been the least reliable brand.

25▷ KENMORE (Sears) 4204[2] **Strong performer.** Similar: 4214[ ], 4205[ ].

26▷ FRIGIDAIRE Gallery GLTR1670A[S] **A very good machine.** Similar: GLTF1670A[ ].GE Profile WPXH214A[WW] Much like #25; some minor differences.

27▷ GE Profile WPXH214A[WW] **Much like #25; some minor differences.**

When space is tight

Sometimes you just don't have room to fit a full-sized washer and dryer side by side. In such tight quarters, a compact stackable duo might be the answer. When stacked, these pairs are about 5½ feet tall and less than 2 feet wide, enabling them to fit into a closet. However, their compact size limits their capacity to only 8 pounds or so–a little more than half that of a full-sized machine. Aside from that, you can expect decent performance. Before buying any stacked pair, measure your floor space; some are wider and/or deeper than a typical stand-alone washer or dryer. Keep in mind that electric dryers usually require 240 volts. The models we tried in our labs did a fine job with washing and drying. Here are some specifics:

• The Miele Novotronic W1926A washer, $1,700, and T1526A dryer, $1,400, are top performers. Among other things, the high price gets you a stainless-steel drum on the dryer, porcelain tops on both pieces, and excellent efficiency. But washes take longer than most (95 minutes), and the dryer is somewhat noisy.

• The Bosch WFK2401UC washer, $970, and WTZ3500UC dryer, $650, are also noteworthy. The washer is quiet and efficient. The dryer has a stainless-steel drum but is noisy.

• The GE Spacemaker WSLS1100A washer, $530, and DSKS433EB dryer, $390, performed well and were relatively quiet. The water efficiency was poor, though, and the dryer has no moisture sensor.

FINDING RELIABLE BRANDS

BRAND REPAIR HISTORIES FOR HOUSEHOLD PRODUCTS

In general, products today are pretty reliable. But CONSUMER REPORTS surveys have found that some brands are more reliable than others. By buying the brands that have been the most reliable, you can improve your chances of getting a less repair-prone product. We know about trends in product reliability because every year, CONSUMER REPORTS asks its readers to report on repairs and problems they encounter with household products. From responses to the Annual Questionnaire, we are able to derive the percentage of each brand's products that have been repaired or suffered a serious problem.

Some product categories are more repair-prone than others, as the chart on page 314 shows. Desktop computers top the list—nearly half have needed repair in their first five years. Other products that have a relatively high number of problems are self-propelled lawn mowers and lawn

tractors—largely mechanical devices that require a lot of maintenance.

Products with complicated mechanisms typically need more repairs than simpler devices. Gas ranges break down more than electric ranges. Self-propelled mowers fail nearly twice as often as push models. The presence of an icemaker or a water dispenser in a refrigerator increases the chances of needing a repair.

These reliability findings can shed light on the dilemma that you face when a product breaks. Should you fix it or replace it? Two factors conspire to make obtaining repairs difficult. Prices are plummeting for many products, notably electronics and computers, often making repair the more expensive option. Also, repairs may be harder to obtain—parts and repairers may be scarce, their fees are high, and repair times are long.

Many people decide to get a model with

new features when a product breaks. And you can sometimes get a lot more for less. Electronics products are the best example. For instance, a typical 27-inch TV set currently costs about $400 and has more features than did TVs that cost $560 five years ago. With appliances, you might reap cost savings due to newer models' greater efficiency. Appliances have greatly improved efficiency over the years, especially refrigerators and washers. The most frugal cost the most, but they can save enough in energy over the long term to make replacing a broken older model a smarter option than repairing it.

➤ IF YOU REPAIR IT

Here's a way to assess whether or not to repair something. Consider its original cost, repair cost, and the technology velocity—the speed of improvement and innovation. Thus replacing a broken product may be worthwhile if a new model brings major new technology and if the cost of repair is high. With many electronic products, a repair often involves replacing an entire circuit board—a costly proposition. Complexity and proprietary parts can be a disincentive to fixing a laptop computer, for example.

You should probably fix nearly anything in its first year—especially if it's under warranty. Items such as pro-style ranges, lawn tractors, and projection TVs are usually worth repairing long into their lives because new ones are so expensive. Otherwise consider replacing products if their repair cost exceeds 50 percent of replacement.

When something breaks, a few simple steps can help make the repair process easier. First, determine if you can fix it yourself. Most owners' manuals have a troubleshooting section, and manufacturers' web sites sometimes include repair instructions. The Help for Problem PCs guide in the computers section of our web site ConsumerReports.org has a set of self-help tips, plus steps to take to get PC manufacturers and retailers to correct a problem quickly. Other helpful sites include:

• *www.pcappliancerepair.com.* Provides solutions to common problems and free help with diagnosing trickier ones. Step-by-step instructions help you find and identify parts as well as buy do-it-yourself repair manuals.

• *www.repairclinic.com.* Primarily a source for appliance parts—available overnight if needed. The site covers nearly 90 brands and includes troubleshooting hints, care tips, and a "RepairGuru" you can query via e-mail.

• *www.livemanuals.com.* This site includes simulations of how appliances and electronics equipment work, along with lists of manufacturers' addresses, phone numbers, and web links. Some of these web links allow you to e-mail the manufacturer for help with diagnosing and repairing a problem.

If the item is still not working, you may have to call the manufacturer. This can be frustrating: In a recent survey, about one quarter of those who tried had difficulty getting through, and almost half found the assistance wanting. Persistence can sometimes pay: Nearly 10 percent of those who tried to call the manufacturer got an offer to fix or replace an out-of-warranty item for free.

Manufacturers generally train authorized service technicians on the latest equipment and hold them to certain standards. Independent repairers can be a viable choice, especially for products out of warranty. Ask if the repairer belongs to a trade association such as the Professional Service Association or the International Society of Certified Electronics Technicians

Which products are most likely to need repair?

The chart below shows the percentage of five-year-old products with and without warranty that have ever been repaired or had a serious problem. (The charts on the following pages cover products from one to five years old, some still under warranty.) Gas ranges have more breakdowns than electric ranges, for example, while self-propelled mowers fail nearly twice as often as push models. Also listed are brands that have been among the more repair-prone over the past few years.

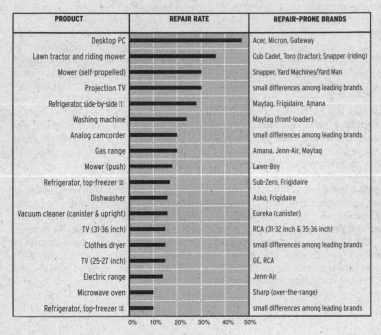

PRODUCT	REPAIR RATE	REPAIR-PRONE BRANDS
Desktop PC		Acer, Micron, Gateway
Lawn tractor and riding mower		Cub Cadet, Toro (tractor); Snapper (riding)
Mower (self-propelled)		Snapper, Yard Machines/Yard Man
Projection TV		small differences among leading brands
Refrigerator, side-by-side [1]		Maytag, Frigidaire, Amana
Washing machine		Maytag (front-loader)
Analog camcorder		small differences among leading brands
Gas range		Amana, Jenn-Air, Maytag
Mower (push)		Lawn-Boy
Refrigerator, top-freezer [2]		Sub-Zero, Frigidaire
Dishwasher		Asko, Frigidaire
Vacuum cleaner (canister & upright)		Eureka (canister)
TV (31-36 inch)		RCA (31-32 inch & 35-36 inch)
Clothes dryer		small differences among leading brands
TV (25-27 inch)		GE, RCA
Electric range		Jenn-Air
Microwave oven		Sharp (over-the-range)
Refrigerator, top-freezer [3]		small differences among leading brands

0%   10%   20%   30%   40%   50%

Source: Consumer Reports 2001 Annual Questionnaire

[1] with icemaker and dispenser
[2] with icemaker
[3] no icemaker

(ISCET), both of which cover appliance and electronics repairs. While membership doesn't guarantee integrity, it may mean repairers have had special training, as they must with ISCET.

If you feel victimized by a repairer, you can file a complaint with your local community affairs department, the Better Business Bureau *(www.bbb.org)*, or your state's attorney general's office. You can also take the repairer to small-claims court. Keep all receipts and records. And ask to keep any parts that are replaced.

➤ IF YOU TOSS IT

Disposing of broken products may make economic sense for the individual consumer, but the environmental costs for communities include burdening landfills and the risk that hazardous materials will enter the waste stream. Examples of dangerous waste include lead in circuit boards and picture tubes; mercury in laptops and digital cameras; and cadmium in some rechargeable batteries. Electronics products pose a particular challenge, since only about 15 percent of them are recycled.

While most municipalities recycle "white goods" such as refrigerators and washing machines, proper disposal of electronics is not standard practice. Some manufacturers offer options, though they're rarely free. IBM and Hewlett-Packard, for example, will ship any maker's PC and peripherals to a recycler for a fee, which covers shipping. Gateway will pay up to $50 for proof that you took a used PC to a reclamation center. Some web sites provide recycling information. Among them:

- *www.iaer.org* (International Association of Electronics Recyclers). Features a searchable database in which you can look up the address of the nearest recyclers of computers, large-screen TV sets, cellular phones, and other electronics products.

- *www.eiae.org* (Electronic Industries Alliance). Connects you with charities, needy schools, neighborhood "demanufacturers," and recycling programs that collect electronics products.

- *www.recycle-steel.org/database/main.html* (the Steel Alliance Steel Recycling Institute). Helps you track down local appliance recyclers through its searchable database of 30,000 listings.

- *www.rbrc.org* (Rechargeable Battery Recycling Corp.) Working with leading retailers, this nonprofit organization has implemented a nationwide recycling program for all types of rechargeable batteries. You can return worn-out batteries at BellSouth, CellularOne, Circuit City, RadioShack, Sears, Target, and Wal-Mart, among others.

BRAND REPAIR HISTORIES

To help you gauge reliability, the graphs that follow give brand repair rates for 26 product categories. CONSUMER REPORTS has been asking about brands' reliability for more than 30 years. The findings have been quite consistent, though they are not infallible predictors. A brand's repair history includes data on many models, some of which may have been more or less reliable than others. And surveys of past products can't anticipate design or manufacturing changes in new products.

Product categories include appliances such as refrigerators and vacuum cleaners, electronic products such as TV sets, cam-corders, and computers, as well as lawn mowers and tractors, and desktop computers. Histories for different kinds of products aren't directly comparable because they cover products of different ages, and older products tend to break more often than newer ones. In addition to the guidance provided by our survey, CONSUMER REPORTS engineers have noted the kinds of problems likely to occur.

Because the quality of technical support may be the deciding factor when you're shopping for a desktop computer, we include a recent assessment of PC manufacturers' technical support as well.

Camcorders Compact analog models

Camcorders are used only about 12 hours per year, which may influence their repair rate. Things that go wrong include temporary problems caused by moisture condensation or clogged heads and more serious problems involving the motors or loading mechanism. Digital models are too new for us to give brand histories, but overall, digital models purchased within the past two years seem to have been about as reliable as analog models. Differences of 3 or more points are meaningful.

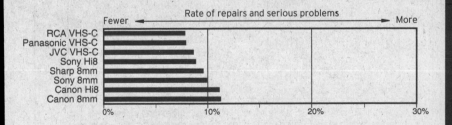

Based on more than 35,000 responses on compact analog camcorders purchased in 1996 to 2001. Data have been standardized to eliminate differences between brands due to age and usage.

Computers Desktop models

Computers are the most repair-prone products that we ask about. Things that go wrong include problems with the CD-ROM drive, system board, or monitor. Differences of 5 or more points are meaningful.

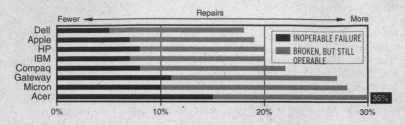

Based on more than 35,000 responses on desktop models purchased between 1997 and the first four months of 2001. Data have been standardized to eliminate differences between brands due to age and usage.

Computer tech support

Overall, just over 40 percent of the people who used a computer manufacturer's technical support were highly satisfied with the service, in a recent CONSUMER REPORTS survey based on experiences from January 2001 to May 2002. That's lower than most other service industries CONSUMER REPORTS measures. One in three who tried phoning had a problem getting through to the company.

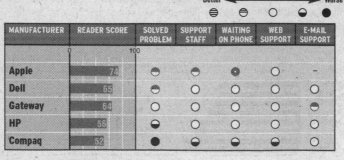

Based on more than 4,600 responses from subscribers to ConsumerReports.org surveyed in May 2002. Results refer to computers purchased since 1998. If everyone were completely satisfied, the **reader score** would be 100; 80 very satisfied on average; 60, very well satisfied. **Solved problem** indicates how many respondents said the manufacturer solved the problem. **Support staff** represents how many said the staff on the phone seemed knowledgeable. **Waiting on phone** indicates whether respondents waited on hold too long or had other problems. **Web and e-mail support** indicate whether respondents had problems with those avenues of contact. A dash (–) means insufficient data.

Dishwashers

Asko and Frigidaire were the most repair-prone brands. In general, things that go wrong include door-lock assembly problems, excessive water in unit (pump assembly), and no water or overflow (water valve). Differences of 4 or more points are meaningful.

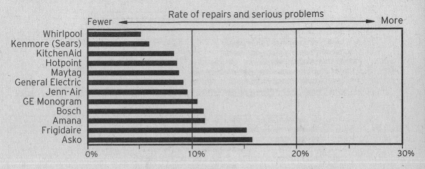

Based on more than 108,000 responses on built-in dishwashers purchased in 1996 to 2001. Data have been standardized to eliminate differences between brands due to age and usage.

Dryers

Clothes dryers are simpler machines than washers. Gas and electric models have been equally reliable. Things that go wrong include motor failure, problems with the igniter or heating element causing the dryer not to heat, and problems with rollers or belts. Differences of 4 or more points are meaningful.

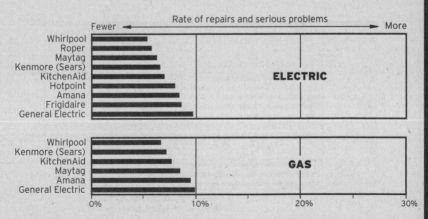

Based on nearly 95,000 responses on gas and electric dryers purchased in 1996 to 2001. Data have been standardized to eliminate differences between brands due to age and usage.

Lawn mowers Push and self-propelled

Push models have been generally more reliable than self-propelled ones because they're less complex. Things that go wrong include problems with starting, cables, controls, wheels, belts and drive systems. We don't have sufficient data to give reliability for electric models. Differences of 4 or more points are meaningful.

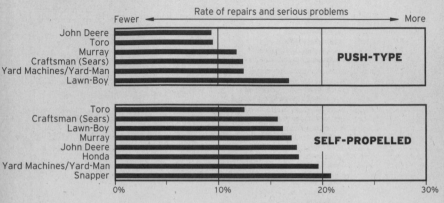

Based on more than 49,000 responses on push and self-propelled mowers purchased in 1997 to 2001. Data have been standardized to eliminate differences between brands due to age and usage.

Lawn tractors and riding mowers

These products, which have many moving parts, have typically been very repair-prone. Things that go wrong include problems with starting, batteries, cables, controls, pulleys, belts, and drivetrain. Differences of 6 or more points are meaningful.

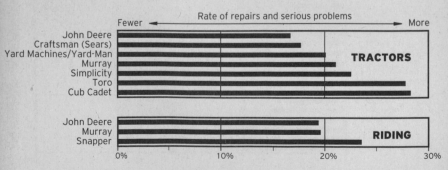

Based on more than 17,000 responses on lawn tractors and riding mowers purchased in 1997 to 2001. Data have been standardized to eliminate differences between brands due to age and usage.

Microwave ovens

Microwave ovens have historically shown low repair rates. A simple failure to operate can be caused by a power surge. (Restart by unplugging and plugging back in.) Differences of 4 or more points are meaningful.

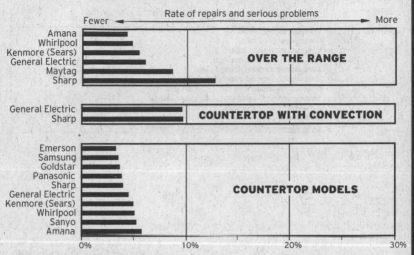

Based on more than 89,000 responses on microwave ovens or combination microwave/convection ovens purchased in 1997 to 2001. Data have been standardized to eliminate differences between brands due to age and usage.

Ranges Electric models

In general, electric ranges have required fewer repairs than gas ranges. Smoothtop models have been about as reliable as conventional coil-burner models. Things that do go wrong include failed heating elements. Differences of 3 or more points are meaningful.

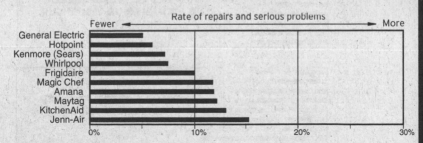

Based on more than 55,000 responses on coil and smoothtop electric ranges purchased in 1996 to 2001. Data have been standardized to eliminate differences between brands due to age.

Ranges Gas models

In general, gas ranges have required more repairs than electric ranges. Things that go wrong include failed igniters. Differences of 5 or more points are meaningful.

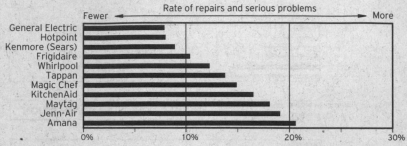

Based on more than 29,000 responses on gas ranges purchased in 1996 to 2001. Data have been standardized to eliminate differences between brands due to age.

Refrigerators

Regardless of configuration—top-freezer, bottom-freezer, and side-by-side—the presence of an icemaker increases the chances of needing a repair. All side-by-side models included an outside ice and water dispenser, features that considerably increase the chances of needing a repair. Of models so equipped, Maytag has been the least reliable. In general, things that go wrong with all types of refrigerators include cooling problems caused by the compressor or motor. Differences of 3 or more points are meaningful.

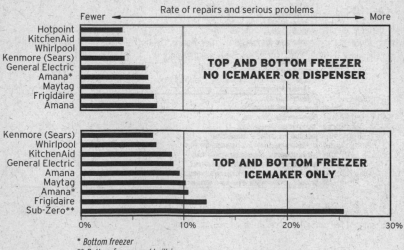

* Bottom freezer
** Bottom freezer and built-in

Refrigerators continued

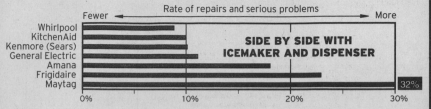

Rate of repairs and serious problems

Fewer ←——————————→ More

Whirlpool
KitchenAid
Kenmore (Sears)
General Electric
Amana
Frigidaire
Maytag

**SIDE BY SIDE WITH
ICEMAKER AND DISPENSER**

32%

0%   10%   20%   30%

Based on more than 93,000 responses on refrigerators bought in 1996 to 2001. Data have been standardized to eliminate differences between brands due to age.

TV sets 25- to 27-inch

These models tend to be a bit older than sets in the 31- to 36-inch range. GE and RCA have been significantly more troublesome than other brands. In general, things that go wrong with this size set are
no picture or sound (which may be related to the power supply), deteriorating picture quality (picture
tube or tuner), and inability to get channels (tuner). Differences of 3 or more points are meaningful.

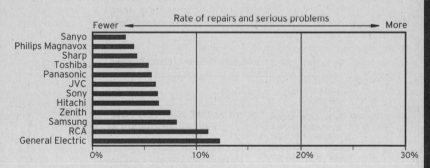

Rate of repairs and serious problems

Fewer ←——————————→ More

Sanyo
Philips Magnavox
Sharp
Toshiba
Panasonic
JVC
Sony
Hitachi
Zenith
Samsung
RCA
General Electric

0%   10%   20%   30%

Based on more than 84,000 responses on 25- to 27-inch TV sets purchased in 1996 to 2001. Data have been standardized to eliminate differences between brands due to age and usage.

TV sets 31-, 32-, 35-, and 36-inch

Most models in our survey were fairly new and were used more often than smaller-sized TVs. RCA has been significantly more troublesome than other brands. In general, things that go wrong with this size set are much the same as with smaller sets. Differences of 3 or more points are meaningful.

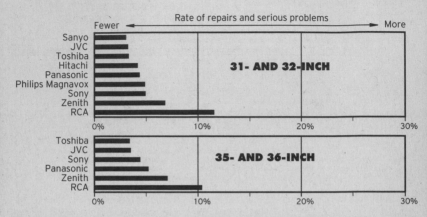

Based on more than 44,000 responses on 35- and 36-inch TV sets purchased in 1997 to 2001. Data have been standardized to eliminate differences between brands due to age and usage.

TV sets Projection

Beyond the types of things that generally go wrong with TV sets, projection sets tend to have problems with the projection and lens systems. Because of these sets' high price tag, it's usually worth repairing them—even sets as old as 6 years. Differences of 3 points are meaningful.

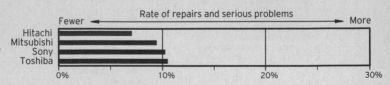

Based on more than 5,600 responses on projection TV sets purchased in 1996 to 2001. Data have been standardized to eliminate differences between brands due to age and usage.

Vacuum cleaners

Things that go wrong include inability to run (motor), unusually loud noise or vibration (impeller, rotating brush, or bearing), and self-propelling problems. The results shown here don't include broken belts—a frequent but inexpensive problem. Broken belts were more common for Eureka, Panasonic, and Dirt Devil as compared with other brands of uprights. Eureka and Hoover canisters had more belt problems than other brands. Differences of 4 points are meaningful.

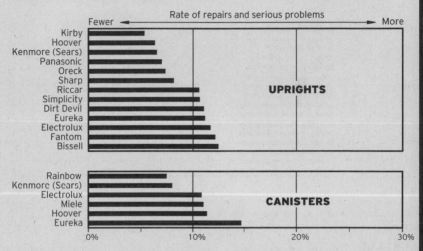

Based on more than 119,000 responses on full-sized upright and canister vacuum cleaners purchased in 1997 to 2001. Data have been standardized to eliminate differences between brands due to age and usage.

VCRs

Most models in our survey were purchased recently and show only modest differences between brands. Things that go wrong include inability to load or reject a tape (related to the loading mechanism), deteriorating picture quality (video heads), and problems caused by loose or failed belts. Differences of 3 or more points are meaningful.

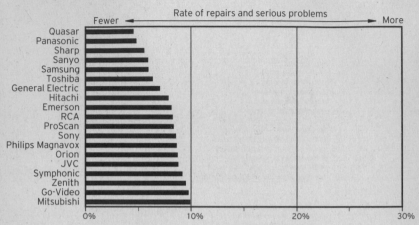

Based on more than 210,000 responses on VCRs purchased in 1996 to 2001. Data have been standardized to eliminate differences between brands due to age and usage.

Washing machines Top and front loaders

Things that go wrong with washing machines included problems with the timer, pump, valves, motor, transmission, and drive belt. Differences of 4 points or more are meaningful.

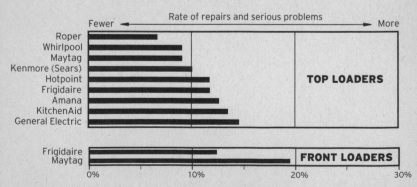

Based on more than 90,000 responses on top- and front-loading full-sized washing machines purchased in 1997 to 2001. Data have been standardized to eliminate differences between brands due to age and usage.

BRAND LOCATOR

Phone numbers and web addresses of selected manufacturers.

A

Acoustic Research	800 969-2748	www.acoustic-research.com
Acura	800 382-2238	www.acura.com
Advent	800 732-6866	www.recoton.com
AGFA	888 988-2432	www.AGFA.com
Aiwa	800 289-2492	www.aiwa.com
Allison	859 236-8298	www.allisonacoustics.com
Amana	800 843-0304	www.amana.com
Apple	800 538-9696	www.apple.com
Ariens	800 678-5443	www.ariens.com
Asko	800 898-1879	www.askousa.com
AT&T	800 222-3111	www.att.com
Audi	800 367-2834	www.audiusa.com
Audiovox	800 229-1235	www.audiovox.com

B

B&W	978 664-2870	www.bwspeakers.com
BellSouth	800 338-1694	www.bellsouth.com
B.I.C.	888 461-4628	www.bicamerica.com
Bionaire	800 253-2764	www.bionaire.com
Bissell	800 237-7691	www.bissell.com
Black & Decker	800 544-6986	www.blackanddecker.com
BMW	800 334-4269	www.bmwusa.com
Bosch	800 944-2904	www.boschappliances.com
Bose	800 444-2673	www.bose.com
Boston Acoustics	800 246-7767	www.bostonacoustics.com
Broilmaster	800 255-0403	www.broilmaster.com
Buick	800 422-8425	www.buick.com

C

Cadillac	800 333-4223	www.cadillac.com
Cambridge Soundworks	800 367-4434	www.cambridgesoundworks.com
Canon	800 652-2666	www.usa.canon.com
Carrier	800 227-7437	www.carrier.com
Casio	800 962-2746	www.casio.com
Cerwin Vega	805 584-5300	www.cerwinvega.com
Char-Broil	800 241-7548	www.charbroil.com
Chevrolet	800 950-0540	www.chevrolet.com
Chrysler	800 422-4797	www.chrysler.com
Coleman	800 356-3612	www.bbqhq.com
Compaq	800 345-1518	www.compaq.com
Craftsman	Call local Sears store	www.sears.com
Creative	800 998-5227	www.creative.com
Cub Cadet	877 282-8684	www.cubcadet.com
Cuisinart	800 726-0190	www.cuisinart.com

D

Dacor	800 793-0093	www.dacor.com
Daewoo	888 643-2396	www.daewoous.com

Dell .... 800 879-3355 .... www.dell.com
DeLonghi .... 800 322-3848 .... www.delonghiusa.com
Denon .... 973 396-0810 .... www.del.denon.com
DeWalt .... 800 433-9258 .... www.dewalt.com
Diamond .... 800 468-5846 .... www.diamondmm.com
DirecTV .... 800 347-3288 .... www.direcTV.com
Dirt Devil .... 800 321-1134 .... www.dirtdevil.com
Dish Network (EchoStar) .... 800 333-3474 .... www.dishnetwork.com
Dodge .... 800 423-6343 .... www.4adodge.com
Ducane .... 800 382-2637 .... www.ducane.com
Dynamic Cooking Systems (DCS) .... 800 433-8466 .... www.dcsappliances.com

E

Echo .... 800 673-1558 .... www.echo-usa.com
EchoStar .... 800 333-3474 .... wwww.dishnetwork.com
Electrolux .... 800 243-9078 .... www.electroluxusa.com
Emerson .... 800 898-9020 .... www.emersonradio.com
Epson .... 800 463-7766 .... www.epson.com
Ericsson .... 800 374-2776 .... www.ericsson.com
Eureka .... 800 282-2886 .... www.eureka.com

F

Fantom .... 800 668-9600 .... www.fantom.com
Fedders .... 217 342-3901 .... www.fedders.com
Fiesta .... 800 396-3838 .... www.fiestabbq.com
Fisher & Paykel .... 888 936-7872 .... www.fisherpaykel.com
Ford .... 800 392-3673 .... www.fordvehicles.com
Friedrich .... 800 541-6645 .... www.friedrich.com
Frigidaire .... 800 374-4432 .... www.frigidaire.com
Fujifilm .... 800 800-3854 .... www.fujifilm.com

G

Gateway 2000 .... 800 846-2000 .... www.gateway.com
GE (appliances) .... 800 626-2000 .... www.geappliances.com
GE (electronics) .... 800 447-1700 .... www.home-electronics.net
Gibson .... 800 245-0100 .... www.frigidaire.com
GMC .... 800 462-8782 .... www.gmc.com
Goldstar .... 800 243-0000 .... www.lgeus.com
Great Outdoors Grill Company .... 888 869-5454 .... www.gogrills.com
Grizzly .... 570 546-966 .... www.grizzly.com

H

Hamilton Beach .... 800 851-8900 .... www.hambeach.com
Haier .... 888 764-2437 .... www.haier.com
Handspring .... 888 565-9393 .... www.handspring.com
Harman/Kardon .... 800 422-8027 .... www.harmankardon.com
Hewlett Packard .... 800 752-0900 .... www.hp.com
Hitachi .... 800 448-2244 .... www.hitachi.com
Holland .... 800 880-9766 .... www.hollandgrill.com
Holmes .... 800 546-5637 .... www.holmesproducts.com
Homelite .... 800 242-4672 .... www.homelite.com
Honda (autos) .... 800 334-6632 .... www.honda.com
Honda (mowers) .... 800 426-7701 .... www.hondapowerequipment.com
Hoover .... 800 944-9200 .... www.hoover.com
Hotpoint .... 800 626-2000 .... www.hotpoint.com
Hughes .... 800 274-8995 .... www.hns-usa.com
Husqvarna .... 800 487-5962 .... www.husqvarna.com
Hyundai .... 800 826-2277 .... www.hyundaiusa.com

I

IBM	800 426-7235	www.ibm.com
Infiniti	877 647-7266	www.infiniti.com
Infinity	800 553-3332	www.infinitysystems.com
Isuzu	800 726-2700	www.isuzu.com

J

Jaguar	800 452-4827	www.usjaguar.com
JBL	800 336-4525	www.jbl.com
Jeep	800 925-5337	www.jeepunpaved.com
Jenn-Air	800 688-1100	www.jennair.com
John Deere	800 537-8233	www.deere.com
Jonsered	877 693-7729	www.usa.jonsered.com
JVC	800 252-5722	www.jvc.com

K

Kenmore	Call a local Sears store	www.sears.com
Kenwood	800 536-9663	www.kenwoodusa.com
Kia	800 333-4542	www.kia.com
KitchenAid	800 422-1230	www.kitchenaid.com
KLH	818 767-2843	www.klhaudio.com
Kodak	800 235-6325	www.kodak.com
Kyocera	800 349-4188	www.qualcomm.com

L

Land Rover	800 346-3493	www.landrover.com
Lawn-Boy	800-526-6937	www.lawnboy.com
Lexmark	800 539-6275	www.lexmark.com
Lexus	800 872-5398	www.lexus.com
Lincoln	800 521-4140	www.lincolnvehicles.com

M

Magic Chef	800 688-1120	www.maytag.com
Magnovox	800 531-0039	www.philipsusa.com
Makita	800 462-5482	www.makita.com
Maxim	800 233-9054	www.salton-maxim.com
Maytag	800 688-9900	www.maytag.com
Mazda	800 639-1000	www.mazdausa.com
McCulloch	800 521-8559	www.mccullochpower.com
Melitta	888 635-4882	www.melitta.com
Mercedes-Benz	800 367-6372	www.mbusa.com
Mercury	800 392-3673	www.mercuryvehicles.com
Microsoft	800 426-9400	www.microsoft.com/actimates
Miele	800 289-6435	www.mieleusa.com
Milwaukee	877 279-7819	www.mil-electric-tool.com
Minolta	800 808-4888	www.minoltausa.com
Mission	310 974-1010	www.missionaudio.com
Mitsubishi	888 648-7820	www.mitsubishicars.com
Motorola	800 331-6456	www.motorola.com
MTD	800 800-7310	www.mtdproducts.com
Murray	800 224-8940	www.murrayinc.com

N

NEC	800 338-9549	www.necus.com
Newpoint	800 639-7646	www.newpoint.com
Nikon	800 645-6687	www.nikonusa.com
Nissan	800 419-7520	www.nissandriven.com
Nokia	888 665-4228	www.nokia.com

O

Oki	800 654-3282	www.okidata.com
Oldsmobile	800 442-6537	www.oldsmobile.com
Olympus	800 622-6372	www.olympusamerica.com
Omnifilter	800 937-6664	www.omnifilter.com
Onkyo	201 785-2600	www.onkyousa.com
Optimus	Call local RadioShack	www.radioshack.com
Oreck	800 989-3535	www.oreck.com
Oster	800 597-5978	www.sunbeam.com

P

Palm	800 881-7256	www.palm.com
Panasonic	800 211-7262	www.panasonic.com
Pella	888 847-3552	www.pella.com
Pentax	800 877-0155	www.pentax.com
Phase Technology	888 742-7385	www.phasetech.com
Philips	800 531-0039	www.philipsusa.com
Pioneer	800 421-1404	www.pioneerelectronics.com
Polaroid	800 432-5355	www.polaroid.com
Polk Audio	800 377-7655	www.polkaudio.com
Pontiac	800 276-6842	www.pontiac.com
Porsche	800 767-7243	www.porsche.com
Porter-Cable	800 487-8665	www.porter-cable.com
Poulan	800 238-9333	www.poulan.com
Pozzi	800 257-9663	www.pozzi.com
Precor	800 477-3267	www.precor.com
Precisionaire	800 347-2220	www.precisionaire.com
Princeton	800 747-6249	www.princetongraphics.com
Proctor-Silex	800 851-8900	www.proctorsilex.com
ProForm	800 291-0994	www.proform.com
PSB	888 772-0000	www.psbspeakers.com
Psion	800 997-7466	www.psioninc.com

Q

Quasar	800 211-7262	www.panasonic.com

R

RadioShack	800 843-7422	www.radioshack.com
RCA	800 336-1900	www.rca.com
Regal	262 626-2121	www.regalware.com
Regina	228 867-8507	www.reginavac.com
Remington	616 791-7325	www.remingtonchainsaw.com
Research Products	800 545-2219	www.resprod.com
Ricoh	800 225-1899	www.ricohcpg.com
Rival	800 557-4825	www.rivco.com
Roper	800 447-6737	www.roperappliances.com
Rowenta	781 396-0600	www.rowentausa.com
Royal	800 321-1134	wwww.dirtdevil.com
Ryobi	800 345-8746	www.ryobi.com

S

Saab	800 722-2872	www.saabusa.com
Sabre by John Deere	800 537-8233	www.deere.com
Salton	800 233-9054	www.salton-maxim.com
Samsung	800 726-7864	www.samsungusa.com
Sanyo	818 998-7322	www.sanyo.com
Saturn	800 522-5000	www.saturn.com
Sensory Science	480 998-3400	www.sensoryscience.com

Sharp	800 237-4277	www.sharp-usa.com
Siemens	888 777-0211	www.icm.siemens.com
Simplicity (yard equipment)	262 284-8669	www.simplicitymfg.com
Simplicity (vacuum cleaners)	888 974-6759	www.simplicityvac.com
Skil	877 754 5999	www.skiltools.com
Snapper	800 762-7737	www.snapper.com
Sonicblue	800 468-5846	www.sonicblue.com
Sony	800 222-7669	www.sony.com
Southwestern Bell	800 366-0937	www.southwesternbell.com
Stanley	800 788-7766	www.stanleylawnmowers.com
Stihl	800 467-8445	www.stihl.com
Subaru	800 782-2783	www.subaru.com
Sub-Zero	800 222-7820	www.subzero.com
Sunbeam	800 458-8407	www.sunbeam.com
Suzuki	877 697-8985	www.suzukiauto.com

T

Tappan	800 537-5530	www.frigidaire.com
Technics	800 211-7262	www.panasonic.com
Thermador	800 735-4328	www.thermador.com
Toastmaster	800 947-3744	www.toastmaster.com
Toro	800 348-2424	www.toro.com
Toshiba	800 631-3811	www.toshiba.com
Toyota	800 468-6968	www.toyota.com
Tripp Lite	773 869-1234	www.tripplite.com
Trion	800 338-7466	www.fedders.com
Troy-Bilt	866 840-6483	www.troybilt.com

U

Umax	214 342-9799	www.umax.com
Uniden	800 297-1023	www.uniden.com

V

ViewSonic	800 688-6688	www.viewsonic.com
Viking	800 467-2643	www.vikingrange.com
Vivitar	805 498-7008	www.vivitar.com
Volkswagen	800 444-8987	www.vw.com
Volvo	800 458-1552	www.volvocars.com
VTech	800 624-5688	www.vtech.com

W

Walker	800 843-7422	www.radioshack.com
Waring	800 492-7464	www.waringproducts.com
Weber	800 446-1071	www.weber.com
Weed Eater	800 554-6723	www.weedeater.com
West Bend	800 367-0111	www.westbend.com
Whirlpool	800 253-1301	www.whirlpool.com
White Outdoor	800 949-4483	www.whiteoutdoor.com
White-Westinghouse	800 245-0600	www.frigidaire.com
Wood's	800 523-0075	www.wcwoods.com

X

Xerox	800 832-6979	www.xerox.com

Y

Yamaha	800 492-6242	www.yamaha.com
Yard Machines by MTD	800 800-7310	www.mtdproducts.com
Yashica	800 526-0266	www.yashica.com

Z

Zenith	256 772-1515	www.zenith.com

PRODUCT RECALLS

Products ranging from child-safety seats to chain saws are recalled when there are safety defects. Various federal agencies—the Consumer Product Safety Commission (CPSC), the National Highway Traffic Safety Administration (NHTSA), the U.S. Coast Guard, and the Food and Drug Administration (FDA)—monitor consumer complaints and injuries and, when there's a problem, issue a recall.

But the odds of hearing about an unsafe product are slim. Manufacturers are reluctant to issue a recall in the first place because they can be costly. And getting the word out to consumers can be haphazard. If you return the warranty card that comes with a product, you might receive notification on a recalled product.

A selection of the most far-reaching recalls appear monthly in CONSUMER REPORTS. The following lists products recalled from December 2001 through November 2002 issues of CONSUMER REPORTS. For details on these products and hundreds more, go to our website, *www.consumerreports.org*, to access our free, comprehensive list of product recalls.

If you wish to report an unsafe product or get recall information, call the CPSC's hotline, 800-638-2772 or visit its web site, *www.cpsc.gov*. Recall notices about your automobile can be obtained from a new-car dealer or by calling the NHTSA hotline at 800-424-9393 or go to *www.nhtsa.dot.gov*. Questions about food and drugs are handled by the FDA's Office of Consumer Affairs, 301-827-4420 or *www.fda.gov*.

Major product recalls in 2002

VEHICLES

- '01 BMW cars (various models)
- '02 Chevrolet TrailBlazer, GMC Envoy, and Oldsmobile Bravada
- '02 Chrysler PT Cruiser and Jeep Grand Cherokee
- '01 Dodge Dakota Quad Cab pickup truck
- '00-01 Dodge Ram van
- '98 Ford Contour and Mercury Mystique
- '00-01 Ford, Lincoln, and Mercury cars and SUVs
- '95 Ford Mustang and Taurus, and Mercury Sable
- '02 Ford SVT Focus
- '99-01 Ford Windstar
- '97-98 Ford Windstar
- '95-96 Ford Windstar
- '01 GM minivans
- '00-02 GM SUVs (various makes)
- '01-02 Harley Davidson motorcycles (various models)
- '00-01 Honda Accord and Civic
- '02 Honda CR-V
- '01 Hyundai Santa Fe
- '99-01 Hyundai Sonata
- '97-01 Hyundai Tiburon
- '99-02 Jeep Cherokee, Grand Cherokee, and Wrangler
- '02 Jeep Liberty
- '02 Lexus ES300 and Toyota Camry
- '98-99 Mercedes Benz C-Class

'02 Mini Cooper (with manual transmission)

'01-02 Mitsubishi Montero

'00-01 Nissan Sentra

'95-99 Subaru Legacy sedan, wagon, and
Outback

'96-98 Toyota 4Runner

'01-02 Volkswagen Beetle, Golf, and Jetta

'97-00 Volkswagen Jetta and Passat

CHILDREN'S PRODUCTS

Baby Buzz'r interactive infant toy

Brio "Curious George" monkey plush toy

Britax Roundabout convertible
child-safety seat

Fisher-Price Smart Response infant swing

Graco SnugRide car seat/infant carrier

Lifetime and Escalade Sports portable basketball
hoops

Peg Perego infant safety seats

Safety 1st Fold-up booster seat

Safety 1st and Beatrix Potter "designer 22"
infant safety seats/carriers

Snuggle Bear plush toy distributed as a premium
with Snuggle fabric softener

Stride Rite "Munchkin" T-strap girls' shoes

"Time Out" folding mini beach chair

"Vacation Station" children's cooler/chairs given
to guests at Doubletree, Hilton, and Hilton
Garden Inn hotels and resorts

Various "fun-kart" type go-karts with Briggs &
Stratton engine

"Wiggly Giggler" baby rattles

HOUSEHOLD, FOOD & RECREATIONAL

Andersen 200 Series Tilt-Wash double-
hung window

Black & Decker VersaToast two- and
four-slice wide-slot toasters

Calphalon stainless steel tea kettle

Coleman Mosquito Deleto mosquito traps

Cozy Coupe computer mouse

Dansk ice cream scoop

Diving Unlimited Int'l. scuba devices

Dynasty pro-style gas ranges

Hamilton Beach juice extractor

Hewlett-Packard DeskJet and PhotoSmart inkjet
printers

Hunter Fan Carefree and Carefree Plus humidi-
fiers

In-Sink-Erator and other brands of instant hot-
water dispensers

Kodak DC5000 zoom digital camera

Martha Stewart Everyday potpourri
simmering pots

Maximus scuba regulator

Motorola DCT2000 digital cable TV boxes

Murray, Murray Select, Wizard, and Yard King riding mowers

NordicTrack and ProForm hiker exercise equipment

Poulan Pro, Weed Eater, Husqvarna, and Jonsered
lawn tractors

Presto "CoolDaddy" electric deep fryers

Rain-X glass cleaner and washer fluid

Roto Zip "Revolution," "Rebel," and "Solaris"
spiral saws

Ryobi circular saws (various models)

Stewart's and Mistic soda in glass bottles

Various brands of gas-fired boilers

Various electric blankets

Whirlpool, Kenmore, and Comfort-Aire
dehumidifiers

Whirlpool, KitchenAid, and Kenmore over-the-
range microwave ovens

Zep Commercial and Enforcer drain cleaners

8-YEAR INDEX

8-YEAR INDEX TO CONSUMER REPORTS

This index includes selected reports published in CONSUMER REPORTS since 1995. Note: Beginning with Volume 61 (January 1996), CONSUMER REPORTS stopped using continuous pagination throughout each volume year. From January 1996 forward, each issue begins on page 1. **Bold type** indicates Ratings reports or brand-name discussions; *italic type* indicates corrections, followups, or Updates.

BUYING GUIDE INDEX

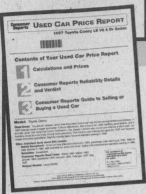